Automotive Electrical and Electronic Systems

Third Edition

**By Chek-Chart Publications,
a Division of
H. M. Gousha**

Rick DuPuy, *Editor*
Alan Ahlstrand,
Kalton C. Lahue, *Contributing Editors*

HarperCollins*Publishers*

Acknowledgments

In producing this series of textbooks for automobile technicians, Chek-Chart has drawn extensively on the technical and editorial knowledge of the nation's carmakers and suppliers. Automotive design is a technical, fast-changing field, and we gratefully acknowledge the help of the following companies and organizations who provided us with help and information, so that we could create the most up-to-date text and illustrations possible. These companies and organizations are not responsible for changes in procedures of specifications made by the carmakers or suppliers, or for any errors or omissions in the instructions or illustrations contained in this book or in any other Chek-Chart product:

Allen Testproducts
Bear Automotive Service Equipment Co.
Borg-Warner Corporation
Champion Spark Plug Company
Chrysler Motors Corporation
Ford Motor Company
Fram Corporation, A Allied Signal
    Company
Don Mullens, Dan Sylvester, and Bryan
    Wilson; General Motors Training Center,
    Burbank, CA
Ellen Clark; AC-Delco, Los Angeles, CA
Delco-Remy Division, General Motors
Rochester Products Division
Saginaw Steering Gear Division
Buick Motor Division
Cadillac Motor Car Division
Chevrolet Motor Division
Oldsmobile Division
Pontiac Division
Jaguar Cars, Inc.
Mazda Motor Corporation
Nissan Motors
Robert Bosch Corporation
Snap-On Tools Corporation, and
    Sun Electric Corporation
Toyota Motor Company
Volkswagen of America

The authors have made every effort to ensure that the material in this book is as accurate and up-to-date as possible. However, neither Chek-Chart nor HarperCollins, nor any related companies can be held responsible for mistakes or omissions, or for changes in procedures or specifications by the carmakers or suppliers.

The comments, suggestions, and assistance of the following reviewers were invaluable:

Daniel S. Boyer, Prairie State College
Mark White, ATI
Ray Winiecki, Oklahoma State University

At Chek-Chart, Ramona Torres managed the production of this book. Type was set by Maria Glidden and Diane Maurice. Original art and photographs were produced by Dave Douglass, Kalton C. Lahue, and Gerald A. McEwan. The project is under the direction of Roger L. Fennema.

With respect, this work is dedicated to **Kalton C. Lahue:** 1934-1993. He wrote all the books.

Library of Congress Cataloging-in-Publication Data

```
Automotive electrical and electronic systems / by Chek-Chart
 Publications, a division of H.M. Gousha ; Richard DuPuy, editor. --
 3rd ed.
      p.   cm.
   Includes indexes.
   Contents: [1] Classroom manual -- [2] Shop manual.
   ISBN 0-06-500759-X (set)
   1. Automobiles--Electric equipment--Maintenance and repair.
 2. Automobiles--Electronic equipment--Maintenance and repair.
 I. DuPuy, Richard    II. Chek-Chart Publications (Firm)
 TL272.A786  1994
 629.25'4'0288--dc20                              93-47370
                                                      CIP
```

Contents

On the Cover:
Front — The Tektronix 222 Digital Storage Oscilloscope.
Rear — The Snap-on MT2500 Scanner

Contents

Introduction to Automotive Electrical and Electronic Systems

Automotive Electrical and Electronic Systems is part of the HarperCollins/Chek-Chart Automotive Series. The package for each course has two volumes, a *Classroom Manual* and a *Shop Manual*.

Other titles in this series include:

- Automatic Transmissions and Transaxles
- Automotive Brake Systems
- Automotive Heating, Ventilation, and Air Conditioning
- Automotive Steering, Suspension, and Wheel Alignment
- Automotive Engine Repair and Rebuilding
- Engine Performance, Diagnosis, and Tune-Up
- Fuel Systems and Emission Controls.

Each book is written to help the instructor teach students to become competent and knowledgeable professional automotive technicians. The two-manual texts are the core of a learning system that leads a student from basic theories to actual hands-on experience.

The entire series is job-oriented, designed for students who intend to work in the car service profession. A student will be able to use the knowledge gained from these books and from the instructor to get and keep a job in automotive repair. Learning the material and techniques in these volumes is a giant leap toward a satisfying, rewarding career.

The books are divided into *Classroom Manuals* and *Shop Manuals* for an improved presentation of the descriptive information and study lessons, along with representative testing, repair, and overhaul procedures. The manuals are to be used together: the descriptive material in the *Classroom Manual* corresponds to the application material in the *Shop Manual*.

Each book is divided into several parts. Instructors will find the chapters to be complete, readable, and well thought-out. Students will benefit from the many learning aids included, as well as from the thoroughness of the presentation.

The series was researched and written by the editorial staff of Chek-Chart and was produced by HarperCollins*Publishers*. For over 60 years, Chek-Chart has provided car and equipment manufacturers' service specifications to the automotive service field. Chek-Chart's complete, up-to-date automotive data bank was used extensively to prepare this textbook series.

Because of the comprehensive material, the hundreds of high-quality illustrations, and the inclusion of the latest automotive technology, instructors and students alike will find that these books will form the core of the master technician's professional library.

How To Use This Book

Why Are There Two Manuals?

Unless you are familiar with the other books in this series, *Automotive Electrical and Electronic Systems* will not be like any other textbook you've used before. It is actually two books, the *Classroom Manual* and the *Shop Manual*. They have different purposes and should be used together.

The *Classroom Manual* teaches you what you need to know about electrical and electronic theory, systems, and components. The *Classroom Manual* will be valuable in class and at home, for study and for reference. You can use the text and illustrations for years to refresh your memory — not only about the basics of automotive electrical and electronic systems but also about related topics in automotive history, physics, and technology.

In the *Shop Manual*, you learn test procedures, troubleshooting, and how to repair the systems and parts you read about in the *Classroom Manual*. The *Shop Manual* provides the practical, hands-on information you need to work on automotive electrical and electronic systems. Use the two manuals together to understand fully how the systems work and how to fix them when they don't work.

What's in These Manuals?

These key features of the *Classroom Manual* make it easier for you to learn and to remember what you learn:

- Each chapter is divided into self-contained sections for easier understanding and review. This organization shows you clearly which parts make up which systems, and how various parts or systems that perform the same task differ or are the same.
- Most parts and processes are fully illustrated with drawings or photographs. Important topics appear in several different ways, to make sure you can see other aspects of them.
- Important words in the *Classroom Manual* text are printed in **boldface type** and are defined on the same page and in a glossary at the end of the manual. Use these words to build the vocabulary you need to understand the text.
- Review questions are included for each chapter. Use them to test your knowledge.
- Every chapter has a brief summary at the end to help you review for exams.
- Every few pages you will find sidebars — short blocks of ''nice to know'' information — in addition to the main text.

The *Shop Manual* has detailed instructions on test, service, and overhaul procedures for modern components and current electrical and electronic systems. These are easy to understand and usually have step-by-step explanations to guide you through the procedures. The *Shop Manual* contains:

- Helpful information that tells you how to use and maintain shop tools and test equipment
- Safety precautions
- Clear illustrations and diagrams to help you locate trouble spots while you learn to read service literature
- Test procedures and troubleshooting hints that will help you work better and faster
- Tips the professionals use that are presented clearly and accurately
- A sample test at the back of the manual that is similar to those given for Automotive Service Excellence (ASE) certification; use this test to help study and prepare yourself when you are ready to be certified as a automotive electrical and electronic systems expert.

Where Should I Begin?

If you already know something about automotive electrical and electronic systems and know how to repair them, you will find that this book is a helpful review. If you are just starting in car repair, then the book will give you a solid foundation on which to develop professional-level skills.

Your instructor will design a course to take advantage of what you already know and what facilities and equipment are available to work with. You may be asked to read certain chapters of these manuals out of order. That's fine. The important thing is to really understand each subject before you move on to the next.

Study the vocabulary words in boldface type. Use the review questions to help you understand the material. When you read the *Classroom Manual*, be sure to refer to your *Shop Manual* to relate the descriptive text to the service procedures. And when you are working on actual car systems and components, look back to the *Classroom Manual* to keep the basic information fresh in your mind. Working on such a complicated piece of equipment as a modern car isn't always easy. Use the information in the *Classroom Manual*, the procedures in the *Shop Manual*, and the knowledge of your instructor to help you.

The *Shop Manual* is a good book for work, not just a good workbook. Keep it on hand while you're working on equipment. It folds flat on the workbench and under the car, and can stand quite a bit of rough handling.

When you perform test procedures and overhaul equipment, you will need a complete and accurate source of manufacturer's specifications, and the techniques for pulling computer codes. Most auto shops have either the carmaker's annual shop service manuals, which lists these specifications, or an independent guide, such as the Chek-Chart *Car Care Guide*. This unique book, with ten-year coverage, is updated each year to give you service instructions, capacities, and troubleshooting tips that you need to work on specific cars.

PART ONE

Electrical Fundamentals

1

Basic Electricity and Basic Circuits

A car may be thought of as a large electrical system on wheels. This is a bit different from the more common conception of cars. But cars use electricity not only to get started, but to keep running.

To know enough about electrical systems to work on them, you will have to know about electricity. Perhaps you already do. If so, these first few chapters will be a good review. If not, study them carefully. You will soon find that some of the best examples of electrical science exist in your own automobile.

Unlike the fuel and oil for your car, electricity cannot be seen, heard, touched, or smelled. We cannot weigh or measure it either. We can, however, measure its actions, and we can see, hear, touch, or smell many of its effects. Our knowledge and use of electricity are based on some scientific theories which describe the features of electricity that we cannot see. When you use a voltmeter to test a circuit you cannot see the voltage. But the meter tells you some facts about the circuit based on theories that define voltage.

Because our knowledge of electricity is based on science, we will begin with a quick look at the chemistry and atomic structure of the materials used in electrical systems.

ATOMIC STRUCTURE

''Matter'' is the general name given to everything in the physical universe. The only place in the physical universe where matter does not exist is in a total vacuum. Matter is made up of chemical building blocks called **elements**.

An element is matter that cannot be reduced to anything simpler by chemical means. Scientists have so far discovered 103 elements in our world. Of these, 92 exist in nature and the others have been created by scientists. Some are familiar elements such as oxygen, gold, and copper. Others are ones we seldom hear of, such as antimony, lithium, and gallium.

The smallest part of an element that still has all the features, or characteristics, of that element is the **atom**. Atoms of each element are distinctly different from those of any other element.

What makes the atom of one element different from those of another are the same characteristics that cause electricity. To learn more about electricity, we must look inside the atom.

Protons, Electrons, and Neutrons

As small as it is, the atom is made of several other, much smaller units: the **proton**, the **electron**, and the **neutron**. Compare the atom

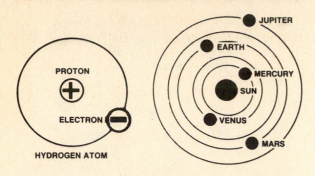

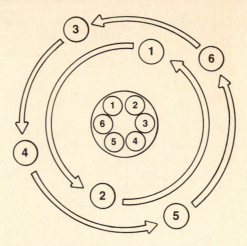

Figure 1-1. In an atom (left), electrons orbit protons in the nucleus just as planets orbit the sun in our solar system (right).

Figure 1-3. A balanced atom.

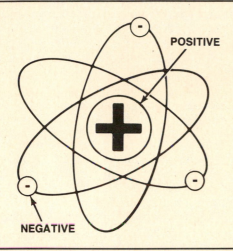

Figure 1-2. The charges within an atom.

to our solar system. Our earth and the other planets go around (orbit) the sun in fixed paths, figure 1-1.

In the atom, the electrons orbit in fixed paths around the central core, or **nucleus**, which contains the protons and the neutrons. The only difference between atoms of different kinds of matter is the number of protons and neutrons in the nucleus and the number and spacing of the orbiting electrons.

Positive and Negative Charges

The parts of the atom have different charges. The orbiting electrons are negatively charged, while the protons are positively charged. Positive charges are indicated by the ''plus'' sign (+), negative charges by the ''minus'' sign (–), figure 1-2. As you will soon see, we use these same + and – signs to identify parts of an electrical circuit. Neutrons have no charge at all — they are neutral. In a normal, or balanced, atom, the number of negative particles equals the number of positive particles. That

is, there are as many electrons as there are protons, figure 1-3. The number of neutrons varies according to the type of atom.

An ordinary magnet has two ends, or poles. One end is called the south pole, and the other is called the north pole. If two magnets are brought close to each other with like poles together (south to south or north to north), the magnets will push each other apart. This is because like poles repel each other. If the opposite poles of the magnets are brought close to each other, south to north, the magnets will snap together. This is because unlike poles attract each other.

The positive and negative charges within an atom are like the north and south poles of a magnet. Charges that are alike will repel each other, similarly to the poles of a magnet, figure 1-4. That is why the negative electrons continue to orbit around the positive protons.

Elements: Chemical building blocks that make up all types of matter in the physical universe.

Atom: The smallest part of a chemical element that still has all the characteristics of that element.

Proton: A positively charged particle within an atom.

Electron: A negatively charged particle within an atom.

Neutron: A particle in an atom that has no charge and is electrically neutral.

Nucleus: The center core of an atom that contains the protons and neutrons.

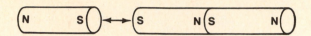

Figure 1-4. Unlike and like charges.

They are attracted and held by the opposite charge of the protons. The electrons keep moving in orbit because they repel each other.

When an atom loses any electrons, it becomes unbalanced. It will have more protons than electrons, and therefore will have a positive charge. If it gains more electrons than protons, the atom will be negatively charged. When an atom is not balanced, it becomes a charged particle called an **ion**. Ions try to regain their balance of equal protons and electrons. They do this by exchanging electrons with neighboring atoms, figure 1-5. This is the flow of electric current, or electricity.

Electron Shells

Electrons orbit around the nucleus in definite paths. These paths form shells, like **concentric** rings, around the nucleus. Only a specific number of electrons can orbit within each shell. If there are too many electrons for the first and closest shell to the nucleus, the others will orbit in additional shells until all electrons have an orbit within a shell. There can be as many as seven shells around a single nucleus.

Free and Bound Electrons

The outermost electron shell, or ring, is the most important to our study of electricity. It is called the **valence ring**. The number of electrons in this ring determines the valence of the atom, and indicates its capacity to combine with other atoms. From now on, we will be concerned only with the valence ring and the action of the electrons in that ring.

If the valence ring of an atom has three or fewer electrons in it, it has room for more. The electrons there are held very loosely, and it is easy for a drifting electron to join the valence ring and push another electron away. These loosely held electrons are called **free electrons**. When the valence ring has five or more electrons in it, it is fairly full. The electrons are held tightly, and it is hard for a drifting electron to push its way into the valence ring. These tightly held electrons are called **bound electrons**.

The movement of these drifting electrons is called current. Current flow can be small, with

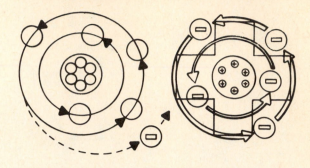

Figure 1-5. An unbalanced, positively charged atom will attract electrons from neighboring atoms.

only a few electrons moving, or it can be large, with a tremendous number of electrons moving. However, current only flows in a conductor. Electric current is the controlled, directed flow of electrons from atom to atom within a conductor.

Conductors, Insulators, and Semiconductors

When a material has many free electrons, it is easy for electrons to move from atom to atom. Materials whose atoms have from one to three free electrons and easy electron flow are good **conductors**. That is, electric current can pass through them easily. Many metals are good conductors, especially silver, copper, and aluminum.

When a material has many bound electrons, it is hard for electrons to move from atom to atom. These materials that do not conduct electricity well are called **insulators**. Rubber, glass, and certain plastics are good insulators, as are gaseous elements such as nitrogen and oxygen. Insulators are used in electrical systems to ensure that the electron flow stays within the conductor and is directed to the proper place in the system.

Some materials are neither good conductors nor good insulators. They have just four electrons in the valence ring. These are called **semiconductors**. They are important in some parts of electrical systems, as we will see when we study diodes, transistors, and other solid-state electronic devices.

ELECTRON FLOW (CURRENT)

If electrons simply move about in various directions, no electricity will flow. This is called random drift of electrons. Only a directed, concentrated flow of electrons from one point to another is called current flow.

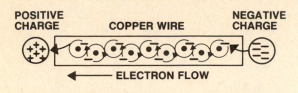

Figure 1-6. Movement of electrons through a wire. (Delco-Remy)

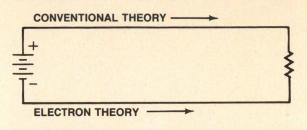

Figure 1-7. Two theories of current flow.

To illustrate the flow of electric current, let's look at a length of copper wire. Copper is a good conductor because it has only one electron in its valence ring. Electrons can be made to move easily from one atom to another. To do this, we must have a positive charge at one end of the wire and a negative charge at the other. How this is done is explained later in this text. For now, assume that these charges do exist and that they remain unchanged.

The outer electron of an atom near the positive end of the wire will be attracted by the positive charge. As it leaves its atom and moves toward the positive charge, the atom becomes unbalanced. It becomes positively charged and attracts the outer electron from a neighboring atom. The outer electrons of neighboring atoms will move in order toward the positive charge. The negative charge at one end of the wire repels the electrons with the same force that the positive charge at the other end attracts them. The net result is a controlled flow of electrons from the negative end of the wire to the positive end, figure 1-6. This flow will continue as long as the positive and negative charges are at the opposite ends of the wire. This brings us back to our definition of electricity, or electric current, namely:

The controlled, directed flow of electrons from atom to atom in a conductor.

Current-Flow Theories

There are two theories that describe electrical current. They are called the conventional theory and the electron theory, figure 1-7. Either theory can be used with equal accuracy, as long as it is used consistently.

Conventional theory
When scientists first began to make discoveries about electricity, they thought it flowed from positive to negative. This became what is now called the **conventional theory** of current flow. In the past, the conventional theory was always used to describe automotive electrical systems.

Electron theory
The **electron theory** of current flow says that current moves from negative to positive. It is this theory we have used so far in talking about basic electricity. It is the theory used in electronic communications, computers, and other areas of the electronics industry.

In recent years, the electron flow theory has been used for the most part to describe systems on automobiles. Whenever the electron flow theory is used in this book, it will be clearly identified. Our continuing study of current, voltage, and resistance in *this* chapter is based on the electron theory.

Ion: An atom which has become unbalanced by losing or gaining an electron. It can be positively or negatively charged.

Concentric: Having the same center, such as two circles drawn around a common centerpoint.

Valence Ring: The outermost electron shell of an atom.

Free Electrons: Three or fewer loosely held electrons in an atom's valence ring.

Bound Electrons: Five or more tightly held electrons in an atom's valence ring.

Conductors: Materials that allow easy electron flow because of their many free electrons.

Insulators: Materials that oppose electron flow because of their many bound electrons.

Semiconductors: Materials that have four electrons in their valence ring and are neither good conductors nor good insulators.

Conventional Theory: The current flow theory that says electricity flows from positive to negative. Also called the positive current flow theory.

Electron Theory: The current flow theory that says electricity flows from negative to positive.

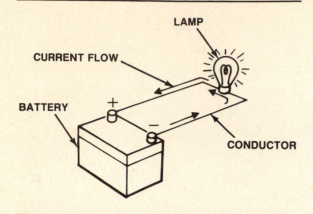

Figure 1-8. A simple circuit.

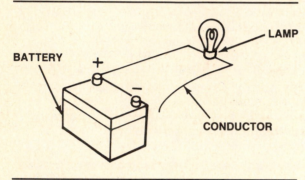

Figure 1-9. An incomplete (open) circuit.

Current Path (Circuit)

An electrical current needs a path to flow. This path is called a **circuit**, which means around. If there is any break in the circuit, no current can flow through it. The electrons have nowhere to go.

One of the simplest circuits contains an energy source (battery), conductors (wires), and a lamp, figure 1-8. The current flows from the negative side, or terminal, of the battery through the wires and the lamp, lighting the lamp, and back to the positive terminal of the battery. If one wire is taken off of its battery terminal, figure 1-9, the circuit is not complete. Current will not flow, and the lamp will not light. Breaking the circuit by removing one wire from its terminal is the same as using a switch to break the circuit.

Ampere (Amp)

Current flowing in a conductor can be compared to water flowing in a pipe, figure 1-10. When measuring water flow, we can count how many gallons flow past a point in a certain period of time. When measuring electrical charges, we count electrons instead of gallons.

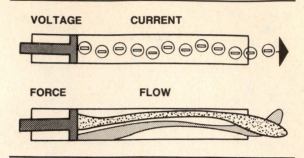

Figure 1-10. Voltage pushes current flow; force pushes water flow.

When 6.28 billion electrons pass a point in one second, we say that one **ampere**, or amp, of current is flowing. The ampere is the unit that indicates the rate of electric current flow. Remember that current (amperes) flows *through* a circuit.

VOLTAGE

Current cannot flow unless some sort of force pushes all the randomly drifting electrons in one direction. This is called electromotive force. It is measured in units called **volts**. The force that causes a current to flow through a conductor is called **voltage**. It can be compared to the force that moves water through a pipe, figure 1-10. Voltage is also the measurement of a **potential** difference in force that exists between two points. One point must be negatively charged, and the other must be positively charged, figure 1-11, such as the two terminals of a battery. The strength of the force depends upon the strength of the charges at each point. If the charges are strong, the voltage is high. If the charges are weak, the voltage is low.

Voltage exists even when there is no current flowing, such as when we disconnect one wire from its battery terminal in our simple circuit. Voltage is present at the terminals of the battery in figure 1-11, but no current can flow without a complete circuit.

Voltage Sources

In automobiles, voltage is supplied by the battery and the alternator. In the battery, chemical action creates a difference in electromotive force (potential) between the positive and negative terminals. In an alternator, mechanical energy is converted to electrical energy (electromotive force, or voltage). Remember that voltage is the force applied *to*, or impressed *on*, a circuit.

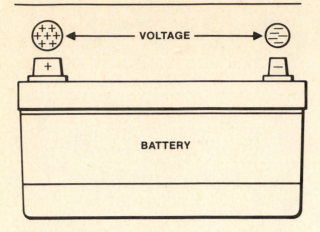

Figure 1-11. Voltage is a potential difference in electromotive force.

RESISTANCE TO CURRENT FLOW

Voltage is required to force current through a conductor. All conductive materials oppose current flow to some extent. This opposition is called **resistance**. More important than the resistance of a conductor is the resistance of an electrical device. The lamp in figure 1-8 is an electrical device that has more resistance than the wire conductors. Other electrical devices, such as starter motors, radios, or ignition coils, also offer resistance.

Resistance can be present in places other than the wires and devices of a circuit. A break in the circuit, such as in figure 1-9, creates infinite resistance. Loose or corroded connections also cause resistance to current flow. Remember that resistance exists *in* a circuit.

Ohm — The Unit of Resistance

Resistance is measured in units called **ohms**. There is an important relationship between volts (electromotive force), amperes (current), and ohms (resistance) that must be understood in order to troubleshoot an electrical circuit effectively:

> When a force of *one volt* pushes *one ampere* of current through a circuit, the resistance present is *one ohm*, figure 1-12.

This statement is an expression of Ohm's Law, named after the German scientist George Simon Ohm. Ohm's Law is one of your most important electrical troubleshooting tools.

Factors of Resistance

Five factors, or characteristics, determine how much resistance is present in any part of an electrical circuit. The examples below refer to

wire conductors. Conductors also exist in circuit devices. The filament of a bulb and the windings of a motor are conductors, so the examples apply to all electrical devices. The electrical devices in a circuit, such as bulbs and motors, are also called ''loads''. These are the

Circuit: A circle or unbroken path through which an electric current can flow.

Ampere: The unit for measuring the rate of electric current flow.

Volt: The unit for measuring the amount of electrical force.

Voltage: The electromotive force that causes current flow. The potential difference in electrical force between two points when one is negatively charged and the other is positively charged.

Potential: Possible, but not yet in use. The voltage between two points.

Resistance: Opposition to electrical current flow.

Ohm: The unit for measuring electrical resistance. When one volt pushes one ampere through a circuit, the resistance present is one ohm.

■ Compounds

Some of the materials used in electrical systems are pure chemical elements, such as copper. Other materials, like rubber and plastic insulation, are combinations of several elements. These combinations of elements are called compounds.

Just as the atom is the smallest identifiable part of an element, the molecule is the smallest identifiable part of a compound. Atoms join into molecules because they seek to complete their outer (valence) rings of electrons. They do this by sharing their valence electrons with each other.

Some compounds, like water and rubber, exist in nature. Others, like various plastics, are man-made. A molecule of water consists of two atoms of hydrogen joined to one atom of oxygen. Each hydrogen atom has one electron in its valence ring, but each could have two. The oxygen atom has six electrons in its valence ring, but it could have eight. By sharing the electrons of the two hydrogen atoms, the oxygen atom completes its valence ring. Similarly, each atom of hydrogen borrows one electron from the oxygen atom to complete its valence ring.

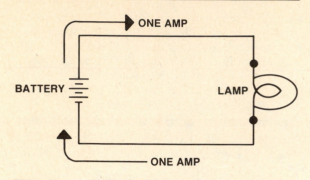

Figure 1-12. If this battery provides one volt of pressure, the resistance of the lamp must be one ohm.

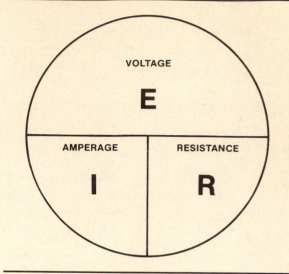

Figure 1-13. This diagram will help you remember the Ohm's Law formula. Cover the unknown value and multiply or divide the other two.

devices that do work — produce light, heat, or motion.

- *The atomic structure of the material* — If the material has few free electrons, it is a poor conductor. Resistance to current flow will be high. All conductors have some resistance, but the resistance of a good conductor is so small that a fraction of a volt will cause current flow.
- *The length of the conductor* — Electrons in motion are constantly colliding with the atoms of the conductor. The longer a piece of wire, the greater the number of collisions that will occur, and the higher the resistance of the conductor.
- *The cross-sectional area of the conductor* — The thinner a piece of wire is, the higher its resistance will be.
- *The temperature of the conductor* — In most cases, the higher the temperature of the conducting material, the higher its resistance will be. That is why alternator regulators are tested at normal operating temperature for accurate readings.
- *The condition of the conductor* — If a wire is partially cut, it will act almost as if the entire wire were of a smaller diameter, offering a high resistance at the damaged point. Loose or corroded connections have the same effect. High resistance at connections is a major cause of electrical problems.

Voltage Drop and Resistance

Because every electrical load in a circuit offers some resistance, voltage is reduced as it moves the current through each load. Voltage is electrical energy, and as it moves current through a load, some of the electrical energy is changed to another form of energy, such as light, heat, or motion.

If you measure the voltage on both sides of a load, you can see how much voltage has been used to move current through the load. This is called **voltage drop**. If you measure the voltage drop at every load in a circuit and add the measurements, they will equal the original voltage available. No voltage disappears; it is just changed into a different form of energy by the resistance of the load.

The resistance of any electrical part (load or conductor) can be measured in two ways:

- Direct measurement with an instrument called an **ohmmeter**, which measures the resistance (in ohms) offered by the part.
- Indirect measurement with an instrument called a **voltmeter**, which measures the voltage drop through the part.

These measurements are explained in Chapter Two of the *Shop Manual*, along with the use of an **ammeter** to measure current flow. While voltage and resistance are measured in different units, they are directly related. As the resistance of a load increases, the voltage drop across the load also increases. If you know either the voltage drop or the resistance (plus the amperage), you can calculate the other, using Ohm's Law, as explained in the next section. If you know *both* the voltage drop and the resistance, you can also calculate the current.

OHM'S LAW

We introduced one way of stating Ohm's Law when we said:

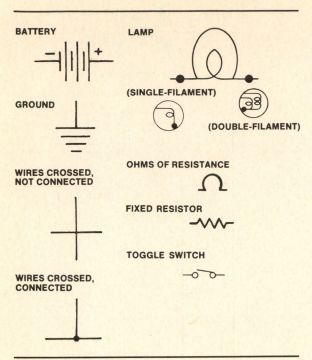

Figure 1-14. Some common electrical symbols.

When a force of *one volt* pushes *one ampere* of current through a circuit, the resistance present is *one ohm*, figure 1-12.

Ohm stated this relationship as a simple mathematical formula that can be written three ways:

- Volts = amperes multiplied by ohms
  $$E = I \times R$$
- Amperes = volts divided by ohms
  $$I = E \div R$$
- Ohms = volts divided by amperes
  $$R = E \div I$$

Traditionally, the equations are shown with amperes (current) abbreviated as I, for "intensity", voltage as E, for "electromotive force", and resistance as R. When any two of the values are known for a circuit, the third can be found using Ohm's Law. The law will make electrical testing easier if you know how to use it. An easy way to remember Ohm's Law is shown in figure 1-13. If you cover the unknown factor, you will see the formula to use in finding it.

We will now look at the three types of circuits — series, parallel, and series-parallel — and see how to apply Ohm's Law to each of them. We will illustrate these circuits in pictures and use symbols to represent different parts. These illustrations are called diagrams. Some common symbols and their meanings are shown in figure 1-14.

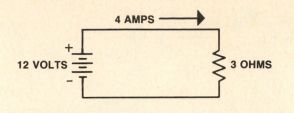

Figure 1-15. A simple series circuit.

SERIES CIRCUIT

In a **series circuit**, the current has only one path to follow. In figure 1-15, using conventional current flow theory, you can see that the current must flow from the battery, through the resistor, and back to the battery. The circuit must be continuous, or have **continuity**. If one wire is disconnected from the battery, the circuit is broken and no current can flow. If electrical loads are wired in series, they must all be switched on and working, or the circuit will be broken and none of them will work. A simplified example of a series circuit in a car is shown in figure 1-16. Current flows from the battery, through the horn switch, through the horn, and then back to the battery.

Series Circuits and Ohm's Law

Ohm's Law can easily be applied to a series circuit. If any two of the values are known, the third can be figured out using Ohm's Law. Some features of a series circuit are:

- Current is the same everywhere in the circuit. Since there is only one path for current flow, the same amount of current must be flowing in all parts of the circuit.

Voltage Drop: The measurement of the loss of voltage caused by the resistance of a conductor or a circuit device.

Ohmmeter: A meter used to measure resistance to current flow.

Voltmeter: A meter used to measure electromotive force in volts.

Ammeter: A meter used to measure electrical current flow in amperes.

Series Circuit: A circuit that has only one path through which current can flow.

Continuity: Continuous, unbroken. Used to describe a working electrical circuit or component that is not open.

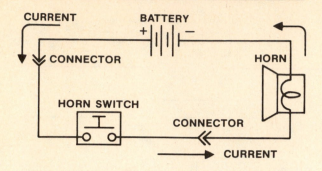

Figure 1-16. This horn circuit diagram illustrates a simple series circuit.

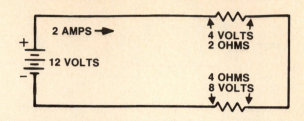

Figure 1-17. A series circuit with more than one resistor.

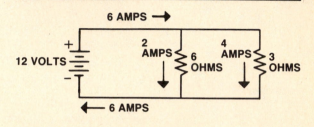

Figure 1-18. A parallel circuit.

- Voltage drops may vary from load to load if the individual resistances vary, but the sum of all the voltage drops in the series equals the original source voltage.
- The total resistance (R_t) is the sum of all the individual resistances in the series.

In figure 1-15, the simple circuit consists of a 3-ohm resistor connected to a 12-volt battery. The amperage can be found by using Ohm's Law:

$$E \div R = I$$
$$12 \div 3 = 4 \text{ amperes}$$

When we know the current and the individual resistances of a series circuit, we can calculate the voltage drop across each load. The sum of these drops equals the source voltage. For the two-ohm resistor in figure 1-17:

$$I \times R = E$$
$$2 \times 2 = 4 \text{ volts}$$

For the four-ohm resistor in figure 1-17:

$$I \times R = E$$
$$2 \times 4 = 8 \text{ volts}$$

The sum of the voltage drops is 4 volts + 8 volts = 12 volts, which is the source voltage.

PARALLEL CIRCUITS

When current can follow more than one path to complete a circuit, that circuit is called a **parallel circuit**. The points where current paths split and rejoin are called junction points. The separate paths which split and meet at junction points are called branch circuits or **shunt** circuits. A parallel circuit is shown in figure 1-18. In an automobile, the headlamps are wired in parallel with each other, figure 1-19.

Parallel Circuits and Ohm's Law

The features of a parallel circuit are:

- The voltage applied to, or measured across, each branch of the circuit is the same.
- The total current in a parallel circuit is the sum of the current in each branch.
- The total resistance (R_t) of a parallel circuit is always less than the lowest individual resistance. The reason is that when you add resistors in parallel, you are actually adding more conductors, or paths in which current can flow, which reduces the total resistance.

There are two ways to calculate the total resistance, or **equivalent resistance**, in a parallel circuit. One formula for any number of resistors is:

$$R_t = \frac{1}{\dfrac{1}{R_1} + \dfrac{1}{R_2} + \dfrac{1}{R_3} + \cdots + \dfrac{1}{R_n}}$$

For the circuit illustrated in figure 1-18:

$$R = \frac{1}{\dfrac{1}{6} + \dfrac{1}{3}} = \frac{1}{\dfrac{1}{6} + \dfrac{2}{6}} = \frac{1}{\dfrac{3}{6}} = \frac{1}{\dfrac{1}{2}} = \frac{1}{0.5} = 2 \text{ ohms}$$

Another way to calculate total resistance is the product-over-the-sum method:

$$R_1 = \frac{R_1 \times R_2}{R_1 + R_2}$$

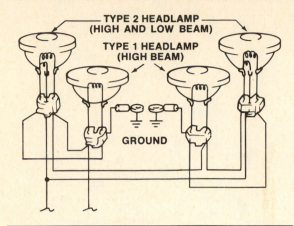

Figure 1-19. The headlamps are wired in parallel with each other in all headlamp circuits.

This formula can only be used for two resistances at a time. If more than two are wired in parallel, you must calculate their values in pairs until you determine one total resistance for the circuit. For the circuit in figure 1-18:

$$R_1 = \frac{6 \times 3}{6 + 3} = \frac{18}{9} = 2 \text{ ohms.}$$

To apply Ohm's Law to a parallel circuit, sometimes you must treat branches as independent circuits and sometimes you must deal with the entire circuit, depending upon which values are unknown.

To find current, you must treat each branch separately because of the different current flow in each branch. Voltage is applied equally across all branches, so the source voltage is divided by the branch resistance to determine the current through that branch. Adding the current in all the branches gives the total current in the circuit. In the circuit shown, figure 1-18, current through the six-ohm resistor is:

$$E \div R = I$$
$$12 \text{ volts} \div 6 \text{ ohms} = 2 \text{ amps}$$

Through the 3-ohm resistor, it is:

$$E \div R = I$$
$$12 \text{ volts} \div 3 \text{ ohms} = 4 \text{ amps}$$

Total circuit current is 2 amps + 4 amps = 6 amps.

If resistance of a branch is unknown, dividing the source voltage by the branch current gives the branch resistance. In figure 1-18, for the first branch:

$$R_1 = 12 \text{ volts} \div 2 \text{ amps} = 6 \text{ ohms}$$

For the second branch:

$$R_2 = 12 \text{ volts} \div 4 \text{ amps} = 3 \text{ ohms}$$

Total resistance of the circuit can be calculated using the product-over-the-sum method:

$$R_t = \frac{6 \text{ ohms} \times 3 \text{ ohms}}{6 \text{ ohms} + 3 \text{ ohms}} = \frac{18}{9} = 2 \text{ ohms}$$

Or, if all you need is the equivalent circuit resistance, divide the source voltage by the total circuit amperage as follows:

$$R_t = 12 \text{ volts} \div 6 \text{ amps} = 2 \text{ ohms}$$

Parallel Circuit: A circuit that has more than one path through which current can flow.

Shunt: Parallel. An electrical connection or branch circuit in parallel with another branch circuit or connection.

Equivalent Resistance: The total resistance of a parallel circuit. The single mathematical equivalent of all the parallel resistance.

■ Kirchoff's Laws

Another 19th-century German physicist, named Gustav Robert Kirchoff, discovered two laws about the actions of current and voltage. Knowing these laws can help your understanding of electrical circuits. Kirchoff's *voltage law* says:

> The sum of the voltage drops across all the devices in a series circuit must equal the source voltage.

Remember when you test a circuit that all of the voltage delivered to the circuit by the battery or alternator must be used up in doing work in the circuit. If you have a 12-volt battery connected to one lamp bulb, the voltage drop across the bulb must be the whole 12 volts. If the battery is connected to two or more bulbs, the drops across all the bulbs and the wires and connectors, must add up to 12 volts. No voltage can be left over at the end of the circuit.

Kirchoff's *current law* deals with current flow at any point in a circuit. It says:

> The sum of the currents flowing into any point in a circuit equals the sum of the currents flowing out of that point.

This is seen easiest in a parallel circuit. It simply means that the sum of the currents flowing in the branches of a circuit must equal the total current flowing to and from the source. Kirchoff's current law is a statement of the conservation of matter. Electrical current is electron flow, and electrons are matter. You can't create or destroy electrons in a circuit. Remember when testing a parallel circuit, all the amperage in the branch circuits must add up to the amperage leaving and returning to the source.

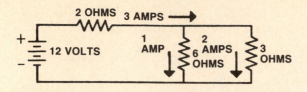

Figure 1-20. A series-parallel circuit.

To determine source voltage, multiply the total circuit current by the total circuit resistance. Or, since the voltage is the same across all branches, multiply one branch current by the same branch resistance. In figure 1-18:

$$I \times R = E$$
$$6 \text{ amps} \times 2 \text{ ohms} = 12 \text{ volts}$$

Or, (branch I) $\times$ (branch R) = E:

Branch 1: $2 \times 6 = 12$ volts
Branch 2: $4 \times 3 = 12$ volts

SERIES-PARALLEL CIRCUITS

As the name suggests, **series-parallel circuits** combine the two types of circuits already discussed. Some of the loads are wired in series, but there are also some loads wired in parallel, figure 1-20. The entire headlamp circuit of an automobile is a series-parallel circuit, figure 1-21. The headlamps are in parallel with each other, but the switches are in series with the battery and with each lamp. Both lamps are controlled by the switches, but one lamp will still light if the other is burned out. Most of the circuits in an automobile electrical system are series-parallel.

Series-Parallel Circuits and Ohm's Law

Values in a series-parallel circuit are figured by reducing the parallel branches to equivalent values for single loads in series. Then the equivalent values and any actual series loads are combined.

To calculate total resistance, first find the resistance of all loads wired in parallel. If the circuit is complex, it may be handy to group the parallel branches into pairs and treat each pair separately. Then add the values of all loads wired in series to the equivalent resistance of all the loads wired in parallel. In the circuit shown in figure 1-20:

$$R_t = \left(\frac{6 \times 3}{6 + 3}\right) + 2 = \frac{18}{9} + 2 = 4 \text{ ohms}$$

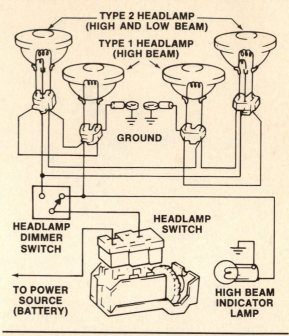

Figure 1-21. A complete headlamp circuit, with all bulbs and switches, is a series-parallel circuit.

In the illustration, the equivalent resistance of the loads in parallel is:

$$\frac{6 \times 3}{6 + 3} = \frac{18}{9} = 2 \text{ ohms}$$

The total of the branch currents is $1 + 2 = 3$ amps, so the voltage drop is:

$$I \times R = E$$
$$3 \times 2 = 6$$

The voltage drop across the load in series is $2 \times 3 = 6$ volts. Add these voltage drops to find the source voltage:

$$6 + 6 = 12 \text{ volts}$$

To determine the source voltage in a series-parallel circuit, you must first find the equivalent resistance of the loads in parallel, and the total current flowing through this equivalent resistance. Figure out the voltage drop across this equivalent resistance and add it to the voltage drops across all loads wired in series.

To determine total current, find the currents in all parallel branches and add them together. This total is equal to the current flowing at any point in the series circuit. In figure 1-20:

$$I = \frac{E}{R_1} + \frac{E}{R_2} = \frac{6}{6} + \frac{6}{3} = 1 + 2 = 3 \text{ amps}$$

Notice that there are only six volts across each of the branch circuits because another six volts

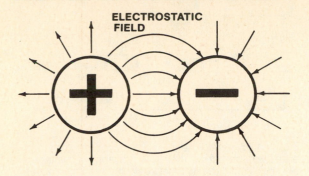

ELECTROSTATIC FIELD

Figure 1-22. An electrostatic field exists between two charged bodies.

have already been "dropped" across the two-ohm series resistor.

WATTS — ELECTRIC POWER

We have learned that voltage is the ability to do work. It is the electromotive force that causes current to flow. Voltage, however, is not the same as power. Power is the *rate* of doing work, or the amount of work done per unit of time. The basic formula for calculating any type of power, mechanical or electrical, is the amount of work divided by the time taken to do the work.

Electric power can be calculated easily by multiplying the current by the voltage. The unit for measuring electric power is called the **watt**. The abbreviation for watt is W; however, in power formulas, P is usually used as the symbol for power.

Electric power (watts, or wattage) equals voltage times current. This formula, using abbreviations we have already used, is written simply:

$$P = E \times I$$

We can substitute other values from Ohm's Law into the power formula, if necessary. We know that E = IR, so we can substitute IR for E in the power formula and write:

$$P = (IR)I, \text{ or simply, } P = I_2 R$$

Similarly, we know that I = E ÷ R, so we can substitute E ÷ R for I in the power formula and write:

$$P = \frac{EE}{R}, \text{ or simply, } P = \frac{E2}{R}$$

Up to this point, we have talked about resistors and other electrical devices in terms of their resistance in ohms. Electrical devices, particularly resistors, can be rated in two ways: in ohms of resistance, and in watts of power capacity.

Wattage measurement and wattage ratings in an automotive electrical system are most commonly applied to lighting and accessory circuits and to batteries. The wattage formula can be applied to an entire circuit by multiplying the applied voltage by the total current. It can also tell you the power used by one separate part of a circuit, when the voltage drop across that section is multiplied by the current flowing through that section.

CAPACITANCE

There is another important concept for our understanding of electricity; the concept of an **electrostatic field**. Earlier, we learned about positive and negative charges. We saw that like charges repel each other, while unlike charges attract each other. This action of like and unlike charges leads to the assumption that each charged body has an electrostatic field around it consisting of invisible lines of

Series-Parallel Circuit: A circuit that has some parts in series with the voltage source and some parts in parallel with each other and with the voltage source.

Watt: The unit of measurement for electric power. One way to measure the rate of doing work. Watts equals volts times amperes.

Electrostatic Field: The area around an electrically charged body resulting from the difference in voltage between two points or surfaces.

■ **Watts = Metric Horsepower**

When it comes to automobiles, the unit traditionally used to measure the rate of doing work has been the horsepower. It does not relate to the work done by a single horse, but it has become a standardized unit of measure.

While "horsepower" is still commonly used, there is another way to describe the rate of doing work, and that is the "watt". Since it is part of the metric system, the watt is beginning to come into use as the system is gradually adopted.

One horsepower contains (equals) 746 watts. A Chevrolet 4.1-liter (250-cid) engine, for example, would be rated at 110 kW at 3,800 rpm. That equals 147 horsepower. The abbreviation "kW" stands for kilowatt (1,000 watts). The prefix "kilo" (k) is used in the metric system to mean 1,000.

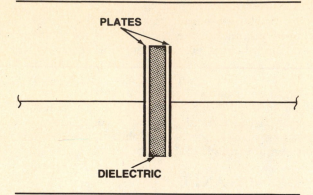

Figure 1-23. A simple capacitor.

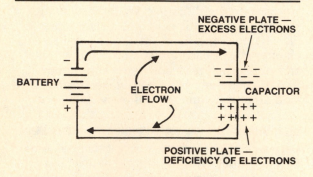

Figure 1-24. As the capacitor is charging, the battery forces electrons through the circuit.

force, figure 1-22. According to the laws affecting charged bodies, the closer they are to each other, the stronger the force becomes between them. As the bodies move farther apart, the force weakens. An electrostatic field results from a difference in potential, or voltage, between two points or surfaces.

Capacitance is the ability of two conducting surfaces (charged bodies), separated by some kind of insulator, to store an electric charge (voltage). A capacitor, then, is a device that will store electricity when it is installed in a circuit.

Capacitor Construction and Operation

A capacitor consists of two conductive plates with an insulating material between them, figure 1-23. The insulating material is commonly called a **dielectric**. It may be air, mica, ceramic, glass, paper, plastic, or any similar nonconductive material. When a capacitor is placed in a closed circuit, the voltage source (battery) forces electrons around the circuit, figure 1-24. Because electrons cannot flow through the dielectric of the capacitor, excess electrons collect on what becomes the negatively charged plate.

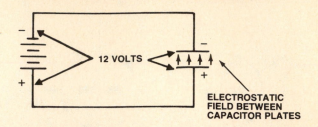

Figure 1-25. When the capacitor is charged, there is equal voltage across the capacitor and the battery. An electrostatic field exists between the capacitor plates. No current flows in the circuit.

At the same time the other plate loses electrons and becomes, therefore, positively charged.

Current flows until the voltage charge across the capacitor plates becomes the same as the source voltage. At that time, the negative plate of the capacitor and the negative terminal of the battery are at the same negative potential. The positive plate of the capacitor and the positive terminal of the battery are also at equal positive potentials. There is then a voltage charge across the battery terminals and an equal voltage charge across the capacitor plates, figure 1-25. The circuit is in balance, and no current will flow. An electrostatic field now exists between the capacitor plates because of their opposite charges. It is this field that stores energy.

At this point, the circuit can be opened, and the capacitor will hold its charge until it is connected into an external circuit through which it can discharge, figure 1-26. When the charged capacitor is connected to an external circuit, it will discharge. After discharging, both plates of the capacitor are neutral. It is important to remember that a capacitor does not change any energy or consume any power, as a circuit load does. All the energy from a circuit stored in a capacitor is returned when it is discharged.

Theoretically, a capacitor will hold its charge indefinitely. Actually, the charge will slowly leak off the capacitor through the dielectric. The better the dielectric, the longer the capacitor will hold its charge. To avoid an electrical shock, any capacitor should be treated as if it were charged until it is proven to be discharged.

Capacitors are also called **condensers**. This term developed because electric charges collect, or condense, on the plates of a capacitor much like water vapor collects and condenses on a cold bottle or glass.

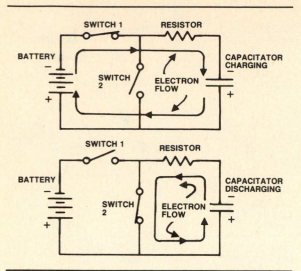

Figure 1-26. The capacitor is charged through one circuit (top) and discharged through another (bottom).

Capacitor Ratings

Capacitors are rated in units called **farads**. The abbreviation for farad is: F. In reality, one farad is a very large charge, and a capacitor rated at one farad might be the size of a railroad box car. Capacitors used in automotive electrical systems are rated in microfarads, or one-millionth (0.000001) of a farad, abbreviated: μF.

Just as resistors are rated in terms of their resistance (ohms) and their power-handling capabilities (watts), capacitors are rated in terms of their maximum safe working voltage, as well as their capacitance.

We learned earlier that resistance is a physical property of a resistor. A single resistor will have the same ohm rating in any circuit in which it is used. Similarly, capacitance is a physical property of a capacitor, and this value will not change in any circuit. We also learned that there are physical factors that affect the resistance of a resistor. There are similar factors that affect the capacitance of a capacitor.

Factors of Capacitance

Capacitance is governed by three factors:

- The surface area of the plates
- The distance between the plates
- The dielectric material.

The larger the surface area of the plates, the greater the capacitance will be. This is because more electrons can collect on a large plate area than on a small one.

The closer the plates are to each other, the greater the capacitance will be. This is because a stronger electrostatic field exists between charged bodies that are close together.

The insulating qualities of the dielectric material also affect capacitance. The capacitance of a capacitor is higher if the dielectric is a very good insulator.

Types of Capacitors

Capacitors are designed with either fixed or variable capacitance. The common symbols for fixed and variable capacitors are shown in figure 1-27. The capacitance of a variable capacitor is usually changed by altering the plate area or the distance between the plates.

Some fixed capacitors used in radio and electronic circuits are small ceramic units with short wire leads that are soldered into a circuit. The most common fixed capacitor found in automotive electrical systems in the days of igni-

Capacitance: The ability of two conducting surfaces, separated by an insulator, to store an electric charge.

Dielectric: The insulating material between the two conductive plates of a capacitor.

Condenser: A capacitor. Usually refers to an automotive capacitor constructed of two pieces of tinfoil, separated by an insulator, within a metal can.

Farad: The unit of measurement of capacitance.

■ **Capacitance Is All Around Us**

The ignition condenser is probably the most familiar capacitor in an automobile, but the largest is the car's battery. A 12-volt automotive battery is also a 12-volt capacitor. Because a difference in potential exists between the positive and negative plates of a battery, they act as a capacitor. This is one reason why a battery stores a voltage charge.

High-tension electric power lines can also act as a capacitor. The power lines carry very high voltages and act like the plates of a capacitor. The air space between the lines acts as a dielectric. During a rainstorm, when water vapor reduces the insulating qualities of the air space, you can often see a blue halo around power lines. This is the "corona effect" of the electrostatic field between the lines.

A similar halo can sometimes be seen around the spark plug cables of an automobile. Spark plug cables carry high ignition voltages and can also act like the plates of a capacitor, particularly when they lie parallel and close to each other. The glow often seen around the cables is another example of an electrostatic field.

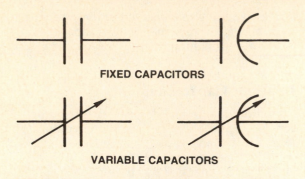

FIXED CAPACITORS

VARIABLE CAPACITORS

Figure 1-27. You will see these capacitor symbols on electrical diagrams. The negative plate is often shown curved.

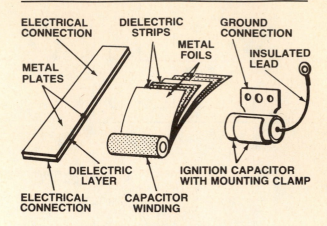

Figure 1-28. Cylindrical capacitors are the most common fixed capacitors for automotive use.

tion points was the cylindrical type, figure 1-28. The plates were two layers of metal foil, with a dielectric between them, rolled into a cylinder. Contacts were attached to the plates, and the capacitor sealed in a metal shell. A wire lead was attached to the contact for one plate for connection to the insulated side of the circuit. The contact for the other plate was attached to the capacitor shell and connected to the ground side of the circuit through a mounting clamp.

Capacitor Uses

Because a capacitor will store a voltage charge, it will oppose, or slow down, any voltage change in a circuit. Therefore, capacitors are often used as voltage "shock absorbers". You will sometimes find a capacitor attached to one terminal of an ignition coil. In this application, it absorbs and damps changes in ignition voltage that can interfere with radio reception.

Probably the most familiar capacitor in an automobile is the ignition condenser in breaker-point ignition systems. The condenser is installed in parallel with the ignition breaker points. The points are a rotating switch that opens and closes the circuit to the ignition coil. When the points open, self-induced voltage in the coil tries to keep current flowing across the opening points. This would cause an arc across the points and burn them up very quickly. However, the condenser, in parallel with the points, provides an easier path for current flow and reduces or eliminates point arcing.

The self-induced voltage from the coil charges the condenser instead of arcing across the point. As the condenser is charged, coil primary voltage drops. The condenser then discharges back into the coil. This current flow from the condenser to the coil aids the buildup

of the coil magnetic field as the points close and primary current flow resumes.

SUMMARY

Materials used in electrical systems are conductors, insulators, or semiconductors. Conductors have three or fewer free electrons in the outer shell of their atoms. Electric current is the controlled, directed flow of electrons from atom to atom in a conductor. Insulators have five or more bound electrons in their outer shells. Current does not flow easily in an insulator. Semiconductors have four electrons in their outer shells. Current can be made to flow in a semiconductor under certain conditions.

There are two theories of electric current flow. The conventional current flow theory says that current flows from positive to negative. The electron current flow theory says that current flows from negative to positive. Either theory can be used to describe current flow in a circuit.

A circuit is a complete path from an electrical energy source, through wires and electrical loads, and back to the source. A complete circuit is necessary for current to flow. Current is measured in amperes and flows *through* a circuit. Voltage is *applied to*, or *impressed on* a circuit. Resistance, measured in ohms, opposes current flow and is *contained within* the circuit.

There are three kinds of electrical circuits: series, parallel, and series-parallel. In a series circuit, there is only one current path. In a parallel circuit, there are two or more current paths. A series-parallel circuit has several current paths in parallel with each other, but in series with other parts of the circuit.

Ohm's Law is the foundation of electrical circuit troubleshooting. It says, "When one volt forces one ampere of current through a circuit, one ohm of resistance is present." Mathematically, Ohm's Law says:

Voltage (E) = Current (I) × Resistance (R)
Current (I) = Voltage (E) ÷ Resistance (R)
Resistance (R) = Voltage (E) ÷ Current (I)

Capacitance is the ability of two conducting surfaces (charged bodies), separated by an insulator, to store an electric charge. A capacitor is a device that will store electricity when it is installed in a circuit. An electrostatic field is formed by the difference in potential between the two charged plates of the capacitor. Because a capacitor will store a voltage charge, it will oppose, or slow down, any voltage change in a circuit. Therefore, they are often used as voltage "shock absorbers".

Review Questions

Choose the single most correct answer.
Compare your answers with the correct answers on page 431.

1. The general name given every substance in the physical universe is:
   a. Mass
   b. Matter
   c. Compound
   d. Nucleus

2. The smallest part of an element that retains all of its characteristics is:
   a. An atom
   b. A proton
   c. A compound
   d. A neutron

3. The particles that orbit around the center of an atom are:
   a. Electrons
   b. Molecules
   c. Nucleus
   d. Protons

4. An atom which loses or gains one electron is called:
   a. Balanced
   b. An element
   c. A molecule
   d. A charged particle or ion

5. A material with many free electrons is a good:
   a. Compound
   b. Conductor
   c. Insulator
   d. Semiconductor

6. A material with four electrons in the valence ring is a:
   a. Compound
   b. Insulator
   c. Semiconductor
   d. Conductor

7. The conventional theory of current flow says that current flows:
   a. Randomly
   b. Positive to negative
   c. Negative to positive
   d. None of the above

8. An ampere is a measure of:
   a. Charge
   b. Resistance
   c. Current flow
   d. Difference in potential

9. Voltage is:
   a. Applied to a circuit
   b. Flowing in a circuit
   c. Built into a circuit
   d. Flowing out of a circuit

10. The unit that represents resistance to current flow is:
    a. Ampere
    b. Volt
    c. Ohm
    d. Watt

11. In automotive systems, voltage is supplied by the:
    a. Alternator
    b. Battery
    c. Generator
    d. All of the above

12. Which of the following does *not* affect resistance?
    a. Diameter of the conductor
    b. Temperature of the conductor
    c. Atomic structure of the conductor
    d. Direction of current flow in the conductor

13. The resistance in a longer piece of wire is:
    a. Higher
    b. Lower
    c. Unchanged
    d. Higher, then lower

14. According to Ohm's Law, when one volt pushes one ampere of current through a conductor, the resistance is:
    a. Zero
    b. One ohm
    c. One watt
    d. One coulomb

15. What circuit does this figure illustrate?
    a. Series
    b. Parallel
    c. Series-parallel
    d. Broken

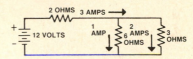

16. Which of the following is an example of a series circuit that might be used in an automobile?
    a. Headlamp
    b. Horn
    c. Taillamp
    d. Stereo

17. The amperage in a series circuit is:
    a. Always the same anywhere
    b. Always the same at certain points
    c. Sometimes the same, under some conditions
    d. Never the same anywhere

18. The sum of the voltage drops in a series circuit equals:
    a. The amperage
    b. The resistance
    c. The source voltage
    d. The shunt circuit voltage

19. The total resistance is equal to the *sum* of all the resistance in:
    a. Series circuits
    b. Parallel circuits
    c. Series-parallel circuits
    d. Series and parallel circuits

20. Where E = volts, I = amperes, and R = resistance, Ohm's Law is written:
    a. $I = E \times R$
    b. $E = I \times R$
    c. $R = E \times I$
    d. $E = I_2 \times R$

21. Where current can follow more than one path to complete the circuit, the circuit is called:
    a. Branch
    b. Series
    c. Complete
    d. Parallel

22. If resistance in a parallel circuit is unknown, dividing the voltage by the branch _____ equals branch resistance.
    a. Amperage
    b. Conductance
    c. Voltage drops
    d. Wattage

23. In a closed circuit with a capacitor, current will continue to flow until the voltage charge across the capacitor plates:
    a. Becomes less than the source voltage
    b. Becomes equal to the source voltage
    c. Becomes greater than the source voltage
    d. Becomes equal to the resistance of the plates

24. Capacitors are also called:
    a. Diodes
    b. Resistors
    c. Condensers
    d. Dielectrics

25. Capacitors are rated in:
    a. Microcoulombs
    b. Megawatts
    c. Microfarads
    d. Milliohms

2

Magnetism, Electro-magnetism, and EMI Suppression

SOURCES OF ELECTRICITY

So far, in discussing voltage sources, we have used automobile batteries and alternators as examples. We have not gone into detail on how voltage and current are created. There are several sources of electrical energy, but only a few of them are used in automotive electrical systems.

Friction

When certain different materials are rubbed together, the friction causes electrons to be transferred from one to the other. Both materials become electrically charged. These charges are not in motion, but stay on the surface where they were deposited. Because the charges are stationary, or static, this type of voltage is called **static electricity**. Vehicle tires rolling on pavement often create static electricity that interferes with radio reception. This is one form of electromagnetic interference, or EMI, as we will see later in this chapter.

Heat

When pieces of two metals are joined together at both ends and one junction is heated, current will flow through the metals. The current is very small, only millionths of an ampere, but this is enough to use in a temperature measuring device called a thermocouple. Some engine temperature sensors operate in this manner. This form of voltage is called **thermoelectricity**.

Light

When certain metals are exposed to light, some of the light energy is transferred to the free electrons of the metal. This excess energy breaks the electrons loose from the surface of the metal. They can be collected and made to flow in a conductor. This **photoelectricity** is widely used in light-measuring devices such as photographers' exposure meters and automatic headlamp dimmers.

Pressure

When subjected to pressure, certain crystals, such as quartz, will develop a potential difference, or voltage, on the crystal faces. This current is used in phonograph pickups, crystal microphones, underwater hydrophones, and certain stethoscopes. The voltage created is called piezoelectricity. Many automobile engine control sensors use **piezoelectricity** to create voltage or to vary resistance and control a computer input signal.

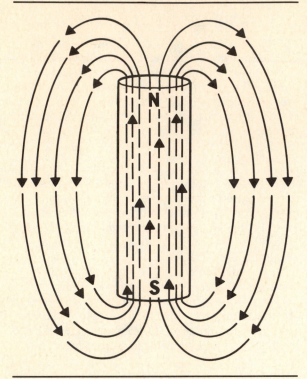

Figure 2-1. Magnetic lines of force surrounding a bar magnet.

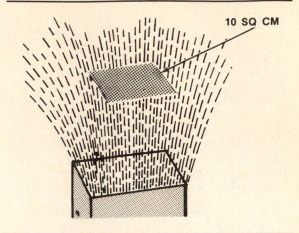

Figure 2-2. Flux density equals the number of lines of force per unit of area.

Chemistry

Two different materials (usually metals) placed in a conducting and reactive chemical solution can create a difference in potential, or voltage, between them. This principle is called **electrochemistry** and is the basis of the automotive battery. We will study this in depth in Chapter Seven.

Magnetism

The lines of force which surround magnetic materials can cause current to flow in a conductor. This chapter will explain magnetism and electromagnetism in detail, because they are vital parts of the automotive electrical system.

FUNDAMENTALS OF MAGNETISM

Magnetism is a form of energy that is caused by the motion of electrons in some materials. It is recognized by the attraction it exerts on other materials. Like electricity, magnetism cannot be seen. It can be explained in theory, and we can see the results of magnetism and recognize the actions that it causes.

Iron ore can exist as a magnet in nature. Many other materials can be artificially magnetized to some degree, depending upon their

atomic structure. Soft iron is very easy to magnetize, while some materials — such as aluminum, glass, wood, and plastic — cannot be magnetized at all.

Lines of Force

The lines that create a field of force around a magnet are believed to be caused by the way groups of atoms are aligned in the magnetic material. In a bar magnet, the lines are concentrated at both ends of the bar and form closed, parallel loops in three dimensions around the magnet, figure 2-1. Force does not flow along these lines like electrical current flows, but the lines *do* have direction. They come out of one end, or pole, and enter at the other end.

The stronger a magnet is, the more lines of force will be formed. The magnetic lines of force form a **magnetic field**. These lines of force are also called **magnetic flux**, or **flux lines**. You will often see the terms ''magnetic field'', ''lines of force'', ''flux'', and ''flux lines'' used interchangeably. In this chapter, we will use ''flux lines''.

Flux density refers to the number of flux lines per unit of area. To determine flux density, divide the number of flux lines by the area in which the flux exists. For example, 100 flux lines divided by an area of 10 square centimeters equals a flux density of 10, figure 2-2.

Polarity

The **poles** of a magnet are called north (N) and south (S) because, when a magnet is suspended freely, the poles tend to point toward the north and south magnetic poles of the earth, figure 2-3. The discovery of this property in

Figure 2-3. A freely suspended natural magnet. (Delco-Remy)

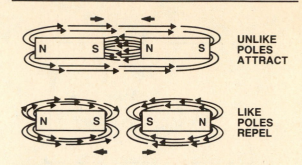

Figure 2-4. Magnetic poles behave like electrically charged particles.

natural magnets led to the development of the compass.

Magnetic flux lines exit from the north pole and bend around to enter the south pole. An equal number of lines exit and enter, so magnetic force is equal at both poles of a magnet. Flux lines are concentrated at the poles, and therefore magnetic force (flux density) is stronger at the ends.

Magnetic poles behave like positively and negatively charged particles. When unlike poles are placed close together, the lines will exit from one magnet and enter the other. The two magnets will be pulled together by the flux lines. If like poles are placed together, the curving flux lines will meet head on, forcing the magnets apart. The like poles of a magnet will repel and the unlike poles will attract, figure 2-4.

Permeability

Magnetic flux lines cannot be insulated. There is no known material through which magnetic force will not pass, if the force is strong enough. However, some materials will allow the force to pass through more easily than others. This ease of passage is called **permeability**. Iron will let magnetic flux lines pass through much more easily than will air, so iron is very permeable.

Reluctance

While there is no absolute insulation for magnetism, certain materials resist the passage of magnetic force. This can be compared to resistance within an electrical circuit. Air does not allow easy passage, so air has a high **reluctance**. Magnetic flux lines will tend to concentrate in permeable materials and avoid reluctant materials, following the path of least resistance.

Static Electricity: Voltage resulting from the transfer of electrons from the surface of one material to the surface of another material. The electrons are "static", meaning at rest.

Thermoelectricity: Voltage resulting from an unequal transfer of electrons from one metal to another, when one of the metals is heated.

Photoelectricity: Voltage caused by the energy of light as it strikes certain materials.

Piezoelectricity: Voltage caused by physical pressure applied to the faces of certain crystals.

Electrochemistry: In a battery, voltage caused by the chemical action of two dissimilar materials in the presence of a conductive chemical solution.

Magnetism: A form of energy caused by the alignment of atoms within certain materials. The ability of a metal to attract iron.

Magnetic Field: The area surrounding a magnet that is influenced by the magnet's energy.

Magnetic Flux: The invisible directional lines of force which make up a magnetic field.

Flux Lines: Another term for magnetic flux.

Flux Density: The number of flux lines in a magnetic field area. The more flux lines in a unit of area, the stronger the magnetic field at that point.

Pole: The areas of a magnetized body where the lines of magnetic force are concentrated. One end of a magnet.

Permeability: A measure of the ease with which materials can be penetrated by magnetic flux lines. Iron is more permeable than air.

Reluctance: The tendency of some materials to resist penetration by magnetic flux lines.

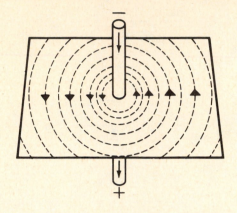

Figure 2-5. A magnetic field surrounds a straight current-carrying conductor. (Delco-Remy)

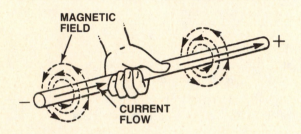

Figure 2-6. The left-hand rule for field direction, used with the electron-flow theory.

Electromagnetism

Not until 1820 did scientists discover that current-carrying conductors also are surrounded by a magnetic field. These fields can be made many times stronger than those surrounding conventional magnets. Also, the magnetic field strength around a conductor can be controlled by changing the current flow. As current flow increases, more flux lines are created and the magnetic field expands. As current flow decreases, the magnetic field contracts, or collapses. These discoveries greatly broadened the practical uses of magnetism and opened an area of study known as **electromagnetics**.

Straight Conductor

The magnetic field surrounding a straight, current-carrying conductor consists of several concentric cylinders of flux the length of the wire, figure 2-5. The strength of the current determines how many flux lines (cylinders) there will be and how far out they will extend from the surface of the wire.

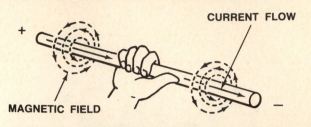

Figure 2-7. The right-hand rule for field direction, used with the conventional theory of electron flow.

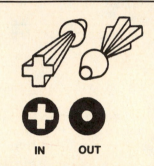

Figure 2-8. Current direction symbols. (Delco-Remy)

Left- and right-hand rules

Magnetic flux cylinders have direction, just as the flux lines surrounding a bar magnet have direction. The **left-hand rule** is a simple way to determine this direction. When you grasp a conductor with your left hand so that your thumb points in the direction of electron flow (– to +) through the conductor, your fingers will curl around the wire in the direction of the magnetic flux lines, figure 2-6.

It is important to note at this point that if we were using the conventional theory of current flow (+ to –), we would use the **right-hand rule** to determine the direction of the magnetic flux lines, figure 2-7. For the rest of this chapter, we will continue to use electron-flow theory and the left-hand rule.

Field Interaction

The cylinders of flux surrounding current-carrying conductors will interact with other magnetic fields. In the following illustrations, the cross symbol (+) indicates current flowing inward, or away from you. It represents the tail of an arrow. The dot symbol (•) represents an arrowhead and indicates current flowing outward, or toward you, figure 2-8. If two conductors carry current in opposite directions, their magnetic fields will be in opposite directions (according to the left-hand rule). If they are placed side by side, figure 2-9, the oppos-

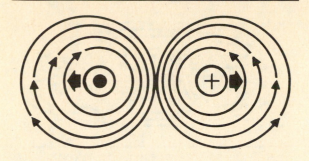

Figure 2-9. Conductors with opposing magnetic fields.

Figure 2-10. Conductors will move apart into weaker fields. (Delco-Remy)

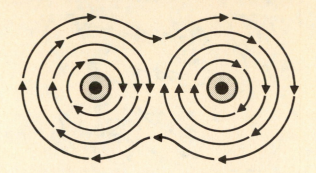

Figure 2-11. Conductors with the same magnetic field direction.

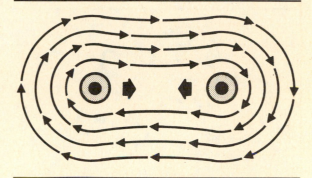

Figure 2-12. Conductors will move together into the weak field.

ing flux lines between the conductors will create a strong magnetic field. Current-carrying conductors tend to move out of a strong field into a weak field, so the conductors will move away from each other, figure 2-10.

If the two conductors carry current in the same direction, their fields will be in the same direction. As you can see in figure 2-11, the flux lines between the two conductors cancel each other out, leaving a very weak field. The conductors will move into this weak field; that is, they will move closer together, figure 2-12.

Motor principle

Electric motors, such as automobile starter motors, use this field interaction to change electrical energy into mechanical energy, figure 2-13. If two conductors carrying current in opposite directions are placed between strong north and south poles, the conductors' magnetic fields will interact with the poles' magnetic fields. The clockwise field of the top conductor will add to the fields of the poles and create a strong field beneath the conductor. The conductor will try to move up to get out of this strong field. The counterclockwise field of the lower conductor will add to the field of the poles and create a strong field above the conductor. The conductor will try to move down to get out of this strong field. These forces will cause the center of the motor, where the conductors are mounted, to turn clockwise.

Loop Conductor

The field around a straight conductor can be strengthened by bending the wire into a loop. This is because, as the wire is bent, the fields

Electromagnetics: The study of the relationship of magnetic energy to electrical energy.

Left-Hand Rule: A method of determining the direction of the magnetic flux lines surrounding a current-carrying conductor, when the electron theory of current flow (– to +) is used. If the conductor is grasped with the left hand so the thumb points in the direction of current flow, the fingers will point in the direction of magnetic flux.

Right-Hand Rule: A method of determining the direction of magnetic flux lines surrounding a current-carrying conductor, when the conventional theory of current flow (+ to –) is used. If the conductor is grasped with the right hand so the thumb points in the direction of conventional current flow, the fingers will point in the direction of magnetic flux.

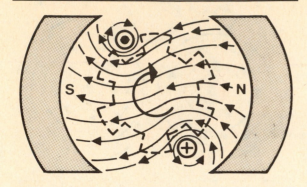

Figure 2-13. Electric motors use field interaction to produce mechanical energy.

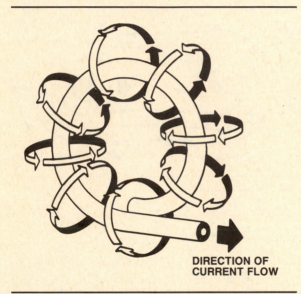

DIRECTION OF CURRENT FLOW

Figure 2-14. The magnetic field surrounding a looped conductor. (Delco-Remy)

which meet in the center of the loop will combine their strengths, figure 2-14. The left-hand rule also applies to loop conductors.

Coil Conductor

If several loops of wire are made into a coil, the magnetic flux density is further strengthened. Flux lines around a coil are the same as the flux lines around a bar magnet, figure 2-15. They exit from the north pole and enter at the south pole. You can use the left-hand rule to determine the north pole of a coil. If you grasp a coil with your left hand so that your fingers point in the direction of electron flow, your thumb will point toward the north pole of the coil, figure 2-16. The magnetic field of a coil can be strengthened by increasing the number of turns in the wire, by increasing the current flow through the coil, or both.

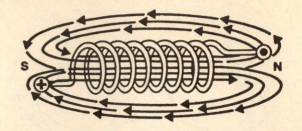

Figure 2-15. The flux lines surrounding a coil look much like those surrounding a bar magnet.

Electromagnets

There is a third way to strengthen the magnetic field surrounding a current-carrying conductor. Because soft iron is very permeable, magnetic flux lines will pass through it easily. If a piece of soft iron is placed inside a coiled conductor, the flux lines will concentrate in the iron core, figure 2-17, rather than pass through the air, which is less permeable. This concentration of force greatly increases the strength of the magnetic field inside the coil. Coils with an iron core are called **electromagnets**.

Relays

One common use of electromagnets is in a device called a **relay**. A relay is a control device which allows a small amount of current to trigger the flow of a large amount of current. You can think of it as a remote-control switch. A simple relay, figure 2-18, would contain an electromagnetic coil in series with a battery and a switch. Near the electromagnet is a movable flat blade, or **armature**, of some material which is attracted by a magnetic field. The armature pivots at one end and is held a small distance away from the electromagnet by a spring (or by the spring steel of the armature itself). A contact point, made of a good conductor, is attached to the free end of the armature. Another contact point is fixed a small distance away. The two contact points are wired in series with an electrical load and the battery.

When the switch in figure 2-18 is closed:

1. Current flows from the battery through the electromagnet.
2. The magnetic field created by the current attracts the armature, bending it down until the contact points meet.
3. Closing the contacts allows current to flow in the second circuit from the battery to the load.

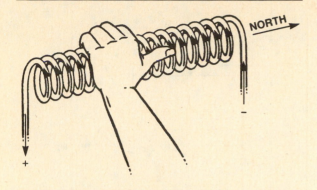

Figure 2-16. The left-hand rule for a coil.

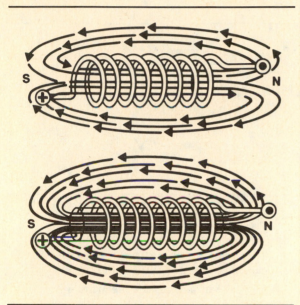

Figure 2-17. An iron core concentrates the magnetic flux lines surrounding a coil.

When the switch is open:

1. The electromagnet looses its current and its magnetic field.
2. Spring pressure brings the armature back.
3. The second circuit is broken by the opening of the contact points.

Relays can also be designed with normally closed contacts that open when current flows through the electromagnet.

ELECTROMAGNETIC INDUCTION

Only a decade after the discovery of magnetic fields surrounding current-carrying conductors, more discoveries were made about the relationship between electricity and magnetism. The modern automotive electrical system is based in great part upon the principles of **electromagnetic induction**, discovered in the 1830s.

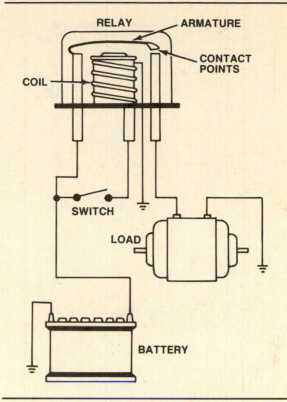

Figure 2-18. An electromagnetic relay.

Magnetic flux lines can create an electromotive force, or voltage, in a conductor if either the flux lines or the conductor is moving. This movement is called **relative motion**. This process is called induction, and the resulting elec-

Electromagnet: A soft iron core wrapped in a coil of a current-carrying conductor.

Relay: An electromagnetic switch. A relay uses a small amount of current flow to control the flow of a larger amount of current through a separate circuit.

Armature: The movable part in a relay. The revolving part in a generator or motor.

Electromagnetic Induction: The creation of a voltage within a conductor when relative motion exists between the conductor and a magnetic field.

Relative Motion: Movement of a conductor in relation to magnetic flux lines or movement of magnetic flux lines in relation to a conductor.

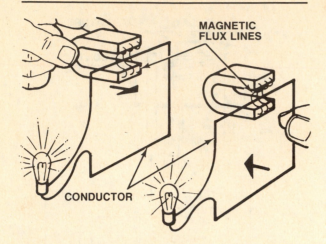

Figure 2-19. Voltage can be induced by the relative motion between a conductor and magnetic flux lines.

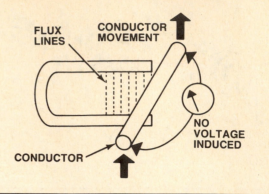

Figure 2-20. No voltage is induced if no flux lines are cut. (Delco-Remy)

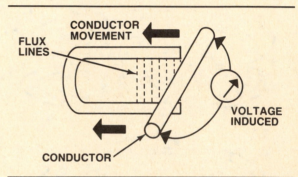

Figure 2-21. Maximum voltage is induced when the flux lines are cut at a 90-degree angle. (Delco-Remy)

tromotive force is called **induced voltage**. If the conductor is in a complete circuit, current will flow.

Voltage is induced when magnetic flux lines are cut by a conductor. This relative motion can be a conductor moving across a magnetic field (as in a d.c. generator), or a magnetic field moving across a stationary conductor (as in a.c. generators and alternators, and ignition coils), figure 2-19. In both cases, the induced voltage is caused by relative motion between the conductor and the magnetic flux lines.

Voltage Strength

Induced voltage depends upon magnetic flux lines being cut by a conductor. The strength of the voltage depends upon the rate at which the flux lines are cut. The more flux lines cut per unit of time, the greater will the be be the induced voltage. If a single conductor cuts one million flux lines per second, one volt will be induced.

There are four ways to increase induced voltage:

• Increase the strength of the magnetic field, so there are more flux lines to be cut.
• Increase the number of conductors which are cutting the flux lines.
• Increase the speed of the relative motion between the conductor and the flux lines so that more lines are cut per time unit.
• Increase the angle between the flux lines and the conductor to a maximum of 90 degrees. There will be no voltage induced if the conductors move parallel to, and do not cut any, flux lines, figure 2-20. Maximum voltage is induced if the conductors cut flux lines at 90 degrees, figure 2-21. In-

duced voltage varies proportionately at angles between zero and 90 degrees.

We know voltage can be electromagnetically induced, and we can measure it and predict its behavior. Induced voltage can cause current to flow. The direction of induced voltage (and the direction in which current flows) is called **polarity** and depends upon the direction of the flux lines and the direction of relative motion.

An induced current will flow so that its magnetic field opposes the motion which induced the current. This principle, called Lenz's Law, is based upon Newton's observation that every action has an equal and opposite reaction. The relative motion of a conductor and a magnetic field is opposed by the magnetic field of the current it has induced. This is why induced current can flow in either direction, and it is an important factor in the design and operation of voltage sources such as alternators.

Generator Principles

As we said earlier, voltage can be induced by the motion of a conductor across a stationary magnetic field. This is the principle used to change mechanical energy to electrical energy in a generator. A looped conductor is mechani-

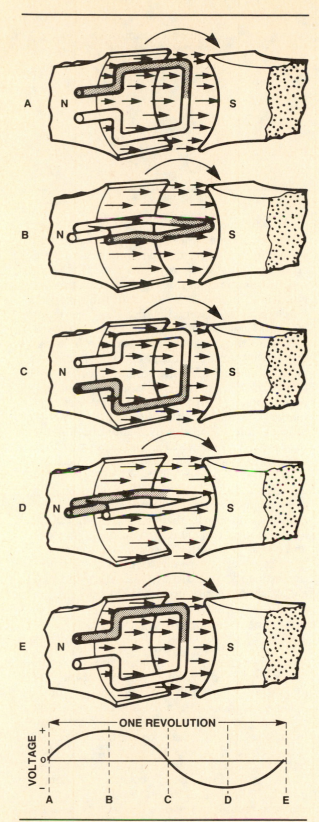

Figure 2-22. Alternating current voltage generated in a rotating loop conductor.

cally moved within the magnetic field created by stationary magnets, figure 2-22. In figure 2-22A, the voltage is zero because the conductor motion is parallel to the flux lines. As the conductor moves from A to B, the voltage increases because it is cutting across the flux lines. At B, the voltage is at a maximum because the conductor is moving at right angles to the flux lines, cutting the maximum number.

From position B to C, the voltage decreases to zero again because fewer lines are cut. At C, the conductor is again parallel to the flux lines. As the conductor rotates from C to D, voltage increases. However, the induced voltage is in the opposite direction because the conductor is cutting the flux lines in the opposite direction. From position D to E, the cycle begins to repeat.

Figure 2-22 shows how voltage is induced in a loop conductor through one complete revolution in a magnetic field. The induced voltage is called **alternating current** (a.c.) voltage because it reverses direction every half cycle, as shown on the graph at the bottom of the figure.

Induced Voltage: The voltage which appears in a conductor when relative motion exists between it and magnetic flux lines.

Polarity: Having poles, such as the north and south poles of a magnet. The poles of a battery or an electrical circuit are its positive and negative terminals.

Alternating Current: A flow of electricity through a conductor, first in one direction and then in the opposite direction.

■ Benjamin Franklin's Theory

When the science of electricity was still young, the men who studied it were able to use electricity without really understanding why and how it worked. In the early 1700s, Benjamin Franklin, the American printer, inventor, writer, and politician brought his famed common sense to the problem.

Although he was not the first to think that electricity and lightning were the same, he was the first to prove it. He also thought that electricity was like a fluid in a pipe that flowed from one terminal to the other. He named the electrical terminals *positive* and *negative* and suggested that current moved from the positive terminal to the negative terminal.

It was Benjamin Franklin who created what we now call the *Conventional Theory of Current Flow*.

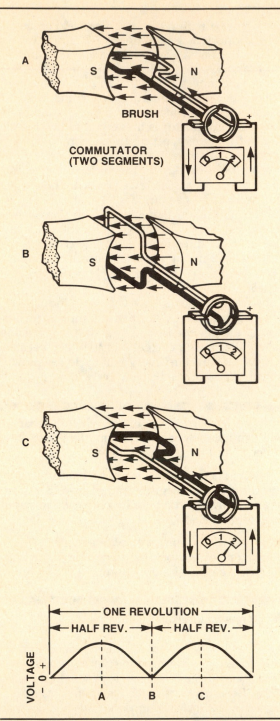

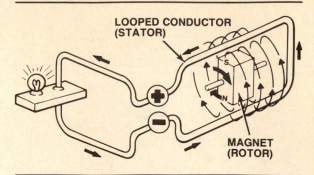

Figure 2-24. A simplified alternator.

single-loop generator, the commutator would be a split ring of conductive material connected to the ends of the conductor. Brushes of conductive material ride on the surface of the two commutator segments. Induced current flows from the conductor through the commutator and out through the brushes, figure 2-23A. At the instant the looped conductor is turned so that the induced current changes direction, figure 2-23B, the commutator also rotates under the brushes so that the brushes now contact the opposite commutator segments. Current now flows out of the other half of the commutator, but the same brush is there to receive it, figure 2-23C. This design is called a brush-rectified, or commutator-rectified, generator, and the output is called pulsating direct current.

Simple pulsating d.c. from one generator winding and a pair of commutator segments would not work well to run electrical devices and recharge a battery. Actual d.c. generators have many armature windings and commutator segments. The d.c. voltages overlap to create an almost continuous d.c. output.

Alternator Principles

Since 1960 virtually all automobiles have used an a.c. generator, or alternator, in which voltage is generated by the movement of magnetic lines through a stationary conductor, figure 2-24. A magnet called a rotor is turned inside a stationary looped conductor called a stator, figure 2-24. The induced current, like that of a d.c. generator, is constantly changing its direction of flow. The rotation of the magnetic field causes the stator to be cut by flux lines, first in one direction and then the other. The a.c. must be rectified to match the battery d.c. This is done with diodes, small electronic devices which conduct current in only one direction. This design is called a diode-rectified alternator. We will study diodes in Chapter Three and alternators in Chapter Eight.

Figure 2-23. The commutator and brushes conduct pulsating direct current from the looped conductor.

Because automotive battery voltage is always in one direction, the current it produces always flows in one direction. This is called **direct current** (d.c.). Alternating current cannot be used to charge the battery, so the a.c. must be changed, or **rectified** to d.c. This is done in a generator by the **commutator**. In a simple,

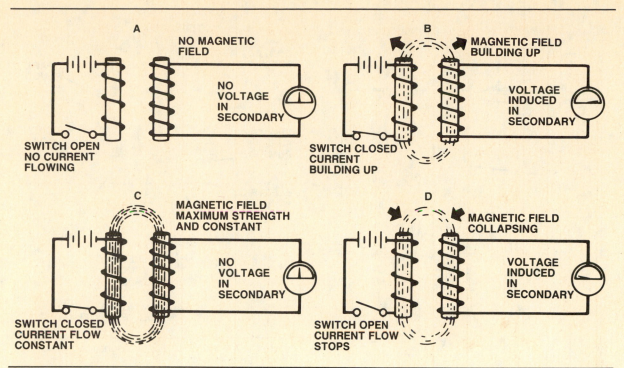

Figure 2-25. Mutual induction.

Self-Induction

Up to this point, our examples have depended upon mechanical energy to physically move either the conductor or the magnetic field. Another form of relative motion occurs when a magnetic field is forming or collapsing. When current begins to flow in a coil, the flux lines expand as the magnetic field forms and strengthens. As current increases, the flux lines continue to expand, cutting through the wires of the coil and actually inducing another voltage within the same coil. Following Lenz's Law, this **self-induced voltage** will tend to *oppose any damage* in the current that produces it. If the current continues to increase, the second voltage will oppose the increase. When the current stabilizes, the countervoltage will no longer be induced because there are no more expanding flux lines (no relative motion). When current to the coil is shut off, the collapsing magnetic flux lines will self-induce a voltage in the coil that tries to keep the original current flowing. The self-induced voltage *opposes* and *slows down* the *decrease* in the original current. The self-induced voltage that opposes the source voltage is called **counter-electromotive force (cemf)**.

Mutual Induction

When two coils are close together, energy can be transferred from one to the other by mag-

netic coupling called mutual induction. **Mutual induction** means that the expansion or collapse of the magnetic field around one coil will induce a voltage in the second coil.

Usually, the two coils are wound on the same iron core. One coil winding is connected

Direct Current: A flow of electricity in one direction through a conductor.

Rectify: To change alternating current to direct current.

Commutator: A segmented ring attached to one end of an armature in a d.c. generator or a motor, providing an electrical connection between the armature and the brushes. In a generator, it rectifies the alternating current. In a motor, it provides a direct current path to the armature.

Self-Induced Voltage: Voltage created in a conductor by the magnetic lines of a current through that same conductor.

Counterelectromotive Force (CEMF): An induced voltage that opposes the source voltage and any change (increase or decrease) in the charging current.

Mutual Induction: Creation of voltage in one conductor by the rise and collapse of the magnetic field surrounding another conductor.

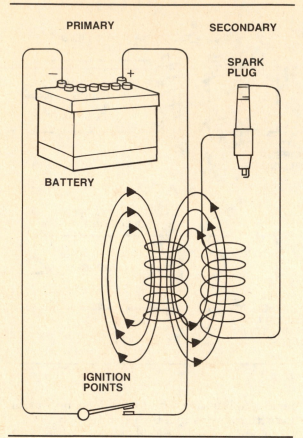

Figure 2-26. Mutual induction in the ignition coil produces voltage to the spark plugs.

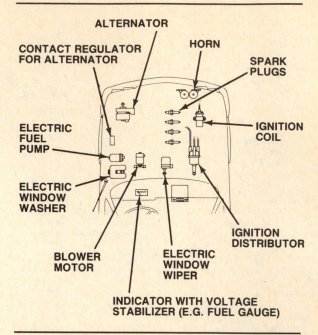

Figure 2-27. Sources of electromagnetic interference (EMI) in an automobile.

to a battery through a switch and is called the **primary winding**. The other coil winding is connected to an external circuit and is called the **secondary winding**.

When the switch is open, figure 2-25A, no current flows in the primary winding. There is no magnetic field and, therefore, no voltage in the secondary winding. When the switch is closed, figure 2-25B, current starts to flow and a magnetic field builds up around both windings. The primary winding thus changes electrical energy from the battery into magnetic energy of the expanding field. As the field expands, it cuts across the secondary winding and induces a voltage in it. A meter connected to the secondary circuit shows current flowing.

When the magnetic field has expanded to its full strength, figure 2-25C, it remains steady as long as the same amount of current continues to flow. The flux lines have stopped their cutting action. There is no relative motion and no voltage in the secondary winding, as shown on the meter.

When the switch is opened, figure 2-25D, primary current flow stops, and the field col-

lapses. As it does, flux lines cut across the secondary winding, but in the opposite direction. This induces a secondary voltage with current flow in the opposite direction, as shown on the meter.

Mutual induction is used in ignition coils, figure 2-26. In an ignition coil, low-voltage primary current induces a very high secondary voltage because of the different number of turns in the primary and secondary windings. We will study ignition coils in detail in Chapter Fourteen.

ELECTROMAGNETIC INTERFERENCE (EMI) SUPPRESSION

Until the advent of the on-board computer, **electromagnetic interference (EMI)** was not a source of real concern to automotive engineers. The problem was mainly one of **radio-frequency interference (RFI)**, caused primarily by the use of secondary ignition cables containing a low-resistance metal core. These cables produced electrical impulses that interfered with radio and television reception.

The problem was recognized in the 1950s and brought under control by the use of secondary ignition cables containing a high-resistance, nonmetallic core made of carbon, linen, or fiber glass strands impregnated with graphite. In addition, some carmakers even installed a metal shield inside their distributors to further reduce RFI radiation from the breaker points, condensers, and rotors.

As the use of electronic components and systems on cars increased, the problem of electromagnetic interference reappeared with broader implications. The low-power digital integrated circuits now in use are extremely sensitive to EMI signals that were of little or no concern before the late 1970s.

Interference Generation and Transmission

Whenever current flows in a conductor, an electromagnetic field is created. When current stops and starts, as in a spark plug cable or a switch that opens and closes, field strength changes. Each time this happens, it creates an electromagnetic signal wave. If it happens rapidly enough, the resulting high-frequency signal waves, or EMI, will interfere with radio and television transmission or with other electronic systems such as those under the hood of the car. This is an undesirable side effect of the phenomenon of electromagnetism. Figure 2-27 shows common sources of EMI on an automobile.

EMI can also be caused by static electric charges caused by friction of the tires with the road or the friction resulting from engine drive belts contacting their pulleys. Drive axles, drive shafts, and clutch or brake lining surfaces are other sources of static electric charges.

There are four ways of transmitting EMI, all of which can be found in an automobile:

- Conductive coupling through circuit conductors, figure 2-28
- Capacitive coupling through an electrostatic field between two conductors, figure 2-29
- Inductive coupling as the magnetic fields between two conductors form and collapse, figure 2-30
- Electromagnetic radiation, figure 2-31.

EMI Suppression Devices

Just as there are four methods of EMI transmission, there are four general ways in which EMI can be reduced:

- By the addition of resistance to conductors that will suppress conductive transmission and radiation
- By the use of capacitors and **choke coil** combinations to reduce capacitive and inductive coupling

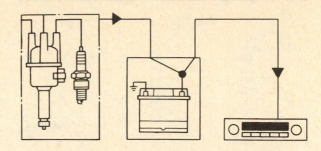

Figure 2-28. Conductive-coupling interference is transmitted by wiring from the source of interference to the receiver.

- By the use of metal or metalized plastic shielding, which reduces EMI radiation in addition to capacitive and inductive coupling
- By an increased use of ground straps to reduce conductive transmission and radiation by bypassing the unwanted signals to ground.

Resistance suppression
Adding resistance to a circuit to suppress RFI works only for high-voltage systems (for example, changing the conductive core of ignition cables). The use of resistance to suppress interference in low-voltage circuits creates too much voltage drop and power loss to be efficient.

The only high-voltage system on most cars is the ignition secondary circuit. While this can be the greatest single source of EMI, it is also the easiest to control. This has been done in

Primary Windings: The coil winding made of a few turns of a heavy wire, which uses battery current to create a magnetic field.

Secondary Windings: The coil winding made of many turns of a fine wire, in which voltage is induced by the rise and collapse of the magnetic field of the primary winding.

Electromagnetic Interference (EMI): An undesirable form of electromagnetism created by rapid changes in field strength whenever current stops and starts.

Radiofrequency Interference (RFI): A form of electromagnetic interference created in the ignition secondary circuit which disrupts radio and television transmission.

Choke Coil: A coil wound with fine wire and installed in a circuit to absorb oscillations that occur when the circuit is closed or opened.

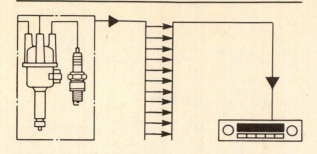

Figure 2-29. Capacitive-coupling interference is transmitted by a capacitive field between adjacent wiring.

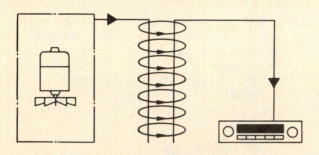

Figure 2-30. Inductive-coupling interference is transmitted by an electromagnetic field between adjacent wiring.

large part by the use of resistance spark plug cables, resistor spark plugs, and the silicone grease used on the distributor cap and rotor of some electronic ignitions.

Suppression capacitors and coils
Capacitors can be installed across many circuits and switching points absorb voltage fluctuations. Among other applications, they are used:

- Across the primary circuit of some electronic ignition modules, figure 2-32
- Across the output terminal of most alternators
- Across the armature circuit of electric motors.

Choke coils reduce current fluctuations resulting from self-induction. They are often combined with capacitors to act as EMI filter circuits for wiper motors and electric fuel pump motors, figure 2-33. Filters may also be incorporated in wiring connectors.

Shielding
Metal shields, such as the ones used in breaker point distributors, can be used to block the waves from components that create RFI signals. The circuits of onboard computers are protected to some degree from external electromagnetic waves by their metal housings.

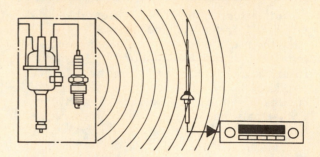

Figure 2-31. Radiation interference occurs when EMI waves travel through space and are picked up by wiring that acts as a receiving antenna.

Ground straps
Ground or bonding straps between the engine and chassis of an automobile help suppress EMI conduction and radiation by providing a low-resistance circuit ground path. Such suppression ground straps are often installed between rubber-mounted components and body parts, figure 2-34. Carmakers are now installing ground straps between body parts such as the hood and a fender panel where no electrical circuit exists, figure 2-34. In such a case, the strap has no other job than to suppress EMI. Without it, the car body and hood could function as a large capacitor. The space between the fender and hood could form an electrostatic field and couple with the computer circuits in the wiring harness routed near the fender panel.

EMI Suppression on Late-Model Cars

Interference suppression is now a critical automotive engineering task. The modern automobile has increased the need for EMI suppression. The increasing use of citizens band (CB) radios and mobile telephones, as well as onboard computer systems, are only a few of the factors that have made interference suppression extremely important.

EMI can disrupt the operation of the vehicle's digital computer, which operates on voltage signals of a few millivolts (thousandths of a volt) and milliamperes (thousandths of an ampere) of current.

Any of the interference transmission modes discussed earlier can create false voltage signals and excessive current in the computer systems. False voltage signals disrupt computer operation, while excessive current can permanently damage the microelectronic circuitry.

As the complexity and number of electronic systems on cars continues to increase, carmak-

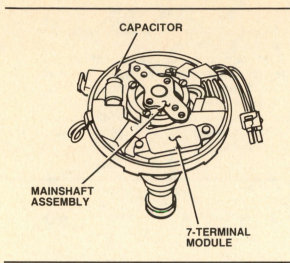

Figure 2-32. This capacitor attached to an HEI ignition module protects the module from EMI.

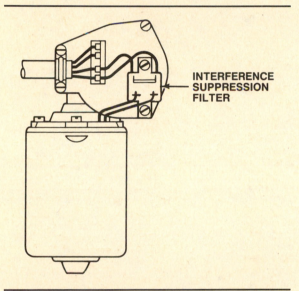

Figure 2-33. Interference-suppression capacitors and choke coils are attached to many electric motors, like this wiper motor. (Bosch)

ers are using multiplex wiring systems to reduce the size and number of wiring harnesses, which also reduces EMI. Multiplexing is a method of sending more than one electrical signal over the same channel. Multiplex circuits are described in detail in Chapter Five.

SUMMARY

Electricity can be generated in several ways. The most important way for automotive use is by magnetism. Magnetism is a form of energy caused by the alignment of atoms in certain materials. It is the ability of metal to attract iron. Some magnetic materials exist in nature; others can be artificially magnetized.

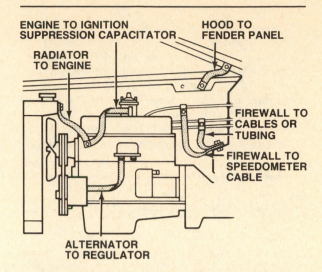

Figure 2-34. Ground straps are installed in many areas of late-model engine compartments to suppress EMI. (Bosch)

Lines of force, called flux lines, form a magnetic field around a magnet. Flux lines exit the north pole and enter the south pole of a magnet. Electrical conductors are also surrounded by magnetic flux lines. As current flow increases, the magnetic field of a conductor becomes stronger. Voltage can be generated by the interaction of magnetic fields around conductors.

■ Squeeze a Rock, Get a Volt

In 1880, the French physicists, Pierre and Jacques Curie, discovered the phenomenon of piezoelectricity, which means, "electricity through pressure". They found that when pressure is applied to a crystal of quartz, tourmaline, or Rochelle salt, a voltage is generated between the faces of the crystal. Although the effect is only temporary, while the pressure lasts, it can be maintained by alternating the pressure between compression and tension.

Piezoelectricity is put to practical use in phonograph pickups and crystal microphones, where mechanical vibrations (sound waves) are converted into varying voltage signals. Similar applications are used in underwater hydrophones and piezoelectric stethoscopes.

A reverse piezoelectric effect can be created by applying a high-frequency alternating voltage to a crystal. The crystal then produces mechanical vibrations at the same frequency. The vibrations are called ultrasonic sound waves because their vibrations are above our range of hearing. These ultrasonic vibrations are used, among other things, for sonar reflections from submarines and to drill holes in diseased teeth.

Voltage is generated by the relative movement of a conductor and a magnetic field. This process is called induction. Either the conductor or the magnetic field may be moving. The strength of the induced voltage depends on the strength of the magnetic field, the number of conductors, the speed of the relative motion, and the angle at which the conductors cut the flux lines. Electromagnetic induction is used in generators, alternators, electric motors, and coils.

Electromagnetism can also generate electromagnetic interference (EMI) and radiofrequency interference (RFI). Such interference can disrupt radio and television signals, as well as electronic systems in the car. Many devices are used to suppress this interference in automotive systems.

Review Questions

Choose the single most correct answer.
Compare your answers with the correct answers on page 431.

1. Current flows through a heated thermocouple because of:
   a. The two-way flow of electrons between dissimilar materials
   b. The blockage of free electrons between the metals
   c. The one-way transfer of free electrons between the metals
   d. Random electron flow

2. Which of the following forms of generating electricity is *not* widely used in an automobile?
   a. Heat
   b. Pressure
   c. Chemistry
   d. Magnetism

3. The lines of force of a magnet are called:
   a. Flux lines
   b. Magnetic polarity
   c. Magnetic lines
   d. Flux density

4. A material through which magnetic force can easily flow has a high:
   a. Reluctance
   b. Permeability
   c. Capacitance
   d. Magnetic attraction

5. The "left-hand rule" says that if you grasp a conductor in your left hand with your thumb pointing in the direction of the electron (– to +) flow:
   a. Your fingers will point in the direction of the magnetic flux lines
   b. Your fingers will point in the opposite direction of the magnetic flux lines
   c. Your fingers will point at right angles to the magnetic flux lines
   d. Your fingers will point at a 45°-angle to the magnetic flux lines

6. The "left-hand rule" is useful to determine:
   a. The direction of current flow
   b. The length of the magnetic flux lines
   c. The strength of the magnetic field
   d. Flux density

7. When two parallel conductors carry electrical current in opposite directions, their magnetic fields will:
   a. Force them apart
   b. Pull them together
   c. Cancel each other out
   d. Rotate around the conductors in the same direction

8. The motor principle of changing electrical energy into mechanical energy requires:
   a. Two semiconductors carrying current in opposite directions
   b. Two semiconductors carrying current in the same direction
   c. Two conductors carrying current in opposite directions
   d. Two conductors carrying current in the same direction

9. Which of the following will *not* increase induced voltage?
   a. Increase the strength of the magnetic field
   b. Increase the number of conductors cutting flux lines
   c. Increase the speed of the relative motion between the conductor and the flux lines
   d. Increase the angle between the flux lines and the conductor beyond 90 degrees

10. The _____ in an automobile d.c. generator rectifies a.c. to d.c.
    a. Armature
    b. Commutator
    c. Field coil
    d. Loop conductor

11. In an ignition coil, low-voltage primary current induces a very high secondary voltage because of:
    a. Different number of wire turns in the two windings.
    b. An equal number of turns in the two windings
    c. The constant current flow through the primary winding
    d. Bigger wire in the secondary winding

12. To reduce EMI, carmakers have done all of the following *except:*
    a. Use low resistance in electrical systems
    b. Install metal shielding in components
    c. Increase the use of ground straps
    d. Use capacitors and choke coils

3

Semiconductors and Solid-State Electronics

SEMICONDUCTORS

In Chapter One, we examined the atom's valence ring, the outermost electron shell. We learned that elements whose atoms have three or fewer electrons in their valence rings are good conductors because the free electrons in the valence ring readily join with the valence electrons of other, similar atoms. We also learned that elements whose atoms have five or more electrons in their valence rings are good insulators (poor conductors) because the valence electrons do not readily join with those of other atoms.

Elements whose atoms have four electrons in their valence rings are neither good insulators nor good conductors. Their four valence electrons cause special electrical properties which give them the name ''semiconductors''. Germanium and silicon are two widely used semiconductor elements.

When semiconductor elements are in the form of a crystal, they bond together so that each atom has eight electrons in its valence ring. It has its own four electrons and shares four with surrounding atoms, figure 3-1. In this form it is an excellent insulator, because there are no free electrons to carry current flow.

Other elements can be added to silicon and germanium to change this crystalline structure. This is called **doping** the semiconductor. The ratio of doping elements to silicon or germanium is about 1 to 10,000,000. The doping elements are often called **impurities** because their addition to the silicon or germanium makes the semiconductor materials impure.

N-material

If silicon or germanium is doped with an element such as phosphorus, arsenic, or antimony, each of which has five electrons in its valence ring, there will not be enough space for the ninth electron in any of the shared valence rings. This extra electron is free, figure 3-2. This type of doped material is called negative, or **N-material**, because it already has excess electrons and will repel additional negative charges.

P-material

If silicon or germanium is doped with an element such as boron or indium, each of which has only three electrons in its outer shell, some of the atoms will have only seven electrons in their valence rings. There will be a **hole** in these valence rings, figure 3-3. This type of

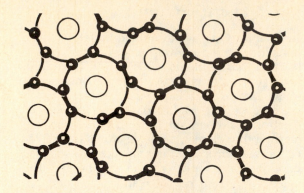

Figure 3-1. Crystalline silicon is an excellent insulator. (Delco-Remy)

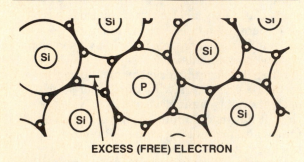

EXCESS (FREE) ELECTRON

Figure 3-2. N-material has an extra, or free, electron. (Delco-Remy)

doped material is called positive or **P-material**, because it will attract a negative charge (an electron).

HOLE FLOW

We have explained the electron flow theory of electricity as the movement of electrons from negative to positive. We can also visualize the movement of the holes which these electrons move into and out of. If you imagine a line of cars moving ahead one car length at a time, the car length of empty space can be seen to move from the front to the back of the line, figure 3-4. Just as the car-length of empty space moves in the opposite direction from traffic flow, holes move in the direction opposite from electron flow, or from positive to negative. The hole can be thought of as a positive charge of electricity. Holes can move from atom to atom just as electrons move from atom to atom. The hole flow theory is an easy way to understand the operation of diodes and transistors, as we will see.

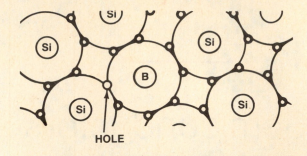

HOLE

Figure 3-3. P-material has a hole in some of its valence rings. (Delco-Remy)

Figure 3-4. Space flow moves opposite to traffic flow just as hole flow moves opposite to electron flow.

VOLTAGE AND SEMICONDUCTORS

Doping silicon or germanium causes it to behave in unusual but predictable ways when voltage is applied to it. The behavior depends upon which charge of the voltage is connected to which type of doped material (P or N). To use this behavior in solid-state devices, P-material and N-material are placed side by side. The line along which they meet is called the **junction**. The application of voltage to the two doped semiconductor materials is called **biasing**. To begin our description of doped material behavior, let us look at a P-material and N-material junction, with positive voltage connected to the P-material and negative voltage connected to the N-material, figure 3-5. A simple device consisting of P-material and N-material joined at a junction is called a **diode**.

Diode Bias Voltage

The negative battery voltage in figure 3-5 will repel the free electrons in the N-material, causing them to move toward the junction. The positive battery voltage will repel the holes in the P-material, moving them toward the junction also. With enough voltage, the electrons of the N-material will move across the junction into the holes of the P-material. This leaves behind positively charged holes in the N-material,

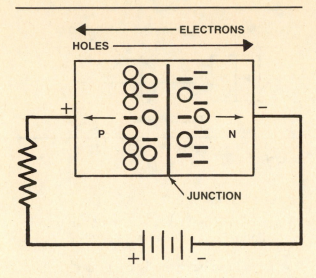

Figure 3-5. Current will flow through this forward-bias connection. (Delco-Remy)

which attract more electrons from the negative voltage source. At the same time, the free electrons which moved into the P-material continue to be attracted toward the positive battery voltage, leaving behind holes in the P-material at the junction. This area near the junction where the N-type material is depleted of electrons and the P-material is depleted of holes is called the **depletion region**. As long as battery voltage is maintained, this chain of events will be repeated, and current will flow through the doped materials. The application of voltage to maintain current flow as described here is called **forward bias**.

A diode cannot withstand unlimited forward bias voltage and current flow. If the forward current flow is too strong or flows for too long, the doped materials can be damaged or destroyed.

If the battery polarity is reversed, so that the negative battery voltage is connected to the P-material and the positive battery voltage is connected to the N-material, the doped materials' behavior changes, figure 3-6. The positive battery voltage attracts the free electrons in the N-material, causing them to move away from the junction. The negative battery voltage attracts the holes in the P-material, causing them to move away from the junction. At the junction, there will be no holes and no free electrons. No current can flow under these conditions. Voltage applied in this way is called **reverse bias**, figure 3-6. If reverse bias voltage is very high, the diode will break down and current will flow. One of the most common ways to rate a diode is in terms of its **peak inverse voltage (piv)**. This refers to the amount of voltage a diode can withstand be-

fore it breaks down and allows reverse current flow. A diode can withstand reverse bias voltage below its piv rating indefinitely, but reverse current flow caused by voltage higher than the piv rating can quickly damage the diode. This is the reason that diodes in alternators can be damaged if a battery is hooked up backwards or if high voltage from a battery charger is applied to a battery without disconnecting it from a car's electrical system. We will learn more about diode uses when we

Doping: The addition of a small amount of a second element to a semiconductor element.

Impurities: The doping elements added to pure silicon or germanium to form semiconductor materials.

N-material: A semiconductor material that has excess (free) electrons because of the type of impurity added. It has a negative charge and will repel additional electrons.

Hole: The space in a valence ring where another electron could fit.

P-material: A semiconductor material that has holes for additional electrons because of the type of impurity added. It has a positive charge and will attract additional electrons.

Junction: The area where two types of semiconductor materials (P- and N-material) are joined.

Biasing: Applying voltage to a junction of semiconductor materials.

Diode: An electronic device made of P-material and N-material bonded at a junction. A diode allows current flow in one direction and blocks it in the other.

Depletion Region: An area near the junction of a diode where P-material is depleted of holes and N-material is depleted of electrons.

Forward Bias: The application of a voltage to produce current flow across the junction of a semiconductor.

Reverse Bias: The application of a voltage so that normally no current will flow across the junction of a semiconductor.

Peak Inverse Voltage (PIV): The highest reverse bias voltage that can be applied to a junction of a diode before its atomic structure breaks down and allows current to flow.

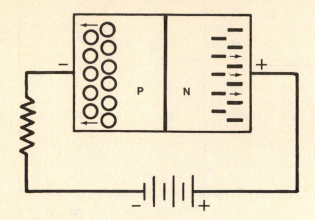

Figure 3-6. No current will flow through this reverse-bias connection. (Delco-Remy)

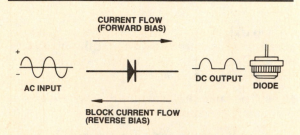

Figure 3-7. A diode blocks one-half of the current wave and transmits the other half. (Chrysler)

study charging systems, ignition systems, and other electronic circuits in an automobile.

Junction Diode Applications

Diodes operate as electrical one-way check valves. They allow current flow in one direction but not in the other. For example, they can allow one-half of an alternating current (a.c.) wave to flow in one direction while blocking flow of the remaining half of the current wave in the other direction, figure 3-7. The diode polarity may be either positive or negative, depending upon the direction of forward bias. Bias direction is determined by the direction in which the P-material or N-material is connected into the circuit.

The symbol for a simple PN diode is shown in figure 3-8. The arrowhead represents the P section, and the vertical bar represents the N section. Hole flow, or conventional current flow, is in the direction of the arrowhead. Electron flow is in the *opposite* direction.

One of the first major uses of diodes in automotive electrical systems was in a.c. generators, or alternators, which we will study in Chapter Eight. An early alternator diode is shown in figure 3-9, along with smaller diodes used in radios and other electronic systems.

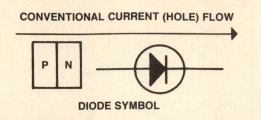

Figure 3-8. The electrical symbol for a diode. (Delco-Remy)

Zener Diodes

We said before that reverse current can damage a diode. **Zener diodes** are heavily doped to withstand reverse current without damage. The doping can be carefully controlled so that a zener diode will only conduct reverse current if the voltage is higher than a specific level. For instance, a certain zener diode might be designed to conduct reverse current if the voltage is more than six volts. At any voltage below six volts, the zener acts as a normal junction diode and does not conduct reverse flow. At six volts and above, the zener will conduct reverse current with no damage to the doping materials if the current flow is kept within specified limits. Six volts is then called the diode's **breakdown voltage** or zener voltage.

Zener diodes are often used in control circuits, especially in the charging system, which we will study in Part Two. The symbols for a zener diode are shown in figure 3-10. Like the junction diode symbol, the arrowhead shows the direction in which conventional current is allowed to flow freely. Zener diodes are carefully rated as to the reverse voltage necessary for reverse current to flow. This rating is often expressed as the amount of voltage the zener diode will regulate in a circuit.

SILICON-CONTROLLED RECTIFIERS

The silicon-controlled rectifier (SCR) is basically a four-layer PNPN device which normally allows current flow in both directions. It can be triggered to block current flow in one direction or the other. Its importance lies in this ability to control current flow. Silicon-controlled rectifiers may be found in some solid-state ignition systems and solid-state regulators for charging systems. An SCR is often called a thyristor. Its symbol is shown in figure 3-11.

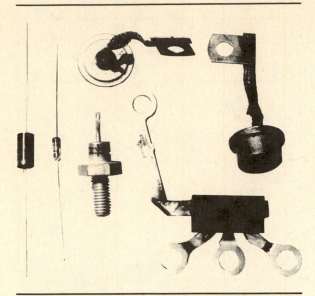

Figure 3-9. Alternator diodes (top center and top right) and radio diodes (left and center). At lower right is a diode trio (three diodes in one unit) from a late-model alternator.

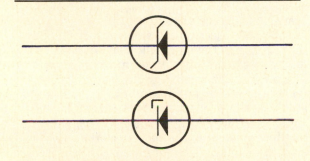

Figure 3-10. A zener diode is represented by either of these symbols.

LIGHT-EMITTING DIODES

A light-emitting diode (LED), figure 3-12, is a diode made of a particular type of crystal that glows when current is passed through it. Light-emitting diodes are used in the display faces of many ''digital'' instruments, such as digital clocks and digital tachometers or speedometers. These are called digital instruments because the LEDs are arranged in the display face to light up as numbers (digits) when current is passed through different combinations of the LEDs.

TRANSISTORS

A transistor is a three-element semiconductor, produced by adding another layer of doped material to a basic PN diode. The three materials are combined so that the two outer layers

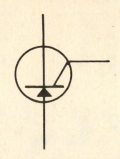

Figure 3-11. The symbol for a silicon-controlled rectifier (SCR), also called a thyristor.

are the same (either P-material or N-material) and are doped with the same impurity. The inner layer is the opposite type of material and doped with a different impurity.

Zener Diode: A junction of semiconductor materials that has been heavily doped so that the junction will allow reverse current flow without damage at any voltage above a specific value.

Breakdown Voltage: The voltage above which a zener diode will allow reverse current flow.

■ Semiconductor Doping

Adding impurities to a semiconductor material, or doping, must be a carefully controlled process. Manufacturing methods are constantly changing as better doping processes are developed. Early semiconductor technology called for painting layers of doping elements onto either side of a semiconductor wafer and baking it at temperatures above 2,000°F (1,093°C). The ratio of impurity to the pure semiconductor was not easily controlled, and new uses for semiconductors demanded more precise production.

Some newer processes use a gas of the doping material. A process called diffusion passes this gas over the surface of a semiconductor wafer, which has been heated to 2,000°F. The doping elements are slowly absorbed into the wafer. The doping ratios can be carefully controlled during this slow absorption.

Ion implantation uses a 100-kV force to create an arc through the doping gas. The flow of electrons through the gas ionizes it, causing the gas particles to become positively and negatively charged. A semiconductor wafer is bombarded with the ionized gas, and doping elements are deeply implanted in the wafer. This method can be combined with the diffusion method to create a very deep but controlled layer of doped material.

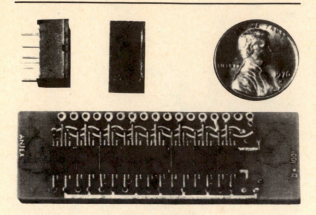

Figure 3-12. Light-emitting diodes, like these, are used in the digital displays of instruments like clocks and tachometers. Light-emitting diodes light up when current is passed through them.

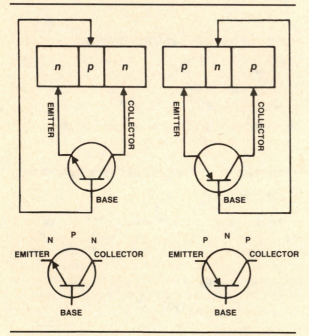

Figure 3-13. Transistor symbols and construction.

The three parts of a transistor are called the **base**, the **emitter**, and the **collector**. The emitter and the collector are the outer layers, and the base is the inner layer. If the emitter and the collector are N-material, the base is P-material. If the emitter and the collector are P-material, the base is N-material. Transistors are described as either PNP construction or NPN construction. The circuit diagram symbols for the two kinds of transistors are shown in figure 3-13, along with illustrations of how the materials are joined together in their construction. Note that the arrowhead is always shown on the emitter branch of the symbol and indicates the direction of hole flow. The emitter al-

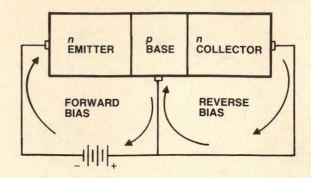

Figure 3-14. Forward and reverse biasing for an NPN transistor.

ways produces the majority current carriers, either holes (P-material) or free electrons (N-material), and transfers them to the base. Because this type of transistor uses both holes and electrons to carry current, it is called a **bipolar** transistor.

Transistor Operation

Transistors can be used to control current flow in solid-state electronic systems. In this way, they work like the mechanical relays discussed in Chapter Two, but with no moving parts. The most common automotive uses of transistors are as relays, although they can be used to amplify voltage or current in electronic systems. In the following paragraphs, we will briefly look at how a transistor works as a solid-state relay. These are the basic principles on which many electronic ignition systems and voltage regulators work.

To use a transistor as a simple solid-state relay, the emitter-base junction must be forward biased, and the collector-base junction must be reverse biased. Figure 3-14 shows this arrangement for an NPN transistor.

Input and output circuits

The input circuit for a NPN transistor is the emitter-base circuit, figure 3-15. Because the base is thinner and doped less than the emitter, it has fewer holes than the emitter has free electrons. Therefore, when forward bias is applied, the numerous free electrons from the emitter do not find enough holes to combine with in the base. In this condition, the free electrons accumulate in the base and eventually restrict further current flow.

The output circuit for this NPN transistor is shown in figure 3-16 with reverse bias applied. The base is thinner and doped less than the

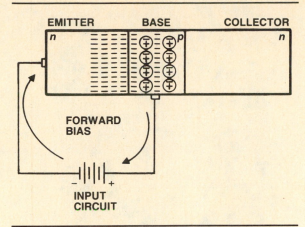

Figure 3-15. Free electrons cannot find enough holes to join with in the base. Therefore, electrons accumulate in the base, and little forward current flows.

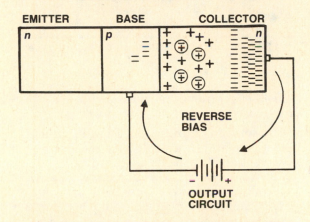

Figure 3-16. The base does not have enough free electrons to combine with holes in the collector, and little reverse current flows.

collector. Therefore, under reverse bias, it has few minority carriers (free electrons) to combine with many minority carriers (holes in the collector). When the collector-base output circuit is reverse biased, very little reverse current will flow. This is similar to the effect of forward biasing the emitter-base input circuit, in which very little forward current will flow.

When the input and output circuits are connected, with the forward and reverse biases maintained, the overall operation of the NPN transistor changes, figure 3-17. Now, the majority of free electrons from the emitter, which could not combine with the base, are attracted through the base to the holes in the collector. The free electrons from the emitter are moved by the negative forward bias toward the base, but most pass through the base to the holes in the collector, where they are attracted by a positive bias. Reverse current flows in the

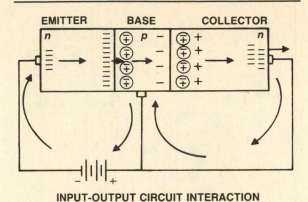

Figure 3-17. Electrons from the emitter pass through the base to the collector, and greater overall forward current flows. Note that greater reverse current flows in the output circuit because more holes in the collector are filled by free electrons.

collector-base output circuit, but the overall current flow in the transistor is forward.

A slight change in the emitter-base bias causes a large change in emitter-to-collector current flow. This is similar to a small amount of current flow controlling a large current flow through a relay. As the emitter-base bias changes, either more or fewer free electrons

Base: The center layer of semiconductor material in a transistor.

Emitter: The outside layer of semiconductor material in a transistor that conducts current to the base.

Collector: The outside layer of semiconductor material in a transistor that conducts current away from the base.

Bipolar: A transistor which uses both holes and electrons as current carriers.

■ **Tran(sfer) + (Re)sistor**

The word "transistor" was originally a business trademark used as a name for an electrical part that transferred electric signals across a resistor. The point-contact transistor was invented by two scientists, John Bardeen and Walter H. Brattain, at Bell Telephone Laboratories in 1948. In 1951, the junction transistor was invented by their colleague, William Shockley. As a result of their work, these three men received the 1956 Nobel Prize for physics.

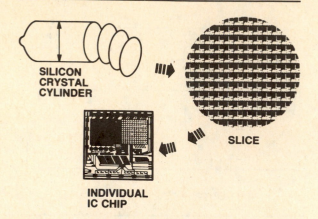

Figure 3-18. Each small square on the silicon slice or wafer is a complete IC chip. (Chrysler)

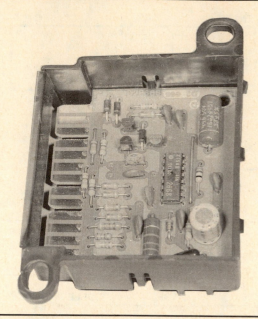

Figure 3-20. A hybrid circuit contains several discrete devices and integrated circuits.

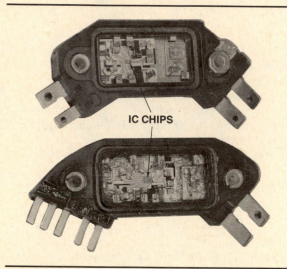

Figure 3-19. The Delco HEI and HEI-EST ignition modules use integrated circuit (IC) chips.

are moved toward the base. This causes the collector current to increase or decrease. If the emitter-base circuit is opened or the bias is removed, no forward current will flow through the transistor because the base-collector junction acts like a PN diode with reverse bias applied.

FIELD-EFFECT TRANSISTORS

The field-effect transistor (FET) is a three-element solid-state device which controls high voltage and large current flow with a small signal voltage. This means that it can be used as an amplifier when installed in the proper circuit. As we have just seen, the bipolar transistor is controlled by altering the current through the emitter-base junction. To control a field-effect transistor, we change the voltage in a capacitive field.

A field-effect transistor consists of three parts:

- The **source**, which is similar to the emitter of a bipolar transistor. It supplies the current-carrying holes or electrons.
- The **drain**, which is similar to the collector. It collects the current carriers.
- The **gate**, which is similar to the bipolar transistor base. It creates a capacitive field which permits current to flow from source to drain.

Field-effect transistors are generally installed in a circuit to either improve (amplify) the current flow from the source to the drain, or to deplete (shut off) current flow. An easy-to-understand analogy is to compare them to normally open or normally closed switches. Field-effect transistors are used to do much of the switching, processing, and amplifying work required in an electronic circuit.

DISCRETE DEVICES VS. INTEGRATED CIRCUITS

Each of the electronic devices we have seen so far is an individual component with its own leads for installing it in a circuit. Such solid-state components are often called **discrete devices**. Good examples are the rectifying diodes used on older alternators; each diode is an individual unit and is connected into the circuit by itself.

Discrete devices are still in use, but they are being replaced in many cases by the **integrated**

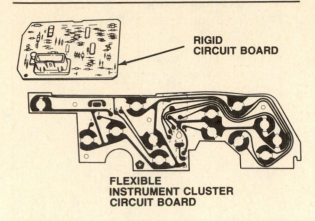

RIGID
CIRCUIT BOARD

FLEXIBLE
INSTRUMENT CLUSTER
CIRCUIT BOARD

Figure 3-21. Printed circuits may use a rigid or flexible circuit board to connect the components into a complete circuit. (Chrysler)

circuit (IC). This is a very complex and very small electronic circuit that contains hundreds (or in some cases, thousands) of transistors and other devices on a tiny silicon chip. This has allowed a drastic reduction in the size and cost of electronic components.

An IC is made from a slice or wafer of silicon crystal. Its circuit pattern is reproduced by a photographic and diffusion process to create hundreds of identical circuits, each containing transistors, diodes, conductors, and capacitors within a tiny ''chip'' on the wafer. Once the ICs have been formed, each chip is cut from the wafer. Figure 3-18 summarizes the major steps in IC manufacture. The individual chip is then incased in its own packaging device and installed in a larger circuit. Figure 3-19 shows integrated circuit use in ignition control modules.

HYBRID CIRCUITS

A hybrid circuit is one that contains several discrete devices and several ICs. Figure 3-20 shows a hybrid circuit as used in a barometric/ manifold absolute pressure (B/MAP) sensor. Like discrete devices, hybrid circuits are being replaced by one or two ICs.

PRINTED CIRCUITS

Printed circuits are often used to connect individual solid-state components. An etched conductor is used on one or both sides of a circuit board to connect the various electronic components. The components are then soldered to the circuit board. Automotive instrument clusters often use a flexible type of circuit board. Figure 3-21 shows both rigid and flexible types of circuit boards.

SUMMARY

Elements with four valence-ring electrons are neither good conductors nor good insulators. They are called semiconductors. Adding small amounts of other elements to semiconductors is called doping. Doping creates either N-material or P-material, depending on whether the doping element has five electrons or three electrons in its valence ring. Doped semiconductor materials behave in unusual but predictable ways when exposed to voltage. A simple PN material junction, called a diode, acts as a one-way electrical check valve. It allows current flow in one direction but not the other. Applying voltage to a semiconductor device is called biasing.

Transistors are three-part semiconductor devices. They are made of layers of positive-negative-positive (PNP) or negative-positive-negative (NPN) materials. The three parts of a transistor are called the emitter, the base, and the collector. Transistors can be used to amplify current or voltage, but in automobiles, transistors are generally used as solid-state relays.

Other semiconductor devices commonly used in automotive applications are zener diodes, silicon-controlled rectifiers, light-emitting diodes, and integrated circuits. An integrated circuit contains many transistors, diodes, and other discrete devices on a small metallic chip. Hybrid circuits combine discrete devices with IC chips. Printed circuit boards are often used to form a circuit with discrete devices.

Source: The field-effect transistor (FET) layer which supplies current-carrying holes or electrons (similar to the emitter of a bipolar transistor).

Drain: The field-effect transistor (FET) layer which collects current carriers (similar to the collector of a bipolar transistor).

Gate: The field-effect transistor (FET) layer which creates a capacitive field that lets current flow from the source to the drain (similar to the base of a bipolar transistor).

Discrete Device: A complete, separately manufactured, individual component with wire leads for connection into a circuit.

Integrated Circuit (IC): A very small, complex electronic circuit that contains hundreds or thousands of transistors and other devices on a tiny silicon chip.

Review Questions

Choose the single most correct answer.
Compare your answers with the correct answers on page 431.

1. Semiconductors are elements which have _____ electrons in their valence rings.
   a. Two
   b. Four
   c. Six
   d. Eight

2. A diode is a simple device which joins:
   a. P-material and N-material
   b. P-material and P-material
   c. N-material and N-material
   d. P-material and a conductor

3. Which of the following is *not* true of forward bias in a diode?
   a. Free electrons in the N-material and holes in the P-material both move toward the junction
   b. N-material electrons move across the junction to fill the holes in the P-material
   c. Negatively charged holes left behind in the N-material attract electrons from the negative voltage source
   d. The free electrons which moved into the P-material continue to move toward the positive voltage source

4. When reverse bias is applied to a simple diode, which of the following will result?
   a. The free electrons will move toward the junction
   b. The holes of the P-material move toward the junction
   c. No current will flow across the junction
   d. The voltage increases

5. Under normal use, a simple diode acts to:
   a. Allow current to flow in one direction only
   b. Allow current to flow in alternating directions
   c. Block the flow of current from any direction
   d. Allow current to flow from either direction at once

6. ''Breakdown voltage'' is the voltage at which a Zener diode will:
   a. Allow reverse current to flow
   b. Stop the flow of reverse current
   c. Sustain damage as a result of current overload
   d. Stop the flow of either forward or reverse current

7. Which of the following combinations of materials can exist in the composition of a transistor?
   a. NPN
   b. PNP
   c. Both a and b
   d. Neither a nor b

8. To use a transistor as a simple solid-state relay:
   a. The emitter-base junction must be reverse biased, and the collector-base junction must be forward biased
   b. The emitter-base junction must be forward biased, and the collector-base junction must be reverse biased
   c. The emitter-base junction and the collector-base junction both must be forward biased
   d. The emitter-base junction and the collector-base junction both must be reverse biased

9. Which of the following is *not* commonly used as a doping element?
   a. Arsenic
   b. Antimony
   c. Phosphorus
   d. Silicon

10. The display faces of digital instruments are often made of:
    a. Silicon-controlled rectifiers
    b. Integrated circuits
    c. Light-emitting diodes
    d. Thyristors

11. All of the following are parts of a field-effect transistor (FET), *except* the:
    a. Drain
    b. Source
    c. Base
    d. Gate

12. All of the following are characteristics of an integrated circuit (IC), *except*:
    a. It is extremely small
    b. It contains thousands of individual components
    c. It is manufactured from silicon
    d. It is larger than a hybrid circuit

4

Automotive Computer Systems

Revolutionary changes have occurred in automotive technology during the past decade. These changes are the result of the onboard computer, which may control from one to a dozen or more functions that range from fuel metering to suspension leveling. In this chapter, we will look at what an automotive computer is, what it does, and how it performs its functions.

WHAT IS A COMPUTER?

We often use the term ''computer'' without really understanding what it means. A computer is nothing more than a machine that receives information, which it uses to make a series of decisions, and that acts as a result of the decisions made. A computer cannot think on its own; it does everything according to a detailed set of instructions called a **program**. The old mechanical calculator was a primitive form of computer.

The earliest electronic computers and those in use today all use identical principles. They use voltage to send and receive information. As we have learned, voltage is electrical pressure and does not flow through circuits. It causes current flow, which does the real work in an electrical circuit. However, voltage can be used as a signal. A computer converts input information, or data, into voltage signal combinations that represent number combinations. The number combinations can represent a wide variety of information — temperature, speed, or even words and letters. A computer handles or processes the input voltage signals it receives by computing what they represent and then delivering data in computed or processed form.

Most people are unaware that they are using simple computers every day when they set the cooking time on their microwave oven or set their VCR to tape a favorite program while they are away from home.

Computer Functions

The operation of every computer, regardless of its size or the use to which it is put, can be divided into four basic functions:

- Input
- Processing
- Storage
- Output.

These basic functions are not unique to computers; they can be found in many noncomputer systems. However, we need to know how the functions work in a computer.

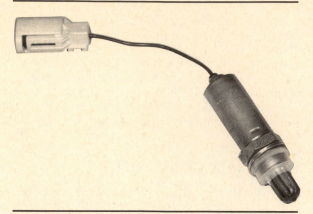

Figure 4-1. This is an example of an automotive sensor, providing input to the onboard computer.

Figure 4-2. An actuator on a Ford engine that controls air intake.

Input

The computer receives a voltage signal (input) from an input device. The device can be as simple as a button or switch on an instrument panel. It can also be a **sensor** on an automobile engine, figure 4-1. The keyboard on your personal computer or the programming keyboard of a VCR are other examples of an input device.

Modern automobiles use various mechanical, electrical, and magnetic sensors to measure a variety of things, including vehicle and engine speed, air pressure, oxygen content of exhaust gas, airflow, and temperature. Each sensor transmits its information in the form of voltage signals which the computer can understand. Sensors are described more fully later in this chapter.

Processing

The computer receives input voltage signals and switches them through a series of electronic logic circuits according to its programmed instructions. These processing logic circuits change the input voltage signals, or data, into output voltage signals, or commands.

Storage

The program instructions for a computer are stored in its electronic memory. Some programs may require that certain input data be stored for later reference or future processing. In others, output commands may be delayed or stored before they are transmitted to devices elsewhere in the system. Computers use a number of different memory devices which we will look at later in this chapter.

Output

After the computer has processed the input signals, it sends output voltage signals, or commands, to other devices in the system, such as a solenoid or a display screen. The output devices used on automobiles vary from a display on an instrument panel to a system actuator. An **actuator** is an electrical or mechanical device that performs a desired operation, figure 4-2, whether it is adjusting engine idle speed, changing suspension height, or regulating fuel metering.

To make matters slightly more complicated for the automotive technician, computers can communicate with, and control, each other through their output and input functions. This means that the output signal from one computer system can act as an input signal for another computer system. For instance, on some 1986 and later GM cars, a body computer module (BCM) acts as a master control unit by managing a network containing all sensors, switches, and other vehicle computers, figure 4-3.

As an example, let's suppose the BCM sends an output signal to disengage the air conditioning compressor clutch. That same output signal can become an input signal to the electronic control module (ECM) that controls engine operation. Based on the signal from the BCM, the ECM tells an actuator to adjust engine speed to compensate for the decreased load when the compressor is disengaged.

The four basic functions just described are common to all computers, regardless of size or purpose. They also form an organizational pat-

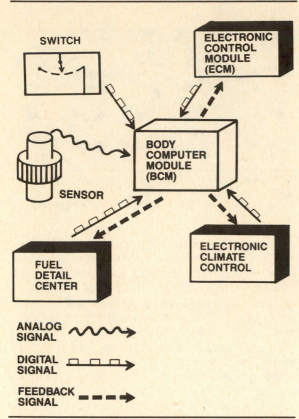

ANALOG SIGNAL

DIGITAL SIGNAL

FEEDBACK SIGNAL

Figure 4-3. The body computer module reads data from various input devices, while sending commands to other devices. (GM)

tern for troubleshooting a malfunctioning system. While most input and output devices may be adjusted or repaired, the processing and storage functions can only be replaced.

Computer Sizes

The first computers were huge, occupying entire rooms and even buildings with the vacuum tubes and connecting wiring that formed their processing and storage equipment. Since the development of the transistor after World War II, electronics has evolved toward microminiature components. Today, we can identify three major sizes or classes of computers:

- Mainframe computers
- Minicomputers
- Microcomputers.

Mainframe computers, figure 4-4, are used to design automobiles and control automatic factory equipment or robots. These can do several jobs at the same time, receiving and sending thousands of separate inputs and outputs, and often supporting dozens or hundreds of users simultaneously.

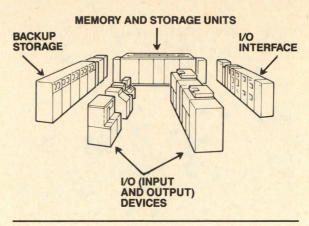

Figure 4-4. A mainframe computer, such as used in a large industrial or commercial operation. (GM)

Minicomputers also can do several jobs at once using dozens of inputs and outputs, but they do not have the capacity or speed of a mainframe computer. Among other functions, they are used by businesses and schools to maintain records.

Microcomputers, or personal computers, are generally used by one person at a time, although they can serve as input terminals for larger computer systems or can be connected together in some applications. Most microcomputers can only do one job at a time, but they can do many different jobs, depending upon the programs used.

Onboard Computers

In Chapter Three, we looked at solid-state silicon chips containing entire circuits. A single chip, or several chips on a single board, may form a computer for a specific function. An example is an engine control computer, figure 4-5. The continuing development of the silicon chip has taken us through various phases from the single transistor to what we now call very large scale integration (VLSI), in which tens of thousands of logic circuits are incorporated on

Program: The instructions a computer uses to do its job. The program consists of mathematical instructions and may include fixed data and require variable data from vehicle sensors.

Sensor: A device which provides input data in the form of voltage signals to a computer.

Actuator: A device which translates the computer output voltage signal into mechanical energy.

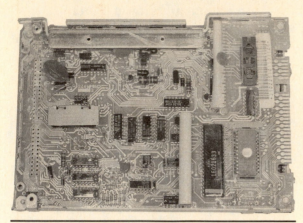

Figure 4-5. This engine control computer is a printed circuit board containing dozens of integrated circuit chips, transistors, diodes, capacitors, and other circuit devices.

Figure 4-6. While this Delco microprocessor is about an inch and a half (40 mm) long, the actual chip inside the packaging is no bigger than a fingernail.

a single silicon chip about one-quarter of an inch (6 mm) square. The end result is what we call a microprocessor, or the central processing unit (CPU) of a microcomputer.

When the microprocessor is enclosed in its circuit package with the necessary leads attached, it is no larger than a couple sticks of chewing gum or a small eraser, figure 4-6. The computer receives the input signals and sends them to the microprocessor, where calculation and logic decisions are made, and output commands are sent to the actuators.

ANALOG AND DIGITAL SYSTEMS

A computer has to be told how to do its job. The instructions and data necessary to do this are called a program. Since a computer cannot read words, the information must be translated into a form the computer can understand — voltage signals. This can be done by using an analog or digital system.

Analog Computers

The first automotive computer application was Chrysler's Electronic Lean-Burn (ELB) system used from 1976 through 1978, figure 4-7. Since it received, processed, and sent analog signals, it is called an analog computer. **Analog** means that the voltage signal or processing function varies relative to the field being measured or the adjustment required, position A, figure 4-8.

The majority of operating conditions affecting an automobile, such as engine speed, are analog variables. Such operating conditions can be measured by thermistors or potentiom-

eters acting as sensors. For example, engine speed doesn't change abruptly from idle to wide-open throttle; it varies in clearly defined, finite steps — 1,500 rpm, 1,501 rpm, 1,502 rpm, etc. — which can be measured. The same holds true for temperature, fuel metering, airflow, vehicle speed, and other factors.

If a computer is to measure engine speed changes from 0 rpm through 6,500 rpm, it can be programmed to respond to an analog voltage that varies from 0 volts at 0 rpm to 6.5 volts at 6,500 rpm. Any analog signal between 0 and 6.5 volts will represent a proportional engine speed between 0 and 6,500 rpm.

Analog computers have several shortcomings, however. They are affected by temperature changes, supply voltage variations, and signal interference. They also are slower in operation, more expensive to manufacture, and more limited in what they can do than digital computers.

Digital Computers

Digital computers first appeared on automotive applications in 1980. **Digital** means that the voltage signal or processing function is a simple high/low, yes/no, or on/off condition. The digital signal voltage is limited to two voltage levels. One is a positive voltage, the other is no voltage. Since there is no stepped range of voltage or current in between, a digital signal is a square wave, position B, figure 4-8.

Using our example dealing with engine speed, suppose that the computer needs to know that engine speed is either above or below a specific level, say 1,800 rpm. Since it doesn't need to know the exact engine speed, but only whether it is above or below 1,800 rpm, the digital signal could be zero volts below 1,800 rpm and one volt above 1,800 rpm. As you can see, a digital signal acts like a simple switch to open and close a circuit.

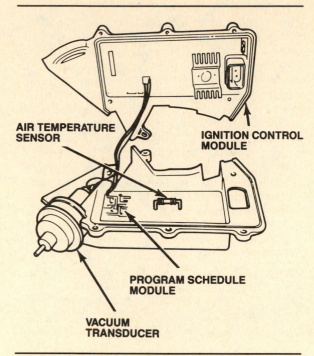

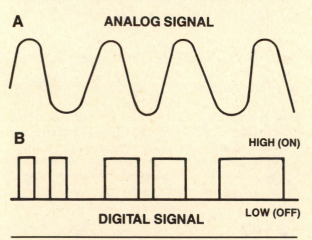

Figure 4-7. Chrysler's Lean-Burn system in 1976 was the first onboard automotive computer. (Chrysler)

Figure 4-8. Signal patterns of analog and digital signals. (GM)

The signal is called ''digital'' because the on and off signals are processed by the computer as the digits or numbers 0 and 1. The number system containing only these two digits is called the **binary system**. Any number or letter from any number system or language alphabet can be translated into a combination of binary 0s and 1s for the digital computer, figure 4-9.

A digital computer changes the analog input signals (voltage) to digital **bits** (*binary digits*) of information through an analog-to-digital (AD) converter circuit, figure 4-10. The binary digital number is used by the microprocessor in its

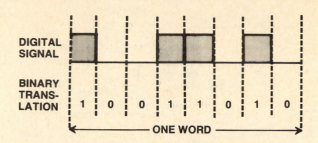

Figure 4-9. All information, data, or signals must be converted to an on/off binary system for the computer. (GM)

calculations or logic networks to come up with the appropriate output signal. Since the output signal is a binary digital number, it often must go through a digital-to-analog (DA) converter circuit to produce a voltage output to operate the actuator device, figure 4-10.

The digital computer can process thousands of digital signals per second because its circuits are able to switch voltage signals on and off in billionths of a second.

Binary Numbers

Digital computer switching circuits are characterized by either being off or on. This state can be represented by a 0 (off) or a 1 (on). If a digital computer is to understand a command, that command must be stated in binary form, as zeros or ones. A binary number system represents all numbers as sequences of zeros or ones. Therefore, off and on voltage signals can represent the 0 and 1 of the binary number system.

Analog: A voltage signal or processing action that varies relative to the operation being measured or controlled.

Digital: A voltage signal or processing function that has only two levels, on/off or high/low.

Binary System: A mathematical system containing only two digits (0 and 1), which allows a digital computer to read and process input voltage signals.

Bits: A digital input or output signal. One bit roughly equals one computer keystroke, or one discrete piece of information. The word comes from binary digit.

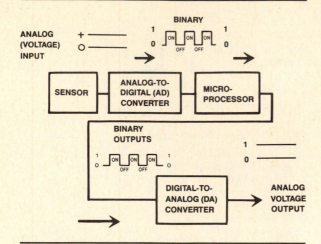

Figure 4-10. An analog-to-digital converter changes input signals into a binary system the microprocessor can understand. (Chrysler)

We call our number system a decimal, or base 10, system; it uses the digits 0 through 9 written in a single column. When numbers above 9 are used, another column is added to the left — the ten's position. Therefore, the number 10 is equal to one ten and zero ones; 18 equals one ten and eight ones. Each additional position to the left multiplies the number by a power of ten:

$1 = 10^0$
$10 = 10^1$
$100 = 10^2$
$1000 = 10^3$

Using the binary system, we group whole numbers from right to left, just as in the decimal system. Since the system uses only two digits, the first one must equal either 0 or 1. To indicate the value of 2, we use the second position and write it as 10, since it equals one two and zero ones. Each additional position to the left multiplies the number by a power of two:

$1 = 2^0$ or decimal 1
$10 = 2^1$ or decimal 2
$100 = 2^2$ or decimal 4
$1000 = 2^3$ or decimal 8

In this way, we can change any decimal number to a binary number:

Decimal	Binary
1	1
2	10
3	11
4	100
5	101
6	110
7	111
8	1000
9	1001

This exercise in translating decimals into their binary equivalents has a very practical application in a digital computer. It allows the computer to understand exactly what we wish it to do. With several thousand circuits arranged in various series and parallel combinations inside the microprocessor, they can switch on and off in combinations that equal any binary number in a microsecond (0.000001 second). You will never have to do this conversion, but understanding it gives you a better insight into how a digital computer works and how it can handle so much information in so little time.

How does the computer know where one binary number (voltage pulse) ends and another one begins? How does it differentiate between a 01 and a 0011? A clock generator inside the computer provides constant pulses. Each pulse is the length of one bit. The computer's memory (or memories) monitors these clock pulses while reading or sending data. In this way, it knows how long each voltage pulse should last.

Analog-to-Digital Conversion

Earlier, we mentioned that most operating conditions affecting an automobile are analog variables. When our computer needs to know whether an operating condition is above or below a specified level or point, a digital sensor can be used as a simple off/on switch. Below the specified point, the switch is open. The computer receives no voltage signal until the condition reaches the specified point, at which time the switch closes. This is an example of a simple digital off/on circuit: off = 0, on = 1.

Let's use engine coolant temperature as an example and specify that the computer needs to know the exact temperature within one degree. This requires analog input signals. Suppose our sensor measures temperature from 0 degrees to 300 degrees and sends an analog signal that varies from 0 to 6 volts. Each 1-volt change in the sensor signal is the equivalent of a 50-degree change in temperature. If 0 volt equals 0 degrees temperature and 6 volts equals 300 degrees:

1.00 volt = 50 degrees
0.50 volt = 25 degrees
0.10 volt = 5 degrees
0.02 volt = 1 degree

In order for the computer to determine temperature within 1 degree, it must react to a sensor voltage change as small as 0.020 volt or 20 millivolts. For example, if the temperature is 125 degrees, the sensor signal will be 2.50 volts. If the temperature rises to 126 degrees, sensor voltage will increase to 2.52 volts. In re-

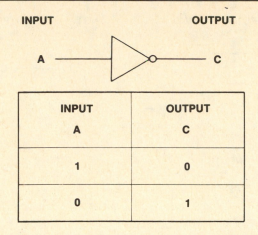

INPUT A	OUTPUT C
1	0
0	1

Figure 4-11. Logic symbol and truth table for a NOT gate.

ality, temperature does not pass directly from one degree to another; it passes through many smaller increments, as does voltage as it changes from 2.50 to 2.52 volts.

Our digital computer, however, processes only signals equaling 1-degree changes in temperature. To do so, the computer sends the signal through analog-to-digital (AD) conversion circuits, where the analog sensor voltage is converted to a series of 0.020-volt changes for each degree. This is called "digitizing" an analog signal.

The analog-to-digital conversion process brings us back to binary numbers. As we have learned, transistors can be designed to switch on and off at different voltage levels or with differing combinations of voltage signals. In the computer we are discussing, transistor groups must switch from off to on at 20-millivolt increments. The input signal is created by varying the transistor combinations that are on or off. In binary numbers, the 125 degree temperature is:

1111101

When the temperature increases to 126 degrees, the binary number also changes:

1111110

Since the computer can read the various voltage signal combinations as binary numbers, it performs its calculations. It does so almost instantly because the current travels through the miniature circuits at the speed of light.

DIGITAL LOGIC

Digital computers all handle data bits with three basic logic circuits called **logic gates**: the NOT, AND, and OR gates. This terminology is used to describe the circuit switching functions

only and has nothing to do with their physical construction. They are called "gates" because the circuits act as routes or "gates" for output voltage signals according to different input signal combinations. A voltage signal enters the input terminal of a logic gate where it is processed according to the internal circuit switching pattern and then exits through the logic gate's output terminal.

The thousands of field-effect transistors (FETs) in a microprocessor function as logic gates. Figures 4-11 through 4-15 show the symbols used to represent each type of logic gate. The table contained within each figure is

Logic Gates: Circuit switching functions within a computer which act as routes for output voltage signals according to differing combinations of input signals.

■ Other Number Systems

Digital computers require the use of binary digits to perform their processing. However, working with the binary equivalents of decimal numbers can be awkward. For example, 150 in binary is 10010110. That's not bad, but suppose you wish to represent an engine speed of 2179 rpm; its binary equivalent is 100010000011. Binary numbers are usually long and their length introduces the possibility of human error when working with them.

Since any number system can be used to represent any measurable value, computer engineers simplify matters by working with other number systems. Those most often used are the octal system (base 8), the hexadecimal system (base 16) and one called the binary coded decimal (BCD) system.

Using one of these other number systems allows the computer to be loaded with less complex number combinations. The computer changes the octal, hexadecimal, or BCD numbers into binary numbers for its own use. Octal and hexadecimal systems work quite satisfactorily since they are based on numbers that are whole number powers of 2: $8 = 2^3$, and $16 = 2^4$. A digital computer can make the required conversions between base 8 or base 16 numbers and binary numbers with relative ease.

Converting from decimal (base 10) to binary numbers is not as convenient for a computer, because 10 is not a whole number power of 2. To make the more complicated calculations, the computer requires additional circuits. Binary coded decimal (BCD) numbers can be used for some operations. In the BCD system, groups of four binary numbers are used to represent each digit of a decimal number.

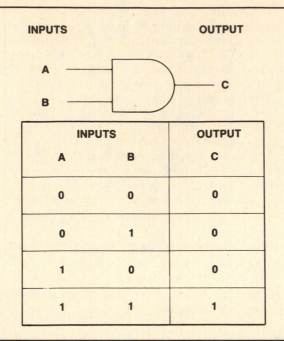

Figure 4-12. Logic symbol and truth table for an AND gate.

INPUTS   OUTPUT

INPUTS		OUTPUT
A	B	C
0	0	0
0	1	0
1	0	0
1	1	1

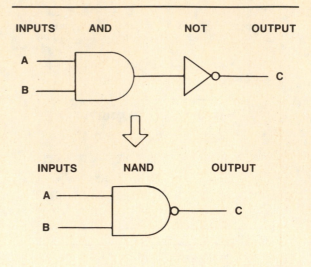

Figure 4-14. Logic symbol and truth table for a NAND gate.

INPUTS		OUTPUT
A	B	C
0	0	1
0	1	1
1	0	1
1	1	0

INPUTS   OUTPUT

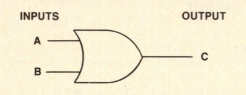

INPUTS		OUTPUT
A	B	C
0	0	0
0	1	1
1	0	1
1	1	1

Figure 4-13. Logic symbol and truth table for an OR gate.

the "truth table", showing the logical or truthful combination of input and output signals for that logic gate.

As we have seen, a digital computer works by switching output voltage on and off according to the input voltage signals. When input voltage enters a logic gate, its transistors change from a cutoff state (no voltage) to full saturation (voltage). This is equivalent to an off, or low, signal and an on, or high, signal (in binary terms, a 0 or a 1). By combining input and output signals in logical combinations, they can be made to equal binary numbers.

The most elementary logic gate inverts the signal. This is called a NOT gate, figure 4-11. When voltage to its single input terminal is high or on (binary 1), output voltage is low or off (binary 0).

The AND gate, figure 4-12, has two inputs and one output. Its output is high (1) only if both inputs are high. If one or both of the inputs are low (0), output is low.

The OR gate also has two inputs and one output, figure 4-13. However, it differs from the AND gate in that output is high (1) when one or both inputs are high. OR gate output is low (0) when both inputs are low (0).

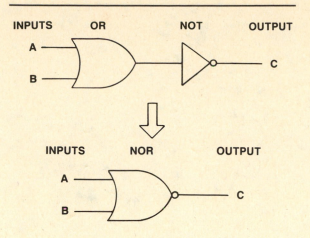

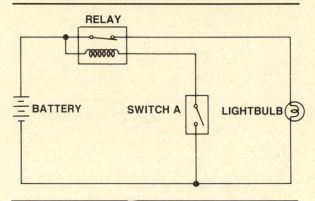

INPUTS		OUTPUT
A	B	C
0	0	1
0	1	0
1	0	0
1	1	0

Figure 4-15. Logic symbol and truth table for a NOR gate.

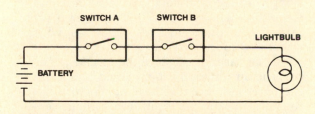

Figure 4-16. Two switches wired in series, similar to an AND gate. Both must be closed for the bulb to light.

These gates can be combined to produce other logic functions. By placing an invertor or NOT gate after an AND or an OR gate, we can invert the signal and create a NAND (NOT AND) gate, figure 4-14, or a NOR (NOT OR) gate, figure 4-15.

Relay and Switch Logic

You may find it difficult to visualize the computer logic operations just described. You can't

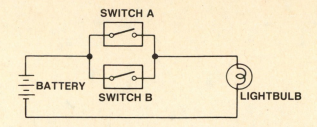

Figure 4-17. Two switches wired in parallel, similar to an OR gate. Either one or both may be closed for the bulb to light.

Figure 4-18. A circuit similar to a NOT gate, in which the output is opposite to the input.

watch anything happen because the circuits are so small that they can't be seen with the naked eye and the current moves at literally lightning speed. To help you understand what is happening, let's demonstrate digital logic by using mechanical relays and switches.

Suppose we connect two switches in series to a light bulb and a power source as shown in figure 4-16. The bulb will only light if both switches are closed; if either or both switches are open, the bulb cannot light. We have constructed a circuit equal in function to an AND gate. Switch A and switch B are equal to the input (A and B) of the AND gate; the bulb is equal to the output (C) of the AND gate.

Now let's connect the two switches in parallel to the light bulb and power source, figure 4-17. The bulb will light if (a) one switch is closed, or (b) both switches are closed. This is a basic OR gate.

What happens when we connect a normally closed relay, a switch, and a light bulb as shown in figure 4-18? When the switch is open, the relay is closed and the bulb lights. The bulb will not light if the switch is closed, since this opens the relay and shuts off current flow to the bulb. This is a basic NOT gate, in

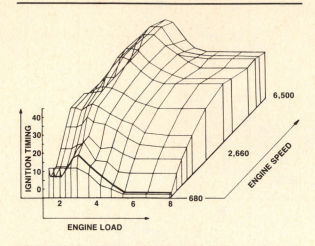

Figure 4-19. Engine mapping is used to program an automotive computer. (Porsche)

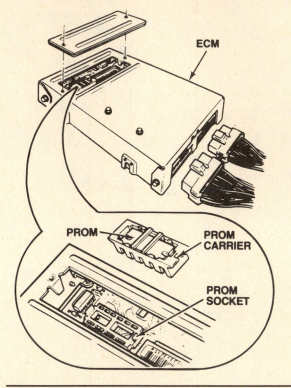

Figure 4-20. An engine computer with a replaceable PROM. (GM)

which the output is always opposite to the input, or inverted.

Series and parallel connections can be combined in various ways to produce different logic functions. The same thing can be done by arranging thousands of transistors in various combinations to produce thousands of logic gates.

COMPUTER PROGRAMS

Every computer needs instructions to do its job. These instructions are called a computer program. The program for an engine control computer consists of several elements. First are the mathematical instructions that tell the computer how to process, or ''compute'', the information it receives. Second is information that pertains to *fixed* vehicle values such as the number of cylinders, engine compression ratio, transmission type and gear ratios, firing order, and emission control devices. Finally, there is data that pertains to *variable* vehicle values such as engine speed, car speed, coolant temperature, intake airflow, fuel flow, ignition timing, and others.

Since the mathematic instructions and engine data are constant values, they are fixed and are easily placed into computer memory. To place the variable values into memory, it is necessary to simulate the vehicle and its system in operation. A large mainframe computer at the factory is used to calculate all of the possible variable conditions for any given system. This provides the control program for the individual onboard computers.

This is called system simulation and involves a process called **engine mapping**. By operating a vehicle on a dynamometer and manually ad-

justing the variable factors such as speed, load, and spark timing, it is possible to determine the optimum output settings for the best driveability, economy, and emission control.

The vehicle information obtained is stored along with the mathematical instructions in a computer memory chip called a **programmable read-only memory (PROM)**, figure 4-6, which is installed in the central computer for that particular car model. Since the PROM remembers the information programmed into it, the computer uses the PROM as its memory for comparison with the input from various sensors and then adjusts the systems under its control accordingly.

Engine mapping creates a three-dimensional performance graph which applies to a given vehicle and powertrain combination, figure 4-19. Each combination is mapped in this manner to produce a PROM. This allows a carmaker to use one basic computer for all models; the unique PROM individualizes the computer for a particular model. Also, if a driveability problem can be resolved by a change in the program, the carmaker can release a revised PROM to supersede the earlier part. Some PROMs are made in such a way that they can be erased by exposure to ultraviolet light and

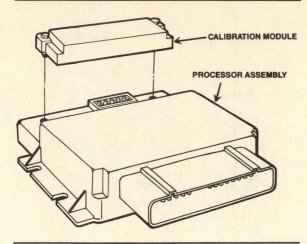

Figure 4-21. A Ford calibration module containing the system PROM. (Ford)

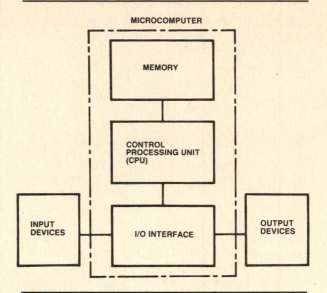

Figure 4-22. The basic structure of a microcomputer. (Toyota)

reprogrammed. These are called EPROMs, or erasable PROMs.

Most carmakers use a single PROM which plugs into the computer, figure 4-20. Some Ford computers use a larger ''calibration module'' that contains the system PROM, figure 4-21. If the onboard computer needs to be replaced, the PROM or calibration module must be removed from the defective unit and installed in the replacement computer.

PARTS OF A COMPUTER

We have dealt with the functions, logic, and **software** used by a computer. The software consists of the programs and logic functions stored in the computer's circuitry. The **hardware** is the mechanical and electronic parts that physically make up a computer. Figure 4-22 shows the basic structure of a microcomputer.

Central Processing Unit (CPU)

As mentioned earlier, the microprocessor is the **central processing unit (CPU)** of a microcomputer. Since it performs the essential mathematical operations and logic decisions that make up its processing function, the CPU can be considered the brain of a microcomputer. Some microcomputers use more than one microprocessor.

Computer Memory

The computer storage or memory function is provided by other integrated circuit (IC) devices. These simply store the computer operating program, system sensor input data, and system actuator output data for use by the CPU. Computers use two different types of

memory for their storage functions, read-only memory (ROM) and random-access memory (RAM).

Read-only memory (ROM)

Permanent memory is called **read-only memory (ROM)** because the central computer can only ''read'' the contents of the memory, but cannot change the information contained within it. Da-

Engine Mapping: A process of vehicle and engine simulation used to establish variable values for the computer to work with in determining system control.

Programmable Read-Only Memory (PROM): An integrated circuit chip installed in the onboard computer which has been programmed with operating instructions and database information for a particular vehicle.

Software: The programs and logic functions that are stored in the computer.

Hardware: The mechanical and electronic components that physically make up a computer.

Central Processing Unit (CPU): The processing and calculating portion of a microcomputer.

Read-Only Memory (ROM): The permanent part of a computer's memory storage function. The ROM can be read but not changed and is retained when power to the computer is shut off.

ta stored in ROM is retained even when power to the computer is turned off. The computer control program and specific vehicle data are stored in ROM so they will not be lost if power to the computer is interrupted. Part of the ROM is built into the computer and the remainder is in the PROM described earlier.

Random-access memory (RAM)

Temporary memory is called **random-access memory (RAM)** because the central computer can both "read" information from it and "write" new information into it as dictated by the computer program. However, data contained in RAM is lost whenever power to the computer is shut off. Depending upon the computer design, RAM can provide either short- or long-term memory. Short-term memory is lost every time the ignition switch is turned off; long-term memory is retained until the computer power supply is completely disconnected. System trouble codes and diagnostic test results are usually stored in RAM.

Adaptive memory (computer learning ability)

The control program stored in the central computer unit and PROM is designed to regulate ignition timing, fuel delivery, and other variables on an engine in proper working order. However, production variations, engine wear, variable fuel quality and other factors often combine to make an engine's real needs different from the ideal design values used to establish the initial program.

To compensate for these variables, many late-model engine control systems have an "adaptive memory" that monitors the operation of the engine and related systems. When a controlled value regularly falls outside design limits, the adaptive memory makes a small modification to the control program to reestablish proper operation.

Adaptive memory program modifications are stored in RAM and are lost when power to the computer is disconnected. When this occurs on an older or high-mileage vehicle, the car must be driven long enough to let the adaptive memory again fine-tune the engine operation. This usually requires approximately 20 miles of driving under varied operating conditions.

Input and Output Circuits

A microprocessor is not directly connected to every input or output device. The signals are received and sent by other IC devices, many of which provide the microprocessor with parallel

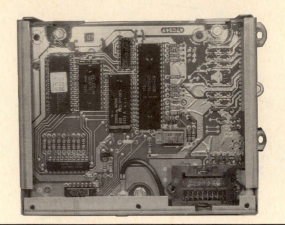

Figure 4-23. A GM onboard computer module.

connections. This allows it to receive several input signals while it is sending several output signals.

Converter Circuits

The computer must have circuits to convert input data into a form that the computer can work with. The analog signals which we have discussed must be digitized, or changed to digital signals. This conversion is done by separate IC devices called analog-to-digital (AD) converter circuits.

Similarly, the computer's output signals must be converted into a form which the output device can recognize and act upon. Since some of the output devices are analog, the digital signals to these devices must be changed to analog signals. This conversion is done by digital-to-analog (DA) converter circuits. Because the circuits that perform these functions "interface" the CPU with the input and output devices, they are sometimes called the input/output (I/O) interface, figure 4-22.

Computer Installations

The onboard automotive computer may be called an electronic control unit, module, or assembly, depending upon the carmaker and the computer application. The computer hardware is mounted on one or more circuit boards, figure 4-23, and installed in a metal case to help shield it from electromagnetic interference (EMI). The wiring harnesses that link the computer to sensors and actuators connect to multipin connectors or edge connectors on the circuit boards.

Onboard computers range from single-function units that control a single operation to

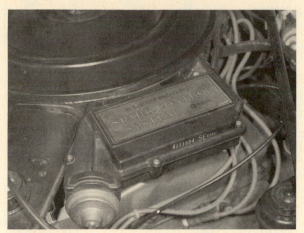

Figure 4-24. This Chrysler engine computer is mounted next to the air cleaner housing.

Figure 4-25. A GM engine computer mounted in the passenger compartment.

multifunction units that manage all of the separate but linked electronic systems in the vehicle. They vary in size from a small module to a notebook-sized box. Some Chrysler computers are installed in the engine compartment, figure 4-24. Most computers are installed in the passenger compartment either under the instrument panel or in a side kick panel, figure 4-25, where they can be shielded from possible damage caused by temperature extremes, dirt and vibration, or interference from the high electrical currents and voltages of various underhood systems.

INSTRUMENTATION AND CONTROL SYSTEMS

Automotive computer systems have two purposes, instrumentation and control. An instrumentation system is one which measures variables and displays the output in a form the driver can use. Speedometers, odometers, tachometers, gauges and warning lamps are examples of instrumentation devices.

Chrysler's Electronic Navigator is a good example of a computerized instrumentation system. The computer receives input data from various sensors as well as an analog input from the fuel gauge. By pressing a series of momentary contact pushbutton switches, the driver selects the processed information to be displayed. This can be clock functions, distance to destination, estimated time of arrival, current fuel mileage, and other factors relating to the trip on the instrument panel display.

When a computer is used as a control system, it regulates the operation of another system or systems. While there are several types of computer control systems in use today, the engine control computer is common to virtually all late-model vehicles. This computer re-

ceives input data concerning vehicle speed, engine speed and load, ignition timing, exhaust gas composition, fuel metering, and various other factors. After processing the data, the computer sends output signals to various actuators to control ignition timing, fuel metering, and operation of the emission devices.

Computers can perform dual functions by acting as both instrumentation and control systems. A multifunction computer can perform as a trip computer while regulating the speed or cruise control system. An automatic climate control system that regulates heating and air conditioning also can display temperature information. The same basic microprocessor can receive and process an input signal in different systems for different purposes. The output signals it produces can be used for different instrumentation and control purposes.

CONTROL SYSTEM OPERATING MODES

A computer control system can be selective, with different operating modes. It does not have to respond to data from all of its sensors, nor does it have to respond in the same way each time. It may ignore sensor input under specified conditions. It also may respond in different ways to the same input signal, based on inputs from other sensors. Because of this, control systems are often designed with two operating modes: open loop and closed loop.

Random-Access Memory (RAM): Computer memory in which information can be written (stored) and read. Whatever is stored in RAM is lost whenever power to the computer is shut off.

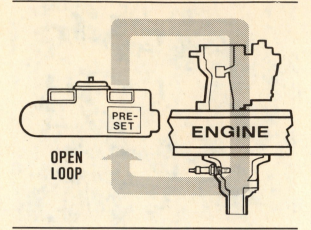

Figure 4-26. In open loop control, the computer operates according to preset specifications. (Chrysler)

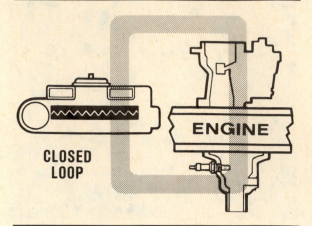

Figure 4-27. In closed loop control, the computer monitors the oxygen sensor and sends corrections to the carburetor. (Chrysler)

Open Loop Control

Open loop control means that our computer functions according to pre-established conditions in its program. It gives the orders and the output actuators carry them out. The computer ignores sensor input (feedback) as long as the pre-established conditions exist.

An engine control computer, for example, is programmed to furnish a specified amount of fuel and spark timing when the engine is first started. It will ignore signals (feedback) from the exhaust gas oxygen (EGO) sensor until coolant temperature reaches a predetermined level. Figure 4-26 is a simple diagram of open loop control.

Closed Loop Control

When the system goes into **closed loop**, the computer reads and responds to signals from all of its sensors, figure 4-27. Our engine control computer ignored the EGO sensor when the engine was first started. Once coolant temperature reaches a predetermined level, the computer accepts this sensor input and adjusts the fuel and spark timing accordingly. We say that the computer is responding to a ''feedback'' signal, that is, the sensor is feeding information back to the computer that there is an error factor in its operation that must be corrected.

INTRODUCTION TO TRANSDUCERS

A **transducer** converts, or transduces, one form of energy into another. All sensors and actuators are transducers. Sensors convert light, temperature, motion, and other types of energy into voltage signals. Actuators convert voltage signals into mechanical energy or

work. Sensors and actuators used with modern automotive computer systems often do the same work that mechanical transducers such as vacuum diaphragms did on older vehicles.

Sensors

Engine control system sensors fall into several basic categories including switches, timers, resistors, transformers and generators. With the exception of generators, all automotive sensors are resistive devices; they cannot create a voltage, they can only modify a voltage applied to them. This voltage is controlled by the microprocessor and is called the **reference voltage**.

The computer sends the reference voltage to the sensors, and receives a different voltage back. The returning signal is determined by the changing sensor resistance. The computer interprets the altered return voltage as a sign of specific changes in the engine operating condition and adjusts engine operation accordingly.

Engine control systems use either a 5-volt or a 9-volt reference voltage. In all cases, the reference voltage must always be less than minimum battery voltage so it can be maintained at a constant level at all times to prevent faulty input signals from the sensors.

Sensor characteristics and features

Automotive sensors are designed for long-term, reliable operation in a severe environment while providing reliable signals. For a sensor to function properly, it must have certain characteristics or operating features. These not only affect the selection of a particular sensor for a given function, they also set the specifications for troubleshooting and service.

These characteristics are:

- Repeatability — the sensor must function consistently. This means that a temperature switch must open and close at the design points thousands of times (repeatedly) without deviation. If the sensor produces a voltage in proportion to the condition being measured, it must do so throughout its operating range.
- Accuracy — the sensor must function within the tolerances or limits designed into it. Our temperature switch may close at 195 degrees ±1 degree, or it may close at 195 degrees ±10 degrees. The tolerances depend upon the use to which the sensor is put, but once established, the sensor must function consistently. These tolerances are used to design sensor test specifications for troubleshooting.
- Operating range — an operating or dynamic range is established for the sensor for it to function within. A digital sensor has only one or two switching points. The operating range of an analog sensor is wider and must be proportional. Signals outside the operating range are ignored by the computer.
- Linearity — this refers to sensor accuracy throughout its dynamic range. Within this range, an analog sensor must be as consistently proportional as possible to the measured value. Sensor linearity is most accurate near the center of its dynamic range, but no sensor has perfect linearity. Therefore, computer programs rely on memory data to compensate for this.

Switches and timers

Switches are the simplest form of sensors; they signal either an on or an off condition. When the switch is closed, full reference voltage is returned to the computer. When the switch is open, no return voltage signal is sent. Not all switches relay reference voltage back to the computer; some send a battery voltage signal directly to the computer when the monitored condition is met.

A common use for switch sensors is to signal the computer when a high-load accessory such as an air conditioning compressor or rear window defogger is turned on or off. The computer uses the switch signal to adjust the idle speed to compensate for the added load. Coolant temperature switches that close when the engine has reached a certain temperature are also used in some systems.

A timer, when combined with a switch, can delay a signal for a predetermined length of time. Timers prevent the computer from hav-

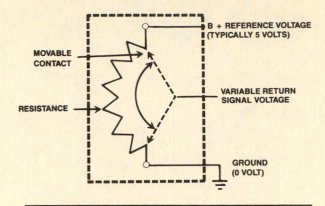

Figure 4-28. A potentiometer is a three-terminal variable resistance sensor.

ing to compensate for momentary conditions that do not significantly affect engine operation. The timer may be built into the computer, or it can be part of the switch itself.

Potentiometers

A potentiometer is a variable resistance sensor with three terminals, figure 4-28. Reference voltage is applied to one end of the resistor and the other end is grounded. The third terminal is attached to a movable contact that slides across the resistor to vary its resistance. Depending on whether the contact is near the supply or the ground end of the resistor, return voltage will be high or low.

Throttle position sensors are among the most common potentiometer-type sensors. The computer uses their input to determine the amount of throttle opening and the rate of

Open Loop: An operational mode in which the computer adjusts a system to function according to pre-determined instructions and does not always respond to feedback signals from its sensors.

Closed Loop: An operational mode in which the computer reads and responds to feedback signals from its sensors, adjusting system operation accordingly.

Transducer: A device that converts (transduces) one form of energy to another. A sensor is such a device, converting light or other energy into a voltage signal.

Reference Voltage: Voltage applied to a sensor to which a microprocessor compares the sensor's output voltage and makes any adjustments.

change. Vane-type intake airflow meters use a potentiometer to signal the amount of air entering the engine. Exhaust gas recirculation (EGR) valve flow sensors use a potentiometer to signal the valve position and thus the amount of flow.

Thermistors

A thermistor is a variable resistor with a **negative temperature coefficient (NTC)**. This means that as its temperature *increases*, its resistance *decreases*. In other words, its resistance is high at low temperatures, and low at high temperatures. The computer applies the reference voltage to one sensor terminal and receives the signal voltage from the other. As the thermistor warms up, the signal voltage increases. Coolant and cylinder head temperature sensors are the most common type of NTC thermistor sensors.

Piezoresistive devices

A piezoresistive sensor is one whose signal voltage varies with the amount of pressure or force applied to it. Like a thermistor, a piezoresistive sensor has two terminals, one to receive the reference voltage and the other to return the signal voltage to the computer. Many barometric and manifold pressure sensors are piezoresistive devices, as are engine detonation sensors.

Transformers

A transformer sensor has input and output windings with a movable core in between. The electric coupling between the two cores varies with the core position. Reference voltage is applied to the input winding. The transformer is designed so the signal voltage generated in the output winding is the same as that in the input winding when the core is centered. As the core moves away from the center position, the return signal voltage changes. Transformer sensors are used as one type of manifold pressure sensor.

Generators

Generator-type sensors do not depend upon a reference voltage. They generate a low voltage that is sent to the computer as the signal voltage. There are several types of generator sensors, including magnetic-pulse generators, Hall-effect switches, and galvanic batteries. You will study magnetic-pulse and Hall-effect sensors in detail in *Part Five* of this book.

Magnetic pulse generators are similar to the pickup coil and reluctor used in many electronic ignition systems. Hall-effect switches are used in some newer applications. These sensors are

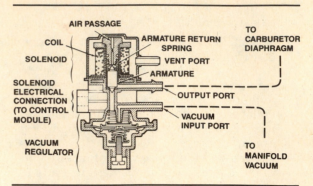

Figure 4-29. This feedback solenoid controls vacuum on carburetor diaphragms. (GM)

commonly used to provide an ignition trigger signal, or crankshaft or camshaft position information. They may be located in the distributor or mounted in the block to respond to a tooth or cutout on the harmonic damper or flywheel. Some engines use separate sensors to signal crankshaft and camshaft position.

A galvanic battery is a generator-type sensor that produces a voltage by comparing the oxygen level in the ambient air to that in the engine exhaust. The only galvanic battery on modern cars is the oxygen sensor, figure 4-1, used to help control the air-fuel mixture.

Actuators

Once the central computer has received the inputs and calculated which engine systems must be adjusted to meet the demands of the moment, it sends electrical control signals to the output control devices, or actuators.

Some of the computer's electronic output signals, such as those that regulate ignition timing, provide direct engine control. However, whenever the output must regulate a mechanical device, an actuator is required. Remember that an actuator converts the computer's electrical signal into a mechanical action. Most engine actuators are solenoids, but some are stepper motors.

Solenoids

A solenoid is essentially a digital actuator; it is either on or off. Battery voltage is applied to one terminal on the solenoid and the computer opens and closes the ground circuit attached to the other terminal, figure 4-29. In most applications, the solenoid is energized for varying lengths of time as determined by the computer program. When energized, a solenoid may extend a plunger or an armature to control engine speed. Other types of solenoids regulate vacuum flow to various emission-related systems such as air injection, vapor canister

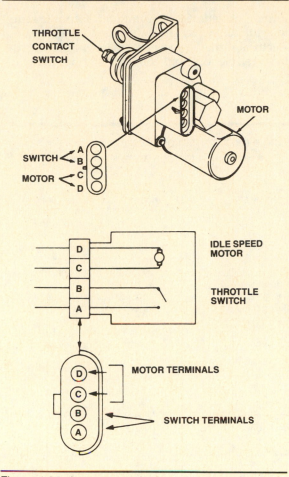

THROTTLE
CONTACT
SWITCH

MOTOR

SWITCH
MOTOR

A
B
C
D

IDLE SPEED
MOTOR

THROTTLE
SWITCH

D
C
B
A

MOTOR TERMINALS

SWITCH TERMINALS

Figure 4-30. A stepper motor is a digital actuator that moves in fixed increments. (GM)

purge, and EGR. Solenoid-controlled hydraulic valves are used in some automatic transmissions to control torque converter lockup.

Pulse width and duty cycle
Solenoids are more precisely controlled on some late-model cars through the use of a procedure called **pulse width modulation (PWM)**. In this design, the solenoid is continuously cycled on and off a fixed number of times per second. The solenoid is on (energized) for part of each cycle, and off for the remainder of that cycle. The percentage of the total cycle time that the solenoid is energized is called its **duty cycle**. The duty cycle is determined by a timed voltage pulse from the computer. The computer varies, or modulates, this pulse width to establish the duty cycle and achieve the desired solenoid output.

Pulse width modulation allows a digital output signal to provide varied or analog control of a mechanical device. It is also used to control fuel injectors and carburetor mixture control solenoids.

Stepper motors
A stepper motor, figure 4-30, is also a digital actuator. Stepper motors are d.c. motors that move in fixed increments from deenergized (no voltage) to fully energized (full voltage). A stepper motor can have as many as 120 discrete steps of motion, allowing it to serve as an analog output operated by a digital signal.

The most common uses for stepper motors are as idle speed controls. On carbureted engines, the motor often acts directly on the throttle linkage, but in most fuel injection systems, it controls an idle air bypass built into the throttle body.

SUMMARY

Every computer works on four principal functions: input, processing, storage and output. Computers can operate on analog or digital signals. An analog signal is infinitely variable. A digital signal is an on/off or high/low signal. Most variable measurements on an automobile produce analog signals which must be changed to digital signals for computer processing.

Digital computers use the binary system in which on/off or high/low voltage signals are represented by combinations of 0s and 1s. These voltage signals are switching pulses for thousands of transistor logic gates. The basic NOT, AND, and OR logic gates are the building blocks of all digital computers.

Onboard computers are used in automotive instrumentation and control systems. An instrumentation system measures variable quantities and displays its output to the driver. A control system regulates the operation of a vehicle system. One computer system can perform both functions.

A control system operates in open or closed loop modes. In an open loop mode, the sys-

Negative Temperature Coefficient (NTC): A type of sensor (also called a thermistor) that has less resistance as its temperature increases.

Pulse Width Modulation (PWM): The continuous on/off cycling of a solenoid a fixed number of times per second.

Duty Cycle: The percentage of the total time that a solenoid is energized during pulse width modulation as determined by a timed voltage pulse from the computer.

tem does not respond to an output feedback signal. In a closed loop mode, the computer responds to the feedback signal and adjusts the output value accordingly.

Computer input is provided by sensors. Sensors can be switches, timers, resistors, trans-

former, or generators. Computer output is sent to actuators, which transduce or convert the electrical signal to mechanical action. Most actuators are solenoids but some are stepper motors.

Review Questions

Choose the single most correct answer.
Compare your answers with the correct answers on page 431.

1. Technician A says that an engine computer receives input information from its actuators, processes data, stores data, and sends output information to its sensors.
   Technician B says that most late-model computers are based on analog microprocessors.
   Who is correct?
   a. A only
   b. B only
   c. Both A and B
   d. Neither A nor B

2. The operational program for a specific engine and vehicle is stored in the computer's:
   a. Logic module
   b. Programmable read-only memory (PROM)
   c. Random access memory (RAM)
   d. I/O interface

3. An exhaust gas oxygen (EGO) sensor is an example of a:
   a. Resistor
   b. Potentiometer
   c. Generator
   d. Solenoid

4. An engine detonation sensor uses a:
   a. Piezoresistive crystal
   b. Voltage divider pickup
   c. Potentiometer
   d. Thermistor

5. The binary system used by a digital computer consists of:
   a. 5 numbers
   b. 4 numbers
   c. 3 numbers
   d. 2 numbers

6. NOT gates can be added to AND gates and OR gates to create NAND gates and NOR gates because they:
   a. Invert the signal
   b. Have two inputs and one output
   c. Are binary in nature
   d. Convert the signal

7. The result of engine mapping is:
   a. A clean engine compartment
   b. Easy-to-service component locations
   c. A three-dimensional performance graph
   d. Lower design profile of the vehicle hood

8. The computer can read but not change the information stored in:
   a. ROM
   b. RAM
   c. Adaptive memory
   d. Output circuits

9. An onboard computer can act as:
   a. An instrumentation system
   b. A control system
   c. Both a and b
   d. Neither a nor b

10. Technician A says that analog input data must be digitized by an AD converter.
    Technician B says that output data must be changed to analog signals by a DA converter.
    Who is right?
    a. A only
    b. B only
    c. Both A and B
    d. Neither A nor B

11. A computer control system can do all of the following except:
    a. Ignore sensor input under certain conditions
    b. Respond in different ways to the same input signal
    c. Accept an input signal from another computer
    d. Ignore its program instructions under certain conditions

12. When the engine control computer is in open loop operation, it:
    a. Controls fuel metering to a predetermined value
    b. Ignores the temperature sensor signals
    c. Responds to the EGO sensor signal
    d. All of the above

13. The reference value sent to a sensor by the computer must:
    a. Be above battery voltage
    b. Be exactly the same as battery voltage
    c. Be less than minimum battery voltage
    d. Be ± 10 volts of the battery voltage

14. The simplest digital sensor is a:
    a. Solenoid
    b. Switch
    c. Timer
    d. Generator

15. A variable resistance sensor is called a:
    a. Potentiometer
    b. Thermistor
    c. Transformer
    d. Varactor diode

16. The percentage of time a solenoid is energized relative to total cycle time is the:
    a. Pulse width modulation (PWM)
    b. Frequency
    c. Duty cycle
    d. EPROM

17. A stepper motor:
    a. Is either on or off
    b. Is one form of solenoid
    c. Is used to operate the EGR valve
    d. Has discrete steps of movement

18. Most onboard computers work with:
    a. Binary numbers
    b. Voltage signals
    c. Both a and b
    d. Neither a nor b

19. Technician A says that throttle position sensors are analog devices.

    Technician B says that manifold absolute pressure (MAP) sensors are digital devices.

    Who is right?
    a. A only
    b. B only
    c. Both A and B
    d. Neither A nor B

20. An engine coolant temperature sensor:
    a. Receives no voltage from the microprocessor
    b. Acts as a thermistor
    c. Is a potentiometer
    d. Provides the microprocessor with a variable frequency signal

PART TWO

Basic Automotive Electrical Systems and Components

5

Automotive Wiring and Basic Circuit Components

WIRING AND HARNESSES

Now that we have discussed current flow, voltage sources, electrical loads, and simple circuits, we can start to build some automotive circuits in this chapter and the next. To build a complete circuit, we must have conductors to carry the current from the voltage source to the electrical loads. The conductors are the thousands of feet of wire and cable used in the complete electrical system. The vehicle chassis is also a conductor for the ground side of the circuits, as we will see later. We will begin our study by looking at the **wiring harnesses**, connectors, and terminals of the system.

An automobile may contain as much as half a mile of wiring, in as many as 50 harnesses, with more than 500 individual connections, figure 5-1. This wiring must perform under very poor working conditions. Engine heat, vibration, water, road dirt, and oil can damage the wiring and its connections. If the wiring or connections break down, the circuits will fail.

To protect the many wires from damage and to keep them from becoming a confusing tangle, the automotive electrical system is organized into wiring harnesses. These are bundles of wires which serve various areas of the automobile. The wires are generally wrapped with tape or plastic covering, or they may be enclosed in insulated tubing. Simple harnesses are designed to connect two components; complex harnesses are collections of simple harnesses bound together, figure 5-2.

Main wiring harnesses are located behind the instrument panel, figure 5-3, in the engine compartment, figures 5-4 and 5-5, and along the body floor. Branch harnesses are routed from the main harness to other parts of the system. The colored insulation used on individual wires makes it easier to trace them through these harnesses, especially where sections of the wire are hidden from view.

A loose or corroded connection, or a replacement wire that is too small for the circuit, will add extra resistance and an additional voltage drop to the circuit. For example, a 10-percent extra drop in voltage to the headlamps will cause a 30-percent voltage loss in candlepower. The same 10-percent voltage loss at the power windows or windshield wiper motor can reduce, or even stop, motor operation.

All automotive electrical circuits, except the secondary circuit of the ignition system (from the coil to the spark plugs), operate on 12 to 14 volts and are called low-voltage systems. (Six-volt systems on older cars and 24-volt systems on trucks also are considered low-voltage sys-

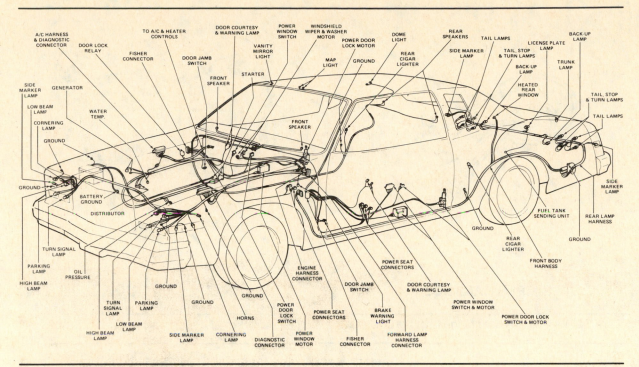

Figure 5-1. The wiring harnesses in this Buick are typical of those in late-model cars. (Buick)

tems.) The low-voltage wiring of a vehicle, with the exception of the battery cables, is called the **primary wiring**. This usually includes all lighting, accessory, and power distribution circuits.

WIRE TYPES AND MATERIALS

Almost all automotive wiring consists of a conductor covered with an insulator. Copper is the most common conductor used. It has excellent conductivity, is flexible enough to be bent easily, solders readily, and is relatively inexpensive.

A conductor must be surrounded with some form of protective covering to prevent it from contacting other conductors. This covering is called insulation. High-resistance plastic compounds have replaced the cloth or paper insulation used on older wiring installations.

Stainless steel is used in some heavy wiring, such as battery cables and some ignition cables.

Some General Motors cars use aluminum wiring in the main body harness. Although less expensive, aluminum is also less conductive and less flexible. For these reasons, aluminum wires must be larger than comparable copper wires and they generally are used in the lower forward part of the vehicle where flexing is not a problem. Aluminum wiring in GM cars can be recognized by its brown plastic wrapping; copper wiring harnesses in the cars have a black wrapping.

Wire Types

Automotive wiring or circuit conductors are used in one of three forms:

- Solid wires (single-strand)
- Stranded wires (multistrand)
- Printed circuitry.

Solid or single-strand wire is used where current is low and flexibility is not required. In automotive electrical systems, it is used inside components such as alternators, motors, relays, and other devices with only a thin coat of enamel or shellac for insulation.

Stranded or multistrand wire is made by braiding or twisting a number of solid wires together into a single conductor insulated with a covering of colored plastic, figure 5-6. Most automotive electrical system wiring uses stranded wire, either as single conductors or grouped together in harnesses or looms.

Wiring Harness: A bundle of wires enclosed in a plastic cover and routed to various areas of the vehicle. Most harnesses end in plug-in connectors. Harnesses are also called looms.

Primary Wiring: The low-voltage wiring in an automobile electrical system.

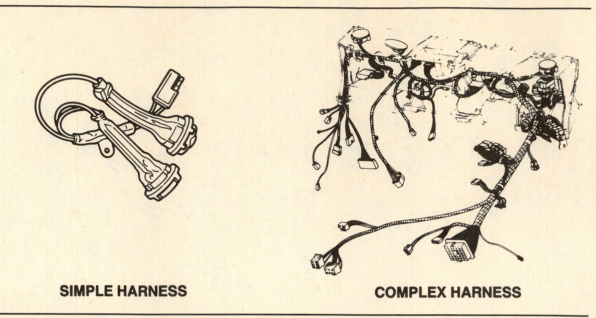

SIMPLE HARNESS   **COMPLEX HARNESS**

Figure 5-2. Wiring harnesses range from the simple to the complex. (Chrysler)

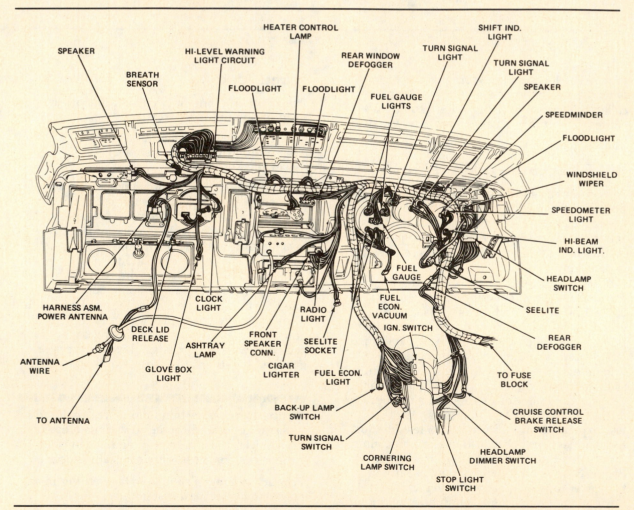

Figure 5-3. This Buick instrument panel wiring harness has 41 different connectors. (Buick)

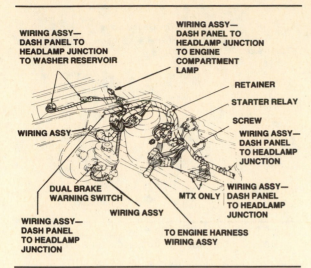

Figure 5-4. The engine compartment wiring harness on a Ford Escort connects to the headlamps and the engine harness shown in Figure 5-5. (Ford)

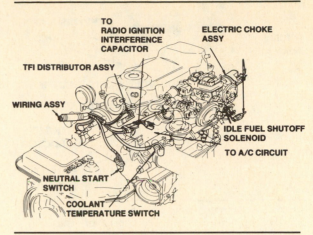

Figure 5-5. This Ford Escort engine harness connects the individual engine components to the engine compartment harness in Figure 5-4. (Ford)

Printed circuitry is a thin film of copper or other conductor that has been etched or imbedded on a flat insulating plate, figure 5-7. A complete printed circuit consists of conductors, insulating material, and connectors for lamps and other components, and is called a printed circuit (PC) board. It is used in places where space for individual wires or harnesses is limited, such as behind instrument panels.

WIRE SIZE

Automotive electrical systems are very sensitive to changes in resistance. This makes the selection of properly sized wires critical whenever systems are designed or circuits repaired. There are two important factors to consider, wire gauge number and wire length.

Wire Gauge Number

A **wire gauge** number is an expression of the cross section area of the conductor. The most common system for expressing wire size is the American Wire Gauge (AWG) system. Figure 5-8 is a table of AWG wire sizes commonly used in automotive systems.

Wire cross section area is measured in circular mils. A mil is one-thousandth of an inch (0.001″). A circular mil is the area of a circle 1 mil (0.001″) in diameter. A circular mil measurement is obtained by squaring the diameter of a conductor measured in mils. For example, a conductor ¼″ in diameter is 0.250″, or 250 mils, in diameter. The circular mil cross section area of the wire is 250 squared, or 62,500 circular mils.

Gauge numbers are assigned to conductors of various cross section areas. As gauge number increases, area decreases and the conductor becomes smaller, figure 5-9. A 6-gauge conductor is smaller than a 3-gauge conductor, and a 12-gauge conductor is smaller than a 6-gauge conductor. You learned in Chapter One that as the cross section area of a conductor decreases, its resistance increases. As resistance increases, so does the gauge number, figure 5-9. Also, because the current-carrying ability of a conductor decreases as the resistance increases, a conductor with a higher gauge number will carry less current than a conductor with a lower gauge number, figure 5-9.

Remember that the wire gauge number refers to the size of the conductor, not the size of the complete wire (conductor plus insulation). For example, it is possible to have two 16-gauge wires of different outside diameters because one has a thicker insulation than the other.

Twelve-volt automotive electrical systems generally use 14-, 16-, and 18-gauge wire. Main power distribution circuits between the battery and alternator, ignition switch, fuse box, headlamp switch, and larger accessories use 10- and 12-gauge wire. Low-current electronic circuits may use 20-gauge wire. Lighting other than the headlamps, as well as the cigarette lighter, radio, and smaller accessories, use 14-, 16-, and 18-gauge wire. Battery cables,

Wire Gauge: Wire size numbers based on the cross section area of the conductor. Larger wires have lower gauge numbers.

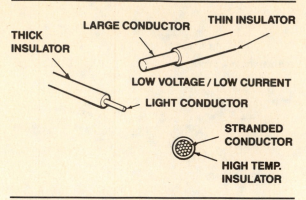

Figure 5-6. Automotive wiring may be a solid wire conductor or a multistrand wire conductor. (Chrysler)

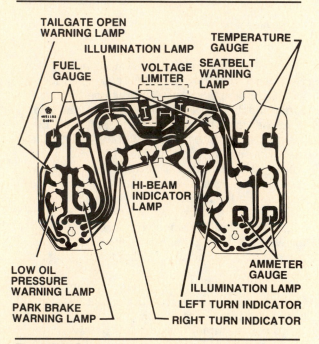

Figure 5-7. Printed circuit boards are used in automotive instrument panels. (Chrysler)

American Wire Gauge Sizes		
Gauge size	Conductor diameter (inches)	Cross-section area (circular mils)
20	.032	1,020
18	.040	1,620
16	.051	2,580
14	.064	4,110
12	.081	6,530
10	.102	10,400
8	.128	16,500
6	.162	26,300
4	.204	41,700
2	.258	66,400
1	.289	83,700
0	.325	106,000
2/0	.365	133,000
4/0	.460	211,600

Figure 5-8. This table lists the most common wire gauge sizes used in automotive electrical systems.

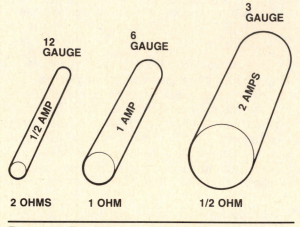

Figure 5-9. This figure shows the relationship between current capacity and resistance as the cross section of a conductor changes. (Chrysler).

however, generally are listed as 2, 4, or 6 wire, although they may be identified by an AWG wire size.

The gauge sizes used for various circuits in an automobile are generally based on the use of copper wire. A larger gauge size is required when aluminum wiring is used, because aluminum is not as good a conductor as copper. Similarly, 6-volt electrical systems require larger-gauge wires than 12-volt systems for the same current loads. This is because the lower source voltage requires lower resistance in the conductors to deliver the same current. Generally, 6-volt systems use wires two sizes larger than 12-volt systems for equivalent current loads.

While wire sizes are based on current capacity, the voltage of a system has an effect on wire selection. A low source voltage needs less resistance to transmit the same current that a higher source voltage would deliver. For example, a 24-volt electrical system can use smaller gauge wiring than a 12-volt system and still deliver equal current. In the same way, a computer sensor circuit that functions on 5 volts would need heavier wiring than a similar 12-volt circuit if the current flow were the same.

Wire Length

Wire length also must be considered when designing electrical systems or repairing circuits. As conductor length increases, so does resistance. An 18-gauge wire can carry a 10-ampere load for 10 feet without an excessive voltage drop. However, to carry the same 10-ampere load for 15 feet, a 16-gauge wire will be required. Figure 5-10 is a table showing the

Total approximate circuit amperes (12 volts)

Wire Gauge Table

Circuit length (feet)

	3	5	7	10	15	20	25	30	40	50	75	100
1	18	18	18	18	18	18	18	18	18	18	18	18
1.5	18	18	18	18	18	18	18	18	18	18	18	18
2	18	18	18	18	18	18	18	18	18	18	16	16
3	18	18	18	18	18	18	18	18	18	18	14	14
4	18	18	18	18	18	18	18	18	16	16	12	12
5	18	18	18	18	18	18	18	16	14	12	12	12
6	18	18	18	18	18	16	16	16	14	12	12	10
7	18	18	18	18	18	16	16	16	14	14	10	10
8	18	18	18	18	18	16	16	16	14	12	10	10
10	18	18	18	18	16	16	16	14	12	12	10	10
11	18	18	18	18	16	16	14	14	12	12	10	8
12	18	18	18	18	16	16	14	14	12	12	10	8
15	18	18	18	18	14	14	12	12	12	10	8	8
18	18	18	18	16	14	14	12	12	10	10	8	8
20	18	18	16	16	14	12	10	10	10	10	8	6
22	18	18	16	16	12	12	10	10	10	8	6	6
24	18	18	16	16	12	12	10	10	10	8	6	6
30	18	16	16	14	10	10	10	10	10	6	4	4
40	18	16	14	12	10	10	8	8	6	6	4	2
50	16	14	12	12	10	10	8	8	6	6	2	2
100	12	12	10	10	6	6	4	4	4	2	1	1/0
150	10	10	8	8	4	4	2	2	2	1	2/0	2/0
200	10	8	8	6	4	4	2	2	1	1/0	4/0	4/0

Figure 5-10. As wire length increases, larger gauge wire must be used to carry the same amount of current.

gauge sizes required for wires of different lengths to carry various current loads. Wire lengths are based on circuits that are grounded to the vehicle chassis.

SPECIAL WIRING

While most of the electrical system is made up of low-voltage primary wiring, special wiring is required for the battery and the spark plugs. Since these wires are larger in size than primary wiring, they are often called cables. Battery cables are low-resistance, low-voltage conductors. Ignition cables are high-resistance, high-voltage conductors.

Battery Cables

The battery is connected to the rest of the electrical system by very large cables. Large cables are necessary to carry the high current required by the starter motor. Figure 5-11 shows several kinds of battery cables. Twelve-volt systems generally use number 4 or number 6 wire cables; 6-volt systems and some 12-volt diesel systems require number 0 or number 1 wire cables. Cables designed for a 6-volt system can be used on a 12-volt system, but the smaller cable intended for a 12-volt system cannot be used on a 6-volt system without causing too much voltage drop.

Battery installations may have an insulated ground cable or one made of braided, uninsu-

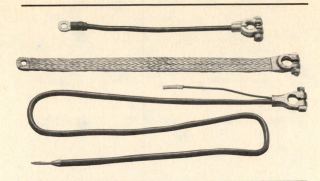

Figure 5-11. Assorted battery cables.

lated wire. The braided cables or straps are flat instead of round; however, they have the same resistance and other electrical properties of a round cable of equivalent gauge.

Most battery cables are fitted at one end with a lead terminal clamp to connect to the battery, although many import cars use a spring-clamp terminal. The lead terminal is used to reduce corrosion when attached to the lead battery

■ Metric Wire Sizes

Look at a wiring diagram or a service manual for an imported car, and you may see wire sizes listed in metric measurements. For example, if you look at a wiring diagram for a Volkswagen Rabbit or Golf, you will see wire sizes listed as 0.5, 1.0, 1.5, 4.0, 6.0, and so on. These numbers are the cross section area of the conductor in square millimeters (mm^2).

These metric measurements are not the same as circular-mil measurements. They are determined by calculating the cross section area of the conductor by the formula:

$$\text{Area} = \text{Radius}^2 \times 3.14$$

A wire with a 1-mm^2 cross section area actually has a 1.128-mm diameter.

The table below lists AWG sizes and equivalent metric wire sizes.

AWG Size (Gauge)	Metric Size (mm^2)
20	0.5
18	0.8
16	1.0
14	2.0
12	3.0
10	5.0
8	8.0
6	13.0
4	19.0

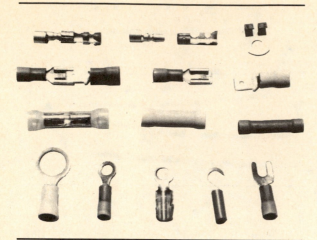

Figure 5-12. Some common single-wire terminals (connectors).

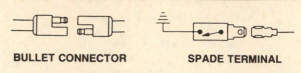

BULLET CONNECTOR   **SPADE TERMINAL**

Figure 5-13. Male and female bullet connectors and spade terminals are common automotive connectors. (Chrysler)

post. A tinned copper terminal is attached to the other end of the cable to connect to the starter motor or ground, as required.

Ignition Cables

The ignition cables, or spark plug cables, are often called high-tension cables. They carry current at 10,000 to 40,000 volts from the coil to the distributor cap, and then to the spark plugs. Because of the high voltage, these cables must be very well insulated.

Years ago, all ignition cables were made with copper or steel wire conductors. During the past 30 years, however, metallic conductor cables have been replaced by high-resistance, non-metallic cables as original equipment on cars and light trucks. While metallic-conductor ignition cables are still made, they are sold for special high-performance or industrial applications and are not recommended for highway use.

The conductors used in high-resistance, non-metallic ignition cables are made of carbon, or of linen or fiber glass impregnated with carbon. These cables evolved for two reasons:

- High-voltage ignition pulses emit high-frequency electrical impulses or radio frequency interference (RFI) that interfere with radio and television transmission, as we saw in Chapter Two. The principal method used to limit this interference is the use of high-resistance ignition cables, often referred to as suppression cables.
- The extra resistance in the cable decreases the current flow and thus reduces the burning of spark plug electrodes. The higher resistance also helps take advantage of the high-voltage capabilities of the ignition system, as we will learn in Part Five of this manual.

The high-voltage current carried by ignition cables requires that they have much thicker insulation than low-voltage primary wires. Ignition cables are 7 or 8 millimeters in diameter, but the conductor in the center of the cable is only a small core. The rest of the cable diameter is the heavy insulation used to contain the high voltage and protect the core from oil, dirt, heat, and moisture.

One type of cable insulation material is known by its trade name, "Hypalon", but the type most commonly used today is silicone rubber. Silicone is generally thought to provide greater high-voltage insulation while resisting heat and moisture better than other materials. However, silicone insulation is softer and more pliable than other materials and thus more likely to be torn or damaged by rough handling. Cables often have several layers of insulation over the conductor to provide the best insulating qualities with strength and flexibility.

CONNECTORS AND TERMINALS

Electrical circuits can be broken by the smallest gap between conductors. The gaps can be caused by corrosion, weathering, or mechanical breaks. One of the most common wear points in an automobile electrical system is where two conductors have been joined. Their insulation coats have been opened and the conductive material exposed. Special connectors are used to provide strong, permanent connections and to protect these points from wear.

These simple connectors are usually called wiring terminals. They are metal pieces that can be crimped or soldered onto the end of a wire. Terminals are made in many shapes and sizes for the many different types of connections required. They can be wrapped with plastic electrical tape or covered with special pieces of insulation. The simplest wire terminals join a single wire to a device, to another single wire, or to a few other wires, figure 5-12. Terminals for connecting to a device often have a lug ring, a spade, or a hook which can be bolted onto the device. Male and female spade terminals or

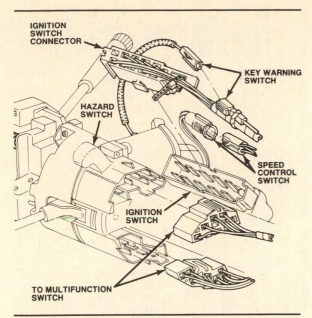

Figure 5-14. Multiple connectors are used to make complex switch connections. (Ford)

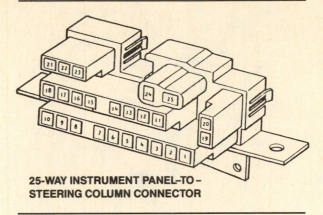

25-WAY INSTRUMENT PANEL-TO-STEERING COLUMN CONNECTOR

Figure 5-15. This junction block accepts individual wires on one side and connectors on the other. (Chrysler)

bullet connectors are often used to connect two individual wires, figure 5-13.

Multiple Wire Connectors

While the simple wiring terminals just described are really wire connectors, the term "connector" is normally used to describe multiple-wire connector plugs. This type of plug is used to connect wiring to switches, figure 5-14, or to other components. It also is used to join wiring harnesses.

Multiple wire connectors are sometimes called junction blocks. On older vehicles, a junction block was a stationary plastic connector with terminals set into it, in which individual wires were plugged or screwed in place. Because of the time required to connect this type of junction block on the assembly line, it has been replaced by a modern version which accepts several plugs from different harnesses, figure 5-15.

Some multiple connector plugs have as many as 40 separate connections in a single plug. They provide a compact, efficient way to connect wires for individual circuits while still grouping them together in harnesses. Wiring connections can be made quickly and accurately with multiple connectors, an important consideration in assembly line manufacturing.

Such connector plugs generally have hard plastic shells, with one half of the connector containing the male terminals or pins, and the other half containing the female terminals or sockets. Circuit operation can be tested by

probing the rear of the individual connections without separating the connector. A locking tab of some type is used to prevent the connector halves from separating. Separation or removal of the plug may require the locking tab to be lifted or depressed, figure 5-16.

Although many hard-shell connector designs allow removal of the individual wires or their terminals for repair, figure 5-17, carmakers are now using plugs that are serviced as an assembly. If a wire or terminal is defective, the entire plug is cut from the harness. The replacement

■ Early Wiring Problems

Early automobiles had many problems with their electrical systems. Usually these problems were the result of poor electrical insulation. For example, high-tension cable insulation, made by wrapping cotton or silk around wire and then coating it with rubber, was easily hardened by heat. The insulation often broke off, leaving bare wire exposed.

A common problem in cars that used dry cell batteries was moisture penetration through the batteries' paper insulation. Current would flow to ground, and the batteries would become discharged.

Even washing a car sometimes caused trouble. Water got into the distributor terminals and made the engine hard, if not impossible, to start. Some mechanics poured melted wax into the space between the plug wires and the distributor cap terminals.

For protection from heat, moisture, oil, and grease, wiring was often run through a metal conduit. Armored cable — insulated wire enclosed in a permanent, flexible metal wrapping — was also used, especially in a circuit where any voltage drop was critical.

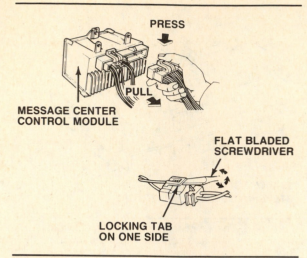

Figure 5-16. Connectors have some form of lock to prevent accidental separation. (Ford)

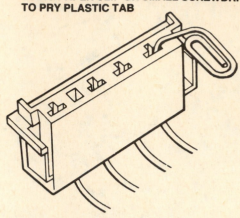

Figure 5-17. Individual terminals and wires can be removed from some connectors; other connectors are replaced as an entire assembly. (Ford)

plug is furnished with two or three inches of wires extending from the rear of the plug. These plugs are designed to be replaced by matching and soldering their wire leads to the harness.

Bulkhead Connectors

A special multiple connector, called a bulkhead connector or bulkhead disconnect, is used where a number of wiring circuits must pass through a barrier such as the firewall, figure 5-18. The bulkhead connector is installed in the firewall and multiple connectors are plugged into each side of it to connect wires from the engine and front accessories to wires in the rest of the car.

Weatherproof Connectors

Special weatherproof connectors are used in the engine compartment and body harnesses of late-model GM cars. This type of connector has a rubber seal on the wire ends of the terminals, with secondary sealing covers on the rear of each connector half. Such connectors are particularly useful in electronic systems where moisture or corrosion in the connector can cause a voltage drop. Some Japanese carmakers use a similar design, figure 5-19.

GROUND PATHS

We have spoken as if wiring carried all the current in an automotive electrical system. In fact, wiring is only about half of each circuit. The other half is the automobile engine, frame, and body, which provide a path for current flow. This side of the circuit is called the ground, figure 5-20. Automotive electrical sys-

tems are called single-wire, or ground-return systems.

The cable from one battery post, or terminal, is bolted to the car engine or frame. This is called the **ground cable**. The cable from the other battery terminal provides current for all the car's electrical loads. This is called the **insulated, or hot, cable**. The insulated side of every circuit in the vehicle is the wiring running from the battery to the devices in the circuit. The ground side of every circuit is the vehicle chassis, figure 5-20.

The hot battery cable is always the insulated type of cable described earlier. The ground cable may be an insulated type of cable, or it may be a braided strap. On many vehicles additional grounding straps or cables are connected between the engine block and the vehicle body or frame. The battery ground cable may be connected to either the engine or the chassis, and the additional ground cable ensures a good, low-resistance ground path between the engine and the chassis. This is necessary for proper operation of the circuits on the engine and elsewhere in the vehicle. Late-model vehicles which rely heavily on computerized components often use additional ground straps whose sole purpose is to minimize or eliminate electromagnetic interference (EMI), as we saw in Chapter Two.

The resistances in the insulated sides of all the circuits in the vehicle will vary depending on the number and kinds of loads and the length of the wiring. The resistance on the ground side of all circuits, that is, between each load and its ground connection, must be virtually zero. For this reason, every ground

CAVITY	DESCRIPTION
1	WINDSHIELD WIPER
2	WINDSHIELD WIPER
3	BRAKE WARNING LAMP
4	VACANT
5	WINDSHIELD WIPER
6	WINDSHIELD WIPER
7	BACK-UP LAMP
8	BACK-UP LAMP
9	WINDSHIELD WIPER
10	HAZARD FLASHERS
11	RIGHT TURN SIGNAL
12	HORN
13	LEFT TURN SIGNAL
14	HIGH BEAM
15	LOW BEAM
16	TACHOMETER
17	IGNITION RUN
18	VACANT
19	IGNITION SWITCH
20	AMMETER
21	AMMETER
22	VACANT
23	IGNITION SWITCH
24	VACANT
25	HEADLAMP SWITCH
26	IGNITION SWITCH
27	HEADLAMP SWITCH
28	A/C HIGH BLOWER
29	OIL PRESSURE
30	VACANT
31	A/C CLUTCH
32	TEMPERATURE

Figure 5-18. A bulkhead connector, or disconnect, is mounted on many firewalls. Multiple-wire connectors plug into both sides. (Chrysler)

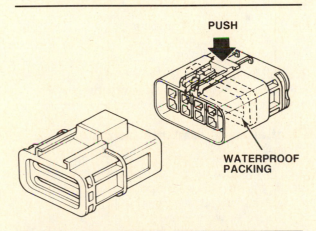

Figure 5-19. Nissan uses this type of waterproof connector. (Nissan)

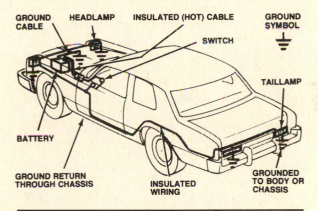

Figure 5-20. Half of the automotive electrical system is the ground path through the vehicle chassis.

connection on the vehicle is electrically the same as a connection directly to the ground terminal of the battery. This is an important point to remember. It may be helpful at this time to review the explanations in Chapter One of voltage drops and current flow in various circuits from the source, through all the loads, and back to the source.

Every electrical load is attached to the chassis so that current can pass through the ground and back to the grounded battery ter-

minal. Grounding connections must be secure for the circuit to be complete. In older cars where plastics were rarely used, most loads

Ground Cable: The battery cable that provides a ground connection from the vehicle chassis to the battery.

Insulated, or Hot, Cable: The battery cable that conducts battery current to the automotive electrical system.

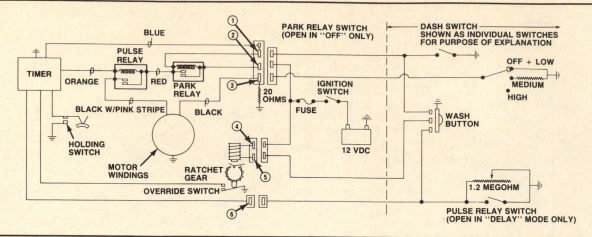

Figure 5-21. Parallel data transmission through differentiated voltage levels reduces the amount of wiring in this multiplex wiper-washer circuit. (GM)

had a direct connection to a metal ground. With the increased use of various plastics, designers have had to add a ground wire from some loads to the nearest metal ground. The ground wires in most circuits are black for easy recognition.

MULTIPLEX CIRCUITS

The use of multiplexing, or multiplex circuits, is becoming a necessity in late-model automobiles because of the increasing number of conventional electrical circuits required by the use of electronic control systems. Wiring harnesses used on such vehicles have ballooned in size to 60 or more wires in a single harness, with the use of several harnesses in a vehicle not uncommon. Simply put, there are too many wires and too limited space in which to run them for convenient service. With so many wires in close proximity, they are subject to the problem of electromagnetic interference (EMI), which you learned about in Chapter Two. To meet the almost endless need for electrical circuitry in the growing and complex design of automotive control systems, engineers are gradually reducing the size and number of wire and wiring harnesses by using a **multiplex wiring system**.

The term ''multiplexing'' means different things to different people, but generally it is defined as a means of sending two or more messages simultaneously over the same channel. Different forms of multiplexing are used in automotive circuits. For example, windshield wiper circuits often use multiplex circuits. The wiper and washer functions in such circuits work though a single input circuit by means of different voltage levels. In this type of application, data is sent in parallel form.

However, the most common form of multiplexing in automotive applications is serial data transmission, also known as time-division multiplex. In the time-division type of circuit, information is transmitted between computers through a series of digital pulses in a program sequence that can be read and understood by each computer in the system. The three major approaches to a multiplex wiring system presently in use are:

- Parallel data transmission
- Serial data transmission
- Optical data links.

We will look at each of these types of system, and then we will discuss the advantages of multiplexing over older systems of wiring.

Parallel Data Transmission

The most common parallel data multiplexing circuits use differentiated voltage levels as a means of controlling components. The multiplex wiring circuit used with a Type C General Motors pulse wiper-washer unit is shown in figure 5-21. The circuit diagram shows several major advantages over other types of pulse wiper circuits:

- Eliminating one terminal at the washer pump reduces the wiring required between the wiper and control switch
- Using a simple grounding-type control switch eliminates a separate 12-volt circuit to the fuse block
- Eliminating a repeat park cycle when the wash cycle starts with the control switch in the Off position — in standard circuits, the blades begin a wash cycle from the park position and return to park before continuing the cycle — simplifies operation.

An electronic timer controls the park and pulse relays. The timer consists of a capacitor, a variable resistor in the control switch, and electronic switching circuitry. The variable resistor controls the length of time required to charge the capacitor. Once the capacitor reaches a certain level of charge, it energizes the electronic switching circuit, completing the ground circuit to the pulse relay. This energizes the 12-volt circuit to the motor windings and the motor operates. When the driver presses the wash button, it grounds the washer pump ratchet relay coil circuits, starting a wash cycle. The electronic timer circuity uses a high-voltage signal for wiper operation and a low-voltage signal for the wash cycle.

A multiplex circuit that functions with parallel data transmission is a good tool for simple circuit control. However, transmitting data in parallel form is slower and more cumbersome than transmitting in serial form. This is important when the signal is to be used by several different components or circuits at the same time.

Serial Data Transmission

Serial data transmission has become the most frequently used type of multiplex circuit in automotive applications. It is more versatile than parallel transmission but also more complex. A single circuit used to transmit data in both directions also is called a bus data link.

Several different components, or elements within a single component, can be operated by sequencing voltage inputs transmitted in serial form. This allows each component or element to receive input for a specified length of time before the input is transmitted to another component or element. A four-element **light-emitting diode (LED)** display in the instrument cluster is a typical example. By rotating the applied voltage from left to right rapidly enough, each segment of the display is illuminated 25 percent of the time, but the human eye cannot detect that fact. To the eye, the entire display appears to be uniformly illuminated 100 percent of the time.

To prevent interference between the various signals transmitted, a multiplex system using bus data links must have a central transmitter (microprocessor) containing a special encoder. The system also requires a receiver with a corresponding decoder at each electrical load to be controlled. The transmitter and each receiver are connected to battery power and communicate through a two-way data link called a peripheral serial bus. Operational switches for each circuit to be controlled have an individual

digital code or signal and are connected to the transmitter. When the transmitter receives a control code, it determines which switch is calling and sends the control signal to the appropriate receiver. The receiver then carries out the command. Suppose a driver operates the headlamp switch. The transmitter will signal the proper receiver to turn the headlights on or off, according to the switch position.

On the Chrysler application shown in figure 5-22, each module has its own microprocessor connected to the data bus through the Chrysler Collision Detection (C2D) integrated circuit which sends and receives data. The C2D circuit acts like a traffic control officer at a four-way intersection. If the data bus is not in use, it allows unrestricted transmission from a module. However, if one module is transmitting, it blocks the transmission of data from another module until the bus (intersection) is clear. If two or more modules start to transmit at the same time, or almost at the same time, the C2D circuit assigns a priority to the messages according to the identification code at the beginning of the transmission. If a message is blocked by the C2D circuit, the module which originally sent it retransmits the signal until it is successful.

Multiplex Wiring System: An electrical circuit in which several devices share signals on a common conductor. Signals may be transmitted in parallel form by a solid-state switching device or in serial form over a peripheral data bus or fiber optic cable.

Light-Emitting Diode (LED): A gallium-arsenide diode that emits energy as light. Often used in automotive indicators.

■ **Connection Protection**

It's a well-known fact that salt and calcium used on icy roads take their toll on the underside of vehicles. They can also cause trouble with exposed electrical connections, and the Prestolite Company offers a tip for protecting these connections. When repairing broken wires or adding a splice for an accessory circuit, place a two-inch length of plastic soda straw over one end. Then join the wires, making sure you have a good solder joint. After the soldered splice has cooled, coat it freely with silicone rubber sealant. Slide the plastic straw over the splice, ensuring that the straw is completely filled with the sealing material. After it has cured, the sealed splice will be corrosion-proof.

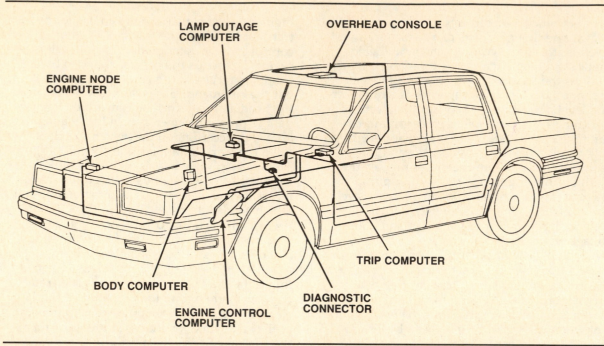

LAMP OUTAGE
COMPUTER

OVERHEAD CONSOLE

ENGINE NODE
COMPUTER

TRIP COMPUTER

BODY COMPUTER

ENGINE CONTROL
COMPUTER

DIAGNOSTIC
CONNECTOR

Figure 5-22. The Chrysler EVIC system is an example of a vehicle data communications network which allows separate computers to share data and communicate with each other through serial data transmission. (Chrysler)

Receivers work in one of two ways: they operate the electrical load directly, or they control a relay in the circuit to operate the load indirectly. They are not capable of making decisions on their own, but only carry out commands from the transmitter. However, they can send a feedback signal informing the transmitter that something is wrong with the system.

Optical Data Links

A variation of the serial data transmission approach to multiplexing substitutes optical data links or fiber optic cables for the peripheral serial bus. The concept is the same, but light signals are substituted for voltage signals. An optical data link system operates with the transmitter and receivers described above, but a light-emitting diode (LED) in the transmitter sends light signals through the fiber optic cables to a photo diode in the receiver. The light signals are decoded by the receiver, which then performs the required control function.

This form of multiplexing has been used primarily by Toyota and other foreign carmakers. Since it uses light instead of voltage to transmit signals, system operation is not affected by EMI, nor does the system create interference that might have an adverse influence on other electrical systems in the vehicle.

Multiplex Advantages

Regardless of the type of multiplex system used, such a circuit offers several advantages over conventional wiring circuits used in the past:

- The size and number of wires required for a given circuit can be greatly reduced. As a result, the complexity and size of wiring harnesses also are reduced.
- The low-current capacity switches used in a multiplex circuit allow the integration of various touch-type switches into the overall vehicle design.
- The master computer or transmitter can be programmed with timing functions for convenience features, such as locking doors above a given speed or unlocking them when the ignition is shut off.

ELECTRICAL SYSTEM POLARITY

We discussed positive (+) and negative (–) electrical charges in Chapter One. We learned that like charges repel each other and unlike charges attract each other. We also noted that the terminals of a voltage source are identified as positive and negative. In Chapter Two, we defined magnetic polarity in terms of the north and south poles of a magnet and observed that unlike poles of a magnet attract each other, just as unlike charges do. Similarly, like poles repel each other.

Figure 5-23. Many different types of switches are used in the complete electrical system of a modern automobile.

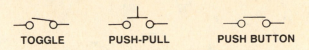

Figure 5-24. These symbols for normally open switches are used on electrical system diagrams.

The polarity of an electrical system refers to the connections of the positive and negative terminals of the voltage source, the battery, to the insulated and ground sides of the system. All domestic cars and trucks manufactured since 1956 have the negative battery terminal connected to ground and the positive terminal connected to the insulated side of the system. These are called negative-ground systems and are said to have positive polarity.

Before 1956, 6-volt Ford and Chrysler vehicles had the positive battery terminal connected to ground and the negative terminal connected to the insulated side of the system. These are called positive-ground systems and are said to have negative polarity. Foreign carmakers used positive-ground systems as late as 1969. In both kinds of systems, we say that current leaves the hot side of the battery and returns through the ground path to the grounded battery terminal.

In your service work, it is very important to recognize system polarity negative or positive ground before working on the electrical system. Some electrical components and test equipment are sensitive to the system polarity and must be installed with their connections matching those of the battery. Reversing polarity can damage alternators, cause motors to run backwards, ruin electronic modules, and cause relays or solenoids to malfunction. We will learn more about this in later chapters.

COMMON ELECTRICAL PARTS

Many common electrical parts are used in various circuits in an electrical system. All circuits have switches of some kind to control current flow. Most circuits have some form of protective device, such as a fuse or circuit breaker, to protect against too much current flow. Various kinds of solenoids, relays, and motors are used in many circuits, and whatever their purpose, they operate in similar ways wherever they are used.

Before we look at complete circuits and system diagrams in the next chapter, we should learn about some of the common devices used in many circuits. The following paragraphs describe these items.

Switches

Switches are used in automobile electrical systems to start, stop, or redirect current flow. They can be operated manually by the driver or remotely through mechanical linkage. Manual switches, such as the ignition switch and the headlamp switch, allow the driver to control the operation of the engine and accessories. Examples are shown in figure 5-23. A remotely operated switch is controlled indirectly by the driver or the passengers. For example, a mechanical switch called a neutral safety switch on automatic transmission gear selectors will not let the engine start if the automobile is in gear. Switches operated by opening and closing the doors control the interior lights.

Switches exist in many forms but have common characteristics. They all depend upon physical movement for operation. A simple switch contains one or more sets of contact points, with half of the points stationary and the other half movable. When the switch is operated, the movable points change position.

Switches can be designed so that the points are normally open and switch operation closes them to allow current flow. Normally closed switches allow the operator to open the points and stop current flow. For example, in an automobile with a seatbelt warning buzzer, the switch points are opened when the seatbelt is buckled. This stops current flow to the buzzer. Figure 5-24 shows the electrical symbols for some simple normally open switches.

A switch may lock in the desired position, or it may be spring-loaded so that a constant pressure is required to keep the points out of

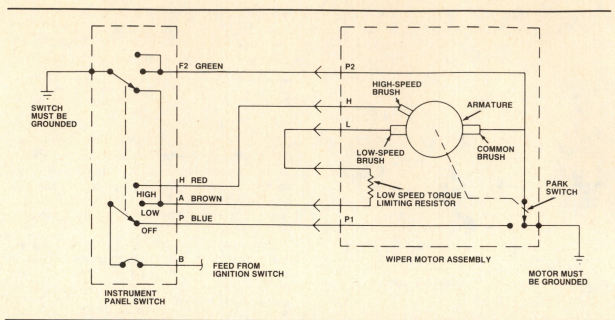

Figure 5-25. The instrument panel switch in this two-speed windshield wiper circuit has two sets of contacts linked together as shown by the broken line. The Park switch is operated by mechanical linkage from the wiper motor armature. (Chrysler)

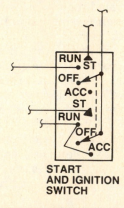

Figure 5-26. This starting and ignition switch has two sets of contacts linked together by the dashed line. Triangular terminals in the Start (ST) position indicate that this position is spring-loaded and that the switch will return to RUN when the key is released. (Chrysler)

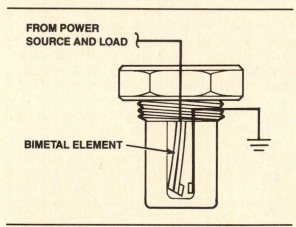

Figure 5-27. A coolant temperature switch in its normally open position. (Ford)

their normal position. Switches with more than one set of contact points can control more than one circuit. For example, a windshield wiper switch might control a low, medium, and high wiper speed, as well as a windshield washer device, figure 5-25.

Switches are shown in simplified form on electrical diagrams so that current flow through them can easily be traced, figure 5-26. Triangular contact points generally indicate a spring-loaded return, with circular contacts indicating a locking-position switch. A dashed line between the movable parts of a switch

means that they are mechanically connected and operate in unison, figure 5-26.

In addition to manual switches, automotive electrical circuits use a variety of other switch designs. Switches may be operated by temperature or pressure. Switches designed to sense engine coolant temperature contain a bimetal arm that flexes as it heats and cools, opening or closing the switch contacts, figure 5-27. Oil pressure and vacuum switches respond to changes in pressure.

Mercury and inertia switches are motion detector switches, that is, they open and close circuits automatically when their position is disturbed. A mercury switch uses a capsule containing two electrical contacts at one end.

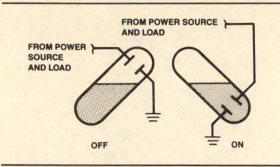

Figure 5-28. A mercury switch is activated by motion. (Ford)

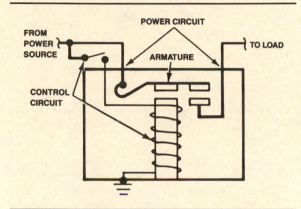

Figure 5-29. A relay contains a control circuit and a power circuit. (Ford)

The other end is partially filled with mercury, which is a good conductor, figure 5-28. When the capsule moves a specified amount in a given direction, the mercury flows to the opposite end of the capsule and makes a circuit between the contacts. This type of switch often is used to turn on engine compartment or trunk lamps. It can also be used as a rollover switch to open an electric fuel pump or other circuit in an accident.

An inertia switch is generally a normally closed switch with a calibrated amount of spring pressure or friction holding the contacts together. Any sharp physical movement (a sudden change in inertia) sufficient to overcome the spring pressure or friction will open the contacts and break the circuit. This type of switch is used to open the fuel pump circuit in an impact collision. After the switch has opened, it must be reset manually to its normally closed position.

Relays

A relay is a switch that uses electromagnetism to physically move the contacts. It allows a small current to control a much larger one. As

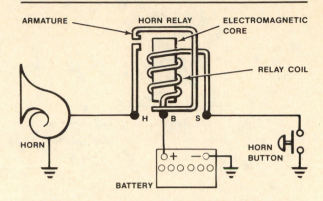

Figure 5-30. When the horn button is pressed, low current through the relay coil magnetizes the core. This pulls the armature down and closes the contacts to complete the high-current circuit from the battery to the horn.

you remember from our introduction to relays in Chapter Two, a small amount of current flow through the relay coil moves an armature to open or close a set of contact points. This is called the control circuit because the points control the flow of a much larger amount of current through a separate circuit, called the power circuit, figure 5-29.

A relay with a single control winding is generally used for a short duration, as in a horn circuit, figure 5-30. Relays designed for longer periods or continuous use require two control windings. A heavy winding creates the magnetic field necessary to move the armature; a lighter second winding breaks the circuit on the heavy winding and maintains the magnetic field to hold the armature in place with less current drain.

Solenoids

A solenoid is similar to a relay in the way it operates. The major difference is that the solenoid core moves instead of the armature, as in a relay. This allows a solenoid to change current flow into mechanical movement.

Solenoids consist of a coil winding around a spring-loaded metal plunger, figure 5-31. When the switch is closed and current flows through the windings, the magnetic field of the coil attracts the movable plunger, pulling it against spring pressure into the center of the coil toward the plate. Once current flow stops, the magnetic field collapses and spring pressure moves the plunger out of the coil. This type of solenoid is used to operate remote door locks and to control vacuum valves in emission control and air conditioning systems.

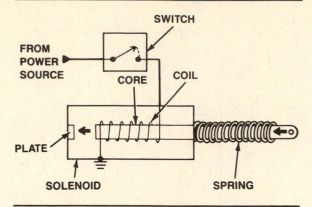

Figure 5-31. Energizing a solenoid moves its core, converting current flow into mechanical movement. (Ford)

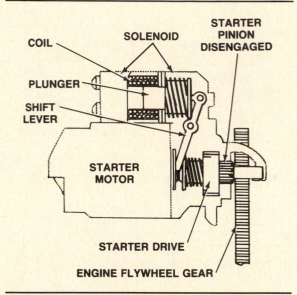

Figure 5-32. A starter solenoid mounted on the starter motor. Solenoid movement engages the starter drive with the engine flywheel gear.

The most common automotive use of a solenoid is in the starter motor circuit. In many systems, the starter solenoid is designed to do two jobs. The movement of the plunger engages the starter motor drive gear with the engine flywheel ring gear so that the motor can crank the engine, figure 5-32. The starter motor requires high current, so the solenoid also acts as a relay. When the plunger moves into the coil, a large contact point on the plunger meets a large stationary contact point, figure 5-33. Current flow across these contact points completes the battery-to-starter motor circuit. The plunger must remain inside the coil for as long as the starter motor needs to run.

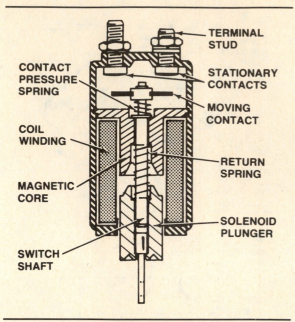

Figure 5-33. A starter solenoid also acts as a relay.

A large amount of current is required to draw the plunger into the coil, and the starter motor also requires a large amount of current. To conserve battery energy, starting circuit solenoids have two coil windings, the primary or **pull-in winding** and the secondary or **hold-in winding**, figure 5-34. The pull-in winding is made of very large diameter wire which creates a magnetic field strong enough to pull the plunger into the coil. The hold-in winding is made of much smaller diameter wire. Once the plunger is inside the coil, it is close enough to the hold-in winding that a weak magnetic field will hold it there. The large current flow through the pull-in winding is stopped when the plunger is completely inside the coil, and only the smaller hold-in winding draws current from the battery. The pull-in winding on a starter solenoid may draw from 25 to 45 amperes. The hold-in winding may draw only 7 to 15 amperes.

Some starter motors do not need the solenoid movement to engage gears. Circuits for these motors use a solenoid primarily as a current switch. The physical movement of the plunger brings it into contact with the battery and starter terminals of the solenoid, figure 5-35, allowing full battery current to flow to the starter motor. This type of solenoid can be designed to provide an alternate path to the ignition coil during starting. This bypasses the resistance wire normally used to lower coil voltage during engine operation and provides a hotter spark during starting.

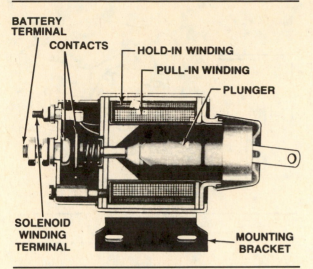

Figure 5-34. A starter solenoid, showing the pull-in and hold-in windings. (Delco-Remy)

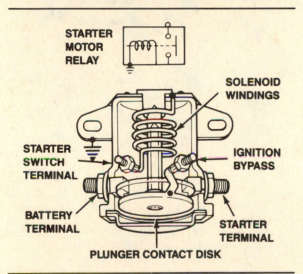

Figure 5-35. When the Ford starter relay is energized, the plunger contact disk moves against the battery and starter terminals to complete the circuit. (Ford)

Buzzers and Chimes

Buzzers are used in some automotive circuits as warning devices. Seatbelt buzzers and door-ajar buzzers are good examples. A buzzer is similar in construction to a relay but its internal connections differ. Current flow through a coil magnetizes a core to move an armature and a set of contact points. However, in a buzzer, the coil is in series with the armature and the contact points are normally closed.

When the switch is closed, current flow through the buzzer coil reaches ground through the normally closed contacts. However, current flow also magnetizes the buzzer core to move the armature and open the con-

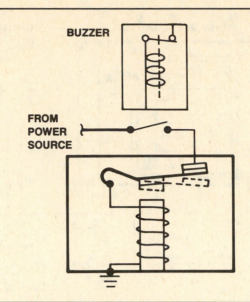

Figure 5-36. Armature spring tension is the key to buzzer operation. (Ford)

tacts. This breaks the circuit, and current flow stops. Armature spring tension then closes the contacts, making the circuit again, figure 5-36. This action is repeated several hundred times a second, and the vibrating armature creates the buzzing sound.

Most simple automotive buzzers are sealed units and simply plug into their circuits. Some buzzers are combined in a single assembly with a relay for another circuit, figure 5-37, such as a horn relay. This application is used on some General Motors cars. While mechanical buzzers are still in use, they are comparatively heavy and draw a relatively high current compared to the lighter solid-state chimes and buzzers provided by electronic technology and tone generators.

Motors

The typical automotive electrical system includes a number of motors which perform various jobs. The most common is the starter motor (also called a cranking motor) which ro-

Pull-In Winding: The coil of large-diameter wire in a solenoid that is used to create a magnetic field to pull the solenoid plunger into the coil.

Hold-In Winding: The coil of small-diameter wire in a solenoid that is used to create a magnetic field to hold the solenoid plunger in position inside the coil.

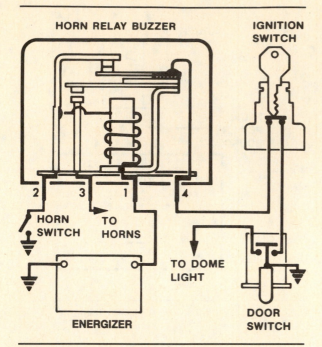

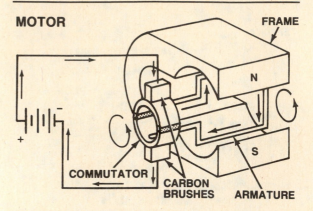

Figure 5-39. A simple motor.

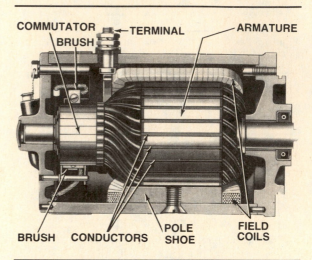

Figure 5-40. An electric motor. (Delco-Remy)

Figure 5-37. Typical horn relay and buzzer circuits. (Delco-Remy)

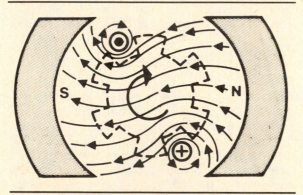

Figure 5-38. The motor principle.

tates the automobile's crankshaft until the engine starts and can run by itself. Other smaller motors run windshield wipers, power windows, and other accessories. Whatever job they do, all electric motors operate on the same principles of electromagnetism.

We explained the motor principle in terms of magnetic field interaction in Chapter Two. When a current-carrying conductor is placed in an external magnetic field, it tends to move out of a strong field area and into a weak field area, figure 5-38. This motion can be used to rotate an armature. Now we will see how automotive electrical motors are constructed and used.

A simple picture of electric motor operation, figure 5-39, looks much like the operation of a simple generator. Instead of rotating the looped conductor to induce a voltage, however, we are applying a current to force the conductor to rotate. As soon as the conductor has made a half-revolution, the field interaction would tend to force it back in the opposite direction. To keep the conductor rotating in one direction, the current flow through the conductor must be reversed. This is done by the split-ring commutator, which rotates with the conductor, figure 5-39.

Current is carried to the conductor through carbon brushes. At the point where current direction must be reversed, the commutator has rotated so that the opposite half of the split ring is in contact with the current-feeding brush. Current flow is reversed in the conductor and rotation continues in the original direction. In actual motors, many more conductor loops are mounted on an armature, figure 5-40.

Electric motors can be manufactured with several brushes and varying combinations of series and parallel connections for armature

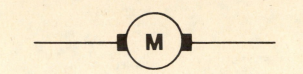

Figure 5-41. The electrical symbol for a motor.

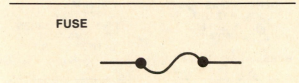

Figure 5-42. The electrical symbol for a motor.

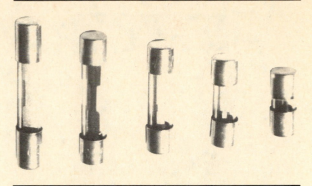

Figure 5-43. The lengths of SFE fuses vary with the current ratings.

windings and electromagnetic field windings. The design depends upon the use to which the motor will be put.

Electric motors generally use electromagnetic field poles because they can produce a strong field in a limited space. Field strength in such a motor is determined by the current flow through the field windings. The starter motor is the most common automotive application of this design.

Most small motors used in automotive applications, however, are built with permanent magnet fields. These motors are inexpensive, lightweight, can reverse direction of operation if necessary and be equipped with up to three operating speeds. They are ideal for constant light loads such as a small electric fan.

Regardless of how they are built, all motors work on these principles. Understanding the internal connections of a motor is essential for testing and repair. Figure 5-41 shows the circuit symbol for a motor.

Circuit Protection Devices

Any amount of current flow through a conductor will raise the temperature of the conductor. The amount of heat generated depends upon the gauge of the conductor, its resistance, and the amount of current present. If a wire carries too much current, the heat could damage or destroy the insulation, the conductor, and nearby wires. Similarly, too much current flow can damage other electrical devices. Circuit protection devices are designed to keep circuitry from being overloaded with current. Automotive electrical systems use three types of protectors:

- Fuses
- Circuit breakers
- Fusible links.

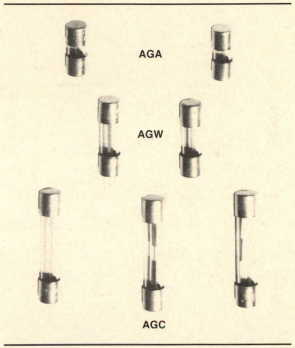

Figure 5-44. Regardless of the current ratings, all AGA (top) fuses are the same length, as are AGW (center) and AGC (bottom) fuses.

A circuit protection device "blows", or opens the circuit, because of a problem somewhere in the circuit. Installing a new device will not solve the problem, as whatever caused the first device to blow will quickly do the same to the replacement. You must always determine and correct the cause of the blown device before the circuit can be restored to working order.

Fuses

A fuse contains a fine piece of metal that can carry a specified current without damage. Any current higher than that rating will melt, or fuse, the metal and open the circuit. Figure 5-42 shows the electrical symbol for a fuse. Fuses may be cylindrical or blade-type.

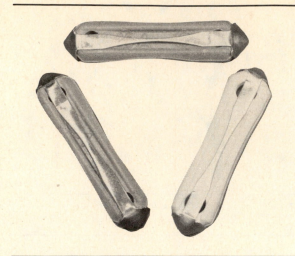

Figure 5-45. These ceramic cartridge fuses are used in European cars.

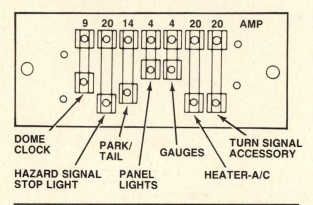

Figure 5-46. Front view of a typical fuse panel. (Chrysler)

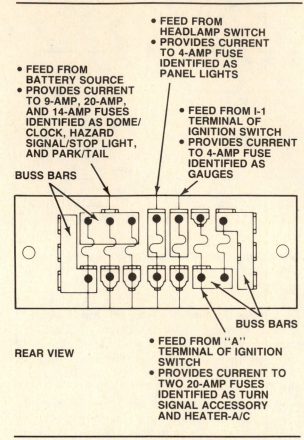

- FEED FROM HEADLAMP SWITCH
- PROVIDES CURRENT TO 4-AMP FUSE IDENTIFIED AS PANEL LIGHTS

- FEED FROM BATTERY SOURCE
- PROVIDES CURRENT TO 9-AMP, 20-AMP, AND 14-AMP FUSES IDENTIFIED AS DOME/CLOCK, HAZARD SIGNAL/STOP LIGHT, AND PARK/TAIL

- FEED FROM I-1 TERMINAL OF IGNITION SWITCH
- PROVIDES CURRENT TO 4-AMP FUSE IDENTIFIED AS GAUGES

BUSS BARS

BUSS BARS

REAR VIEW

- FEED FROM "A" TERMINAL OF IGNITION SWITCH
- PROVIDES CURRENT TO TWO 20-AMP FUSES IDENTIFIED AS TURN SIGNAL ACCESSORY AND HEATER-A/C

Figure 5-47. Rear of the same fuse panel, showing buss bars and electrical connections. (Chrysler)

Cylindrical fuses

Cylindrical automotive fuses contain a fine strip of zinc, housed either in a glass cylinder or on a ceramic cartridge. Glass fuses are uniform in diameter, but vary in length according to current rating. The narrow section in the middle of the fuse strip is its weak point, and it is this section that will melt if current higher than the rating passes through the fuse. The wide sections at each end of the strip and the end caps of the fuse dissipate the heat of brief current overloads that are not serious enough to harm the circuit.

Fuses are rated by current capacity. It is excessive current, not voltage, that causes a fuse to burn out or blow. As long as the current passing through it is within the limit tolerated by its design, a fuse can operate with varying voltages. For example, a 10-ampere fuse will work in a 10-ampere 6-volt circuit or a 10-

ampere 12-volt circuit. Automotive fuse ratings range from 0.5 to 35 amperes, with those in the 4- to 20-ampere range most commonly used. Fuse identification is provided on one or both end caps.

Fuses are made in a range of standard sizes and ampere ratings established by the Society of Fuse Engineers (SFE). All SFE fuses have the same diameter, but the length varies according to the current rating. Figure 5-43 shows several SFE fuses. The Bussman Division of McGraw-Edison makes several types of automotive fuses, known as the AGA, AGW, and AGC series, figure 5-44. These also are made in various current ratings, but the lengths of the fuses in each series are the same. Therefore, an AGC 5-ampere fuse will fit in the same fuse holder as an AGC 20-ampere fuse.

Many European vehicles use ceramic cartridge fuses, figure 5-45. These work exactly like cylindrical glass fuses, but have exposed elements and pointed ends that fit into special fuse holders. Ceramic cartridge fuses are manufactured in a limited number of amperage ratings, and are color-coded accordingly for

Cavity	Fuse	Items fused
1	5 amp	Cluster w/wiper and headlamp switch, ashtray lamp, oil gauge, temperature gauge, tailgate lock switch, rear window defogger, heated back-light, stereo tape, radio, clock, heater-A/C control lamps
2	5 amp	Dual brake, oil pressure, door ajar indicator, seatbelt lamps w/lift safety relay, seatbelt time delay relay and buzzer, high-temperature lamp, voltage limiter, radio capacitor, fuel and temperature gauge, oil gauge
3	5 amp	Radio w/tape
4	20 amp	Back-up and left turn signal lamps, turn signal flasher, speed control, rear window defogger, A/C clutch, cornering lamps, power antenna
5	20 amp	Hazard flasher
6	20 amp	Stop, dome, rear dome, trunk, glove box, map, courtesy, headlamp switch, ignition switch, vanity, and visor lamps; time delay relay, key-in and headlamp-on buzzer, clock, cigarette lighter
7	20 amp	Side marker, tail, license, parking, and instrument lamps
8	20 amp	Horn (dual) and horn relay
9	30 amp C/B	Power window, power seat, tailgate window lift, tailgate lock
10	30 amp	A/C blower motor, heater blower motor, heated back-light relay, electric deck lid

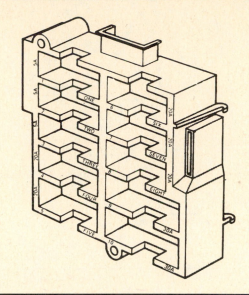

Figure 5-48. Fuse panel codes indicate fuse sizes and circuit connections. (Chrysler)

visual identification. Cylindrical glass fuses designed with pointed ends are available to replace this type of fuse.

Most of the fuses in an automotive electrical system are located in a fuse box or panel, figure 5-46, located under the instrument panel, behind a side kick panel, or in the engine compartment. Current to the plastic fuse panel comes directly from the battery or through the accessory circuit of the ignition switch. The power leads are attached to **buss bars**, which are solid metal strips to which fuse holders are riveted, figure 5-47.

A circuit which has a frequent heavy current demand, such as for the windshield wipers, the hazard flasher, or the radio, will have its own fuse. Other circuits may have inline fuses installed in plastic fuse holders and spliced into the circuit wiring. Low-current circuits that are used infrequently, such as courtesy lamps, cigarette lighters, and glove box lamps, can be grouped together and protected by a single fuse. Fuse panels generally have some kind of coding used to identify the fuse sizes and circuit connections, figure 5-48.

Some fuse panels even have a built-in test circuit, figure 5-49. With the ignition and light switches on, the technician moves a slide knob to each detented position and a check light comes on if the fuse is good.

ATO, ATC, and ATM blade-type fuses
The blade-type, or Autofuse, was first introduced in 1977 on General Motors cars and has been adopted by all domestic and most foreign carmakers to reduce the size of the fuse block. The fuse element is similar to that used in cylin-

drical fuses, but one continuous piece of metal serves both as the element and blade terminals, and is sealed in a flat plastic body. When inserted in a fuse panel, the tops of the terminals are exposed. This allows a technician to check the fuse condition with a test probe without removing the fuse from the fuse block.

Autofuses are color-coded according to current rating (3 to 30 amperes), which also is stamped on the plastic body. Some darker colors, however, make it difficult to visually determine if the fuse is good or bad, while it is sometimes difficult to tell the difference between the pastel colors, especially in bad lighting. Figure 5-50 shows the Autofuse design and the difference between a good and a bad fuse.

The Minifuse was introduced in 1990 with current ratings of 5 to 30 amperes. This blade-type fuse is identical in design and appearance to the original Autofuse, but only two-thirds its size, figure 5-51. Its smaller size allows more specific circuit fusing for a given size fuse block. As an example, standard Chrysler fuse blocks holding 20 Autofuses would provide enough space for 28 Minifuses.

Circuit breakers
Circuit breakers are mechanical devices that use the different rates of expansion in heated

Buss Bar: A solid metal strip, or bar, used as a conductor in a fuse panel.

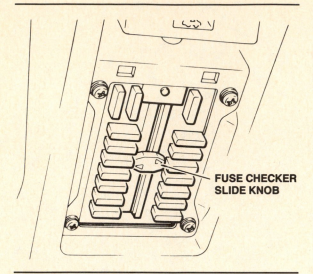

Figure 5-49. The built-in fuse tester used in some imported vehicles. (Mitsubishi)

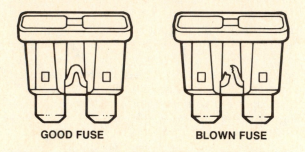

GOOD FUSE   **BLOWN FUSE**

Figure 5-50. A visual inspection will determine the condition of an Autofuse. (GM)

metals to protect circuitry. Unlike fuses, they last through repeated uses. They are used in circuits where temporary overloads are more frequent and where power must be restored rapidly, as in the headlamp circuit.

A circuit breaker consists of a set of contact points, one on a fixed mounting and the other on a bimetallic strip, figure 5-52. As current flows across the bimetallic strip, the metals heat and expand at different rates. If too much current flows, the expansion will be great enough to bend the strip and open the contact points, stopping current flow. The strip cools in a few seconds and the points close. If current flow is still too high, the strip will again heat and open the points. This process will continue until the excessive current is stopped. These are called self-resetting, cycling, or Type I circuit breakers.

Manual resettable or non-cycling, Type II breakers do not reset automatically, but remain open once the current has gone too high. A

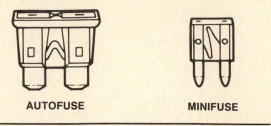

AUTOFUSE   **MINIFUSE**

Figure 5-51. Autofuse and Minifuse comparison. (GM)

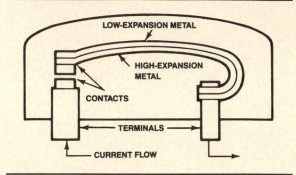

Figure 5-52. A typical circuit breaker. (Ford)

button pops out of the breaker case to indicate that the circuit has been broken. After correcting the source of the problem, the technician can reset the breaker by simply pressing the button.

A second type of non-cycling circuit breaker is a solid-state device called an Electronic Circuit Breaker (ECB). The device has a positive temperature coefficient. The resistance of the ECB increases greatly whenever it is subjected to excessive current flow. When the resistance reaches a predetermined point, the circuit is effectively open, and the ECB will not reset until voltage is removed from its terminals. When voltage is removed, the ECB will reset within one or two seconds.

Type I circuit breakers are commonly used in the headlamp circuit. If the headlamp circuit receives too much current, the repeated opening and closing of the breaker will flash the head lamps so that the car can be safely stopped. Circuit breakers also can be found inside some electrical devices, to protect the innards, and in other lamp circuits. The electrical symbols for a circuit breaker are shown in figure 5-53.

Fusible links
In addition to fuses and circuit breakers, fusible links can protect circuits. These are short lengths of smaller-gauge wire installed in the circuit they are to protect. Fusible links are used when it would be awkward to run wiring from the voltage source to the fuse panel and back to the load. They also are used in circuits

CIRCUIT BREAKER

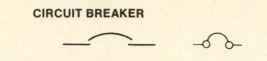

Figure 5-53. The electrical symbols for a circuit breaker.

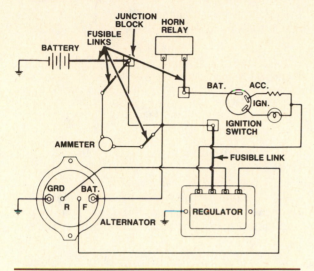

Figure 5-54. Fusible links in an automotive electrical circuit.

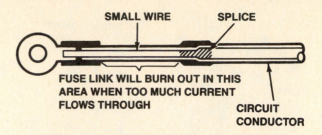

FUSE LINK WILL BURN OUT IN THIS AREA WHEN TOO MUCH CURRENT FLOWS THROUGH

Figure 5-55. Construction of a typical fuse link. (Ford)

Fuse elements and maxifuses

The Pacific Fuse Element was the first real advance in fusible link design in decades, making its domestic vehicle appearance on the 1988 Lincoln Continental. Often called a fuse link or auto link, this plug-in device looks somewhat like a long, fat blade-type fuse. The fuse link is designed to protect wiring from a direct short to ground, just as the fusible link does. The housing contains a short link of wire appropriate for the rated current load. The transparent top of the housing allows you to see the link inside, figure 5-56.

Fuse links are available in three configurations. The most commonly used, Series 0 (zero), has a female receptacle at one end, figure 5-56, and plugs into a fuse block containing male terminals. Series 1 has male terminals and plugs into the fuse block like a blade-type fuse. Series 2 has bent terminal legs. Series 1 and 2 can be bolted in place and have a predrilled hole in each terminal leg for this purpose. Like Autofuses, fuse links are color-coded according to amperage value. They are used, however, in high-amperage circuits (30 to 100 amperes), and are easier to inspect or service than a standard fusible link.

not otherwise protected, and at junction connections or near a circuit splice. Figure 5-54 shows common fusible link locations in a typical circuit.

A current overload will melt the link before it damages the rest of the circuit, figure 5-55. Links are usually four wire-gauge sizes smaller than the rest of the circuit wiring. For example, a circuit using 12-gauge wiring would be protected by a 16-gauge fusible link. The link is covered with a very heavy insulation which will blister and bubble when the conductor melts, showing that the link has fused. However, you cannot always see an open fusible link. Check for battery voltage beyond the fusible link to verify continuity.

Melted links are replaced by soldering or connecting a new one in place after the problem in the circuit has been corrected. Some fusible links are prefabricated and need only be installed. These often are color-coded to indicate current-carrying capacity. Others must be fabricated from a spool of special wire; never use ordinary wire to make a fusible link. When fabricating a fusible link, do not make it longer than nine inches, or it will not provide the required overload protection.

■ Circuit Breakers as Test Aids

Finding a problem in a circuit that keeps blowing fuses as fast as you put them in can be a real problem. You can keep the circuit operating long enough to locate the fault, however, by temporarily substituting a circuit breaker for the fuse. Simply take a 20- to 25-ampere circuit breaker and solder two short leads with alligator clips to the breaker terminals. Then, attach the clips to the fuse clips in the fuse panel. Operate the circuit, and the breaker will pop on and off to keep the circuit working long enough for you to find the trouble spot. After fixing the problem, install a new fuse of the correct current rating.

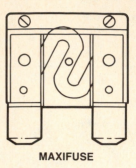

MAXIFUSE

Figure 5-56. The transparent top of the Pacific Fuse Element on the left has been removed to show the element inside. The one on the right shows the legs with the female receptacles that fit over blades in the fuse block or power distribution center.

Figure 5-57. The Maxifuse looks like a large Autofuse. About the same overall size of a Pacific Fuse Element, it is much thinner and requires less space in the fuse block or power distribution center. (GM)

The Maxifuse is the latest design to appear as a replacement for fusible links. It looks and acts like a giant Autofuse, figure 5-57, but has a slightly longer average opening time. It was designed as a slower-blowing fuse to prevent nuisance blows. Maxifuses are available in ten-degree increments for circuits from 20 to 80 amperes.

SUMMARY

Many of the conductors in an automobile are grouped together into harnesses to simplify the electrical system. The conductors are usually made of copper, stainless steel, or aluminum covered with an insulator. The conductor can be a solid or single-strand wire, multiple or multistrand wire or printed circuitry.

The wire size or gauge depends on how much current must be carried for what distance. Wire gauge is expressed as a number —

the larger the number, the smaller the wire's cross section.

Cars use some special types of wire, especially in battery cables and ignition cables. Different wires in the car are joined by terminals and connectors. These can join single wires or 40 or more wires.

Part of every automotive circuit is the ground path through the car's frame and body. The battery terminal that is connected to ground determines the electrical system's polarity. Most modern automobiles have a negative-ground system.

Multiplexing simplifies wiring by sending two or more electric signals over a single channel.

Along with conductors, connectors and the ground path, each automotive circuit has controlling or working parts. These include switches, relays, solenoids, buzzers and motors. Most circuits are protected by at least one fuse, circuit breaker, or fusible link.

Review Questions

Choose the single most correct answer.
Compare your answers with the correct answers on page 431.

1. Which of the following is *not*
   considered part of the primary
   wiring system of an automobile?
   a. Spark plug cables
   b. Lighting circuits
   c. Accessory wiring circuits
   d. Power distribution circuits

2. Automotive wiring, or circuit
   conductors, exist as all of the
   following, *except*:
   a. Single-strand wire
   b. Multistrand wire
   c. Printed circuitry
   d. Enameled chips

3. Which of the following wires are
   known as suppression cables?
   a. Turn signal wiring
   b. Cables from the battery to the
      starter motor
   c. Cables from the distributor
      cap to the spark plugs
   d. Wiring harnesses from the
      fuse panel to the accessories

4. High-resistance ignition cables
   are used to do all of the following,
   except:
   a. Reduce radiofrequency
      interference
   b. Provide extra resistance to
      reduce current flow to the
      spark plugs
   c. Provide more current to the
      distributor
   d. Boost the voltage being
      delivered to the spark plugs

5. One of the most common wear
   points in an automobile electrical
   system is:
   a. At the ground connecting side
   b. The point where a wire has
      been bent
   c. Where two connectors have
      been joined
   d. At a maxifuse connection

6. The symbol below indicates a:

   a. Battery
   b. Capacitor
   c. Diode
   d. Ground

7. Which of the following is *not* a
   term used to describe an
   automobile wiring system?
   a. Hot-return system
   b. Single-wire system
   c. Ground-return system
   d. Negative-ground system

8. For easy identification, ground
   wires on most automotive
   electrical systems are
   color-coded:
   a. Red
   b. White
   c. Black
   d. Brown

9. Which of the following is *not* used
   to switch current flow?
   a. Relay
   b. Solenoid
   c. Transistor
   d. Coil Windings

10. Two separate windings are used
    in starter solenoids to:
    a. Increase resistance in the
       circuit
    b. Decrease resistance in the
       circuit
    c. Increase current being drawn
       from the battery
    d. Decrease current being drawn
       from the battery

11. Which of the following reverses
    the flow of current through the
    conductor of a motor?
    a. The armature
    b. The terminals
    c. The field coils
    d. The commutator

12. The symbol shown is for a:

    a. Fuse
    b. Relay
    c. Motor
    d. Transistor

13. Which of the following is *not* used
    to protect a circuit from too much
    current flow?
    a. Fuse
    b. Buss bar
    c. Fusible link
    d. Circuit breaker

14. What usually causes a fuse to
    "blow"?
    a. Too much voltage
    b. Too much current
    c. Too little voltage
    d. Too little resistance

15. Fuses are rated by _____
    capacity.
    a. Current
    b. Voltage
    c. Resistance
    d. Power

16. Which of the following is true of
    circuit breakers?
    a. Made of a single metal strip
    b. Must be replaced after excess
       current flow
    c. Less expensive than fuses
    d. Used for frequent temporary
       overloads

6

Introduction to Electrical Circuit Diagrams

In the preceding chapters, we have been using symbols, figure 6-1, to show some of the components used in an automotive electrical system. Now that we have studied the basic parts of the system (voltage source, conductors, and loads), we can begin to put them together into complete circuits. First, however, we must add some more symbols to our list. Figure 6-2 shows additional symbols for many of the electrical devices that you will see on the diagrams in this chapter. These symbols and variations of them are used by automobile manufacturers to show you on paper what the electrical systems of their vehicles contain.

Figure 6-3 illustrates symbols used by Chrysler Corporation. Figure 6-4 shows symbols used by Volkswagen on wiring diagrams for vehicles it manufactured in the United States. Chrysler Corporation, General Motors Corporation (GM), and Ford Motor Company are the major domestic carmakers. We will be using some of their illustrations, as well as representative diagrams from Toyota and Nissan, so that you can see how different manufacturers present electrical information.

COLOR CODING

Manufacturers also show you what their electrical systems look like by using **color coding**. We learned in Chapter Five that most automotive wires are covered with a colored polyvinyl chloride (PVC) or plastic insulation. The color of the insulation can help you find a particular wire in the system. Some drawings of a circuit have letters and numbers printed near each wire, figure 6-5. By looking at the code table that accompanies the drawing, you can find out what the letters and numbers stand for. As you can see, the Chrysler code contains information on wire gauge and circuit numbers, as well as wire color. (We will discuss circuit numbers soon.) Figures 6-6, 6-7, and 6-8 show how GM, Ford, and Toyota may present color code information. Note that the Toyota diagram simply has the color name printed on the wires; wire gauge is not identified in the drawing, figure 6-8.

Some GM shop manuals contain individual electrical circuit or Valley Forge diagrams (named after the company that originally devised them) in which the color of the lines matches the color of the wires. In addition, the name of the color is printed beside the wire, figure 6-9. The wire gauge may also be printed (in metric) immediately before the color name. Other GM drawings contain a statement that all wires are of a certain gauge, unless otherwise identified. If this is the case, only some wires in the drawing will have a gauge number printed on them.

The Ford circuit and table in figure 6-7 are for a heater and air conditioner electrical circuit. The wire numbers are indicated by code numbers, which are also circuit numbers. Again, no wire gauges are identified in this example.

Color Coding: The use of colored insulation on wire to identify an electrical circuit.

■ 60 Years of Color-Coding

The sixth edition of the Reo Motor Car Instruction Book shows wiring diagrams for both the left- and right-hand drive models of the 1923-27 E-Roadster. On the left-hand drive model, shown here, the wire from the ignition switch to the generator cutout is identified as 10-gauge wire having a green insulation with a red tracer. The same wire on the right-hand drive model is identified as 10-gauge with yellow insulation.

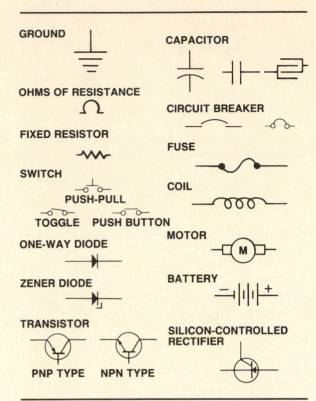

Figure 6-1. The electrical symbols we have used so far.

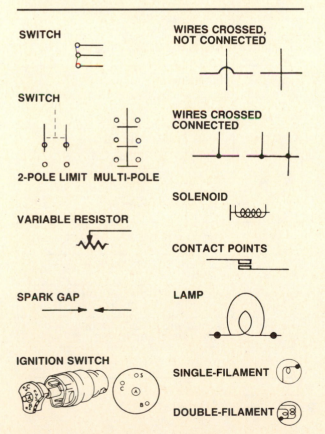

Figure 6-2. Some other common symbols.

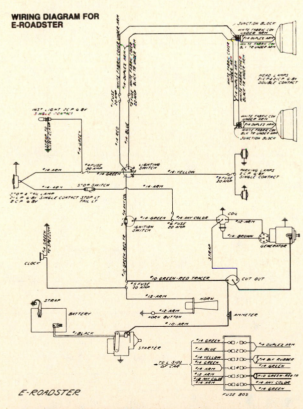

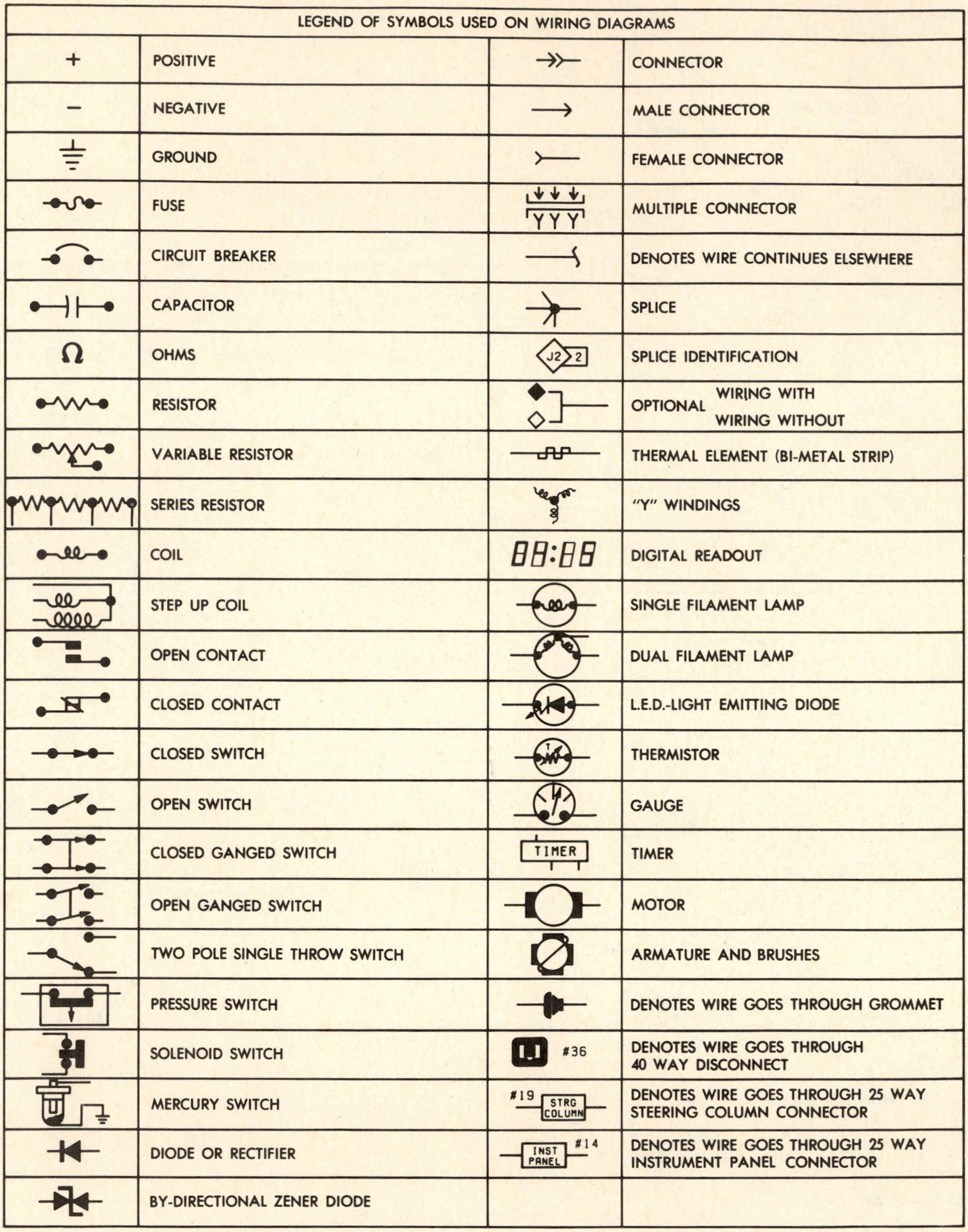

LEGEND OF SYMBOLS USED ON WIRING DIAGRAMS			
+	POSITIVE	⟶≫⟶	CONNECTOR
−	NEGATIVE	⟶→	MALE CONNECTOR
⏚	GROUND	⟩—	FEMALE CONNECTOR
⟍⟋	FUSE	↓↓↓ YYY	MULTIPLE CONNECTOR
⟍⌒⟋	CIRCUIT BREAKER	—⎤	DENOTES WIRE CONTINUES ELSEWHERE
⊢⊣	CAPACITOR	→⟨	SPLICE
Ω	OHMS	◇J2⟩2	SPLICE IDENTIFICATION
⟋\/\/\⟍	RESISTOR	◆⎤ ◇⎦	OPTIONAL WIRING WITH / WIRING WITHOUT
⟋\/\/\⟍	VARIABLE RESISTOR	⟶ᴖᴖ⟶	THERMAL ELEMENT (BI-METAL STRIP)
W\/W\/W	SERIES RESISTOR	⟍⟋	"Y" WINDINGS
⟶ℓℓℓ⟶	COIL	88:88	DIGITAL READOUT
⟶ℓℓ⟶	STEP UP COIL	⟶⦿⟶	SINGLE FILAMENT LAMP
⟍ℓℓ⟋	OPEN CONTACT	⟶⦿⟶	DUAL FILAMENT LAMP
⟍◻⟋	CLOSED CONTACT	⟶⦿⟶	L.E.D.-LIGHT EMITTING DIODE
⟶•⟶	CLOSED SWITCH	⟶⦿⟶	THERMISTOR
⟶╱⟶	OPEN SWITCH	⦿	GAUGE
⟶⟶	CLOSED GANGED SWITCH	⎡TIMER⎤	TIMER
⟶⟶	OPEN GANGED SWITCH	⊣◯⊢	MOTOR
⟶⟶	TWO POLE SINGLE THROW SWITCH	⊘	ARMATURE AND BRUSHES
⊓	PRESSURE SWITCH	⟶▪⟶	DENOTES WIRE GOES THROUGH GROMMET
⊟	SOLENOID SWITCH	▮ ▮ #36	DENOTES WIRE GOES THROUGH 40 WAY DISCONNECT
⊟	MERCURY SWITCH	#19 ⎡STRG COLUMN⎤	DENOTES WIRE GOES THROUGH 25 WAY STEERING COLUMN CONNECTOR
⟶◄⟶	DIODE OR RECTIFIER	⎡INST PANEL⎤ #14	DENOTES WIRE GOES THROUGH 25 WAY INSTRUMENT PANEL CONNECTOR
⟶◄►⟶	BY-DIRECTIONAL ZENER DIODE		

Figure 6-3. Some electrical symbols used by Chrysler Corporation. (Chrysler)

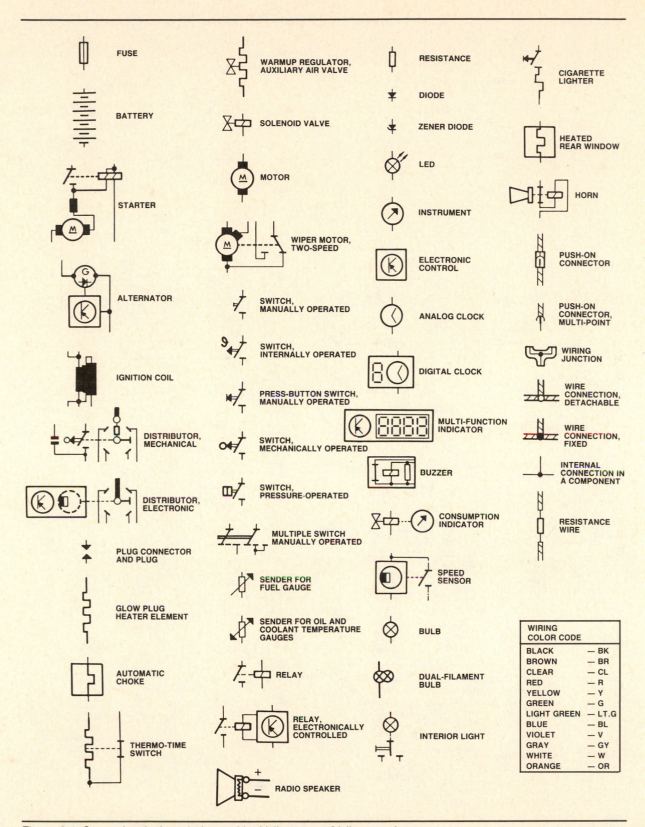

Figure 6-4. Some electrical symbols used by Volkswagen. (Volkswagen)

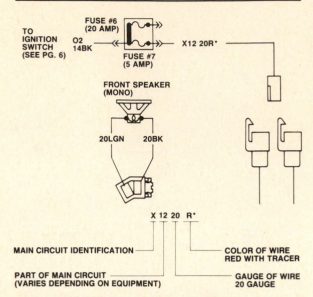

Figure 6-5. In this example from Chrysler, the "20R*" in the wire code stands for a 20-gauge, red with tracer wire. (Chrysler)

WIRE IDENTIFICATION CHART

COLOR	SYMBOL	COLOR	SYMBOL
ALUMINUM	AL	NATURAL	NAT
BLACK	BLK	ORANGE	ORN
BLUE-LIGHT	BLU LT	PINK	PINK
BLUE-DARK	BLU DK	PURPLE	PPL
BROWN	BRN	RED	RED
GLAZED	GLZ	TAN	TAN
GREEN-LIGHT	GRN LT	VIOLET	VLT
GREEN-DARK	GRN DK	WHITE	WHT
GRAY	GRA	YELLOW	YEL
MAROON	MAR		

Figure 6-6. This General Motors diagram is printed in color in the factory manual but includes this table of color abbreviations.

Circuit Numbers

If the wire is labeled with a **circuit number**, such as in figures 6-5 and 6-7, those circuits will be identified in an accompanying table. Figure 6-10 shows a Chrysler circuit with the letter and number that identify the circuits. Any two wires with the same circuit number will be connected within the same circuit.

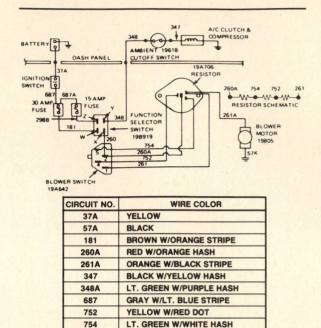

CIRCUIT NO.	WIRE COLOR
37A	YELLOW
57A	BLACK
181	BROWN W/ORANGE STRIPE
260A	RED W/ORANGE HASH
261A	ORANGE W/BLACK STRIPE
347	BLACK W/YELLOW HASH
348A	LT. GREEN W/PURPLE HASH
687	GRAY W/LT. BLUE STRIPE
752	YELLOW W/RED DOT
754	LT. GREEN W/WHITE HASH

Figure 6-7. This Ford accessory circuit is color coded by circuit number. (Ford)

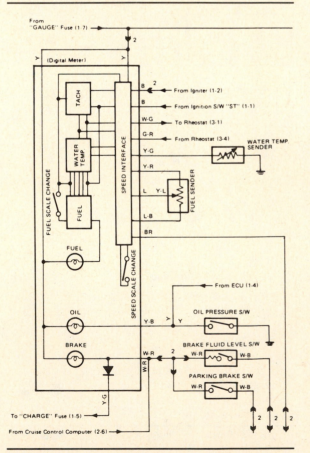

Figure 6-8. This Toyota diagram has no color code table, printing the color directly on the drawing. (Toyota)

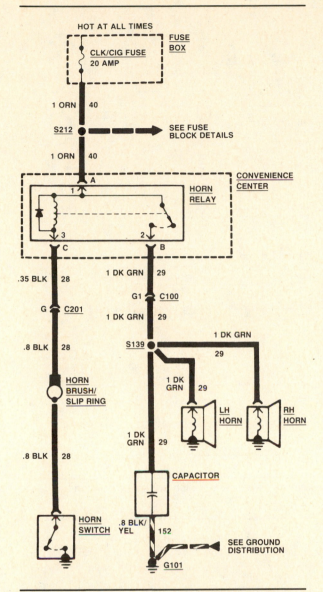

Figure 6-9. General Motors Valley Forge schematics are provided in color with the name of the color printed beside the wire. (Pontiac)

Component and Logic Symbols

We have already looked at basic component symbols used by some carmakers in figures 6-1, 6-2, 6-3, and 6-4. Nissan and other manufacturers often include the symbols with their components and include connector identification and switch continuity positions, figure 6-11.

The increasing use of sophisticated electronics in automobiles has brought about the appearance of a new type of electrical circuit diagram, containing logic symbols. It might be well at this point for you to go back and review our discussion of the various types of logic gates and their functions in Chapter Four.

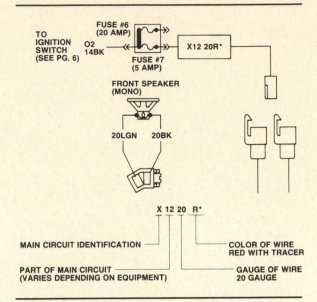

Figure 6-10. In this example from Chrysler, the "X12" in the wire code stands for the #12 part of the main circuit X. (Chrysler)

Logic symbols are used to simplify a complex electrical circuit and describe its operation under specified conditions. Figure 6-12 is a basic diagram of a Toyota Celica sunroof control relay which controls the sunroof motor operation. Figure 6-13 shows how the circuit is activated to tilt the sunroof open — current flows to the motor through relay No. 1 and transistor 1 when the "up" side of the tilt switch is pressed.

DIAGRAMS

The color codes, circuit numbers, and symbols we have illustrated can be combined to create a variety of electrical diagrams. Most people tend to refer to any electrical diagram as a "wiring diagram", but there are at least three distinct types with which you should be familiar:

- System diagrams
- Schematic diagrams
- Installation diagrams.

Circuit Number: The number, or number and letter, that carmakers use to identify an electrical circuit in a diagram.

Logic Symbol: A symbol identifying the type of gate in a digital or logic circuit.

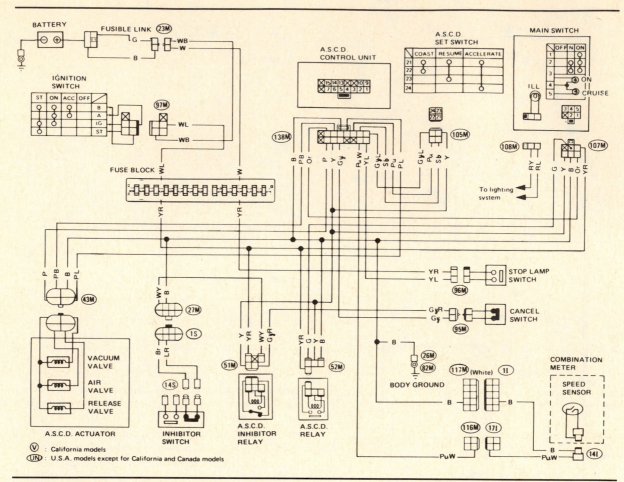

Figure 6-11. Some manufacturers include symbols, components, connector and switch continuity position identification. (Nissan)

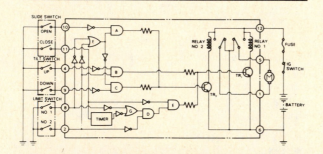

Figure 6-12. The advance of computer technology in cars makes logic symbols like these a typical part of an automotive wiring diagram. (Toyota)

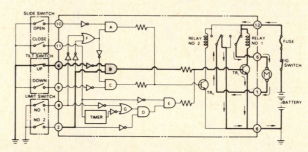

Figure 6-13. This circuit uses logic symbols to show how the sunroof motor operates to tilt the mechanism open. (Toyota)

System Diagrams

A **system diagram** is a drawing of the entire automobile electrical system. This also can properly be called a "wiring diagram". System diagrams show the wires, connections to loads and switches and the type of connectors used, but not how the loads or switches work. Figures 6-14, 6-15, 6-16, and 6-17 show portions of typical system diagrams. These may cover many pages of a manual or they may be printed on special oversize, fold-out pages.

Most system diagrams present current flow horizontally, that is, they are read from left to right. Some European carmakers' diagrams,

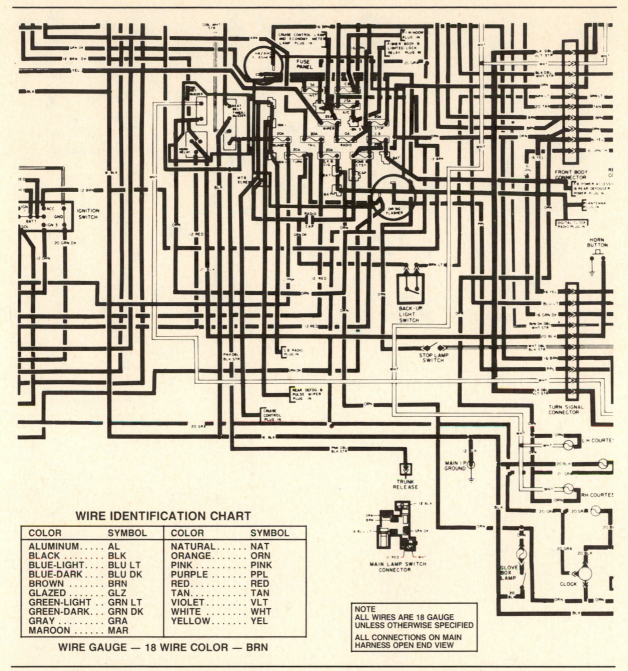

WIRE IDENTIFICATION CHART

COLOR	SYMBOL	COLOR	SYMBOL
ALUMINUM	AL	NATURAL	NAT
BLACK	BLK	ORANGE	ORN
BLUE-LIGHT	BLU LT	PINK	PINK
BLUE-DARK	BLU DK	PURPLE	PPL
BROWN	BRN	RED	RED
GLAZED	GLZ	TAN	TAN
GREEN-LIGHT	GRN LT	VIOLET	VLT
GREEN-DARK	GRN DK	WHITE	WHT
GRAY	GRA	YELLOW	YEL
MAROON	MAR		

WIRE GAUGE — 18 WIRE COLOR — BRN

NOTE
ALL WIRES ARE 18 GAUGE
UNLESS OTHERWISE SPECIFIED

ALL CONNECTIONS ON MAIN
HARNESS OPEN END VIEW

Figure 6-14. Portion of a GM system diagram. Note the gauge-size statement (boxed). (Oldsmobile)

such as Volkswagen's, present current flow vertically, reading from top to bottom.

A useful feature provided by some manufacturers on their system diagrams are reference coordinates along the edges. An index is included listing system components alphabetically along with the specific grid coordinates. This system is similar to that found on a road map and is used in the same manner.

In figure 6-14, the color names are printed on the wires. This GM diagram contains the

statement, ''All wires are 18-gauge unless otherwise specified.''

Volkswagen arranges its system diagrams differently from those of American manufac-

System Diagram: A drawing that shows all of the different circuits in a complete electrical system.

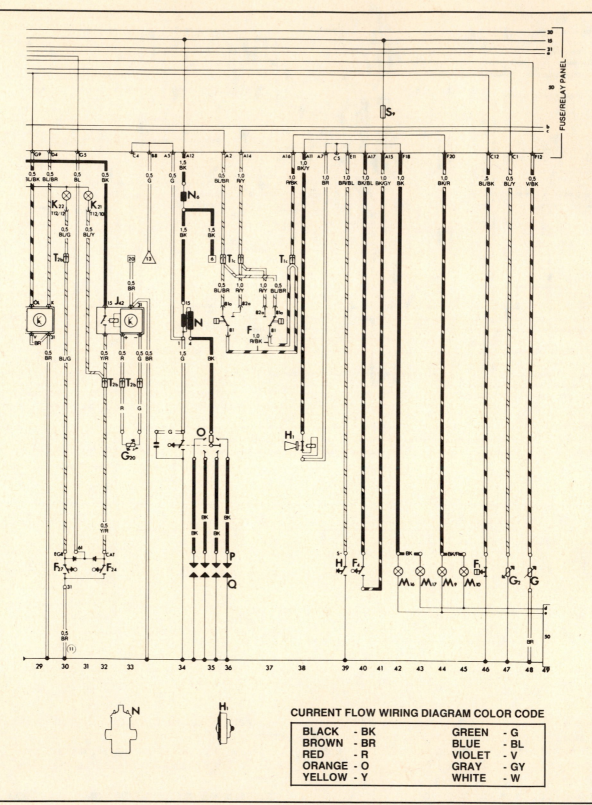

Figure 6-15. Portion of a Volkswagen system diagram for vehicles manufactured in Germany. (Volkswagen)

CURRENT FLOW WIRING DIAGRAM COLOR CODE

BLACK	- BK	GREEN	- G
BROWN	- BR	BLUE	- BL
RED	- R	VIOLET	- V
ORANGE	- O	GRAY	- GY
YELLOW	- Y	WHITE	- W

turers. Figure 6-15 is part of a Volkswagen system diagram from the 1970s and is typical of German manufacturers' electrical diagrams.

Figure 6-16 is part of a system diagram for a Volkswagen Golf manufactured in the United States and differs in style, content, and layout.

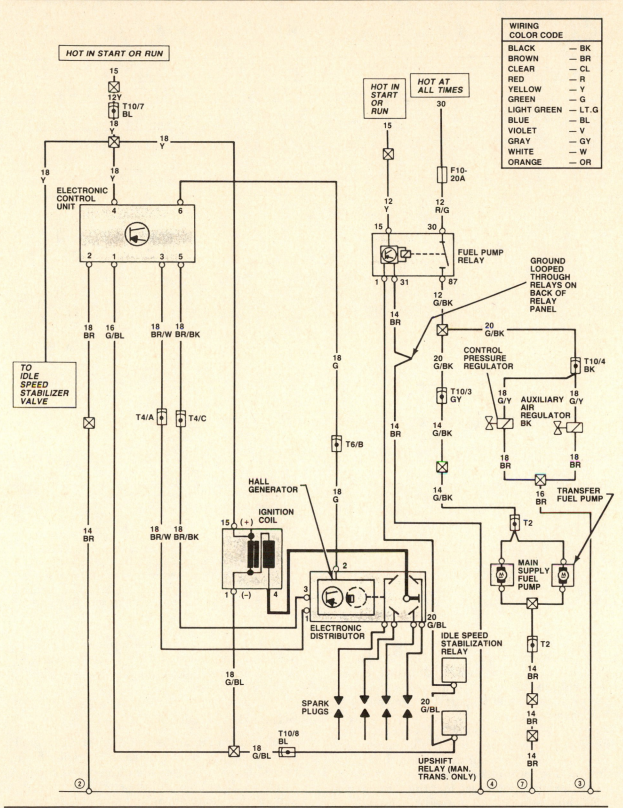

Figure 6-16. Volkswagen systems diagrams differ for vehicles manufactured in the United States. (Volkswagen)

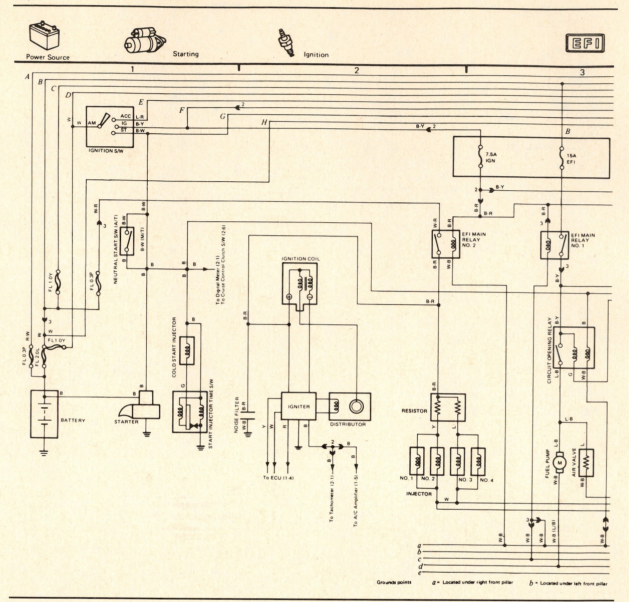

Figure 6-17. Toyota system diagrams are organized by individual systems and include ground points. (Toyota)

In both, however, current flows from the top to the bottom of the page. The German diagrams use lines across the top of the page to represent the fuse panel connections and identify wires by the metric gauge system and a color abbreviation.

Figure 6-17 is a portion of a Toyota system diagram. As we saw earlier, Toyota simply prints the color name on the wire in the drawing, and does not indicate wire gauge. Note that the ground points are identified for all circuits. The diagram is also organized by individual subsystems at the top. This variation on the grid theme mentioned earlier helps you to quickly locate that part of the diagram in which you are interested.

A Chrysler Corporation shop manual may not supply an entire system diagram for a product, but may illustrate all circuits separately, figure 6-18.

Schematic Diagrams

A **schematic diagram** is a portion of the overall system diagram that details the operation of an individual circuit. They are often called circuit diagrams, figure 6-9. All the electrical information about a complete automotive circuit, including the switches, connectors, loads, and other devices is included in a single drawing. Figures 6-18, 6-19, and 6-20 show diagrams of individual circuits from the major domestic au-

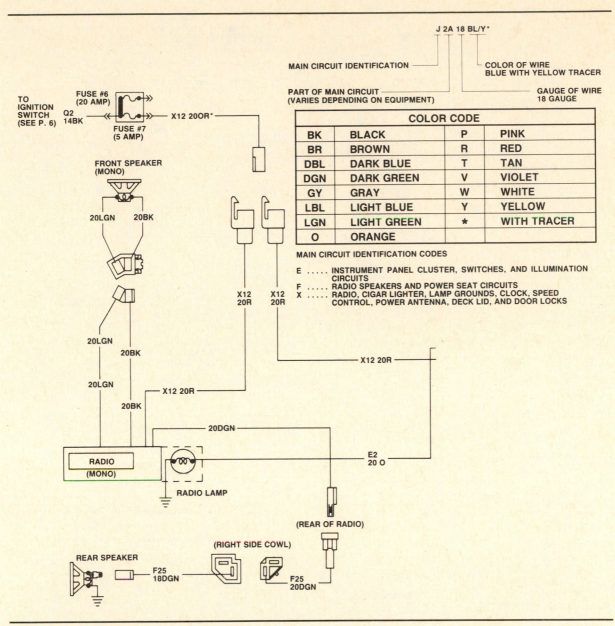

Figure 6-18. A Chrysler radio circuit. (Chrysler)

tomobile manufacturers. The color code tables are included where needed so you may identify the wires and follow them through the circuits shown.

Figure 6-18 illustrates the circuit for a Chrysler radio system. Some of the wires are fully identified with two circuit numbers, wire gauge and wire color. Other wires, such as the two wires connected to the front speaker, are identified only by wire gauge and color. The "20LGN" indicates a 20-gauge, light green wire.

Figure 6-19 is the fuel economy lamp circuit in a GM vehicle. Here, neither wire gauge nor wire color is indicated; the "green" and "amber" refer to the color of the lamp bulbs.

Figure 6-20 shows a Ford side marker lamp circuit. Again, wire size and color are not identified. The numbers on the wires are circuit numbers. Note that the ground wires on the front and rear lamps may not be present, depending upon the type of lamp socket used on the automobile.

Schematic Diagram: A drawing of a circuit or any part of a circuit that shows how it works.

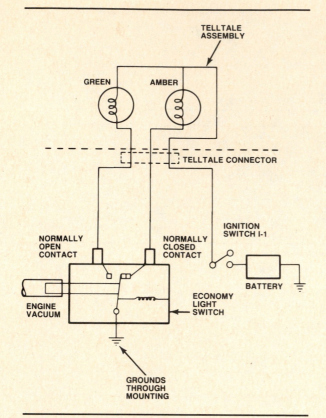

Figure 6-19. A GM fuel economy lamp circuit. (Cadillac)

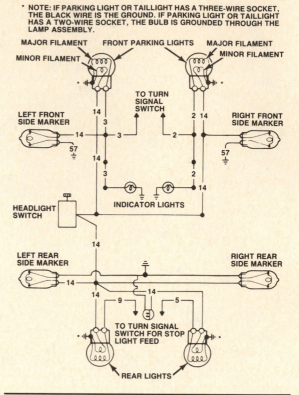

Figure 6-20. A Ford side marker lamp circuit. (Ford)

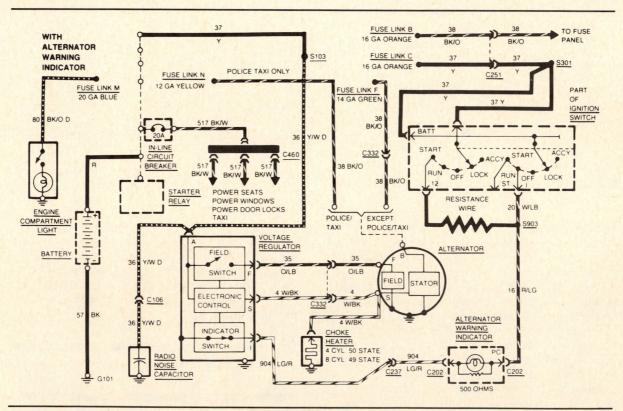

Figure 6-21. This Ford circuit schematic is read horizontally. (Ford)

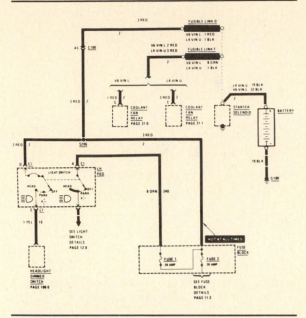

Figure 6-22. A typical GM power distribution schematic. (Pontiac)

Troubleshooting with schematics

It is quicker and easier to diagnose and isolate an electrical problem using a schematic diagram than by working with a systems diagram. You are not distracted or confused by wiring that is not part of the circuit on which you are working. A schematic diagram shows the paths that electrical current takes in a properly functioning circuit. You need to understand how the circuit is supposed to work before trying to determine why it isn't working properly.

Each division of General Motors incorporates a special troubleshooting section in its shop manual for a given vehicle. This section contains current flow schematics of that vehicle's entire electrical system, figure 6-9. These schematics are often referred to as Valley Forge diagrams and are read from top to bottom. Each schematic contains all of the basic information necessary to trace the circuit it covers: wire size and color, components, connector and

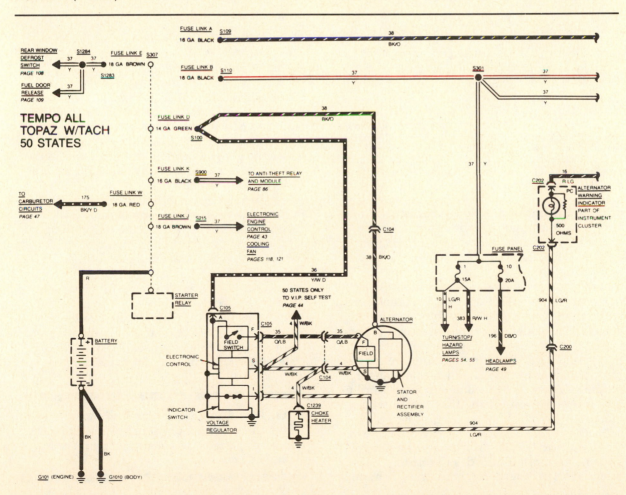

Figure 6-23. A Ford power distribution schematic. (Ford)

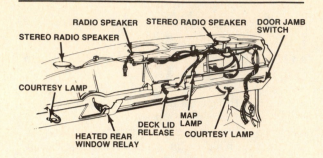

Figure 6-24. A Chrysler installation diagram. (Chrysler)

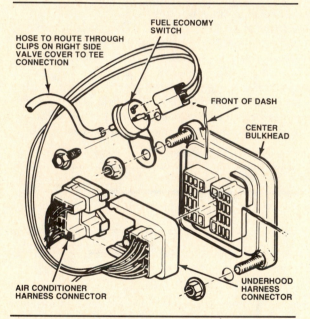

Figure 6-25. A GM installation diagram. (Cadillac)

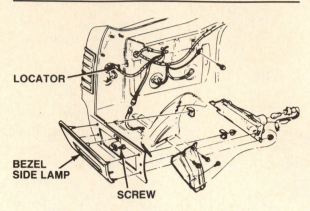

Figure 6-26. A Ford installation diagram. (Ford)

fuse panel. By following the power distribution wiring to the first component in each major circuit, this diagram can be useful in locating short circuits that blow fusible links or fuses.

Installation Diagrams

None of the diagrams shown so far has indicated *where* or *how* the wires and loads are installed in the automobile. Many carmakers provide **installation diagrams**, which show these locations. Installation diagrams are sometimes called pictorial diagrams. Figures 6-24, 6-25, and 6-26 show different styles of installation diagrams. These diagrams can help you to locate the general harness or circuit within the car before you look at the system diagram for more detailed information.

The Chrysler installation diagram in figure 6-24 includes the wiring for the radio speakers. This particular diagram illustrates the major wiring for this area of the car. The circuit diagram for the speakers was shown in figure 6-18.

Figure 6-25 is GM's installation diagram for its fuel economy indicator switch. The circuit diagram for this accessory was given in figure 6-19.

Ford's installation diagram for a side lamp assembly, figure 6-26, also details the placement of the bulbs and lenses. Figure 6-20 illustrated the circuit diagram for these lamps.

Installation Diagram: A drawing that shows where the wires, loads, attachment hardware, and other parts of an electrical circuit are installed in a car.

---

ground references, and where necessary, references to other circuits. In addition, a quick summary of system operation is provided to tell you what should happen when the system is working properly.

Ford provides a similar troubleshooting aid in the form of its Electrical and Vacuum Troubleshooting Guide (EVTG) published for each vehicle in a model year. The Ford circuit schematics contain much the same information as those used by GM, figure 6-21, but are organized in a more traditional horizontal manner.

Both GM and Ford include a power distribution diagram as one of the first overall schematics for troubleshooting, figures 6-22 and 6-23. The power distribution diagram represents the "front end" of the overall electrical system. As such, it includes the battery, starter solenoid/relay, alternator, ignition switch, and

SUMMARY

A variety of electrical symbols are used to represent electrical components. Logic symbols are used to simplify the operation of electronic circuits. The color insulation on automotive wiring can be used to identify particular wires. The wires also can be identified by a circuit number. Electrical diagrams are necessary to service a circuit and the technician must understand how to read and use such diagrams. Carmakers pub-

lish diagrams of each vehicle's electrical systems, often using these color codes and circuit numbers. The diagrams may be system or wiring diagrams, schematic or circuit diagrams, or installation diagrams. System diagrams present an overall view, while schematics isolate a single circuit and are more useful for troubleshooting individual problems. Installation diagrams show locations and harness routing.

Review Questions

Choose the single most correct answer.
Compare your answers with the correct answers on page 431.

1. This symbol represents a:

   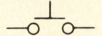

   a. Fixed resistor
   b. Variable resistor
   c. Capacitor
   d. Solenoid

2. This symbol represents which type of switch?

   a. Push-pull
   b. Toggle
   c. Push button
   d. Single-pole, double-throw

3. The following two symbols represent which two devices?

   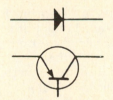

   a. A Zener diode and a PNP transistor
   b. A Zener diode and a NPN transistor
   c. A one-way diode and a PNP transistor
   d. A one-way diode and a NPN transistor

4. A lamp is indicated by which of the following electrical symbols?

   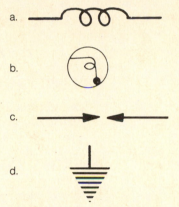

5. In this section of a Ford Motor Company circuit diagram, what does the number "14" (circled) indicate?

   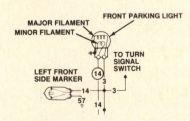

   a. 14 amps
   b. 14 volts
   c. Wire size 14
   d. Circuit number 14

6. The electrical diagram that shows where the wires and loads are installed is the:
   a. Schematic diagram
   b. Electrical system diagram
   c. Installation diagram
   d. Alternator circuit diagram

7. Automobile manufacturers color-code the wires in the electrical system to:
   a. Help trace a circuit
   b. Identify wire gauge
   c. Speed the manufacturing process
   d. Identify replacement parts

8. Which of the following is *not* shown on power distribution or current flow diagrams?
   a. Current flow direction
   b. Circuit numbers
   c. Grounds
   d. Circuit part location

7

Batteries

The automotive battery does not actually store electricity, as is often believed. It converts electrical energy into chemical energy, which is stored until the battery is connected to an external circuit. The stored chemical energy is then converted back to electrical energy, which flows from one battery terminal, through the circuit, and back to the other battery terminal.

We will begin our study of batteries by listing their functions and looking at the chemical action and construction of a battery.

An automotive battery:

- Operates the starter motor
- Provides current for the ignition system during cranking
- Supplies power for the lighting systems and electrical accessories when the engine is not operating
- Acts as a voltage stabilizer for the complete electrical system
- Provides current when the electrical demand of the vehicle exceeds the output of the charging system.

ELECTROCHEMICAL ACTION

All automotive wet-cell batteries operate because of the chemical action of two dissimilar metals in the presence of a conductive and reactive solution called an **electrolyte**. Because this chemical action produces electricity, it is called electrochemical action. The chemical action of the electrolyte causes electrons to be removed from one metal and added to the other. This loss and gain of electrons causes the metals to be oppositely charged, and a potential difference, or voltage, exists between them.

The metal piece which has lost electrons is positively charged, and is called the positive plate. The piece which has gained electrons is negatively charged, and is called the negative plate. If a conductor and a load are connected between the two plates, current will flow through the conductor, figure 7-1. For simplicity, battery current flow is assumed to be conventional current flow (+ to –) through the external circuit connected to the battery.

Primary and Secondary Batteries

There are two general types of batteries: primary and secondary.

The action within a **primary battery** causes one of the metals to be totally destroyed after a period of time. When the battery has delivered all of its voltage to an outside circuit, it is useless and must be replaced. Many small dry-cell batteries, such as those for flashlights and radios, are primary batteries.

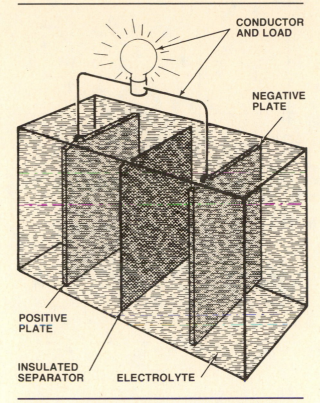

CONDUCTOR AND LOAD

NEGATIVE PLATE

POSITIVE PLATE

INSULATED SEPARATOR   ELECTROLYTE

Figure 7-1. The potential difference between the two plates of a battery can cause current to flow in an outside circuit. (Chevrolet)

In **secondary batteries**, both the electrolyte and the metals change their atomic structure as the battery supplies voltage to an outside circuit. This is called discharging. The action can be reversed, however, by applying an outside current to the battery terminals and forcing current to flow through the battery in the opposite direction. This current flow causes chemical action which restores the battery materials to their original condition, and the battery can again supply voltage. This is called charging the battery. The condition of the battery materials is called the battery's state of charge.

Electrochemical Action in Automotive Batteries

A fully charged automotive battery contains a series of negative plates of chemically active sponge lead (Pb), positive plates of lead dioxide (PbO_2), and an electrolyte of sulfuric acid (H_2SO_4) and water (H_2O), figure 7-2.

As the battery discharges, figure 7-2, the chemical action taking place reduces the acid content in the electrolyte and increases the water content. At the same time, both the nega-

tive and the positive plates gradually change to lead sulphate ($PbSO_4$).

A discharged battery, figure 7-2, has a very weak acid solution because most of the electrolyte has changed to water. Both series of plates are mostly lead sulfate. The battery now stops functioning because the plates are basically two similar metals in the presence of water, rather than two dissimilar metals in the presence of an electrolyte.

During charging, figure 7-2, the chemical action is reversed. The lead sulfate on the plates gradually decomposes, changing the negative plates back to sponge lead and the positive plates to lead dioxide. The sulfate is redeposited in the water, which increases the sulfuric acid content and returns the electrolyte to full strength. The battery is now again able to supply voltage.

Electrolyte: The chemical solution in a battery that conducts electricity and reacts with the plate materials.

Primary Battery: A battery in which chemical processes destroy one of the metals necessary to create electrical energy. Primary batteries cannot be recharged.

Secondary Battery: A battery in which chemical processes can be reversed. A secondary battery can be recharged so that it will continue to supply voltage.

■ Other Secondary Cells

The Edison (nickel-iron alkali) cell and the silver cell are two other types of secondary cells. The positive plate of the Edison cell is made of pencil-shaped, perforated steel tubes that contain nickel hydroxide. These tubes are held in a steel grid. The negative plate has pockets that hold iron oxide. The electrolyte used in this cell is a solution of potassium hydroxide and a small amount of lithium hydroxide.

An Edison cell weighs about one-half as much as a lead-acid cell of the same ampere-hour capacity. This cell has a long life and is not damaged by short circuits or overloads. It is however, more costly than a lead-acid cell.

The silver cell has a positive plate of silver oxide and a negative plate of zinc. The electrolyte is a solution of potassium hydroxide or sodium. For its weight, this cell has a high ampere-hour capacity. It can withstand large overloads and short circuits. It, too, is more expensive than a lead-acid cell.

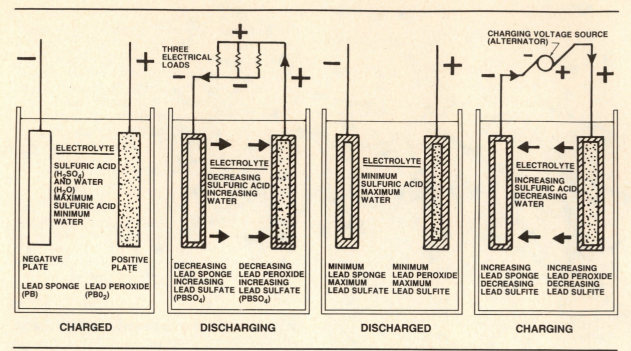

Figure 7-2. Battery electrochemical action from charged, to discharged, and back to charged.

This electrochemical action and battery operation from fully charged to discharged and back to fully charged is called **cycling**.

A safety note is important here. Hydrogen and oxygen gases are formed during battery charging. Hydrogen gas is explosive. Never strike a spark or bring a flame near a battery, particularly during or after charging. *This could cause the battery to explode.*

Battery Construction

There are four types of automotive batteries currently in use:

- Vent-cap (requires maintenance)
- Low-maintenance (requires limited maintenance)
- Maintenance-free (requires no maintenance)
- Recombinant (requires no maintenance).

The basic physical construction of all types of automotive batteries is similar, but the materials used are not. We will look at traditional vent-cap construction first and then explain how the other battery types differ.

Vent-cap batteries

Battery construction begins with the positive and negative plates. The plates are built on grids of conductive materials, figure 7-3, which act as a framework for the dissimilar metals. These dissimilar metals are called the active materials of the battery. The active materials, sponge lead and lead dioxide, are pasted onto the grids. When dry, the active materials are very porous, so that the electrolyte can easily penetrate and react with them.

A number of similar plates, all positive or all negative, are connected together into a plate group, figure 7-4. The plates are joined to each other by welding them to a plate strap through a process called lead burning. The plate strap has a connector or a terminal post for attaching plate groups to each other.

A positive and a negative plate group are interlaced so that their plates alternate, figure 7-5. The negative plate group normally has one more plate than the positive group. To reduce the possibility of a short between plates of the two groups, they are separated by chemically inert separators, figure 7-5. Separators are usually made of plastic or fiber glass. The separators have ribs on one side next to the positive plates. These ribs hold electrolyte near the positive plates for efficient chemical action.

A complete assembly of positive plates, negative plates, and separators is called an **element**. It is placed in a cell of a battery case. Because each **cell** provides approximately 2.1 volts, a 12-volt battery has six cells and actually produces approximately 12.6 volts when fully charged.

The elements are separated from each other by cell partitions, and rest on bridges at the bottom of the case which form chambers where sediment can collect. These bridges prevent ac-

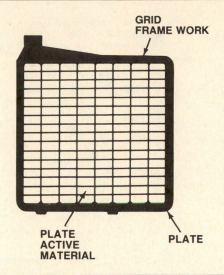

Figure 7-3. The grid provides a support for the plate active material.

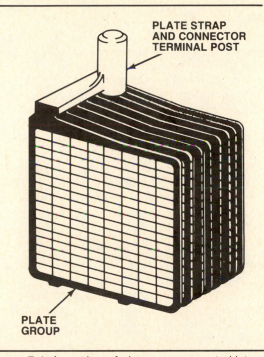

Figure 7-4. A number of plates are connected into a group.

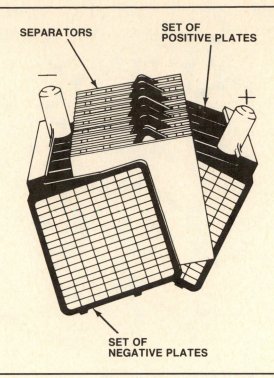

Figure 7-5. Two groups are interlaced to form a battery element.

cape of gases that form during charging and discharging. The battery is connected to the car's electrical system by two external terminals. These terminals are either tapered posts on top of the case or internally threaded connectors on the side. The terminals, which are connected to the ends of the series of elements inside the case, are marked positive (+) or negative (–), according to which end of the series each terminal represents.

Low-maintenance and maintenance-free batteries
Most new batteries today are either semi-sealed, low-maintenance or sealed, maintenance-

cumulated sediment from shorting across the bottoms of the plates. Once installed in the case, the elements (cells) are connected to each other by connecting straps which pass over or through the cell partitions, figure 7-6. The cells are connected alternately in series (positive to negative to positive to negative, etc.), and the battery top is bonded onto the case to form a watertight container.

Vent caps in the battery top provide an opening for adding electrolyte and for the es-

Cycling: Battery electrochemical action and operation from charged to discharged and back. One complete cycle is operation from fully charged to discharged and back to fully charged.

Element: A complete assembly of positive plates, negative plates, and separators making up one cell of a battery.

Cell: A case enclosing one element in an electrolyte. Each cell produces approximately 2.1 to 2.2 volts. Cells are connected in series.

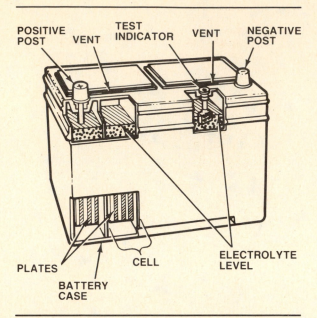

Figure 7-6. A cutaway view of an assembled battery. (Chrysler)

free batteries. Low-maintenance batteries provide some method of adding water to the cells, such as:

- Individual slotted vent caps installed flush with the top of the case
- Two vent panel covers, each of which exposes three cells when removed
- A flush-mounted strip cover which is peeled off to reveal the cell openings.

Maintenance-free batteries have only small gas vents that prevent pressure buildup in the case. A low-maintenance battery requires that water be added much less often than with a traditional vent-cap battery, while a maintenance-free battery will never need to have water added during its lifetime.

These batteries differ from vent-cap batteries primarily in the materials used for the plate grids. For decades, automotive batteries used antimony as the strengthening ingredient of the grid alloy. In low-maintenance batteries, the amount of antimony is reduced to about three percent. In maintenance-free batteries, the antimony is eliminated and replaced by calcium or strontium.

Reducing the amount of antimony or replacing it with calcium or strontium alloy results in lowering the battery's internal heat and reduces the amount of gassing that occurs during charging. Since these are the principal reasons for battery water loss, these changes reduce or eliminate the need to periodically add water.

Reduced water loss also minimizes terminal corrosion, since the major cause of this corrosion is condensation from normal battery gassing.

In addition, non-antimony lead alloys have better conductivity, so a maintenance-free battery has about a 20-percent higher cranking performance rating than a traditional vent-cap battery of comparable size.

Sealed maintenance-free batteries

More recently, completely sealed maintenance-free batteries were introduced. These new batteries do not require — and do not have — the small gas vent used on previous maintenance-free batteries. Although these batteries are basically the same kind of lead-acid voltage cells used in automobiles for decades, a slight change in plate and electrolyte chemistry reduces hydrogen generation to almost nothing.

During charging, a vent-cap or maintenance-free battery releases hydrogen at the negative plates and oxygen at the positive plates. Most of the hydrogen is released through electrolysis of the water in the electrolyte near the negative plates as the battery reaches full charge. In the sealed maintenance-free design, the negative plates never reach a fully charged condition and therefore cause little or no release of hydrogen. Oxygen is released at the positive plates, but it passes through the separators and recombines with the negative plates. The overall effect is virtually no gassing from the battery. Because the oxygen released by the electrolyte recombines with the negative plates, some manufacturers call these batteries "recombination" or **recombinant electrolyte** batteries.

Recombinant batteries

Recombination electrolyte technology and improved grid materials allow some sealed, maintenance-free batteries to develop fully charged, open-circuit voltage of approximately 2.2 volts per cell, or a total of 13.2 volts for a six-cell battery. Microporous fiber glass separators reduce internal resistance and contribute to higher voltage and current ratings.

In addition, the electrolyte in these new batteries is contained within plastic envelope-type separators around the plates, figure 7-7. The entire case is not flooded with electrolyte. This eliminates the possibility of damage due to sloshing or acid leaks from a cracked battery. This design feature reduces battery damage during handling and installation, and allows a more compact case design. Because the battery is not vented, terminal corrosion from battery gassing and electrolyte spills or spray is also eliminated.

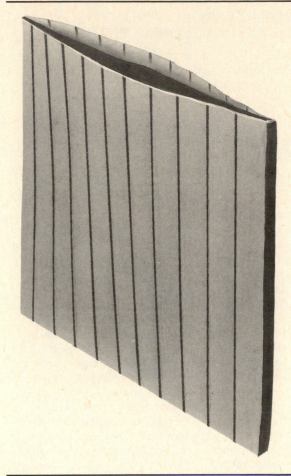

Figure 7-7. Many maintenance-free batteries have envelope separators that hold active material near the plates.

The envelope design also catches active material as it flakes off the positive plates during discharge. By holding the material closer to the plates, envelope construction ensures that it will be more completely redeposited during charging.

Although recombinant batteries are examples of advanced technology, test and service requirements are basically the same as for other maintenance-free, lead-acid batteries. Some manufacturers caution, however, that fast charging at high current rates may overheat the battery and can cause damage. Always check the manufacturer's instructions for test specifications and charging rates before servicing one of these batteries.

BATTERY ELECTROLYTE

For the battery to become chemically active, it must be filled with an electrolyte solution. The electrolyte in an automotive battery is a solution of sulfuric acid and water. In a fully

charged battery, the solution is approximately 35 to 39 percent acid by weight (25 percent by volume) and 61 to 65 percent water by weight. The state of charge of a battery can be measured by checking the **specific gravity** of the electrolyte.

Specific gravity is the weight of a given volume of liquid divided by the weight of an equal volume of water. Since the acid is heavier than water, and water has a specific gravity of 1.000, the specific gravity of a fully charged battery is approximately 1.260 when weighed in a hydrometer. As the battery discharges, the specific gravity of the electrolyte decreases because the acid is changed into water. The specific gravity of the electrolyte can tell you approximately how discharged the battery has become:

1.265 specific gravity	100% charged
1.225 specific gravity	75% charged
1.190 specific gravity	50% charged
1.155 specific gravity	25% charged
1.120 specific gravity or lower	discharged

These values may vary slightly, according to the design factors of a particular battery.

Specific gravity measurements are based on a standard temperature of 80°F (26.7°C). At higher temperatures, specific gravity is lower. At lower temperatures, specific gravity is higher. For every change of 10°F, specific gravity changes by four points (0.004). That is:

- For every 10°F above 80°F, add 0.004 to the specific gravity reading
- For every 10°F below 80°F, subtract 0.004 from the specific gravity reading.

When you study battery service in the *Shop Manual*, you will learn to measure specific gravity of a vent-cap battery with a tool called a hydrometer.

STATE-OF-CHARGE INDICATORS

Many low-maintenance and maintenance-free batteries have a visual state-of-charge indicator installed in the battery top. The indicator

Recombinant: A nongassing battery design in which the oxygen released by the electrolyte recombines with the negative plates.

Specific Gravity: The weight of a volume of liquid divided by the weight of the same volume of water at a given temperature and pressure. Water has a specific gravity of 1.000.

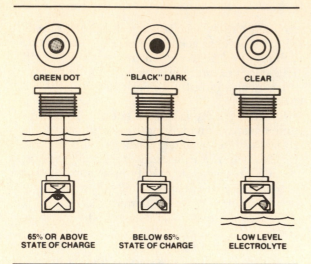

GREEN DOT   "BLACK" DARK   CLEAR

65% OR ABOVE   BELOW 65%   LOW LEVEL
STATE OF CHARGE   STATE OF CHARGE   ELECTROLYTE

Figure 7-8. Delco "Freedom" batteries have this integral hydrometer built into their tops.

shows whether the electrolyte has fallen below a minimum level, and it also functions as a go/no-go hydrometer.

The indicator, figure 7-8, is a plastic rod inserted in the top of the battery and extending into the electrolyte. In the design used by Delco, a green plastic ball is suspended in a cage from the bottom of the rod. Depending upon the specific gravity of the electrolyte, the ball will float or sink in the cage, changing the appearance of the indicator "eye" from green to dark. When the eye is dark, the battery should be recharged.

Other manufacturers either use the "Delco Eye" under license, or one of several variations of the design. One variation contains a red and blue ball side by side in the cage. When the specific gravity is high, only the blue ball can be seen in the "eye". As the specific gravity falls, the blue ball sinks in the cage, allowing the red ball to take its place. When the battery is recharged, the increasing specific gravity causes the blue ball to move upward, forcing the red ball back into the side of the cage.

Another variation is the use of a small red ball on top of a larger blue ball. When the specific gravity is high, the small ball is seen as a red spot surrounded by blue. As the specific gravity falls, the blue ball sinks, leaving the small ball to be seen as a red spot surrounded by a clear area. The battery then should be recharged.

If the electrolyte drops below the level of the cage in batteries using a state-of-charge indicator, the "eye" will appear clear or light yellow. This means that the battery must be replaced because it has lost too much electrolyte.

WET-CHARGED AND DRY-CHARGED BATTERIES

Batteries may be manufactured and sold as either wet-charged or dry-charged batteries. Before maintenance-free batteries became widely used, dry-charged batteries were very common. A wet-charged battery is completely filled with an electrolyte when it is built. A dry-charged battery is shipped from the factory without electrolyte. During manufacture, the positive and negative plates are charged and then completely washed and dried. The battery is then assembled and sealed to keep out moisture. It will remain charged as long as it is sealed, and it can be stored for a long time in any reasonable environment. A dry-charged battery is put into service by adding electrolyte, checking the battery state of charge, and charging if needed.

Even when a wet-charged battery is not in use, a slow reaction occurs between the plates and the electrolyte. This is a self-discharging reaction, and will eventually discharge the battery almost completely. Because this reaction occurs faster at higher temperatures, wet-charged batteries should be stored in as cool a place as possible when not in use. A fully charged battery stored at a room temperature of 100°F (38°C) will almost completely discharge after 90 days. If the battery is stored at a temperature of 60°F (16°C), very little discharge will take place.

BATTERY CHARGING VOLTAGE

A battery is charged by forcing current to flow through it in the direction opposite to its discharge current. In an automobile, this charging current is supplied by the generator or alternator. The battery offers some resistance to this charging current, because of the battery's chemical voltage and the resistance of the battery's internal parts. The battery's chemical voltage is another form of counterelectromotive force (CEMF) that you studied in Chapter Two.

When a battery is fully charged, its CEMF is very high. Very little charging current can flow through it. When the battery is discharged, its CEMF is very low, and charging current flows freely. For charging current to enter the battery, the charging voltage must be higher than the battery's CEMF *plus* the voltage drop caused by the battery's internal resistance.

Understanding this relationship of CEMF to the battery state of charge is helpful. When the battery is nearly discharged, it needs — and will accept — a lot of charging current. When the battery is fully charged, the high CEMF will resist charging current. Any additional charging current could overheat and damage the battery materials. Charging procedures are explained in Chapter Three of your *Shop Manual*.

The temperature of the battery affects the charging voltage because temperature affects the resistance of the electrolyte. Cold electrolyte has higher resistance than warm electrolyte, so a colder battery is harder to charge. The effects of temperature must be considered when servicing automotive charging systems and batteries, as we will see later in this chapter and in Part Three.

BATTERY SELECTION AND RATING METHODS

Automotive batteries are 12-volt, wet-cell, lead-acid batteries and are available in a variety of sizes, shapes, and current ratings. They are called ''starting batteries'' and are designed to deliver a large current output for a brief time to start an engine. After starting, the charging system takes over to supply most of the current required to operate the car. The battery acts as a system stabilizer and provides current whenever the electrical loads exceed the charging current output. An automotive battery must provide good cranking power for the car's engine and adequate reserve power for the electrical system in which it is used.

Manufacturers also make 12-volt automotive-type batteries that are not designed for automotive use. These are called ''cycling batteries'' and are designed to provide a power source for a vehicle or accessory without continual recharging. Cycling batteries provide a constant low current for a long period of time. They are designed for industrial, marine, and recreational vehicle (RV) use. Most of their current capacity is exhausted in each cycle before recharging.

The brief high-current flow required of a starting battery is produced by using relatively thin plates, compared to those used in a cycling battery. The thicker plates of the cycling battery will provide a constant current drain for several hours. Using a starting battery in an application calling for a cycling battery will shorten its life considerably, as we will see later in the chapter. The use of a cycling battery to start and operate a car will cause excessive internal heat from the brief but high current draw, resulting in a shorter service life.

Test standards and rating methods devised by the Battery Council International (BCI) and the Society of Automotive Engineers (SAE) are designed to measure a battery's ability to meet the requirements for which it is to be used.

The BCI publishes application charts that list the correct battery for any car. Optional heavy-duty batteries are normally used in cars with air conditioning or several major electrical accessories or in cars operated in cold climates. To ensure adequate cranking power and to meet all other electrical needs, a replacement battery may have a higher rating, but never a lower rating, than the original unit. The battery must also be the correct size for the car, and have the correct type of terminals. BCI standards include a coding system, called the group number. BCI battery rating methods are explained in the following paragraphs.

Ampere-Hour Rating

The oldest battery rating method, no longer used to rate batteries, was the ampere-hour rating. This rating method was the industry standard for decades. It was replaced, however, years ago by the cranking performance and reserve capacity ratings, which provide better indications of a battery's performance.

The ampere-hour method was also called the 20-hour discharge rating method. This rating represented the steady current flow which a battery delivered at a temperature of 80°F (27°C) without cell voltage falling below 1.75 volts (a total of 10.5 volts for a 12-volt battery). For example, a battery that continuously delivered 3 amperes for 20 hours was rated as a 60 ampere-hour battery (3 amperes × 20 hours = 60 ampere-hours).

Cranking Performance Rating

The **cranking performance rating** indicates the power a battery can supply for engine cranking

---

Cranking Performance Rating: A battery rating based on the amperes of current that a battery can supply for 30 seconds at 0°F, with no battery cell falling below 1.2 volts.

■ **Don't Pull the Plugs**

Do you make a practice of removing the vent plugs from a battery before charging it? Prestolite says you shouldn't, at least with many late-model batteries. ''A great number of batteries manufactured today will have safety vents,'' says Prestolite. ''If these are removed, the batteries are open to external sources of explosion ignition.'' Prestolite recommends that, on batteries with safety vents, the vent plugs should be left in place when charging.

Figure 7-9. This Ford Escort diesel battery is encased in a protective bag and housed in the trunk.

at 0°F (–18°C). The rating figures for car and light truck batteries range from 165 to 1,050 cold-cranking amperes. These figures represent the current flow a battery can deliver for 30 seconds at 0°F (–18°C) while maintaining at least 1.2 volts per cell, for a minimum terminal voltage of 7.2 volts for a 12-volt battery.

Reserve Capacity Rating

The **reserve capacity rating** indicates the long-term power available from a battery for ignition, lighting, and accessories required in emergencies. Reserve capacity (listed in minutes) is the time a fully charged battery at 80°F (27°C) can deliver 25 amperes and maintain at least 1.75 volts at every cell, or 10.5 volts total for a 12-volt battery. Battery reserve capacity ratings range from 30 to 175 minutes, and correspond approximately to the length of time a vehicle can be driven after the charging system has failed.

Group Number

Carmakers provide a designated amount of space in the engine compartment to accommodate the battery. Since battery companies build batteries of various current-capacity ratings in a variety of sizes and shapes, it is useful to have a guide when replacing a battery, because it must fit into the space provided. The BCI size **group number** identifies a battery in terms of its length, width, height, terminal design, and other physical features.

BATTERY INSTALLATIONS

Most automobiles use one six-cell, 12-volt battery installed in the engine compartment. Certain factors influence battery location:

- The distance between the battery and the alternator or starter motor determines the length of the cables used. Cable length is important because of electrical system resistance. The longer the cables, the greater the resistance.
- The battery should be located away from hot engine components in a position where it can be cooled by airflow.
- The battery should be in a location where it can be securely mounted as protection against internal damage from vibration.
- The battery should be positioned where it can be easily serviced.

The decrease in size of late-model vehicles has resulted in lighter, smaller batteries with greater capacity. The use of new plastics and improved grid and plate materials have contributed to the new battery designs.

Some older cars and a few new imported and domestic models have the battery located in the trunk. For example, the battery used with the Ford Escort diesel is mounted in the trunk beneath a trim cover and encased in a protective bag, figure 7-9. The bag will retain battery acid in case of an accident which might damage it. A tube and seal assembly connected to the battery vents allows gassing to the atmosphere. This venting device should be inspected periodically and replaced, if necessary, because proper venting is essential for safety. Such locations require the use of long cables of heavy gauge wire. The size of such cables offsets their greater length in keeping resistance manageable, but increases cost and weight while reducing convenience.

Late-model GM diesel cars and Ford light trucks use two 12-volt batteries connected in parallel, figure 7-10. Both battery + terminals are connected to each other and to the + battery cable attached to the starter motor (GM) or to the relay (Ford). The battery – terminals are connected to each other in a similar manner, and to the ground cable. The use of a parallel installation doubles the current available for starting the high-compression diesel without increasing voltage (if they were connected in series, the voltage would double). The two batteries provide 12 volts to the electrical system and are charged simultaneously by the alternator.

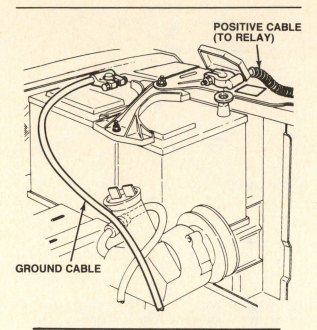

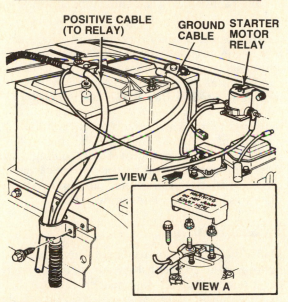

Figure 7-10. Diesel vehicles generally have two 12-volt batteries for better cranking with a 12-volt starter. (Ford)

BATTERY INSTALLATION COMPONENTS

Selecting and maintaining properly designed battery installation components are a prerequisite for good battery operation and service life.

Connectors, Carriers, and Holddowns

As we saw in Chapter Five, battery cables are very large-diameter multistrand wire, usually no. 0 to no. 6 gauge. Diesel engine vehicles

generally use the larger no. 0, while gasoline engine vehicles use no. 6. A new battery cable should always be the same gauge as the one being replaced.

Battery terminals may be tapered posts on the top or internally threaded terminals on the side of the battery. To prevent accidental reversal of battery polarity (incorrectly connect-

Reserve Capacity Rating: A battery rating based on the number of minutes a battery at 80°F can supply 25 amperes, with no battery cell falling below 1.75 volts.

Group Number: A battery identification number that indicates battery dimensions, terminal design, holddown location, and other physical features.

■ Parasitic Losses

Parasitic losses are small current drains required to operate electrical systems, such as the clock, that continue to work when the car is parked and the ignition is off. The current demand of a clock is small and not likely to cause a problem.

The advent of computer controls, however, has made parasitic losses more serious. Many late-model cars have computers to control such diverse items as engine operation, radio tuning, suspension leveling, climate control, and more. Each of these microprocessors contains random access memory (RAM) that stores information relevant to its job. To "remember", RAM requires a constant supply of power, and therefore puts a continuous drain on the car's electrical system.

The combined drain of several computer memories can discharge a battery to the point where there is insufficient cranking power after only a few weeks. Vehicles with these systems that are driven infrequently, put into storage, or awaiting parts for repair will require battery charging more often than older cars with lower parasitic voltage losses.

Because of the higher parasitic current drains on late-model cars, the old test of removing a battery cable connection and tapping it against the terminal while looking for a spark is both dangerous and no longer a valid check for excessive current drain. Furthermore, every time the power source to the computer is interrupted, the information programmed into memory is lost and will have to be reprogrammed when the battery cables are reconnected.

On engine control systems with learning capability, like GM's Computer Command Control, driveability may also be affected until the computer relearns the engine calibration modifications that were erased from its memory when the battery was disconnected.

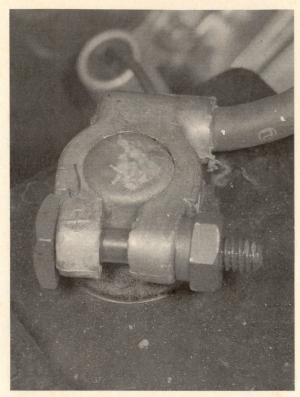

Figure 7-11. The most common type of top terminal battery clamp.

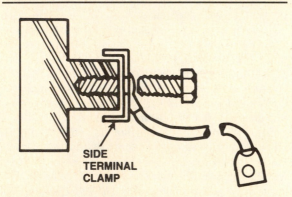

Figure 7-12. The side terminal clamp is attached with a bolt. (Chrysler)

ing the cables), the positive terminal is slightly larger than the negative terminal. Three basic styles of connectors are used to attach the battery cables to the battery terminals:

- A bolt-type clamp is used on top-terminal batteries, figure 7-11. The bolt passes through the two halves of the cable end into a nut. When tightened, it squeezes the cable end against the battery post.
- A bolt-through clamp is used on side-terminal batteries. The bolt threads through the cable end and directly into the battery terminal, figure 7-12.

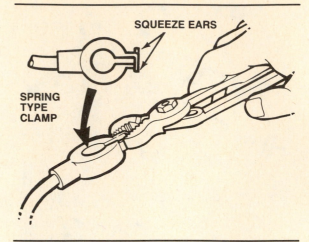

Figure 7-13. The spring-type clamp generally is found on non-domestic cars.

- A spring-type clamp is used on some top-terminal batteries. A built-in spring holds the cable end on the battery post, figure 7-13.

Batteries are usually mounted on a shelf or tray in the engine compartment, although some manufacturers place the battery in the trunk, under the seat, or elsewhere in the vehicle. The shelf or tray that holds the battery is called the carrier, figure 7-14. The battery is mounted on the carrier with brackets called holddowns, figures 7-14 and 7-15. These keep the battery from tipping over and spilling acid. A battery must be held securely in its carrier to protect it from vibration that can damage the plates and internal plate connectors.

Battery Heat Shields

Many late-model cars use battery heat shields, figure 7-16, to protect batteries from high under-hood temperatures. Most heat shields are made of plastic, and some are integral with the battery holddown. Integral shields are usually large plastic plates that sit alongside the battery.

Heat shields do not require removal for routine battery inspection and testing, but must be removed for battery replacement.

BATTERY LIFE AND PERFORMANCE FACTORS

All batteries have a limited life, but certain conditions can shorten that life. The important factors that affect battery life are discussed in the following paragraphs.

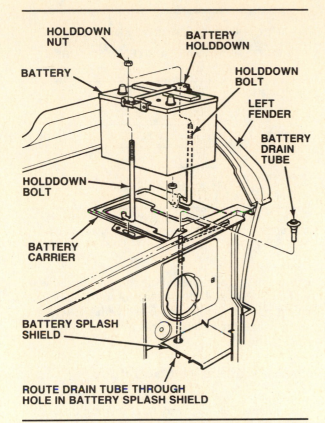

ROUTE DRAIN TUBE THROUGH
HOLE IN BATTERY SPLASH SHIELD

Figure 7-14. A common type of battery carrier and holddown.

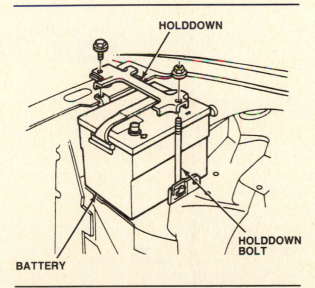

Figure 7-15. Another common battery holddown.

Electrolyte Level

As we have seen, the design of maintenance-free batteries has minimized the loss of water from electrolyte so that battery cases can be sealed. Given normal use, the addition of water to such batteries is not required during

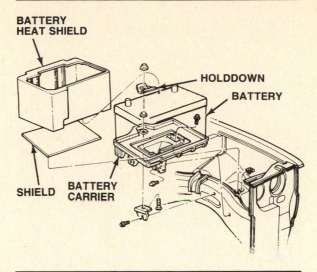

Figure 7-16. A molded heat shield that fits over the battery is used by Chrysler and some other carmakers.

their service life. However, even maintenance-free batteries will lose some of their water to high temperature, overcharging, deep cycling, and recharging — all factors in battery gassing and resulting water loss.

With vent-cap batteries, and to some extent, low-maintenance batteries, water is lost from the electrolyte during charging in the form of hydrogen and oxygen gases. This causes the electrolyte level to drop. If the level drops below the top of the plates, active material will be exposed to the air. The material will harden and resist electrochemical reaction. Also, the remaining electrolyte will have a high concentration of acid, which can cause the plates to deteriorate quickly. Even the addition of water will not restore such hardened plates to a fully active condition.

■ How the Battery Got Its Name

The word "battery" means a group of like things used together. An automobile battery is a group of electrochemical cells connected and working together. Battery voltage is determined by the number of cells connected in series in the battery.

Early automobile batteries could be taken apart for service. Cases were made of wood, and the tops were sealed with tar or a similar material. The top could be opened and the plate element could be removed from a single cell and replaced with a new one.

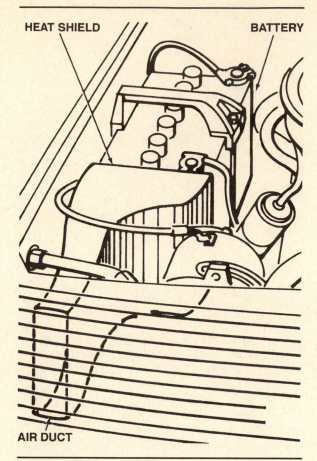

HEAT SHIELD   BATTERY

AIR DUCT

Figure 7-17. Battery power decreases as temperature decreases.

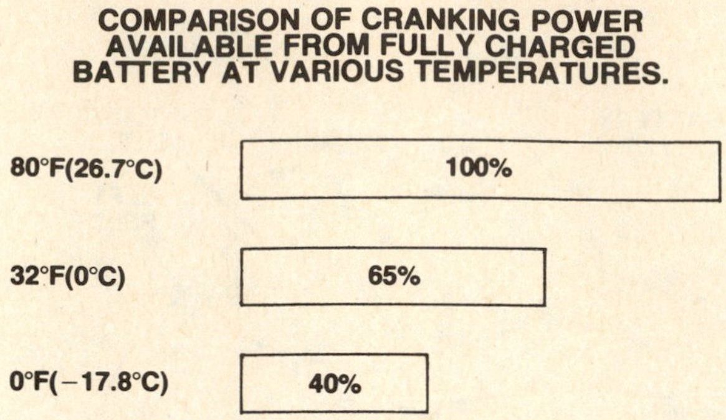

COMPARISON OF CRANKING POWER AVAILABLE FROM FULLY CHARGED BATTERY AT VARIOUS TEMPERATURES.

80°F(26.7°C)	100%
32°F(0°C)	65%
0°F(−17.8°C)	40%

Figure 7-18. This graph represents the increased power required to crank an engine at low temperatures.

Corrosion

Battery corrosion is caused by spilled electrolyte and by electrolyte condensation from gassing. The sulfuric acid attacks and can destroy not only connectors and terminals, but metal holddowns and carriers, as well. Corroded connectors increase resistance at the battery connections. This reduces the applied voltage for the car's electrical system. Corrosion also can cause mechanical failure of the holddowns and carrier, which can damage the battery. Spilled electrolyte and corrosion on the battery top also can create a current leakage path, which can allow the battery to discharge.

Overcharging

Batteries can be overcharged either by the automotive charging system or by a separate battery charger. In either case, there is a violent chemical reaction in the battery. The water in the electrolyte is rapidly broken down into hydrogen and oxygen gases. These gas bubbles can wash active material off the plates, as well as lower the level of the electrolyte. Overcharging can also cause excessive heat, which can oxidize the positive grid material and even buckle the plates.

Undercharging and Sulfation

If an automobile is not charging its battery, either because of stop-and-start driving or a fault in the charging system, the battery will be constantly discharged. As we saw in the explanation of electrochemical action, a discharged plate is covered with lead sulfate. The amount of lead sulfate on the plate will vary according to the state of charge. As the lead sulfate builds up in a constantly undercharged battery, it can crystallize and not recombine with the electrolyte. This is called battery **sulfation**. The crystals are difficult to break down by normal recharging and the battery becomes useless. Despite the chemical additives sold as ''miracle cures'' for sulfation, a completely sulfated battery cannot be effectively recharged.

Cycling

As we learned at the beginning of this chapter, the operation of a battery from charged to discharged and back to charged is called cycling. Automotive batteries are not designed for continuous deep-cycle use (although special marine and RV batteries are). If an automotive battery is repeatedly cycled from a fully charged condition to an almost discharged condition, the active material on the positive plates may shed and fall into the bottom of the case. If this happens, the material cannot be restored to the plates. Cycling thus reduces the capacity of the battery and shortens its useful service life.

Temperature

Temperature extremes affect battery service life and performance in a number of ways. High temperature, caused by overcharging or excessive engine heat, increases electrolyte loss and shortens battery life.

Low temperatures in winter can also harm a battery. If the electrolyte freezes, it can expand and break the case, ruining the battery. The freezing point of electrolyte depends upon its specific gravity and thus, on the battery's state of charge. A fully charged battery with a specific gravity of 1.265 to 1.280 will not freeze until its temperature drops below –60°F (–51°C). A discharged battery with an electrolyte which is mostly water can freeze at –18°F (–8°C).

As we saw earlier, cold temperatures make it harder to keep the battery fully charged, yet this is when a full charge is most important. Figure 7-17 compares the energy levels available from a fully-charged battery at various temperatures. Figure 7-18 compares the energy required to crank an engine at those temperatures. As you can see, the colder a battery is, the less energy it can supply. Yet the colder an engine gets, the more energy it requires for cranking. This is why battery care is especially important in cold weather.

Vibration

As mentioned earlier, a battery must be securely mounted in its carrier to protect it from vibration. Vibration can shake the active materials off the plates and severely shorten a battery's life. Vibration can also loosen the plate connections to the plate strap and damage other internal connections. Some manufacturers now build batteries with plate straps and connectors in the center of the plates to reduce the effects of vibration. Severe vibration can even crack a battery case and loosen cable connections.

SUMMARY

Automotive batteries are lead-acid secondary batteries containing a number of electrochemical cells which can be recharged after discharging. Batteries not only store power, they generate voltage and current through the electrochemical action between dissimilar plates in the presence of an electrolyte.

Each lead-acid cell generates about 2.1 volts regardless of the number of positive and negative plates. Cells are connected in series, allowing six cells to produce about 12.6 volts in a fully charged 12-volt battery. Current output of a cell depends upon the total surface area of all the plates. Batteries with higher current or capacity ratings have larger plate areas.

The battery state of charge is determined by electrolyte specific gravity. In a fully charged battery, electrolyte should have a specific gravity of 1.260 to 1.265. Maintenance-free batteries contain calcium-alloy grids to reduce battery heat and water loss. Since such batteries are sealed, their electrolyte cannot be checked and water cannot be added to their cells.

Automotive batteries are designed for starting the engine, not for continual cycling from fully charged to discharged and back to fully charged.

Batteries have cranking performance and reserve capacity ratings, and their size and physical characteristics are indicated by BCI size group numbers.

Battery service life is affected by electrolyte level, corrosion, overcharging or undercharging, cycling, vibration, and temperature variations.

Sulfation: The crystallization of lead sulfate on the plates of a constantly discharged battery.

■ Deep-Cycle Service

Some batteries, like those in golf carts and electric vehicles, are used for deep-cycle service. This means that as they provide electrical power they go from a fully charged state to an almost fully discharged state, and are then recharged and used again.

Maintenance-free batteries should never be used in deep-cycle service. Deep-cycle service promotes shedding of the active materials from the battery plates. This action drastically reduces the service life of a maintenance-free battery.

Review Questions

Choose the single most correct answer.
Compare your answers with the correct answers on page 431.

1. Which of the following occurs within an automobile battery?
   a. The positive plate gains electrons and is positively charged
   b. The negative plate loses electrons and is negatively charged
   c. The positive plate loses electrons and the negative plate gains electrons
   d. The positive plate gains electrons and the negative plate loses electrons

2. Battery electrolyte is a mixture of water and:
   a. Lead peroxide
   b. Sulfuric acid
   c. Lead sulfate
   d. Sulfur crystals

3. The plates of a *discharged* battery are:
   a. Two similar metals in the presence of an electrolyte
   b. Two similar metals in the presence of water
   c. Two dissimilar metals in the presence of an electrolyte
   d. Two dissimilar metals in the presence of water

4. Which of the following is true about a "secondary" battery?
   a. It can be recharged
   b. Neither the electrolyte nor the metals change their atomic structure
   c. One of the metals is totally destroyed by the action of the battery
   d. The action of the battery cannot be reversed

5. Which of the following does *not* occur during battery recharging?
   a. The lead sulfate on the plates gradually decomposes
   b. The sulfate is redeposited in the water
   c. The electrolyte is returned to full strength
   d. The negative plates change back to lead sulfate

6. Each cell of an automobile battery can produce about _____ volts.
   a. 1.2
   b. 2.1
   c. 4.2
   d. 6.0

7. Which of the following is true of a six-volt automobile battery?
   a. It has six cells connected in series
   b. It has three cells connected in series
   c. It has six cells connected in parallel
   d. It has three cells connected in parallel

8. The correct ratio of water to sulfuric acid in battery electrolyte is *approximately*:
   a. 80 percent water to 20 percent sulfuric acid
   b. 60 percent water to 40 percent sulfuric acid
   c. 40 percent water to 60 percent sulfuric acid
   d. 20 percent water to 80 percent sulfuric acid

9. At 80°F, the correct specific gravity of electrolyte in a fully charged battery is:
   a. 1.200 to 1.225
   b. 1.225 to 1.265
   c. 1.265 to 1.280
   d. 1.280 to 1.300

10. A specific gravity of 1.170 to 1.190 at 80°F indicates that a battery's state of charge is about:
    a. 75 percent
    b. 50 percent
    c. 25 percent
    d. 10 percent

11. Which of the following materials is *not* used for battery separators?
    a. Lead
    b. Wood
    c. Paper
    d. Plastic

12. Batteries are rated in terms of:
    a. Amperes at 65°F
    b. Resistance at 32°F
    c. Voltage level at 80°F
    d. Cranking performance at 0°F

13. Maintenance-free batteries:
    a. Have individual cell caps
    b. Require water infrequently
    c. Have three pressure vents
    d. Use non-antimony lead alloys

14. Which of the following statements is *not* true of a replacement battery?
    a. It may have the same rating as the original battery
    b. It may have a higher rating than the original battery
    c. It may have a lower rating than the original battery
    d. It should be selected according to an application chart

15. An automobile battery with a cranking performance rating of 380 can deliver 380 amps for:
    a. 30 seconds at 0°F
    b. 60 seconds at 0°F
    c. 90 seconds at 32°F
    d. 90 seconds at 0°F

16. The principal cause of battery water loss is:
    a. Spillage from the vent caps
    b. Leakage through the battery case
    c. Conversion of water to sulfuric acid
    d. Evaporation due to heat of the charging current

17. Which of the following is *not* true of a maintenance-free battery?
    a. It will resist overcharging better than a vent-cap battery
    b. It will lose water slower than a vent-cap battery
    c. It will produce a greater voltage than a vent-cap battery
    d. It has a greater electrolyte capacity than a vent-cap battery

18. The electrolyte in a fully charged battery will generally not freeze until the temperature drops to:
    a. 32°F
    b. 0°F
    c. −20°F
    d. −50°F

19. The grid material used in a maintenance-free battery is alloyed with:
    a. Silicon
    b. Antimony
    c. Calcium
    d. Germanium

20. Low-maintenance batteries:
    a. Have no cell caps
    b. Have a higher proportion of sulfuric acid
    c. Have no gas pressure vents
    d. Require infrequent water addition

21. Recombinant batteries are:
    a. Rebuilt units
    b. Completely sealed
    c. Vented to release gassing
    d. Able to produce a higher cell voltage

PART THREE

The Charging System

Chapter Eight
A.C. Charging Systems
and Alternators

Chapter Nine
Regulators and Indicators

8

A.C. Charging Systems and Alternators

The charging system converts the engine's mechanical energy into electrical energy. This electrical energy is used to maintain the battery's state of charge and to operate the loads of the automotive electrical system. During our study of the charging system, we will use the conventional theory of current flow (+ to –).

During cranking, all electrical energy for the car is supplied by the battery. Once the engine is running, the charging system must produce enough electrical energy to recharge the battery and to supply the demands of other loads in the electrical system.

If the starting system is in poor condition and draws too much current, or if the charging system cannot recharge the battery and supply the additional loads, more energy must be drawn from the battery for short periods of time.

CHARGING SYSTEM DEVELOPMENT

For many years, automotive charging systems used only d.c. generators to provide electrical energy. Internally, generators produce an alternating current voltage which is mechanically rectified by the commutator into direct current voltage. Systems using d.c. generators are called d.c. charging systems.

Alternators also produce alternating current, but there was no simple way to rectify the current until semiconductor technology finally provided the answer in the form of diodes, or one-way electrical valves. By the mid-1960s, almost all new automobiles were using a diode-rectified alternator in their charging system. Systems using alternators are commonly called a.c. charging systems.

Alternators have replaced the generator in the automotive charging system because they have several advantages; they:

- Weigh less per ampere of output
- Can be operated at much higher speed
- Pass less current through the brushes (only a few amperes of field current), reducing brush wear
- Govern their own maximum current output, requiring no external current regulation
- Can produce current when rotated in either direction, although their cooling fans usually are designed for one-way operation.

CHARGING VOLTAGE

Although the automotive electrical system is called a 12-volt system, the alternator must produce more than 12 volts. We learned in Chapter Seven that each battery cell produces about 2.1

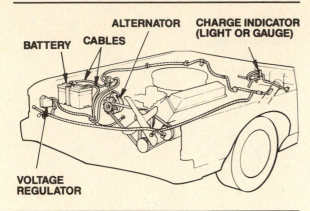

Figure 8-1. The major components of an automotive charging system. (Chrysler)

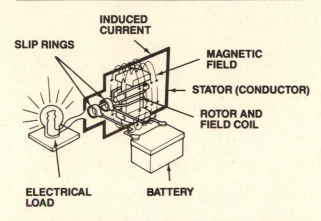

Figure 8-2. An alternator is based on the rotation of a magnet inside a fixed-loop conductor. (Chrysler)

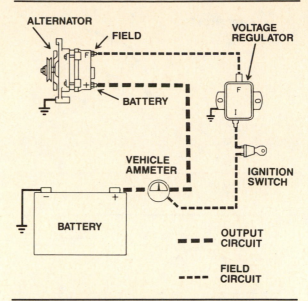

Figure 8-3. The output circuit and the field circuit make up the automotive charging system. (Prestolite)

volts when fully charged. This means that the open-circuit voltage of a fully charged 12-volt battery (six cells) is approximately 12.6 volts. If the alternator cannot produce more than 12 volts, it cannot charge the battery until system voltage drops under 12 volts. This would leave nothing extra to serve the other electrical demands put on the system by lights, air conditioning, and power accessories.

Alternating-current charging systems are generally regulated to produce a maximum output of 14.5 volts. Output of more than 16 volts will overheat the battery electrolyte and shorten its life. High voltage also can damage components that rely heavily on solid-state electronics, such as fuel injection and engine control systems. On the other hand, low voltage output will cause the battery to become sulfated. As you can see, the charging system must be maintained within the voltage limits specified by the carmaker if the vehicle is to perform properly.

A.C. Charging System Components

The automotive charging system, figure 8-1, contains:

- A battery, which provides the initial field current required to operate the alternator and, in turn, is charged and maintained by the alternator.
- An alternator, which is belt driven by the engine and converts mechanical motion into charging voltage and current. A simple alternator, figure 8-2, consists of a magnet rotating inside a fixed-loop stator, or conductor. The alternating current produced in the conductor is rectified by diodes for use by the electrical system.

■ Heat Sinks

The term "heat sink" is commonly used to describe the block of aluminum or other material in which the alternator diodes are mounted. The job of the heat sink is to absorb and carry away the heat in the diodes caused by electrical current through them. This action keeps the diodes cool and prevents damage.

An internal combustion engine is also a heat sink. The engine is designed so that the combustion and friction heat will be carried away and dissipated to the atmosphere.

Although they are not thought of as heat sinks, many individual parts of an automobile — such as the brake drums — are designed so that they will also do this important job.

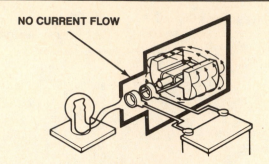

Figure 8-4. No current flows when the rotor's magnetic field is parallel to the stator. (Chrysler)

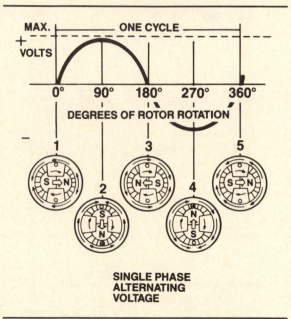

SINGLE PHASE
ALTERNATING
VOLTAGE

Figure 8-5. These are the voltage levels induced across the upper half of the conductor during one rotor revolution. (Chrysler)

- A regulator, which limits the field current flow and thus the alternator's voltage output according to the electrical system demand. A regulator can be either an electromechanical or a solid-state device. Some late-model solid-state regulators are part of the vehicle's onboard computer.
- An ammeter, a voltmeter, or an indicator warning lamp mounted on the instrument panel to give a visual indication of charging system operation.

Charging System Circuits

The charging system consists of two major circuits, figure 8-3:

- The **field circuit**, which delivers current to the alternator field

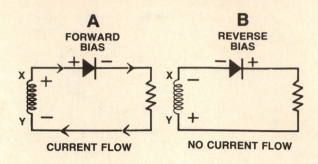

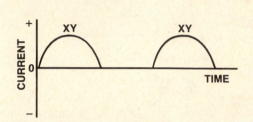

Figure 8-6. A single diode in the circuit results in half-wave rectification. (Delco-Remy)

- The **output circuit**, which sends voltage and current to the battery and other electrical components.

SINGLE-PHASE CURRENT

Alternators induce voltage by rotating a magnetic field inside a fixed conductor. The greatest current output is produced when the rotor is parallel to the stator with its magnetic field at right angles to the stator, figure 8-2. When the rotor makes one-quarter of a revolution and is at right angles to the stator with its magnetic field parallel to the stator, figure 8-4, there is no current output. Figure 8-5 shows the voltage levels induced across the upper half of the looped conductor during one revolution of the rotor.

The constant change of voltage, first to a positive peak and then to a negative peak, produces a **sine wave voltage**. This name comes from the trigonometric sine function. The wave shape is controlled by the angle between the magnet and the conductor. The sine wave voltage induced across one conductor by one rotor revolution is called a **single-phase voltage**. Positions 1 through 5 of figure 8-5 show complete sine wave single-phase voltage.

This single-phase voltage causes alternating current to flow in a complete circuit, because the voltage switches from positive to negative as the rotor turns. The alternating current caused by a single-phase voltage is called **single-phase current**.

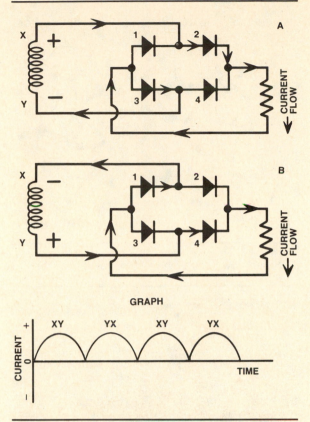

GRAPH

Figure 8-7. More diodes are needed for full-wave rectification. (Delco-Remy)

DIODE RECTIFICATION

If the single-phase voltage shown in figure 8-5 made current flow through a simple circuit, the current would flow first in one direction and then in the opposite direction. As long as the rotor turned, the current would reverse its flow with every half revolution. We know that the battery cannot be recharged with alternating current. Alternating current must be rectified to direct current. This is done with diodes.

We saw in Chapter Three that a diode acts as a one-way electrical valve. If we insert a diode in a simple circuit, figure 8-6, one-half of the a.c. voltage will be blocked. That is, the diode will allow current to flow from X to Y, as shown in position A. In position B, the current cannot flow from Y to X because it is blocked by the diode. The graph in figure 8-6 shows the total current flow.

The first half of the current flow, from X to Y, was allowed to pass through the diode. It is shown on the graph as curve XY. The second half of the flow, from Y to X, was not allowed to pass through the diode. It does not appear on the graph because it never flowed through the circuit. When the voltage reverses at the

start of the next rotor revolution, the current is again allowed through the diode from X to Y.

An alternator with only one conductor and one diode would show this current output pattern. However, this output would not be very useful, because half of the time there is no current available. This is called **half-wave rectification**, since only half of the a.c. sine wave voltage produced by the alternator is allowed to flow as d.c. voltage.

If we add more diodes to the circuit, figure 8-7, more of the a.c. voltage can be rectified to d.c. In position A, current is flowing from X to Y. It flows from X, through diode 2, through the load, through diode 3, and back to Y. In position B, current is flowing from Y to X. It flows from Y, through diode 4, through the load, through diode 1, and back to X.

Notice that in both cases, current flowed through the load in the same direction. The a.c. has been rectified to d.c. The graph in figure 8-7 shows the current output of an alternator with one conductor and four diodes. There is more current available because all of the voltage has been rectified. This is called **full-wave rectification**. There are still moments, however, when current flow is at zero. Most automotive alternators use three conductors and six diodes to produce overlapping current waves so that current output is *never* at zero. We will see how this is done shortly.

Field Circuit: The charging system circuit that delivers current to the alternator field.

Output Circuit: The charging system circuit that sends voltage and current to the battery and other electrical systems and devices.

Sine Wave Voltage: The constant change, first to a positive peak and then to a negative peak, of an induced alternating voltage in a conductor.

Single-Phase Voltage: The sine wave voltage induced within one conductor by one revolution of an alternator rotor.

Single-Phase Current: Alternating current caused by a single-phase voltage.

Half-Wave Rectification: A process by which only one-half of an a.c. sine wave voltage is rectified and allowed to flow as d.c.

Full-Wave Rectification: A process by which all of an a.c. sine wave voltage is rectified and allowed to flow as d.c.

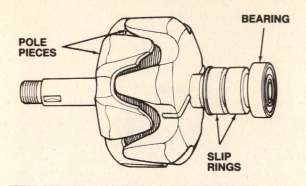

Figure 8-8. A typical 12-pole rotor. (Chrysler)

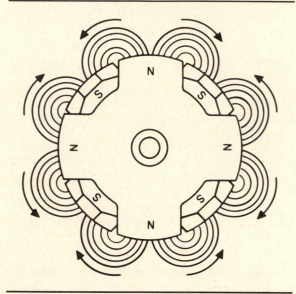

Figure 8-9. The flux lines surrounding an eight-pole rotor. (Prestolite)

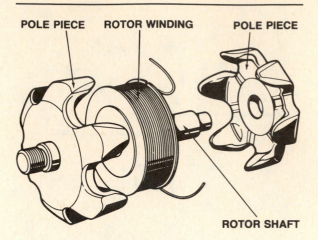

Figure 8-10. The magnetic field of the rotor is caused by current flow through the rotor winding. (Bosch)

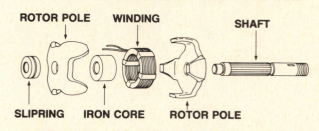

Figure 8-11. An exploded view of the parts of the complete rotor assembly. (Prestolite)

ALTERNATOR CONSTRUCTION

Our simple illustrations have shown the principles of alternator operation. To provide enough direct current for an automobile, alternators must have a more complex design. But no matter how the design varies, the principles of operation remain the same.

We mentioned that the design of an alternator limits the maximum current output of the alternator. To change this maximum value for different applications, manufacturers change the design of the stator, rotor, and other components. The following paragraphs describe the major parts of an automotive alternator.

Rotor

The rotor carries the alternator's magnetic field. Unlike a generator, which usually has only two magnetic poles, the alternator rotor has several N and S poles. This increases the number of flux lines within the alternator and increases the voltage output. A typical automotive rotor, figure 8-8, has 12 poles: 6 N and 6 S. The rotor consists of two steel rotor halves, or pole pieces, with fingers that interlace. These fingers are the poles. Each pole piece has either *all* N or *all* S poles. The magnetic flux lines travel between adjacent N and S poles, as you can see from the eight-pole rotor shown in figure 8-9.

As you look along the outside of the rotor, note that the flux lines point first in one direction and then in the other. This means that as the rotor spins inside the alternator, the fixed conductors are being cut by flux lines which point in alternating directions. The induced voltage will alternate, just as in our example of a simple alternator with only two poles. Automotive alternators may have any number of poles, as long as they are placed N-S-N-S. Common alternator designs use eight to 14 poles.

The rotor poles may retain some magnetism when the alternator is not in operation, but this residual magnetism is not strong enough to induce any voltage across the conductors. The

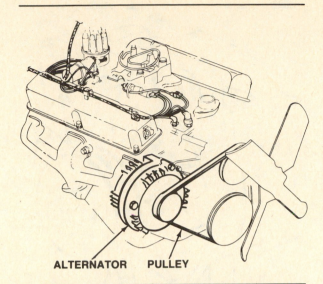

ALTERNATOR   PULLEY

Figure 8-12. The alternator and drive pulley. (Chrysler)

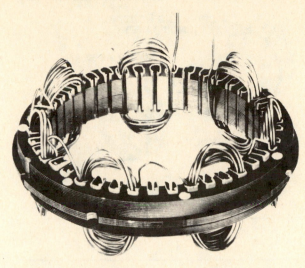

Figure 8-14. A stator with only one conductor installed. (Delco-Remy)

Figure 8-13. An alternator stator.

magnetic field of the rotor is produced by current flow through the rotor winding, a coil of wire between the two pole pieces, figure 8-10. This is also called the excitation winding, or the field winding. Varying the amount of field current flow through the rotor winding will vary the strength of the magnetic field. This affects the voltage output of the alternator.

A soft iron core is mounted inside the rotor winding, figure 8-11. One pole piece is at-tached to either end of the core. When field current flows through the winding, the iron core is magnetized. The pole pieces take on the magnetic polarity of the end of the core to which they are attached. Current is supplied to the winding through sliprings and brushes.

The combination of a soft iron rotor core and steel rotor halves provides better localization and permeability of the magnetic field. The rotor pole pieces, winding, core, and sliprings are pressed onto a shaft. The ends of this shaft are held by bearings in the alternator housing. Outside the housing, a drive pulley is attached to the shaft, figure 8-12. A belt from the automobile engine passes around this pulley to turn the alternator shaft and rotor assembly.

Stator

The three alternator conductors are wound onto a cylindrical, laminated core. The lamination prevents unwanted eddy currents from forming in the core. The assembled piece is called a stator, figure 8-13. Each conductor, called a stator winding, is formed into a number of coils spaced evenly around the core. There are as many coils in each conductor as there are pairs of N-S rotor poles. Figure 8-14 shows an incomplete stator with only one of its conductors installed. In this example, there are seven coils in the conductor, so the matching rotor would have seven pairs of N-S poles (a total of 14 poles). There are two ways in which the three stator windings can be connected. These methods will be explained later in this chapter.

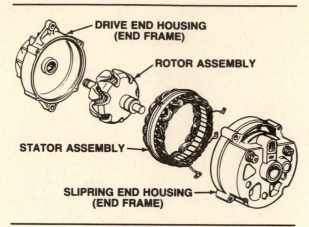

Figure 8-15. The alternator housing encloses the rotor and stator.

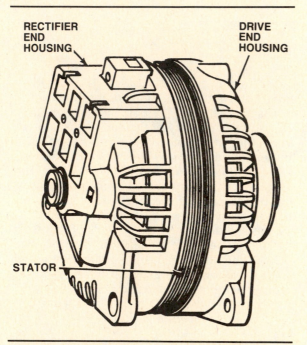

Figure 8-16. An alternator with exposed stator core.

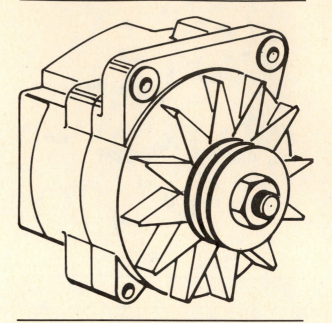

Figure 8-17. An alternator with the stator core enclosed.

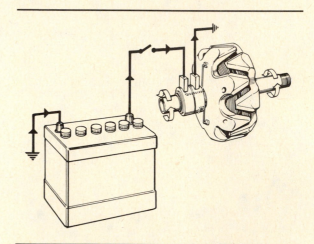

Figure 8-18. The sliprings and brushes carry current to the rotor windings.

Housing

The alternator housing, or frame, is made of two pieces of cast aluminum, figure 8-15. Aluminum is lightweight and nonmagnetic and conducts heat well. One housing piece holds a bearing for the end of the rotor shaft where the drive pulley is mounted. This is often called the drive-end housing, or front housing, of the alternator. The other end holds the diodes, the brushes, and the electrical terminal connections. It also holds a bearing for the slipring end of the rotor shaft. This is often called the slipring-end housing, or rear housing. Together, the two pieces totally enclose the rotor and the stator windings.

The end housings are bolted together. Some stator cores have an extended rim that is held between the two housings, figure 8-16. Other stator cores provide holes for the housing bolts, but do not extend to the outside of the housings, figure 8-17. In both designs, the stator is bolted rigidly in place inside the alternator housing.

Because the alternator housing is bolted directly to the engine, it is part of the electrical ground path. Anything connected to the housing, which is not insulated from the housing, is grounded.

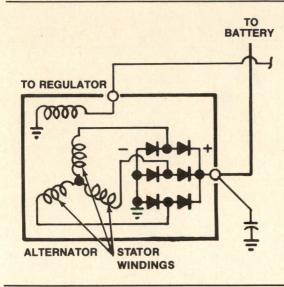

Figure 8-19. Each conductor is attached to one positive and one negative diode.

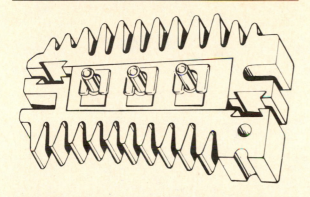

Figure 8-20. Positive and negative diodes can be mounted in a heat sink for protection.

Sliprings and Brushes

The sliprings and brushes conduct current to the rotor winding. Most automotive alternators have two sliprings mounted on the rotor shaft. The sliprings are insulated from the shaft and from each other. One end of the rotor winding is connected to each slipring, figure 8-18. One brush rides on each ring under spring tension from its brush holder to carry current to and from the winding. The brushes are connected in parallel with the alternator output circuit. They draw some of the alternator current output and route it through the rotor winding. Current flow through the winding must be d.c. We will see later how this is supplied.

Field current in an alternator is usually about 1.5 to 3.0 amperes. Because the brushes carry so little current, they do not require as much maintenance as generator brushes, which must conduct all of the generator's current output.

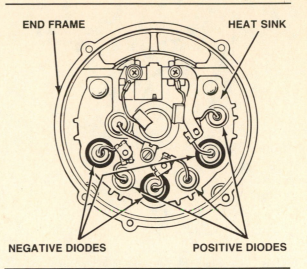

Figure 8-21. Negative diodes may be pressed into the rear housing.

Diode Installation

Automotive alternators that have three stator windings generally use six diodes to rectify the current output. The connections between the conductors and the diodes vary slightly, but each conductor is connected to one positive and one negative diode, figure 8-19.

The three positive diodes are always insulated from the alternator rear housing. They are connected to the insulated terminal of the battery and to the rest of the automotive electrical system. The battery cannot discharge through this connection because the bias of the diodes blocks any current flow from the battery. The positive diodes will conduct only that current flowing from the conductors toward the battery. The positive diodes are mounted together on a conductor called a heat sink, figure 8-20. The heat sink carries heat away from the diodes, just as the radiator carries heat away from the engine. Too much heat from current flow could damage the diodes.

The three negative diodes may be pressed or threaded into the alternator rear housing, figure 8-21. On high-output alternators, they may be mounted in a heat sink for added protection. In either case, the connection to the alternator housing is a ground path. The negative diodes will conduct only that current flowing from ground into the conductors.

Each group of three or more negative or positive diodes can be called a diode bridge, a diode trio, or a diode plate.

Some manufacturers use complete rectifier assemblies containing all the diodes and connections on a printed circuit board, figure 8-22.

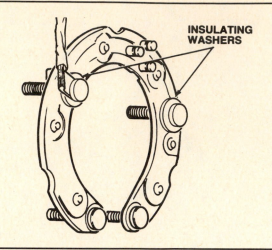

Figure 8-22. All diodes and connections may be included in a single printed circuit board. (Ford)

This assembly is replaced as a unit if any of the individual components fail.

Each stator winding connects to its proper negative diode through a circuit in the rectifier. A capacitor generally is installed between the output terminal at the positive diode's heat sink to ground at the negative diode's heat sink. This capacitor is used to eliminate voltage switching transients at the stator, to smooth out the a.c. voltage fluctuations, and to reduce EMI.

CURRENT PRODUCTION IN AN ALTERNATOR

Now that we have studied the principles of alternator operation and the components of an alternator, we can see the total picture of how an automotive alternator produces current.

Three-Phase Current

The alternator stator has three windings. Each is formed into a number of coils, which are spaced evenly around the stator core. The voltages induced across each winding by one rotor revolution are shown in the graphs of figure 8-23. The total voltage output of the alternator is three overlapping, evenly spaced, single-phase voltage waves, as shown in the bottom graph of the illustration. If the stator windings are connected into a complete circuit, the three phase voltages cause an a.c. flow called **three-phase current**.

Stator Types

When the three conductors are completely wound on the stator core, six loose ends remain. The way in which these ends are con-

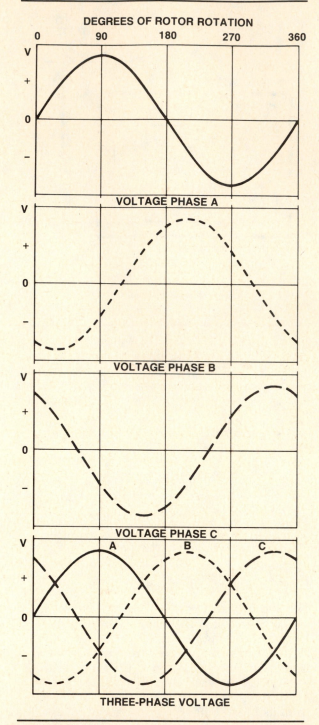

Figure 8-23. The single-phase voltages of the three conductors create a three-phase voltage output. (Bosch)

nected to the diode rectifier circuitry determines if the stator is a Y-type or a delta-type, figure 8-24. Both kinds of stators produce three-phase current and the rectification produces d.c. output. However, the voltage and current levels within the stators differ.

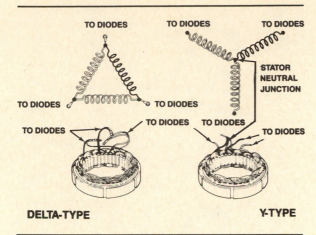

Figure 8-24. The two types of stator windings. (Chrysler)

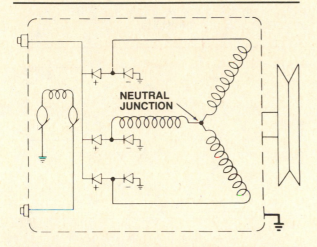

Figure 8-25. A Y-type stator circuit diagram. (Prestolite)

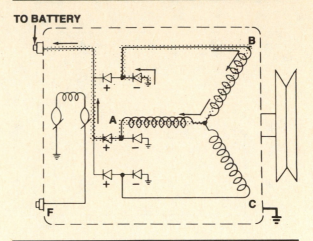

Figure 8-26. A typical current path during rectification in a Y-type stator. (Prestolite)

Y-type stator design

In the **Y-type** stator, or Y-connected stator, one end of each of the three windings is connected at a **neutral junction**, figure 8-24. The circuit diagram of the Y-type stator, figure 8-25, looks like the letter ''Y''. This is also sometimes called a wye or a star connection. The free end of each conductor is connected to a positive and a negative diode.

In a Y-type stator, two windings always will form a series circuit between a positive and a negative diode. At any given instant, the position of the rotor will determine the direction of current flow through these two windings. Current will flow from the negative voltage to the positive voltage. As shown in figure 8-26, current will flow from ground, through a negative diode, through two of the windings, and through a positive diode to the alternator out-put terminal. The induced voltages across the two windings will add together to produce the total voltage at the output terminal. Y-type

Three-Phase Current: Three overlapping, evenly spaced, single-phase currents that make up the total a.c. output of an alternator.

Y-Type Stator: An alternator stator design in which one end of each of the three windings in a three-phase alternator is connected at a neutral junction. This design is used in alternators that require high voltage at low alternator speed.

Neutral Junction: The center connection of the three windings in a Y-type stator.

■ Unrectified Alternators

Although the battery cannot be recharged with a.c., other automotive accessories can be designed to run on unrectified alternator output. Motorola has made alternators with separate terminals for a.c. output. Ford has offered a front-and-rear-window defroster that heats the windows with three-phase, 120-volt a.c. The high-voltage current is supplied by an additional alternator, mounted above the standard 12-volt a.c. alternator and driven by the same belt.

The Ford high-voltage alternator has a Y-type stator. Field current draw is more than four amps, and there is no regulator in the field circuit. Output is 2,200 watts at high engine speed. All of the wiring between the alternator and the defrosters is special, shielded wiring with warning tags at all connectors. Ford's test procedures use only an ohmmeter, because trying to test such high output could be dangerous.

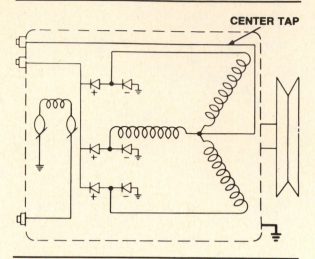

Figure 8-27. A Y-type stator with center tap. (Prestolite)

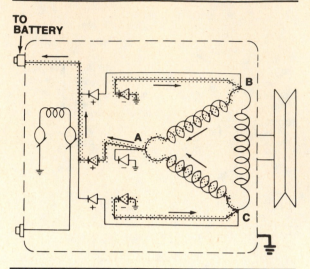

Figure 8-29. A typical current path during rectification in a delta-type stator. (Prestolite)

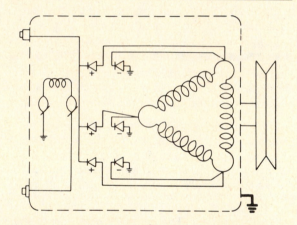

Figure 8-28. Circuit diagram of a delta-type stator. (Prestolite)

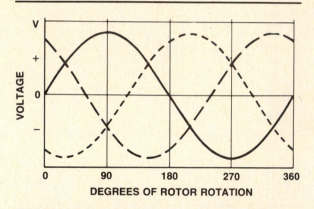

Figure 8-30. The three-phase voltage from one revolution of the rotor. (Bosch)

stators are used in alternators that require high-voltage output at low alternator speeds.

Some alternators include a center tap lead from the neutral junction to an insulated terminal on the housing, figure 8-27. The center tap can be used in controlling the field current, to activate an indicator lamp, to control the electric choke on a carburetor, or for other functions.

Delta-type stator design

The **delta-type stator**, or delta-connected stator, has the three windings connected end-to-end, figure 8-24. The circuit diagram of a delta-type stator, figure 8-28, looks like the Greek letter Delta (△), a triangle. There is no neutral junction in a delta-type stator. The windings will always form two parallel circuit paths between a negative and two positive di-

odes. Current will flow through two different circuit paths between the diodes, figure 8-29. Because there are two parallel circuit paths, more current can flow. Delta-type stators are used when a high-current output is needed.

Phase Rectification

The current flow pattern during rectification is similar in any automotive alternator. The only differences are specific current paths through Y- and delta-type stators, as we saw in figures 8-26 and 8-29.

Rectification with Multiple-Pole Rotors

The three-phase voltage output we have used in our examples, figure 8-30, is the voltage which would result if the alternator rotor had only one N and one S pole. As we have seen,

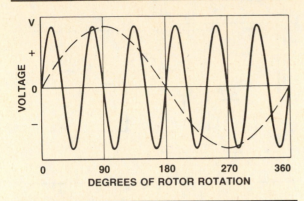

Figure 8-31. An alternator with six pairs of N-S poles would produce the solid line voltage trace. (Bosch)

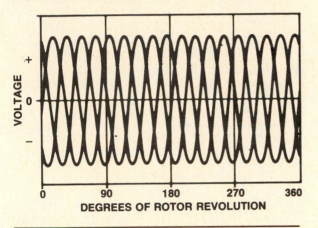

Figure 8-32. This is the total output of a three-winding, multiple-pole alternator.

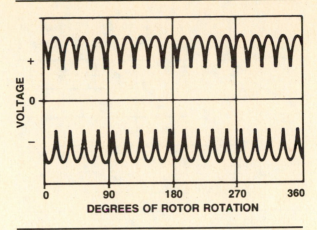

Figure 8-33. The diodes receive the maximum voltage values.

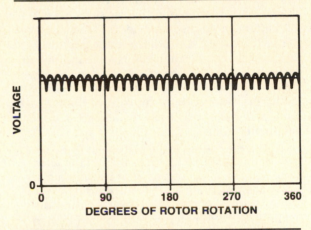

Figure 8-34. Rectified output is a pulsating d.c. current.

actual alternator rotors have many N and S poles. Each of these N-S pairs produces one complete voltage sine wave per rotor revolution, across each of the three windings. In figure 8-31, the sine wave voltage caused by a single pole is shown as a dashed line. The actual voltage trace from one winding of a 12-pole alternator is shown as a solid line. The entire stator output is three of these waves, evenly spaced and overlapping, figure 8-32. The maximum voltage value from these waves causes current flow through the diodes, figure 8-33.

After rectification, the voltage output is a pulsating d.c. voltage, figure 8-34, formed from the maximum voltage peaks of the stator output.

Excitation Field Circuit

We have said that the magnetic field of the rotor is caused by field current flow through the rotor winding. Field current can be drawn from the alternator output circuit once the alternator has begun to produce current. But when the automotive engine first begins to turn the alternator, there is not enough residual magnetism in the rotor poles to induce voltage. Unlike the generator, an alternator cannot start operation independently. Field current must be drawn from another source in order to magnetize the rotor and begin alternator output.

The other source is the car battery. It is connected to the alternator rotor winding through the excitation, or field, circuit. Battery voltage

Delta-Type Stator: An alternator stator design in which the three windings of a three-phase alternator are connected end-to-end. The beginning of one winding is attached to the end of another winding. Delta-type stators are used in alternators that must give high-current output.

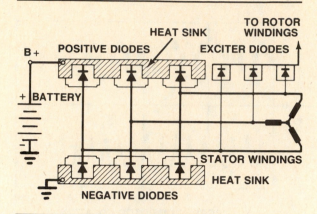

Figure 8-35. Some alternators have additional diodes to rectify field current. (Bosch)

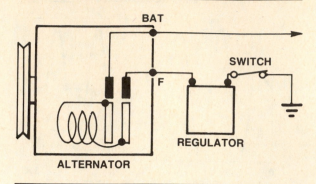

Figure 8-36. An A-circuit.

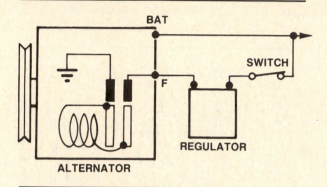

Figure 8-37. A B-circuit.

''excites'' the rotor magnetic field and begins alternator output. When the car's engine is off, the battery must be disconnected from the excitation circuit. If it is not disconnected, it could discharge through the rotor windings to ground. Some alternators use a relay to control this circuit. The voltage regulator or a part of the ignition switch also can control the excitation circuit. We will study this circuit in depth in Chapter Nine.

Once the alternator has started to produce current, field current is drawn from the alternator output. The current may be drawn after it has been rectified by the output diodes. Some alternators draw field current from unrectified a.c. alternator output, which is then rectified by three additional diodes before it flows through the rotor winding, figure 8-35. These additional diodes are called the exciter diodes or the field diodes.

Circuit Types

Alternators are designed with different types of field circuits. The three most common types are:

- A-circuit (externally grounded field)
- B-circuit (internally grounded field)
- Isolated-field circuit.

Circuit types are determined by where the voltage regulator is connected and from where the field current is drawn.

A-circuit

The A-circuit alternator, figure 8-36, also can be called an externally grounded field alternator. Both brushes are insulated from the alternator housing. One brush is connected to the voltage regulator, where it is grounded. The second brush is connected to the alternator output circuit within the alternator, where it draws current for the rotor winding. The regulator lies

between the rotor field winding and ground. This type of circuit is often used with solid-state regulators, which can be small enough to be mounted on the alternator housing.

B-circuit

The B-circuit alternator, figure 8-37, also can be called an internally grounded field alternator. One brush is grounded within the alternator housing. The other brush is insulated from the housing and connected through the insulated voltage regulator to the alternator output circuit. The rotor field winding is between the regulator and ground. This type of circuit is most often used with electromagnetic voltage regulators, which are mounted away from the alternator housing.

Isolated-field circuit

The **isolated-field circuit**, figure 8-38, is a variation of the A-circuit. The rotor winding is again grounded through the voltage regulator. Current for the rotor winding is drawn from the alternator output circuit outside the alternator housing and comes through a third terminal on the housing. Current flow through this third terminal can be controlled by an external switch or a field relay. This type of circuit is used mainly by Chrysler Corporation.

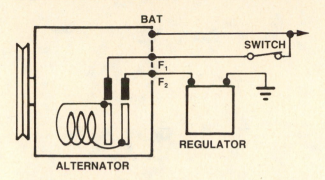

Figure 8-38. An isolated-field circuit.

SPECIFIC ALTERNATORS

Manufacturers use various alternator designs for specific applications. We have seen that such factors as maximum current output and field circuit types affect alternator construction. The following paragraphs describe some commonly used automotive alternators.

Delco-Remy

Delco-Remy, a division of General Motors Corporation, supplies most of the electrical devices used on GM vehicles, as well as those of some other carmakers. The trademark name for Delco-Remy's alternators is Delcotron® generators. The alternator model number and current output can be found on a plate attached to, or stamped into, the housing.

10-DN series

Internally mounted regulators were not commonly used with Delcotrons until the early 1970s. Before that time, 10-DN series alternators were widely used. Six individual diodes are mounted in the rear housing, figure 8-39, with a capacitor for protection. A 14-pole rotor and Y-type stator provide current output. Field current is drawn from rectified output and travels through a B-circuit.

The terminals on a 10-DN are labeled BAT, GRD, R, and F. If the alternator is used with an electromagnetic regulator:

- BAT connects alternator output to the insulated terminal of the battery
- GRD, if used, is an additional ground path
- R, if used, is connected to a separate field relay controlling the indicator lamp
- F connects the rotor winding to the voltage regulator.

Some 10-DN alternators are used with a remotely mounted solid-state regulator. The voltage control level of this unit is usually ad-

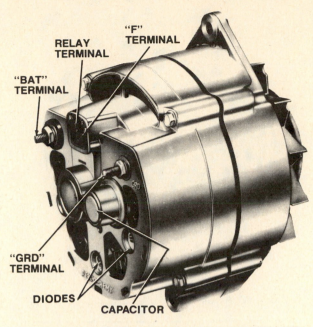

Figure 8-39. The Delcotron 10-DN. (Delco-Remy)

justable. The terminal connections are the same for electromagnetic and solid-state regulators.

10-, 12-, 15-, and 27-SI series

The most common late-model Delcotron alternators are part of the SI series, figure 8-40. A 14-pole rotor is used in most models. The 10- and 12-SI models have Y-type stators, and the 15- and 27-SI models have delta-type stators.

Two general SI designs have been used, with major differences appearing in the rear housing diode installation, regulator appearance, field circuitry, and ground path.

Early SI alternators have six separate diodes mounted in the rear housing, figure 8-41. The regulator has individual leads secured with screws. Field current is drawn from rectified alternator output. These early types can be identified by the separate ground terminal on the rear housing.

Most SI models have a rectifier bridge that contains all six rectifying diodes, figure 8-42. The regulator is a fully enclosed unit attached by screws to the housing. Field current is drawn from unrectified alternator output and rectified by an additional diode trio.

Isolated Field Circuit: A variation of the A-circuit. Field current is drawn from the alternator output outside of the alternator and sent to an insulated brush. The other brush is grounded through the voltage regulator.

Figure 8-40. A 10-SI series alternator. (Delco-Remy)

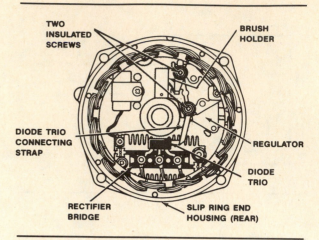

Figure 8-42. The rear end housing of the later model 10-SI Delcotron. (Delco-Remy)

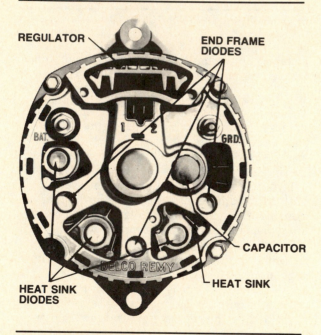

Figure 8-41. The rear housing of the early 10-SI Delcotron. (Delco-Remy)

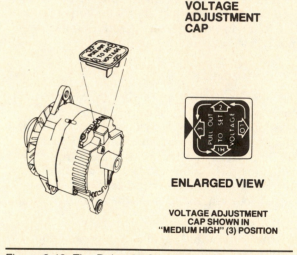

Figure 8-43. The Delco 27-SI alternator has an adjustable voltage regulator. (Delco-Remy)

All SI models have A-circuits. Their terminals are labeled BAT, No. 1, and No. 2:

- The BAT terminal connects alternator output to the insulated terminal of the battery
- The No. 1 terminal conducts battery current to the rotor winding for the excitation circuit and is connected to the indicator lamp

- The No. 2 terminal receives battery voltage so that the voltage regulator can react to system operating conditions.

All SI models have a capacitor installed in the rear housing to protect the diodes from sudden voltage surges and to filter out voltage ripples that could produce EMI.

The 27-SI is intended principally for commercial vehicles. It has an adjustable voltage regulator, figure 8-43. The voltage is adjusted by removing the adjustment cap, rotating it until the desired setting (low, medium, medium-high, or high) is opposite the arrow on the alternator housing, and reinstalling it in the new position. Repair or replace a 27-SI alternator only if it fails to pass an output test after the regulator has been adjusted.

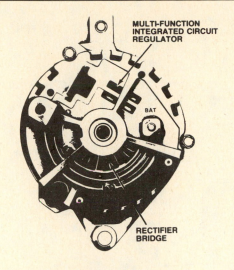

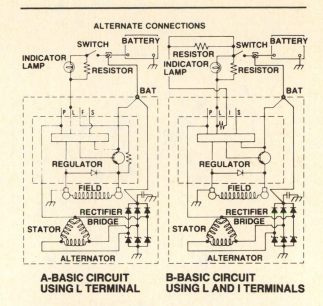

Figure 8-45. Two basic circuits for the Delco-Remy CS series alternators. (Delco-Remy)

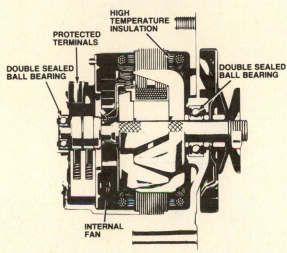

Figure 8-44. Typical Delco-Remy CS series alternator construction. (Delco-Remy)

CS-121, CS-130, and CS-144 series
The smaller Delco-Remy CS series alternators introduced on some 1986 GM cars, figure 8-44, maintain current output similar to larger alternators. The number following the CS designation denotes the outer diameter of the stator lamination in millimeters. All models use a delta-type stator. Field current is taken directly from the stator, eliminating the diode trio. An integral cooling fan is used on the CS-121 and CS-130.

CS alternators have a conventional BAT output terminal and either a one- or two-wire connector for the regulator. Figure 8-45 shows the two basic circuits for CS alternators, but you must check carmakers' diagrams for complete charging system circuits. The use of the P, F, and S terminals shown in figure 8-45 is optional:

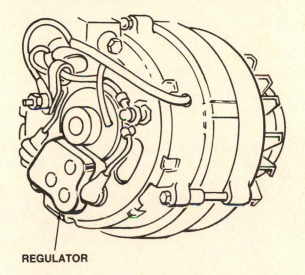

Figure 8-46. The Motorcraft 55-ampere alternator of 1969-1971 had a solid-state regulator mounted on the rear housing.

- The P terminal, connected to the stator, may be connected to a tachometer or other such device
- The F terminal connects internally to field positive and can be used as a fault indicator
- The S terminal can be externally connected to battery voltage to sense the voltage to be controlled
- The L terminal connects the regulator to the indicator lamp and battery.

The indicator lamp in a CS charging system works differently than in other Delco-Remy

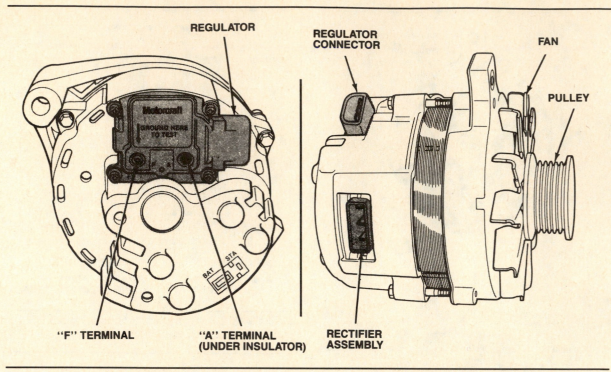

Figure 8-47. The 1985 and later Motorcraft IAR alternator also has a rear-mounted regulator.

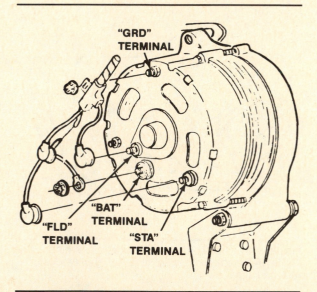

Figure 8-48. A Motorcraft rear-terminal alternator. (Ford)

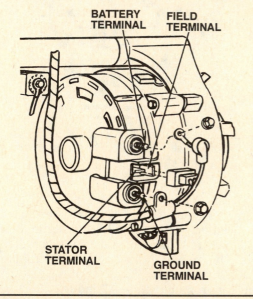

Figure 8-49. The Motorcraft side-terminal alternator. (Ford)

systems. Any defect causes it to light at full brilliance. The lamp will also light if charging voltage is either too low or too high.

If the regulator has an I terminal, its wire supplies field current (in addition to that applied internally), either directly from the switch or through a resistor. The parallel connections at the top of figure 8-45 are alternate circuits.

Motorcraft

Motorcraft, a division of Ford Motor Company, makes most of the alternators used on domestic Ford vehicles. The alternators used the name Autolite until the early 1970s. Model and current rating identifications for later models are stamped on the front housing with a color code. Motorcraft alternators prior to 1985 are

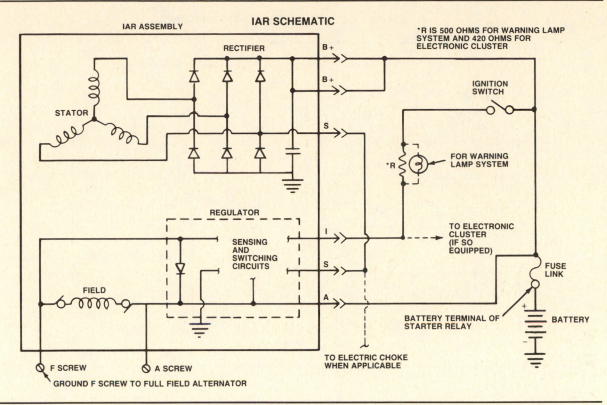

Figure 8-50. A circuit diagram of the Motorcraft IAR alternator.

used with either an electromechanical voltage regulator or a remotely mounted solid-state regulator. One exception to this is the 55-ampere model of 1969-1971, which has a solid-state regulator mounted on the rear housing, figure 8-46. This model has an A-circuit; all others are B-circuit. The Motorcraft IAR (integral alternator/regulator) model was introduced on some front-wheel-drive Ford Motor Company cars in 1985. This alternator also has a solid-state regulator mounted on its rear housing, figure 8-47. Some Motorcraft charging systems continue to use an external solid-state regulator with either a rear-terminal, figure 8-48, or side-terminal alternator, figure 8-49. These charging systems are called external voltage regulator (EVR) systems to differentiate them from IAR systems.

Integral alternator/regulator (IAR) models

The Motorcraft IAR alternators, figure 8-47, are rated at 40 to 80 amperes. The sealed rectifier assembly is attached to the slipring-end housing. On early models, the connecting terminals (BAT and STA) protruded from the side of the alternator in a plastic housing. Current models use a single pin stator (STA) connector and separate output stud (BAT). The brushes are attached to, and removed with, the regulator. A Y-type stator is used with a 12-pole rotor.

Some applications are equipped with an internal cooling fan.

Turning the ignition on sends voltage to the regulator I terminal through a resistor in the I circuit. System voltage is sensed and field current is drawn through the regulator A terminal until the ignition is turned off, which shuts off the control circuit. Figure 8-50 shows the basic IAR alternator circuit.

If the vehicle is equipped with a heated windshield, output is switched from the battery to the windshield by an output control relay, figure 8-51. This allows output voltage to increase above the normal regulated voltage and vary with engine speed. The regulator I circuit limits the voltage increase to 70 volts, which is controlled by the heated windshield module during the approximately four-minute cycle of heated windshield operation. When the cycle times out, the charging system returns to normal operation.

Chrysler

Chrysler Corporation manufactured all of the alternators for its domestic cars until the late 1980s, when it phased in Bosch and Nippondenso alternators for use on all vehicles.

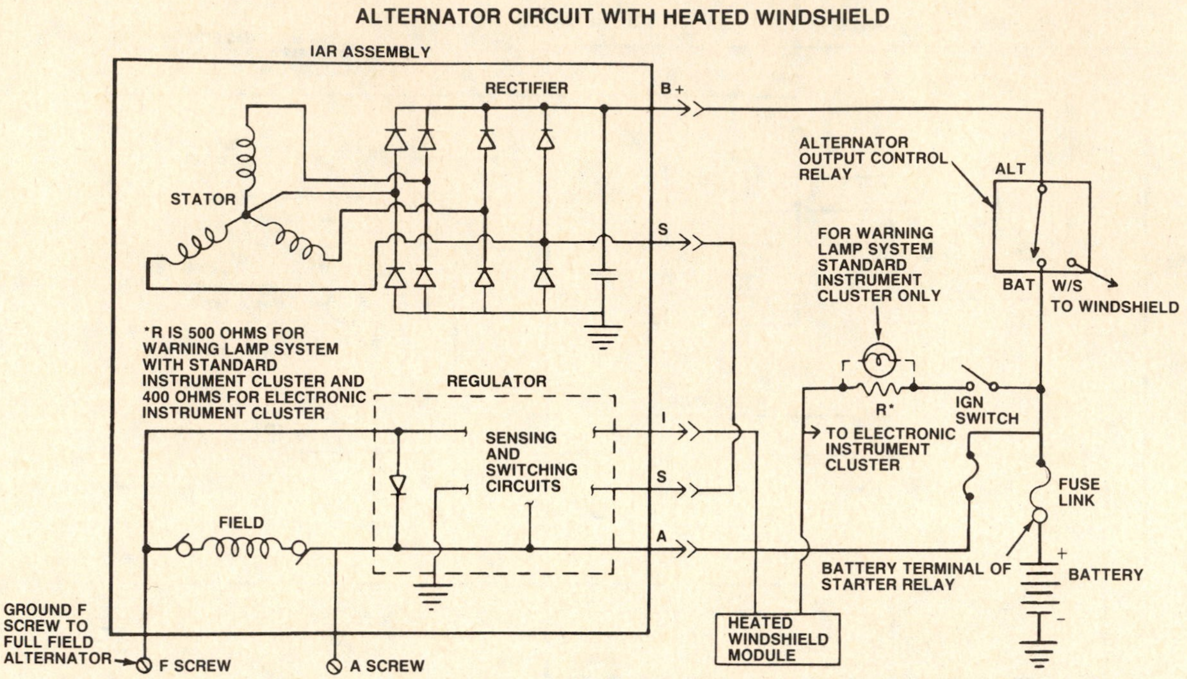

ALTERNATOR CIRCUIT WITH HEATED WINDSHIELD

Figure 8-51. A circuit diagram of the Motorcraft IAR alternator used with heated windshields. (Ford)

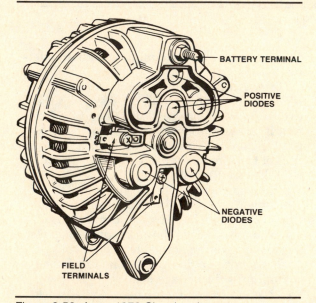

Figure 8-52. A pre-1972 Chrysler alternator.

Chrysler alternators

Prior to 1972, Chrysler alternators had six individual diodes pressed into a heat sink in the rear housing, figure 8-52. The alternator was used with an electromechanical regulator and a B-circuit until 1968. In some 1968 and all 1969 models, the alternator had an A-circuit and used the remotely mounted solid-state regulator. The isolated-field circuit was introduced in

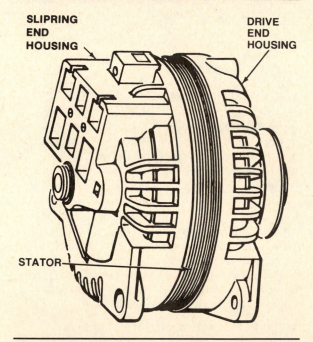

Figure 8-53. Chrysler's standard corporate alternator from 1972 to 1984.

1970 and is used in the current computer-controlled regulator models.

Two alternator designs were used from 1972 through 1984. The standard-duty alternator, rated from 50 to 65 amperes, can be identified by an internal cooling fan and the stator core

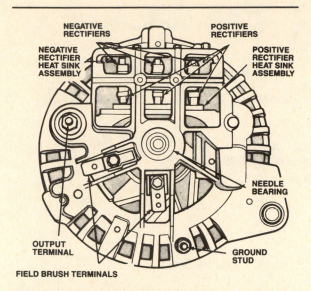

Figure 8-54. The terminals on a Chrysler standard-duty alternator. (Chrysler)

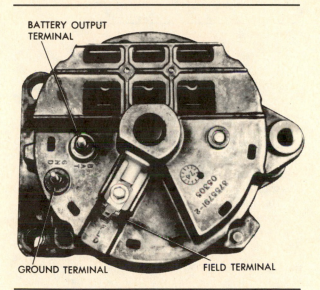

Figure 8-55. The terminals on a Chrysler 100-ampere alternator. (Chrysler)

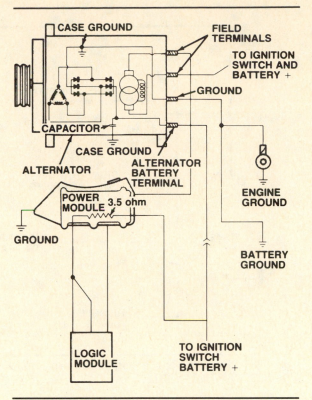

Figure 8-56. Typical Chrysler computer voltage regulation with Chrysler 40/90-ampere alternator. Circuit connections vary on different models.

extension between the housings, figure 8-53. The heavy-duty 100-ampere alternator has an external fan and a totally enclosed stator core. Identification also is stamped on a color-coded tag on the housing.

All models have a 12-pole rotor and use a remotely mounted solid-state regulator. The brushes can be replaced from outside the housing. Individual diodes are mounted in positive and negative heat sink assemblies, and are protected by a capacitor. The terminals on the standard-duty alternator are labeled BAT, GRD, and FLD, figure 8-54:

- The BAT terminal connects alternator output to the insulated terminal of the battery
- The GRD terminal is the ground connection
- Two FLD terminals connect to the insulated brushes. On the 100-ampere model, the FLD terminal has two separate prongs that fit into a single connector, figure 8-55. The additional GRD terminal is a ground path.

Chrysler's standard-duty alternators have a Y-type stator connected to six diodes. Although both brush holders are insulated from the housing, one is indirectly grounded through the negative diode plate, making it a B-circuit.

The 100-ampere alternator has a delta-type stator. Each of the conductors is attached to two positive and two negative diodes. These 12 diodes create additional parallel circuit branches for high-current output.

Chrysler eliminated the use of a separate voltage regulator on most 1985 and later fuel injected and turbocharged engines by incorporating the regulator function in the engine control computer, figure 8-56.

The computer-controlled charging system was introduced with the standard Chrysler alternator on GLH and Shelby turbo models. All

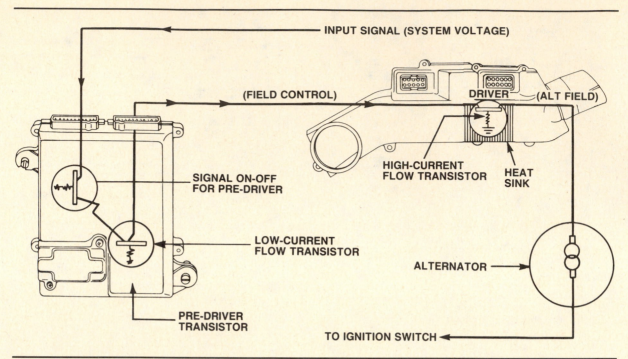

Figure 8-57. The Chrysler charging system with computer-controlled voltage regulation uses integrated circuitry to provide internal field control. (Chrysler)

other four-cylinder engines used a new Chrysler 40/90-ampere alternator or a modified Bosch 40/90-ampere or 40/100-ampere model.

The Chrysler-built alternator uses a delta-type stator. The regulator circuit is basically the isolated-field type shown in figure 8-38, but field current is controlled by integrated circuitry in the logic and power modules, figure 8-57, or the logic and power circuits of the single-module engine control computer (SMEC) or single-board engine control computer (SBEC). In addition to sensing system voltage, the logic module or circuit senses battery temperature as indicated by system resistance. The computer then switches field current on and off in a duty cycle that regulates charging voltage as in any other system.

The Chrysler computer-controlled charging system has two important features:

- It varies charging voltage relative to ambient temperature and/or the system voltage requirements
- The engine computer can detect charging system problems and record fault codes in system memory. Some codes will light the POWER LOSS, POWER LIMITED, or MALFUNCTION INDICATOR lamp on the instrument panel; others will not.

Turning the ignition on causes the logic circuit to check battery temperature to determine the control voltage. A predriver transistor in the logic module or logic circuit signals a driver translator in the power module or power circuit to turn on the alternator field current, figure 8-58. The logic module or logic circuit constantly monitors system voltage and battery temperature to tell the driver in the power module or power circuit when field current adjustment is necessary to keep output voltage within the specified 13.6 to 14.8 volt range.

Bosch alternators

Modified Bosch 40/90-ampere and 40/100-ampere alternators were introduced in 1985 for use with the Chrysler computer-controlled charging system. These Bosch dual-output alternators have a Y-type stator and were modified by removing their internal voltage regulators and changing the external leads. They are fully interchangeable with Chrysler dual-output alternators of the same rating.

Use of dual-output alternators was phased out in favor of a single-output Bosch alternator when Chrysler ceased manufacture of its own alternators in 1989. Current Chrysler charging systems with a Bosch alternator (84 or 86 amperes) are essentially the same design as those used with the dual-output alternators, figure 8-59, but an engine controller replaces the separate logic and power modules.

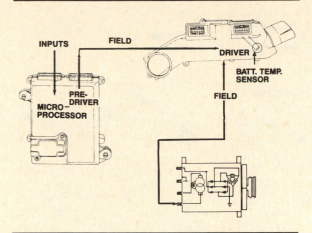

Figure 8-58. Chrysler computer regulated charging system internal field control. (Chrysler)

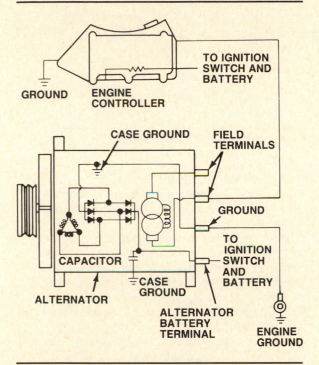

Figure 8-59. Current Chrysler vehicles equipped with a SBEC or SMEC use the same charging system wiring as earlier models equipped with the logic and power modules. (Chrysler)

Nippondenso alternators

Some current Chrysler vehicles also use Nippondenso alternators with an output range of 68 to 102 amperes. These are virtual clones of the Bosch design, even to the external wiring connections, figure 8-60. Charging system circuitry is the same, as are test procedures.

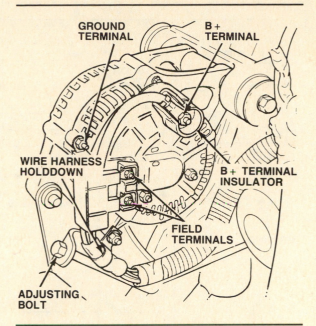

Figure 8-60. Nippondenso and Bosch alternators used on Chrysler vehicles have identical wiring connections. (Chrysler)

Import Vehicle Charging Systems

The charging systems of most import cars use the same design, construction, and operating principles that we have seen in the domestic systems we have studied.

Many European vehicles have Bosch alternators featuring Y-type stators. Bosch models with a remote regulator use six rectifiers and have a threaded battery terminal and two-way spade connector on the rear housing. Those with an integral regulator contain 12 rectifiers and have a threaded battery stud marked B + and a smaller threaded stud marked D + . This smaller stud is used for voltage from the ignition switch. Models with internal regulators also have a diode trio to supply field current initially and a blocking diode to prevent current from flowing back to the ignition system when the ignition is turned off.

Several manufacturers such as Hitachi, Nippondenso and Mitsubishi provide alternators for Japanese carmakers. While all function on the same principles we have just studied, the design and construction of some units are unique. For example, figure 8-61 shows a Mitsubishi alternator that uses an integral regulator with double Y-stator and 12 diodes in a pair of rectifier assemblies to deliver high current with high voltage at low speeds. A diode trio internally supplies the field, and a 50-ohm resistor in the regulator performs the same function as the Bosch blocking diode.

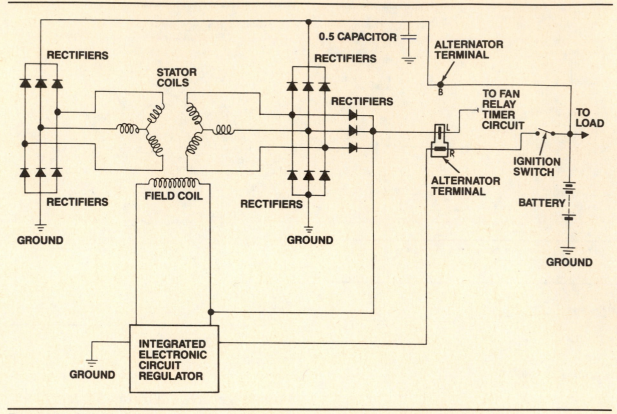

Figure 8-61. A circuit diagram of the Mitsubishi charging system using the double Y-stator alternator.

SUMMARY

The sine wave voltage induced across one alternator conductor causes single-phase current flow. By connecting the alternator conductor diodes, the a.c. flow can be fully rectified to d.c. In an actual automotive alternator, there are more than two magnetic poles and one conductor. Common alternators have from eight to 14 poles on a rotor, and three conductors wound to create a stator. The rotor and stator are held in a two-piece housing. Two brushes attached to the housings, but often insulated from it, ride on sliprings to carry current to the rotor winding. The diodes are installed in the same end housing as the brushes. Three positive diodes are insulated from the housing; three negative diodes are grounded to the housing.

Stators with three conductors produce three-phase current. The three conductors can be connected to make a Y-type or a delta-type stator. The rectification process is the same for both types, although the current paths through the stators differ. Rectified output from a multiple-pole alternator is a rippling d.c. voltage.

Because the rotor does not retain enough magnetism to begin induction, an excitation circuit must carry battery current to the rotor winding. The rotor winding can be part of an externally grounded field, or A-circuit; an internally grounded field, or B-circuit; or an isolated-field circuit.

Common alternators used by domestic manufacturers include the Delco-Remy DN, SI, and CS series used by GM; the Motorcraft IAR, rear-terminal, and side-terminal models used by Ford; and the Chrysler-built, Bosch, and Nippondenso models used by Chrysler. Most European imports use Bosch alternators, while Asian imports use alternators made by several manufacturers, including Hitachi, Nippondenso and Mitsubishi.

Review Questions

Choose the single most correct answer.
Compare your answers with the correct answers on page 431.

1. Alternators induce voltage by rotating:
   a. A magnetic field inside a fixed conductor
   b. A conductor inside a magnetic field
   c. Either a or b
   d. Neither a nor b

2. In an alternator, induced voltage is at its maximum value when the angle between the magnetic lines and the looped conductor is:
   a. 0°
   b. 45°
   c. 90°
   d. 180°

3. The sine wave voltage induced across one conductor by one rotor revolution is called:
   a. Single-phase current
   b. Open-circuit voltage
   c. Diode rectification
   d. Single-phase voltage

4. Alternating current in an alternator is rectified by:
   a. Brushes
   b. Diodes
   c. Slip rings
   d. Transistors

5. An alternator with only one conductor and one diode would show which of the following current output patterns?
   a. Three-phase current
   b. Open-circuit voltage
   c. Half-wave rectification
   d. Full-wave rectification

6. An alternator consists of:
   a. A stator, a rotor, slip rings, brushes, and diodes
   b. A stator, an armature, slip rings, brushes, and diodes
   c. A stator, a rotor, a commutator, brushes, and diodes
   d. A stator, a rotor, a field relay, brushes, and diodes

7. A typical automotive alternator has _____ poles.
   a. 2 to 4
   b. 6 to 8
   c. 16 to 20
   d. 8 to 14

8. The three alternator conductors are wound onto a cylindrical, laminated metal-piece called:
   a. A rotor core
   b. A stator core
   c. An armature core
   d. Any of the above

9. Automotive alternators that have three conductors generally use _____ diodes to rectify the output current.
   a. Two
   b. Three
   c. Four
   d. Six

10. Which of the following is not true of the positive diodes in an alternator?
    a. Connected to the insulated terminal of the battery
    b. Conduct only the current flowing from ground into the conductor
    c. Mounted in a heat sink
    d. The bias of the diodes prevents the battery from discharging

11. A group of three or more like diodes may be called:
    a. Diode wing
    b. Diode triplet
    c. Diode dish
    d. Diode bridge

12. Y-type stators are used in alternators that require:
    a. Low voltage output at high alternator speed
    b. High voltage output at low alternator speed
    c. Low voltage at low alternator speed
    d. High voltage at high alternator speed

13. Which of the following is true of a delta-type stator?
    a. There is no neutral junction
    b. There is no ground connection
    c. The windings always form a series circuit
    d. The circuit diagram looks like a parallelogram

14. Delta-type stators are used:
    a. When high-voltage output is needed
    b. When low-voltage output is needed
    c. When high-current output is needed
    d. When low-current output is needed

15. Which of the following is a commonly used type of field circuit in automotive alternators?
    a. X-circuit
    b. Y-circuit
    c. Connected-field circuit
    d. A-circuit

Chapter

9

Regulators and Indicators

Alternator regulators limit voltage output by controlling field current flow. The regulator's location in the field circuit determines whether the alternator is an A-circuit, a B-circuit, or an isolated-field circuit, as we learned in Chapter Eight.

SELF-REGULATION OF CURRENT

The maximum current output of an alternator is limited by the design of the alternator. We learned in Chapter Two that as induced voltage causes current flow in a conductor, a counter-voltage also is induced in the same conductor. The countervoltage is caused by the expanding magnetic field of the original induced current. The countervoltage will tend to oppose any change in the original current flow.

When induced voltage causes current flow in the conductors of the stator, a countervoltage also appears. The countervoltage opposes any increased current flow in the stator windings. The more current the alternator puts out, the greater this countervoltage becomes. At a certain point, the countervoltage is great enough to totally stop any further increase in the alternator's current output. At this point, the alternator has reached its maximum current output. Therefore, because the two voltages will continue to increase as alternator speed increases, a method of regulating alternator voltage is required.

VOLTAGE REGULATION

Alternator output voltage is directly related to field strength and rotor speed. An increase in either factor will increase voltage output. Similarly, a decrease in either factor will decrease voltage output. Rotor speed is controlled by engine speed and cannot be changed simply to control the alternator. Field strength can be changed by controlling the field current in the rotor windings. This is how both alternator and generator voltage regulators work. Figure 9-1 shows how the field current (dashed line) is lowered to keep alternator output (solid line) at a constant maximum, even when the rotor speed increases.

At low rotor speeds, the field current is allowed to flow at full strength for relatively long periods of time, and is reduced only for short periods, figure 9-2A. This causes a high average field current. At high rotor speeds, the field current is reduced for long periods of time and flows at full strength only for short periods, figure 9-2B. This causes a low average field current.

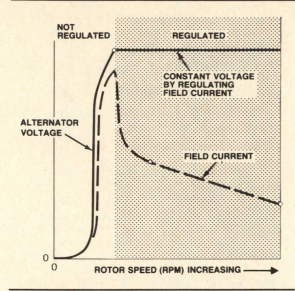

Figure 9-1. Field current is decreased as rotor speed increases to keep alternator output voltage at a constant level.

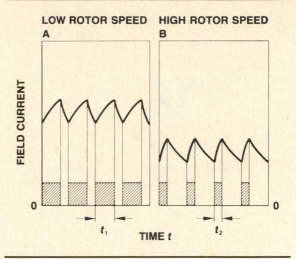

Figure 9-2. The field current flows for longer periods of time at low speeds (t1) than at high speeds (t2). (Bosch)

The field circuit can be controlled by an electromagnetic regulator. In the last decade, however, semiconductor technology has made solid-state voltage regulators possible. Because they are smaller and have no moving parts, solid-state regulators have replaced the older electromagnetic type in a.c. charging systems.

Some solid-state regulators are mounted on the inside or outside of the alternator housing, as we saw in Chapter Eight. This eliminates exposed wiring and connections that could be damaged. Remotely mounted voltage regulators often use a multiple-plug connector, figure 9-3, to ensure that all connections are properly made. In the mid-1980s, many carmakers moved the regulator function into the engine control computer of fully integrated electronic engine control systems.

ELECTROMAGNETIC REGULATORS

Electromagnetic voltage regulators (sometimes called electromechanical regulators) operate the same whether they are used with d.c. generators or a.c. generators (alternators). The electromagnetic coil of the voltage regulator is connected from the ignition switch to ground. This forms a parallel branch that receives system voltage, either from the alternator output circuit or from the battery. The magnetic field of the coil acts upon an armature to open and close contact points that control current to the field.

Double-Contact Voltage Regulator

At high rotor speeds, the alternator may be able to force too much field current through a single-contact regulator, exceeding the desired output. This is called **voltage creep (voltage drift)**. Single-contact regulators are used only with low-current-output alternators. Almost all electromagnetic voltage regulators used with automotive alternators are double-contact units, figure 9-4. When the first set of contacts opens at lower rotor speeds, a resistor is inserted in series with the field circuit. These contacts are called the **series contacts**. The value of the regulating resistor is kept very low to permit high field currents when needed. At higher rotor speeds, the armature is further attracted by the coil and a second set of contacts is closed. This grounds the field circuit, stopping the field current. These contacts are called the **shorting contacts**, because they short-circuit the field to

Voltage Creep (Voltage Drift): Excessive voltage at high speeds due to excessive field current flow through a single-contact regulator.

Series Contacts: The normally closed set of contacts in a double-contact regulator. When they open, field current must flow through a resistor.

Shorting Contacts: The normally open set of contacts in a double-contact regulator. When closed, they short-circuit the field to ground.

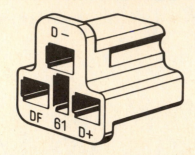

Figure 9-3. Most regulators use a multiple-plug connector to ensure that connections are properly made. (Bosch)

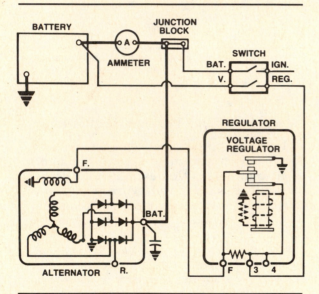

Figure 9-4. The circuit diagram of a double-contact regulator. (Delco-Remy)

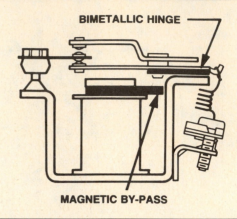

Figure 9-5. Temperature compensating devices in an electromagnetic regulator. (Delco-Remy)

Figure 9-5 shows the use of the bimetallic hinge and a **magnetic shunt (magnetic by-pass)**. The magnetic field required to operate these devices and to open the series contacts varies with temperature. The colder it is, the greater the voltage output. Conversely, as the temperature increases, the voltage output is reduced. Installing a ballast resistor in series with the regulator coil provides a constant resistance value regardless of temperature.

Field Relay Uses

Many a.c. charging systems include a **field relay** along with the voltage regulator, figure 9-6. The field relay is used to energize the field circuit when the ignition switch is turned on. It also controls the charging system indicator lamp, if one is used. The field relay may be housed with the voltage regulator or in a separate unit.

Using a field relay reduces the amount of wiring needed in the field circuit, as well as the voltage drop across the field circuit. The field current can be more accurately controlled at different temperatures and current flow rates.

When the ignition switch is closed in a system using an indicator lamp, figure 9-6A, current flows from the battery, through the indicator lamp, through the voltage regulator, and through the alternator field circuit to ground.

This current flow lights the indicator lamp and partly energizes the alternator field. As the engine begins to run and the alternator begins to supply voltage, the voltage is impressed on the field relay coil. This *closes* the relay contacts and completes a circuit that provides a direct path for system voltage to the regulator. It also applies system voltage to the opposite terminal of the indicator lamp. With

ground. The double-contact design offers consistent regulation over a broad range of alternator speeds.

Temperature compensation
The temperature of the regulator coil can increase both from the heat of current flow and from outside temperature. As the coil's temperature increases, so does its resistance. Higher resistance means more voltage is needed to create a strong enough magnetic field at higher temperatures, or just the opposite of what is desired.

A combination of three types of temperature compensation often is used to take advantage of the best characteristics of each:

- A bimetallic hinge
- A magnetic shunt
- A ballast resistor.

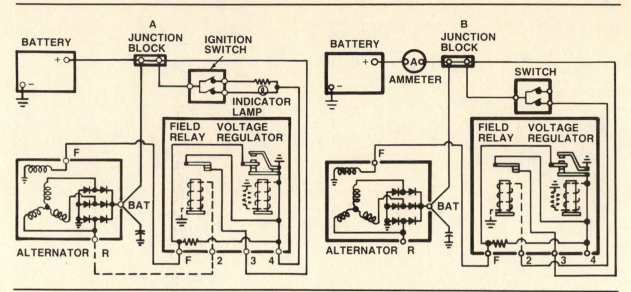

Figure 9-6. Field relays can control an indicator lamp and field circuit, or the battery to field circuit only.

Figure 9-7. An example of the latest integrated circuit regulator design, Ford's IAR regulator and brush holder are combined.

no voltage drop across the lamp, no current flows through the lamp, and it goes out. The field relay remains closed as long as the alternator is operating.

In a charging system with an ammeter and a field relay, figure 9-6B, current flows from the battery, through the ammeter and the ignition switch, to the field relay coil. The energized coil *closes* the relay contacts. Battery current then flows through the relay, through the voltage regulator, and to the alternator field. The relay remains closed as long as the ignition switch is closed.

SOLID-STATE REGULATORS

Solid-state regulators have completely replaced the older electromagnetic design on late-model cars. They are compact, have no moving parts, and are not seriously affected by temperature changes. The early solid-state designs combined transistors with the electromagnetic field relay. The latest and most compact is the integrated-circuit (IC) regulator, figure 9-7. This combines all control circuitry and components on a single silicon chip. Attaching terminals are added, and the chip is sealed in a small plastic module that mounts inside, or on the back of, the alternator. Because of their construction, however, all solid-state regulators are nonserviceable and must be replaced if defective. No adjustments are possible.

We have already looked at most of the components of a solid-state regulator. They are:

- Diodes
- Transistors
- Zener diodes
- Thermistors
- Capacitors.

Magnetic Shunt (Magnetic Bypass): A piece of metal on a voltage regulator coil that controls voltage output at varying temperatures by affecting the coil's magnetic field.

Field Relay: A magnetic switch used to open and close the alternator field circuit or, in a charging circuit with a warning lamp, to control the lamp circuit.

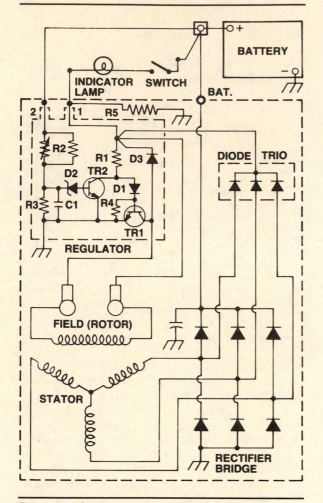

Figure 9-8. Circuit diagram of a typical solid-state voltage regulator. (Delco-Remy)

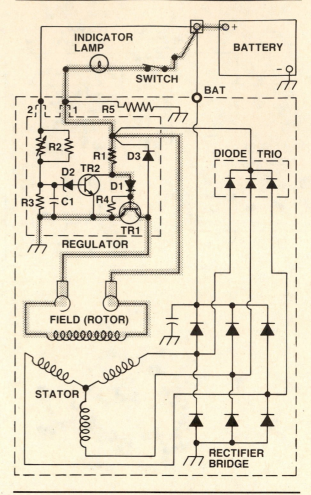

Figure 9-9. Field current in a typical solid-state regulator during starting. (Delco-Remy)

Diodes are one-way electrical check valves. Transistors act as relays. A zener diode is specially doped to act as a one-way electrical check valve until a specific reverse voltage level is reached. At that point, the zener diode reverse current will be conducted.

The electrical resistance of a **thermistor (thermal resistor)**, decreases as its temperature increases. Such resistors used in automotive applications are called negative temperature coefficient (NTC) resistors. As we learned in Chapter Four, this is because their resistance decreases as temperature increases. The thermistor in a solid-state regulator reacts to temperature to ensure proper battery charging voltage.

A capacitor is used by some manufacturers to smooth out any abrupt voltage surges and protect the regulator from damage. Diodes can also be used as circuit protection.

General circuit operation

Figure 9-8 is a simplified circuit diagram of a solid-state regulator. This A-circuit regulator is contained within the alternator housing. The No. 2 terminal on the alternator is always connected to the battery, but battery discharge is limited by the high resistance of R2 and R3. The circuit allows the regulator to sense battery voltage.

When the ignition switch is closed, figure 9-9, current flows from the battery to ground through the base of TR1. This makes TR1 conduct current through its emitter-collector circuit from the battery to the low-resistance rotor winding. The alternator field is energized, and the warning lamp is turned on.

When the alternator begins to produce current, figure 9-10, field current is drawn from unrectified alternator output and rectified by the diode trio. No current flows through the warning lamp.

When the alternator has charged the battery to a maximum safe voltage level, figure 9-11,

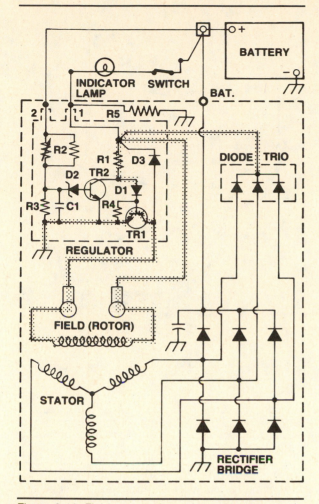

Figure 9-10. Field current drawn from alternator output. (Delco-Remy)

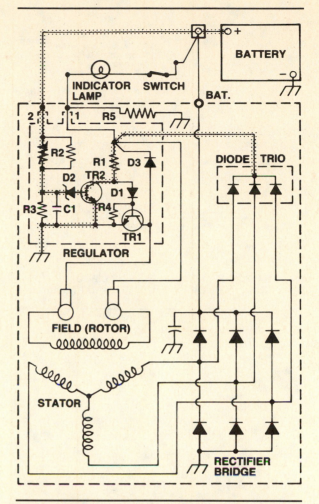

Figure 9-11. When alternator output voltage reaches a maximum safe level, no current is allowed in the rotor winding. (Delco-Remy)

the battery voltage between R2 and R3 causes zener diode D2 to conduct current. TR2 is turned on and field current flows directly to ground. TR1 is turned off, so no current reaches the rotor winding.

With TR1 off, the field current decreases and system voltage drops. D2 then blocks current flow in the base of TR2, and TR1 turns back on. The field current and system voltage increase. This cycle repeats many times per second to limit the alternator voltage to a predetermined value.

The other components within the regulator perform various functions. Capacitor C1 provides smooth voltage across R3, and R4 prevents excessive current through TR1 at high temperatures. To prevent circuit damage, D3 bypasses high voltages induced in the field windings when TR1 turns off. Resistor R2 is a thermistor that causes the regulated voltage to vary with temperature.

Specific Solid-State Regulator Designs

Delco-Remy
The Delco-Remy solid-state automotive regulator was used in figures 9-8 through 9-11 to explain the basic operation of these units. This is the integral regulator unit of the 10-, 12,- and 15-SI series alternators. The No.1 and No.2 terminals on the alternator housing connect directly to the regulator. The No.1 terminal conducts field current from the battery or the alternator, and controls the indicator lamp. The No.2 terminal receives battery voltage and allows the zener diode to react to it.

Thermistor (Thermal Resistor): A resistor specially constructed so that its resistance decreases as its temperature increases.

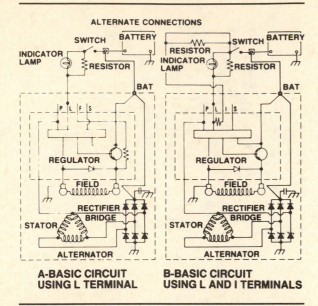

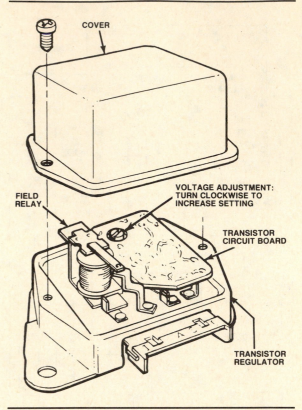

Figure 9-12. Two basic circuits for the Delco-Remy CS series alternators. (Delco-Remy)

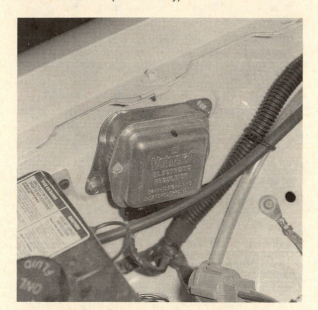

Figure 9-13. The Ford remote solid-state regulator.

Figure 9-14. The Ford solid-state voltage regulator with electromagnetic field relay. (Ford)

regulator for full-field testing. The regulator cannot be tested with an ohmmeter; a special tester is required.

Motorcraft

Motorcraft alternators use both remote-mounted, figure 9-13, and integral solid-state regulators, figure 9-14. The earlier remote-mounted unit had both a transistorized voltage regulator and an electromagnetic field relay in the same housing. Motorcraft regulator terminals are designated as follows:

- A + or A connects the battery to the field relay contacts
- S connects the alternator output to the field relay coil
- F connects the field coil to the regulator transistors
- I is used only with a warning lamp to connect the ignition switch to the field relay and regulator contacts.

In 1978, Ford began using a remote-mounted, fully solid-state regulator, figure 9-13, on its intermediate and large cars. The functions of the I, A +, S, and F terminals, figure 9-15, are identical to those of the transistorized regulator shown in figure 9-14 and figure 9-15B. On systems with an ammeter, the regulator is

Unlike other voltage regulators, the multi-function IC regulator used with Delco-Remy CS-series alternators, figure 9-12, switches the field current on and off at a fixed frequency of 400 Hz. The regulator varies the current duty cycle (percentage of on-time to total cycle time) to control the average field current and to regulate voltage. At high speeds, the on-time might be 10 percent with the off-time 90 percent. At low speeds with high electrical loads, this ratio could be reversed: 90 percent on-time and 10 percent off-time. Unlike the SI series, CS alternators have no test hole to ground the

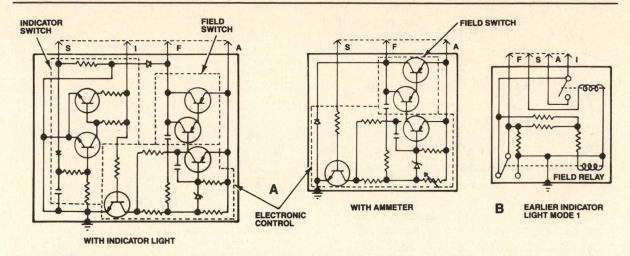

Figure 9-15. Electrical schematic of Ford's current solid-state regulator (A) and its earlier transistorized model (B). (Ford)

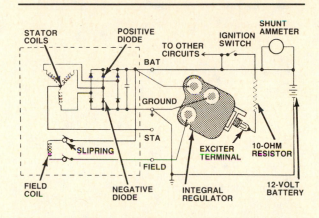

Figure 9-16. The early Ford integral solid-state regulator. (Ford)

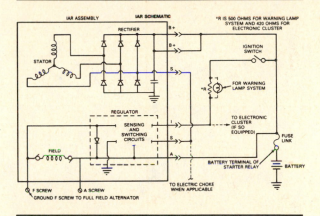

Figure 9-17. A circuit diagram of the Motorcraft IAR alternator. (Ford)

color-coded blue or gray, and the I terminal is not used. On warning lamp systems, the regulator is black, and all terminals can be used. The two models are not interchangeable, and cannot be substituted for the earlier solid-state unit with a relay or for an electromagnetic regulator. However, Ford does provide red or clear service replacement solid-state regulators, which can be used with both systems.

The early Motorcraft integral regulator, figure 9-16, used on the 1969-1971 55-ampere alternator, is mounted on the outside of the alternator rear housing. The ignition switch opens and closes the field circuit, and the regulator internal circuitry controls the field current level. The terminals are connected to the battery, to ground, to the ignition switch, and to the field. This regulator forms an A-circuit field.

The Motorcraft integral alternator/regulator (IAR) introduced in 1985 uses an IC regulator

which also is mounted on the outside of the rear housing. This regulator differs from others in that it contains a circuit to tell when the battery is being overcharged, figure 9-17. It turns on the charge indicator lamp if terminal A voltage is too high or too low, or if the terminal S voltage signal is abnormal.

Chrysler

The Chrysler solid-state regulator depends on a remotely mounted field relay to open and close the isolated-field or the A-circuit alternator field. The relay closes the circuit only when the ignition switch is in the RUN position. The voltage regulator, figure 9-18, contains two transistors that are turned on and off by a zener diode. The zener diode reacts to system voltage to start and stop field current. The field current flows through what Chrysler calls a field-suppression diode, which limits the flow to control alternator output. The regulator also

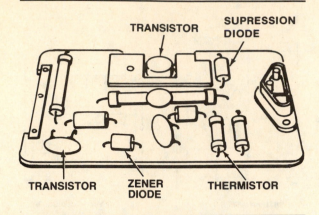

Figure 9-18. The Chrysler solid-state regulator.

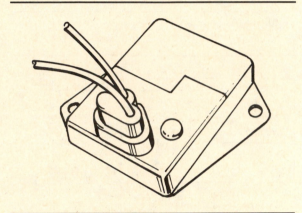

Figure 9-19. The Chrysler solid-state regulator is mounted on the firewall or shock tower.

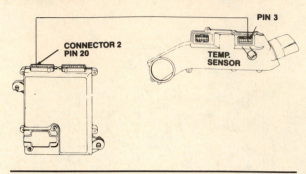

Figure 9-20. Battery temperature circuit of the Chrysler computer-regulated charging system. (Chrysler)

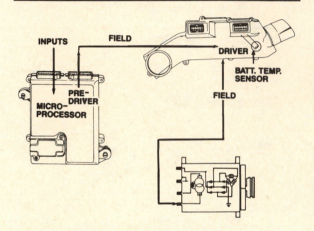

Figure 9-21. Chrysler computer-regulated charging system internal field control. (Chrysler)

contains a thermistor to control battery charging voltage at various temperatures. The regulator has two terminals, figure 9-19. One is connected to the ignition system, and the other is connected to the alternator field.

Computer-Controlled Regulation

Chrysler Corporation eliminated the separate regulator by moving its function to the engine control computer in 1985. When the ignition is turned on, the engine controller logic module or logic circuit checks battery temperature to determine the control voltage, figure 9-20. A predriver transistor in the logic module or logic circuit then signals the power module or power circuit driver transistor to turn the alternator field current on, figure 9-21. The logic module or logic circuit continually reads battery temperature and system voltage. At the same time, it instructs the power module or power circuit driver to adjust the field current as required to maintain output voltage between 13.6 and 14.8 volts, ±0.3 volt. Figure 9-22 shows the complete circuitry involved.

General Motors has taken a different approach to regulating CS charging system voltage electronically. Turning the ignition switch to the run position supplies voltage to alternator terminals L and F (or F/I). This voltage activates a solid-state digital regulator which uses pulse-width modulation (PWM) to supply rotor current and thus control output voltage. The rotor current is proportional to the PWM pulses from the digital regulator. With the ignition on, narrow width pulses are sent to the rotor, creating a weak magnetic field. As the engine starts, the regulator senses alternator rotation through a.c. voltage detected on an internal wire. Once the engine is running, the regulator switches the field current on and off at a fixed frequency of about 400 cycles per second (hertz). By changing the pulse width, or on-off time of each cycle, the regulator provides a correct average field current for proper system voltage control.

A lamp driver in the digital regulator controls the indicator warning lamp, turning on the bulb when it detects an under- or overvoltage condition, or a non-rotating alternator.

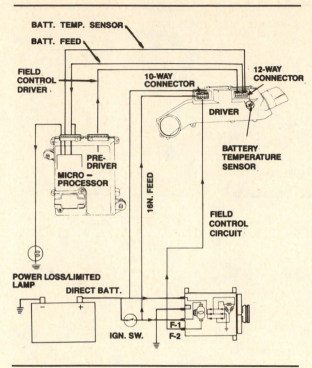

Figure 9-22. Chrysler computer-regulated charging system voltage control. (Chrysler)

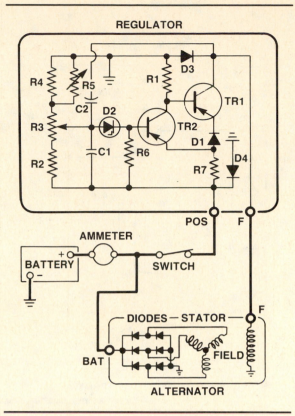

Figure 9-23. A typical ammeter installation. (Delco-Remy)

The powertrain control module (PCM) does not directly control charging system voltage, as in the Chrysler application. However, it does monitor battery and system voltage through an ignition switch circuit. If the PCM reads a voltage above 17 volts, or less than 9 volts for longer than 10 seconds, it sets a code 16 in memory and turns on the SERVICE ENGINE SOON or MALFUNCTION INDICATOR lamp.

Fault codes

On late-model Chrysler vehicles, the onboard diagnostic system capability of the engine control system detects charging system problems and can record up to five fault codes in the system memory. Some of the codes will light a POWER LOSS, POWER LIMITED, or MALFUNCTION INDICATOR lamp on the instrument panel; others will not. The Chrysler fault codes and their use are described in the test procedures in Chapter Four of the *Shop Manual*. Problems in the General Motors CS charging system cause the PCM to turn on the indicator lamp and set a single code in memory.

INDICATORS

A charging system failure cripples an automobile. Therefore, most manufacturers provide some way for the driver to monitor the system operation. The indicator may be an ammeter, a voltmeter, or an indicator (warning) lamp.

Ammeter

An instrument panel ammeter measures charging system current into and out of the battery and the rest of the electrical system, figure 9-23. When current is flowing from the alterna-

■ Motor-Generators

Motors and generators are similar in construction. In fact, it is possible to use the same unit as both a motor and as a generator by changing the external circuitry.

In the late 1910s, motor-generators were built by Delco, Simms-Huff, North East, and others. A Simms-Huff model used on the 1915-1917 Maxwell acted as a 12-volt starter motor and a six-volt generator. The Maxwell had two six-volt batteries. A special switch connected them in series during cranking and in parallel during running and charging. The motor-generator had six pole pieces, with shunt windings on all six and series windings on every other one. The electromagnetic voltage regulator that controlled the field current of the generator had two sets of contact points; one set was for voltage regulation, the other set acted as cutout points.

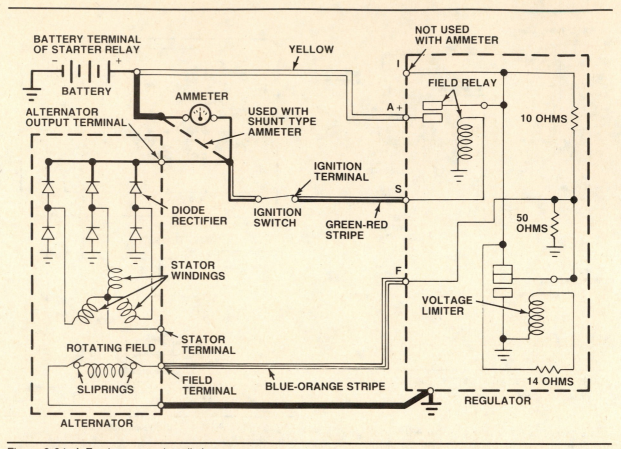

Figure 9-24. A Ford ammeter installation.

Figure 9-25. An automotive voltmeter for the instrument panel.

tor into the battery, the ammeter needle moves in the CHARGE direction. When the battery takes over the electrical system's load, current flows in the opposite direction and the needle moves into the DISCHARGE zone. The ammeter simply indicates which is doing the most work in the electrical system, the battery or the alternator. Some ammeters are graduated to indicate the approximate current in amperes, such as 5, 10, or 20. Others simply show an approximate rate of charge or discharge, such as high, medium, or low.

Some ammeters have a resistor in parallel so that the meter does not carry all of the current. These are called shunt ammeters.

While the ammeter tells the driver whether the charging system is functioning normally, it does not give a good picture of the battery condition. Even when the ammeter indicates a charge, the current output may not be high enough to fully charge the battery while supplying other electrical loads. Figure 9-24 shows a typical ammeter circuit, including a shunt resistor.

Voltmeter

The instrument panels of many late-model cars contain a voltmeter instead of an ammeter, figure 9-25. A voltmeter measures electrical pressure, and indicates regulated alternator voltage output or battery voltage, whichever is greater. System voltage is applied to the meter through the ignition switch contacts. Figure 9-26 shows a typical voltmeter circuit.

The voltmeter tells a driver more about the condition of the car's electrical system than an ammeter. When a voltmeter begins to indicate lower-than-normal voltage, it's time to check the battery and the voltage regulator.

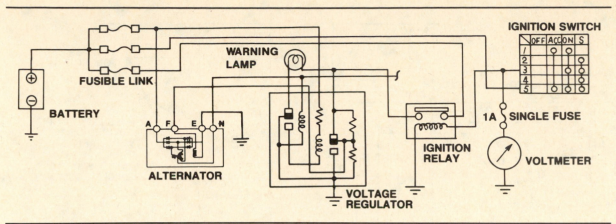

Figure 9-26. The circuit diagram of a typical voltmeter installation.

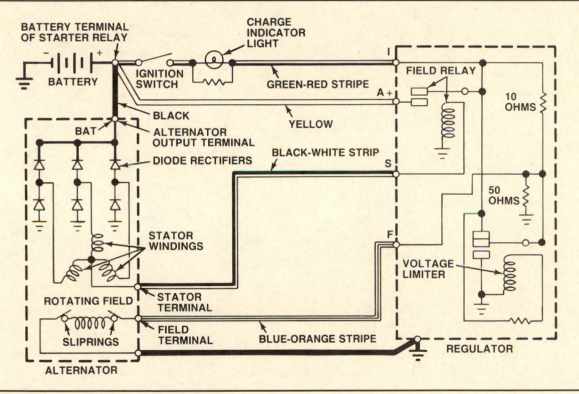

Figure 9-27. A Ford warning lamp installation.

Indicator Lamps

Most charging systems use an instrument panel indicator, or warning lamp, to show general charging system operation. Although the lamp usually does not warn the driver of an overcharged battery or high charging voltage, it will light to show an undercharged battery or low voltage from the alternator.

The lamp also lights when the battery supplies field current before the engine starts. The lamp is often connected in parallel with a resistor, so that field current will flow even if the bulb fails. The lamp is wired so that it lights when battery current flows through it to the alternator field. When the alternator begins to produce voltage, this voltage is applied to the side of the lamp away from the battery. When the two voltages are equal, there will be no voltage drop across the lamp and it will go out.

Figures 9-17, 9-27, and 9-28 show typical warning lamp circuit installations. In Figure 9-17, a 500-ohm resistor is used for warning lamp systems and a 420-ohm resistor for electronic display clusters. In Figure 9-28, a 40-ohm resistor (R5) has been installed near the

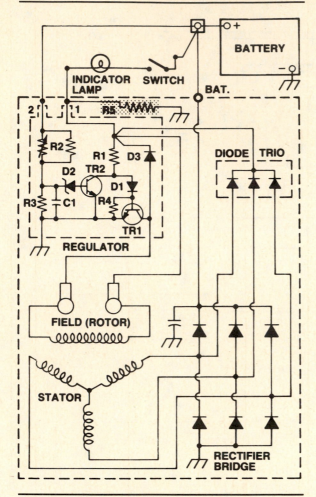

Figure 9-28. The Delco-Remy warning lamp installation. (Delco-Remy)

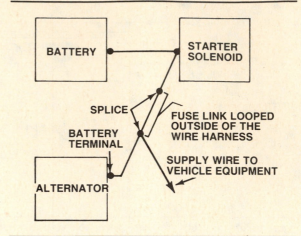

Figure 9-29. A wiring diagram showing fusible link locations. (Ford)

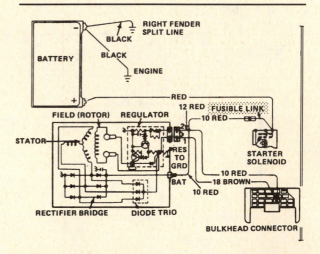

Figure 9-30. A circuit diagram showing fusible link location. (Buick)

integral regulator. In each case, the grounded path ensures that the warning lamp will light if an open occurs in the field circuitry.

Indicator lamps also can be controlled by the field relay, as we saw earlier.

The indicator lamp for a Delco-Remy CS system works differently from most others. It lights if charging voltage is *either* too low or *too high*. Any problem in the charging system causes the lamp to light at full brilliance.

CHARGING SYSTEM PROTECTION

If a charging system component fails or malfunctions, wiring and other units in the system could be damaged by excessive current or heat, voltage surges, and other uncontrolled factors. To protect the system from high current flow, fusible links are often wired in series at various places in the circuitry. Figures 9-29 and 9-30 show some typical fusible link locations.

SUMMARY

Because a countervoltage is induced in the stator windings, an alternator's current output is self-limiting. Voltage regulation is still needed. Electromagnetic voltage regulators can be used. They generally are double-contact units with temperature-compensating designs. Field relays are also sometimes used to decrease the voltage drop across the field circuit.

Early solid-state regulator designs combined the use of transistors with electromagnetic regulators. Voltage regulators now in use are completely solid-state designs.

Indicators that allow the driver to monitor the performance of the charging system can be ammeters, voltmeters, or warning lamps. Fusible links are installed in the charging system to protect against high current flow.

Review Questions

Choose the single most correct answer.
Compare your answers with the correct answers on page 431.

1. Alternator output voltage is directly related to:
   a. Field strength
   b. Rotor speed
   c. Both field strength and rotor speed
   d. Neither field strength nor rotor speed

2. Double-contact voltage regulators contain all of the following *except*:
   a. An armature
   b. An electromagnet
   c. Two sets of contact points
   d. A solenoid

3. The shorting contacts of a double-contact regulator:
   a. Increase voltage creep
   b. Short the field circuit to the alternator
   c. React to battery temperature changes
   d. Reduce field current to zero

4. Field relays are often used to:
   a. Control an indicator lamp
   b. Regulate alternator voltage output
   c. Control the alternator-output-to-battery circuit
   d. Control the headlights

5. Which of the following can *not* be used in a totally solid-state regulator?
   a. Zener diodes
   b. Thermistors
   c. Capacitors
   d. Circuit breakers

6. Which of the following is used to smooth out any abrupt voltage surges and protect a regulator?
   a. Transistor
   b. Capacitor
   c. Thermistor
   d. Relays

7. Which of the following is used to monitor the charging system?
   a. Ammeter
   b. Ohmmeter
   c. Voltmeter
   d. Fusible link

8. Warning lamps are installed so that they will *not* light when:
   a. The voltage on the battery side of the lamp is higher
   b. Field current is flowing from the battery to the alternator
   c. The voltage on both sides of the lamp is equal
   d. The voltage on the resistor side of the lamp is higher

9. Maximum current output in an alternator is reached when:
   a. It reaches maximum designed speed
   b. Electrical demands from the system are at the minimum
   c. Induced countervoltage becomes great enough to stop current increase
   d. Induced countercurrent becomes great enough to stop voltage increase

10. The regulator is a charging system device that can control _____ circuit opening and closing.
    a. Ignition-to-battery
    b. Alternator-to-thermistor
    c. Battery-to-accessory
    d. Voltage source-to-battery

11. The regulator component that controls the voltage-source-to-battery circuit is:
    a. Cutout relay
    b. Voltage regulator
    c. Current regulator
    d. Field relay

PART FOUR

The Starting System

10

Starting System Overview

The automotive starting system is also called the cranking system. Its only job is to crank the engine fast enough for the engine to fire and run. The ignition and fuel systems must supply the spark and fuel for the engine to start and run, but the starting system cranks the engine to get it going.

SYSTEM OPERATION

The starting system draws a large amount of current from the battery to power the starter motor. The starter circuit on a large gasoline powered V8 engine must carry as much as 300 amperes under some conditions. Large V8 diesel engines require even more current. To handle this current safely and with a minimum voltage loss from resistance, the cables must be the correct size, and all connections must be clean and tight.

The starting system is controlled by the driver through the ignition switch. If the heavy cables that carry current to the starter were routed to the instrument panel and the switch, they would be so long that the starter would not get enough current to operate properly. To avoid such a voltage drop, the starting system has two circuits, figure 10-1:

- The starter circuit
- The control circuit.

Starter Motor Circuit

The starter circuit, or motor circuit, shown as the solid lines of figure 10-1, consists of:

- The battery
- A magnetic switch
- The starter motor
- Heavy-gauge cables.

The circuit between the battery and the starter motor is controlled by a magnetic switch (a relay or solenoid). Switch design and function vary from system to system.

A gear on the starter motor armature engages with gear teeth on the engine flywheel. When current reaches the starter motor, it begins to turn. This turns the car's engine, which can quickly fire and run by itself. If the starter motor remained engaged to the engine flywheel, the starter motor would be spun by the engine at a very high speed. This would damage the starter motor. To avoid this, there must be a mechanism to disengage the starter motor from the engine. There are several different designs that will do this, as we will see in the next chapter.

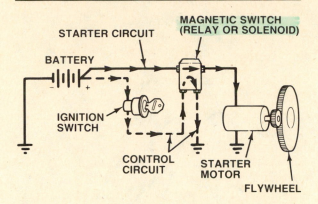

Figure 10-1. In this diagram of the starting system, the starter circuit is shown as a solid line and the control circuit is shown as a dashed line. (Delco-Remy)

Control Circuit

The control circuit is shown by the dashed lines in figure 10-1. It allows the driver to use a small amount of battery current, about three to five amperes, to control the flow of a large amount of battery current to the starter motor. Control circuits usually consist of an ignition switch connected through normal-gauge wiring to the battery and the magnetic switch. When the ignition switch is in the start position, a small amount of current flows through the coil of the magnetic switch. This closes a set of large contact points within the magnetic switch and allows battery current to flow directly to the starter motor.

BASIC SYSTEM PARTS

We have already studied the battery, which is an important part of the starting system. The other circuit parts are the:

- Ignition switch
- Starting safety switch (on some systems)
- Relays or solenoids (magnetic switches)
- Starter motor
- Wiring.

Ignition Switch

The ignition switch has jobs other than controlling the starting system. The ignition switch normally has at least four positions:

- Accessories
- Off
- On (Run)
- Start.

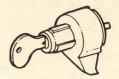

Figure 10-2. This ignition switch acts directly on the contact points. (Bosch)

Switches on late-model cars also have a lock position to lock the steering wheel. All positions except start are **detented**. That is, the switch will remain in that position until moved. When the ignition key is turned to start and released, it will return to the on (run) position. The start position is the actual starter switch part of the ignition switch. It applies battery voltage to the magnetic switch.

There are two types of ignition switches in use. On older cars, the switch is mounted on the instrument panel and contains the contact points, figure 10-2. The newer type, used on cars with locking steering columns, is usually mounted on the column. Many column-mounted switches operate remotely mounted contact points through a rod, figure 10-3. Other column-mounted switches operate directly on contact points, figure 10-4. Older domestic and imported cars sometimes used separate push button switches or cable-operated switches that controlled the starting system separately from the ignition switch.

Detented: Positions in a switch that allow the switch to stay in that position. In an ignition switch, the On, Off, Lock, and Accessory positions are detented.

■ The Beginning

The automobile became common in America in the early 1900s. The first automobiles had no electric starting systems. The driver had to insert a crank into the front of the engine and turn it by hand until the engine fired and ran. This required both skill and physical strength. Without a self-starting system, engines were limited in displacement and compression ratios. Operating an automobile was very inconvenient for those who could not crank the engine themselves.

In 1910, Charles F. Kettering began work on a practical automotive self-starter. The system first appeared on the 1912 Cadillac, and was quickly adopted by other manufacturers.

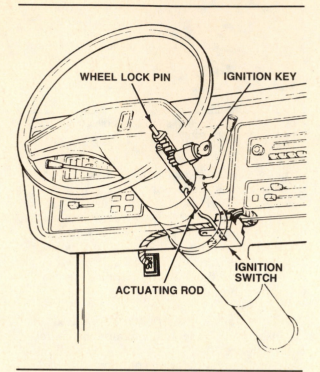

Figure 10-3. Many column-mounted ignition switches act on the contact points through the movement of a rod. (Ford)

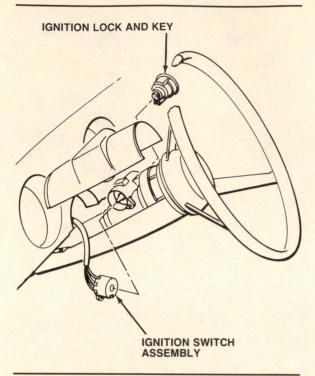

Figure 10-4. This column-mounted ignition switch acts directly on the contact points.

Starting Safety Switch

The **starting safety switch** is also called a neutral start switch. It is a normally open switch that prevents the starting system from operating when the automobile's transmission is in gear. If the car has no starting safety switch, it is possible to spin the engine with the transmission in gear. This will make the car lurch forward or backward which could be dangerous. Safety switches or interlock devices are now required by law with all automatic and manual transmissions.

Starting safety switches can be connected in two places within the starting system control circuit. The safety switch can be placed between the ignition switch and the magnetic switch, figure 10-5, so that the safety switch must be closed before current can flow to the magnetic switch. The safety switch also can be connected between the magnetic switch and ground, figure 10-6, so that the switch must be closed before current can flow from the magnetic switch to ground.

Where the starting safety switch is installed depends upon the type of transmission used and whether the gear shift lever is column mounted or floor mounted.

Automatic transmissions

The safety switch used with an automatic transmission can be either an electrical switch or a mechanical device. Electrical switches have contact points that are closed only when the gear lever is in Park or Neutral, as shown in figure 10-5. The switch can be mounted near the gear shift lever, figures 10-7 and 10-8, or on the transmission housing, figure 10-9. The contacts are in series with the control circuit, so that no current can flow through the magnetic switch unless the transmission is out of gear.

Mechanical interlock devices physically block the movement of the ignition key when the transmission is in gear, figures 10-10 and 10-11. The key can be turned only when the gear shift lever is in Park or Neutral.

Some manufacturers use an additional circuit in the neutral start switch to light the backup lamps when the transmission is placed in Reverse, figures 10-8 and 10-9.

Ford vehicles equipped with an electronic automatic transmission or transaxle use an additional circuit in the neutral safety switch to inform the microprocessor of the position of the manual lever shaft. This signal is used to determine the desired gear and electronic pressure control. The switch is now called a manual lever position sensor or switch (MLPS).

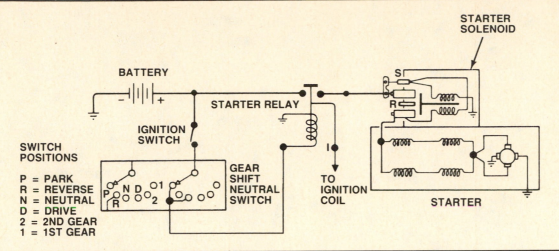

Figure 10-5. This starting safety switch must be closed before battery current can reach the magnetic switch. (Ford)

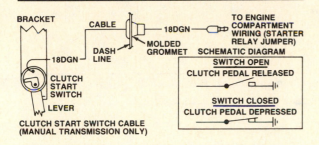

Figure 10-6. The clutch switch must be closed before battery current can flow from the magnetic switch to ground. (Chrysler)

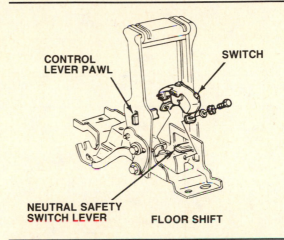

Figure 10-7. An electrical safety switch installed near the floor-mounted gear shift lever. (Chevrolet)

General Motors has done essentially the same as Ford, renaming the Park/Neutral switch used on its THM 4T60-E transaxle. It now is called either a PRNDL switch or a Park/Neutral position switch and provides input to the control module regarding torque converter clutch slip. This input allows the control module to make the necessary calculations to control clutch apply and release feel.

Manual transmissions
The starting safety switch used with a manual transmission on older vehicles is usually an electrical switch similar to those shown in figures 10-7 and 10-8. A **clutch start switch** (also called an interlock switch) is commonly used with manual transmissions and transaxles on late-model vehicles. This is an electric switch mounted on the floor or firewall near the clutch pedal. Its contacts are normally open and close only when the clutch pedal is fully depressed, figure 10-12.

Starting Safety Switch: A neutral start switch. It keeps the starting system from operating when a car's transmission is in gear.

Clutch Start Switch: A starting safety switch that is operated by the clutch pedal.

■ **Crank Lost?**

In 1935, if a car's electric starter wouldn't work, and if the starting crank had been misplaced, motorists were advised that they could jack up a rear wheel, put the clutch in, place the transmission gears in "high", let the clutch out, and start the engine by turning the rear wheel.

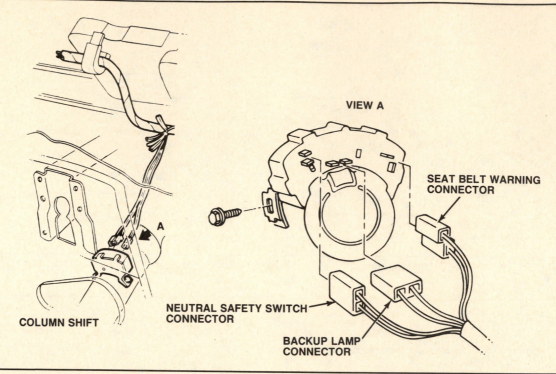

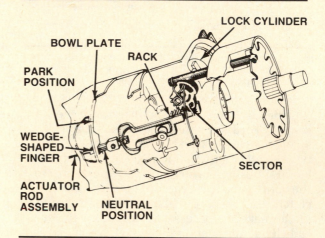

Figure 10-8. An electrical safety switch installed near the column-mounted gear shift lever. (Chevrolet)

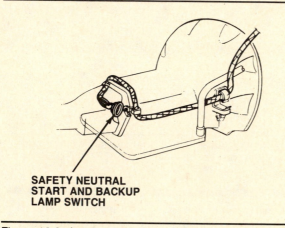

Figure 10-9. An electrical safety switch mounted on the transmission housing. (Chrysler)

Figure 10-10. A mechanical device within the steering column blocks the movement of the ignition switch actuator rod when the transmission is in gear. (Buick)

Relays and Solenoids

A magnetic switch in the starting system allows the control circuit to open and close the starter circuit. The switch can be a:

- Relay, which uses the electromagnetic field of a coil to attract an armature and close the contact points
- Solenoid, which uses the electromagnetic field of a coil to pull a plunger into the coil and close the contact points

In addition to closing the contact points, solenoid-equipped circuits often use the move-

ment of the solenoid to engage the starter motor with the engine flywheel. We will explain this in the next chapter.

The terminology used with relays and solenoids is often confusing. Technically, a relay operates with a hinged armature and does only an electrical job. A solenoid operates with a movable plunger and usually does a mechanical job. Sometimes, a solenoid is used only to open and close an electric circuit. The movement of the plunger is not used for any me-

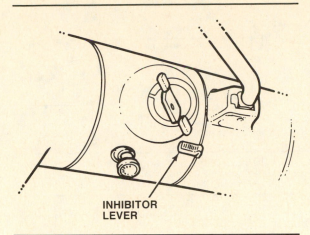

Figure 10-11. A lever on the steering wheel blocks the movement of the ignition key when the transmission is in gear.

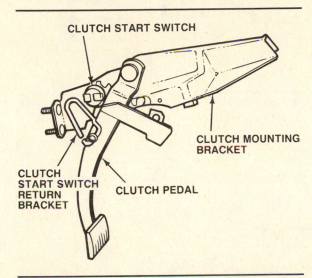

Figure 10-12. The clutch pedal must be fully depressed to close the clutch switch and complete the control circuit. (Buick)

Figure 10-13. The Ford starter relay or magnetic switch.

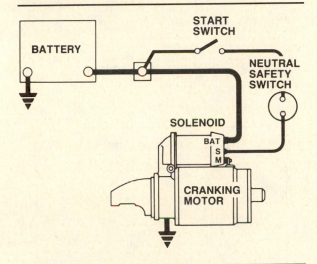

Figure 10-14. A typical GM starting circuit. (Delco-Remy)

chanical work. Manufacturers sometimes call these solenoids "starter relays". Figure 10-13 shows a commonly used Ford starter relay. We will continue to use the general term "magnetic switch", and will tell you if the manufacturer uses a different name for the device.

Starter Motor

The starter motors used by various carmakers are explained in detail in Chapter Eleven.

Wiring

The starter motor circuit uses heavy-gauge wiring to carry current to the starter motor. The control circuit carries less current and thus uses lighter-gauge wires.

SPECIFIC STARTING SYSTEMS

Various manufacturers use different starting system components. The following paragraphs briefly describe the circuits used by major manufacturers. We will study the starter motors used by each carmaker in the next chapter.

Delco-Remy and Bosch

Delco-Remy and Bosch starter motors are used by General Motors. The most commonly used Delco-Remy and Bosch automotive starter motor depends upon the movement of a solenoid

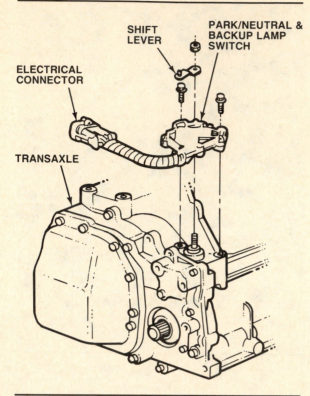

Figure 10-15. Location of the park/neutral or PRNDL switch on GM THM transaxles. (Oldsmobile)

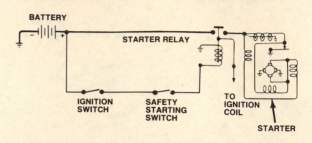

Figure 10-16. The Ford starting system with the positive engagement starter. (Ford)

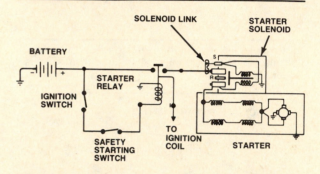

Figure 10-17. The Ford solenoid-actuated system uses the starter-mounted solenoid only for a mechanical job, not for an electrical job. (Ford)

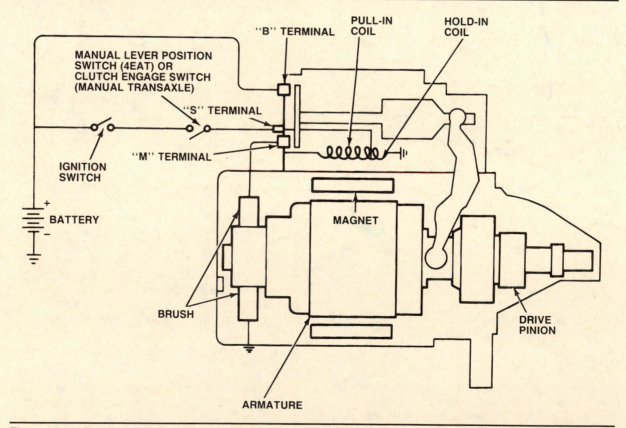

Figure 10-18. The Ford PMGR starter circuit may use only a solenoid instead of a solenoid and a relay. (Ford)

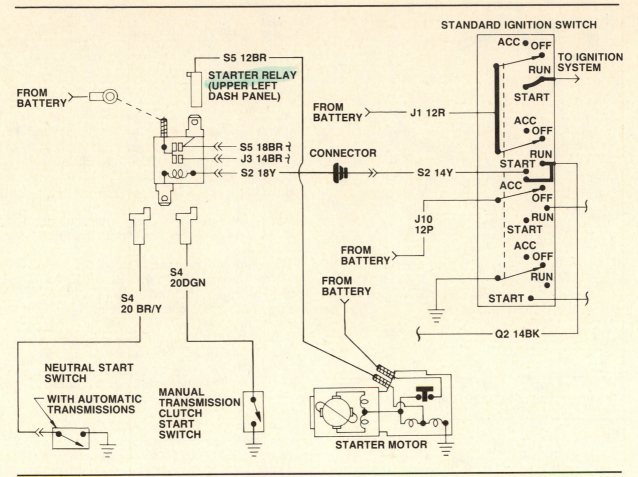

Figure 10-19. A typical Chrysler starting system. (Chrysler)

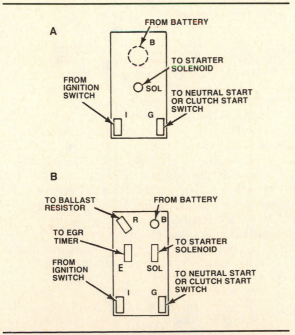

Figure 10-20. Comparison of the terminals on a pre-1977 Chrysler starter relay (A) and a 1977 or later relay. (Chrysler)

both to control current flow in the starter circuit and to engage the starter motor with the engine flywheel. This is called a **solenoid-actuated starter**. The solenoid is mounted on, or enclosed with, the motor housing, figure 10-14.

The type and location of starting safety switches vary within the GM divisions and carlines. Larger-size GM cars use a mechanical blocking device in the steering column, figure 10-10. The intermediate and smaller cars with automatic transmissions have electrical switches mounted near the shift lever. These are either on the column, figure 10-8, or on the floor, figure 10-7. On front-wheel-drive (FWD) cars with automatic transmissions, the Park/Neutral or PRNDL switch is an electrical

Solenoid-Actuated Starter: A starter that uses a solenoid both to control current flow in the starter circuit and to engage the starter motor with the engine flywheel.

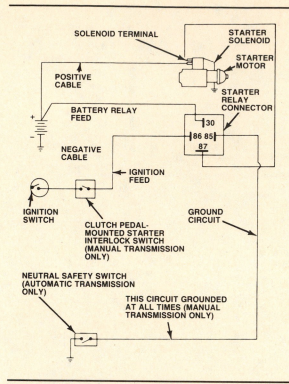

Figure 10-21. The Chrysler starting system with a five-terminal Bosch relay. (Chrysler)

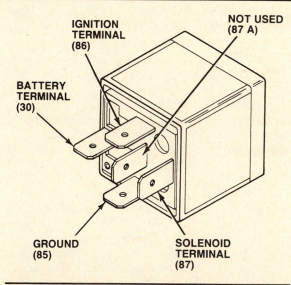

Figure 10-22. Only four of the five relay terminals are used when the Bosch relay is installed in the Chrysler starting system. (Chrysler)

switch mounted on the transaxle case manual lever shaft, figure 10-15. GM cars with floor-shift manual transmissions use a clutch pedal-operated safety switch. With column-shift manual transmissions, an electric switch is mounted on the column.

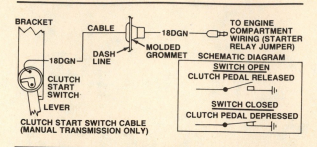

Figure 10-23. The Chrysler clutch switch. (Chrysler)

Motorcraft

Ford has used three types of starter motors, and therefore has several different starting system circuits.

The Motorcraft positive engagement starter has a movable pole shoe that uses electromagnetism to engage the starter motor with the engine. This motor does not use a solenoid to *move* anything, but it uses a solenoid to open and close the starter circuit as a magnetic switch, figure 10-16. Ford calls this solenoid a starter relay, figure 10-13.

The Motorcraft solenoid-actuated starter is very similar to the Delco-Remy and depends upon the movement of a solenoid to engage the starter motor with the engine, figure 10-17. The solenoid is mounted within the motor housing and receives battery current through the same type of starter relay used in the positive engagement system. Although the motor-mounted solenoid could do the job of this additional starter relay, the second relay is installed on many Ford automobiles to make the cars easier to build. Motorcraft solenoid-actuated starters were used on Ford cars and trucks with large V8 engines.

The Motorcraft permanent magnet gear-reduction (PMGR) starter is a solenoid-actuated design that operates much like the Motorcraft solenoid-actuated starter described above. However, the starter circuit may or may not use a starter relay, depending on the car model, figure 10-18.

Rear-wheel-drive (RWD) Ford automobiles with manual transmissions have no starting safety switch. Front-wheel-drive (FWD) models with manual transaxles have a clutch interlock switch. If a Ford car with an automatic transmission has a column-mounted shift lever, a blocking interlock device prevents the ignition key from turning when the transmission is in gear. If the automatic transmission shift lever is mounted on the floor, an electrical switch prevents current from flowing to the starter relay when the transmission is in gear. The switch may be mounted on the transmission case or near the gear shift lever.

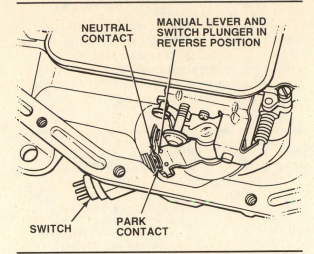

Figure 10-24. When the automatic transmission is in park or neutral, a transmission lever touches the contact and completes the control circuit to ground. (Chrysler)

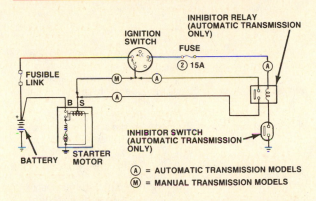

(A) = AUTOMATIC TRANSMISSION MODELS
(M) = MANUAL TRANSMISSION MODELS

Figure 10-25. A typical Nissan starting system used on gasoline engines.

Chrysler

Chrysler uses a solenoid-actuated starter motor. The solenoid is mounted inside the motor housing and receives battery current through a starter relay, figure 10-19.

Chrysler starter relays used prior to 1977 have four terminals, as shown in figure 10-20A. In 1977, a second set of contacts and two terminals were added, figure 10-20B. The extra contacts and terminals allow more current to flow through the relay to the ignition system and to the exhaust gas recirculation (EGR) timer. This has no effect on the operation of the relay within the starting system. These starter relays generally were mounted on the firewall.

Current Chrysler starting systems use a standard five-terminal Bosch relay, figure 10-21, but only four terminals are used in the circuit, figure 10-22. The relay is located at the front of

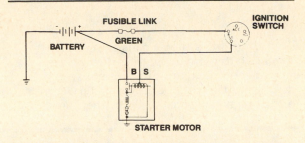

Figure 10-26. A typical Nissan diesel starting system.

the driver's side strut tower in a power distribution center or cluster.

Chrysler automobiles with manual transmissions have a clutch interlock switch, figure 10-23. Current from the starter relay can flow to ground only when the clutch pedal is fully depressed. Cars with automatic transmissions have an electrical neutral start switch mounted on the transmission housing, figure 10-24. When the transmission is out of gear, the switch provides a ground connection for the starter control circuit.

Toyota and Nissan

Toyota and Nissan use a variety of solenoid-actuated direct drive and reduction gear starter designs manufactured primarily by Hitachi and Nippondenso, figures 10-25 and 10-26. The neutral start switch (called an inhibitor switch by the Japanese) incorporates a relay in its circuit.

■ **Vacuum Control Switches**

Magnetic switches are not the only control devices that have been used in the starting system's control circuit. Before the 1950s, some GM cars had a vacuum control switch that was mounted in the carburetor. To start the car, the driver turned on the ignition switch and depressed the accelerator pedal. The pedal movement was transmitted through a linkage to the vacuum control switch, closing its contacts. Current flowed from the battery, through the vacuum switch contacts, to the starter motor.

When the engine started and ran, carburetor vacuum opened the vacuum switch contacts to stop cranking. If the carburetor vacuum was not great enough to do this, a secondary system would stop the cranking. Generator voltage was applied to the ground side of the motor. When generator voltage equalled battery voltage, there would be no voltage drop across the motor and the motor would not crank.

SUMMARY

Electric starting systems consist of a high-current starter circuit controlled by a low-current control circuit. The ignition switch includes contacts that conduct battery current to the magnetic switch. The magnetic switch may be a relay or a solenoid and may have other jobs besides controlling the starter circuit current flow. The starter motor and connecting wires are also included in the system. Variations are common among the starting systems used by the various carmakers.

Review Questions

Choose the single most correct answer.
Compare your answers with the correct answers on page 431.

1. The first practical automotive self-starter was introduced in:
   a. 1895
   b. 1902
   c. 1912
   d. 1916

2. The starting system has _____ circuits to avoid excessive voltage drop.
   a. Two
   b. Three
   c. Four
   d. Six

3. The starter circuit consists of which of the following?
   a. Battery, ignition switch, starter motor, large cables
   b. Battery, ignition switch, relays or solenoids, large cables
   c. Battery, magnetic switch, starter motor, primary wiring
   d. Battery, magnetic switch, starter motor, large cables

4. Which of the following is *not* part of the starter control circuit?
   a. The ignition switch
   b. The starting safety switch
   c. The starter relay
   d. The starter motor

5. The ignition switch will *not* remain in which of the following positions?
   a. Accessories
   b. Off
   c. On (run)
   d. Start

6. The starting safety switch is also called a:
   a. Remote-operated switch
   b. Manual-override switch
   c. Neutral-start switch
   d. Single-pole, double-throw switch

7. Safety switches are most commonly used with:
   a. Automatic transmissions
   b. Imported automobiles
   c. Domestic automobiles
   d. Manual transmissions

8. Starting safety switches used with manual transmissions are usually:
   a. Electrical
   b. Mechanical
   c. Floor-mounted
   d. Column-mounted

9. Which of the following is *not* true of solenoids?
   a. They use the electromagnetic field of a coil to pull a plunger into the coil
   b. They are generally used to engage the starter motor with the engine flywheel
   c. They operate with a movable plunger and usually do a mechanical job
   d. They send electronic signals to the control module and have no moving parts

Chapter

11

Starter Motors

We learned in Chapter Two that the interaction of magnetic fields can be used to convert electrical energy to mechanical energy. Positions A and B of figure 11-1 show that a current-carrying conductor placed in a magnetic field will tend to move from the stronger field area to the weaker field area. Position C shows that two conductors carrying current in opposite directions will tend to move in opposite directions. The simple motor in position D uses this movement to rotate an armature.

We can now look at automotive starter motors and see how they are constructed to put the motor principle to work.

FRAME AND FIELD ASSEMBLY

The frame, or housing, of a starter motor, figure 11-2, encloses all of the motor's moving parts. It supports the parts and protects them from dirt, oil, and other contamination. The part of the frame that encloses the pole shoes and field windings is made of iron to provide a path for magnetic flux lines, figure 11-3. To reduce weight, other parts of the frame may be made of cast aluminum.

One end of the housing holds one of the two bearings or bushings in which the armature shaft turns. On most motors, it also contains the brushes that conduct current to the armature, figure 11-4. This is called the brush, or commutator, end housing. The other end housing holds the second bearing or bushing in which the armature shaft turns. It also encloses the gear that meshes with the engine flywheel. This is called the drive end housing. The drive end housing often provides the motor's mounting points. These end pieces can be made of aluminum because they do not have to conduct magnetic flux.

The magnetic field of the starter motor is provided by two or more pole shoes and field windings. The pole shoes are made of iron and are attached to the frame with large screws, figure 11-5. Figure 11-6 shows the paths of magnetic flux lines within a four-pole motor. The field windings are usually made of a heavy copper ribbon, figure 11-7, to increase their current-carrying capacity and electromagnetic field strength. Automotive starter motors usually have four pole shoes and two to four field windings to provide a strong magnetic field within the motor. Pole shoes that do not have field windings are magnetized by flux lines from the wound poles.

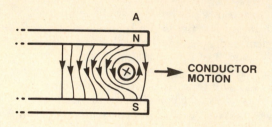

A

CONDUCTOR MOTION

B

DIRECTION OF CURRENT

CONDUCTOR MOTION

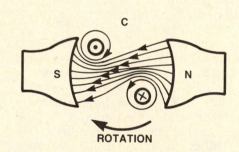

C

S N

ROTATION

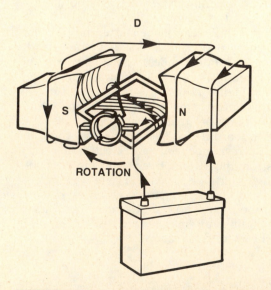

D

S N

ROTATION

Figure 11-1. The motor principle. (Prestolite)

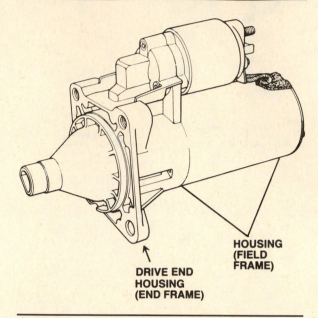

HOUSING (FIELD FRAME)

DRIVE END HOUSING (END FRAME)

Figure 11-2. The starter motor housing. (Chrysler)

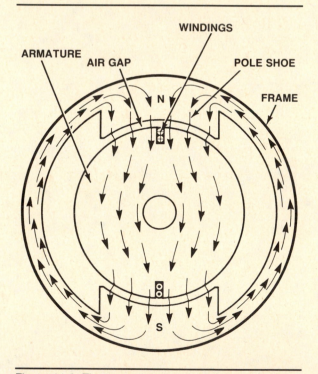

WINDINGS

ARMATURE   AIR GAP   POLE SHOE

FRAME

N

S

Figure 11-3. The motor frame is a path for flux lines. (Bosch)

Torque is the force of a starter motor, a force applied in a rotary, or circular, direction. A motor's torque, speed, and current draw are related. As speed increases in most automotive starter motors, torque and current draw decrease. These motors will develop maximum torque just before the engine begins to turn.

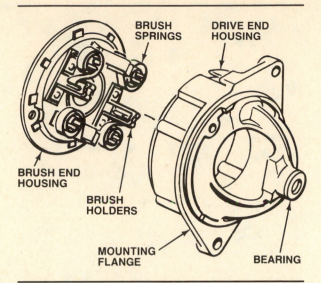

Figure 11-4. The brush end and drive end housings.

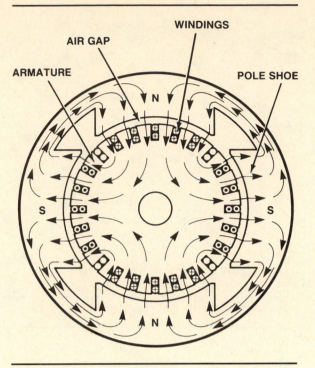

Figure 11-6. Flux line paths in a four-pole motor. (Bosch)

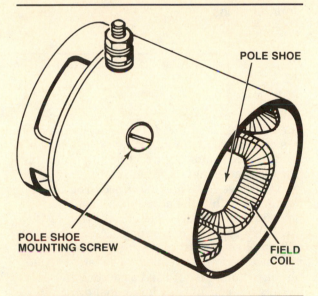

Figure 11-5. Pole shoes and field windings are installed in the housing.

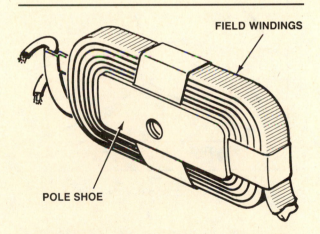

Figure 11-7. A pole shoe and field winding.

Once the engine begins to turn, the motor's speed increases and its torque decreases. The maximum amount of torque produced by a motor depends upon the strength of its magnetic fields. As field strength increases, torque increases.

Because field current and armature current flow to the motor through one terminal on the housing, the field and armature windings must be connected in a single complete circuit. The internal circuitry of the motor (the way in which the field and armature windings are connected) gives the motor some general oper-

ating characteristics. Figure 11-8 shows the three general types of motor internal circuitry:

- Series
- Shunt (parallel)
- Compound (series-parallel).

Torque: Twisting or rotating force; usually expressed in foot-pounds, inch-pounds, or Newton-meters.

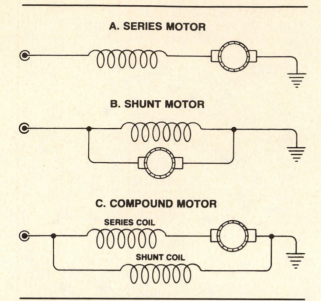

A. SERIES MOTOR

B. SHUNT MOTOR

C. COMPOUND MOTOR

SERIES COIL

SHUNT COIL

Figure 11-8. Basic motor circuitry. (Ford)

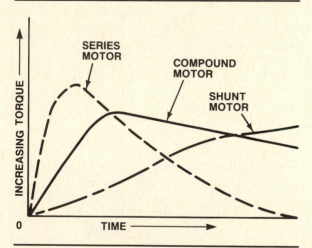

Figure 11-9. The torque output characteristics of series, shunt, and compound motors.

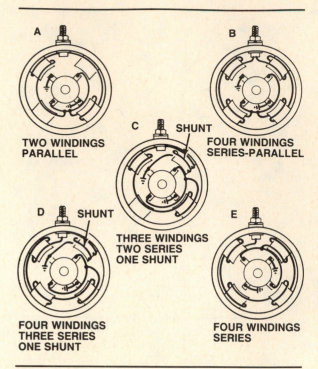

A

TWO WINDINGS PARALLEL

B

FOUR WINDINGS SERIES-PARALLEL

C   SHUNT

THREE WINDINGS TWO SERIES ONE SHUNT

D   SHUNT

FOUR WINDINGS THREE SERIES ONE SHUNT

E

FOUR WINDINGS SERIES

Figure 11-10. Actual motor circuit connections. (Prestolite)

All automotive starter motors in use today are the series type or the compound type. The **series motor**, figure 11-8A, has only one path for current flow. As the armature rotates, its conductors cut magnetic flux lines. A countervoltage will be induced in the armature windings, opposing the original current flow through them. The countervoltage decreases the total current flow through both the field and the armature windings, because they are connected in series. This reduction of current flow reduces the motor's magnetic field and its torque. Series motors produce a great amount of torque when they first begin to operate, but torque decreases as the engine begins to turn, figure 11-9. Series motors can be used as auto-

motive starters because cranking an engine requires a great amount of torque at first, and less torque as cranking continues.

The **shunt motor**, figure 11-8B, does not follow the increasing-speed/decreasing-torque relationship we have just described. The countervoltage within the armature does not affect field current, because field current travels through a separate circuit path. A shunt motor will, in effect, adjust its torque output to the imposed load and operate at a constant speed. Shunt motors are not used as automotive starters because of their low initial torque, figure 11-9, but they are used to power other automotive accessories.

The **compound motor**, figure 11-8C, has both series and shunt field windings. It combines both the good starting torque of the series-type and the relatively constant operating speed of the shunt-type motor, figure 11-9. A compound motor is often used as an automotive starter.

Figure 11-10 shows the actual relationships of field and armature windings in different types of motors.

ARMATURE AND COMMUTATOR ASSEMBLY

The motor armature, figure 11-11, has a laminated core. Insulation between the laminations helps to reduce eddy currents in the core. For

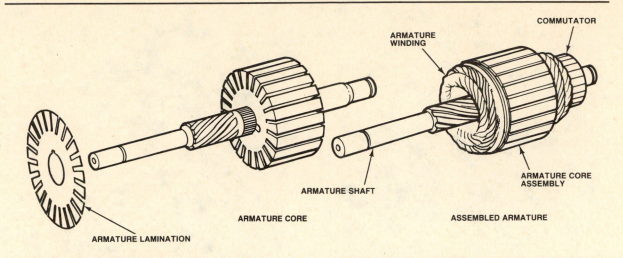

Figure 11-11. The motor armature. (Bosch)

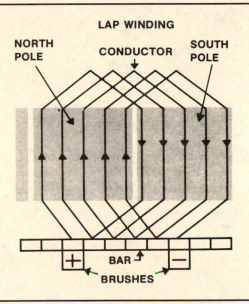

Figure 11-12. Armature lap winding. (Delco-Remy)

reduced resistance, the armature conductors are made of a thick copper wire. Motor armatures can be connected to the commutator in two ways. In a **lap winding**, the two ends of each conductor are attached to two adjacent commutator bars, figure 11-12. In a **wave winding**, the two ends of a conductor are attached to commutator bars that are 180 degrees apart (on opposite sides of the commutator), figure 11-13. A lap-wound armature is more commonly used because it offers less resistance.

The commutator is made of copper bars insulated from each other by mica or some other insulating material. The armature core, windings, and commutator are assembled on a long

armature shaft. This shaft also carries the pinion gear that meshes with the engine's flywheel ring gear, figure 11-14. The shaft is supported by bearings or bushings in the end housings.

To supply the proper current to the armature, four-pole motors must have four brushes riding on the commutator, figure 11-15. Most automotive starters have two grounded and two insulated brushes. The brushes are held against the commutator by spring pressure.

Series Motor: A motor that has only one path for current flow through the field and armature windings. Commonly used for starter motors.

Shunt Motor: A motor that has its field windings wired in parallel with its armature. Not used as a starter motor, but often used to power vehicle accessories.

Compound Motor: A motor that has both series and shunt field windings. Often used as a starter motor.

Lap Winding: A method of wiring a motor armature. The two ends of a conductor are attached to two commutator bars that are next to each other.

Wave Winding: A method of wiring a motor armature. The two ends of a conductor are attached to two commutator bars that are opposite each other.

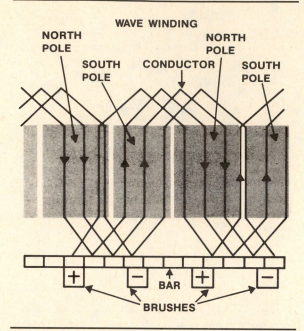

Figure 11-13. Armature wave winding. (Delco-Remy)

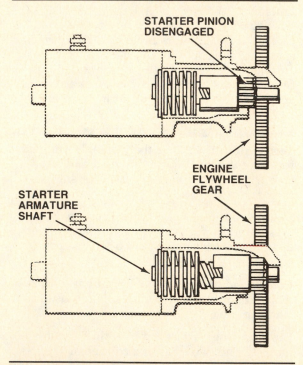

Figure 11-14. The pinion gear meshes with the flywheel ring gear.

PERMANENT-MAGNET FIELDS

The permanent-magnet (PM), planetary-drive starter motor is the first significant advance in starter design in decades. It was introduced first on some 1986 Chrysler and GM models,

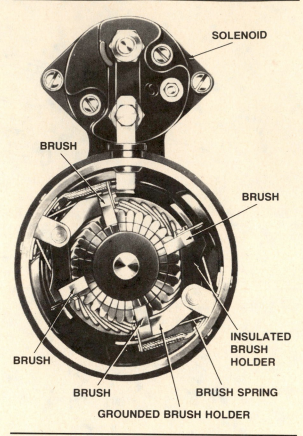

Figure 11-15. A four-brush motor. (Delco-Remy)

and in 1989 by Ford on Continental and some Thunderbird models. Permanent magnets are used in place of the electromagnetic field coils and pole shoes. This eliminates the motor field circuit, which in turn eliminates the potential for field wire-to-frame shorts, field coil welding, and other electrical problems. The motor has only an armature circuit. Because the smaller armature in PM starters uses reinforcement bands, it has a longer life than the armature in wound-field starter motors.

The magnetic field of the starter motor is provided by four or six small permanent magnets. These magnets are made of a new alloy of iron and rare-earth materials that produces a magnetic field strong enough to operate the motor without relying on traditional current-carrying field coil windings around iron pole pieces. Removing the field circuit not only minimizes potential electrical problems, the use of permanent-magnet fields allows engineers to design a gear reduction motor half the size and weight of a conventional wound-field motor without compromising cranking performance.

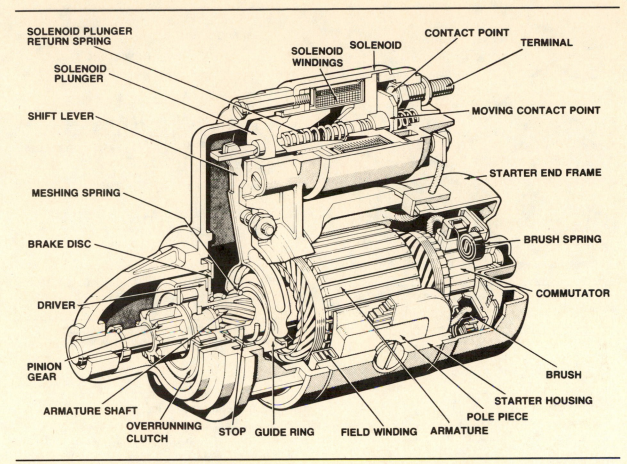

Figure 11-16. A cutaway view of a typical starter motor.

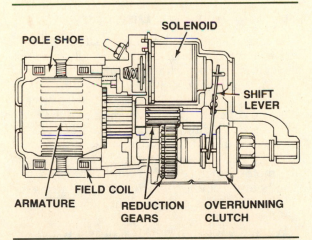

Figure 11-17. The Chrysler reduction gear starter motor. (Chrysler)

STARTER MOTOR AND DRIVE TYPES

Starter motors, figure 11-16, are direct-current motors that use a great amount of current for a short time. As we saw in Chapter Ten, the starter motor circuit is a simple one containing just the starter motor and a solenoid or relay. This circuit is a direct path for delivering the momentary high current required by the starter motor from the battery.

The starter motor cranks a car's engine through a pinion gear that engages a ring gear on the engine flywheel. The pinion gear is driven directly off the starter armature, figure 11-16, or through a set of reduction gears, figure 11-17, that provide greater starting torque, although at a lower rpm.

■ The Compressed Air Starter

This early starting system used fresh air stored in a tank to supply the power to crank the engine. The starting "motor" was an air-tight chamber mounted on the front of the car. A rod from the starter was attached to the crankshaft. When the driver operated a foot pedal mounted on the floorboard, air rushed from the supply tank to the starter. A revolving vane inside the starter was turned by the air, turning the crankshaft at the same time.

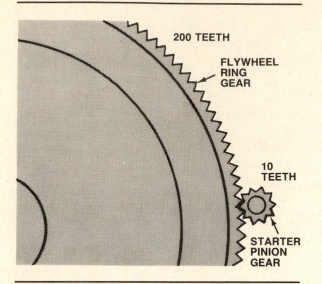

Figure 11-18. The ring gear to pinion gear ratio is about 20:1.

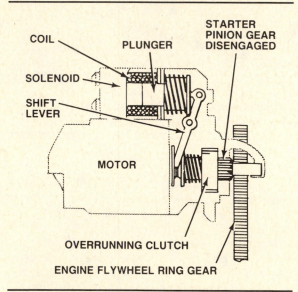

Figure 11-19. A typical solenoid-actuated drive.

For the starter motor to be able to turn the engine quickly enough, the number of teeth on the flywheel ring gear, relative to the number of teeth on the motor pinion gear, must be between 15 and 20 to one, figure 11-18.

When the engine starts and runs, its speed increases. If the starter motor were permanently engaged to the engine, the motor would be spun at a very high speed. This would throw armature windings off the core. Thus, the motor must be disengaged from the engine as soon as the engine turns more rapidly than the starter motor has cranked it. This job is done by the starter motor drive.

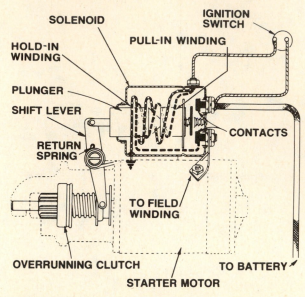

Figure 11-20. The solenoid has a heavy-gauge pull-in winding and a lighter-gauge hold-in winding. (Delco-Remy)

Four general kinds of starter motors are used in late-model automobiles:

- Solenoid-actuated, direct drive
- Solenoid-actuated, reduction drive
- Movable pole shoe
- Permanent-magnet, planetary drive.

Solenoid-Actuated, Direct Drive

The main parts of a solenoid-actuated, direct-drive starter, figure 11-19, are the solenoid, the shift lever, the overrunning clutch, and the starter pinion gear.

The solenoid used to actuate a starter drive has two coils: the pull-in winding and the hold-in, or holding, winding, figure 11-20. The pull-in winding consists of few turns of a heavy wire. The winding is grounded through the motor armature and grounded brushes. The hold-in winding consists of many turns of a fine wire and is grounded through the solenoid case.

When the ignition switch is turned to the start position, current flows through both windings. The solenoid plunger is pulled in, and the contacts are closed. This applies battery voltage to both ends of the pull-in winding, and current flow through it stops. The magnetic field of the hold-in winding is enough to keep the plunger in place. This circuitry reduces the solenoid's current draw during cranking, when both the starter motor and the ignition system are drawing current from the battery.

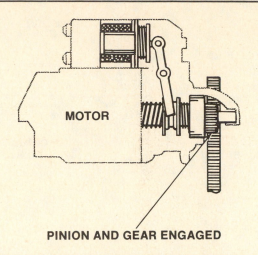

PINION AND GEAR ENGAGED

Figure 11-21. The movement of the solenoid plunger meshes the pinion gear and the flywheel ring gear.

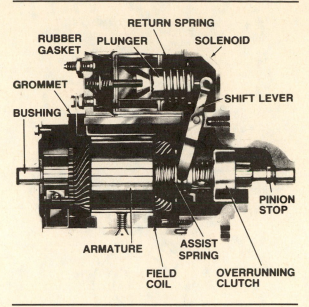

Figure 11-22. The Delco-Remy solenoid-actuated drive motor. (Delco-Remy)

The solenoid plunger action, transferred through the shift lever, pushes the pinion gear into mesh with the flywheel ring gear, figure 11-21. When the starter motor receives current, its armature begins to turn. This motion is transferred through the overrunning clutch and pinion gear to the engine flywheel.

The teeth on the pinion gear may not immediately mesh with the flywheel ring gear. If this happens, a spring behind the pinion compresses so that the solenoid plunger can complete its stroke. When the motor armature begins to turn, the pinion teeth will line up with the flywheel, and spring pressure will force the pinion to mesh.

The Delco-Remy MT series, figure 11-22, is the most common example of this type of starter motor and has been used for decades on almost all GM cars and light trucks. While this motor is manufactured in different sizes for different size engines, figure 11-23, the most common application is a four-pole, four-brush design. The solenoid plunger action, in addition to engaging the pinion gear, closes contact points to complete the starter circuit. To avoid closing the contacts before the pinion gear is fully engaged, the solenoid plunger is in two pieces, figure 11-24. When the solenoid windings are magnetized, the first plunger moves the shift lever. When the pinion gear reaches the flywheel, the first plunger has moved far enough to touch the second plunger. The first plunger continues to move into the solenoid, pushing the second plunger against the contact points.

A similar starter design, figure 11-25, has been used by Ford on its diesel engines and older large displacement V8 gasoline engines. It operates in the same way as the typical starter just described. The solenoid action closes a set of contact points, figure 11-26. Because Ford installs a remotely mounted magnetic switch in all of its starting circuits, the

■ Bendix Drive

Bendix drive starter motors were very common before the 1960s, but have been almost completely replaced by the three other types of drives. Some imported cars use a Bendix drive starter manufactured in England by Lucas. Delco-Remy and Autolite also have made a Bendix drive unit.

The Bendix drive relies on inertia to engage and disengage the pinion and ring gear. The Bendix drive pinion gear rides loosely on threads in the armature shaft. The inside of the pinion has matching threads.

When the motor armature begins to rotate, the pinion does not pick up speed as quickly as the armature. The pinion moves along the shaft threads and meshes with the ring gear. As the pinion hits the pinion stop, it begins to rotate with the armature to crank the engine.

When the engine fires and runs, the flywheel begins to turn the pinion faster than the armature. This makes the pinion move back along the shaft threads, disengaging it from the flywheel ring gear. A drive spring attached to the pinion helps this disengagement.

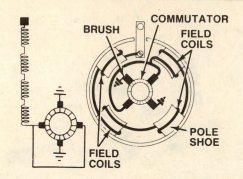

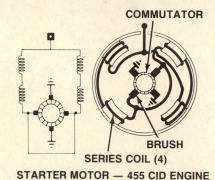

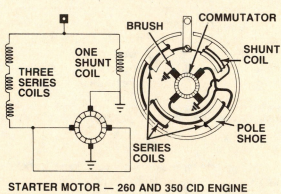

Figure 11-23. Delco-Remy provides differently connected starter motors for use with various engines. (Oldsmobile)

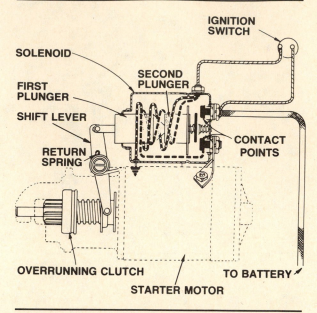

Figure 11-24. The Delco-Remy solenoid plunger is in two pieces. (Delco-Remy)

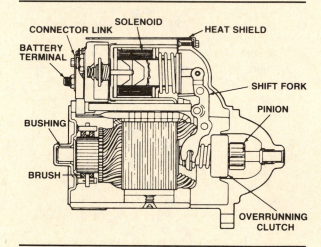

Figure 11-25. The Ford solenoid-actuated drive starter. (Ford)

solenoid contact points are not required to control the circuit. The solenoid contact points are physically linked, so that they are always "closed".

In the early 1970s, Chrysler also manufactured a fully-enclosed direct-drive starter motor, figure 11-23. It works in the same way as the typical solenoid-actuated starter described above. The solenoid plunger closes contact points to complete the motor circuitry, but the system also has a remotely mounted starter relay. Reduction drive starters are usually compound motors.

Most Bosch and virtually all Japanese starter motors operate on the same principles.

Solenoid-Actuated, Reduction Drive

The Chrysler solenoid-actuated, reduction-drive starter uses a solenoid to engage the pinion with the flywheel and close the motor circuit. The motor armature does not drive the pinion directly, however. It drives a small gear that is permanently meshed with a larger gear, figure 11-17. The armature gear to reduction gear ratio is from 2 to 3.5:1, depending upon the engine application. This allows a small, high-speed motor to deliver increased torque

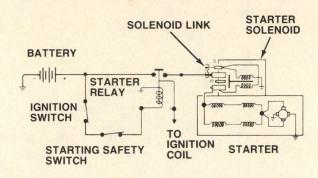

Figure 11-26. Ford solenoid-actuated starter circuitry. (Ford)

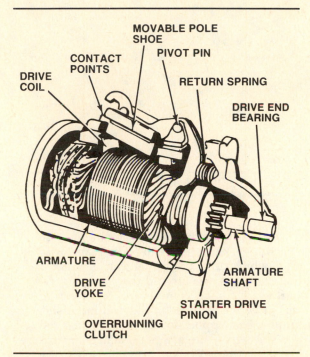

Figure 11-27. The Ford movable-pole-shoe starter.

at a satisfactory cranking rpm. Solenoid and starter drive operation is basically the same as a solenoid-actuated, direct drive starter.

Movable Pole Shoe Drive

Manufactured by the Motorcraft Division of Ford, the movable pole shoe starter motor is used on most Fords. One of the motor pole shoes pivots at the drive end housing, figure 11-27. The field winding of this shoe also contains a holding coil, wired in parallel and independently grounded, figure 11-28. When the starter relay is closed, battery current flows through the field windings and the holding coil of the pole shoe to ground. This creates a strong magnetic field, and the pole shoe is

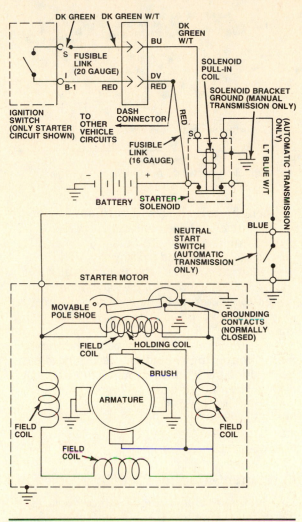

Figure 11-28. Circuit diagram of a system using a movable-pole-shoe starter.

pulled down into operating position. The motion is transferred through a shift lever, or drive yoke, to mesh the pinion gear with the ring gear.

■ Starter Drive Lubrication

The 1936 Hudson Terraplane Shop Manual recommends that once a year, before cold weather, the starter be removed and the starter drive cleaned and lubricated. This will make sure that the drive will engage the flywheel all through the winter months.

The Shop Manual cautions that only kerosene should be used as a cleaner. Gasoline will remove all of the lubricant. If Gredag No. 31-1/4 is not available, use a few drops of SAE 10 engine oil for relubrication. Do not try to clean or lubricate the screw threads of the starter drive.

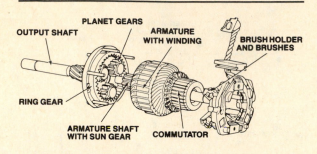

Figure 11-29. Bosch permanent-magnet, gear-reduction starter components. (Chrysler)

When the pole shoe is in position, it opens a set of contacts. These contacts break the ground connection of the field windings. Battery current is allowed to flow through the motor's internal circuitry, and the engine is cranked. During cranking, a small amount of current flows through the holding coil directly to ground to keep the shoe and lever assembly engaged.

An overrunning clutch prevents the starter motor from being turned by the engine. When the ignition switch moves out of the start position, current no longer flows through the windings of the movable pole shoe or the rest of the motor. Spring tension pulls the shoe up, and the shift lever disengages the pinion from the flywheel.

Permanent-Magnet Planetary Drive

This high-speed, low-torque motor operates the drive mechanism through gear reduction provided by a simple planetary gearset, not two spur gears as in the older Chrysler design. Figure 11-29 shows the Bosch gear reduction design used in the Chrysler starters. Figure 11-30 shows the gear reduction design used in the Delco-Remy permanent-magnet, gear-reduction (PMGR) starter. Figure 11-31 shows the PMGR design used by Ford, and compares PM starters to those of a typical wound-field starter.

All PMGR starter designs use a solenoid to operate the starter drive and close the motor armature circuit. The drive mechanism is identical to that used on other solenoid-actuated starters already described. Some models, however, use lightweight plastic shift levers.

The planetary gearset between the motor armature and the starter drive reduces the speed and increases the torque at the drive pinion. The compact gearset is only 1/2 to 3/4 inch (13 to 19 mm) deep and is mounted inline with the armature and drive pinion. An internal ring gear is keyed to the field frame and held stationary in the motor. The armature shaft

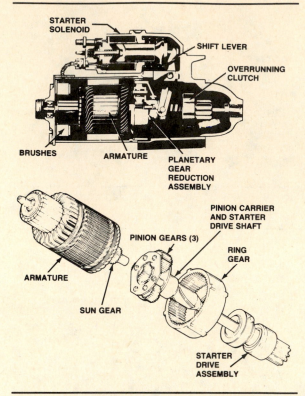

Figure 11-30. Delco-Remy permanent-magnet, gear-reduction starter components.

drives the sun gear for the planetary gearset. The sun gear meshes with three planetary pinions, which drive the pinion carrier in reduction as they rotate around the ring gear. The starter drive shaft is mounted on the carrier and driven at reduced speed and increased torque. This application of internal gear reduction through planetary gears delivers armature speeds in the 7,000 rpm range. The armature and drive shaft ride on roller or ball bearings rather than bushings.

Permanent-magnet, planetary-drive starters differ mechanically in how they do their job, but their electrical wiring is the same as that used with field-coil designs, figure 11-32. Field circuit testing and service are not required, but brush, commutator, and armature testing and service are basically the same as for any other motor.

Although PMGR motors are lighter in weight and simpler to service than traditional designs, they do require special handling precautions. The material used for the permanent magnet fields is quite brittle. A sharp impact caused by hitting or dropping the starter can destroy the fields.

Overrunning Clutch

Regardless of the type of starter motor used, when the engine starts and runs, its speed increases. The motor must be disengaged from the engine as soon as the engine is turning more rapidly than the starter motor that has cranked it. With a movable-pole-shoe or solenoid-actuated drive, however, the pinion remains engaged until power stops flowing to the starter. In these applications, the starter is protected by an overrunning clutch, figure 11-33.

The overrunning clutch consists of rollers that ride between a collar on the pinion gear and an outer shell. The outer shell has tapered slots for the rollers so that the roller can either ride freely or wedge tightly between the collar and the shell. Figure 11-34 shows the operation of an overrunning clutch. In figure 11-34A, the armature is turning, cranking the engine. The rollers are wedged against spring pressure into their slots. In figure 11-34B, the engine has started and is turning faster than the motor armature. Spring pressure pushes the rollers so that they float freely. The engine's motion is not transferred to the motor armature. These devices are sometimes called one-way clutches, because they transmit motion in one direction only.

Once the engine runs by itself, the ignition switch can be released from the start position. The solenoid hold-in winding is demagnetized, and a return spring moves the plunger out of the solenoid. This moves the shift lever back so that the overrunning clutch and pinion gear can slide away from the flywheel.

■ Kick Starter

Solenoid-operated and movable-pole shoe starters have been standard equipment for so long that a lot of people have forgotten that engines didn't always start at the turn of a key. The standard starter motor on Chevrolets from the 1930s through the 1940s was a "kick starter".

The motor and drive pinion were quite similar to the Delco-Remy starters used by GM today. In place of a solenoid, however, a large lever moved the pinion into mesh with the flywheel and closed the motor switch contacts. The lever pivoted on the engine bellhousing and had a large "button" that projected through the floorboard to the right of the accelerator. The driver turned the ignition key to Run and kicked the starter with his or her right foot. Because the starter "button" was close to the accelerator, the driver could operate the throttle and the starter at the same time.

The Chevrolet kick starter was simple and direct, but motorists demanded more convenience on modern cars. The kick starter disappeared from cars in 1948 and from trucks in the mid-1950s.

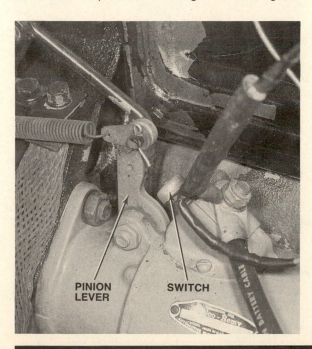

PINION LEVER   SWITCH

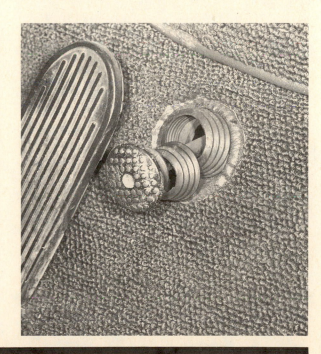

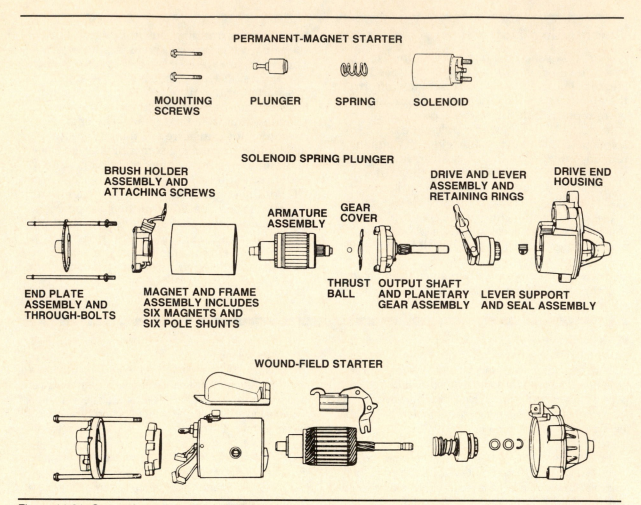

PERMANENT-MAGNET STARTER

MOUNTING SCREWS   PLUNGER   SPRING   SOLENOID

SOLENOID SPRING PLUNGER

BRUSH HOLDER ASSEMBLY AND ATTACHING SCREWS   ARMATURE ASSEMBLY   GEAR COVER   DRIVE AND LEVER ASSEMBLY AND RETAINING RINGS   DRIVE END HOUSING

END PLATE ASSEMBLY AND THROUGH-BOLTS   MAGNET AND FRAME ASSEMBLY INCLUDES SIX MAGNETS AND SIX POLE SHUNTS   THRUST BALL   OUTPUT SHAFT AND PLANETARY GEAR ASSEMBLY   LEVER SUPPORT AND SEAL ASSEMBLY

WOUND-FIELD STARTER

Figure 11-31. Comparison of the Ford PMGR starter motor components with those of a typical wound-field starter motor. (Ford)

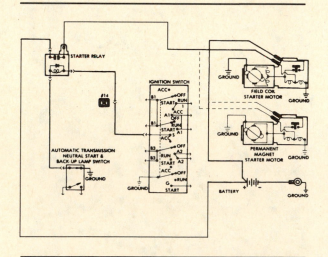

Figure 11-32. Field coils and permanent-magnet starters use the same electrical wiring. (Chrysler)

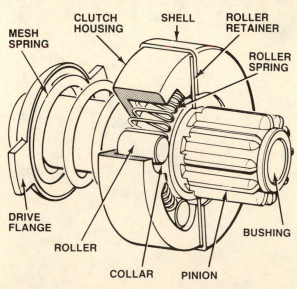

Figure 11-33. A cutaway view of an overrunning clutch.

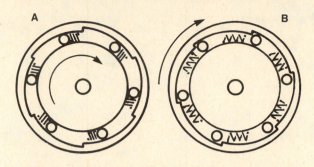

Figure 11-34. The operation of an overrunning clutch.

SUMMARY

Traditional starter motors have pole pieces wound with heavy copper field windings attached to the housing. A new design, the permanent-magnet (PM) planetary drive, uses small permanent magnets to create a magnetic field instead of pole pieces and field windings.

One end housing holds the brushes, the other end housing shield the pinion gear. The motor armature windings are installed on a laminated core and mounted on a shaft. The commutator bars are mounted on, but insulated from, the shaft.

The solenoid-actuated drive uses the movement of a solenoid to engage the pinion gear with the ring gear. Delco-Remy, Chrysler, Motorcraft, and many foreign manufacturers use this type of starter drive. The movable pole-shoe drive, used by Ford, has a pivoting pole piece that is moved by electromagnetism to engage the pinion gear with the ring gear. In the planetary gear drive used by Chrysler, Ford, and GM, an armature shaft sun gear meshes with the planetary pinions, which drive the pinion carrier in reduction as they rotate around the ring gear. The starter drive shaft is mounted on the carrier and driven at reduced speed and increased torque. An overrunning clutch is used with all starter designs to prevent the engine from spinning the motor and damaging it.

Review Questions
Choose the single most correct answer.
Compare your answers with the correct answers on page 431.

1. Starter motors usually have _____ pole shoes.
   a. Two
   b. Four
   c. Six
   d. Eight

2. The rotational force of a starter motor is:
   a. Polarized
   b. Rectified
   c. Torque
   d. Current

3. Which of the following is true of a shunt motor?
   a. It has high initial torque
   b. It operates at variable speeds
   c. It has only one path for current flow
   d. It is not often used as a starting motor

4. Which of the following is true of a compound motor?
   a. It has low initial torque
   b. It operates at variable speeds
   c. It has only one path for current flow
   d. It is often used as a starting motor

5. In a lap-wound motor armature, the two ends of each conductor are attached to commutator segments that are:
   a. Adjacent
   b. 45° apart
   c. 90° apart
   d. 180° apart

6. Most automotive starters have _____ grounded and _____ insulated brushes.
   a. 2,2
   b. 2,4
   c. 4,4
   d. 4,8

7. The ratio between the number of teeth on the flywheel and the motor pinion gear is about:
   a. 1:1
   b. 5:1
   c. 20:1
   d. 50:1

8. The overrunning clutch accomplishes which of the following?
   a. Separates the starter motor from the starter solenoid
   b. Brings the starter motor into contact with the ignition circuit
   c. Lets the starter motor rotate in either direction
   d. Protects the starter motor from spinning too rapidly

9. A starting motor must have _____ brushes as poles.
   a. The same number of
   b. Twice as many
   c. One-half as many
   d. Three times as many

10. The illustration below shows a:

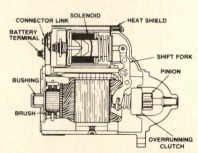

   a. Permanent magnet planetary gear starter
   b. Movable pole shoe starter
   c. Direct drive, solenoid-actuated starter
   d. Reduction gear drive, solenoid-actuated starter

11. Which type of starter drive is *not* used on late-model cars?
    a. Direct drive
    b. Bendix drive
    c. Reduction drive
    d. Planetary drive

12. A solenoid uses two coils. Their windings are called:
    a. Push-in and pull-out
    b. Pull-in and push-out
    c. Push-in and hold-out
    d. Pull-in and hold-in

13. Which of the following is true of a reduction drive?
    a. The motor armature drives the pinion directly
    b. The sun gear is mounted on the armature shaft
    c. The overrunning clutch reduces battery current
    d. The small gear driven by the armature is permanently meshed with a larger gear

14. The planetary drive starter uses:
    a. Permanent magnets
    b. Field coils
    c. Both a and b
    d. Neither a nor b

15. Which of the following is *not* required of a permanent magnet starter?
    a. Brush testing
    b. Commutator testing
    c. Field circuit testing
    d. Armature testing

PART FIVE

The Ignition System and Electronic Engine Controls

12

The Ignition System and Engine Operation

Automobile engines commonly used today burn a mixture of air and gasoline to produce power. The air-fuel mixture must be ignited by a spark before it can burn. This is the job of the ignition system. It must provide a high-voltage spark in the correct cylinder at the correct time for the most efficient combustion. This chapter explains the relationship between the engine and the ignition system. Chapters Thirteen and Fourteen cover the primary and secondary circuits. Chapter Fifteen explains ignition timing. Chapter Sixteen covers the solid-state electronic ignition systems, and Chapter Seventeen deals with electronic engine control systems.

ENGINE OPERATION

Modern automotive engines are called internal combustion engines because fuel burns inside the engine. The engine converts the burning fuel's thermal energy to mechanical energy.

Reciprocating Engine

Except for the Wankel rotary engine, all production automotive engines are the reciprocating, or piston, design. Reciprocating means "up and down" or "back and forth". It is this up and down action of a piston in a cylinder that gives the **reciprocating engine** its name. Almost all engines of this type are built upon a cylinder block, or engine block, figure 12-1. The block is an iron or aluminum casting that contains the engine cylinders. The top of the block is covered with the cylinder head, figure 12-2, which forms the combustion chambers.

Power is produced by the reciprocating motion of a piston in a cylinder, but this power must be changed to rotating power to turn the wheels of a car. The piston is attached to the top of a connecting rod by a pin, called a wristpin, figure 12-3. The bottom of the connecting rod is attached to the crankshaft. The connecting rod transmits the up-and-down motion of the piston to the crankshaft, which changes it to rotating motion.

Most automotive engines are fueled by gasoline. The gasoline is mixed with air and is drawn into the combustion chambers through valves. The mixture is compressed and then ignited by the spark plug. Force from the burning, expanding gases drives the piston down and makes the crankshaft turn.

One complete top-to-bottom or bottom-to-top movement of the piston is called a **stroke**, figure 12-4. One stroke of a piston causes the crankshaft to rotate 180 degrees. Two strokes of the piston cause the crankshaft to make a

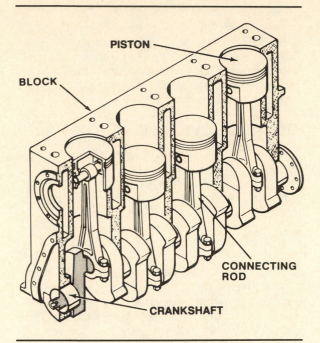

Figure 12-1. The automobile engine block.

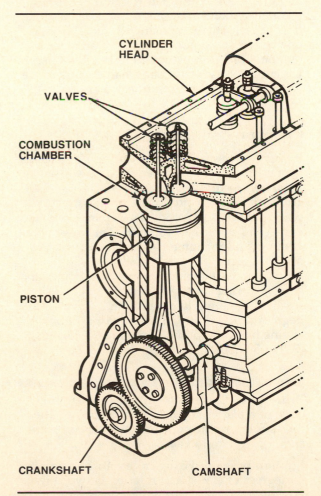

Figure 12-2. The cylinder head forms combustion chambers above the pistons.

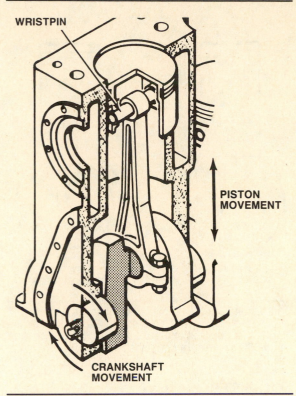

Figure 12-3. The reciprocating motion of the piston is converted to rotary motion of the crankshaft.

complete 360-degree revolution. In previous chapters, we have used the terms ''engine revolution'' and ''revolutions per minute (rpm)''. These terms refer to the complete 360-degree revolution of the crankshaft caused by two piston strokes.

Most automobile engines are a four-stroke, spark-ignition, reciprocating design. Other types of engines include two-stroke and compression-ignition (diesel) engines. Two-stroke engines are used mainly in motorcycles, lawnmowers, outboards, and other types of equipment. They are rarely used in automobiles and they are not covered in this text. Compression-ignition engines do not need a spark to ignite the air-fuel mixture; their high compression causes extreme heat which ignites the fuel. We will not discuss them here, because they do not have an electric ignition system.

Reciprocating Engine: Also called a piston engine. An engine in which the pistons move up and down or back and forth, as a result of combustion on the top of the cylinder.

Stroke: One complete top-to-bottom or bottom-to-top movement of an engine piston.

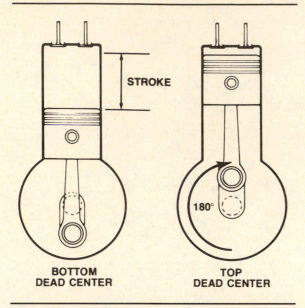

STROKE

BOTTOM DEAD CENTER   **TOP DEAD CENTER**

180°

Figure 12-4. One top-to-bottom or bottom-to-top movement of the piston is called a stroke. One piston stroke equals 180 degrees of crankshaft rotation; two strokes equal 360 degrees of crankshaft rotation.

FOUR-STROKE CYCLE

In the **four-stroke cycle**, four strokes of the piston, figure 12-5, are required to complete one operating cycle:

1. Intake stroke: as the piston moves downward, the air-fuel mixture is drawn into the cylinder through an intake valve.
2. Compression stroke: the intake valve closes and the upward stroke of the piston compresses the mixture, which is ignited by a spark.
3. Power stroke: with both valves closed, the expanding gases of combustion force the piston downward.
4. Exhaust stroke: the piston moves upward and pushes the burned gases out an open exhaust valve. The next stroke will be another intake stroke, and the cycle will repeat.

Ignition Interval

Every two strokes of a piston cause the crankshaft to rotate 360 degrees. Therefore, every four strokes of a piston cause the crankshaft to rotate 720 degrees (360 + 360 = 720). Since four strokes of a piston equal one engine operating cycle, that cycle equals 720 degrees of crankshaft rotation.

During the four strokes of the operating cycle, the spark plug fires only once, at the beginning of the power stroke. In a one-cylinder

engine, there would be only one ignition spark every 720 degrees of crankshaft rotation. These 720 degrees are called the **ignition interval**, or **firing interval**, of the engine. It is the number of degrees of crankshaft rotation that occurs between ignition sparks.

MULTIPLE-CYLINDER ENGINES

Up to this point, we have been talking about a single piston in a single cylinder. However, most car engines have four, six, or eight cylinders, although engines with one, two, three, five, ten, twelve, and sixteen cylinders have been built and used. In automotive engines, all pistons are connected to a single crankshaft, figure 12-1.

The more cylinders an engine has, the more power strokes are produced per engine revolution. A four-cylinder engine produces a power stroke four times as often as a one-cylinder engine. The four-cylinder engine has power strokes that are closer together in terms of time and degrees of crankshaft rotation.

A one-cylinder engine has one power stroke during each engine operation cycle, that is, one power stroke for every two crankshaft revolutions. In a four-cylinder engine, the operating cycles of each cylinder mean that there are four power strokes for every two crankshaft revolutions.

Common Ignition Intervals

If four power strokes occur during 720 degrees of crankshaft rotation, then each power stroke must occur every 180 degrees (720 ÷ 4 = 180). The ignition must produce a spark for every power stroke, so it produces a spark every 180 degrees of crankshaft rotation. This means that a four-cylinder engine has an ignition interval of 180 degrees.

An inline six-cylinder engine has six power strokes during every 720 degrees of crankshaft rotation, resulting in an ignition interval of 120 degrees (720 ÷ 6 = 120). An eight-cylinder engine has an ignition interval of 90 degrees (720 ÷ 8 = 90).

Four-Stroke Cycle: One complete operating cycle of a piston in a four-stroke engine. The four strokes of the cycle are: intake, compression, power, and exhaust.

Ignition Interval (Firing Interval): The number of degrees of crankshaft rotation between ignition sparks.

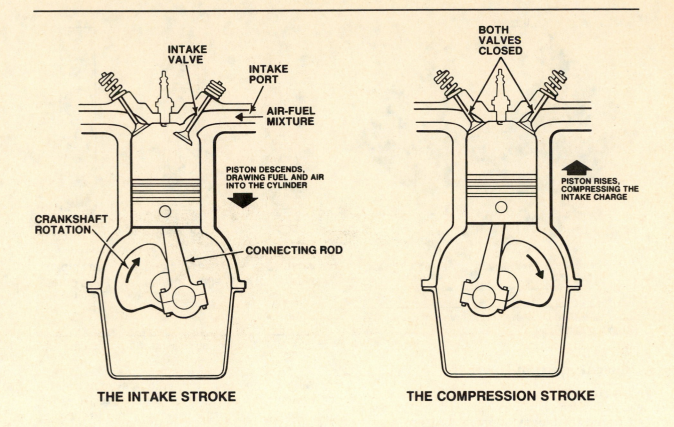

INTAKE VALVE
INTAKE PORT
AIR-FUEL MIXTURE
PISTON DESCENDS, DRAWING FUEL AND AIR INTO THE CYLINDER
CRANKSHAFT ROTATION
CONNECTING ROD

THE INTAKE STROKE

BOTH VALVES CLOSED
PISTON RISES, COMPRESSING THE INTAKE CHARGE

THE COMPRESSION STROKE

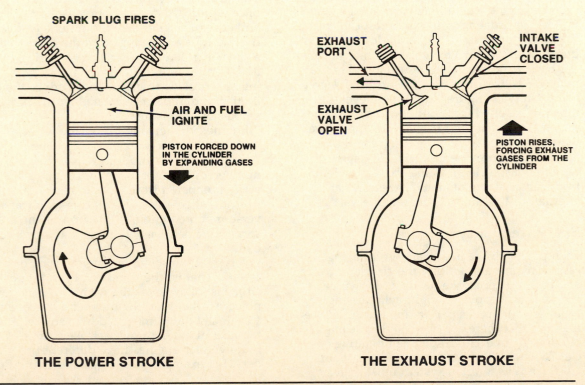

SPARK PLUG FIRES
AIR AND FUEL IGNITE
PISTON FORCED DOWN IN THE CYLINDER BY EXPANDING GASES

THE POWER STROKE

EXHAUST PORT
INTAKE VALVE CLOSED
EXHAUST VALVE OPEN
PISTON RISES, FORCING EXHAUST GASES FROM THE CYLINDER

THE EXHAUST STROKE

Figure 12-5. The four-stroke cycle.

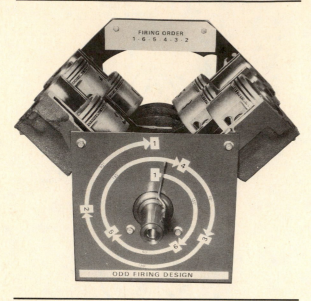

Figure 12-6. The uneven firing intervals of Buick's early V6 engine. (Buick)

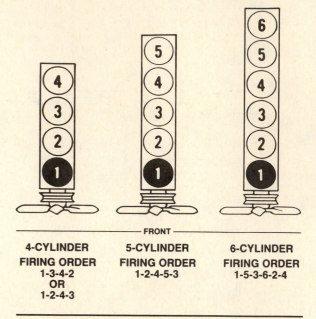

**4-CYLINDER
FIRING ORDER
1-3-4-2
OR
1-2-4-3**

**5-CYLINDER
FIRING ORDER
1-2-4-5-3**

**6-CYLINDER
FIRING ORDER
1-5-3-6-2-4**

Figure 12-7. Cylinder numbering of an inline engine.

Unusual Ignition Intervals

Most automotive engines have four, six, or eight cylinders, but some unusual engines are still being used today. Manufacturers such as Jaguar and Ferrari produce twelve-cylinder engines with a 60-degree firing interval. Audi of Germany has a five-cylinder engine with a 144-degree firing interval. Suzuki uses a three-cylinder engine with a 240-degree firing interval.

Other unusual firing intervals result from particular engine designs. General Motors has produced two different V6 engines from eight-cylinder blocks. A Buick engine developed in the early 1960s has alternating 90- and 150-degree firing intervals, figure 12-6. The uneven firing intervals resulted from building a V6 with a 90-degree crankshaft and block. This engine was modified in mid-1977 by redesigning the crankshaft to provide uniform 120-degree firing intervals, as in an inline six. Chevrolet introduced a V6 engine in 1978 that fires at alternating 108- and 132-degree intervals.

Spark frequency

Each power stroke in a spark-ignition engine is caused by a spark igniting the air-fuel mixture, and each power stroke needs an individual spark. For example, an eight-cylinder engine requires four sparks per engine revolution (remember that there are two 360-degree engine revolutions in each 720-degree operating cycle). When a V8 engine is running at about 1,000 rpm, its ignition system must deliver 4,000 sparks per minute. At an engine speed of about 4,000 rpm, the ignition system must deliver 16,000 sparks per minute. Precise ignition system performance is required to meet such demands.

FIRING ORDER

To cause each cylinder in an engine to fire once within 720 degrees of crankshaft rotation and at regular intervals, the pistons and connecting rods are arranged on the crankshaft in a specific order. This is called the **firing order** and it varies with different engine designs. Firing orders also are designed to reduce the vibration and imbalance created by the power strokes of the pistons.

Engine cylinders are numbered for easy identification. However, the cylinders do not usually fire in the order in which they are numbered. Straight, or inline, engines are generally numbered from front to rear, figure 12-7. In front-wheel-drive (FWD) cars with transverse-mounted engines, the front is the accessory (drive belt) end; the rear is the flywheel end.

A typical four-cylinder engine firing order is 1-3-4-2. That is, the number 1 cylinder power stroke is followed by the number 3 cylinder power stroke, then the number 4 power stroke and finally the number 2 power stroke. Then the next number 1 power stroke occurs. A few four-cylinder engines have different firing orders. For example, the English Ford and Pinto

1,600-cc engines fire 1-2-4-3. The Suzuki three-cylinder firing order is 1-3-2.

The cylinders of inline five- and six-cylinder engines also are numbered from front to rear, but do not fire in that order. The firing order for inline five-cylinder engines is 1-2-4-5-3, and the firing order for inline six-cylinder engines is 1-5-3-6-2-4, figure 12-7.

The cylinders of 90° V-type engines in domestic cars and in some Japanese imports are numbered the same, figure 12-8. The front cylinders are numbered 1 (driver's side) and 2

Firing Order: The order in which combustion occurs in the cylinders of an engine.

■ The Rotary Engine

The constant repetition of the reciprocating engine's two-way motion (up and down or back and forth) makes a piston engine the eventual instrument of its own destruction. Since the reciprocating engine must change the linear movement of its pistons into rotating power, engineers like Dr. Felix Wankel have long reasoned that there must be a more efficient approach. Dr. Wankel did more than reason; he developed the Wankel rotary engine, once used for automotive applications by NSU in Germany and by Curtiss-Wright aircraft in the U.S. Even General Motors once had plans to develop Wankel-powered vehicles. However, Dr. Wankel's rotary engine is best known for its use in Mazda RX-7 automobiles.

A rotary engine uses the same sequence of intake, compression, power, and exhaust as the reciprocating engine, but the power cycle takes place as separate stages in a single revolution of a three-sided or triangular rotor. The rotor revolves around, and turns, an eccentric shaft (equivalent to the reciprocating engine's crankshaft). The rotors ride on eccentric journals on the shaft, with shaft motion turning a flywheel.

Intake, compression, power, and exhaust phases of the rotor's revolution take place as the rotor passes and uncovers the intake port. The side of the rotor then turns to face the top of the housing, enlarging the combustion chamber and creating a vacuum that draws in the air-fuel mixture. As the rotor continues its movement, the air-fuel mixture is compressed and placed next to the spark plugs. One or both of the spark plugs fire, depending upon engine speed, load, and temperature. The expanding gases turn the rotor until its tip passes the exhaust port. As the rotor continues turning, the size

of the combustion chamber is reduced. The exhaust gases are then forced out and the cycle begins again.

A single rotor revolution results in a power phase for each face of the rotor, or a total of three per revolution. Since each rotor face acts as a piston, the ignition intervals of a single rotor engine are approximately equal to those of a three-cylinder reciprocating engine.

Rotary engines can be built with more than one rotor. By properly positioning multiple rotors and combining

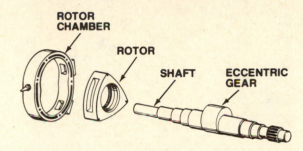

their power phases, it is possible to build a smooth, powerful engine that is considerably smaller than a comparable reciprocating design. The output of a two-rotor engine can equal that of a six-cylinder reciprocating engine. There are no valves, connecting rods, or pistons to self-destruct.

The rotary engine, however, does have its own design limitations and disadvantages. Mazda's initial engines had very poor sealing of the rotor tips, which led to major problems that temporarily gave the rotary engine a bad name. This problem has been solved, but rotary engines are still not as fuel-efficient as a comparable piston engine, although fuel injection and turbocharging have lessened the gap.

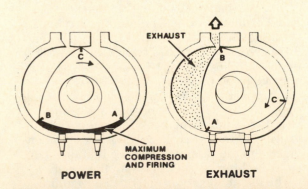

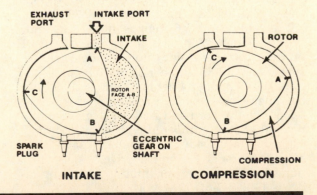

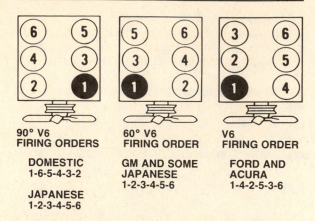

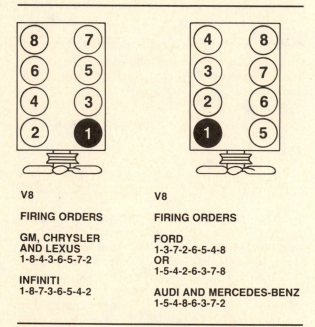

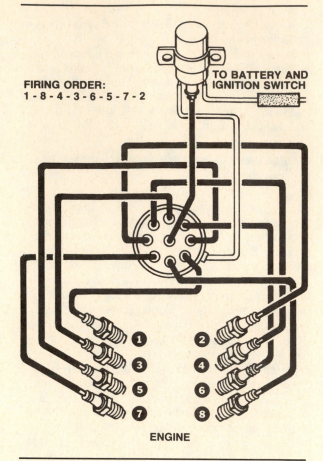

Figure 12-8. V6 engines are numbered in this way.

Figure 12-9. V8s have these firing orders.

Figure 12-10. The spark plug cables must be connected to the distributor in the proper firing order.

(passenger's side). Behind number 1 is number 3; behind number 2 is number 4; and so on. The firing order for most domestic 90° V6 engines numbered this way is 1-6-5-4-3-2. For Japanese versions, the firing order is 1-2-3-4-5-6.

The cylinders in V6 engines in GM cars and in some Japanese models are numbered with 1 on the passenger's side and 2 on the driver's side, figure 12-8. Number 3 comes behind number 1; number 4 behind number 2; and so on. The firing order for these engines is 1-2-3-4-5-6. Finally, Ford and Acura V6 cylinders, figure 12-8, are numbered with number 1 on the passenger's side, and numbers 2 and 3 behind it. Number 4 is on the driver's side, and numbers 5 and 6 come behind it. The firing order is 1-4-2-5-3-6.

V8 engine cylinders are numbered back and forth or straight back, depending on the manufacturer, figure 12-9. In GM, Chrysler, Lexus, and Infiniti engines, the number 1 cylinder is on the driver's side, and number 2 is on the passenger's side. Number 3 comes behind number 1; number 4 behind number 2; and so on. The firing order for the domestics and for Lexus is 1-8-4-3-6-5-7-2. The Infiniti firing order is 1-8-7-3-6-5-4-2. In Ford, Audi, and Mercedes-Benz V8s, the number 1 cylinder is on the passenger's side, and numbers 2, 3, and 4 come behind it. The number 5 cylinder is on the driver's side, and numbers 6, 7, and 8 are behind it. Ford has two possible firing orders: 1-3-7-2-6-5-4-8 or 1-5-4-2-6-3-7-8. The German V8 firing order is 1-5-4-8-6-3-7-2.

Whenever a V-type engine (or a horizontally opposed engine) is numbered from front to rear, the number one bank is located slightly forward of the other. When looking at the engine from the side, you will see that one valve cover is closer to the front than the other.

The distributor rotor must deliver ignition voltage to the correct cylinder at the correct

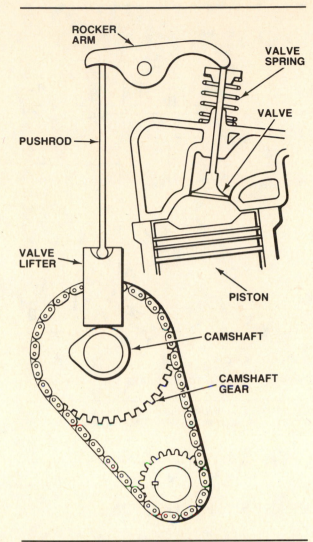

Figure 12-11. Valve mechanism for an overhead-valve engine.

time. To maintain the firing order, the spark plug cables must be attached to the distributor cap in the proper order, figure 12-10.

ENGINE-IGNITION SYNCHRONIZATION

During the engine operating cycle, the intake and exhaust valves open and close at specific times. The ignition system delivers a spark when the piston is near the top of the compression stroke and both valves are closed. These actions must all be coordinated, or engine damage could occur.

Valve Timing

The intake and exhaust valves are operated by the engine camshaft, figure 12-11. As the camshaft turns, its lobes cause the valves to open. The valves are closed by the valve springs.

Each valve opens and closes once per camshaft revolution, which equals one engine operating cycle. The engine crankshaft makes two complete revolutions during one engine operating cycle. Therefore, the camshaft must turn at *one-half* the speed of the engine crankshaft. The two shafts are connected by a chain, by a toothed belt, or by gears, figure 12-12. The gear on the end of the camshaft has twice as many teeth as does the gear on the end of the crankshaft, creating a 1:2 gear ratio.

To coordinate valve action with piston action, the camshaft's rotation must be synchronized with the rotation of the crankshaft. This is called **valve timing**. The gears on the ends of the two shafts are marked by the manufacturer, figure 12-13, and must be aligned during installation.

Valve Timing: A method of coordinating camshaft rotation and crankshaft rotation so that the valves open and close at the right times during each of the piston strokes.

■ The Rarest Firing Order of All

The booming economy of the 1920s encouraged Cadillac to design one of the grandest cars ever to hit the road, the Sixteen. Engines with sixteen cylinders have always been uncommon and this overhead-valve, 452 cubic-inch, V16 powerplant has one of the rarest of all firing orders: 1-8-9-14-3-6-11-2-15-10-7-4-13-12-5-16. Odd-numbered cylinders are on the left bank; even-numbered cylinders are on the right.

Unfortunately, Cadillac announced its new 16-cylinder machine just prior to the stock market crash of 1929 and the beginning of the Great Depression. Even with a large amount of the Sixteen's projected market gone, General Motors' vast financial strength kept the Sixteen alive for nine model years. Such expensive cars were difficult to sell and by 1938 fewer than 300 customers drove home in new Sixteens.

For 1939, Cadillac presented a new design which, though still a V16, was less expensive to produce. Based on the company's successful V8, the new engine was a 431 cubic-inch flat-head design. This engine's wide, 135-degree cylinder block required a new ignition interval, producing a unique firing order: 1-4-12-3-16-11-8-15-14-7-6-13-2-5-10.

Throughout the 1930s, technical advances improved Cadillac's V8 to the point that a V16 had no clear-cut advantages. Management prudently decided to concentrate on V8 engines, a policy they have broken only once in the last 50 years. The flat-head V16 lasted only one more year, until 1940, making it the very last production 16-cylinder automotive powerplant.

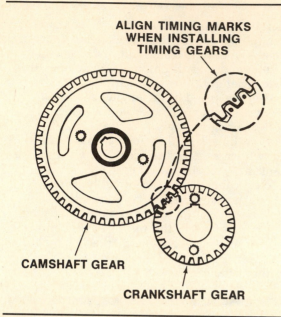

Figure 12-12. The camshaft is driven by the crankshaft at one-half crankshaft speed.

Distributor Drive

The distributor must supply one spark to each cylinder during each cylinder's operating cycle. The distributor cam has as many lobes as the engine has cylinders, or in a solid-state system, the trigger wheel has as many teeth as the engine has cylinders. One revolution of the distributor shaft will deliver one spark to each cylinder. Each cylinder needs only one spark for each *two* crankshaft revolutions. The distributor shaft must turn at one-half engine crankshaft speed. On most engines, therefore, the distributor is driven by the camshaft, which also turns at one-half crankshaft speed.

Distributorless Ignition

Many late-model engines have eliminated the distributor by using a multiple coil pack and the **waste spark** theory of ignition. In a distributorless ignition system, sensors indicate crankshaft and speed information to the engine control computer, which signals the ignition module when to fire a specific coil in the coil pack. Each coil fires two spark plugs at the same time. The plugs are connected to the coil so that when one fires during the compression stroke to ignite the air-fuel mixture, the other fires during the exhaust stroke when the spark is useless or wasted. Thus, a power stroke occurs on each cylinder event, with a wasted spark fired in an exhausting cylinder. The key to this method of engine-ignition synchronization is the ignition module, which determines

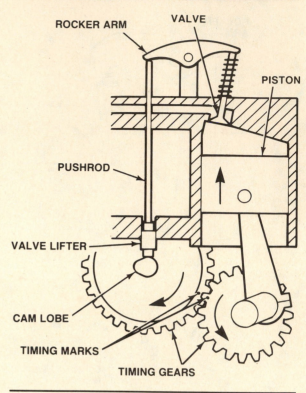

Figure 12-13. Timing marks on the timing gears synchronize valve action with piston movement.

coil turn on and firing time through crankshaft position and cylinder identification sensors.

CRANKSHAFT POSITION

The bottom of the piston stroke is called **bottom dead center (BDC)**, figure 12-14. The top of the piston stroke is called **top dead center (TDC)**. The ignition spark occurs near top dead center, as the compression stroke is ending. As the piston approaches the top of its stroke, it is said to be **before top dead center (BTDC)**. A spark that occurs before top dead center is called an advanced spark. As the piston passes top dead center and starts down, it is said to be **after top dead center (ATDC)**. A spark that occurs after top dead center is called a retarded spark.

Burn Time

Approximately three milliseconds (0.003 second) elapse from the instant the air-fuel mixture ignites until its combustion is complete. Remember that this burn time is a function of *time* and not of piston travel or crankshaft degrees. The ignition spark must occur early enough so that the combustion pressure reaches its maximum just after top dead center, when the piston is beginning its downward

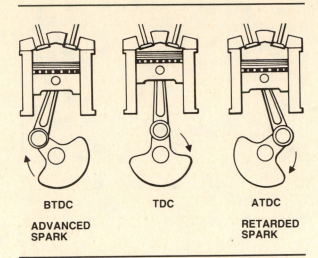

Figure 12-14. Piston position is identified in terms of crankshaft rotation.

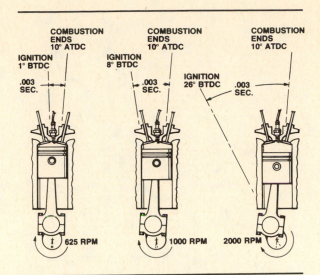

Figure 12-15. As engine speed increases, ignition timing must be advanced.

power stroke. Combustion should be completed by about 10° ATDC.

If the spark occurs too soon before top dead center, the rising piston will be opposed by combustion pressure. If the spark occurs too late, the force on the piston will be reduced. In either case, power will be lost. In extreme cases, the engine could be damaged. Ignition must start at the proper instant for maximum power and efficiency.

Engine Speed

As engine speed increases, piston speed increases. If the air-fuel ratio remains relatively constant, the fuel burning time will remain constant. However, at greater engine speed, the piston will travel farther during this burning time. Ignition timing must be changed to ensure that maximum combustion pressure occurs at the proper piston position.

For example, consider an engine, figure 12-15, that requires 0.003 second for the fuel charge to burn and that achieves maximum power if the burning is completed at 10° ATDC.

- At an idle speed of 625 rpm, figure 12-15A, the crankshaft rotates about 11 degrees in 0.003 second. Therefore, timing must be set at 1° BTDC to allow ample burning time.
- At 1,000 rpm, figure 12-15B, the crankshaft rotates 18° in 0.003 second. Ignition should begin at 8° BTDC.
- At 2,000 rpm, figure 12-15C, the crankshaft rotates 36° in 0.003 second. Spark timing must be advanced to 26° BTDC.

This change in timing is called spark advance, or ignition advance, and is explained in more detail in Chapter Fifteen.

INITIAL TIMING

As we have seen, ignition timing must be set correctly for the engine to run at all. This is called the engine's initial, or basic timing. Initial timing is the correct setting at a specified engine speed. In figure 12-15, initial timing was 1° BTDC. Initial timing is normally within a few degrees of top dead center. For many years, most engines were timed at the speci-

---

Waste Spark: An ignition system without a distributor in which one coil in a coil pack fires two spark plugs at the same time. The spark in the cylinder on compression ignites the air-fuel mixture, while the spark in the cylinder on its exhaust stroke is wasted.

Bottom Dead Center (BDC): The exact bottom of a piston stroke.

Top Dead Center (TDC): The exact top of a piston stroke. Also a specification used when tuning an engine.

Before Top Dead Center (BTDC): The position of a piston as it nears top dead center. Usually expressed in degrees, such as 5° BTDC.

After Top Dead Center (ATDC): The position of a piston after it has passed top dead center. Usually expressed in degrees, such as 5° ATDC.

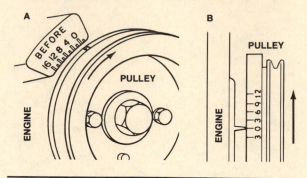

Figure 12-17. Typical timing marks.

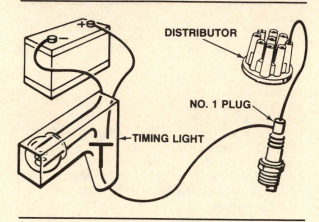

Figure 12-18. A diagram of the timing light connections.

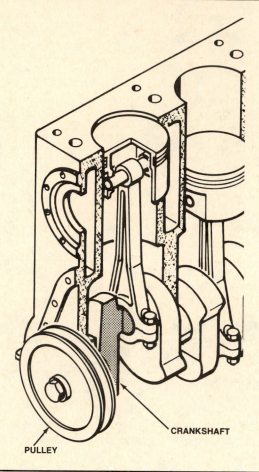

Figure 12-16. Most engines have a pulley bolted to the front end of the crankshaft.

fied slow-idle speed for the engine. However, since about 1974, many Ford, Oldsmobile, and Cadillac engines require timing at speeds either above or below the slow-idle speed.

Initial timing can be adjusted to compensate for mechanical wear, slippage, and other factors. We will learn more about setting the ignition timing in the *Shop Manual*. The following paragraphs describe the basics of initial timing.

Timing Marks

We have seen that initial timing is related to crankshaft position. To properly time the engine, we must be able to determine crankshaft position. The crankshaft is completely enclosed in the engine block, but most cars have a pulley and vibration damper or harmonic balancer bolted to the front of the crankshaft, figure 12-16. This pulley rotates with the crankshaft and can be considered an extension of the shaft.

Marks on the pulley show crankshaft position. For example, when a mark on the pulley is aligned with a mark on the engine block, the number 1 piston is at top dead center.

Timing marks vary widely, even within a manufacturer's product line. There are two common types of timing marks:

- A mark on the crankshaft pulley and marks on the engine block which represent degrees of crankshaft position, figure 12-17A.
- Marks representing degrees of crankshaft position on the pulley and a pointer on the engine block, figure 12-17B.

Some cars have timing marks on the engine flywheel. The flywheel is attached to the end of the crankshaft opposite the pulley. Hondas, some Opels, Dodge Omnis and Plymouth Horizons, Renaults, Saabs, and water-cooled Volkswagens, Audis, and Porsches have this type of timing mark. Some older domestic engines also used a flywheel timing mark.

Ignition Timing Light

A timing light is used with pulley and flywheel timing marks. It usually contains a tran-

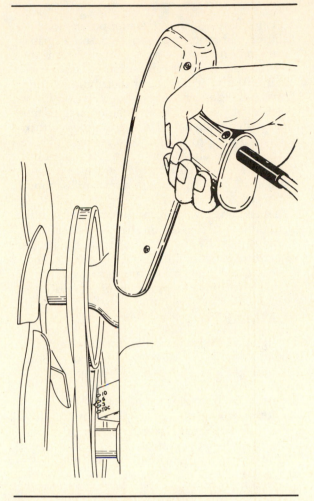

Figure 12-19. Using a timing light.

sistor installed so that a surge of secondary current will make the transistor conduct. The timing light is connected to the automobile battery terminals and the number 1 spark plug circuit, figure 12-18. When the number 1 spark plug receives a surge of ignition voltage, the transistor conducts and the timing bulb is lit by battery current.

When the engine is running, the timing light flashes very rapidly. This is a **stroboscopic effect**, so timing lights are called stroboscopic lights. When the timing light is aimed at the moving timing marks, figure 12-19, the marks appear to stand still with each flash of light. Since the light flashes as the number 1 spark plug fires, the position of the timing mark will show crankshaft position at the instant of ignition. The distributor can be rotated to change this, if necessary, until the correct degree mark appears opposite the pointer when the timing light flashes.

Electromagnetic Timing

Electromagnetic timing was introduced by major manufacturers as a more accurate timing method. Because special equipment for this newer method is required, timing marks are still put on most engines.

The system uses a timing pickup socket on the engine, figure 12-20, and a magnetic probe which is inserted into the socket. The timing socket may be located at the front of the engine, in the side of the engine block, or in the bellhousing. The magnetic probe is inserted into the socket. A tab, notch, or magnetic particle on the crankshaft, the crankshaft damper or harmonic balancer, or on the flywheel alters the magnetic reluctance around the pickup coil as it rotates past the probe. Solid-state electronic circuitry translates the electromagnetic impulses from the crankshaft into a readout of ignition timing on a digital or analog meter.

Electromagnetic timing is more accurate because:

- It eliminates the viewing angle error (parallax) on the part of the mechanic
- The crankshaft position signal comes directly from the crankshaft instead of the distributor.

Manufacturers use this method to time engines when they are assembled at the factory. Mechanics can use the method if they have the correct equipment.

Stroboscopic Effect: The effect caused by a rapidly flashing light as it makes moving objects appear stationary.

■ In Place of a Spark Plug

In the early "make-and-break" ignition system, a movable electrode and a stationary electrode were mounted close to each other and protruded into the side of an engine cylinder. The movable electrode, similar to a lever mounted on a rod, was operated by an outside pushrod that contacted a camshaft. The stationary electrode was insulated from the cylinder wall with mica. Battery current passed through a coil and a switch to reach the stationary electrode. The movable electrode was grounded to complete the electrical circuit.

As the camshaft rotated, it forced the movable electrode to open and close contact with the stationary electrode, "making and breaking" the circuit. Each time the circuit was opened, a spark occurred, igniting the air-fuel mixture in the cylinder.

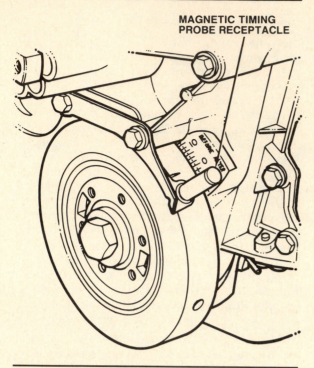

MAGNETIC TIMING
PROBE RECEPTACLE

Figure 12-20. The socket for an electromagnetic timing test probe often is near the pulley timing marks. (Chrysler)

Computer-Controlled Timing

Electromagnetic timing was an interim step between fully adjustable and completely non-adjustable ignition timing. Late-model engines increasingly allow the engine control computer to determine the correct time for combustion. Base ignition timing on such engines is fixed at the factory when the engine is assembled and installed in the vehicle. This eliminates the need for initial timing adjustments. However, as you have learned, constant spark timing adjustment is required for the best engine performance.

Various engine sensors provide the computer with constantly changing data about engine speed, coolant temperature, EGR flow rate, intake air temperature and volume, manifold absolute or barometric pressure, throttle position, and engine knock. Once these inputs are received by the computer, it compares them to its strategy, calibration, and adaptive learning data stored in memory. After processing this data, the computer signals the ignition module which spark plugs to fire and when to fire them.

Computer-controlled timing first eliminated the vacuum and centrifugal advance functions of the distributor. By reassigning these func-

tions to the engine control computer, no distributor calibration was required and adjusting base ignition timing was necessary only if the distributor was physically removed from the engine. With the advent of distributorless ignitions, base ignition timing is referenced to the position of the crankshaft position sensor relative to the crankshaft. During engine startup, the computer provides a fixed amount of fuel at the system's base timing until it picks up the reference signal which allows it to identify crankshaft position. In just a few milliseconds, it can correctly time or sequence fuel injection while sending five-volt, high-low pulses to the ignition module. The high-to-low transition signal is used by the module to fire the proper coil before or after the base timing pulse. In this way, the computer advances or retards timing according to engine requirements.

SUMMARY

The ignition system must be mechanically synchronized with engine operation to deliver an ignition spark to each cylinder at the correct time. Most automobile engines are reciprocating four-stroke engines. The four strokes of the four-stroke cycle are: intake, compression, power, and exhaust. Ignition occurs at the beginning of the power stroke.

One complete four-stroke cycle equals 720 degrees of crankshaft rotation. The sequence in which the cylinders of an engine fire is called the firing order. Firing intervals depend on the number of cylinders in an engine. A three-cylinder engine fires every 240 degrees; a four-cylinder engine fires every 180 degrees; an eight-cylinder engine fires every 90 degrees. Inline six-cylinder engines and even-firing V6 engines fire every 120 degrees. Some V6 engines fire at uneven intervals. The ignition distributor rotates at one-half engine speed to deliver an ignition spark at the right time to each cylinder.

Synchronizing ignition and engine operation is called ignition timing. Engine timing marks are used to set the initial ignition timing near top dead center on the engine's power stroke. The air-fuel mixture requires approximately three milliseconds to burn and deliver full power with the piston and crankshaft in the right position. As engine speed increases, spark timing must be advanced to allow enough burn time for combustion to be complete at the correct position of the piston and crankshaft.

Review Questions

Choose the single most correct answer.
Compare your answers with the correct answers on page 431.

1. How many strokes of a piston are required to turn the crankshaft through 360°?
   a. One
   b. Two
   c. Four
   d. Six

2. Most automobile engines are *not*:
   a. Four-stroke types
   b. Spark ignition types
   c. Reciprocating types
   d. Wankel types

3. One engine cycle equals _____ degrees of crankshaft rotation.
   a. 90°
   b. 180°
   c. 360°
   d. 720°

4. The firing interval of an engine is the number of degrees of crankshaft rotation that:
   a. Takes place in a four-stroke engine
   b. Is required to complete one full stroke
   c. Occurs between ignition sparks
   d. Takes place in a compression ignition engine

5. The sequence in which combustion occurs in an engine's cylinders is called the:
   a. Firing order
   b. Ignition interval
   c. Firing interval
   d. Four-stroke cycle

6. The intake and exhaust valves of each cylinder are operated by:
   a. Reduction gears
   b. Engine camshaft
   c. Firing relays
   d. Engine crankshaft

7. Valve timing is accomplished:
   a. By adjusting setscrews
   b. During camshaft installation
   c. By advancing or retarding spark timing
   d. None of the above

8. The distributor is driven by the:
   a. Crankshaft
   b. Rocker arms
   c. Connecting rods
   d. Camshaft

9. A "retarded spark" is one that occurs:
   a. At top dead center
   b. Before top dead center
   c. After top dead center
   d. At bottom dead center

10. Approximately _____ milliseconds elapse from the instant the air-fuel mixture ignites until its combustion is complete.
    a. 3
    b. 10
    c. 20
    d. 30

11. As engine speed increases, ignition timing:
    a. Must be advanced
    b. Must remain constant
    c. Must be retarded
    d. Varies inversely with the speed

12. Which of the following is *not* true of initial timing?
    a. It is the correct setting for a specified low speed
    b. It is normally within a few degrees of bottom dead center
    c. It can be adjusted to compensate for mechanical wear
    d. All of the above

13. Timing lights are also called _____ lights.
    a. Self-powered
    b. 12-volt test
    c. Power-seeking
    d. Stroboscopic

13

The Ignition Primary Circuit and Components

This chapter explains the components of the low-voltage primary ignition circuit and how the circuit operates. Breaker points were used to open and close the low-voltage primary circuit until the mid-1970s, when solid-state electronic switching devices took their place. Whether breaker points or electronic switches are used, however, the principles of producing high voltage by electromagnetic induction remain the same, as we will see.

NEED FOR HIGH VOLTAGE

Energy is supplied to the automotive electrical system by the battery. The battery can supply about twelve volts, but the voltage required to ignite the air-fuel mixture can range from 5,000 to more than 25,000 volts, depending upon engine operating conditions.

This high voltage is required to cause an arc across the spark plug air gap. The required voltage level increases when the:

- Spark plug air gap increases
- Engine operating temperature increases (resistance increases with greater temperature)
- Air-fuel mixture contains less fuel (fewer volatile fuel particles)
- Air-fuel mixture is at a greater pressure (resistance increases with an increase in pressure).

Since part of the ignition system's job is to provide a high-voltage spark, battery voltage must be greatly increased to meet the needs of the ignition system. This can be done by using electromagnetic induction, which we studied in Chapter Two.

HIGH VOLTAGE THROUGH INDUCTION

We know that a current-carrying conductor or coil is surrounded by a magnetic field. As current in the coil increases or decreases, the magnetic field expands or contracts. If a second coiled conductor is placed within this magnetic field, figure 13-1, the expanding or contracting magnetic flux lines will cut the second coil, causing a voltage to be induced in the second coil. This transfer of energy between two unconnected conductors is called mutual induction, as explained in Chapter Two.

Induction in the Ignition Coil

The ignition coil uses the principle of mutual induction to step up or transform low battery voltage to high ignition voltage. The ignition coil, figure 13-2, contains two windings of cop-

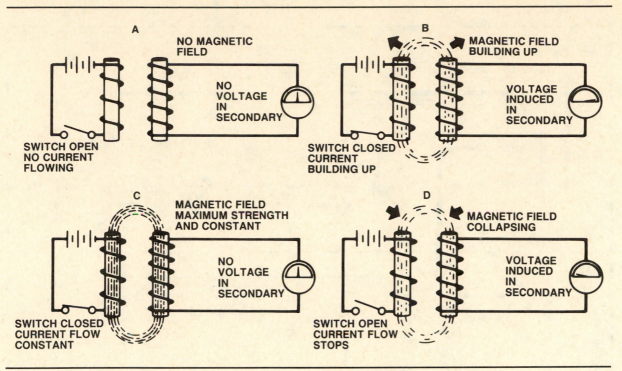

Figure 13-1. Mutual induction in the ignition coil supplies voltage to the spark plugs. (Prestolite)

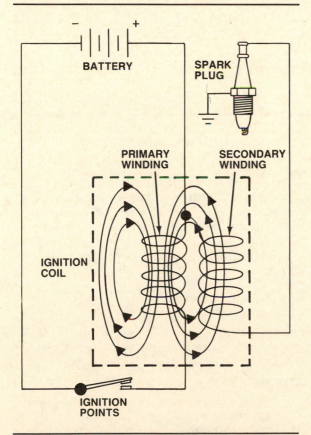

Figure 13-2. The ignition coil produces high-voltage current in the secondary winding when current flow is cut off in the primary winding.

per wire around a soft iron core. The primary winding is made of a hundred or so turns of heavy wire. It is connected to the battery so that current flows through it. The secondary winding is made of many thousand turns of fine wire. When current flow in the primary winding increases or decreases, a voltage is induced in the secondary winding, figure 13-2.

The ratio of the number of turns in the secondary winding to the number of turns in the primary winding can be between 100:1 and 200:1. This ratio is the voltage multiplier. That is, any voltage induced in the secondary winding will be 100 to 200 times the voltage present in the primary winding.

Several factors govern the coil's induction of voltage. Only two of these factors can be controlled easily in an ignition system. Induced voltage will increase with:

- More magnetic flux lines (a stronger magnetic field caused by greater current flow)
- More rapid movement of flux lines (faster collapse of the field caused by an abrupt end to current flow).

Normal voltage applied to the coil primary winding is about nine to ten volts (at high speeds, voltage may rise to twelve volts or more). This voltage causes from one to four amperes of current to flow in the primary winding. When this current is flowing, a magnetic field builds up around the windings.

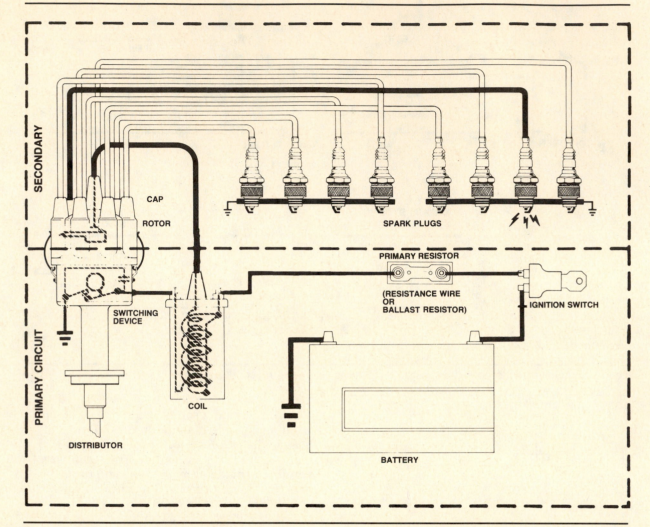

Figure 13-3. The ignition system is divided into the primary circuit and the secondary circuit. (Prestolite)

Building up a complete magnetic field is called **magnetic saturation**, or coil saturation. When this current flow stops, the primary winding's magnetic field collapses. A greater voltage is self-induced in the primary winding by the collapse of its own magnetic field. This self-induction creates from 250 to 400 volts in the primary winding. If it develops 250 volts and the turns ratio multiplies this by 100, then 25,000 volts will be induced in the secondary winding. This is enough voltage to ignite the air-fuel mixture under almost all operating conditions.

This kind of ignition system, based on the induction of a high voltage in a coil, is called an **inductive-discharge ignition** system. An inductive-discharge system using a battery as the source of low-voltage current has been the standard automotive ignition system for about eighty years.

We have seen that the ignition system can transform low battery voltage into high ignition voltage. Now we can look at the ignition system circuitry to see how the system works.

BASIC CIRCUITS AND CURRENT FLOW

The ignition system, figure 13-3, consists of two interconnected circuits:

- The primary (low-voltage) circuit
- The secondary (high-voltage) circuit.

When the ignition switch is turned on, battery current flows:

- Through the ignition switch and the primary resistor
- To and through the coil primary winding
- Through a switching device (breaker points or solid-state device)
- To ground and the grounded terminal of the battery.

Low-voltage current flow in the coil primary winding creates a magnetic field. When the switching device interrupts this current flow:

- A high-voltage surge is induced in the coil secondary winding
- Current flows through an ignition cable from the coil to the distributor
- Current passes through the distributor cap, rotor, across the rotor air gap, and through another ignition cable
- Current flows to the spark plug, where it arcs to ground.

The inductive-discharge battery ignition system was invented by Charles F. Kettering in 1908. He used a set of contact points as a mechanical switch to open and close the circuit to the primary winding of the ignition coil. These contacts are opened by the rotation of a cam on the distributor shaft. They are called **breaker points** because they continually break the primary circuit.

Kettering's ignition system was quickly adopted as the standard for the automotive industry and was used virtually unchanged for over sixty years. By the early 1970s, though, solid-state electronic components began to replace breaker points as switching devices for the primary circuit. The electronic or breakerless ignitions on late-model cars still use the inductive-discharge principles to produce a high-voltage spark. However, the primary circuits are controlled by electronic rather than mechanical switching devices.

PRIMARY CIRCUIT COMPONENTS

The primary circuit, figure 13-3, contains the:

- Battery
- Ignition switch
- Primary (ballast) resistor (in some systems)
- Starting bypass (in some systems)
- Switching device in the distributor
- Coil primary winding.

Battery

The battery supplies low-voltage current to the ignition primary circuit. This current flows when the ignition switch is in the Start or the Run position.

Ignition Switch

The ignition switch controls low-voltage current through the primary circuit. This current can flow when the ignition switch is in the Start or the Run position. Other switch positions route current to accessory circuits and lock the steering wheel in position.

Manufacturers use differing ignition switch circuitry. The differences lie in how battery current is routed to the switch. Regardless of variations, full system voltage is always present at the switch, as if it were connected directly to the battery.

Magnetic Saturation: The condition when a magnetic field reaches full strength and maximum flux density.

Inductive-Discharge Ignition: A method of igniting the air-fuel mixture in an engine cylinder. It is based on the induction of a high voltage in the secondary winding of a coil.

Breaker Points: The metal contact points that act as an electrical switch in a distributor. They open and close the ignition primary circuit.

■ Charles Franklin Kettering (1876-1958)

Charles F. Kettering was a leading inventor and automotive engineer. After graduating from Ohio State University, he became chief of the inventions department at the National Cash Register Company. While there he designed a motor used in the first electrically operated cash register.

In 1909, he helped form a company called Dayton Engineering Laboratories Company, later to be known as Delco. In 1917, he became the president and general manager of the General Motors Research Corporation.

Kettering invented both the automobile self-starter and the inductive-discharge battery ignition system. The accompanying illustration is an early sketch by Kettering of his design for an ignition system. He was involved in the invention and perfection of high-octane gasoline; improvements for engines, especially diesel engines; electric refrigeration; and much more. He also helped establish the Sloan-Kettering Institute for Cancer Research in New York City.

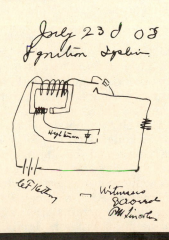

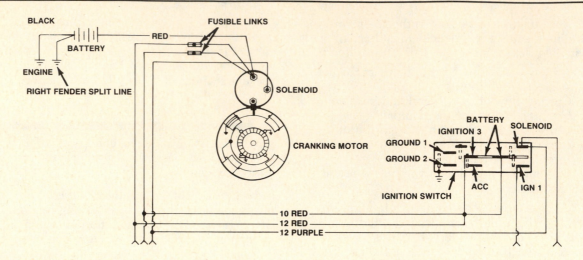

Figure 13-4. General Motors products draw current from a terminal on the starter solenoid. (Buick)

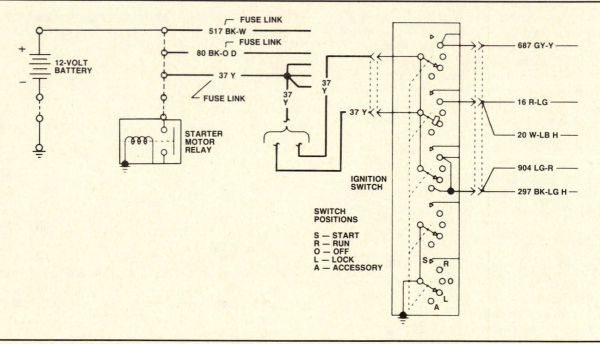

Figure 13-5. Ford products draw ignition current from a terminal on the starter relay. (Ford)

General Motors automobiles draw ignition current from a terminal on the Delco-Remy starter motor solenoid, figure 13-4. Ford Motor Company systems draw ignition current from a terminal on the Motorcraft starter relay, figure 13-5. In Chrysler Corporation cars, ignition current comes through a wiring splice installed between the battery and the alternator, figure 13-6. American Motors cars use the Delco-Remy starter system on some four-cylinder and V6 GM engines. AMC vehicles with AMC engines used the Motorcraft starter relay with one of two different alternators. Ignition cur-

rent was drawn through a wiring splice between the battery and the starter relay to simplify the circuitry, figure 13-7. Older imported and domestic automobiles may use different connections, such as drawing ignition current from a terminal on the voltage regulator.

Ballast (Primary) Resistor

For an ignition coil to have uniform secondary voltage capabilities over a wide range of engine speeds, complete saturation of its mag-

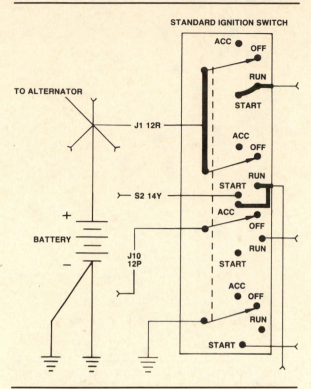

Figure 13-6. Chrysler products draw ignition current from a wiring splice between the battery and the alternator. (Chrysler)

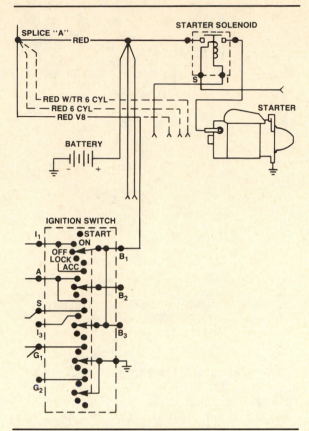

Figure 13-7. AMC products drew ignition current from a wiring splice between the battery and the starter relay. (AMC)

netic fields must be developed at these varying speeds. Magnetic saturation depends on the amount of voltage applied to the coil and the amount of current flowing in the windings. It also depends on the length of time the current flows.

An automotive ignition system does not operate with uniform current and voltage or current flow time. When the starter is cranking, the high current draw of the starter motor drops system voltage to about ten or eleven volts. For this reason, the ignition coil must be able to produce enough secondary voltage to fire the engine with only ten volts of primary voltage applied. Also, at high engine speeds, primary current flow time is reduced to only a few milliseconds. Therefore, uniform coil saturation must develop under extremes of low voltage and short current flow time. To achieve this, most twelve-volt ignition coils are designed to operate on nine or ten volts under most conditions.

As we have mentioned, the starter motor drops ignition system voltage to about ten volts when the engine is cranking. As soon as the engine starts, however, system voltage rises to twelve volts or more. To maintain the ignition primary voltage at the desired level, a

resistor is installed in the primary circuit of all domestic automobile breaker-point ignitions. This is called the **ballast (primary) resistor**, figure 13-8.

The ballast resistor compensates for changes in voltage and current caused by engine speed and temperature changes. The resistor provides about one-half of the total primary circuit resistance (the coil is the other half) and is the only part of the primary circuit that is temperature compensated.

At low speeds, current flows through the circuit for relatively long periods of time. As the current heats the resistor, its resistance increases, dropping the applied voltage at the coil. At higher speeds, the breaker points open more often and current flows for shorter periods of time. As the ballast resistor cools, its resistance drops. Higher voltage is applied to the

---

Ballast (Primary) Resistor: A resistor in the primary circuit that stabilizes ignition system voltage and current flow.

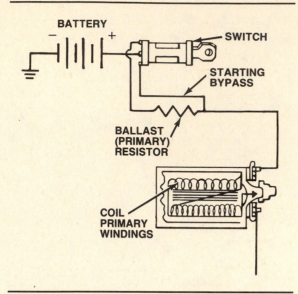

Figure 13-8. A ballast (primary) resistor can protect the primary circuit from excessive voltage.

coil but the shorter current flow duration results in about the same magnetic saturation of the coil.

The ballast resistor simply evens out the voltage and current of the primary circuit. In doing so, it reduces peak voltage at the coil and thus reduces current that would burn the breaker points faster. This is its most noticeable effect.

During cranking, the ballast resistor is bypassed to provide full available battery voltage to the primary circuit. This is done with a low-resistance starting bypass circuit in parallel with the ballast resistor, figure 13-8. When the engine starts, the bypass circuit opens and primary current flows through the resistor. Ignition primary voltage is reduced to the desired level. The ignition, breaker points, and coil are not damaged by this because:

- The ballast resistor is bypassed for a very short time
- The battery voltage available during cranking is already reduced to a safe level.

Bypassing the ballast resistor at times other than cranking would cause rapid burning of the breaker points and could damage the coil primary winding.

Electronic ignitions with fixed dwell use a ballast resistor in the primary circuit to limit current and voltage. Variable dwell electronic ignitions do not require one, because the ignition module or computer regulates primary current and voltage to the coil. The following are descriptions of the installation in late-model domestic cars.

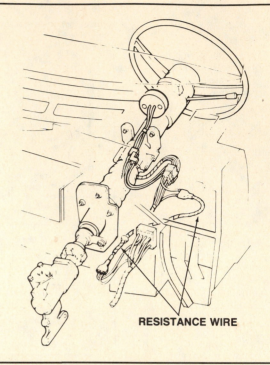

RESISTANCE WIRE

Figure 13-9. Ford products have a length of resistance wire installed near the ignition switch. (Ford)

- Ford products (except those with Dura Spark I or TFI electronic ignitions) have a length of resistance wire installed near the ignition switch, figure 13-9.
- Chrysler products built through 1977 have two ballast resistors in one ceramic holder mounted on the firewall, figure 13-10. A 0.5-ohm resistor is connected between the ignition switch and the coil; a five-ohm resistor is part of the electronic ignition control module circuitry.

The 1977 318-cid V8 and all 1977 and later Chrysler electronic lean burn (ELB) and electronic spark control (ESC) systems have only the 0.5-ohm ballast resistor. With the change from an analog to a digital computer in 1980, Chrysler eliminated the ballast resistor from its six- and eight-cylinder ignitions.

Chrysler front-wheel-drive (FWD) cars from 1978 through 1979 (California) and 1980 (Federal) used an analog computer and the 0.5-ohm ballast resistor. The resistor was eliminated on 1980 California and 1981 Federal FWD cars with the introduction of a digital spark control computer.

- General Motors vehicles using the Prestolite BID or Delco-Remy HEI breakerless ignitions have no ballast resistor.

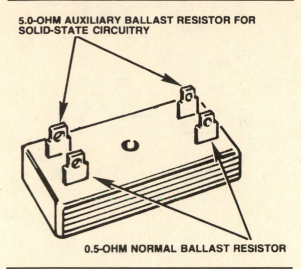

Figure 13-10. Chrysler's dual ballast resistor protects both the primary circuit and the solid-state ignition circuitry.

Starting Bypass

When the ballast resistor is bypassed during cranking, battery current flows to the primary circuit through a parallel circuit branch called the **starting bypass**. Current through this parallel branch can be controlled either by the ignition switch or by the starter relay or solenoid.

When the starting bypass is controlled directly by the ignition switch, figure 13-11, the ballast resistor is connected between the Run position contacts and the coil primary winding. When the ignition switch is in the Start position, full battery voltage is applied to the coil primary winding. Larger Ford automobiles and pre-1977 Chrysler products use this starting bypass method.

When the starting bypass is controlled by a starter relay or solenoid, figure 13-12, the ballast resistor is again connected between the Run ignition switch contacts and the coil. When the ignition switch is turned to Start, current through the starter relay or solenoid closes a set of contact points. Battery current will flow through the relay or solenoid to the coil primary winding through a parallel circuit.

Small Ford automobiles and 1977 and later Chrysler products control the starting bypass through the starter relay. The starting bypass on GM cars is controlled through the starter solenoid.

Switching Devices

The magnetic field of the coil primary winding must collapse totally in order to induce a high

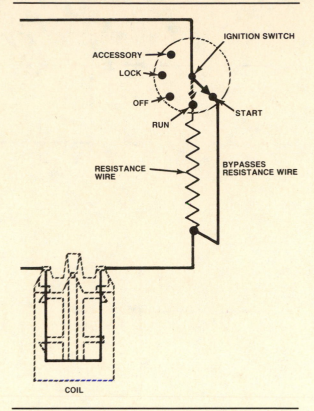

Figure 13-11. The ignition switch can control the starting bypass circuit.

voltage in the secondary winding. For the field to collapse, current through the primary winding must stop very *rapidly*. Current must then start and stop again, to induce the next high-voltage discharge. The primary circuit needs a switching device that rapidly breaks and completes the circuit to start and stop the current. For more than sixty years, ignition systems used breaker points as a mechanical switch. Since the mid-1970s, solid-state electronic devices have replaced breaker points.

Breaker points
The ignition breaker-point assembly, figure 13-13, includes the:

- Fixed contact
- Movable contact
- Movable arm
- Rubbing block
- Pivot
- Spring
- Breaker plate.

Starting Bypass: A parallel circuit branch that bypasses the ballast resistor during engine cranking.

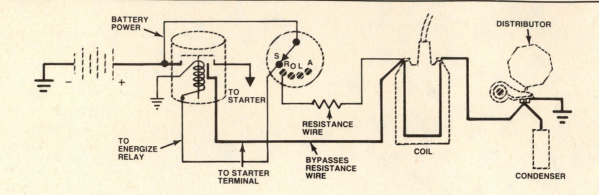

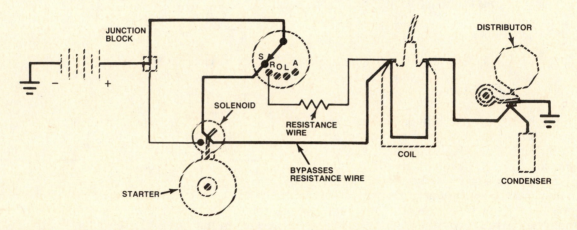

Figure 13-12. The starting bypass circuit can be controlled by the starter relay (top) or the solenoid-point (bottom).

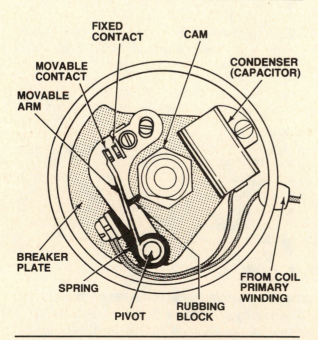

Figure 13-13. Ignition breaker-point (contact) assembly.

Both breaker points are made from tungsten, an extremely hard metal with a high melting point. The fixed contact is grounded through the distributor housing. The movable contact is insulated from the distributor housing and is connected to the negative terminal of the coil primary winding. Because current flows from the movable to the fixed contact, the movable contact can be labeled + and the fixed contact can be labeled – in a negative-ground system.

The movable contact is mounted on a movable arm. The arm also holds a rubbing block, a small piece of plastic or other synthetic nonconductive material that rides on the surface of the distributor cam. As the cam rotates, the lobes push the arm to open the breaker points. The spring closes the points when the cam lobes move away from the rubbing block.

The pivot and spring control the movement of the arm. The entire assembly is mounted on the breaker plate, which is attached to the distributor housing with screws.

The distributor cam is mounted on the centrifugal advance shaft, or driven assembly,

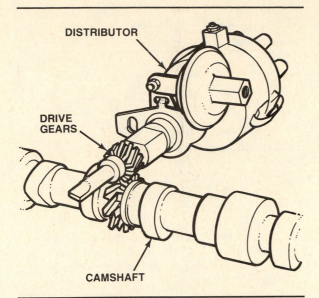

Figure 13-14. The gear on the distributor shaft is driven by another gear on the engine camshaft.

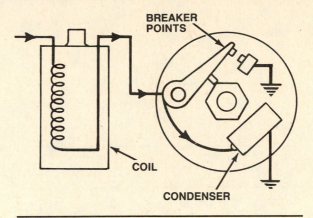

Figure 13-15. The condenser or capacitor prevents arcing as the breaker points open.

which is driven through the centrifugal advance weights by the distributor shaft. The distributor shaft is driven by the engine camshaft through gears, figure 13-14. Every opening of the breaker points induces a pulse of high-voltage current in the secondary circuit, and a spark plug fires. The breaker points must open as many times during one rotation of the cam as the engine has spark plugs. The cam, therefore, has as many lobes as the engine has spark plugs. The cam and points shown in figure 13-13 would be installed on a six-cylinder engine.

When the breaker points open, a voltage is self-induced in the coil primary winding, which would cause a damaging arc across the breaker points. To avoid this, a capacitor, or condenser, is wired in parallel with the breaker points, figure 13-15. The condenser prevents most arcing across the points, as we will see later.

Solid-state switching devices
Breaker-point ignitions make it difficult for an engine to meet today's exhaust emission control standards. Such standards not only require maximum system performance, they also require *consistent performance*. Because breaker points wear during normal operation, ignition system settings and performance change.

Since solid-state switching devices do not wear, ignition system performance remains consistent and emission control can be effectively maintained. Virtually all carmakers now use solid-state ignition systems. Although we will study the more common ignitions in

detail in Chapter Sixteen, we will look now at the most widely used solid-state switching devices.

■ Dual-Point, Dual-Coil, Dual-Plug Ignition

Some early Nash automobiles used a "Twin Ignition" system. This system had two ignition coils, two sets of spark plugs and cables, a distributor with 16 plug terminals and two coil wire terminals, a rotor with offset tips, two sets of breaker points, and two condensers.

The inline engines were designed with the spark plugs on both sides of the cylinders. The overhead valves were located directly over each cylinder in a vertical position.

The breaker points were synchronized by using a dual-bulb test lamp. With the ignition switch on, the distributor cam was turned to just break a stationary set of points, thereby lighting one bulb. A movable set of points was then adjusted to break contact, and light the second bulb, at the same instant. This adjustment assured that both sparks would occur in a cylinder at the same time.

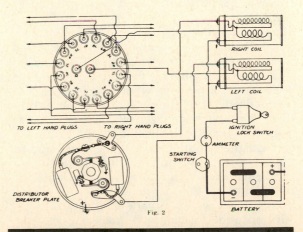

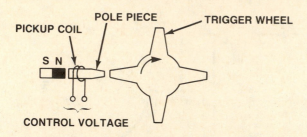

Figure 13-16. A simple magnetic pulse generator. (Bosch)

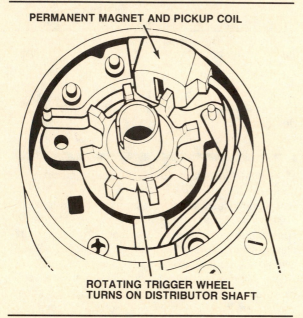

Figure 13-17. A magnetic pulse generator installed in the distributor housing. (Ford)

MANUFACTURER	STATIONARY PICKUP COIL	ROTATING TRIGGER WHEEL
BOSCH	PICKUP COIL & POLE PIECE	TRIGGER WHEEL
CHRYSLER	PICKUP COIL	RELUCTOR
FORD	STATOR	ARMATURE
GM	MAGNETIC PICKUP & POLE PIECE	TIMER CORE
NISSAN	STATOR	RELUCTOR
TOYOTA	PICKUP COIL	SIGNAL ROTOR

Figure 13-18. Manufacturers have different names for the trigger wheels and pickup coils or sensors in breakerless distributors, but all devices serve the same purpose.

A solid-state control module is responsible for switching the primary current on and off. The module must be signalled *when* to turn the current off. Of the four devices commonly used to do this, magnetic pulse generators and Hall-effect switches are the most common. Chrysler and some Japanese carmakers, such as Isuzu, use optical signal generators. A metal-detection switching device was last used by Prestolite from 1975 through 1977.

The **magnetic pulse generator** is installed in the distributor housing where the breaker points used to be. The pulse generator, figure 13-16, consists of a trigger wheel, a permanent magnet, a pole piece affected by the permanent magnet, and a pickup coil wound around the pole piece. The only moving part is the trigger wheel, which rotates as a distributor cam would.

The trigger wheel is made of steel with a low reluctance that cannot be permanently magnetized. Therefore, it provides a low-resistance

path for magnetic flux lines. The trigger wheel has as many teeth as the engine has cylinders.

As the trigger wheel rotates, its teeth come near the pole piece. Flux lines from the pole piece concentrate in the low-reluctance trigger wheel, increasing the magnetic field strength and inducing a voltage in the pickup coil. The pickup coil is connected to the electronic control module, which senses this voltage and switches the primary current off. Each time a trigger wheel tooth comes near the pole piece, the control module is signalled to switch off the primary current. Solid-state circuitry in the module determines when the primary current will be turned on again.

The simple pulse generator shown in figure 13-16 would be installed in a four-cylinder engine. Figure 13-17 shows the typical construction of a pulse generator for an eight-cylinder engine.

We have used the terms "trigger wheel" and "pickup coil" in describing the magnetic pulse generator. Various manufacturers have different names for these components, figure 13-18, but all serve the same purpose.

A **Hall-effect switch** also uses a stationary sensor and rotating trigger wheel (shutter), figure 13-19. Unlike the magnetic pulse generator, it requires a small input voltage in order to generate an output or signal voltage. As used in some Chrysler distributors, the rotor has a shutter blade for each cylinder (Ford and GM use a separate ring of metal blades). The pickup plate in the distributor housing contains a gate which the shutter blades pass as the distributor shaft rotates. An integrated circuit (IC) mounted on the plate faces the switch. As a shutter blade enters the air gap between the IC and the Hall-effect switch, it bypasses the magnetic field around the pickup, causing the Hall-effect output voltage to change. This changes the bias to the ignition module, just as a magnetic pulse generator signal does.

The optical signal generator uses the principle of light beam interruption to generate volt-

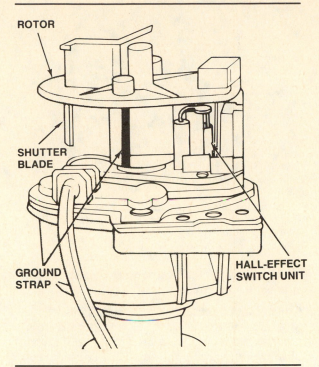

Figure 13-19. Shutter blades rotating through the Hall-effect switch air gap bypass the magnetic field around the pickup and drops the voltage output to zero. (Chrysler)

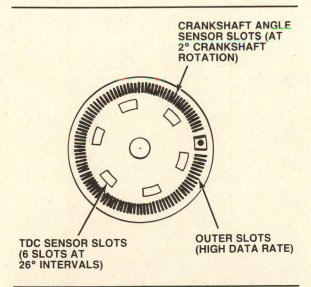

Figure 13-20. The optical signal generator works by interrupting a beam of light passing from the LEDs to photodiodes. (Chrysler)

age signals. As used by Chrysler with its dual-cam 3.0-liter engine, the optical signal distributor contains a pair of light-emitting diodes (LEDs) and photo diodes installed opposite each other, figure 13-20. A disc containing two sets of chemically etched slots is installed between the LEDs and photo diodes. Driven

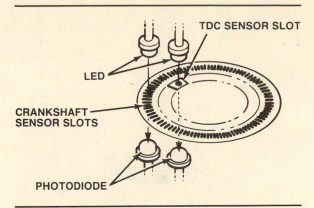

Figure 13-21. Each row of slots in the optical distributor disc acts as separate sensor, creating signals used to control fuel injection, ignition timing, and idle speed. (Chrysler)

by the forward bank camshaft, the disc acts as a timing member and revolves at half engine speed. As each slot interrupts the light beam, an alternating voltage is created in each photo diode. A hybrid integrated circuit converts the alternating voltage into on-off pulses sent to the engine controller.

The high-data-rate slots, or outer set, are spaced at intervals of two degrees of crankshaft rotation, figure 13-21. This row of slots is used for timing engine speeds up to 1,200 rpm. Certain slots in this set are missing, indicating the crankshaft position of the Number 1 cylinder to the engine controller. The low-data-rate slots, or inner set, consists of six slots correlated to the crankshaft top-dead-center angle of each cylinder. The engine computer uses this signal for triggering the fuel injection system and for ignition timing at speeds above 1,200 rpm. In this way, the optical signal generator acts both as the crankshaft position sensor and TDC sensor, as well as a switching device.

Coil Primary Winding

The coil primary winding, figure 13-22, is made of about 100 to 150 turns of a relatively heavy copper wire. The coil turns are insulated from each other by a thin coat of enamel. The

Magnetic Pulse Generator: A signal-generating switch that creates a voltage pulse as magnetic flux changes around a pickup coil.

Hall-Effect Switch: A signal-generating switch that develops a transverse voltage across a current-carrying semiconductor when subjected to a magnetic field.

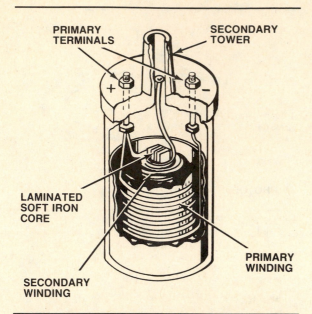

Figure 13-22. An ignition coil cutaway showing the primary and secondary windings.

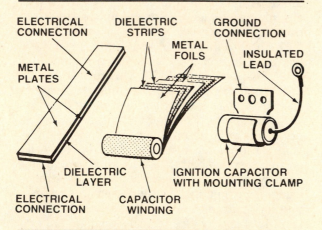

Figure 13-23. The construction of an ignition condenser.

two ends of the winding are connected to two terminals on the top of the coil. With a negative-ground electrical system, the coil + terminal is connected to the battery + terminal; the coil – terminal is connected to the ignition breaker points and through the points to ground. With a positive-ground system, the coil primary connections are reversed. We will look at the coil in greater detail in Chapter Fourteen.

Condensers

We learned in Chapter Two that a condenser or capacitor can absorb and store electrical charges. The condenser acts as an ''electric

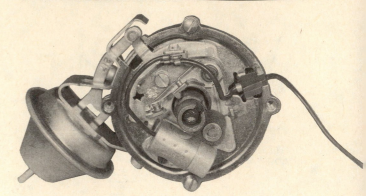

Figure 13-24. A condenser installed inside the distributor housing.

shock absorber'' to dampen any excessive voltage levels in a circuit.

Condenser construction and installation
Most automotive condensers are formed from two thin foil strips separated by several layers of insulating paper, figure 13-23. These layers, each more than eight feet long, are tightly rolled into a cylinder. The foil strips are offset, so that the top edge of one strip protrudes past the paper on one end of the cylinder and the bottom edge of the other strip protrudes from the other end of the cylinder. These edges provide an electrical contact with foil strips. The edges are flattened and the cylinder is installed in a metal canister. The bottom of the canister contacts one foil edge and grounds it. The other foil edge is connected to an insulated lead at the top of the canister.

To ensure ample insulation between the foil strips, the canister is placed in a vacuum. Wax or oil is drawn into the canister and the entire unit sealed. Condensers cannot be adjusted or repaired, but must be replaced if defective.

An assembled condenser is usually installed inside the distributor housing on the breaker plate, figure 13-24. The bracket is held to the breaker plate by a screw. This is the ground connection. The insulated lead from the top of the condenser is attached to the spring of the movable point arm, giving it an electrical connection to the movable breaker point.

The condenser can also be attached to the outside of the distributor housing. The wiring connections look different but provide the same electrical paths.

Some Delco-Remy distributors use a combined points and condenser unit called a Uni-Set, figure 13-25. This is a condenser as described above already attached to the point assembly. The assembly is installed and replaced as one unit. A similar product, the Pre-

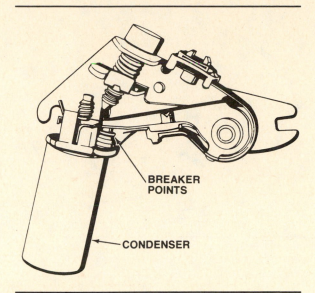

Figure 13-25. Delco-Remy's Uni-Set point and condenser assembly.

stolite Capaci-Point, attaches a ceramic capacitor to the point assembly. Both of these units eliminate the condenser wire lead, a principal cause of radio interference.

Condenser purpose
Self-induction in the coil primary winding can increase the primary voltage to as much as 400 volts. When the breaker points open, figure 13-26, top position, the high voltage would cause current to arc across the air gap. The un-wanted spark would:

- Consume energy at the expense of the secondary circuit energy
- Burn and pit the contacts, causing rapid point failure
- Leave an oxidized coating on the points, increasing primary circuit resistance.

To prevent these problems, the ignition condenser is installed in parallel with the breaker points, figure 13-26, bottom position. When the points open, the condenser is charged by the inductive current from the primary winding. It requires a small amount of time, about 0.1 millisecond, to charge the condenser to the peak voltage of the primary winding. By the time the condenser is fully charged, the contact points have opened far enough so that the current cannot arc across the air gap.

The energy in the condenser is then dis-charged, oscillating between the condenser and the coil primary winding, and dissipated as heat. These voltage oscillations in the primary circuit are shown in figure 13-27.

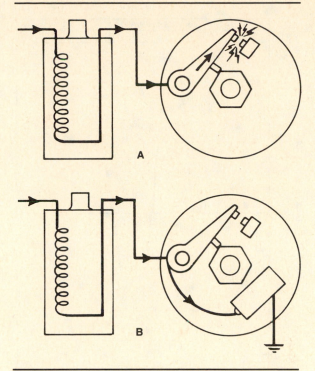

Figure 13-26. In position A, primary current arcs at the breaker points as they open. In position B, primary current flows to the condenser when the breaker points open, eliminating the arc.

Since the condenser allows the primary circuit to be broken quickly and completely, the coil's magnetic field collapses rapidly. The field collapses about 20 times faster than if there was no condenser in the circuit. The faster the collapse, the greater the induced voltage in the secondary winding. The field has fully collapsed by the time the condenser begins its first discharge into the primary circuit.

At low engine speeds, the breaker points open relatively slowly. At engine speeds re-quiring fewer than 3,000 sparks per minute, the primary winding's induced voltage is great enough to cause a slight arc across the slowly opening point air gap, despite the condenser. Automobiles driven mostly at low engine speeds will show more rapid point failure than those used for high-speed travel.

Condenser ratings
Condensers are rated in microfarads (μF), as explained in Chapter Two. Typical automotive condensers have capacities from 0.18 to 0.32 μF.

It is important to follow manufacturers' rec-ommendations when installing ignition con-densers. If a condenser with too little capacity

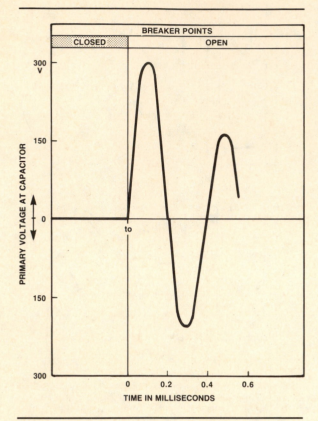

Figure 13-27. The energy stored in the condenser dissipates by oscillating through the primary circuit. (Bosch)

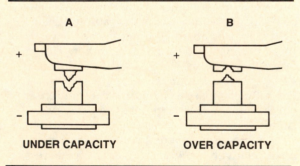

Figure 13-28. Incorrect condenser capacity can cause point pitting.

is used, primary current will charge the condenser and still be able to arc across the point gap. This causes pitting at the points, with metal transfer from the grounded (–) point to the movable (+) point, figure 13-28A. If the condenser has too great a capacity, pitting and metal transfer can occur in the opposite direction, figure 13-28B. The **Minus Rule** may help you to remember these relationships:

> Minus metal on the minus point means a minus-capacity condenser.

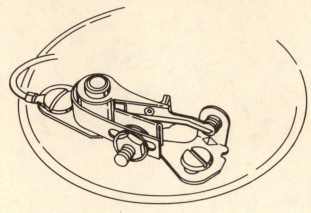

Figure 13-29. Points are normally installed as a complete assembly.

BREAKER-POINT DISTRIBUTORS

Great demands are placed on the ignition breaker points by the rest of the ignition system. Points must be correctly installed and accurately adjusted.

Breaker-Point Installation

Ignition breaker points are normally supplied as a complete unit, figure 13-29. This assembly is fastened to the distributor breaker plate, figure 13-30. The fasteners are either two screws or one screw and a small pin, as illustrated.

One of the mounting holes of the point assembly is elongated, so that the position of the points on the breaker plate can be adjusted. This adjustment has a great effect on breaker-point operation, as we will soon see.

The wiring connections between the points, the condenser, and the primary circuit can be made at one of two places. When the condenser is mounted inside the distributor, the connection is usually made at the bracket where the movable arm's spring is braced, figure 13-31. In some distributors, a nut and bolt hold the two wiring terminals to the bracket. Other distributors have push-on terminals.

When the condenser is mounted outside the housing, the primary lead and the condenser lead may be attached to a single slide terminal. A lead from the movable breaker point attaches to this terminal.

The stationary breaker point and the condenser canister are grounded through the distributor housing and the engine.

Correct ignition point alignment and spring tension are essential for proper ignition operation and long service life. Points are correctly aligned, figure 13-32, when the mating surfaces are in the center of both contacts, the

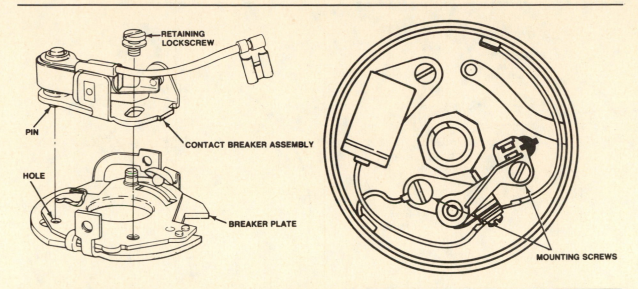

Figure 13-30. Point assemblies are usually mounted with either one screw and a locating pin (left) or with two screws (right). (Ford)

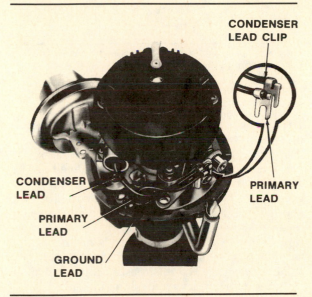

Figure 13-31. When the condenser is inside the distributor, the condenser and primary leads are usually connected to the movable arm spring bracket. (Delco-Remy)

faces are parallel, and the diameters are concentric. This ensures maximum contact area and precise switching action by the points.

Correct spring tension also ensures precise point action. Too much spring tension causes rapid cam and rubbing block wear. In some cases, it even can cause distributor shaft bushing wear or broken points. If spring tension is too light, the points will bounce as they open and close at high speed. This generally results

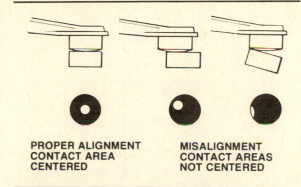

PROPER ALIGNMENT CONTACT AREA CENTERED

MISALIGNMENT CONTACT AREAS NOT CENTERED

Figure 13-32. Breaker points must be properly aligned for proper ignition system performance.

in a loss of engine power. Spring tension is normally between 15 and 25 ounces (425 and 710 grams).

Point Dwell Angle

Point **dwell angle**, or cam angle, is a measurement of how far the distributor cam rotates while the points are closed. In figure 13-33, the

Minus Rule: Minus metal on the minus side of the distributor breaker points means a minus-capacity condenser.

Dwell Angle: The measurement in degrees of how far the distributor cam rotates while the breaker points are closed. Also called cam angle, or dwell.

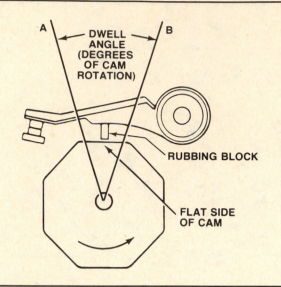

Figure 13-33. Dwell angle is the period during which the ignition points are closed. (Ford)

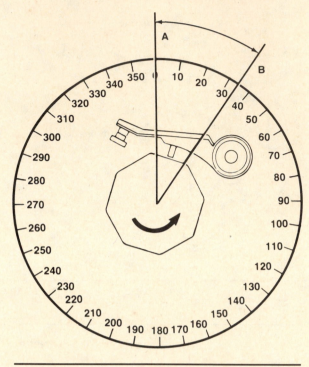

Figure 13-34. Dwell angle is measured in degrees of cam rotation. In this case, dwell is about 33 degrees.

points closed when line A was at the rubbing block. The points will open when line B reaches the rubbing block. Between line A and line B, the points stay closed. The number of degrees that the cam rotates between the point closing (line A) and the point opening (line B) is called the dwell angle.

Distributor rotation, like crankshaft rotation, is measured in degrees. If we superimpose a degree scale onto the point assembly, figure 13-34, we see that this particular dwell measures about 33 degrees.

The cam illustrated has eight lobes, so it is used with an eight-cylinder engine. Four-cylinder or six-cylinder engines require four-lobe or six-lobe cams. This means that the points open four or six times during each cam revolution. The more times the points must open, the less time they can remain closed.

The ignition dwell angle is directly related to an engine's firing intervals. There are 90 degrees of crankshaft rotation between the firing intervals in an eight-cylinder engine. Because the distributor rotates at one-half the crankshaft speed, the distributor cam rotates half as far as the crankshaft between firing intervals, or 45 degrees. The theoretical dwell angle of an eight-cylinder engine would be 45 degrees, but the points must be open during part of that time, and dwell equals the number of degrees during which the points are fully closed. About 12 to 17 degrees are required for the points to open and close on an eight-cylinder engine. Therefore, a typical dwell angle for an eight-cylinder engine is about 28 to 33 degrees.

An even-firing six-cylinder engine fires every 120 degrees of crankshaft rotation (60 degrees of distributor rotation). A four-cylinder engine fires every 180 degrees of crankshaft rotation (90 degrees of distributor rotation). Dwell on a six-cylinder engine could be around 45 degrees; on a four-cylinder engine, it could be about 75 degrees. However, large dwell angles mean that the primary current flows for a long time at low engine speeds. This is not necessary for full coil saturation and could lead to coil overheating. For this reason, four- and six-cylinder distributors are designed for less dwell than the maximum amount they could have. Dwell on a typical four-cylinder engine is usually about 50 degrees; on a six-cylinder engine, it is about 38 degrees.

Dwell and point gap
Point gap is the maximum distance between the breaker points when they are open. Figure 13-35 shows the relationship between point gap and dwell. A small point gap means a large dwell angle. A large point gap means a small dwell angle. Point gap is usually measured in thousandths of an inch or hundredths of a millimeter. Typical point gaps range from 0.015 to 0.025 inches or 0.40 to 0.60 millimeters.

Point gap is adjusted by shifting the position of the breaker point assembly. This changes

NORMAL DWELL

POINTS OPEN AND CLOSE AS SPECIFIED

SMALL DWELL

WIDE GAP

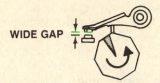

POINTS CLOSE LATE AND OPEN EARLY

LARGE DWELL

SMALL GAP

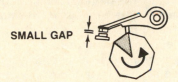

POINTS CLOSE EARLY AND OPEN LATE

 = DWELL ANGLE. POINTS ARE CLOSED DURING THIS PERIOD OF CAM ROTATION.

Figure 13-35. Point gap and dwell angle are related; when one increases, the other decreases.

the position of the points relative to the cam, altering the point gap and the dwell. Point assemblies have elongated mounting holes so that the point gap can be adjusted.

Effect of dwell on the coil
As long as the points are closed, current flows through the coil primary winding. This creates a magnetic field within the coil and makes induction possible.

However, the primary winding magnetic field does not appear instantly. When current first flows through the primary winding, self-induction causes a countervoltage within the winding. This countervoltage opposes primary current flow. The magnetic field of the primary winding does not immediately reach full strength, because the primary current does not immediately reach full strength, figure 13-36. It generally takes from 10 to 15 milliseconds for the primary current to reach full strength.

The breaker points must remain closed long enough for the primary winding's magnetic

■ Dual Breaker Points

In the early days of the automobile, short dwell time was an obstacle to increasing the rpm limit and power of high-performance street engines. Racing engines used magnetos which, by design, increase spark strength with rpm. Street engines, because of cost and starting requirements, were stuck with point-coil ignitions. At high engine speeds, above 4,500 or 5,000 rpm, a typical 33-degree dwell angle on a V8 engine did not allow enough coil saturation time. The result was insufficient voltage, making high-speed misfires a familiar problem. Reducing the point gap to increase dwell time drastically cut point life because the narrow gap caused point arcing and burning at low speeds.

By approximately the 1930s, manufacturers built the first production dual-point distributors that eliminated this problem. The two point sets had staggered openings and closings. The dwell on each set of points might be only 27 to 31 degrees; however, the combined dwell could be 36 to 40 degrees, which provided adequate coil saturation time and voltage for strong ignition at high speeds.

The point sets were connected in parallel, so the primary circuit was complete, or closed, whenever *either or both* point sets were closed. However, *both* sets of points had to be open to break the primary circuit and fire the spark plug. The first set of points to open did not break the circuit because the other set kept voltage flowing through the primary circuit. The second set to open was the ''opening'' set, since both sets were then open simultaneously for a short period. Because the first set to open was also the first to close, it was the ''closing'' set, and vital coil saturation time could begin. Dual-point distributors survived into the 1970s, but were not needed with the universal adoption solid-state swiching devices and electronic ignition.

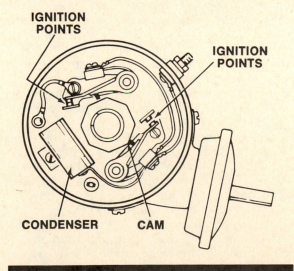

IGNITION POINTS

IGNITION POINTS

CONDENSER   CAM

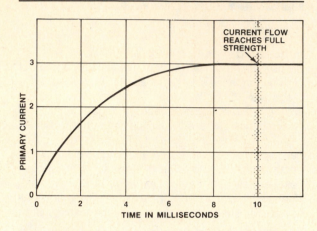

Figure 13-36. Primary winding current flow does not immediately reach full strength. (Bosch)

field to reach nearly full strength. If the field is not at full strength, secondary voltage will be reduced. The point dwell must be great enough to allow nearly maximum coil strength.

However, if the point dwell is too great, the point gap will be very small. Primary current will be able to arc across the air gap, and the magnetic field will not collapse quickly and completely. Point dwell and gap must be adjusted exactly to the manufacturer's specifications if the ignition system is to perform most efficiently.

Dwell and engine speed
As engine speed increases, the distributor cam rotates faster. Dwell angle is unchanged, but the *time* it takes the cam to rotate through this angle is decreased. That is, the amount of time that the points are closed is reduced as engine speed increases.

We have seen that it takes a specific amount of time — about 0.010 second — for primary current flow to reach full strength, figure 13-36. At a 625-rpm idle speed, the 33-degree dwell angle of an eight-cylinder engine lasts about 0.0165 seconds. Primary current flow can reach its full strength before the points open to interrupt it.

As engine speed increases to 1,000 rpm, the 33-degree dwell period decreases to 0.0099 seconds. Primary current is interrupted just before it reaches its maximum strength. Available secondary voltage will be decreased slightly.

At 2,000 rpm, the dwell period is reduced to 0.0045 seconds. Primary current is interrupted well before it reaches its maximum strength. Available secondary voltage will be reduced

considerably. If the engine and ignition system are not in excellent condition, the required voltage level may be greater than the available voltage level. If this occurs, the engine will misfire.

SUMMARY

Through electromagnetic induction, the ignition system transforms the low voltage of the battery into the high voltage required to fire the spark plugs. Induction occurs in the ignition coil where current flows through the primary winding to build up a magnetic field. When the field collapses rapidly, high voltage is induced in the coil secondary winding. All domestic original-equipment ignitions are the battery-powered, inductive-discharge type.

The ignition system is divided into two circuits: the primary and the secondary. The primary circuit contains the battery, the ignition switch, the ballast (primary) resistor, the starting bypass, the coil primary winding, and a switching device in the distributor.

For over sixty years, mechanical breaker points were used as the primary circuit switching device. Solid-state electronic components replaced breaker points as the switching device in the mid-1970s. The two most common solid-state switching devices are the magnetic pulse generator and the Hall-effect switch.

The ignition condenser is a capacitor that absorbs primary voltage when the points open. This prevents arcing across the points and premature burning. Typical ignition condensers are rated at 0.18 to 0.32 microfarads.

The breaker points are a mechanical switch that opens and closes the primary circuit. The period during which the points are closed is called the dwell angle. The dwell angle varies inversely with the gap between the points when they are open. As the gap decreases, the dwell increases.

■ **Useful Distributor Tool**

When you're timing an engine and want to rotate the distributor to advance or retard the spark, you may find that the distributor does not want to budge. This can occur even after the holddown bolt has been loosened. If it does, try using an oil filter wrench around the distributor. It may give you the grip and leverage you need.

Review Questions

Choose the single most correct answer.
Compare your answers with the correct answers on page 431.

1. The voltage required to ignite the air-fuel mixture can range from _____ volts.
   a. 5 to 25
   b. 50 to 250
   c. 500 to 2,500
   d. 5,000 to 25,000

2. Which of the following does *not* require higher voltage levels to cause an arc across the spark plug gap?
   a. Increased spark plug gap
   b. Increased engine operating temperature
   c. Increased fuel in air-fuel mixture
   d. Increased pressure of air-fuel mixture

3. The coil transforms low voltage from the primary circuit to high voltage for the secondary circuit through:
   a. Magnetic induction
   b. Capacitive discharge
   c. Series resistance
   d. Parallel capacitance

4. Voltage induced in the secondary winding of the ignition coil is how many times greater than the self-induced primary voltage?
   a. 1 to 2
   b. 10 to 20
   c. 100 to 200
   d. 1,000 to 2,000

5. The two circuits of the ignition system are:
   a. The "Start" and "Run" circuits
   b. The point circuit and the coil circuit
   c. The primary circuit and the secondary circuit
   d. The insulated circuit and the ground circuit

6. Which of the following components is part of both the primary and the secondary circuits?
   a. Ignition switch
   b. Distributor rotor
   c. Condenser
   d. Coil

7. Which of the following is *not* contained in the primary circuit of an ignition system?
   a. Battery
   b. Spark plugs
   c. Ignition switch
   d. Coil primary winding

8. When the cranking system is operating, the ballast resistor:
   a. Reduces coil primary voltage to about seven volts
   b. Heats up, increasing resistance and reducing voltage
   c. Is bypassed to provide full available voltage
   d. Cools, and increases primary current flow

9. Which of the following is true of the coil primary windings?
   a. They consist of 100 to 150 turns of very fine wire
   b. The turns are insulated by a coat of enamel
   c. The negative terminal is connected directly to the battery
   d. The positive terminal is connected to the breaker points and to ground

10. In order to collapse the magnetic field of the coil, the primary circuit requires a:
    a. Ballast resistor
    b. Switching device
    c. Condenser
    d. Starting bypass circuit

11. Breaker points are usually made of:
    a. Silicon
    b. Tungsten
    c. Aluminum
    d. Copper

12. In the solid-state ignitions used as original equipment on late-model domestic cars, the breaker points and distributor cam have been replaced by:
    a. RFI filter capacitors
    b. Auxiliary ballast resistors
    c. Magnetic pickup triggering devices
    d. Integrated coil and distributor cap assemblies

13. Condensers are rated in:
    a. Ohms
    b. Milliohms
    c. Farads
    d. Microfarads

14. The accompanying illustration shows which of the following situations with respect to the breaker points?

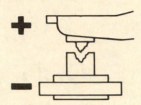

   a. Condenser with too little capacity used
   b. Condenser with too much capacity used
   c. Normal wear of points with correct condenser used
   d. Abnormal wear due to power surges

15. The accompanying illustration shows:

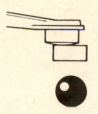

   a. Properly aligned breaker points
   b. Properly offset breaker points
   c. Misaligned breaker points
   d. Breaker points with excessive spring tension

16. Dwell angle is the period during which the ignition points are:
    a. Fully open
    b. Fully closed
    c. Starting to open
    d. Starting to close

17. The point gap is _____ related to the dwell angle:
    a. Directly
    b. Inversely
    c. Proportionately
    d. Reciprocally

18. The distributer rotates at _____ the speed of the crankshaft.
    a. One-half
    b. The same speed as
    c. Twice
    d. One-quarter

14

The Ignition Secondary Circuit and Components

Chapter

We have explained the general operation of the ignition primary circuit and have studied some of the system components. In this chapter, we will look at the secondary circuit and its components.

The secondary circuit must conduct surges of high voltage. To do this, it has large conductors and terminals, and heavy-duty insulation. The secondary circuit, figure 14-1, consists of the:

- Coil secondary winding
- Distributor cap and rotor
- Ignition cables
- Spark plugs.

The secondary circuit has the same components and function whether the primary circuit uses breaker points or a solid-state switching device.

IGNITION COILS

As we have seen, the ignition coil steps up voltage in the same way as a transformer. When the magnetic field of the coil primary winding collapses, it induces a high voltage in the secondary winding.

Coil Secondary Winding and Primary-to-Secondary Connections

Two windings of copper wire compose the ignition coil. The primary winding of heavy wires consists of 100 to 150 turns; the secondary winding is 15,000 to 30,000 turns of a fine wire. The ratio of secondary turns to primary turns is usually between 100 and 200. To increase the strength of the coil's magnetic field, the windings are wrapped around a laminated core of soft iron, figure 14-2.

The coil must be protected from the underhood environment to maintain its efficiency. Three coil designs are used:

- Oil-filled coil
- Laminated E-core coil
- DIS coil packs.

Oil-filled coil

In the oil-filled coil (used with both breaker-point and breakerless ignitions), the primary winding is wrapped around the secondary winding, which is wrapped around the iron core. The coil windings are insulated by layers of paper and the entire case is filled with oil for greater insulation. The top of the coil is molded from an insulating material such as Bakelite. Metal inserts for the winding terminals are installed in the cap. Primary and secondary terminals are generally marked with a + and -, figure 14-3. Leads are attached with nuts and washers on some coils; others use

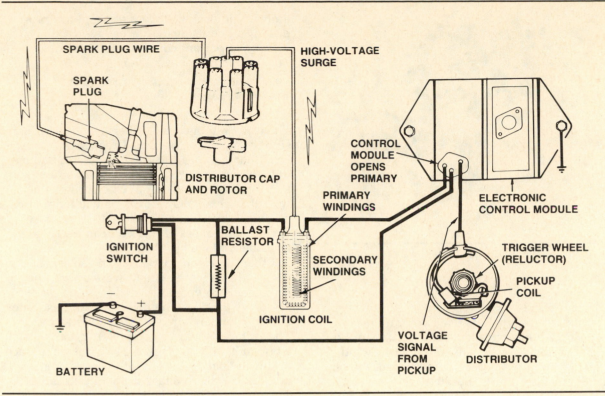

Figure 14-1. Operation of the ignition secondary circuit. (Chrysler)

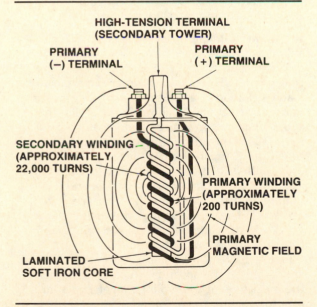

Figure 14-2. The laminated iron core within the coil strengthens the coil's magnetic field.

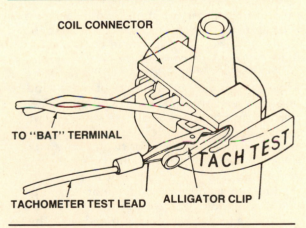

Figure 14-3. The Ford coil used with breakerless ignitions has a polarized slide-on primary terminal connector with a tachometer connection. (Ford)

push-on lead connectors. The entire unit is sealed to keep out dirt and moisture.

Laminated E-core coil

Unlike the oil-filled coil, the E-core coil uses an iron core laminated *around* the windings and potted in plastic, much like a small transform-

er, figure 14-4. The coil is named because of the ''E'' shape of the laminations making up its core. Since the laminations provide a closed magnetic path, the E-core coil has a higher energy transfer. The secondary connection looks much like a spark plug terminal. Primary leads are housed in a single snap-on connector that attaches to the coil's blade-type terminals. The E-core coil has very low primary resistance and is used without a ballast resistor in Ford TFI and some GM HEI ignitions.

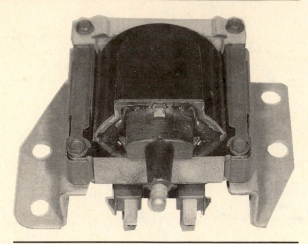

Figure 14-4. The E-core coil is used without a ballast resistor.

DIS coil packs

Distributorless ignitions use two or more coils in a single housing called a coil pack, figure 14-5. Figure 14-6 compares the internal windings of a typical coil pack with those of the oil-filled and E-core coils. Because the E-core coil has a primary and secondary winding on the same core, it uses a common terminal. Both ends of the E-core coil's primary winding connect to the primary ignition circuit; the open end of its secondary winding connects to the center tower of the coil, where the distributor high tension lead connects.

Coil packs are significantly different, using a closed magnetic core with one primary winding for every two high voltage outputs. The secondary circuit of the coil pack is wired in series. Each coil in the coil pack directly provides secondary voltage for two of the spark plugs, which are wired in series with the coil secondary winding. Coil pack current is limited by transistors called output drivers in the ignition module attached to the bottom of the pack. The output drivers open and close the ground path of the coil primary circuit. Timing and sequencing of the output drivers are controlled by other module internal circuits.

Coil Voltage

A coil must supply the correct amount of voltage for any system. Since this amount of voltage varies, depending on engine and operating conditions, the coil's available voltage is generally more than the system's required voltage. If it is less, the engine may not run.

Available voltage

The ignition coil can supply much more secondary voltage than the average engine requires. The peak voltage that a coil can produce is called its **available voltage**.

Three important coil design factors determine available voltage level:

- Secondary-to-primary turns ratio
- Primary voltage level
- Primary circuit resistance.

The turns ratio is a multiplier that creates high secondary voltage output. The primary voltage level that is applied to a coil is determined by the ignition circuit's design and condition. Installing a ballast resistor of the wrong value will affect this voltage level, as will loose and corroded connections. Generally, a primary circuit voltage loss of one volt can decrease available voltage by 10,000 volts.

If there were no spark plug in the secondary circuit (that is, if the circuit were open), the coil secondary voltage would have no place to discharge quickly. The voltage would oscillate in the secondary circuit, dissipating as heat. The voltage would be completely gone in just a few milliseconds. Figure 14-7 shows the trace of this no-load, open-circuit voltage. This is called secondary voltage **no-load oscillation**. The first peak of the voltage trace represents the maximum available voltage from that particular coil. Available voltage is usually between 20,000 and 50,000 volts.

Required voltage

When there is a spark plug in the secondary circuit, the coil voltage creates an arc across the plug air gap. Figure 14-8 compares a typical no-load oscillation to a typical secondary firing voltage oscillation. At about 15,000 volts, the spark plug air gap ionizes and becomes conductive. This is the ionization voltage level, also called the **firing voltage**, or **required voltage**.

As soon as a spark has formed, the energy demands of the spark cause the secondary voltage to drop to the much lower spark voltage level. This is the inductive portion of the spark. **Spark voltage** is usually about one-fourth of the firing voltage level.

Figure 14-9 shows the entire trace of the spark. When the secondary voltage falls below the inductive air-gap voltage level, the spark can no longer be maintained. The spark gap becomes nonconductive. The remaining secondary voltage oscillates in the secondary circuit, dissipating as heat. This is called secondary **voltage decay**. At this time, the primary circuit closes and the cycle repeats, figure 14-10. The traces shown in figures 14-9 and 14-10 are similar to the secondary circuit traces you will see on an oscilloscope screen.

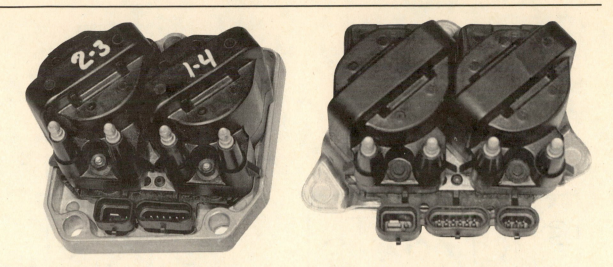

Figure 14-5. Typical DIS coil packs used on four-cylinder engines.

Some conditions that cause required voltage levels to increase are:

- Eroded electrodes in the distributor cap, rotor, or spark plug
- Damaged ignition cables
- Reversed plug polarity
- High compression pressures
- A lean air-fuel mixture that is more difficult to ionize.

Voltage reserve

The physical condition of the automotive engine and ignition system can affect both available and required voltage levels, as we have seen. Figure 14-11 shows available and required voltage levels in a particular ignition system under various operating conditions. **Voltage reserve** is the amount of coil voltage available in excess of the voltage required.

Under certain poor circuit conditions, there may be no voltage reserve. At these times, some spark plugs will not fire, and the engine will run poorly or not at all. Ignition systems must be properly maintained to ensure that there is always some voltage reserve. A well-tuned ignition system should have a voltage reserve of about 60 percent of available voltage under most operating conditions.

Coil Installations

Ignition coils are usually mounted with a bracket on a fender panel in the engine compartment or on the engine, figure 14-12.

Some ignition coils have an unusual design and location. The Delco-Remy High Energy Ignition (HEI) solid-state ignition system used on V6 and V8 engines has a coil mounted in the distributor, figure 14-13. The coil output terminal is connected directly to the center electrode of the distributor cap. The connections to the primary winding are made through a multiple-plug connector.

Distributorless ignitions use an assembly containing two or more separate ignition coils and an electronic ignition module, figure 14-14. Control circuits in the module discharge each coil separately in sequence, with each coil serving two cylinders 360 degrees apart in the firing order. We will learn more about this type of system in Chapter Sixteen.

Available Voltage: The peak voltage that a coil can produce.

No-Load Oscillation: The rapid, back-and-forth, peak-to-peak oscillation of voltage in the ignition secondary circuit when the circuit is open.

Firing Voltage (Required Voltage): The voltage level that must be reached to ionize and create a spark in the air gap between the spark plug electrodes.

Spark Voltage: The inductive portion of a spark that maintains the spark in the air gap between a spark plug's electrodes, usually about one-quarter of the firing voltage level.

Voltage Decay: The rapid oscillation and dissipation of secondary voltage after the spark in a spark plug air gap has stopped.

Voltage Reserve: The amount of coil voltage available in excess of the voltage required to fire the spark plugs.

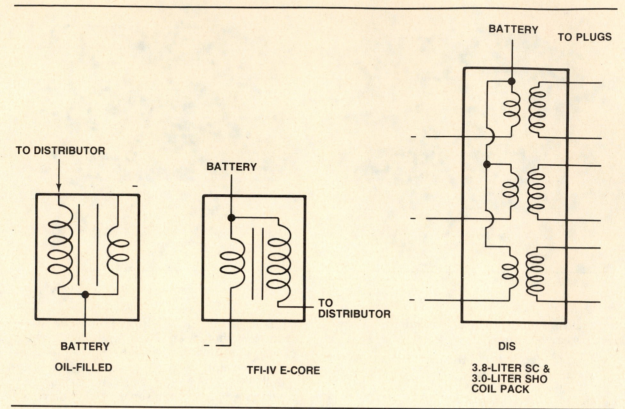

Figure 14-6. Coil Wiring Comparison (Ford Motor Company)

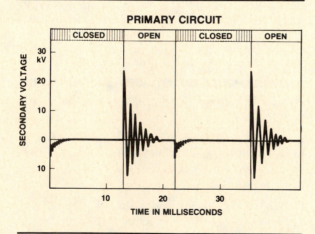

Figure 14-7. A secondary circuit no-load voltage trace. (Bosch)

In any system, the connections to the primary winding must be made correctly. If spark plug polarity is reversed, greater voltage is required to fire the plug. Plug polarity is established by the ignition coil connections.

One end of the coil secondary winding is connected to the primary winding, figure 14-15, so that the secondary circuit is grounded through the ignition primary circuit. When the coil terminals are properly connected to the battery, the grounded end of the second-

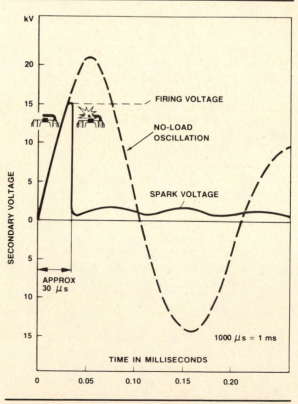

Figure 14-8. The dashed line shows no-load voltage; the solid line shows the voltage trace of firing voltage and spark voltage. (Bosch)

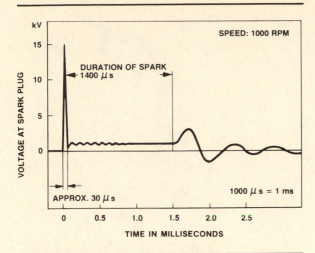

Figure 14-9. The voltage trace of an entire secondary ignition pulse. (Bosch)

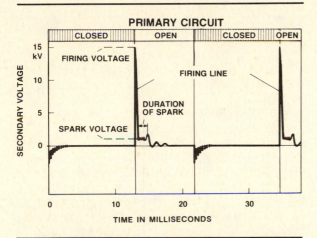

Figure 14-10. As the primary circuit opens and closes, the ignition cycle repeats. (Bosch)

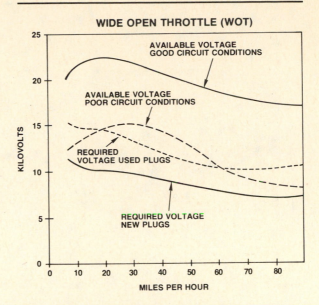

Figure 14-11. Available and required voltage levels under different system conditions.

ary circuit is electrically positive. The other end of the secondary circuit, which is the center electrode of the spark plug, is electrically negative. The plug's grounded side electrode is positive, and plug polarity is correct. Whether the secondary winding is grounded to the primary + or – terminal depends on whether the windings are wound clockwise or counterclockwise.

If the coil connections are reversed, figure 14-16, spark plug polarity is reversed. The grounded end of the secondary circuit is electrically negative. The plug center electrode is electrically positive, and the side electrode is negative. When plug polarity is reversed, 20 to 40 percent more secondary voltage is required to fire the spark plug.

Coil terminals are usually marked BAT or +, and DIST or –. To establish the correct plug polarity with a negative-ground electrical sys-tem, the + terminal must be connected to the positive terminal of the battery (through the ignition switch, starter relay, and other circuitry). The – coil terminal must be connected to the distributor breaker points and condenser or to the ignition control module.

DISTRIBUTOR CAP AND ROTOR

The distributor cap and rotor, figure 14-17, receive high-voltage current from the coil secondary winding. Current enters the distributor cap through the central terminal, called the coil tower. The rotor carries the current from the coil tower to the spark plug electrodes in the rim of the cap. The rotor is mounted on the distributor shaft and rotates with it, so that the rotor electrode moves from one spark plug electrode to another in the cap to follow the designated firing order.

Distributor Rotor

A rotor is made of silicone plastic, **Bakelite**, or a similar synthetic material that is a very good insulator. A metal electrode on top of the rotor conducts current from the carbon terminal of the coil tower.

Bakelite: A synthetic plastic material that is a good insulator. Distributor caps are often made of Bakelite.

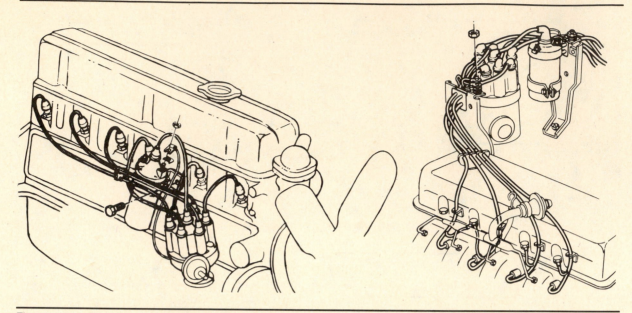

Figure 14-12. Ignition coils are commonly mounted on the engine (left) or on a fender panel (right). (Chevrolet)

The rotor is keyed to the distributor shaft to maintain its correct relationship with the shaft and the spark plug electrodes in the cap. The key may be a flat section or a slot in the top of the shaft. Delco-Remy V6 and V8, shown at the left in figure 14-18, and Ford TFI distributor rotors are keyed in place by two locators and secured by two screws. Most other rotors, shown at the right in figure 14-18, are pressed onto the shaft by hand. The rotor in Chrysler's optically triggered distributor is retained by a horizontal capscrew.

The Ford EEC-I, -II, and -III ignitions have rotors with two pickup arms and two electrodes, figure 14-19. The electrodes are on different levels that correspond to two levels of distributor cap electrodes, which minimizes high-voltage **crossfiring** in the distributor. When the rotor is removed or replaced on 1978 EEC-I systems, figure 14-19, left, it requires alignment. A modification of this design is used on 1979 and later EEC-I, -II, and -III distributors, figure 14-19, right. Rotor alignment is not normally required when replacing this rotor.

Ford's basic rotor design uses a blade-type rotor tip. This was changed to a multiwire or "cat-whisker" rotor tip, figure 14-20, in some 1983-85 systems. This was an attempt to further reduce RFI interference from the secondary circuit without using silicone grease on the rotor tip. However, arcing from the multiwire tip formed ozone and nitrogen oxides from the air inside the distributor. Over a period of time, these combined to form nitric acid that reacted with the distributor cap to create a short-circuit path for secondary voltage.

Ford released replacement caps of a different material in 1985 to counteract the crossfiring problem and discontinued the cat-whisker rotors in 1986. Replacement rotors for 1983-85 models are the blade-type design.

Except for the multiwire-tip rotors, Ford and Chrysler breakerless distributor rotors are coated at the factory with a silicone grease. As the silicone ages, it may look like contamination, but it is not. Do not remove or reapply any coating on a used Ford rotor. Chrysler recommends removing any excess on the tip of the rotor. When a new Ford rotor is installed, apply a 1/8-inch (3-mm) coating of silicone grease (Dow Corning 111, GE G-627, or equivalent) on all sides of the electrode, including the tip. The Ford multiwire-tip rotor *does not* require the silicone grease used on the blade-type rotors.

Rotors used with Hall-effect switches often have the shutter blades attached, figure 14-21, serving a dual purpose. In addition to distributing the secondary current, the rotor blades bypass the Hall-effect magnetic field and create the signal for the primary circuit to fire.

Rotor air gap
An air gap of a few thousandths of an inch, or a few hundredths of a millimeter, exists between the tip of the rotor electrode and the spark plug electrode of the cap. If they actually touched, both would wear very quickly. Because the gap cannot be measured when the distributor is assembled, it is usually described in terms of the voltage required to create an arc across the electrodes. Only about 3,000 volts are required to create an arc across most

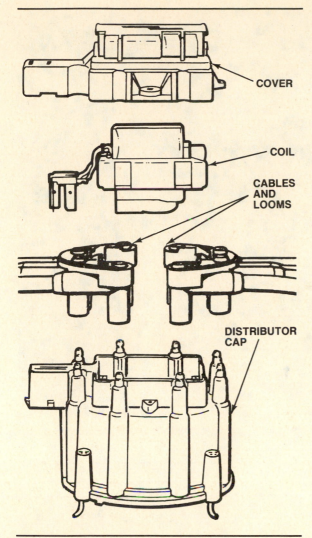

Figure 14-13. Many Delco-Remy HEI solid-state ignition systems used on V6 and V8 engines have a coil mounted in the distributor cap.

breaker-point distributor air gaps, but some Delco-Remy distributors require as much as 9,000 volts. The voltage required to jump the air gap in electronic distributors generally is higher than that required for breaker-point ignitions. As the rotor completes the secondary circuit and the plug fires, the rotor air gap adds resistance to the circuit. This raises the plug firing voltage, suppresses secondary current, and reduces RFI.

Distributor Cap

The distributor cap is also made of silicone plastic, Bakelite, or a similar material that resists chemical attack and protects other distributor parts. Metal electrodes in the spark plug towers and a carbon insert in the coil tower provide electrical connections with the ignition

cables and the rotor electrode, figure 14-22. The cap is keyed to the distributor housing and is held on by two or four spring-loaded clips or by screws.

Delco-Remy HEI caps and all Ford Dura-Spark and TFI caps have male connectors rather than female spark plug towers. When removing a cap from an early 1977 Dura-Spark distributor, unlatch the cap from the adapter ring first. Do not try to lift the cap and adapter from the body together, because the adapter will jam on the rotor. On later Dura-Spark distributors, the adapter ring is held to the body by two screws inside the ring.

HEI distributor caps with an integral coil, figure 14-13, are secured by four spring-loaded clips. When removing this cap, be sure that all four clips are disengaged and clear of the housing. Then lift the cap straight up to avoid bending the carbon button in the cap and the spring that connects it to the coil. If the button

Crossfiring: Ignition voltage jumping from the distributor rotor to the wrong spark plug electrode inside the distributor cap. Also, ignition voltage jumping from one spark plug cable to another due to worn insulation.

■ The Lincoln-Zephyr V12 Ignition System

The ignition system for the Lincoln-Zephyr V12 engines used two coils contained in a single housing mounted on top of a distributor with two distributor caps, two sets of breaker points, a rotor with two contacts, and two condensers. The distributor was mounted on the front of the engine and was connected directly to the camshaft.

Looking at the distributor from the driver's seat position, the right-hand coil and a fixed set of breaker points fired the right bank of cylinders, numbers 2-4-6-8-10-12. The left-hand coil and an adjustable set of breaker points fired the left bank of cylinders, numbers 1-3-5-7-9-11.

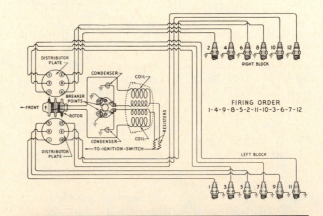

Figure 14-14. The Buick C3I distributorless ignition uses three separate ignition coils, each of which serves two cylinders 360 degrees apart in the firing order.

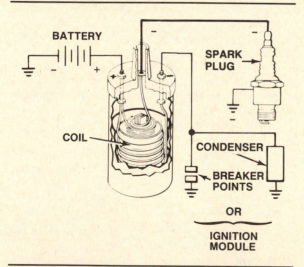

Figure 14-15. When coil connections are made properly, the spark plug center electrode is electrically negative.

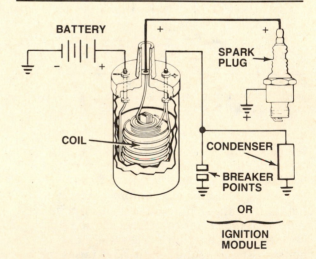

Figure 14-16. When coil connections are reversed, spark plug polarity is reversed.

and spring are distorted, arcing can occur that will burn the cap and rotor.

Positive-engagement spark plug cables are used with some Chrysler and Ford four-cylinder ignition systems. There are no electrodes in distributor caps used with these cables. A terminal electrode attached to the distributor-cap end of the cable locks inside the cap to form the distributor contact terminal, figure 14-23. The secondary terminal of the cable is pressed into the cap.

Ford Motorcraft Dura-Spark III distributors used with some of Ford's electronic engine

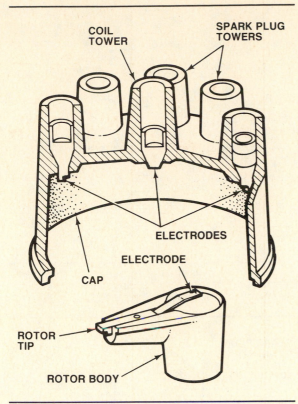

Figure 14-17. A distributor rotor and a cutaway view of the distributor cap.

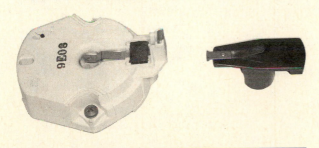

Figure 14-18. Typical distributor rotors.

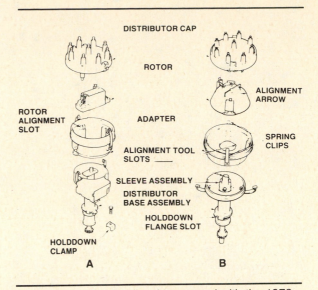

Figure 14-19. Ford's bilevel rotor used with the 1978 EEC-I distributor (left) requires alignment when installed; the style used with 1979 and later EEC-I, -II, and -III distributors (right) normally does not. (Ford)

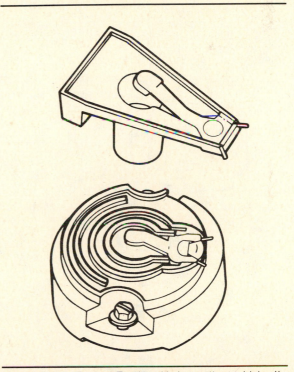

Figure 14-20. Typical Ford multiwire or "cat-whisker" rotors used in some 1983-86 systems. (Ford)

control (EEC) systems have caps and rotors with the terminals on two levels to prevent secondary voltage arcing. Spark plug cables are not connected to the caps in firing order sequence, but the caps are numbered with the engine cylinder numbers, figure 14-24. The caps have two sets of numbers, one set for 5.0-liter standard engines, and the other for 5.7-liter and 302-cid high-performance engines. Cylinder numbers must be checked carefully when changing spark plug cables.

Distributor caps used on some late-model Ford and Chrysler vehicles have a vent to prevent the buildup of moisture and reduce the accumulation of ozone inside the cap, figure 14-23.

IGNITION CABLES

Secondary ignition cables carry high-voltage current from the coil to the distributor (coil wire) and from the distributor to the spark plugs (spark plug cables). They use heavy insulation to prevent the high-voltage current from jumping to ground before it reaches the

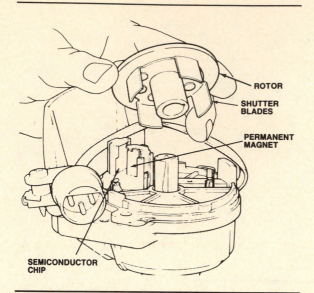

Figure 14-21. A Hall-effect triggering device attached to the rotor. (Chrysler)

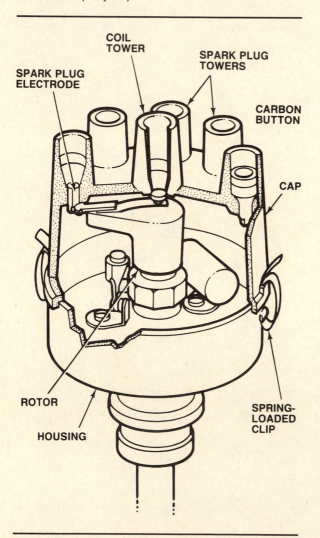

Figure 14-22. The distributor cap and rotor assembled with the distributor housing.

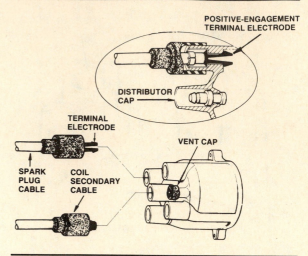

Figure 14-23. Chrysler four-cylinder distributors have used positive locking terminal electrodes as part of the ignition cable since 1980. (Chrysler)

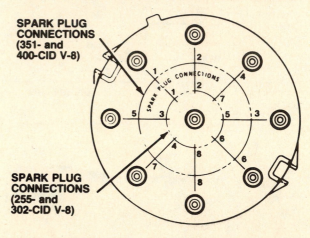

Figure 14-24. Spark plug cable installation order for V8 EEC systems.

spark plugs. Ford, GM, and some other electronic ignitions use an 8-mm cable; all others use a 7-mm cable.

Conductor Types

Spark plug cables originally used a solid steel or copper wire conductor. Cables manufactured with these conductors were found to cause radio and television interference. While this type of cable is still made for special applications such as racing, most spark plug cables have been made of a high-resistance, nonmetallic conductor for the past 30 years. Several nonmetallic conductors may be used, such as carbon, and linen or fiberglass strands impregnated with graphite. The nonmetallic conductor acts as a resistor in the secondary circuit and reduces RFI and spark plug wear due to high current. Such cables are often called **television-radio-suppression (TVRS) cables**, or just suppression cables.

When replacing spark plug cables on vehicles with computer-controlled systems, be sure that the resistance of the new cables is within the carmaker's specifications to avoid possible electromagnetic interference with the operation of the computer.

Terminals and Boots

Secondary ignition cable terminals, figure 14-25, are designed to make a strong contact with the coil and distributor electrodes. They are, however, subject to corrosion and arcing if not firmly seated and protected from the elements.

Positive-engagement spark plug cable terminals, figure 12-23, lock in place inside the distributor cap and cannot come loose accidentally. They can only be removed with the cap off the distributor. The terminal electrode then is compressed with pliers and the wire is pushed out of the cap, figure 14-26.

The ignition cables must have special connectors, often called spark plug boots, figure 14-27. The boots provide a tight and well-insulated contact between the cable and the spark plug.

Television-Radio-Suppression (TVRS) Cables: High-resistance, carbon-conductor ignition cables that suppress RFI.

■ Making Tracks

You often read instructions to inspect ignition parts for carbon tracks. Although you may have heard about or seen carbon tracks, have you ever thought about what they are and what causes them?

Carbon tracks are deposits or defects on distributor rotors, caps, spark plugs, and cables that create a short-circuit pat to ground for secondary high voltage. They also cause crossfiring, in which the high voltage jumps from the distributor rotor to the wrong terminal in the cap.

The problems caused by carbon tracks are all pretty similar, but the causes for these defects are rather complex. A distributor cap or rotor may develop a hairline crack because of rough handling, a manufacturing defect, or some other problem. Under certain conditions, moisture can collect in the crack and create a lower-resistance path for high voltage. High-voltage arcing to ground in a distributor ionizes are molecules and can form conductive deposits along its path. If any dirt or grease is in the short-circuit path, the combination of high voltage and its accompanying current causes carbon deposits to form around the crack. Thus, a carbon track develops.

Carbon tracks can form even without a crack in a cap or rotor. High voltage ionizes air and oil molecules in the distributor and causes deposits to form. The deposits have high resistance, but if they are the least bit conductive, secondary voltage can arc to them. Over a period of time, the deposits build up and can create a short circuit.

Outside a distributor, similar carbon tracks can form on spark plug insulators and ignition cables due to grease deposits and weak points in damaged cable insulation.

Carbon tracks inside a distributor cap often can be tricky to diagnose. Sometimes an engine will run smoothly at idle but misfire at high speed. As the distributor advance mechanisms operate, the rotor moves farther away from the cap terminals as the coil discharges. The high-voltage current must cross an increasing air gap. If a nearby carbon track provides lower resistance, the voltage will jump to ground and the engine will misfire.

A typical carbon track has about the same, or a little less, resistance as a TVRS ignition cable. That's quite conductive enough to cause a misfire or a no-start problem. The accompanying photo shows a classic set of carbon tracks inside a distributor cap.

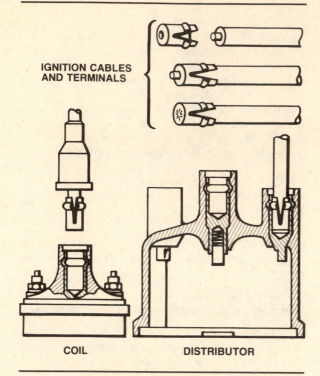

Figure 14-25. Ignition cables and terminals.

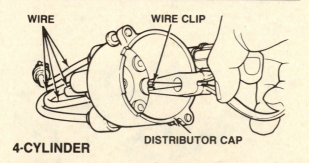

Figure 14-26. Positive locking terminal electrodes are removed by compressing the wire clips with pliers and removing the wire from the cap.

SPARK PLUGS

Spark plugs allow the high-voltage secondary current to arc across a small air gap. The three basic parts of a spark plug, figure 14-28, are:

- A ceramic core, or insulator, which insulates the center electrode and acts as a heat conductor
- Two electrodes, one insulated in the core and the other grounded on the shell
- A metal shell that holds the insulator and electrodes in a gas-tight assembly and which has threads to hold the plug in the engine.

The metal shell grounds the side electrode against the engine. The other electrode is en-

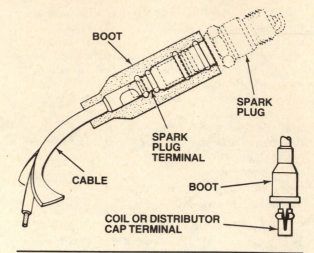

Figure 14-27. Ignition cables, terminals, and boots work together to carry the high-voltage secondary current.

cased in the ceramic insulator. A spark plug boot and cable are attached to the top of the plug. High-voltage current flows through the center of the plug and arcs from the tip of the insulated electrode to the side electrode and ground. This spark ignites the air-fuel mixture in the combustion chamber to produce power.

The burning gases in the engine can corrode and wear the spark plug electrodes. Electrodes are made of metals that resist this attack. Most electrodes are made of high-nickel alloy steel, but platinum and silver alloys have also been used.

Spark Plug Firing Action

The arc of current across a spark plug air gap provides two types of discharge:

- Capacitive
- Inductive.

When a high-voltage surge is first delivered to the spark plug center electrode, the air-fuel mixture in the air gap cannot conduct an arc. The spark plug acts as a capacitor, with the center electrode storing a negative charge and the grounded side electrode storing a positive charge. The air gap between the electrodes acts as a dielectric insulator. This is the opposite of the normal negative-ground polarity, and results from the polarity of the coil secondary winding, as shown in figure 14-29.

Secondary voltage increases, and the charges in the spark plug strengthen until the difference in potential between the electrodes is great enough to **ionize** the spark plug air gap. That is, the air-fuel mixture in the gap is changed from a nonconductor to a conductor by the pos-

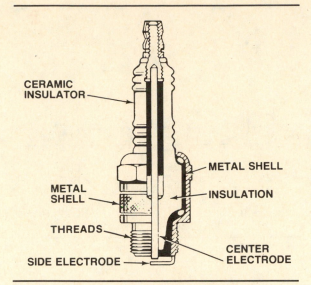

Figure 14-28. A cutaway view of the spark plug.

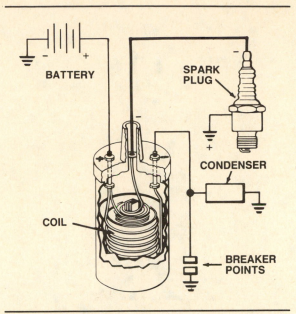

Figure 14-29. The spark plug should have a negative charge at the center electrode and a positive charge at the side electrode.

itive and negative charges of the two electrodes. The dielectric resistance of the air gap breaks down, and current flows between the electrodes. The voltage level at this instant is called ionization voltage. The current that flows across the spark plug air gap at the instant of ionization is the capacitive portion of the spark. It flows from negative to positive and uses the energy stored in the plug itself when the plug was acting as a capacitor, before ionization. This is the portion of the spark that starts the combustion process within the engine.

The ionization voltage level is usually less than the total voltage produced in the coil secondary winding. The remainder of the secondary voltage (that voltage not needed to force ionization) is dissipated as current across the spark plug air gap. This is the inductive portion of the spark discharge, which causes the *visible* flash or arc at the plug. It contributes nothing to the combustion of the air-fuel mixture, but is the cause of electrical interference and severe electrode erosion. High-resistance cables and spark plugs suppress this inductive portion of the spark discharge.

SPARK PLUG CONSTRUCTION

Spark Plug Design Features
Spark plugs are made in a variety of sizes and types to fit different engines. The most important differences among plugs are:

- Reach
- Heat range
- Thread and seat
- Air gap.

These are illustrated in figure 14-30.

Reach
The **reach** of a spark plug is the length of the shell from the seat to the bottom of the shell, including both threaded and unthreaded portions. If an incorrect plug is installed and the reach is too short, the electrode will be in a pocket and the spark will not ignite the air-fuel mixture very well, figure 14-31.

If the spark plug reach is too long, the exposed plug threads could get hot enough to ignite the air-fuel mixture at the wrong time. It may be difficult to remove the plug due to carbon deposits on the plug threads. Engine damage can also result from interference between moving parts and the exposed plug threads.

Heat range
The **heat range** of a spark plug determines its ability to dissipate heat from the firing end. The length of the lower insulator and conductivity of the center electrode are design fea-

Ionize: To break up molecules into two or more oppositely charged ions. The air gap between the spark plug electrodes is ionized when the air-fuel mixture is changed from a non-conductor to a conductor.

Reach: The length of the spark plug shell from the seat to the bottom of the shell.

Heat Range: The measure of a spark plug's ability to dissipate heat from its firing end.

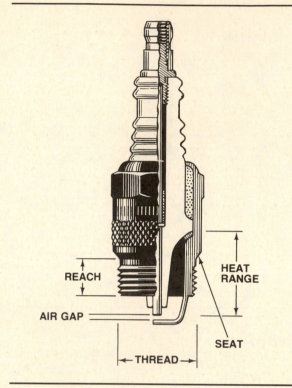

Figure 14-30. The design features of a spark plug.

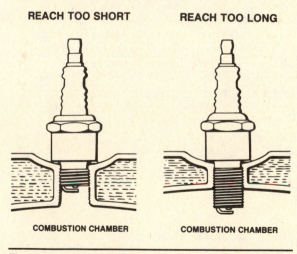

Figure 14-31. Spark plug reach.

tures that primarily control the plug's rate of heat transfer, figure 14-32. A "cold" spark plug has a short insulator tip that provides a short path for heat to travel, and permits the heat to dissipate rapidly to maintain a lower firing tip temperature. A "hot" spark plug has a long insulator tip that creates a longer path for heat to travel. This slower heat transfer maintains a higher firing tip temperature.

Engine manufacturers choose a spark plug with the appropriate heat range required for the

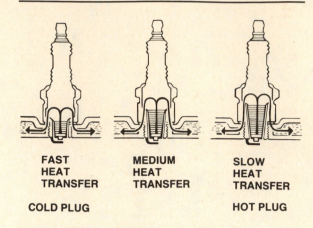

Figure 14-32. Spark plug heat range.

normal or expected service for which the engine was designed. Proper heat range is an extremely important factor because the firing end of the spark plug must run hot enough to burn away fouling deposits at idle, but must also remain cool enough at highway speeds to avoid preignition. It also is an important factor in the amount of emissions an engine will produce.

Current spark plug designations use an alpha-numeric system that identifies, among other factors, the heat range of a particular plug. Spark plug manufacturers gradually are redesigning and redesignating their plugs. For example, a typical A.C. Delco spark plug carries the alpha-numeric designation R45LTS6; the new all-numeric code for a similar AC spark plug of the same length and gap is 41-600. This will make it more difficult for those drivers who attempt to correct driveability problems by installing a hotter or colder spark plug than the carmaker specifies. Eventually, it no longer will be possible for drivers to affect emissions by their choice of spark plugs.

Thread and seat

Most automotive spark plugs are made with one of two thread diameters: 14 or 18 millimeters, figure 14-33. All 18-mm plugs have tapered seats that match similar tapered seats in the cylinder head. No gaskets are used. The 14-mm plugs are made either with a flat seat that requires a gasket or with a tapered seat that does not. The gasket-type, 14-mm plugs are still quite common, but the 14-mm tapered-seat plugs are now used in most late-model engines. A third thread size is 10 millimeters; 10-mm spark plugs are generally used on motorcycles, but some car engines also use them, specifically Jaguar's V12.

The steel shell of a spark plug is hex-shaped so a wrench will fit it. The 14-mm, tapered-seat plugs have shells with a 5/8-inch hex;

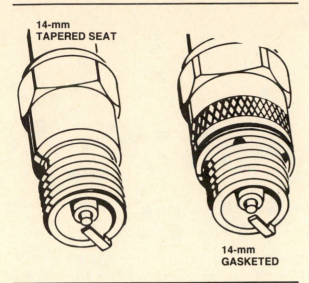

14-mm
TAPERED SEAT

14-mm
GASKETED

Figure 14-33. Spark plug thread and seat types.

14-mm gasketed and 18-mm tapered-seat plugs have shells with a 13/16-inch hex.

Air gap
The correct spark plug air gap is important to engine performance and plug life. A gap that is too narrow will cause a rough idle and a change in the exhaust emissions. A gap that is too wide will require higher voltage to jump it; if the required voltage is greater than the available ignition voltage, misfiring will result.

Special-Purpose Spark Plugs

Specifications for all spark plugs include the design characteristics just described. In addition, many plugs have other special features to fit particular requirements.

Resistor-type spark plugs
This type of plug contains a resistor in the center electrode, figure 14-34. The resistor generally has a value of 7,500 to 15,000 ohms and is used to reduce radiofrequency interference (RFI). **Resistor-type spark plugs** can be used in place of nonresistor plugs of the same size, heat range, and gap without affecting engine performance.

Extended-tip spark plugs
Sometimes called an **extended-core spark plug**, this design uses a center electrode and insulator that extend farther into the combustion chamber, figure 14-35. The extended-tip operates hotter under slow-speed driving conditions to burn off combustion deposits and cooler at high speed to prevent spark plug overheating. This greater efficiency over a wide temperature range has led to increased use in the smaller and less powerful engines used in the 1980s.

Wide-gap spark plugs
The electronic ignition systems on some late-model engines require spark plug gaps in the 0.045- to 0.080-inch (1.0- to 2.0-mm) range. Plugs for such systems are made with a wider gap than other plugs. This wide gap is indicated in the plug part number. Do not try to open the gap of a narrow-gap plug to create the wide gap required by such ignitions.

Resistor-Type Spark Plug: A plug that has a resistor in the center electrode to reduce the inductive portion of the spark discharge.

Extended-Core Spark Plug: Also called power tip. The insulator core and the electrodes in this type of spark plug extend further into the combustion chamber than they do on other types.

■ Spark Plug Design

Many people have tried to redesign the spark plug. Not all of the ''new'' designs have worked out. For example, a plug manufactured before World War I had an insulated handle at the top. By pulling this handle up, an auxiliary gap was opened, presumably to create a hotter spark and stop oil fouling. A window in the side of the plug showed whether the gap was open or closed.

Another ''revolutionary'' type of plug had a screw connector that allowed the inner core assembly to be removed and cleaned quickly.

Still another design had threads and electrodes at each end of the plug. The plug could be removed, the terminal cap installed on the other end, and then reinstalled upside down. All of the photos were provided by Champion Spark Plug Company.

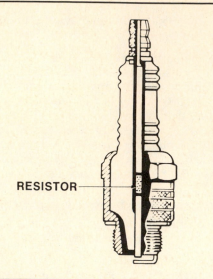

Figure 14-34. A resistor-type spark plug.

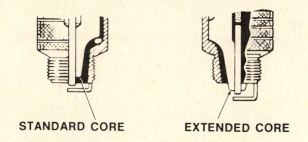

Figure 14-35. A comparison of a standard and an extended-core spark plug.

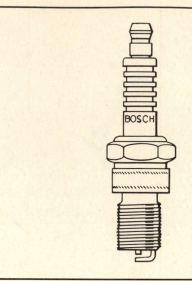

Figure 14-36. A long-reach, short-thread spark plug.

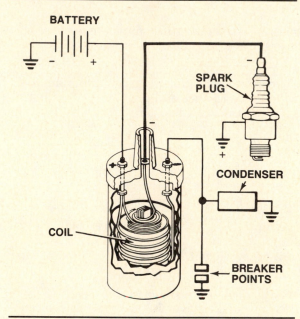

Figure 14-37. Negative, or ground, ignition polarity.

Copper-core spark plugs

Many plug manufacturers are making plugs with a copper segment inside the center electrode. The copper provides faster heat transfer from the electrode to the insulator and then to the cylinder head and engine coolant. Copper-core plugs are also extended-tip plugs. The combined effects are a more stable heat range over a greater range of engine temperatures and greater resistance to fouling and misfire.

Platinum-tip spark plugs

Platinum-tip plugs are used in some late-model engines to increase firing efficiency. The platinum center electrode increases electrical conductivity, which helps prevent misfiring with lean mixtures and high temperatures. Since platinum is very resistant to corrosion and wear from combustion chamber gases and heat, recommended plug life is double that of other plugs.

Long-reach, short-thread spark plugs

Some late-model GM engines, Ford four-cylinder engines, and Ford 5.0-liter V8 engines use 14-mm, tapered-seat plugs with a 3/4-inch reach but which only have threads for a little over half of their length, figure 14-36. The plug part number includes a suffix that indicates the special thread design, although a fully threaded plug can be substituted if necessary.

Advanced combustion igniters

This extended-tip, copper-core, platinum-tipped spark plug was introduced by GM in 1991. It combines all the attributes of the individual plug designs described earlier and uses a nickel-plated shell for corrosion protection.

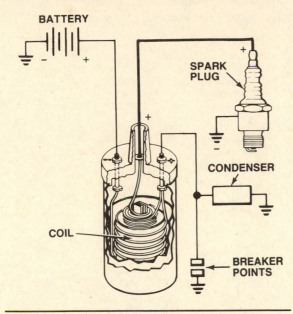

Figure 14-38. Reverse, or positive, ignition polarity.

This combination delivers a plug life in excess of 100,000 miles (160,000 km). No longer called a spark plug, the GM advanced combustion igniter (ACI) has a smooth ceramic insulator with no cooling ribs. The insulator is coated with a baked-on boot release compound that prevents the spark plug wire boot from sticking and causing wire damage during removal.

IGNITION POLARITY

If the ignition coil is correctly connected, figure 14-37, voltage will be delivered to the spark plug so that the center electrode is negatively charged and the grounded electrode is positively charged. Electrons will move from the hotter center electrode to the cooler side electrode at a relatively lower voltage. This is called **negative polarity**. If the coil is incorrectly connected, figure 14-38, electrons will be forced to move from the cooler side electrode to the hotter center electrode. This is called **positive polarity**, or reverse polarity. Figure 14-39 shows how much more voltage is required to fire a spark plug with positive polarity than one with negative polarity.

SUMMARY

The ignition secondary circuit generates the high voltage and distributes it to the engine's spark plugs. This circuit contains the coil secondary winding, the distributor cap and rotor, the ignition cables, and the spark plugs.

The ignition coil produces the high voltage necessary to ionize the spark plug gap through

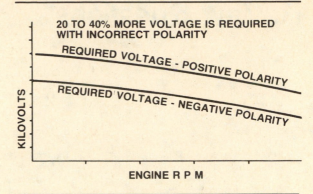

Figure 14-39. More voltage is required to fire a spark plug that has reverse polarity. (Prestolite)

electromagnetic induction. Low-voltage current flow in the primary winding induces high voltage in the secondary winding. A coil must be installed with the same primary polarity as the battery to maintain proper secondary polarity at the spark plugs.

Available voltage is the amount of voltage the coil *can* produce. Required voltage is the voltage necessary to ionize and fire the spark plugs under any given operating condition. Voltage reserve is the difference between available voltage and required voltage. A well-tuned ignition system should have a 60-percent voltage reserve.

The spark plugs allow the high voltage to arc across an air gap and ignite the air-fuel mixture in the combustion chamber. Important design features of a spark plug are its reach, heat range, thread and seat size, and the air gap. Other special features of spark plugs are the use of resistors, extended tips, wide gaps, and copper cores. For efficient spark plug firing, ignition polarity must be established so that the center electrode of the plug is negative and the ground electrode is positive.

Negative Polarity: Also called ground polarity. A correct polarity of the ignition coil connections. Coil voltage is delivered to the spark plugs so that the center electrode of the plug is negatively charged and the grounded electrode is positively charged.

Positive Polarity: Also called reverse polarity. An incorrect polarity of the ignition coil connections. Coil voltage is delivered to the spark plug so that the center electrode of the plug is positively charged and the grounded electrode is negatively charged.

Review Questions

Choose the single most correct answer.
Compare your answers with the correct answers on page 431.

1. Which of the following is used as insulation to protect the windings of coils?
   a. Steel
   b. Wood
   c. Iron
   d. Plastic

2. Which of the following statements is true about ignition coils?
   a. Easily repaired
   b. Adjustments made by setscrews
   c. Requires periodic adjustment
   d. Can be replaced

3. Many of Delco-Remy's solid-state ignition systems have a coil mounted:
   a. On the engine
   b. On a fender panel
   c. On the distributor cap
   d. On the radiator

4. When the coil terminals are properly connected to the battery, the grounded end of the secondary circuit is electrically:
   a. Positive
   b. Negative
   c. Neutral
   d. Ionized

5. A loss of one volt in the primary circuit can decrease available secondary voltage by _____ volts.
   a. 10
   b. 100
   c. 1,000
   d. 10,000

6. The accompanying illustration shows:

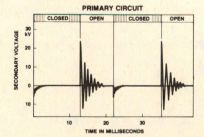

   a. Secondary circuit firing pulse trace
   b. Secondary circuit ignition pulse trace
   c. Secondary circuit no-load voltage trace
   d. Secondary circuit spark voltage trace

7. Firing voltage is usually about _____ as high as spark voltage.
   a. One-fourth
   b. One-half
   c. Four times
   d. Two times

8. The voltage delivered by the coil is:
   a. Its full voltage capacity under all operating conditions
   b. Approximately half of its full voltage capacity at all times
   c. Only the voltage necessary to fire the plugs under any given operating condition
   d. Its full voltage capacity only while starting

9. The voltage reserve is the:
   a. Voltage required from the coil to fire a plug
   b. Maximum secondary voltage capacity of the coil
   c. Primary circuit voltage at the battery side of the ballast resistor
   d. Difference between the required voltage and the available voltage of the secondary circuit

10. A well-tuned ignition system should have a voltage reserve of about _____ of available voltage, under most operating conditions.
    a. 30 percent
    b. 60 percent
    c. 100 percent
    d. 150 percent

11. Bakelite is a synthetic material used in distributors because of its good:
    a. Permeability
    b. Conductance
    c. Insulation
    d. Capacitance

12. Which of the following are basic parts of a spark plug?
    a. Plastic core
    b. Paper insulator
    c. Fiberglass shell
    d. Two electrodes

13. Which of the following is *not* an important design feature among types of spark plugs?
    a. Reach
    b. Heat range
    c. Polarity
    d. Air gap

14. In the illustration below, the dimension arrows indicate the:

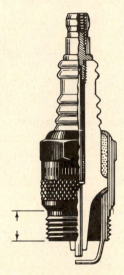

    a. Heat range
    b. Resistor portion of the electrode
    c. Extended core length
    d. Reach

15. All spark plugs have:
    a. A resistor
    b. An extended core
    c. A ceramic insulator
    d. A series gap

15

Ignition Timing and Spark Advance Control

Chapter Twelve dealt with ignition intervals and how the ignition must be synchronized with crankshaft rotation and cylinder firing order. We also have seen that the initial ignition timing is set for the best engine operation at a specific engine speed, usually at or near slow-idle speed. When engine speed changes, ignition timing also must change.

In this chapter, we will learn how ignition timing changes as engine speed and load change and how timing changes are made. This chapter also covers some centrifugal and vacuum advance units and the emission control systems that have been used to modify the vacuum advance operation. With the latest generation of electronic ignition systems, the computer has taken the place of mechanical and vacuum advance devices. Early electronic spark-timing controls are discussed at the end of the chapter.

REVIEWING BASIC TIMING AND BURN TIME

Engine speed and load changes require the ignition timing to advance or to retard. As we have seen, the burn time of an air-fuel mixture is about three milliseconds. Maximum combustion pressure should occur with the piston, connecting rod, and crankshaft in position to produce the most power. At low engine speeds, relatively little spark advance is required to achieve this. However, as engine speed increases, the process of combustion must be started earlier to provide enough burn time.

We have said that burn time is *about* three milliseconds. This means that it does vary somewhat with engine load. When the fuel system provides a lean air-fuel mixture under light load, it takes longer to ignite and burn the mixture. Conversely, richer mixtures ignited under a heavy load burn a little faster.

SPARK ADVANCE

There are two basic factors that govern ignition timing: engine speed and load. All changes in timing are related to these two factors:

- Timing must increase, or advance, as engine speed increases, and it must decrease, or retard, as engine speed decreases
- Timing must decrease, or retard, as load increases, and it must increase, or advance, as load decreases.

Optimum ignition timing under any given combination of these basic factors will result in maximum cylinder pressure. In turn, this delivers maximum power with a minimum of exhaust emissions and the best possible fuel economy.

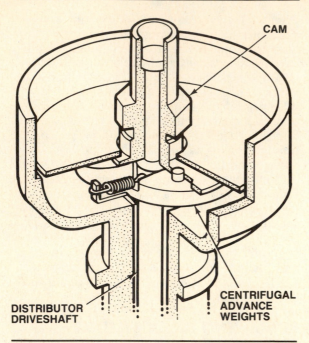

Figure 15-1. The centrifugal advance weights transfer the rotation of the distributor drive shaft to the cam, or trigger wheel, and the rotor.

When ignition takes place too early, the combustion pressure slows down the piston. If timing is too far advanced, the increased combustion pressure causes engine knock. When ignition takes place too late, the piston is too far down on its power stroke to benefit from the combustion pressure, resulting in a power loss.

Before the introduction of computer-controlled timing, most automotive distributors had two spark advance mechanisms to react to engine operating changes and alter ignition timing:

- The centrifugal advance changed ignition timing to match engine speed by altering the position of the distributor cam or trigger wheel on the distributor shaft
- The vacuum advance changed ignition timing to match engine load by altering the position of the breaker points or the magnetic pickup coil (electronic sensor).

These changes in position altered the time, relative to crankshaft position, at which the primary circuit was opened.

Centrifugal Advance — Speed

The **centrifugal advance**, or **mechanical advance**, mechanism consists of two weights connected to the distributor driveshaft by two

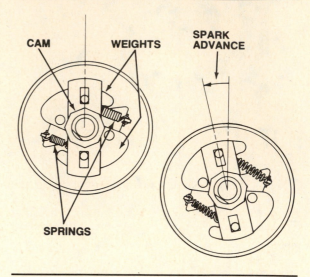

Figure 15-2. When the centrifugal advance weights move, the position of the cam, or trigger wheel, and the rotor changes.

springs, figure 15-1. The distributor cam, or electronic trigger wheel, and the distributor rotor are mounted on another shaft. The second shaft fits over the driveshaft like a sleeve. Driveshaft motion is transmitted to the second shaft through the centrifugal advance weights. When the weights move, the relative position of the driveshaft and the second shaft changes.

As engine speed increases, distributor shaft rotation speed increases. The advance weights move outward because of **centrifugal force**. The outward movement of the weights shifts the second shaft and the cam or the trigger wheel, figure 15-2. The primary circuit opens earlier in the compression stroke, and the spark occurs earlier.

Each advance weight is connected to the distributor driveshaft by a control spring. These springs are selected to allow the correct amount of weight movement and ignition advance for a particular engine.

At low engine speeds, spring tension holds the weights in, so that initial timing is maintained. As engine speed increases, centrifugal force overcomes spring tension and the weights move outward. The advance is not a large, rapid change, but rather a slow, gradual shift. Figure 15-3 shows a typical centrifugal advance curve. The advance curve can be changed by changing the tension of the control springs. Remember that centrifugal advance responds to engine speed.

In most distributors, the centrifugal advance mechanism is mounted below the cam and breaker points, figure 15-1, or below the trigger wheel and pickup coil. Delco-Remy V6 and

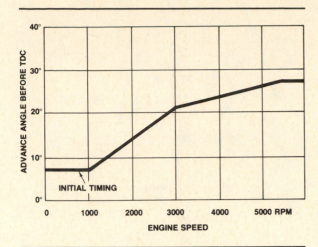

Figure 15-3. A typical distributor advance curve.

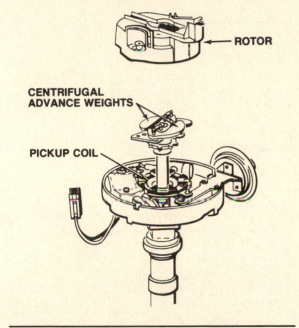

Figure 15-4. Delco-Remy V6 and V8 distributors have the centrifugal advance mechanism above the cam and rotor, or above the pickup coil and trigger wheel, as shown.

V8 distributors, as well as some distributors made in Japan, have the advance mechanism above the cam or trigger wheel, just below the rotor, figure 15-4.

Vacuum Advance — Load

The **vacuum advance** mechanism allows efficient engine performance within a range of air-fuel ratios. These ratios are important, since there are limits to how rich or how lean they can be and still remain fully combustible. The **air-fuel ratio** with which an engine can oper-

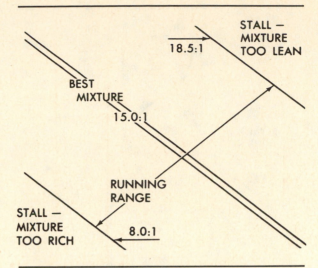

Figure 15-5. Air-fuel ratio limits for a 4-stroke gasoline engine. (Chevrolet)

ate efficiently ranges from 8:1 to 18.5:1 by weight, figure 15-5.

These ratios are generally stated as eight parts of air combined with one part of gasoline (8:1), which is the richest mixture that an engine can tolerate and still fire regularly. A ratio of 18.5 parts of air mixed with one part of gasoline (18.5:1) is the leanest mixture that an engine can tolerate without misfiring.

An average air-fuel ratio is about 15:1. This mixture takes about three milliseconds to burn. A lean mixture (one with more air and less fuel) requires more time to burn. The ignition timing must be advanced to provide maximum combustion pressure at the correct piston position. A rich mixture (one with more fuel and less air) burns more quickly and emits more exhaust pollutants. Ignition timing should be retarded for complete combustion and emission control.

Centrifugal (Mechanical) Advance: A method of advancing the ignition spark using weights in the distributor that react to centrifugal force.

Centrifugal Force: The natural tendency of objects, when rotated, to move away from the center of rotation.

Vacuum Advance: The use of engine vacuum to advance ignition spark timing by moving the distributor breaker plate.

Air-Fuel Ratio: The ratio of air to gasoline by weight in the air-fuel mixture drawn into an engine.

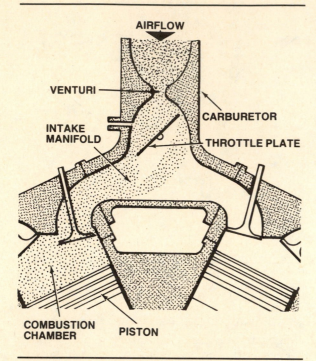

Figure 15-6. Air flows through the carburetor and intake manifold to reach the combustion chamber.

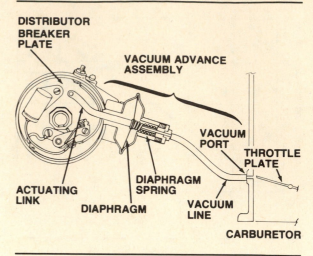

Figure 15-7. The vacuum advance assembly is connected to a port in the carburetor.

Engine Vacuum

The reciprocating engine can be considered as an air pump. As a piston moves downward, air pressure in the cylinder decreases. Air from the atmosphere rushes in to fill the void.

The fuel delivery system uses this air movement to carry fuel to the cylinders. On older cars, the air must travel through a carburetor, figure 15-6, to reach the cylinders. Under several operating conditions, air movement caused by the downstroke of a piston is not great enough to draw fuel into the cylinder. The carburetor forces the air to flow through a restriction called a **venturi**. This increases the speed of the airflow and creates a low-pressure (vacuum) area. Fuel is drawn into the airflow by the vacuum, and the resulting air-fuel mixture enters the cylinder combustion chambers. The air-fuel ratio changes as the **vacuum** in the carburetor changes.

The ignition timing must be changed as the air-fuel ratio changes, so that the mixture has enough time to burn. The vacuum advance mechanism is connected to a small hole or port in the carburetor, figure 15-7, just above the throttle plate. This is called **ported vacuum**. When vacuum exists at the port, timing is advanced. When no vacuum exists at the port, the timing remains at a basic setting or is affected only by the centrifugal advance. The vacuum advance mechanism will be explained

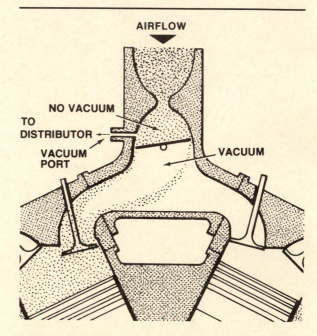

Figure 15-8. When the throttle is closed during idle or deceleration, there is no vacuum at the port.

in more detail later. The following paragraphs explain the relationship between carburetor vacuum and the need for advanced timing.

The driver of a carburetor-equipped automobile controls engine load and carburetor vacuum through the action of the throttle plate, which is a variable restriction in the carburetor airflow. When the engine is at idle, figure 15-8, the throttle plate is almost closed. Very little air flows through the carburetor to mix with the fuel. With this rich air-fuel mixture, no spark advance is necessary. High vacuum exists in the intake manifold, but there is

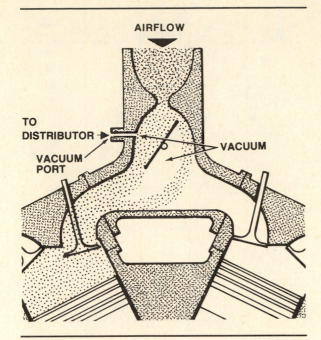

Figure 15-9. When the throttle is partially open, the port is exposed to manifold vacuum.

no vacuum at the port because it is above the closed throttle plate. There is no vacuum-controlled spark advance with a closed throttle. The large amount of vacuum *below* the throttle plate exists because of the small amount of air entering the engine. This is called **manifold vacuum**.

When the throttle plate is partially open, figure 15-9, more air can flow through the carburetor. The air-fuel mixture becomes lean and requires an advanced spark. Since the port is now exposed to vacuum, ignition timing advances.

At medium cruising speeds, the engine operates with a partly open throttle and an air-fuel ratio of approximately 15:1. Airflow velocity is high, and the vacuum signal at the carburetor port is strong enough to provide vacuum advance for this relatively lean air-fuel mixture.

A lean mixture is not the only factor that affects ignition timing requirements. During part-throttle operation, the cylinders are only partially filled with the air-fuel mixture. Because there is less to compress, the compression pressure is less. A less highly compressed mixture takes a longer time to burn.

At wide-open throttle, figure 15-10, the power circuit in the carburetor provides a richer mixture than at part-throttle cruising. Also, the cylinders are more completely filled because airflow volume increases. These factors cause a faster burn that requires the ignition timing to retard or decrease slightly for proper efficiency. Manifold vacuum and ported vacuum drop at wide-open throttle and become approximately

equal. Vacuum may drop to as little as five inches of mercury (17 kPa), and typically seven inches (24 kPa) of vacuum are required to operate a vacuum advance mechanism.

Vacuum advance also decreases when the throttle is opened quickly from idle or a part-throttle position. This occurs because airflow velocity lags behind throttle opening. This reduced vacuum will not draw enough fuel through the main metering circuit of the carburetor, so the accelerator pump supplies extra fuel. This momentarily rich mixture does not need as much spark advance for complete combustion. Because the vacuum at the vacuum port of the carburetor is low when the throttle is first opened quickly, the vacuum advance decreases or retards to meet the needs of the momentarily rich mixture. Remember that vacuum advance responds to engine load.

Venturi: A restriction in an airflow, such as in a carburetor, that increases the airflow speed and creates a reduction in pressure.

Vacuum: A pressure less than atmospheric pressure.

Ported Vacuum: Vacuum immediately above the throttle plate in a carburetor.

Manifold Vacuum: Low pressure in an engine's intake manifold, below the carburetor throttle.

■ **Air Pressure High and Low**

You can think of an internal combustion engine as a big air pump. As the pistons move up and down in the cylinders, they pump in air and pump out the burned exhaust. They do this by creating a difference in air pressure. The air outside an engine has weight and exerts pressure. So does the air inside an engine.

As a piston moves down on an intake stroke with the intake valve open, it creates a larger area inside the cylinder for the air to fill. This lowers the air pressure inside the engine. Because the pressure inside the engine is lower than the pressure outside, air will flow in through the carburetor to try to fill the low-pressure area and equalize the pressure.

We call the low pressure in the engine "vacuum". You can think of vacuum as pulling air into the engine, but it is really the higher pressure on the outside that forces air into the low-pressure area inside. The difference in pressure between two areas is called a "pressure differential". The pressure differential principle has many applications in an automobile engine.

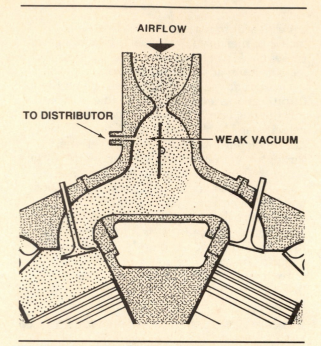

Figure 15-10. When the throttle is fully open, the vacuum at the port is too weak to cause any vacuum advance.

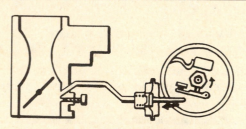

**THROTTLE OPENED
VACUUM PORT UNCOVERED
VACUUM SPARK ADVANCE INTRODUCED**

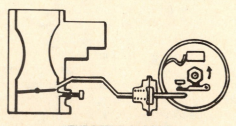

**THROTTLE CLOSED
VACUUM PORT COVERED
NO VACUUM SPARK ADVANCE**

Figure 15-11. Vacuum at the carburetor port causes the position of the breaker plate to shift.

Vacuum advance mechanism
The vacuum advance mechanism at the distributor, figure 15-7, consists of the:

- Movable breaker plate on which the points or electronic pickup coil are mounted

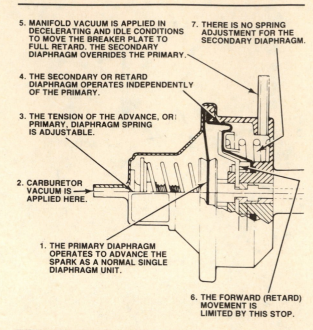

5. MANIFOLD VACUUM IS APPLIED IN DECELERATING AND IDLE CONDITIONS TO MOVE THE BREAKER PLATE TO FULL RETARD. THE SECONDARY DIAPHRAGM OVERRIDES THE PRIMARY.

4. THE SECONDARY OR RETARD DIAPHRAGM OPERATES INDEPENDENTLY OF THE PRIMARY.

3. THE TENSION OF THE ADVANCE, OR PRIMARY, DIAPHRAGM SPRING IS ADJUSTABLE.

2. CARBURETOR VACUUM IS APPLIED HERE.

1. THE PRIMARY DIAPHRAGM OPERATES TO ADVANCE THE SPARK AS A NORMAL SINGLE DIAPHRAGM UNIT.

7. THERE IS NO SPRING ADJUSTMENT FOR THE SECONDARY DIAPHRAGM.

6. THE FORWARD (RETARD) MOVEMENT IS LIMITED BY THIS STOP.

Figure 15-12. Operation of a typical dual-diaphragm vacuum advance assembly. (Ford)

- Vacuum assembly, a housing with a flexible diaphragm and a spring
- Actuating link that connects the vacuum diaphragm to the breaker plate
- Tubing to connect the vacuum unit to the vacuum source.

When the **diaphragm** is pulled toward a vacuum, it pulls the actuating link, figure 15-11. This rotates the breaker plate to change the position of the point rubbing block in relation to the cam. Ignition timing increases or advances. In an electronic system, the pickup is shifted relative to the trigger wheel to advance timing.

Some older vacuum advance units can be adjusted by changing spring tension against the diaphragm.

Some distributors used by Ford, Volkswagen, and AMC had a dual-diaphragm vacuum unit, and this design was also common on Japanese cars. A dual-diaphragm vacuum advance unit retards timing during certain engine operating conditions. In these systems, figure 15-12, one diaphragm acts as described above to advance ignition timing. The second diaphragm is exposed to intake manifold vacuum (between the throttle plate and the combustion chamber), which is high during idle and closed-throttle deceleration. This vacuum acts upon the second diaphragm to shift the breaker plate in the retard direction.

For exhaust emission control, the retard diaphragm can override the advance diaphragm.

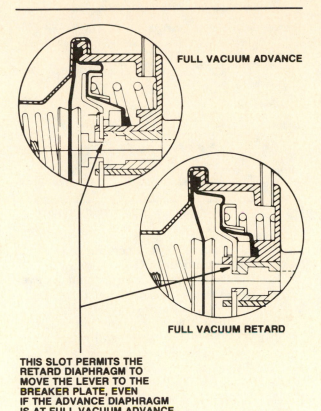

FULL VACUUM ADVANCE

FULL VACUUM RETARD

THIS SLOT PERMITS THE
RETARD DIAPHRAGM TO
MOVE THE LEVER TO THE
BREAKER PLATE, EVEN
IF THE ADVANCE DIAPHRAGM
IS AT FULL VACUUM ADVANCE.

Figure 15-13. In a dual-diaphragm unit, the retard diaphragm can override the action of the advance diaphragm. (Ford)

This causes timing to retard even when the advance diaphragm is at an advanced position, figure 15-13.

Total Ignition Advance

The two types of advance mechanisms we have described work on different parts of the distributor to advance timing. Therefore, their effects are additive: the **total ignition advance** is the sum of the centrifugal advance and the vacuum advance, *plus* the initial ignition timing. This formula determines actual ignition timing under all conditions. Figure 15-14 shows the advance curves of a typical ignition system.

EARLY SPARK-TIMING EMISSION CONTROLS

Spark-timing control systems were introduced in the 1960s to reduce exhaust emissions. Certain types of pollutants are produced under specific engine operating conditions. Spark-timing control systems help reduce **hydrocarbons (HC)**, and to some extent, **oxides of nitrogen (NO$_x$)** emissions. Retarded timing reduces combustion temperature to help re-

duce NO$_x$ formation. At the same time, higher temperatures are created toward the end of combustion. This results in higher exhaust temperatures, which reduce the amount of HC in the exhaust.

Early Distributor Controls

Early emission-control equipment advanced or retarded ignition timing under particular engine operating conditions, usually during starting, deceleration, and idle.

Diaphragm: A thin flexible wall, separating two cavities, such as the diaphragm in a vacuum advance unit.

Total Ignition Advance: The sum of centrifugal advance, vacuum advance, and initial timing; expressed in crankshaft degrees.

Hydrocarbon: A chemical compound of hydrogen and carbon. A major pollutant from an internal combustion engine. Gasoline itself is a hydrocarbon compound.

Oxides of Nitrogen: Chemical compounds of nitrogen and oxygen. Major pollutants produced by an internal combustion engine which combine with hydrocarbons to produce smog.

■ Does a Vacuum Pull Air In?

As you study automotive service, you see many applications for vacuum devices. The engine is a large air pump and the source of vacuum used to operate a variety of accessories. Vacuum diaphragms control ignition advance. EGR operation, carburetor chokes and power valves, air conditioning doors and vents, heater water valves, concealed headlamp mechanisms, power brake boosters, cruise control servos, and many other devices.

It's very easy — and practical for day-to-day use — to think of vacuum as an independent force. But it isn't. Vacuum is simply air pressure that is lower than atmospheric pressure. Vacuum doesn't actually pull air in; air pressure pushes. We talk about connecting a diaphragm to a "vacuum source", but what actually moves the diaphragm? Low pressure (vacuum) on one side allows higher atmospheric pressure on the other to move the diaphragm.

Similarly, we often talk about finding and fixing a "vacuum leak". That concept works just fine for on-the-job troubleshooting, but ask yourself, "Can vacuum actually *leak*?" Not really. What you are actually fixing is an air leak. An unwanted opening allows air to leak *into* the low-pressure area that we call a vacuum.

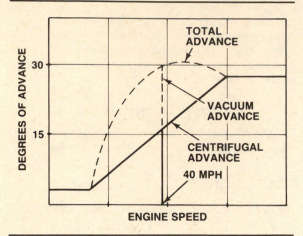

Figure 15-14. This typical advance curve shows that the total advance is the total of vacuum plus centrifugal advances.

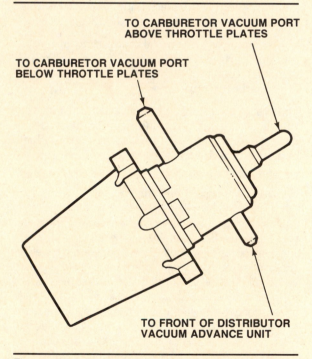

Figure 15-15. A deceleration vacuum advance valve.

The deceleration vacuum advance valve, figure 15-15, was used during the mid-to-late 1960s on Chrysler, Ford, AMC, and Pontiac products with manual transmissions. In a manual-transmission car, the air-fuel mixture becomes extremely rich when decelerating or shifting gears.

This valve momentarily switches the vacuum for the vacuum advance from a low-vacuum source at the carburetor to a high-vacuum source during deceleration, then back to the low-vacuum source. This prevents overly retarded timing during deceleration or gear shift-

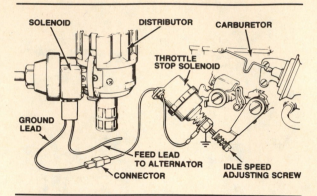

Figure 15-16. A distributor vacuum retard solenoid.

ing, which could cause some engines to emit a lot of **carbon monoxide (CO)**.

While the deceleration vacuum advance valve was effective against CO emissions, it did not limit HC and NO_x emissions. As emission limits for these pollutants became tighter in the early 1970s, use of the device ceased and manufacturers developed other devices that worked against all three major pollutants.

PRINCIPAL SPARK-TIMING CONTROLS OF THE 1970S

These systems were designed primarily to delay vacuum advance at low and intermediate speeds and allow it during high-speed cruising. The most common types of control systems used in the early to mid-1970s are:

- Distributor solenoids
- Vacuum delay valves
- Speed- and transmission-controlled timing.

Distributor Solenoids

A distributor vacuum retard solenoid was used on some 1970-1971 Chrysler products with V8 engines and automatic transmissions. This electric solenoid is attached to and controls the action of the distributor vacuum advance unit, figure 15-16.

The solenoid is energized by contacts mounted on a carburetor throttle stop solenoid. When the throttle is closed, the idle adjusting screw contacts the carburetor solenoid to complete the ground circuit. The contacts in the carburetor solenoid carry current to the distributor solenoid windings. Since the distributor solenoid plunger is connected to the vacuum diaphragm, solenoid movement shifts the breaker plate in the retard direction.

When engine speed increases, the idle adjusting screw breaks contact with the carburetor solenoid. Current to the distributor

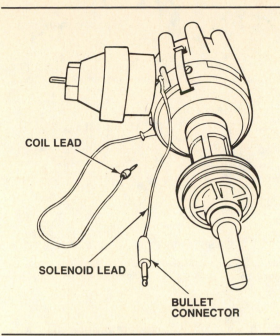

Figure 15-17. The installation of a distributor advance solenoid.

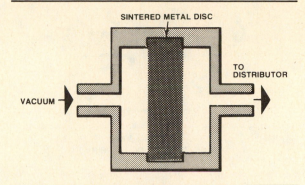

Figure 15-18. A cross-sectional view of a vacuum delay valve containing sintered metal to slow the application of vacuum.

solenoid is stopped, and normal vacuum advance is allowed.

Some 1972-73 Chrysler V8 distributors had a spark-timing advance solenoid that promoted better starting by providing a 7.5-degree spark advance. The solenoid is mounted in the distributor vacuum unit, figure 15-17. It is activated by power from the starter relay at the same terminal that sends power to the starter solenoid. The solenoid is activated only while the engine is cranking.

The starting advance solenoid is not an emission control device by itself, but it allows lower basic timing settings, which help to control emissions while providing advanced timing for quicker starting.

Vacuum Delay Valves

The vacuum delay valve "filters" the carburetor vacuum, slowing its application to the distributor vacuum advance unit. Generally, vacuum must be present in the system for 15-30 seconds before it is allowed to affect the advance mechanism.

One method of vacuum delay was used in Ford's spark delay valve (SDV) system, figure 15-18. In this design, vacuum must work its way through a **sintered**, or sponge-like, metal disc to reach the distributor. Many GM engines also used this type of spark delay valve.

Another method of vacuum delay was used in Chrysler's orifice spark advance control

Carbon Monoxide: An odorless, colorless, tasteless poisonous gas. A pollutant produced by an internal combustion engine.

Sintered: Welded together without using heat to form a porous material, such as the metal disc used in some vacuum delay valves.

■ Starting the Locomobile

If you owned a 1927 or 1928 Locomobile, you had to know how to adjust the spark advance lever when you started your car. The spark lever allowed you to advance or retard spark timing for all conditions. Here are the owner's manual instructions for positioning the lever when starting your Locomobile:

1. Be sure gear shift lever is in neutral position and the hand brake is applied.
2. Retard the spark lever, which is at right center of steering wheel, about one-half way down from the full advance position.
3. The throttle control lever is to the left of center of the steering wheel. Move lever up an inch or more from the closed position.
4. Turn ignition switch arm to the "on" position.
5. Pull choke button as far as it will go, then place the right foot on the starting switch button and press down. On pushing down on the starting switch button, the starter gear will engage itself in the teeth of the flywheel and the motor will start to turn over. As soon as the motor starts, release the starting button and push the choke button part-way in. As the motor warms up a little, push the choke button all the way in. Do this as soon as possible to avoid excessive choking, as any excess gasoline thrown into the cylinders will pass by the rings into the oil in the crankcase, thus diluting and partly destroying its lubricating value.
6. Advance spark by pushing lever up as far as it will go and bring the throttle lever toward the closed position to slow the motor down.

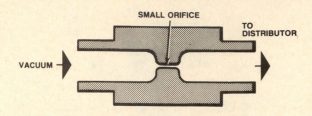

Figure 15-19. A cross-sectional view of a vacuum delay valve using a small orifice to delay the application of vacuum.

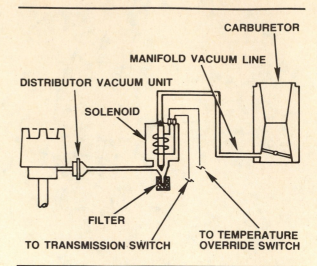

Figure 15-20. A simplified transmission-controlled spark system.

(OSAC) system, figure 15-19. A small **orifice** is placed in the vacuum line to delay vacuum buildup.

Manufacturers have often combined the use of vacuum delay valves with other emission control systems. All valves operate on one of the two principles just described.

Speed- and Transmission-Controlled Timing

These systems prevented any distributor vacuum advance when the vehicle is in a low gear or is traveling slowly. A solenoid controls the application of vacuum to the advance mechanism, figure 15-20. Current through the solenoid is controlled by a switch that reacts to various vehicle operating conditions.

A control switch used with a manual transmission reacts to shift lever position. A control switch used with an automatic transmission will usually react to hydraulic fluid pressure. Both systems prevent any vacuum advance when the car is in a low or intermediate gear.

A speed-sensing switch may be connected to the vehicle speedometer cable, figure 15-21. The switch signals an electronic control module when vehicle speed is below a predetermined level. The module triggers a solenoid that controls engine vacuum at the distributor.

Both vacuum-delay systems and speed- and transmission-controlled systems usually have an engine temperature bypass. This allows normal vacuum advance at high and low engine temperatures. Before March 1973, some systems had an **ambient temperature** override switch. Most of these switches were discontinued at the direction of the Environmental Protection Agency (EPA). Later temperature-override systems sense engine coolant temperature or underhood temperature.

DECLINE AND FALL OF EARLY SPARK-TIMING CONTROLS

Many spark-timing control systems were discontinued when catalytic converters were in-

troduced in 1975. Converters reduce HC and CO emissions, and exhaust gas recirculation (EGR) provides more effective control of NO_x emissions.

Emission standards continued to tighten during the mid-1970s. During this period, fuel mileage requirements also became important. Meeting the challenge of more stringent emission standards and better fuel economy required far more accurate ignition system performance than mechanical devices could deliver. Centrifugal and vacuum advance mechanisms simply could not respond quickly enough to changes in engine operating conditions to provide the necessary accuracy, so major manufacturers turned to computer-controlled ignition systems.

EARLY ELECTRONICALLY CONTROLLED TIMING

In a computer-controlled ignition system, an electronic control module receives signals from various system sensors. These signals may include information on coolant temperature, atmospheric pressure and temperature, throttle position and rate of change of position, and crankshaft position. The central processing unit (CPU) in the control module is programmed to interpret this information and calculate the proper ignition timing for each individual spark.

Early systems worked with the manufacturers' existing solid-state ignition systems. Some changes were made to these ignition systems because they no longer had to control spark timing, but many components remained the same.

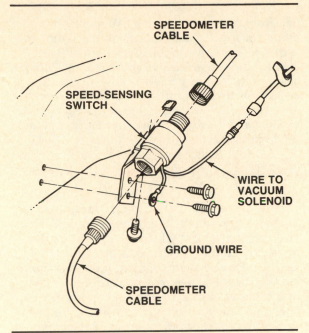

SPEEDOMETER CABLE

SPEED-SENSING SWITCH

WIRE TO VACUUM SOLENOID

GROUND WIRE

SPEEDOMETER CABLE

Figure 15-21. Most speed-controlled spark systems use a speed-sensing switch such as this. (Cadillac)

Early computer-controlled ignition systems used by domestic manufacturers can be divided into two types. In one type, rotation of the distributor shaft sends a crankshaft position signal to the control module. The other type receives crankshaft position information from a sensor mounted near the crankshaft, figure 15-22. The sensor reacts to a trigger attached to the crankshaft itself.

Signals taken directly from the crankshaft are more accurate than those taken from the distributor shaft. The gears or chain driving the camshaft and the gears driving the distributor shaft are manufactured within tolerances. Although the actual measurements are small, these tolerances can combine to cause a significant difference between crankshaft position and ignition timing.

Early systems used by Chrysler, GM, and Ford were called:

- Chrysler Electronic Lean-Burn (ELB)
- GM Microprocessed Sensing and Automatic Regulation (MISAR)
- Ford Electronic Engine Control (EEC).

Orifice: A small opening in a tube, pipe, or valve.

Ambient Temperature: The temperature of the air surrounding a particular device or location.

■ **Vacuum Measurement**

When you work with vacuum devices on late-model cars, you will encounter several different units of measurement used to gauge vacuum. The auto industry customarily has measured air pressure in pounds per square inch (psi) or kilopascals (kPa), and vacuum in inches of mercury (in. Hg) or millimeters of mercury (mm Hg). This is confusing right away, because we're using two different kinds of units to measure essentially the same thing — air pressure. The reason we use both is based on scientific tradition.

Air pressure and vacuum are measured in a laboratory with a device called a manometer. This is a U-shaped glass tube with each end connected to different pressure sources. One end can be opened to the atmosphere, and the other can be connected to a pump or another source of low pressure. The tube is filled with liquid that moves up and down the two columns formed by the two legs of the U. Using two columns joined in a "U" eliminates the effects of gravity and the weight of the liquid. Displacement caused by changes in pressure is read in marks graduated on the columns.

Laboratory manometers ordinarily are filled with mercury because it is stable and flows freely when exposed to pressure differentials. When low pressure on one side drops enough to move the mercury column one inch, vacuum (low pressure) equals 1 in. Hg. When atmospheric pressure is removed completely from one side of the manometer, the mercury column is displaced 29.291 inches at 32°F (0°C). Thus, 29.921 inches of mercury equals one atmosphere of negative pressure, or 14.696 psi. When the manometer column is graduated in millimeters instead of inches, one atmosphere of displacement equals 760 mm Hg.

Another unit you will encounter is the "bar". A bar equals one unit of atmospheric pressure. This is barometric pressure, and that is where we get the term "bar". A standard bar equals one kilogram of force applied to one square centimeter. This equals 750 mm Hg or 14.2 psi. These values are close to the customary atmospheric pressure values of 14.7 psi and 760 mm Hg. All standard pressures are calculated at 32°F (0°C) because pressure drops as temperature rises, and vice versa.

In automobile service, we work with psi and kPa to measure positive pressure. The most common units of vacuum measurement are in. Hg, mm Hg, and bar. Here are some handy conversion factors you can use to switch from one unit to another:

1 psi = 6.895 kPa
1 psi = 2.036 in. Hg = 51.72 mm Hg
1 in. Hg = 0.4912 psi
1 bar = 14.7 psi = 29.9 in. Hg = 760 mm Hg

All these equivalent measurements are at a standard temperature of 32°F (0°C), but the conversions are quite close enough for car service work.

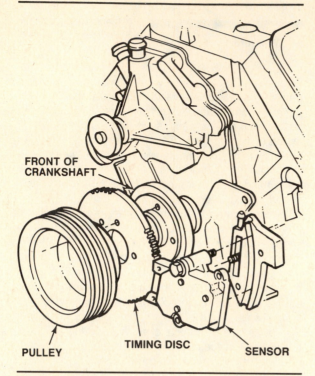

FRONT OF
CRANKSHAFT

PULLEY   TIMING DISC   SENSOR

Figure 15-22. Crankshaft position signals can be taken directly from the crankshaft.

These early electronic timing control systems were partial-function engine control systems. They controlled ignition timing only. They were not fully integrated systems that controlled fuel metering with feedback signals from various engine sensors. Nevertheless, these early systems were the ancestors of the late-model engine control systems that we will study in Chapter Seventeen.

The electronic timing-regulation function of all three systems is similar, but the electronics are fundamentally different. The Lean-Burn system uses an analog computer, while MISAR and EEC use digital microprocessors.

The practical difference between analog and digital electronics in this kind of application is that a digital computer can instantly alter tim-

ing from one to 65 degrees. An analog computer must calculate through all the points on a theoretical curve to make such an adjustment. Since an electronic spark advance adjustment takes only a few milliseconds, this fact is not really significant to the driver or serviceman. However, a digital system is more flexible and more economical to build than an analog system.

SUMMARY

Ignition distributors have used two devices to advance or retard spark timing in response to changing conditions of engine operation. The two primary factors which determine spark advance are engine speed and load. The centrifugal advance alters the position of the distributor cam or trigger wheel on the distributor shaft and changes engine timing as engine speed changes. The vacuum advance alters the position of the breaker points or magnetic pickup coil with respect to the cam or trigger wheel. It changes timing as engine load changes. Many different spark-timing emission control systems have been used. Regardless of their design and operation, these systems all regulated distributor vacuum advance. Vacuum advance is generally allowed only at cold startup, during high gear operation, or if the engine overheats. Development of the exhaust gas recirculation (EGR) systems and catalytic converters, and the expanded use of air injection systems, eliminated the use of transmission-controlled spark and speed-controlled spark systems. Electronic spark-timing systems appeared because more accurate control was required. They regulate ignition timing for the best combination of emission control, fuel economy, and driveability. Early electronic spark-timing systems were the forerunners of late-model, fully integrated electronic engine control systems that we will study in Chapter Seventeen.

Review Questions

Choose the single most correct answer.
Compare your answers with the correct answers on page 431.

1. Distributors commonly have two automatic spark advance mechanisms, which are:
   a. Initial advance and mechanical advance
   b. Initial advance and dynamic advance
   c. Dynamic advance and static advance
   d. Centrifugal advance and vacuum advance

2. Centrifugal advance responds directly to engine:
   a. Load
   b. Horsepower
   c. Speed
   d. Torque

3. The purpose of the venturi in the carburetor is to:
   a. Mix the air and fuel mixture
   b. Speed the airflow and create a low-pressure area
   c. Carry fuel to mix with air
   d. Raise the air pressure sufficiently

4. Vacuum advance responds directly to engine:
   a. Load
   b. Horsepower
   c. Speed
   d. Torque

5. The richest air-fuel ratio with which an engine can operate efficiently is:
   a. 4:1
   b. 6:1
   c. 8:1
   d. 16:1

6. At medium cruising speeds, the engine operates with a partially open throttle and an air-fuel ratio of about:
   a. 8:1
   b. 12:1
   c. 15:1
   d. 18.5:1

7. Which of the following is *not* a component of the vacuum advance mechanism?
   a. Movable breaker plate
   b. Throttle valve
   c. Diaphragm
   d. Actuating link

8. Automotive emission control equipment is designed to reduce exhaust emissions of which pollutants?
   a. Hydrogens
   b. Nitrogens
   c. Carbons
   d. Hydrocarbons

9. Almost all spark timing emission control systems work with the vacuum advance units to:
   a. Increase vacuum advance at low and intermediate vehicle speeds
   b. Cut off vacuum advance during high-speed acceleration
   c. Retard the timing during high-speed deceleration
   d. Cut off vacuum advance at low and intermediate vehicle speeds

10. The dual-diaphragm vacuum unit provides:
    a. Twice as much vacuum advance as a single-diaphragm unit
    b. Faster vacuum retard than does a single-diaphragm unit
    c. Both vacuum advance and vacuum retard
    d. Neither vacuum advance nor vacuum retard

16

Solid-State Electronic Ignition Systems

During the 1960s, solid-state ignition systems were used only on a few high-performance engines. Solid-state systems were not standard on domestic automobiles until the early 1970s; foreign carmakers followed a few years after with their versions. Within less than a decade, solid-state systems completely replaced breaker-point ignitions. Breaker-point and electronic ignition systems do the same thing, except that a breaker-point system switches the primary circuit mechanically while an electronic system does by means of a transistor. The major driving force behind the rapid transition to electronic systems was their ability to help meet stringent emission control standards.

Although solid-state systems are more expensive to produce than breaker-point systems, their advantages greatly outweigh the drawback of increased cost:

- Greater available voltage, especially at high engine speeds
- Reliable system performance at all engine speeds
- Potential for more responsive and variable advance curves
- Decreased maintenance.

In addition, engine operation and exhaust emissions are more accurately controlled by solid-state circuitry.

BASIC SOLID-STATE SYSTEMS

Solid-state systems differ from breaker-point systems in the devices used to control primary circuit current. Breaker-point systems use mechanical breaker points to open and close the primary circuit. The points are operated by a cam on the distributor shaft. Most solid-state systems use an electronic switch in the form of a sealed module to control primary circuit current. This module contains one or more transistors, integrated circuits, or other solid-state control components. A triggering device in the distributor functions with the control module.

As we learned in Chapter Thirteen, this triggering device is usually a magnetic pulse generator or a Hall-effect switch. Solid-state ignitions also can be triggered by a set of breaker points, as will be explained later in this chapter.

Solid-state ignitions can be classified in terms of their primary circuit operation. There are two general types:

- Inductive discharge
- Capacitive discharge.

The difference between these types lies in how they use primary current to produce a high-voltage secondary current.

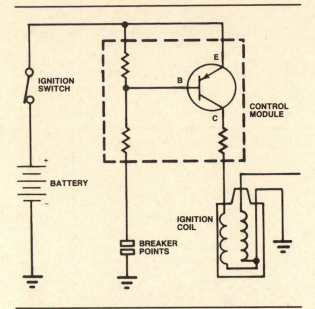

Figure 16-1. A typical breaker-point-triggered electronic ignition system.

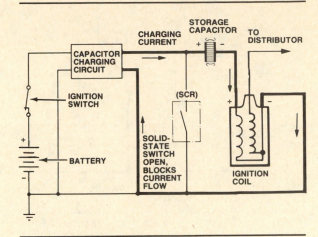

Figure 16-2. When the SCR blocks current, the capacitor is charged. (Bosch)

Inductive Discharge

The inductive discharge system uses battery voltage to create current through the coil primary winding. When a signal is sent by the triggering device, primary current is interrupted. This sudden *decrease* in primary current collapses the coil's magnetic field and induces a high-voltage surge in the secondary circuit.

In an electronic ignition, primary current passes through the ignition control **module**, not through the distributor. Most modules contain one or more large power transistors which switch the primary current. A power or a switching transistor can transmit as much as 10 amperes of current — far more than a set of breaker points can. The power transistor is controlled by a driver transistor that receives voltage signals from the distributor signal generator.

Original equipment solid-state ignitions use inductive discharge to provide about 30,000 volts of available voltage and sustain a spark for about 1.8 milliseconds (a millisecond is one-thousandth of a second, or 0.001 second).

Breaker points

Inductive discharge is used in both electronic and breaker point systems; only the device used to open the circuit differs. The earliest transistorized ignitions used breaker points as a mechanical switch to control voltage applied to a power transistor. Battery voltage causes current to flow through the control module to the breaker points, figure 16-1. This current flow biases the transistor base so that current

can also flow through the coil primary winding. When the points open, current stops. The power transistor will no longer conduct current to the coil primary winding, and an ignition spark is produced.

While full primary current flowed through the transistor, the points carried less than one ampere of current. This minimized the pitting and burning problems encountered with breaker points. However, they were still subject to mechanical wear and bounced at high speeds. Electronic ignitions replaced the points with a solid-state signal generator containing no moving parts.

Capacitive Discharge

The capacitive discharge system uses battery voltage to charge a large capacitor in the control module. The capacitor charging time while the module is on corresponds to dwell in the inductive discharge system. Current flows to the storage capacitor instead of to the coil during this period. The module charging circuit uses a transformer to increase the voltage in the capacitor to as high as 400 volts. The module also contains a **thyristor**, or silicon-

Module: A self-contained, sealed unit that houses the solid-state circuits which control certain electrical or mechanical functions.

Thyristor: A silicon-controlled rectifier (SCR) that normally blocks all current flow. A slight voltage applied to one layer of its semiconductor structure will allow current flow in one direction while blocking current flow in the other direction.

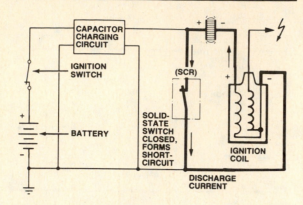

Figure 16-3. When a signal voltage makes the SCR conduct current, the capacitor discharges through the coil primary winding. (Bosch)

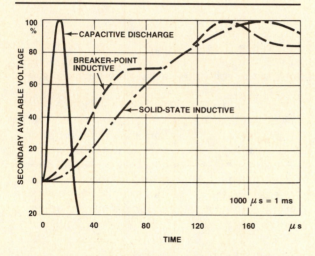

Figure 16-4. A major difference in ignition system performance is the *time* at which maximum secondary voltage is developed. (Bosch)

controlled rectifier (SCR), which functions as an open switch to prevent the capacitor from discharging as it charges, figure 16-2.

When the triggering device signals the module, the SCR closes the capacitor discharge circuit, figure 16-3, which allows the capacitor to discharge through the coil primary winding. This sudden *increase* in primary current expands the coil's magnetic field and induces a high-voltage surge in the secondary circuit.

Capacitive discharge systems are available in the automotive aftermarket, but no major domestic manufacturer installs them as original equipment. A few imported cars such as Audi and Mercedes-Benz have used these ignition systems in the past. They provide a greater available voltage than inductive discharge systems, but can sustain a spark for only about 200 microseconds. The spark is much more in-

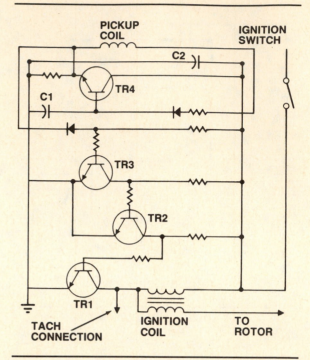

Figure 16-5. A simplified inductive discharge control module. (Chevrolet)

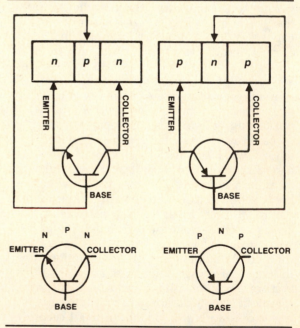

Figure 16-6. Transistor construction and symbols.

tense than that produced by an inductive discharge system and will fire plugs that are in very poor condition. Under certain engine operating conditions, however, a longer spark time is required or the air-fuel mixture will not burn completely.

Figure 16-4 shows the time and voltage characteristics of a breaker-point ignition system, a

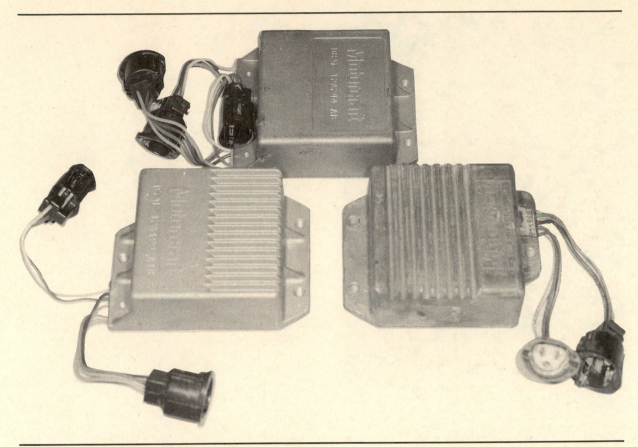

Figure 16-7. Typical external ignition modules from Ford.

capacitive discharge system, and a solid-state inductive system.

CONTROL MODULES AND PRIMARY CIRCUITRY

Although various manufacturers use different circuitry within their ignition system control modules, the basic function of all modules is the same. The following paragraphs explain how these electronic ignition modules work. Because the electronic components within the module are delicate and complex, the modules are sealed during manufacture. If any individual component within the module fails, the entire unit is replaced rather than being repaired. Our explanation of module circuitry and operation will be brief, because you will never need to service module components.

Inductive-Discharge System

Figure 16-5 is a simple inductive-discharge ignition control module circuit. The various triggering devices that can be used in this system all produce the same type of signal: a pulsating voltage. In the illustration, the signal comes from the pickup coil of a magnetic pulse

generator. This pulsating voltage is applied to the control module's transistor and signals the module to turn primary current off.

Primary Circuit Control

Primary circuit control is made possible in an electronic ignition by the ability of transistors to control a high current flow in response to a very small current. The transistor, as we learned in Chapter Three, is like a solid-state relay. It has a base of one type of semiconductor material and an emitter and collector of the other type of material, figure 16-6. A certain amount of current must flow through the base-to-emitter or base-to-collector circuit before any current will flow through the emitter-to-collector circuit. In this way, a small amount of current controls the flow of a large amount of current.

Ignition Transistor Operation

In our illustration, figure 16-5, the module can either be in the dwell mode (when primary current flows) or in the firing mode (when primary current stops).

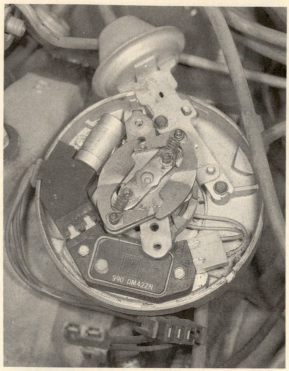

Figure 16-8. The ignition module may be installed inside the distributor, as in the HEI system.

During the dwell mode, TR1 and TR3 are conducting. TR2 is nonconducting. A signal from the pickup coil turns TR3 off, charges C1, and turns TR4 on. This results in the firing mode, as reduced primary current flow causes a high-voltage secondary surge.

TR4 stays on until C1 is discharged. When C1 is discharged, TR3 turns on and the module returns to the dwell mode. At higher engine speeds, C1 will be charged less and less. This results in reduced firing times and longer dwell periods. C2 is a capacitor in the distributor for radio noise suppression.

Actual electronic ignition modules take various forms, but all work on these principles. Some modules are large units, figure 16-7. Others are relatively small integrated circuit (IC) units mounted in the distributor, figure 16-8.

TRIGGERING DEVICES AND IGNITION TIMING

We have seen that all triggering devices produce a pulsating voltage that signals the generation of an ignition spark. Four triggering devices are commonly used in a solid-state ignition:

- Magnetic pulse generator
- Hall-effect switch

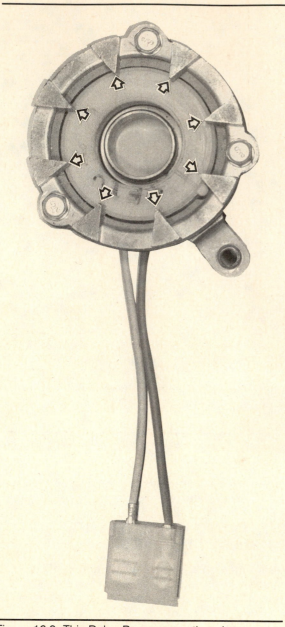

Figure 16-9. This Delco-Remy magnetic pulse generator has a pole piece for each cylinder (arrows), but operates in the same manner as single pole piece units.

- Metal detection
- Optical (light detection) signal generator.

Magnetic Pulse Generator

Magnetic pulse generators are the most common type of original equipment triggering device. They were used in the original Chrysler, GM, and Ford electronic ignitions and are still used today, both by domestic and foreign carmakers.

Most manufacturers use the rotation of the distributor shaft to time voltage pulses. Dis-

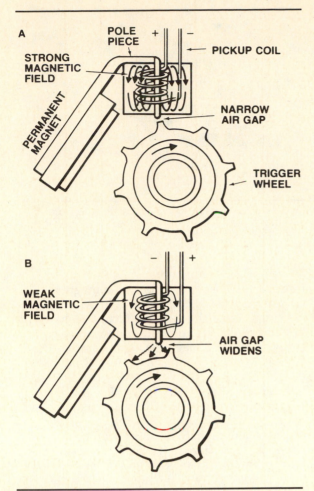

Figure 16-10. The magnetic field expands and collapses as the trigger wheel's teeth move past. This induces a varying strength voltage in the pickup coil.

tributor-mounted magnetic pulse generator designs may have a single pole piece or as many pieces as the trigger wheel has teeth, figure 16-9. Regardless of the design, the pickup coil works in the same way. The pickup coil is wound around the permanent magnet or between the magnet and the pole pieces.

As the nonmagnetic trigger wheel turns with the shaft, figure 16-10, teeth on the wheel approach, align with, and move away from the pole piece of the permanent magnet. The low reluctance of the trigger wheel teeth causes the magnet's field to expand as a tooth approaches, figure 16-10A. The field collapses as the tooth moves away, figure 16-10B. This motion of the magnetic field induces a signal voltage in the pickup coil wound around the pole piece.

Although magnetic field strength is strongest when the trigger wheel tooth is aligned with the pole piece, the rate of expansion or contraction is zero. Pickup coil voltage drops to

zero at this point and changes the bias voltage on the ignition module driver transistor to turn it off. The driver transistor turns off the power transistors to interrupt primary current. The coil then discharges secondary voltage to fire a spark plug.

The point at which the trigger wheel tooth aligns with the pole piece is the ignition timing point for one cylinder and corresponds to the point where breaker points open.

As mentioned in Chapter Fifteen, GM, Ford, and some other carmakers have used magnetic pulse generators that rely on engine crankshaft rotation (instead of distributor shaft rotation) to produce a signal voltage. In GM's 1977 microprocessed sensing and automatic regulation (MISAR) system, the pickup coil, pole piece, and permanent magnet are mounted near a disc on the end of the crankshaft, figure 16-11. Teeth on the disc act like the teeth on a distributor-mounted trigger wheel to induce a single voltage in the pickup coil. In the 1978 MISAR system, the pickup coil and trigger wheel were installed in the distributor.

Ford's EEC-I system takes its crankshaft rotation signal from the flywheel end of the crankshaft. As we will see later in this chapter, Buick's C³I system uses a Hall-effect crankshaft sensor.

Simple Simulator

If you've done much solid-state ignition service, you know that pinpointing an intermittent problem — a random misfire, for example — can be time consuming and frustrating. You often spend a lot of time on the road, driving and waiting for the bug to appear. However, there is an ignition pulse simulator as near as your toolbox that may reduce your troubleshooting time considerably.

An electric engraving tool, driven by a vibrating electromagnet, will produce a high-frequency signal that can trigger the pickup coil in some electronic ignitions. It works fine on Ford solid-state ignitions and may work as well on similar systems.

Simply remove the coil high-voltage lead from the distributor cap and set up about a half-inch (13-mm) gap to ground. Then remove the distributor cap and lay the electric engraver across the top of the distributor near the pickup coil. Be sure it doesn't touch the shaft, pickup coil, or armature (reluctor). Then turn the ignition switch to ON and switch on the engraving tool. A strong, high-frequency spark should be produced at the coil lead. You can use your scope to test coil output and you can poke, wiggle, and otherwise check all connectors while the ignition is "running".

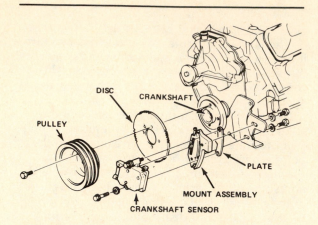

Figure 16-11. This magnetic pulse generator reacts to the movement of a disc mounted on the crankshaft. (Oldsmobile)

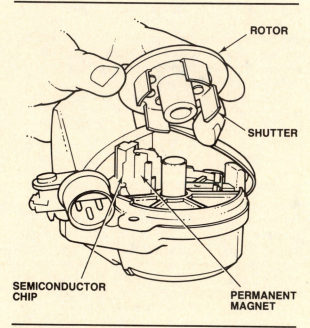

Figure 16-12. A Hall-effect triggering device.

Hall-Effect Switch

The Hall-effect switch is the latest switching technology in electronic ignitions. The Hall-effect triggering assembly uses a small chip of semiconductor material, a permanent magnet, and a ring of low-reluctance shutters, figure 16-12.

The Hall-effect switch does not generate a signal voltage in the same way as a magnetic pulse generator, however. In fact, it requires an input voltage to generate an output voltage.

The Hall effect is the generation of a small voltage in a semiconductor by passing current through it in one direction while applying a magnetic field at a right angle to its surface,

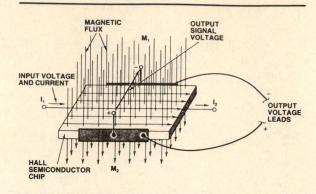

Figure 16-13. The Hall-effect output voltage varies with the strength of the magnetic field, while the input current remains constant.

figure 16-13. When current flows from I_1 to I_2 through the semiconductor and a magnetic field intersects the chip from M_1 to M_2, voltage develops across the semiconductor as shown in figure 16-13. If the input current remains constant and the magnetic field is varied, the signal voltage will vary proportionally to the field strength.

When the shutter blade of a Hall-effect switch enters the gap between the magnet and the Hall semiconductor element, it creates a magnetic shunt that varies the Hall field strength. This changes the Hall signal voltage, which changes the bias on an ignition driver transistor similarly to the signal from a magnetic pulse generator.

A Hall-effect switch is a complex electronic circuit. Figure 16-14 shows the relationships of the Hall-effect switch and ignition operation. An important point to understand is that ignition occurs when the Hall shutter *leaves* the gap between the Hall semiconductor element and the magnet.

The Hall-effect voltage is not affected by changing engine speed. Magnetic pulse generators (and metal-detection units) depend upon induction to create the signal voltage. The strength of an induced voltage varies if the magnetic lines move more quickly or slowly. The Hall effect is not induction, and the speed of the magnetic lines has no effect on the signal voltage. This constant-strength signal voltage offers more reliable ignition system performance throughout a wide range of engine speeds. Moreover, a Hall-effect switch provides a uniform digital voltage pulse regardless of rotation speed. This makes a Hall-effect switch ideal as a digital engine sensor for fuel injection timing and other functions besides ignition control.

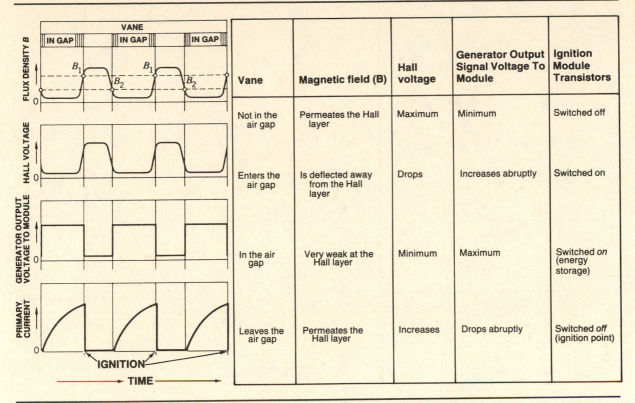

Vane	Magnetic field (B)	Hall voltage	Generator Output Signal Voltage To Module	Ignition Module Transistors
Not in the air gap	Permeates the Hall layer	Maximum	Minimum	Switched off
Enters the air gap	Is deflected away from the Hall layer	Drops	Increases abruptly	Switched on
In the air gap	Very weak at the Hall layer	Minimum	Maximum	Switched *on* (energy storage)
Leaves the air gap	Permeates the Hall layer	Increases	Drops abruptly	Switched *off* (ignition point)

Figure 16-14. The relationship of Hall-effect signal voltage and ignition discharge. (Bosch)

Metal Detection

This triggering device is a variation of the magnetic pulse generator. Instead of a permanent magnet affecting the pole piece, an electromagnet supplies the magnetic field, figure 16-15. The control module applies a small amount of battery voltage to the electromagnet coil. The metal teeth on the trigger wheel affect the electromagnetic field and the voltage within the electromagnetic coil. These voltage changes are sensed by the control module.

This device produces a more reliable signal voltage at lower engine speeds than a magnetic pulse generator. A metal-detection triggering device is used in the Prestolite electronic ignition used by American Motors from 1975 to 1977.

Optical (Light Detection) Signal Generator

The optical signal generator uses a light-emitting diode (LED) and a light-sensitive phototransistor (photocell) to produce signal voltage pulses. When the LED light beam strikes the photocell, voltage is generated. A slotted disc rotating on the distributor shaft, figure 16-16, interrupts the light beam, sending an on-off voltage signal to the control module.

Until Chrysler introduced one on some 1987 models, no domestic carmaker had used an optical signal generator as original equipment. The Isuzu I-TEK and other Japanese ignition systems, however, rely on optical signal generators, which operate in essentially the same way as the Chrysler version.

The slotted timing disc used in the Chrysler optical distributor serves a dual purpose. Two sets of slots are etched along the inner and outer circumference of the disc. Signals produced by the slots also serve as the crankshaft angle sensor (outer slots) and the Top Dead Center (TDC) sensor (inner slots). Because the sensors are self-contained within the distribu-

■ Mind Those Magnets

When you are servicing a distributor from an electronic ignition system, be sure that no metal particles or iron filings get inside. The magnetic pickup coils and pole pieces in the breakerless distributors used by many carmakers will attract metal debris which can really foul up ignition performance. Use a clean, soft-bristled brush or low-pressure compressed air to clean the inside of a distributor and keep scrap metal off the pickup coil.

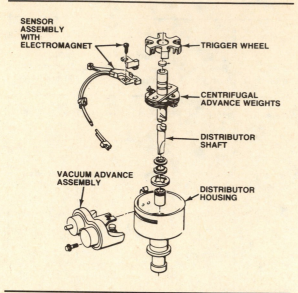

Figure 16-15. A metal-detection triggering device.

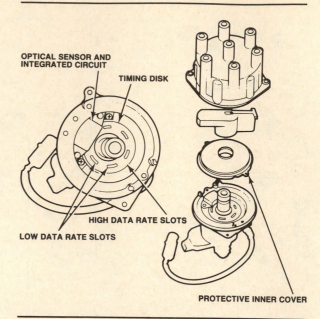

Figure 16-16. Components of the Chrysler optical distributor. The slotted timing disc interrupts the light beam in the optical sensor to produce on-off signals used to control fuel injection, idle speed, and ignition timing. (Chrysler)

tor, a protective inner cover is used to separate them from the high-tension distribution part of the distributor housing. The cover prevents actuation errors caused by electrical noise.

The optical signal generator provides a more reliable signal voltage at much lower engine speeds than either a magnetic pulse or metal-detection unit. However, periodic LED and photocell cleaning may be required. Several aftermarket, or add-on, ignition systems have been produced using this switching device.

ELECTRONIC IGNITION DWELL, TIMING, AND ADVANCE

As you learned in Chapter Thirteen, dwell is the period of time when the breaker points are closed and current is flowing in the primary winding of the coil. Although solid-state ignitions require a dwell period for the same purpose, it is controlled by a timing or current-sensing circuit in the ignition module, rather than by a signal from the distributor.

The initial timing adjustment for most basic electronic ignitions is similar to that for breaker-point ignition systems. Timing is set by rotating the distributor housing with the engine idling at normal operating temperature.

The first generation of electronic ignitions used the same centrifugal and vacuum advance mechanisms to advance timing as breaker-point ignitions use. As carmakers began to equip their engines with computer-controlled systems in the late 1970s, however, timing advance became a function of the computer. Since a computer can receive, process,

and send information very rapidly, it can change ignition timing with far more efficiency and accuracy than any mechanical device.

The distributor in an electronic ignition used with a computer engine control system contains a triggering device for basic timing. Because the computer actually controls ignition timing, however, the distributor's primary function is to distribute secondary voltage.

Fixed vs. Variable Dwell

Although dwell is not adjustable in electronic distributors, electronic ignitions may have one of two kinds of dwell control:

- Fixed dwell
- Variable dwell.

Fixed dwell

A ballast resistor is placed in the primary circuit of a **fixed dwell** electronic ignition to limit current and voltage. Dwell is the length of time the switching transistor sends current to the primary coil windings. It begins once the secondary voltage and current have fallen below predetermined levels. The ballast resistor functions just as it does in a breaker-point system to control primary voltage and current. Dwell measured in distributor degrees remains constant at all engine speeds. Figure 16-17 shows the primary circuit oscilloscope pattern of a typical fixed dwell electronic ignition.

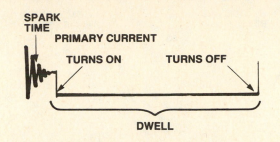

Figure 16-17. Dwell measured in degrees of distributor rotation remains relatively constant at all engine speeds in a fixed-dwell system.

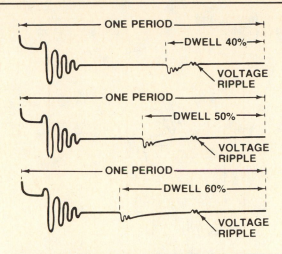

Figure 16-18. The dwell period increases with engine speed in the variable-dwell Delco HEI and some Motorcraft systems.

Chrysler's original electronic ignition is a good example of a fixed dwell system. The original Ford solid-state ignition (SSI) and Dura-Spark II are other examples of fixed dwell systems with ballast resistors, as are some Bosch and Japanese electronic ignitions.

Variable dwell

A ballast resistor is not used in a **variable dwell** system. The coil and ignition module receive full battery voltage. A module circuit senses primary current to the coil and reduces the current when the magnetic field is saturated. Unlike a breaker-point or fixed dwell electronic ignition, dwell measured in distributor degrees changes with speed in a variable dwell ignition, but the dwell *time* remains relatively constant. Figure 16-18 shows the primary circuit oscilloscope pattern of a typical variable dwell electronic ignition.

In general, ignition coils used with variable dwell systems have a higher available voltage capability, lower primary resistance, and a higher turns ratio than the coils used with fixed dwell systems.

All variations of the GM Delco-Remy High Energy Ignition (HEI) are variable dwell systems, as well as Ford Dura-Spark I and thick-film integrated (TFI) ignition systems. Other examples are most Chrysler Hall-effect ignitions, some Bosch, Marelli, and several Japanese electronic ignitions.

Basic Timing and Advance Control

We learned in Chapter Fifteen that ignition takes place at a point just before or just after top dead center is reached during the compression stroke of a piston. This time is measured in degrees of crankshaft rotation and is established in distributor-type ignitions by the mechanical coupling between the crankshaft and distributor. Basic or initial ignition timing is usually state at idle speed.

As engine speed increases, however, ignition must take place earlier. This is necessary to ensure that maximum compression pressure from combustion develops as the piston starts downward on its power stoke, figure 16-19. This change in ignition timing is called spark advance and is controlled in basic electronic ignitions (those not integrated with electronic engine controls) by the same mechanical devices used with a breaker-point ignition:

- Centrifugal advance weights
- Vacuum advance diaphragm.

The centrifugal advance mechanism responds to changes in *engine speed* and moves the position of the trigger wheel relative to the distributor shaft. The vacuum advance mechanism responds to changes in engine load and moves the position of the pickup coil. These changes in position alter the time, relative to crankshaft position, at which the primary circuit is opened.

When electronic ignitions are integrated with electronic control systems, the computer monitors engine speed and load changes, engine temperature, manifold pressure (vacuum), air-

Fixed Dwell: The ignition dwell period begins when the switching transistor turns on and remains relatively constant at all speeds.

Variable Dwell: The ignition dwell period varies in distributor degrees at different engine speeds, but remains relatively constant in duration or actual time.

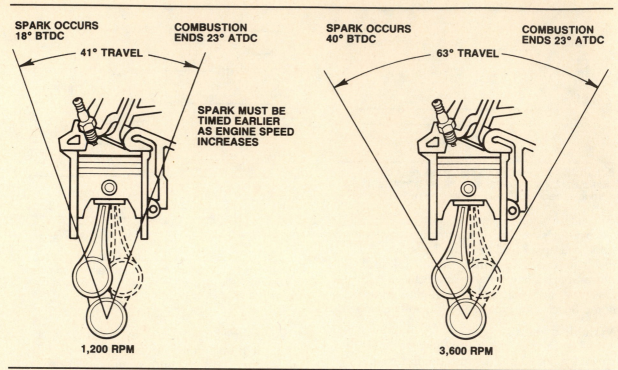

Figure 16-19. As rpm increases, the spark must be advanced to deliver the maximum spark for the best torque.

flow, exhaust oxygen content, and other factors. The computer then changes ignition timing to produce the most efficient combustion. Electronic engine controls are used on most late-model vehicles and will be discussed in the next chapter.

ORIGINAL EQUIPMENT ELECTRONIC DISTRIBUTOR-TYPE IGNITIONS

This section contains brief descriptions of the major distributor-type electronic ignitions used by domestic and foreign carmakers. All are inductive-discharge systems, but their triggering devices and module circuits vary somewhat from manufacturer to manufacturer.

Because these systems have been under constant development, they have been modified from year to year and model to model. The descriptions given in this section summarize the basic changes resulting from this on-going development. Whenever an electronic ignition requires service, you should always refer to the carmaker's shop manual or an appropriate repair manual to determine the exact specifications and whether the system has any unique features you should know about.

Delco-Remy

High energy ignition (HEI)
The Delco-Remy High Energy Ignition (HEI)

system, figure 16-20, was introduced on some 1974 GM V8 engines and became standard equipment on all GM engines in 1975. The HEI system was developed from an earlier Delco-Remy Unitized ignition used on a limited number of 1972-74 engines. The HEI and Unitized ignitions have all of the ignition components built into the distributor.

The HEI system was the first domestic original-equipment manufacturer (OEM) electronic ignition to use a variable dwell primary circuit and no ballast resistor. The control module lengthens the dwell period as engine rpm increases to maintain uniform primary current and coil saturation throughout all engine speed ranges. The HEI module is installed on the breaker plate inside the distributor, and the basic ignition module has four terminals: two connected to the primary circuit and two attached to the pickup coil of a magnetic pulse ignition pickup. The back of the HEI module is coated with a silicone dielectric compound before installation.

The HEI pickup looks different from those of other manufacturers, but it operates in the same basic manner. The rotating trigger wheel of the HEI distributor is called the ''timer core'', while the coil is attached to a fixed ring-shaped magnet called the ''pole piece''. The pole piece and trigger wheel have as many equally spaced teeth as the engine has cylinders, except on uneven-firing V6 engines,

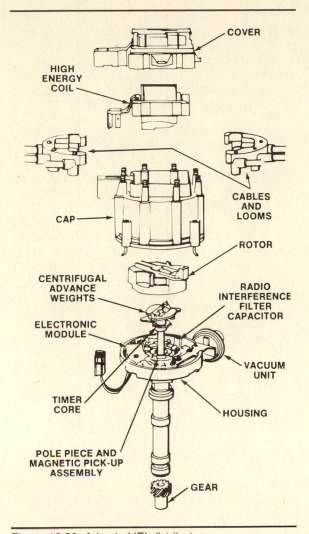

Figure 16-20. A basic HEI distributor.

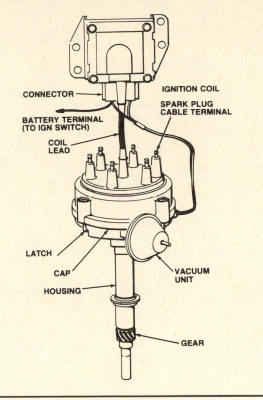

Figure 16-21. The HEI distributor used with some inline and V6 GM engines.

which have three teeth on the trigger wheel and six unevenly spaced teeth on the pole pieces.

The most common HEI system has an integral (built-in) coil mounted in the distributor cap, figure 16-20. Some four- and six-cylinder engines have HEI systems with a separate coil, figure 16-21, that provides additional distributor clearance on the engine. Both designs operate in the same way and have similar wiring connections. All HEI systems use 8-mm spark plug cables with silicone insulation to minimize crossfiring caused by the high secondary voltage capability of the HEI coil. Some engines use wide-gap spark plugs to take advantage of the system's high-voltage capability.

In addition to distributing the spark to the appropriate cylinder, the HEI rotor serves as a fuse to protect the module. If an open circuit occurs in the ignition secondary and voltage rises above a certain level, the center of the rotor will burn through and allow the spark to travel to ground rather than arcing through and destroying the module. Early black rotors have a dielectric strength of approximately 70,000 volts; later white ones are designed to ground the secondary circuit at around 100,000 volts.

The newer design rotor may be used in place of the earlier one, but the cap and rotor must be replaced as a matched set. The air gap between the rotor tip and cap electrodes was 0.090 inch (2.29 mm) on the earlier parts, but the later design has an air gap of 0.125 inch (3.18 mm) to better suppress radiofrequency interference (RFI) that could interfere with the engine control computers of the systems discussed in Chapter Seventeen. Caps and rotors from the early and late designs should never be mixed.

In addition to this basic HEI system, GM has used six other HEI versions with electronic engine controls and for certain spark timing requirements. The six systems are HEI with:

- Electronic spark selection (ESS)
- Electronic spark control (ESC)
- Electronic module retard (EMR)
- Electronic spark timing (EST)
- EST and ESC
- EST and a Hall-effect switch.

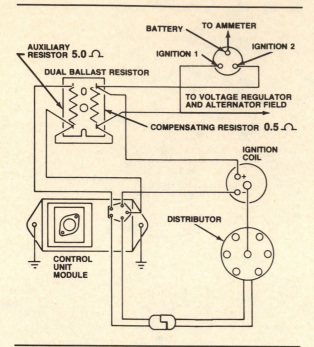

Figure 16-22. A primary circuit diagram of Chrysler's electronic ignition system. (Chrysler)

The HEI system with electronic spark selection (ESS) uses a five-terminal HEI module and was introduced by Cadillac on the Seville in 1978. The system has an electronic decoder that receives inputs from the:

- EGR solenoid that signals coolant temperature
- Ignition switch that signals cranking
- The fuel economy switch that signals engine vacuum level.

The decoder uses these signals to determine the appropriate timing alterations. Timing is retarded by a fixed amount during cranking and during cold-engine operation on California models. Timing is advanced, again by a fixed number of degrees, during cruise.

The HEI system with electronic spark control (ESC) is a detonation-control system used on 1980 and later turbocharged and high-compression engines. The system consists of a knock sensor, a controller unit, and a special five-terminal HEI module.

When detonation occurs, the knock sensor sends a signal to the controller, which then instructs the module to retard the ignition timing by a small amount. If the knock sensor continues to detect detonation, the controller instructs the module to further retard timing by another small increment. This sensor-controller-module cycle goes on continuously, and the controller's instructions to the module are updated many times a second until the

detonation is eliminated. As soon as that happens, the process reverses itself and timing is advanced in small steps as long as detonation does not reoccur. Once the detonation-producing conditions have been eliminated, the timing will return to normal within 20 seconds.

The HEI system with electronic module retard (EMR) is a simple 10-degree timing retard system used for cold starts and was also introduced in 1980. The retard circuitry is contained within the special five-terminal HEI module and is activated by a simple vacuum switch on most models. On cars with the computer-controlled catalytic converter (C-4) system, the module is controlled by the C-4 computer.

The HEI system with electronic spark timing (EST) was introduced on 1981 engines with computer command control (CCC), except those with minimum-function CCC systems (Chevette, Pontiac T1000, and Acadian). The seven-terminal module converts the pickup coil signal into a crankshaft position signal used by the electronic control module (ECM) to advance or retard ignition timing for optimum spark timing. HEI-EST distributors have no centrifugal or vacuum advance units.

The HEI system with EST and ESC was also introduced in 1981 and combines the electronic spark control of EST with the detonation sensor of ESC. It is used primarily with turbocharged engines.

The HEI system with EST and a Hall-effect switch combines the basic magnetic pulse generator of the HEI distributor with a Hall-effect switch and is used with CCC engine control systems. The pickup coil sends timing signals to the HEI module during cranking. Once the engine starts, the Hall-effect switch overrides the pickup coil and sends crankshaft position signals to the computer for electronic control of timing.

Chrysler

Electronic ignition

In 1971, Chrysler became the first domestic carmaker to introduce a basic electronic ignition on some models, figure 16-22. The system became standard on all Chrysler Motors' cars in 1973. The same basic system, with very few modifications, has been used on most six- and eight-cylinder Chrysler engines since.

The Chrysler electronic ignition system, figure 16-23, is a fixed dwell design using a magnetic pulse distributor, a remote-mounted electronic control module, and a unit-type ballast resistor. The control module is mounted on the firewall or inner fender panel and has

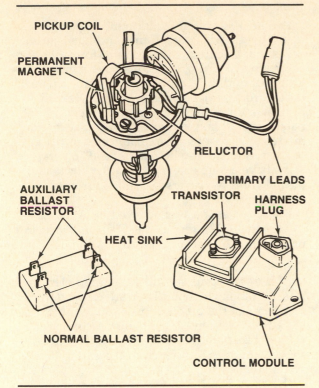

Figure 16-23. The basic Chrysler electronic ignition system.

PICKUP COIL

PERMANENT MAGNET

RELUCTOR

AUXILIARY BALLAST RESISTOR

PRIMARY LEADS

TRANSISTOR

HARNESS PLUG

HEAT SINK

NORMAL BALLAST RESISTOR

CONTROL MODULE

an exposed switching transistor that controls primary current. Don't touch the transistor when the ignition is on, because enough voltage is present to give you a shock. The distributor housing, cap, rotor, and advance mechanisms are all similar to breaker-point components, as are the ignition coil and 7-mm spark plug cables.

All 1972-78 cars and some 1979-80 models have five-pin modules with a matching five-terminal wiring harness connector. Early five-pin module ignition systems used a dual ballast resistor that contained an exposed 0.5-ohm temperature-compensating resistor to control primary circuit current and voltage, and a 5.0-ohm temperature-compensating resistor to protect the module circuitry from high voltage or current surges. This part was superseded in the mid-1970s by a revised dual resistor using a sealed 1.2-ohm non-temperature-compensating resistor in place of the earlier 0.5-ohm part. The later design is the approved replacement part for all dual-resistor systems.

Some 1979-80 and all 1981 and later vehicles with basic electronic ignition have a four-pin module and matching wiring harness connector. The four-pin module contains integral protection circuitry, eliminating terminal 3, which received input voltage from the 5.0-ohm resistor. A single 1.2-ohm unit-type ballast resistor

is used in four-pin module systems to regulate primary circuit current and voltage.

All early Chrysler electronic ignition systems have a single magnetic pickup in the distributor. However, the distributors used with some electronic lean burn (ELB) and electronic spark control (ESC) systems use a dual-pickup distributor containing a start pickup and a run pickup. The run pickup is positioned to advance the ignition trigger signal compared to the start pickup. Under normal engine operation, the module uses the signal from the run pickup. When the ignition switch is in the start position, however, the retarded trigger signal from the start pickup is used to ensure faster starts.

Distributors with early ELB systems had only a centrifugal advance mechanism. Those for later ESC systems have neither centrifugal nor vacuum advance mechanisms; all spark advance is controlled by the computer.

The air gap between the reluctor and pickup coil, or coils, is adjustable, but has no effect on the dwell period, which is determined by the control module. The air gap must be set to a specific clearance with a non-metallic feeler gauge when a new pickup unit is installed. Air gap specifications vary according to model year.

Hall-effect electronic ignition system

Chrysler introduced a different electronic ignition in 1978 on their first four-cylinder, front-wheel-drive (FWD) cars. A Hall-effect switch is used instead of a magnetic pulse generator. The original fixed dwell ignition on 1978 four-cylinder engines was used with an analog computer and had a 0.5-ohm ballast resistor to control primary current and voltage. The 1978 ELB and 1979 ESC system distributors had both centrifugal and vacuum advance mechanisms and were similar in operation to the six- and eight-cylinder versions described above.

A changeover to a digital spark-control computer in 1981 resulted in the electronic spark advance (ESA) system. This meant several changes to the system and its operation. Since the computer took over spark control timing, the distributor had no advance mechanisms. The system uses no ballast resistor, and dwell is variable; that is, it increases as engine speed increases. In 1984, the ESA system was incorporated into the electronic fuel injection (EFI) spark control system used on fuel-injected engines. A logic module and a power module replaced the spark control computer, but the ignition portion of this system works essentially the same as in the ESA system.

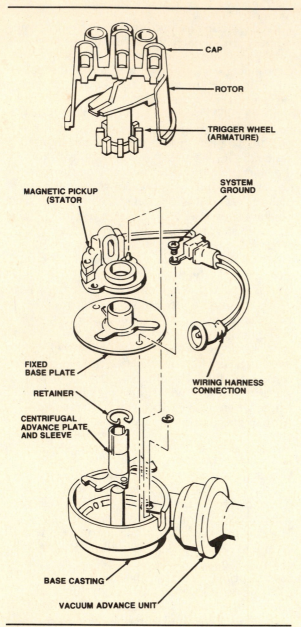

CAP

ROTOR

TRIGGER WHEEL
(ARMATURE)

MAGNETIC PICKUP
(STATOR

SYSTEM
GROUND

FIXED
BASE PLATE

RETAINER

WIRING HARNESS
CONNECTION

CENTRIFUGAL
ADVANCE PLATE
AND SLEEVE

BASE CASTING

VACUUM ADVANCE UNIT

Figure 16-24. Ford's solid-state ignition (SSI)
distributor.

Ford

Motorcraft solid-state ignition (SSI)
The Ford Motorcraft solid-state ignition system
was used in three forms from 1973 through
1976. It consists of a magnetic pulse distributor, figure 16-24, an electronic control module
and a special oil-filled coil that can be identified by its blue case or tower. The coil primary
terminals are labeled BAT and DEC (distributor electronic control) and a standard primary
circuit ballast resistor wire is used, figure
16-25.

The 1973-74 system ignition modules are
identified by a black grommet and have seven
wires that terminate in three- and four-wire
connectors. The 1975 versions have a green
grommet and the three-wire connector shape
differs from earlier systems. In mid-year, the
blue wire for system protection was eliminated, and all later systems (and replacement
modules) have a two-wire connector in place
of the earlier three-wire part. The 1976 versions have a blue grommet and the black and
purple wires are reversed in the four-wire
connector.

The 1976 version was adopted by American
Motors in 1978 to replace the Prestolite system
used from 1975 through 1977.

Dura-Spark I and II
Ford introduced its second generation electronic ignitions in 1977. They are direct de-
scendants of the original SSI ignition. The
Dura-Spark systems have higher secondary
voltage capabilities and the electrical values of
some components differ from the earlier Ford
systems.

The Dura-Spark I system is used on some
1977-79 California engines and can be identified by a red grommet in the control module.
The system does not use a primary resistor
and has a new coil with a gray tower and
unique terminals that prevent its use in other
systems. The Dura-Spark I module adjusts ignition dwell relative to current through the coil
at the time of a spark. The module also has a
stall-shutdown feature for circuit protection. If
the engine stalls, the module opens the primary circuit even though the ignition switch is
in the on position. The switch must be turned
off and then back to start to close the primary
circuit.

Dura-Spark II systems more closely resemble
the 1976 solid-state ignition (SSI). They retain
a primary resistor wire, but the resistance values are changed to provide higher secondary
voltage. The coil is the same as that used with
the 1973-76 systems.

Dura-Spark II systems have been produced
in several variations. The most basic version,
produced from 1977 on, has a blue grommet,
just like the 1976 SSI system. Some 1979 and
later 2.3-liter engines with automatic transmissions have a Dura-Spark II module with a
white grommet. This module has "start retard" circuitry that retards the timing up to 18
degrees at cranking speed. Certain 1979-80
engines use a "dual-mode" module with a
yellow grommet. This module has three additional wires attached to a third connector. The
connector plugs into one of two sensors that

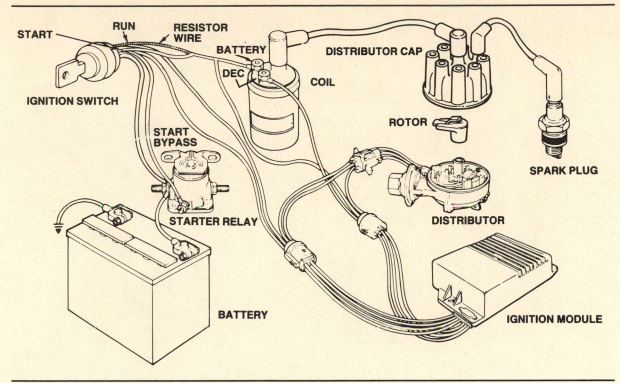

Figure 16-25. Components of Ford's solid-state ignition (SSI). (Ford)

affect ignition timing in different ways, depending upon the application. Some models have a vacuum switch for improved fuel economy, while others use a barometric pressure switch for altitude compensation.

From 1981 on, the dual-mode module is replaced by the universal ignition module (UIM) which also has three connectors and a yellow grommet. This module is smaller and more compact than previous Dura-Spark units and contains a factory-programmable retard feature used for fuel economy calibrations, altitude compensation, or spark knock control, depending upon the application.

All Dura-Spark I and II distributor caps, figure 16-26, use male terminals for the 8-mm spark plug cables. The caps on six- and eight-cylinder distributors are much larger than previous models and have adapter rings to mate with the distributor housing. Large rotors are also used with the bigger caps.

Dura-Spark III

This system was introduced in late 1979 as part of Ford's second generation electronic engine control (EEC-II) system. The Dura-Spark III ignition module can be identified by its brown grommet. Although it appears similar to other Dura-Spark modules, many of its control circuits were eliminated and their functions incorporated in the EEC-II engine control assembly (ECA).

The Dura-Spark III distributor essentially is nothing more than a device to route the spark from the coil to the proper plug. It has no centrifugal or vacuum advance mechanisms. The magnetic pulse generator was removed from the distributor and relocated to the crankshaft in the form of a crankshaft position sensor (pickup coil) and pulse ring (armature), figure 16-27.

Thick-film integrated (TFI) ignition

The TFI-I ignition system, figure 16-28, was introduced in 1982 on the 1.6-liter Escort engine. It differs in many respects from the earlier Ford systems already discussed. Instead of a remote-mounted control module, the TFI-I system uses an integrated circuit control module attached to the outside of the distributor housing. The module connects directly to the distributor stator.

Inside the distributor is the familiar magnetic pulse generator, but TFI-I is a variable dwell system that operates without a ballast resistor. The conventional oil-filled coil is replaced with a special low-resistance E-core part. The distributor cap, rotor, and spark plug cables, however, are similar to those used with Dura-Spark systems.

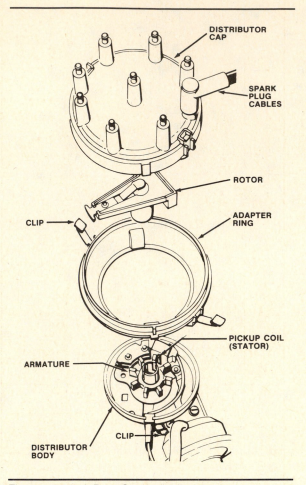

Figure 16-26. A Dura-Spark distributor.

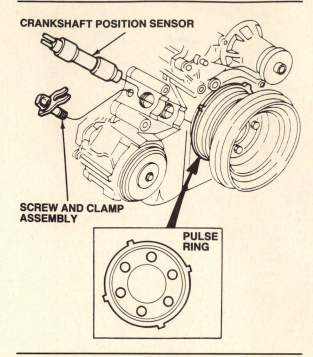

Figure 16-27. The EEC-III crankshaft position sensor replaced the magnetic pulse generator in the Dura-Spark III distributor. (Ford)

There are two different versions of the TFI-I control module. Early production parts were made of blue plastic and are called "non-push-start" modules. They contain protection circuitry that will shut off voltage to the coil if an ignition trigger signal is not detected for a period of 10 to 15 seconds. When shutdown occurs, the ignition switch must be turned off and back on again before the engine will start.

All later modules are made of gray plastic and contain revised circuitry that still turns off the voltage to the coil after a preset period, but switches the power back on as soon as a trigger signal is detected.

A revised TFI ignition system appeared in 1983 as part of Ford's fifth generation of electronic engine controls (EEC-IV). Called TFI-IV, this design uses a gray ignition module which appears similar to the TFI-I module, but has a six-wire connector instead of the TFI-I's three-wire connector. The additional three wires connect the module to the ECA. The TFI-IV module is used with a Universal distributor that contains a Hall-effect switch. The TFI igni-

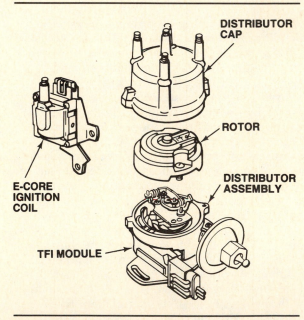

Figure 16-28. Ford TFI ignition system components.

tions have replaced the Dura-Spark ignitions on virtually all new Ford vehicles.

The TFI module attaches to the distributor with several screws and depends on good contact with the distributor housing for its cooling. Whenever a module is replaced, silicone dielectric compound must be applied to its back to improve heat conductivity and prevent

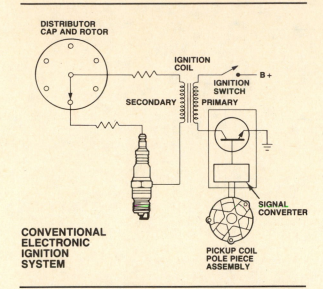

CONVENTIONAL
ELECTRONIC
IGNITION
SYSTEM

Figure 16-29. When a spark plug is fired with forward polarity, current flows from the center to the side electrode. (General Motors)

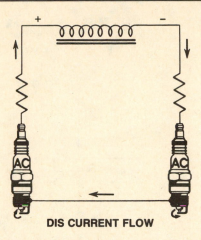

DIS CURRENT FLOW

Figure 16-30. In a DIS system, one spark plug in each pair always fires with forward polarity. The other plug fires with reverse polarity, with current flowing from the side to the center electrode. (General Motors)

premature module burnout. The module should never be used as a handle to turn the distributor when setting the initial timing. This kind of careless handling can cause it to warp and fail soon after.

ORIGINAL EQUIPMENT DISTRIBUTORLESS IGNITIONS

This section contains brief descriptions of the distributorless electronic ignitions used by domestic carmakers. Whenever a distributorless ignition requires service, you should always refer to the carmaker's shop manual or an appropriate repair manual to determine the exact specifications and whether the system has any unique features you should know about.

Principles of Distributorless Ignitions

The term distributorless ignition system (DIS) refers to any ignition system without a distributor. A DIS fires the spark plugs with a multiple coil pack containing two or three separate ignition coils (according to the number of engine cylinders) and an electronic ignition module. Control circuits in the module discharge each coil separately in sequence, with each coil serving two cylinders 360 degrees apart in the firing order. Each coil fires two plugs simultaneously in what is called a **waste spark** method. One spark goes to a cylinder near TDC on the compression stroke, while the other fires the plug in a cylinder near TDC of the exhaust stroke. The plug in the cylinder on the exhaust stroke requires very little voltage (about four kV)

to fire and has no effect on engine operation.

As we learned in Chapter Fourteen, the ignition coil secondary windings in a distributor ignition generally are wound to give the spark plug center electrode positive polarity and the side electrode negative polarity. When the spark plug fires, electrons flow from the coil secondary windings to the center electrode, across the plug gap to the side electrode where they return to the coil secondary windings through the engine block. A spark plug fired in this manner is said to have forward polarity, figure 16-29. If the electrons flow to the side electrode and across the plug gap to the center electrode, the plug is said to have reverse polarity.

In a distributorless ignition, each pair of spark plugs is connected to one coil. In this system, one plug is always fired with forward polarity and the other is always fired with reverse polarity, figure 16-30. Because firing a spark plug with reverse polarity takes about 30 percent more energy, a misfire could result if the DIS coils did not have a different saturation time and primary current flow than a conventional coil. This provides more than 40 kilovolts of available energy — as much as 20 percent more than a conventional coil.

Waste Spark: An ignition system without a distributor in which one coil in a coil pack fires two spark plugs at the same time. The spark in the cylinder on compression ignites the air-fuel mixture, while the spark in the cylinder on its exhaust stroke is wasted.

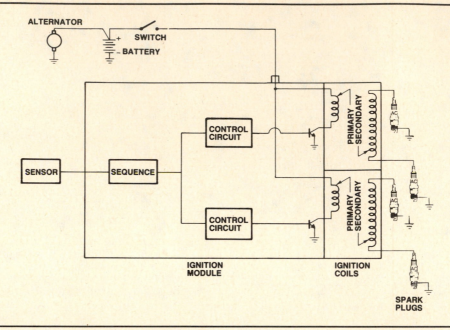

Figure 16-31. A functional schematic of the DIS module, showing the current-limiting control circuitry. (General Motors)

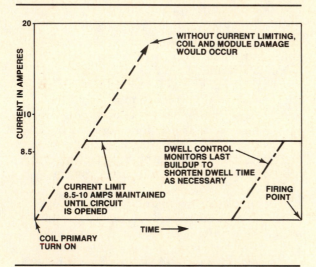

Figure 16-32. Closed loop dwell allows full saturation of the ignition coil by increasing or decreasing dwell time. (General Motors)

The ignition module determines and maintains the coil firing order. When it orders the coil to fire, one spark plug fires forward and the other fires backward. The voltage drop across each plug is determined by firing polarity and cylinder pressure. The ignition module controls primary current flow and limits dwell time. The low resistance of the primary coil winding, combined with an applied voltage of 14 volts, results in a theoretical current flow greater than 14 amperes, helping to decrease the coil's saturation time. Such a high current flow, however, will damage the system components unless it can be limited to a range of 8.5 to 10 amperes. Limiting of the circuit current to the safe range is done by a control circuit inside the module, figure 16-31.

Some modules use a type of **closed loop dwell control**, figure 16-32. In this system, the module continuously monitors coil buildup for maximum current. If maximum current was reached during the previous buildup, the module shortens dwell time to lower the wattage used by the system. If minimum current was not reached during the previous buildup, the module lengthens dwell time to permit full saturation of the coil. When current limiting takes place before coil discharge, the module decreases dwell time for the next cycle.

Delco-Remy

Computer-controlled coil ignition (C³I)
This distributorless ignition was introduced in 1984 and is used on Buick-built V6 engines. There is no distributor with signal generator, rotor, and cap in the C³I system. The ignition trigger signal is provided by Hall-effect crankshaft and camshaft position sensors. The crankshaft sensor provides a signal that indicates basic timing, crankshaft position, and engine speed. The camshaft sensor, figure 16-33, provides a firing order signal. On 3800 and 3.8-liter non-turbo engines, the camshaft sensor is mounted in the timing cover. With 3.8-liter turbocharged engines, the camshaft

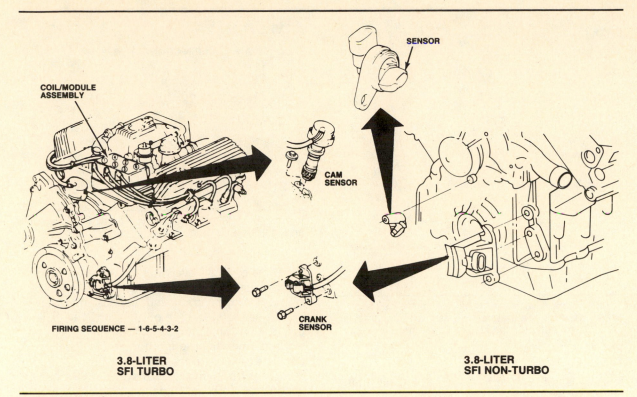

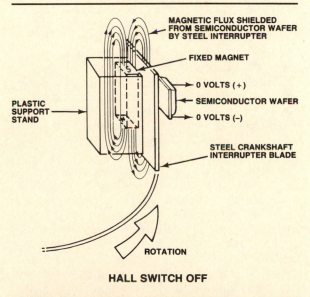

FIRING SEQUENCE — 1-6-5-4-3-2

**3.8-LITER
SFI TURBO**

**3.8-LITER
SFI NON-TURBO**

Figure 16-33. C³I Hall-effect sensors vary in appearance and location, but all use the same electrical circuitry to perform the same job. (General Motors)

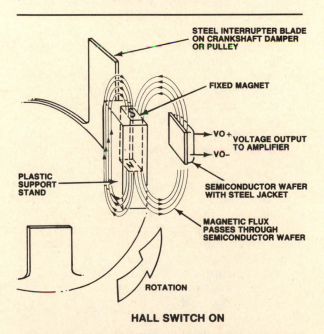

HALL SWITCH ON

Figure 16-34. Hall switch with unbroken field and reference voltage. (General Motors)

HALL SWITCH OFF

Figure 16-35. Hall switch with broken field and voltage drop-off. (General Motors)

sensor replaces the normal distributor and is mounted in the distributor location to drive the oil pump. On 3300 and 3.0-liter engines, the camshaft sensor is combined with the crankshaft sensor at the front of the engine.

Closed Loop Dwell Control: A type of distributorless ignition system in which the control module varies dwell time in response to previous coil current buildup.

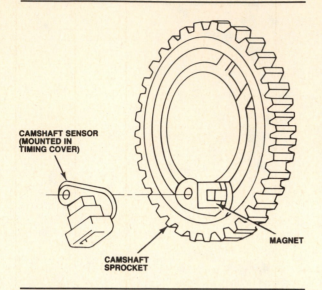

Figure 16-36. A variation of the Hall switch camshaft sensor in which the magnet mounted on the camshaft sprocket rotates past the Hall switch, turning it on and off. (General Motors)

Regardless of their appearance or location, all camshaft sensors have the same purpose and use the same electrical signals.

The crankshaft and camshaft sensors use Hall-effect switches with revolving interrupter rings to synchronize and fire the coils at the required time. The ignition module sends a reference voltage through a semiconductor wafer in the Hall switch. A permanent magnet mounted in line with the semiconductor wafer induces a voltage across the semiconductor, figure 16-34. As a metal blade on the interrupter ring passes between the permanent magnet and semiconductor wafer, the magnetic field is broken and Hall voltage drops, figure 16-35. The 3800 and 3.8-liter non-turbo engines reverse the process. On these engines, the permanent magnet is mounted on the camshaft sprocket and the Hall switch is part of the timing cover sensor, figure 16-36. As the camshaft sprocket revolves, it turns the Hall switch on and off.

The camshaft sensor serves only to establish the initial ignition firing sequence during engine cranking. The ignition module synchronizes the initial cam sensor signal with one of the crankshaft sensor signals during cranking and remembers the crankshaft sensor sequence as long as the ignition remains on.

The operation of the C³I system is very similar to that of the HEI with EST system described earlier. During starting, the ignition module controls both ignition timing and spark distribution. When the engine reaches a programmed speed between 200 and 400 rpm,

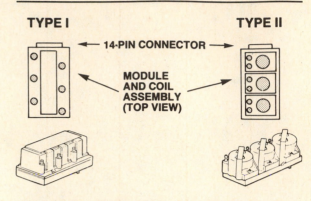

Figure 16-37. Identifying the Type I and Type II coil and ignition module assemblies used by Delco.

the ECM or PCM overrides the ignition module and assumes control of timing based on signals from the crankshaft sensor and other engine sensors. In case of ECM or PCM failure, the ignition module assumes timing control and operates the ignition with a fixed advance of 10 degrees BTDC.

Since introducing the C³I system, GM has used three different variations:

- Type 1 — all three coils are molded into a single housing with a smooth exterior surface, figure 16-37. Three spark plug cable terminals are provided on each side of the housing. If one coil malfunctions, the entire coil pack must be replaced.
- Type 1 Fast Start — the coil pack can be interchanged with a Type 1, but ignition module circuitry differs and connector plugs are not compatible.
- Type 2 — similar to Type I, but the coils can be replaced individually, figure 16-37.

The Type 1 Fast Start system measures crankshaft sensor signals more precisely, resulting in a faster startup. A dual crankshaft sensor is located beside the harmonic balancer/crankshaft pulley on the front of the engine. The harmonic balancer has two sets of interrupter rings. The outside ring consists of 18 evenly spaced interrupter blades that deliver 18 pulses every crankshaft revolution. These pulses are called the 18X signal. The inside ring consists of three blades with gaps of 10, 20, and 30 degrees spaced at 100, 90, and 110 degrees apart respectively. The inside ring pulses are called the 3X signal, figure 16-38.

Variations in the 3X signal allow the ignition module to synchronize the correct coil without need of the camshaft signal or the synchronization signal. Since the module can determine the correct coil within 120 degrees of crankshaft rotation, it starts firing on the first coil

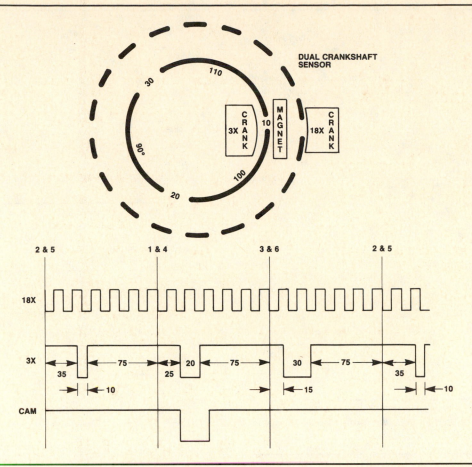

Figure 16-38. Dual Hall switches and two sets of interrupter rings on the harmonic balancer are used in the "fast start" system to measure crankshaft sensor signals with more accuracy. (General Motors)

identified. The 18X pulse acts as a "clock pulse" to measure the length of each 3X pulse. The 18X pulse changes once during the 3X 10-degree gap, twice during the 20-degree gap, and three times during the 3X 30-degree gap. Once the module determines which 3X pulse it is reading, it can energize the correct coil.

Direct ignition system (DIS)

The basic operation of the DIS used on many Chevrolet and Pontiac four-cylinder and V6 engines is quite similar to that of the C³I system, except for the method used to sense crankshaft position. Instead of Hall-effect switches located on the front of the engine, this DIS system uses a magnetic sensor installed in the side of the engine block. When used with the 2.5-liter engine, the sensor is installed on the back of the module. With other four-cylinder and V6 engines, the sensor is installed in the block below the module and is connected externally, figure 16-39.

A notched wheel or reluctor is cast into the crankshaft. The crankshaft reluctor on both four-cylinder and V6 engines is machined with seven notches or slots and serves as the field interrupter. The sensor head consists of a permanent magnet with a wire winding and is positioned a specified distance from the reluctor. As the crankshaft rotates, the reluctor notches interrupt the sensor's magnetic field, causing a small a.c. voltage to be induced in the sensor's wire winding, figure 16-40. Because the sensor is installed in a fixed position in the engine block and the reluctor is an integral part of the crankshaft, there is no timing adjustment possible or required with this system.

Six reluctor notches are evenly spaced around the reluctor surface at 60-degree intervals; the seventh notch is spaced 10 degrees from one of the six notches. The signal from the seventh notch is used by the module to synchronize coil firing sequence to the crankshaft position. While reluctor configuration is the same for four-cylinder and V6 engines, coil firing order and determination of crankshaft position are calculated by the ignition module differently.

In the V6 engine system, figure 16-41, the synchronization notch tells the module to ig-

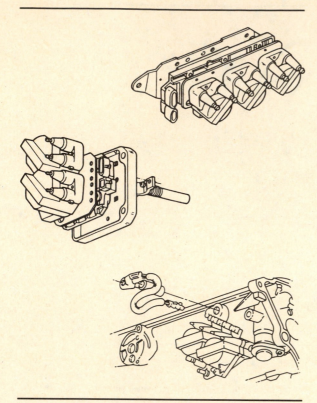

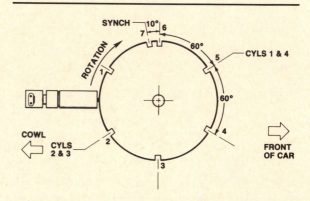

Figure 16-39. Location of DIS block-mounted crankshaft sensors to produce a crankshaft position signal. (General Motors)

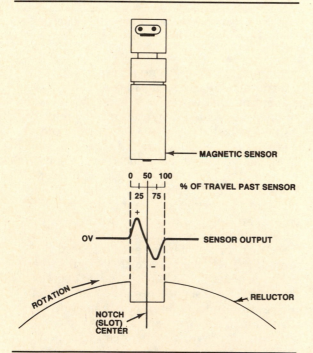

Figure 16-40. A small a.c. voltage is induced in the wire winding of the magnetic sensor when its magnetic field is interrupted by the reluctor. This voltage signal is used by the ignition module to determine firing of each wheel. (General Motors)

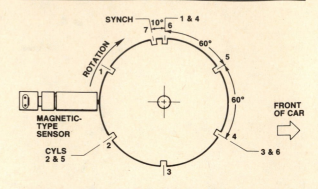

Figure 16-41. The V6 ignition module recognizes notches 2, 4, and 6 as the signal to fire cylinders 2 and 5, 3 and 6, and 1 and 4, in that order. (General Motors)

Figure 16-42. The four-cylinder ignition module recognizes notches 2 and 5 as the signal to fire cylinders 2 and 3, and 1 and 4, in that order. (General Motors)

nore the first notch and establish base timing for cylinders 2 and 5 with the second notch. The module ignores the third notch, and relies on the fourth notch to set base timing of cylinders 3 and 6. The fifth notch also is ignored in favor of the sixth notch for cylinders 1 and 4. After the seventh or synchronization notch passes, the entire sequence is repeated. As a result, the firing order of the first crankshaft revolution is 1-2-3 and 4-5-6 for the second revolution.

With four-cylinder engines, figure 16-42, the module starts the firing sequence on the seventh notch. If engine speed is below a predetermined value, the module fires each coil at a specified interval based only on engine speed. The synchronization notch tells the module to ignore the first notch and use the second notch to establish 10 degrees BTDC timing for cylinders 2 and 3. The module ignores the third and fourth notches, but uses the fifth notch to

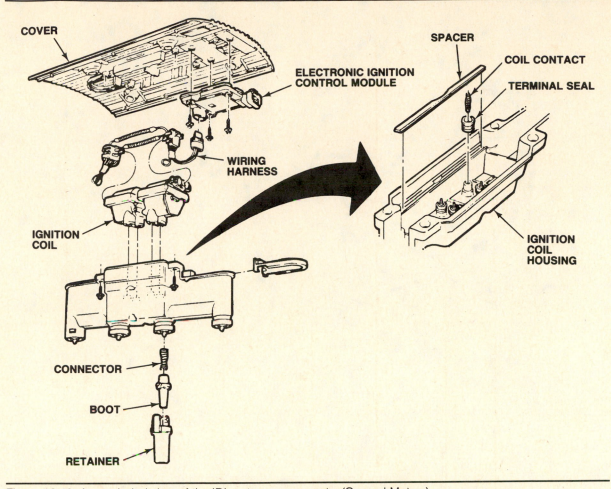

Figure 16-43. An exploded view of the IDI system components. (General Motors)

establish an equivalent timing setting for cylinders 1 and 4. In this way, the 2/3 coil is fired first during startup.

The reference pulse in both systems is pulled low by the notch ahead of the one that is used to fire the cylinder, returning to its high state when the cylinder firing notch passes. The change in reference voltage is sent to the ECM or PCM for use in electronic spark timing (EST) and fuel injection.

Integrated direct ignition (IDI)
This system is used only on the Oldsmobile-built Quad 4 engine and differs from other four-cylinder systems primarily in the configuration of the system components, figure 16-43. The coil pack and module are contained in a unit that connects directly to the spark plugs. This eliminates the use of spark plug cables, but the entire housing must be removed when changing spark plugs. However, the coils can be replaced individually.

Chrysler

Direct ignition system (DIS)
Chrysler uses a direct ignition system, figure 16-44, on its 3.3-liter and 3.5-liter engines. Crankshaft timing is determined by a magnetic sensor installed in the transaxle bellhousing. The single-board engine controller (SBEC) sends an eight-volt reference signal to the sensor. The transaxle drive plate contains three groups of four slots. The groups of slots are positioned 20 degrees apart and provide a signal for two spark plugs. Transaxle drive plate rotation makes and breaks the sensor's magnetic field, causing sensor output voltage to the SBEC engine controller to vary between zero and five volts. The SBEC uses this voltage signal to determine engine speed and calculate both timing advance and the required fuel delivery.

Also a magnetic type, the camshaft sensor is installed in the timing chain case cover and functions in the same way as the crankshaft sensor. The camshaft timing gear contains five

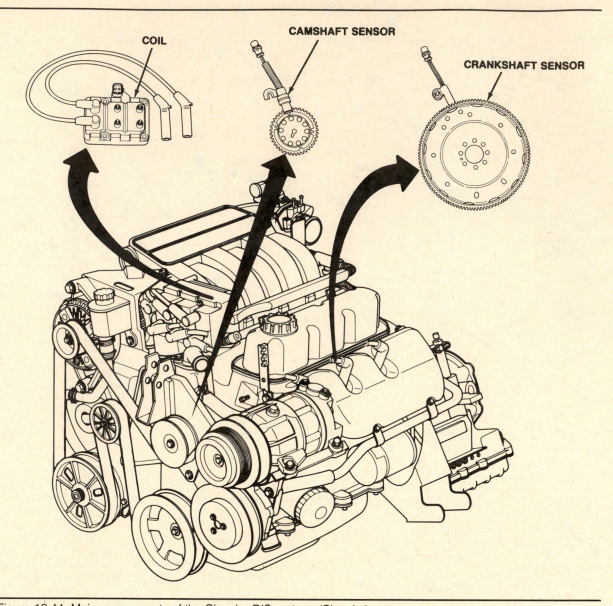

Figure 16-44. Major components of the Chrysler DIS system. (Chrysler)

areas with notched slots. Two areas have a single slot, two areas have two slots, and one area has three slots. These are arranged around the timing gear to produce one long and four short solid unnotched surfaces. This arrangement of notched and solid area produces a predictable sequence of voltage signals sent to the SBEC. The SBEC uses the signals to determine crankshaft position, then calculates which coil and injector pair to energize within one crankshaft revolution during startup.

Ford

All Ford distributorless ignitions operate on the same basic principles as those used by GM

and Chrysler. Each coil fires two spark plugs, with one spark igniting the mixture at the top of the compression stroke and the other spark wasted at the top of the exhaust stroke. One plug of each pair has positive polarity; the other has negative polarity.

4-2 distributorless ignition system (DIS)
Sometimes called the Dual Plug DIS, this unusual distributorless ignition was introduced on 1989 2.3-liter, four-cylinder truck engines, figure 16-45. Each cylinder uses two spark plugs, with one plug installed on each side of the combustion chamber. Those plugs on the right side of the engine form the primary system, and are responsible for engine operation at all times. The plugs on the left side of the engine

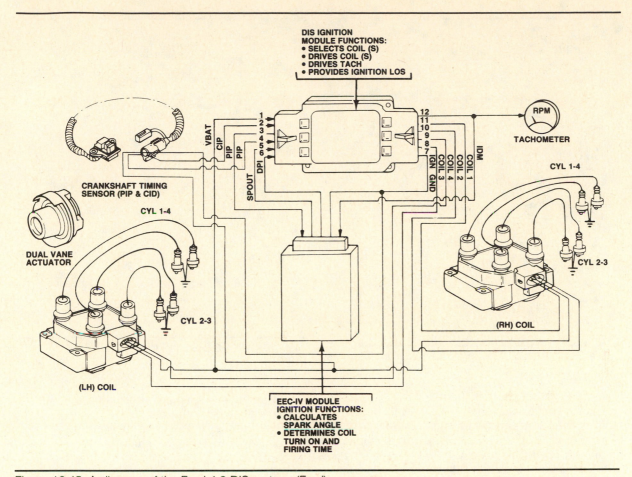

DIS IGNITION
MODULE FUNCTIONS:
• SELECTS COIL (S)
• DRIVES COIL (S)
• DRIVES TACH
• PROVIDES IGNITION LOS

EEC-IV MODULE
IGNITION FUNCTIONS:
• CALCULATES
  SPARK ANGLE
• DETERMINES COIL
  TURN ON AND
  FIRING TIME

Figure 16-45. A diagram of the Ford 4-2 DIS system. (Ford)

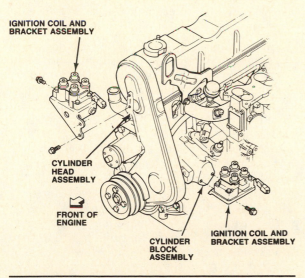

Figure 16-46. 4-2 DIS coil pack locations. (Ford)

form the secondary system and are switched on and off by the EEC-IV computer, according to engine speed and load requirements.

Only the primary plugs fire when the engine is cranking. Once the engine is running, the

EEC-IV computer commands the DIS module through the dual plug inhibit (DPI) circuit to switch from single to dual plug operation. The EEC-IV computer also is responsible for ignition timing and dwell.

The 4-2 DIS uses two four-tower DIS coil packs, figure 16-46, with a single remote DIS module, figure 16-47. A dual Hall-effect crankshaft sensor bracket-mounted near the crankshaft damper, figure 16-48, completes the system. The right coil fires the primary plugs during normal operating conditions; the left coil fires the secondary plugs as directed by the EEC-IV computer and the DIS module.

The crankshaft sensor works on the same principles as other Hall-effect switches you have studied, and is very similar in operation to the dual sensor used by GM in its C^3I ignition. A pair of rotating vane cups on the crankshaft damper produces a profile ignition pickup (PIP) signal for base timing data, and a cylinder identification (CID) signal used by the DIS module to determine which coil to fire.

The EEC-IV module sends a spark output (SPOUT) signal to the DIS module. The leading edge triggers the coil, and the trailing edge

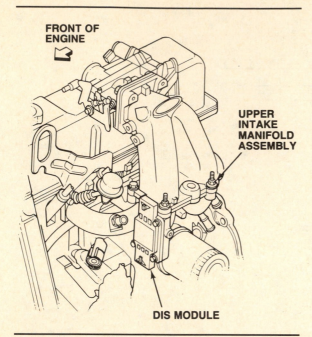

Figure 16-47. 4-2 DIS ignition module location. (Ford)

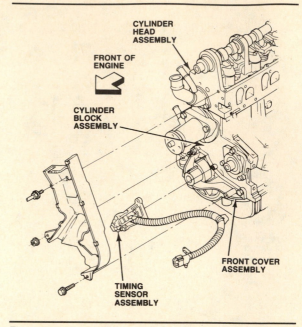

Figure 16-48. 4-2 DIS crankshaft sensor location. (Ford)

controls dwell time. This feature is called computer-controlled dwell (CCD). A buffered tach signal called Ignition Diagnostic Monitor (IDM) supplies ignition system diagnostic information used for self-test.

A CID sensor or circuit failure will not result in a no-start condition, as the DIS module randomly selects and fires one of the two coils under such circumstances. The result of the module's guess may be an engine that is hard to start. However, turning the key off and then back on to crank the engine again allows the module to make another guess. After a few tries, the module will make the right choice and select the correct firing sequence.

If an ignition failure results in the loss of the SPOUT signal, a failure effects management (FEM) program in the EEC-IV computer memory prevents total driveability loss. The EEC-IV computer opens the SPOUT line, allowing the DIS module to fire the coils directly from the PIP output. This results in a fixed spark angle of 10 degrees btdc with fixed dwell.

V6 distributorless ignition system (DIS)
This system also was introduced in 1989 on the 3.0-liter SHO V6 engine and the 3.8-liter supercharged V6 engine. The system functions in essentially the same way as the 4-2 DIS discussed above, but its components differ, figure 16-49:

- A single six-tower coil pack contains three coils with an individual tach wire for each coil; the coil pack is serviced as an assembly

- A single set of spark plugs is used, with one plug per cylinder
- The 3.0-liter cylinder identification (CID) sensor is installed on the end of one camshaft
- The 3.8-liter CID sensor is installed in the engine block where the distributor would normally be located
- A single Hall-effect switch is used as the crankshaft sensor.

When the engine is cranked, the DIS module looks for a change in the CID signal, from high to low or low to high. As soon as the module sees the leading or trailing edge of the CID signal, it prepares to fire coil 2 of the coil pack. Once the change in the CID signal occurs, the module looks for the trailing edge of SPOUT to turn on coil 2. When the module sees the next leading edge of SPOUT, it turns the primary current off to coil 2, which fires coil 2, figure 16-50. The DIS module always fires the coils in one coil pack in a given order. At engine start-up, the coil firing sequence is always 2, 3, 1. Because the coils continue to fire in the same order, they are synchronized with compression and remain synchronized as long as the engine is running, even if the DIS module loses the CID signal. SPOUT tells the DIS module when to fire the next coil as long as the engine is running. If the SPOUT circuit opens, the PIP signal is used by the module to fire the coils.

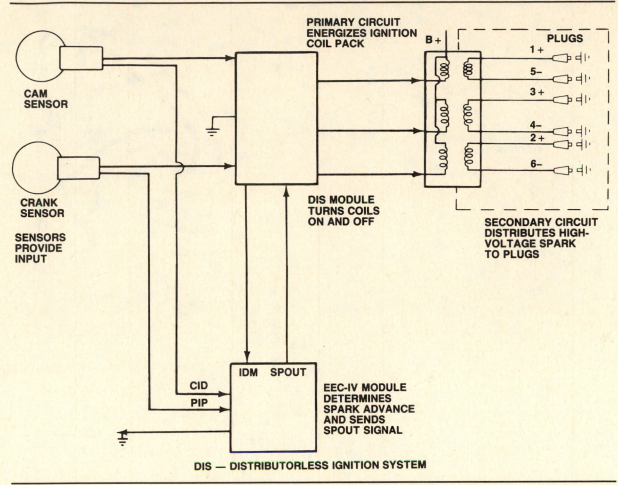

Figure 16-49. A diagram of the Ford V6 DIS. (Ford)

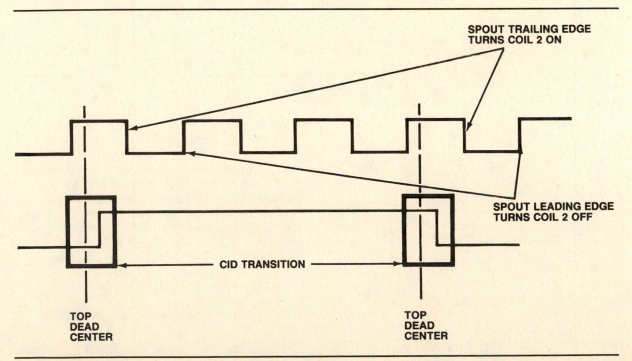

Figure 16-50. Coil selection with the engine cranking. (Ford)

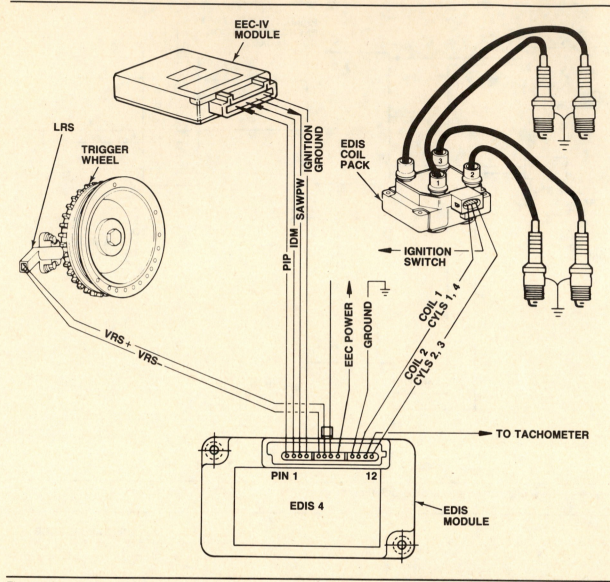

Figure 16-51. The 1.9-liter EDIS ignition system components. (Ford)

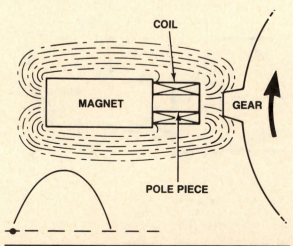

Figure 16-52. A variable reluctance sensor. (Ford)

Electronic direct ignition system (EDIS)
A second-generation DIS, EDIS functions faster and with greater accuracy than the V6 system just described. Because the system has been used on four-cylinder, V6, and V8 engines since its introduction in 1990, the number of coils and coil packs differs according to engine application. Other EDIS components also differ in appearance and location, but the system functions essentially the same regardless of engine application. Figure 16-51 shows the EDIS components used on the 1.9-liter SEFI engine.

There are other differences between EDIS and DIS:

- EDIS does not use a cylinder identification (CID) sensor or crankshaft position (CP)

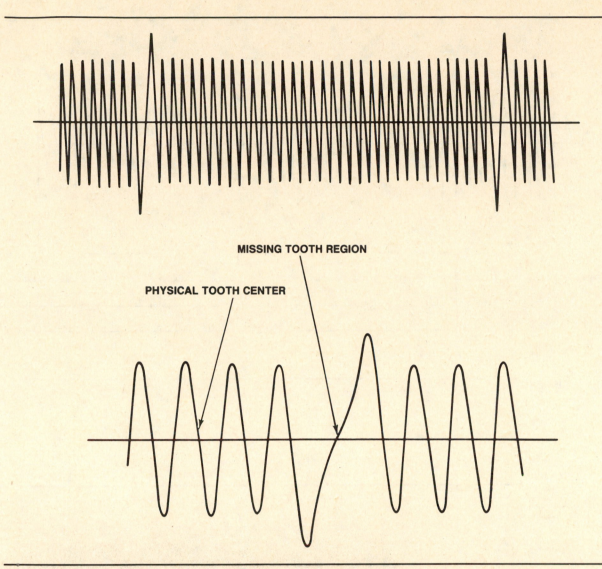

MISSING TOOTH REGION

PHYSICAL TOOTH CENTER

Figure 16-53. The VRS analog signal wave. (Ford)

sensor; a variable reluctance sensor (VRS) and trigger wheel perform the CID and CP sensor functions
- EDIS crankshaft position signals are more sophisticated and complex than those used for DIS
- EDIS uses a spark angle word (SAW) signal in place of the DIS SPOUT signal. The SAW signal also is more complex than a SPOUT signal
- The EDIS module is smarter, faster, has more "thinking" ability and decision-making responsibilities, and better diagnostic ability than the earlier DIS module.

The variable reluctance sensor (VRS) is a magnetic transducer containing a pole piece wrapped with fine wire, figure 16-52. If the transducer is exposed to a change in flux lines,

a differential voltage will be induced across the terminals of the wire windings. Thus, when a ferromagnetic toothed timing wheel on the crankshaft rotates in the presence of the VRS, the passing teeth cause the VRS reluctance to change, resulting in a varying analog voltage signal. The timing wheel has 35 teeth and a blank spot spaced at 10-degree increments. The blank spot for the thirty-sixth tooth serves as a fixed reference point for No. 1 piston travel identification.

During cranking, the EEC-IV module refers to a predetermined fuel control strategy stored in its memory to supply the necessary fuel for starting the engine. At the same time, the EDIS module looks for any significant change in the VRS signal. When it recognizes the missing tooth, figure 16-53, the EDIS module has a reference point and is synchronized to

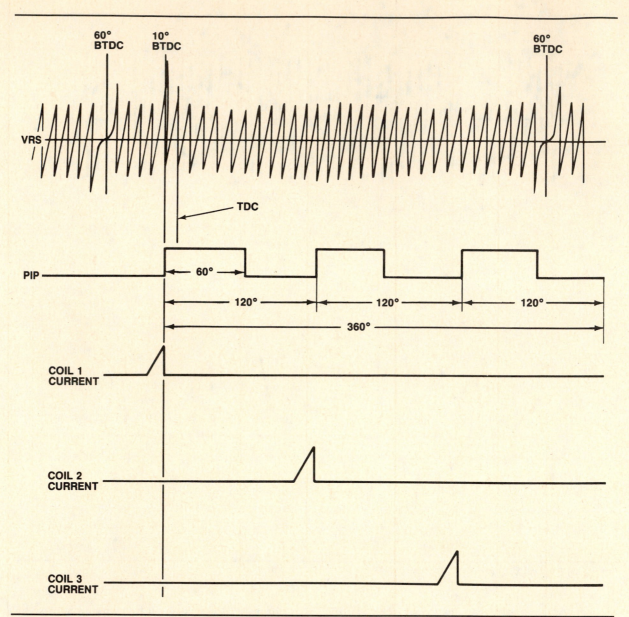

Figure 16-54. Comparison of analog VRS sensor signals with digital PIP signals created by the EDIS module. (Ford)

fire the proper coil. While the engine continues to crank, the EDIS module fires the coil at 10 degrees BTDC (base timing). When the coil for piston No. 1 is fired, a profile ignition pickup (PIP) signal is sent from the EDIS module to the EEC-IV computer. The PIP signal provides the EEC-IV computer with crankshaft position and engine speed data. Because the PIP signal is synthesized by the EDIS module, it takes the form of a digital square wave with a 50-percent duty cycle, figure 16-54. When the EEC-IV computer recognizes the PIP signal, it enables fuel and spark functions. It also processes the PIP signal with other information to determine the spark angle word (SAW) signal.

This signal is sent to the EDIS module, which uses it to determine whether ignition timing should be advanced or retarded.

Imported Car Electronic Ignitions

Imported vehicles appeared on the automotive scene with electronic ignitions about the same time or shortly after the domestic systems we have discussed. All major imported cars now use an inductive-discharge electronic ignition. In most of these systems, timing signals are sent to the ignition module from a magnetic pulse generator in the distributor, although

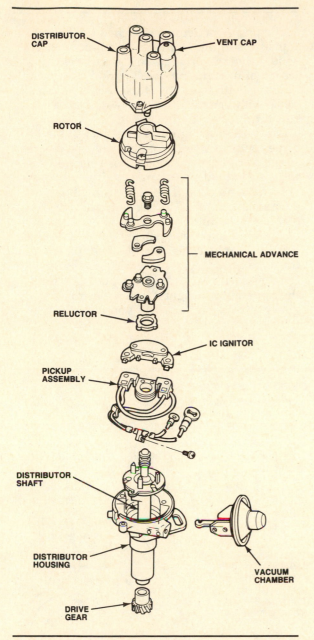

Figure 16-55. The Mitsubishi ignition system used on 2.6-liter engines is typical of the inductive-discharge ignitions used on Japanese vehicles.

Bosch makes a Hall-effect distributor used by Volkswagen.

The electronic ignition used on the Mitsubishi-built 2.6-liter engine in some Chrysler vehicles is typical of most Japanese designs, figure 16-55. The distributor contains a magnetic

pickup with an integral IC ignitor (control module), although some Toyota ignitions use an external ignitor mounted on the coil. The variable dwell ignition contains no ballast resistor. Full battery voltage is supplied to both the coil and ignitor whenever the ignition switch is in the start or the run position.

■ **Individual-Coil DIS**

The distributorless ignition systems (DIS) we have detailed in this chapter commonly employ half as many coils as they have spark plugs to fire. These systems fire each pair of spark plugs simultaneously: one with forward polarity and the other with reverse polarity. Depending on piston position, one spark is a waste spark. These systems eliminate moving parts and reduce the associated friction and wear and tear. They are also economical to produce and quite adequate for their intended use. However, there is a better, though more expensive, way.

Some Acura, BMW, Nissan, and Saab models have distributorless ignition systems that use a single ignition coil for each spark plug. In addition to the advantages of the waste-spark DIS, individual-coil DIS fire all plugs individually with forward polarity for a hotter spark, which

provides better performance at high rpm or under load. These systems further reduce the length of the secondary cable or eliminate it altogether, decreasing the chance of secondary arcing or leakage, improving the long-term reliability of the system, and eliminating the chance of cross-fire. Furthermore, shortening or eliminating the spark plug cable greatly reduces the amount of radiofrequency interference (RFI) emitted by the ignition system.

SUMMARY

Solid-state electronic ignition systems came into widespread use on both domestic and import vehicles in the early 1970s. Today, they are standard on all domestically-built cars and light trucks, as well as imported cars and light trucks. Solid-state ignitions provide greater available voltage, reliable performance for longer periods under varying operating conditions, with decreased maintenance.

Solid-state ignitions are either the inductive discharge type or the capacitive discharge type. Original equipment systems are the inductive discharge type. The primary circuits of solid-state ignitions can be triggered by breaker points, a magnetic pulse generator, a Hall-effect switch, a metal detector, or an optical triggering device. Original equipment systems generally use a magnetic pulse generator or a Hall-effect switch in the distributor to trigger the primary circuit.

The primary circuit is switched on and off by transistors in the ignition control module. The solid-state ignition module also controls the length of the ignition dwell period. Electronic ignitions with fixed dwell use a ballast resistor; those with variable dwell have no ballast resistor.

Basic electronic ignition systems use the same centrifugal and vacuum advance devices as breaker point ignitions. Those electronic ignitions used with electronic engine control systems have no advance mechanisms. Spark advance is controlled by the systems computer.

Electronic ignitions have undergone major change and improvement since their introduction in the mid-1970s. Distributor-type ignitions are being replaced by distributorless ignitions, with increasing responsibility for their operation assigned to the electronic engine control system, which you will study in the next chapter.

Review Questions

Choose the single most correct answer.
Compare your answers with the correct answers on page 431.

1. Which of the following is true of solid-state ignition systems?
   a. Provide less available voltage than breaker-point systems
   b. Provide greater available voltage than breaker-point systems
   c. Give less reliable system performance at all engine speeds
   d. Require more maintenance than breaker point systems

2. Inductive discharge systems use a triggering device to provide a sudden _____ in primary current.
   a. Increase
   b. Decrease
   c. High-voltage surge
   d. Low-voltage pulse

3. Which of the following is true of inductive discharge systems?
   a. Used as original equipment by most car manufacturers
   b. A common aftermarket installation
   b. Provide about 50,000 volts of available voltage
   c. Sustains a spark for about 200 microseconds

4. Capacitive discharge systems provide _____ secondary voltage when compared to inductive discharge systems.
   a. Exactly the same
   b. About the same
   c. Greater
   d. Less

5. Transistors have:
   a. A base of one type of material and an emitter and collector of another
   b. An emitter of one type of material and a base and collector of another
   c. A collector of one type of material and a base and emitter of another
   d. A collector, base, and emitter all of the same material

6. The earliest solid-state ignition systems used which of the following triggering devices?
   a. Metal detectors
   b. Breaker points
   c. Magnetic pulse generators
   d. Light detectors

7. The most common type of original equipment triggering devices are:
   a. Breaker points
   b. Light detectors
   c. Metal detectors
   d. Magnetic pulse generators

8. The accompanying illustration shows a:

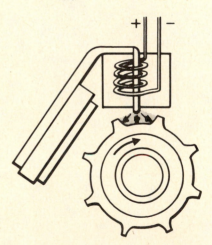

   a. Magnetic pulse generator
   b. Metal detector
   c. Light detector
   d. Breaker point assembly

9. The dwell period of a solid-state system can be measured with:
   a. A voltmeter
   b. An ammeter
   c. An ohmmeter
   d. An oscilloscope

10. In the Delco High-Energy Ignition (HEI) system, the dwell period is controlled by the:
    a. Pole piece
    b. Timer core
    c. RFI filter capacitor
    d. Electronic control module

11. The Delco HEI system uses:
    a. A single ballast resistor
    b. A dual ballast resistor
    c. No ballast resistor
    d. Calibrated resistance wire

12. The Chrysler electronic ignition system uses a:
    a. Dual ballast resistor
    b. Single ballast resistor
    c. No ballast resistor
    d. Calibrated resistance wire

13. The rotating component attached to the distributor shaft in the Chrysler electronic ignition is called the:
    a. Armature
    b. Reluctor
    c. Timer core
    d. Trigger wheel

14. The rotating component attached to the distributor shaft in the Ford electronic ignition is called the:
    a. Armature
    b. Reluctor
    c. Timer core
    d. Trigger wheel

15. Ford's Dura-Spark I system uses:
    a. A single ballast resistor
    b. A dual ballast resistor
    c. No ballast resistor
    d. A calibrated resistance wire

16. A Hall-effect switch requires _____ to generate an output voltage.
    a. A magnetic pulse generator
    b. A varactor diode
    c. A 45-degree magnetic field
    d. An input voltage

17. Thick-film integrated (TFI) ignition modules are:
    a. Mounted inside the distributor
    b. Mounted on the side of the distributor
    c. Mounted on the vehicle fenderwell
    d. Used as a handle to rotate the distributor

18. Dual-mode ignition modules are used with:
    a. Dura-Spark I
    b. TFI-I
    c. Dura-Spark II
    d. TFI-IV

19. A Hall-effect switch is used with which Chrysler electronic ignitions?
    a. Four-cylinder
    b. Inline-six
    c. V6
    d. V8

20. When a distributorless ignition coil fires its two spark plugs, one spark ignites the mixture at the _____ of the compression stroke and the other spark is wasted at the _____ of the exhaust stroke.
    a. Top, top
    b. Top, bottom
    c. Bottom, bottom
    d. Bottom, top

21. The initial firing sequence in a distributorless ignition is established by the _____ sensor.
    a. Vehicle speed
    b. Crankshaft
    c. Electronic engine control module
    d. Camshaft

22. When a DIS module fires the spark plug in a cylinder on its exhaust stroke, there is _____ effect on engine operation.
    a. No
    b. A minor
    c. A stabilizing
    d. A detrimental

23. The Ford Dual Plug DIS system is used on:
    a. 3.0-liter SHO V6 engines
    b. 3.8-liter supercharged V6 engines
    c. 2.3-liter truck engines
    d. Four-cylinder, V6, and V8 engines

17

Electronic Engine Control Systems

ENGINE COMPUTERS

The computers used to control various electrical systems, including engine operation, may be called modules, assemblies, or electronic control units. Some, like the HEI module we saw in Chapter Sixteen, are single-function devices that control a given system — in this case, ignition. Others are multiple-function devices that regulate more than one system. As we learned in Chapter Four, such modules use input signals from various sensors to control a given system, and the output signal from one computer can act as an input signal to another computer.

Computer Functions

Every computer, regardless of its use, does four basic jobs:

- Input
- Processing
- Storage
- Output.

The voltage signals received from various sensors are the computer input. The computer then compares the input data to its operating program and makes a decision. Part of that decision can be the storage of input data for future reference or the delay of an output signal. The computer always stores its own operating instructions, and most automotive computers store additional information concerning vehicle operation. Output is the decision made by the computer and transmitted to a display unit or to a system actuator by another voltage signal.

Analog and Digital Computers

Computer systems, their input, and their output are classified into two categories:

- Analog
- Digital.

Every late-model engine control system has both analog and digital functions.

Analog means that a voltage signal or processing action is continuously variable relative to the operation being measured or controlled. Most engine-related conditions are analog variables. For example, engine temperature does not change abruptly from 0° to 195°F (–18° to 91°C). It varies in an infinite number of amounts from low to high. The same holds true for engine speed, intake airflow, and many other factors.

Digital, however, means that an input or output signal or a processing action is either yes/no, high/low, or on/off. An air condition-

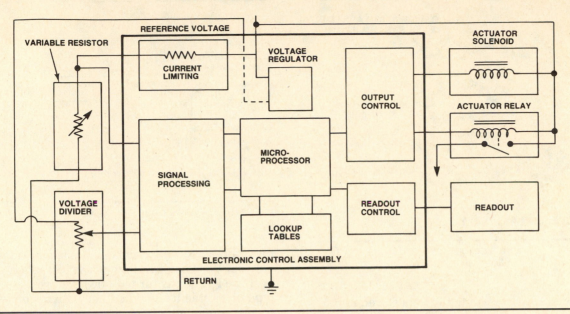

Figure 17-1. The lookup tables in electronic engine control computers contain the computer operating program. (Ford)

ing compressor clutch signal is a digital input; the voltage that engages the clutch is either on or off.

Some early engine control computers, such as those in the mid-1970s Chrysler electronic lean-burn system, were analog units. However, analog computers are susceptible to temperature changes, fluctuations in supply voltage, and signal interference. Digital computers are not. Digital computers are also faster, simpler, and easier to build. Current engine control systems use digital computers.

Digital computers can only act on digital signals, however, so analog inputs are changed into digital form by **analog-to-digital (AD)** conversion circuits in the computer. In a similar manner, **digital-to-analog (DA)** converters change output signals back into analog form when necessary.

Computer Programs and Memory

The central processing unit of any computer is a chip called the microprocessor. This chip is responsible for performing all of the mathematical computations and decision-making logic required of the computer. By itself, a microprocessor is useless without instructions in binary form that it can use to understand input data, perform calculations, and transmit output commands. These instructions are called a program and are stored on an integrated circuit (IC) chip in the form of **lookup tables**. These tables are part of the computer memory. Figure 17-1 shows the relationship of the

lookup tables to the other components of a Ford electronic control assembly (ECA).

A separate set of lookup tables in the memory contains information on fixed and variable vehicle values. This data is used to calibrate the computer for a specific engine and transmission combination and is stored in a separate IC chip called a programmable read-only memory (PROM) or calibration assembly, figure 17-2.

Two basically different types of memory are used for computer storage functions:

- Permanent, read-only memory (ROM)
- Temporary, random-access memory (RAM).

Permanent memory is called read-only because the computer can only read the con-

Analog-to-Digital (AD): An electronic conversion process for changing analog voltage signals to digital voltage signals.

Digital-to-Analog (DA): An electronic conversion process for changing digital voltage signals to analog voltage signals.

Lookup Tables: Part of a computer's program, or instructions. One set of lookup tables is common to all microprocessors of a specific group. Another set of lookup tables is used for specific engine calibrations and is located in the PROM.

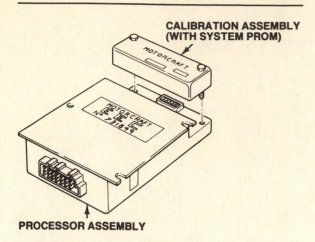

Figure 17-2. Ford's calibration assembly is a PROM containing fixed and variable vehicle values.

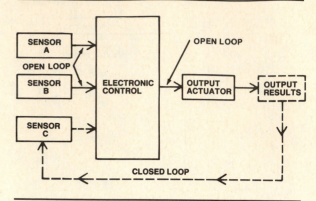

Figure 17-3. Typical open- and closed-loop control.

tents; it cannot change the data stored in it. This data is retained even when power to the computer is shut off. Part of the ROM is built into the computer, and the rest is located in the PROM or calibration assembly just described. PROM is programmed by the chipmaker and can be used only once. If changes need to be made to the information stored in PROM, the chip must be removed from the computer and replaced by another PROM containing the revised information.

PROMs are being replaced gradually by another type of read-only memory called erasable, programmable, read-only memory (EPROM). While the computer can write data into an EPROM for permanent storage, its most important feature is the ability of the EPROM to be erased and reprogrammed by the carmaker. Since EPROM memory is erasable, it can be changed either electrically or by exposure to ultraviolet light. If the EPROM memory can be electrically reprogrammed one byte at a time, it is called an electrically erasable PROM or EEPROM. When the memory is altered by exposure to ultraviolet light, a small window on the top of the chip is exposed for 15 to 20 minutes. Once the chip's memory is clean, it can be reprogrammed with new data in less than four seconds. EPROMs are used to store data such as odometer information; EEPROMs allow a car dealership to update or change the computer memory without having to replace the entire module.

Temporary memory is called random-access memory (RAM) because the computer can write or store new data into it as directed by the computer program, as well as read the data already in it. Automotive computers use

two types of RAM memory: volatile and nonvolatile. Volatile RAM memory is lost whenever the ignition is turned off. However, a type of volatile RAM called keep-alive memory (KAM) can be wired directly to battery power. This prevents its data from being erased when the ignition is turned off. Both RAM and KAM have the disadvantage of losing their memory when disconnected from their power source. One example of RAM and KAM is the loss of station settings in a programmable radio when the battery is disconnected. Since all the settings are stored in RAM, they have to be reset when the battery is reconnected. System trouble codes are commonly stored in RAM and can be erased by disconnecting the battery.

Nonvolatile RAM memory can retain its information even when the battery is disconnected. One use for this type of RAM is the storage of odometer information in an electronic speedometer. The memory chip retains the mileage accumulated by the vehicle. When speedometer replacement is necessary, the odometer chip is removed and installed in the new speedometer unit.

Computer programs increasingly incorporate backup or fail-safe modes, as well as adaptive learning strategies. The backup or fail-safe modes compensate for such things as sensor failure. If a sensor does fail, the computer takes its required signal from another source. For example, fuel pump operation in an electronic fuel injection is controlled by a pump relay. Relay failure means the loss of a signal, but the computer compensates by taking its signal from the oil pressure switch. The process is so sophisticated that few people would notice a difference in vehicle operation. The only clues to the relay failure are the lighting of the malfunction indicator lamp (MIL) and the fault code stored in memory.

Adaptive learning strategies compensate for production variations and gradual wear in sys-

ENGINE OPERATING MODES

Engine Operating Mode	Air-Fuel Ratio	Engine Temperature	Exhaust Gas Sensor Input	Air-Fuel Temperature
Engine Crank	Fixed 2:1 to 12:1	Cold to cool	None	Cold to cool
Engine warmup	Fixed 2:1 to 15:1	Warming	None until engine warmup	Warming
Open loop	Fixed 2:1 to 15:1	Cold or warm	May signal, but ignored by processor	Cold or warm
Closed loop	14.7:1 depends on exhaust gas sensor input	Warm	Signaling	Warm
Hard acceleration	Variable rich mixture, depends on driver demands	Warm	Signals, but ignored by processor	Warm
Deceleration	Variable lean mixture	Warm	Signals, but ignored by processor	Warm
Idle	Rich or lean, depends on calibration	Warm	Signal may be ignored, depending on calibration	Warm

Figure 17-4. Ford computers are programmed for seven different engine operating modes. Sensor input determines the mode selected. (Ford)

tem components. When a controlled value sent to the computer is not within the original design parameters, the adaptive learning strategy modifies the computer program to accept the new value and restore proper operation of the system. Such modifications are stored in RAM and remain in memory when the ignition is turned off, but not when the battery is disconnected. When battery power is restored, vehicle driveability is unsatisfactory until the computer relearns the parameters, which generally requires driving the vehicle several miles under varying conditions.

Vehicle driveability also can be affected when a malfunctioning sensor is replaced in a system with adaptive learning strategies. Since the computer had modified its original program to compensate for the unreliable sensor signals, the signals received from the new sensor are in conflict with the computer's modified program. This means that driveability will remain unsatisfactory until the computer relearns the necessary parameters.

Control System Operating Modes

Every computer control system has two operating modes. The computer can ignore sensor input under certain operating conditions, or it can make one of several different possible decisions based on the input of other sensors. For example, the computer can ignore an exhaust gas recirculation (EGR) sensor if a temperature sensor tells it that the engine is cold. It will also ignore the EGR sensor if the sensor input signal is outside the range which the computer has been given for speed, load, and temperature conditions.

Since a computer has this ability to be selective, engineers program a control system for two basic operating modes: open-loop and closed-loop, figure 17-3. (These modes were discussed in detail in Chapter Four.) The most common application of these modes applies to fuel-metering feedback control, although there are other open- and closed-loop functions. In addition to these two basic modes, a practical fuel control system must handle other operating modes as operating conditions change. Control logic that is programmed into the microprocessor determines the operating mode according to the existing engine condition. Figure 17-4 shows the seven different engine operating modes used by Ford and how the mode control logic selects the proper mode according to sensor input. This chart also is typical of the control systems used by other carmakers.

Open-loop control
When a vehicle is first started, the control system is in open loop. The sensors provide information to the computer. The computer reads these signals and orders the output actuators to operate in a specific manner. The actuators obey the orders they receive without providing any feedback to the computer. This unidirectional operating sequence is shown by the solid lines in figure 17-3.

When you turn on the windshield wipers, you are exercising open-loop control over the wiper system. The wiper blades will move across the windshield at a given rate of speed, regardless of whether the rain falling on the windshield is a light drizzle or heavy downpour. Wiper speed does not change until you readjust the wiper control. The wiper system does not receive an error feedback signal telling it that it is operating too slowly to clean the heavy downpour from the windshield. It relies on an outside force (the driver) for adjustment.

For an engine computer to determine whether the air-fuel mixture is correct, it requires a feedback signal from the exhaust gas oxygen (EGO) sensor. If the computer ignores this signal, it relies on signals from other sensors to make its decision. In this case, suppose the engine coolant sensor tells the computer that the

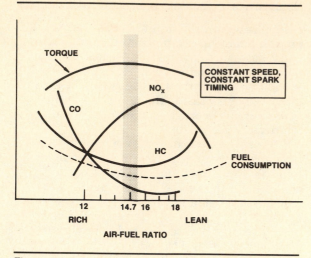

Figure 17-5. Changes in air-fuel ratio produce these fuel consumption, emission, and torque curves.

engine is cold. The throttle position sensor also signals that engine speed is increasing. Based on this information, the computer tells the fuel control actuator to enrich the mixture. It does this under certain specified conditions:

- During a cold start or hot restart
- Under low vacuum conditions
- At wide-open throttle or under full load, regardless of engine speed
- During idle or deceleration conditions (some systems).

Closed-loop control

In closed-loop control, the computer responds to feedback signals provided by sensors and actuators. These feedback signals tell the computer whether the output is too little, too much, or just right. In other words, the feedback signals regulate the output control. This cycle is summarized by the dotted line in figure 17-3.

In our fuel metering example above, the computer will respond to the EGO sensor signal in closed-loop operation. If the sensor measures a low oxygen content, which indicates a rich mixture, it signals this fact to the computer. The computer then directs the fuel control actuator to lean the mixture. If the actuator makes the mixture too lean, the EGO sensor will inform the computer, which then directs the fuel control actuator to again enrich the mixture. This is an ongoing process that occurs many times per second.

Fuel metering is not the only use of closed-loop control. Systems that use a detonation sensor retard ignition timing according to the sensor signal until detonation stops, then return the timing to normal. Idle speed control is still another example. If the engine idle speed

changes from a preset value, the computer receives a signal from the speed sensor and directs the idle speed control (an actuator) to change the idle airflow until idle speed is brought back into specifications.

In essence, a computer operating in closed loop is constantly "retuning" the engine while it is running in order to compensate for changes in various operating factors, such as temperature, speed, load, and altitude.

Adaptive Memory, Integrator, and Block Learn

The newer engine control systems can be programmed to learn from their own experience. This **adaptive memory** feature allows the microprocessor to adjust its memory for computing open-loop operation. When the system is operating in closed loop, the microprocessor compares its open-loop calculated air-fuel ratios against the average duty cycle values in closed loop. If there is a substantial difference, the microprocessor corrects its memory so that it can match closed-loop control as closely as possible when it is in open loop. This data is stored in long-term RAM so that it can be used the next time the vehicle is started, providing more accurate air-fuel ratio control. It also allows a microprocessor to adapt to long-term changes in engine operation resulting from wear.

The electronic control module (ECM) on GM fuel-injected engine control systems contains a pair of functions called **integrator function** and **block-learn function**. These are responsible for making minor adjustments to the air-fuel ratio of a fuel-injected engine. As such, they perform the same function as the mixture control solenoid does on a carbureted engine and represent the injector on-time.

The block learn and integrator functions can be understood by seeing how the ECM calculates fuel injection metering.

The ECM of a fuel-injected engine uses a base fuel calculation. When the EGO sensor tells the ECM to enrich the air-fuel mixture, the ECM adds fuel to the base calculation. If the mixture needs to be leaner, the ECM subtracts fuel from the base calculation.

This information can be obtained from the ECM using a scan tool which connects to the ECM serial data transmission line through the diagnostic connector. Acting like a bystander, the scan tool monitors the inputs and outputs as received and sent by the ECM.

The scan tool reads the base fuel calculation as the number 128. If the scan tool reads a higher number, the ECM is adding fuel to the mixture. If the number is less than 128, the ECM is subtracting fuel. Such corrective action taken by the ECM is the integrator function, but is effective only on a short-term basis. Block learn, or long-term correction, will only change if the integrator sees a condition that remains for a longer, calibrated period of time.

In summary, adaptive memory allows the engine computer to alter its program over the life of the vehicle. The computer can adapt its program to such long-term variables as:

- Engine wear
- Changes in fuel quality
- Changes in regular driving habits
- Changes in environmental conditions.

The integrator capability allows the computer to make short-term — minute-by-minute — corrections in fuel metering. Such corrections may be necessary, for example, when a car is driven from low altitude across a high mountain pass and back to low altitude in an hour or two.

Block-learn represents the long-term effects of integrator corrections. As such, it complements adaptive memory. If the computer continually must overcompensate fuel metering to maintain the stoichiometric ratio, it "learns" the correction and adapts its memory to make the correction factor part of its basic program. The period necessary for block-learn to become part of basic memory may be eight hours, 40 hours, 80 hours, or some other period determined by the system engineers.

AIR-FUEL RATIO, TIMING, AND EGR EFFECTS ON OPERATION

This is a good point to review the effects of air-fuel ratio, timing, and EGR operation on overall engine operation. The review will help you to understand why only a computer can exercise the control necessary for maximum engine efficiency.

Air-Fuel Ratio

Assuming fixed timing and engine speed, variations in air-fuel ratio have a dramatic effect on pollutants, figure 17-5. When the ratio is richer than 14.7, HC and CO emissions are high, as would be expected with the increase in fuel consumption. However, NO_x emissions are low. Torque is greatest at ratios between 12 and 16:1. Above 16, torque falls off, with increases in HC and NO_x. When the ratio is very lean, HC emissions also increase, as does fuel consumption. This is caused by engine misfiring from the lean mixture and passing un-

burned fuel through the cylinders. The result is a reduction in both power and torque.

The stoichiometric air-fuel ratio
As you learned in Chapter Twelve, air-fuel ratios for gasoline engines can range from 8:1 at the richest to about 18.5:1 at the leanest. With more or less fuel, the mixture will not burn. Ratios of approximately 12 to 13.5 produce maximum power. Ratios of approximately 15 to 16 produce maximum fuel economy. Between these two ranges lies the **stoichiometric air-fuel ratio** of 14.7:1.

"Stoichiometric" is a scientific term that indicates the air-fuel ratio which produces the most complete combustion with the fewest unburned byproducts. At a ratio of 14.7, the oxygen molecules in air and the hydrocarbon molecules in gasoline combine almost completely for the best *combination* of power, economy, and emission control.

Adaptive Memory: A feature of computer memory that allows the microprocessor to adjust its memory for computing open-loop operation, based on changes in engine operation.

Integrator Function: The ability of the computer to make short-term — minute-by-minute — corrections in fuel metering.

Block-Learn Function: The long-term effects of integrator corrections. Block-learn complements adaptive memory. If the computer continually makes the same correction, it "learns" the correction and adapts its memory to make the correction factor part of its basic program.

Stoichiometric Air-Fuel Ratio: The air-fuel ratio of approximately 14.7 that provides the most complete combustion and combination of oxygen and hydrocarbon molecules.

■ The Key Number

Do you have a lucky number? Perhaps a set of numbers that are important to your business or your life? Everyone remembers his or her own birthday by the numbers of the day, month, and year. Most people remember their social security number, their car license number, or their driver's license number. Here's a key number for any automotive technician to remember:

14.7

That's the number that represents both atmospheric pressure at sea level (14.7 psi) and the stoichiometric air-fuel ratio: 14.7 pounds of air to each pound of gasoline.

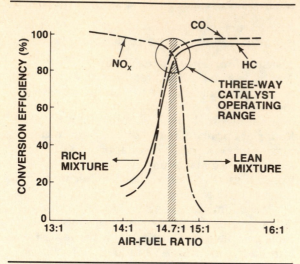

Figure 17-6. Three-way catalyst efficiency is maximized at a 14.7:1 air-fuel ratio. (GM)

Emission control is optimum at the stoichiometric ratio, if a three-way oxidation-reduction catalytic converter is used, figure 17-6. As the mixture gets richer, HC and CO conversion efficiency falls off. With leaner mixtures, NO_x conversion efficiency falls off. As figure 17-6 shows, the conversion efficiency range is very narrow — between 14.65 and 14.75:1. A fuel system without feedback control cannot maintain this narrow range.

Ratio control with carburetors and fuel injection

Two types of fuel control actuators are used with carburetors:

- A solenoid or stepper motor mounted on or in the carburetor to directly control the fuel-metering rods or air bleeds, or both
- A remotely-mounted, solenoid-actuated vacuum valve to regulate carburetor vacuum diaphragms that control the fuel-metering rods or air bleeds.

The computer sends a pulsed voltage signal to the control device, varying the ratio of on-time to off-time according to the signals received from the EGR sensor. As the percentage of on-time is increased or decreased, the mixture is made leaner or richer.

With fuel injection systems, however, the computer exercises ratio control by switching one or more fuel injectors on and off. The switching rate is determined by engine speed, and the computer varies the time the injectors remain open (pulse width) to establish the air-fuel ratio, figure 17-7. As the computer receives data from its input sensors, it lengthens the pulse width to supply additional fuel for situations such as cold running, heavy loads,

and fast acceleration. In a similar manner, it shortens the pulse width to lean the mixture for situations such as idle, cruising, or deceleration.

Ignition Timing

Assuming a fixed air-fuel ratio and engine speed, variations in ignition timing also have a dramatic effect on fuel consumption and pollutants. When timing is at TDC or slightly retarded, emissions are low and fuel consumption is high. As timing is advanced, fuel consumption drops off but emissions increase. Engine computers are programmed to calculate the best timing for any combination of air-fuel ratio and engine speed without detonation problems.

Exhaust Gas Recirculation

Exhaust gas recirculation is considered the most efficient way of reducing NO_x emissions without adversely affecting fuel economy, driveability, and HC emission control. Because the recirculation of exhaust gases lowers the combustion temperature, NO_x emissions drop off sharply when exhaust gas is introduced into the air-fuel mixture. However, excessive reliance on EGR leads to an increase in both HC emissions and fuel consumption. Again, the engine computer is programmed to calculate the percentage of exhaust gas that delivers the best compromise between NO_x control, HC emissions, and fuel economy without detonation problems. On late-model cars, engineers use EGR to control detonation by lowering combustion temperatures. This allows more advanced spark timing for better fuel economy than would be possible without EGR.

Computer Integration

One of the primary values of a computer is its ability to integrate the operation of two or more individual, single-function systems to form a larger, more precise multiple-function system. For example, we have seen that centrifugal and vacuum advance mechanisms can control spark timing relative to engine speed and load. We know that fuel metering through a carburetor is controlled by airflow, and that manifold or ported vacuum can manage basic EGR flow. Integrating such independent systems through a computer provides faster, more precise regulation of each system, and allows the computer to calculate the effect of changing several variables at the same time. Computer integration now is proceeding in two directions: body computer modules (BCM)

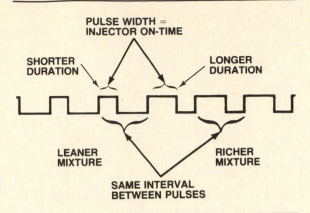

Figure 17-7. Fuel injector pulse width determines the air-fuel ratio.

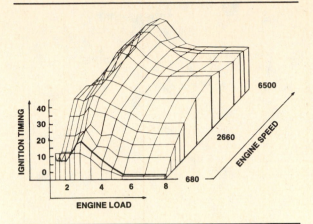

Figure 17-8. Engine mapping is a three-dimensional graph of the optimum fuel, ignition, EGR, and other variables.

with multiplexing, and smarter engine control computers.

Body computer modules

During the mid-1980s, body computer modules and multiplexing appeared to be the trend of the future. A body computer module is one that has been designated a ''master'' computer in an automobile, with various other system computers functioning both on their own, and as ''slaves'' to the BCM. As you learned in Chapter Five, the master computer module uses multiplexing to communicate with other computer modules in the car, and acts as a traffic control officer at a four-way intersection in controlling how and when the modules talk to each other.

Smarter computers

The trend toward multiplexing has cooled somewhat in the face of computers with faster microprocessors and larger memories. While some carmakers continue to link separate computer modules by multiplexing, others have turned to smarter, faster engine control computers as a way of handling multiple functions and systems within a single unit. One example of this approach is the use of electronic automatic transmissions (EATs). The early EATs were controlled by their own module, which interfaced with the engine control computer to determine torque converter clutch application and shift scheduling. More recent EATs have their computer program integrated with that of the engine control computer. This integration has caused some carmakers, like GM, to redesignate its electronic control module (ECM) as a powertrain control module (PCM). In the foreseeable future, it appears that both methods of computer integration will continue to be used.

Engine Mapping

The programs for engine computers consist of three parts:

- The basic mathematical instructions for processing data
- Data on engine and vehicle fixed values such as engine displacement, number of cylinders, fuel system type, compression ratio, transmission type and gear ratios, vehicle weight, and accessories
- Variable data such as combinations of engine and vehicle speed, intake airflow, fuel metering, engine load, and air injection and EGR operation.

The first two groups of data are constant values and are loaded into the computer memory from engineering design information. To load the third category of variable performance values into memory, engineers use a process called engine mapping.

The car is operated on a dynamometer while speed, spark timing, fuel metering, engine load, and other factors are adjusted manually for the best combination of operating conditions. The information derived from this operation is collected by a larger computer and loaded into the vehicle computer PROM.

Engine mapping creates a three-dimensional graph of engine operation, figure 17-8. The computer PROM remembers this performance graph and responds to sensor input data to adjust ignition timing, fuel metering, and emission control for best overall performance.

ELECTRONIC FUEL INJECTION PRINCIPLES

Gasoline fuel injection provides the fuel metering for many late-model engine control sys-

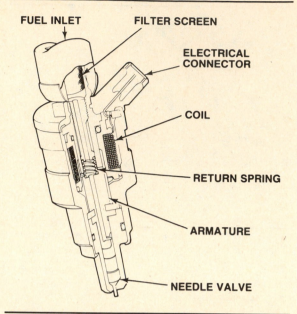

FUEL INLET   FILTER SCREEN

ELECTRICAL
CONNECTOR

COIL

RETURN SPRING

ARMATURE

NEEDLE VALVE

Figure 17-9. Solenoid actions intermittently open the EFI nozzles. (Volvo)

tems. Gasoline injection systems are generally classified as:

- Mechanical or electronic systems
- Continuous or intermittent injection
- Port or manifold injection, or throttle body injection.

These categories are not always clear-cut, however. Mechanical systems have many electronic parts, for example. Most electronic systems provide intermittent (pulsed) injection, but Chrysler's V8 throttle-body system is an electronic continuous-injection system.

Air-Fuel Mixture Control

Fuel metering through a carburetor is controlled by air pressure and air volume (airflow into an engine). These same factors govern fuel injection. In a carburetor, fuel metering is controlled by the difference between air pressure in the fuel bowl and air pressure in the carburetor venturi. Airflow is determined by the pumping capacity of the engine, the airflow capacity of the carburetor, and the position of the throttle. In a fuel injection system, however, the fuel is isolated from intake airflow and pressure behind the injection nozzles. All injection systems, therefore, use one of the following kinds of sensors to measure intake air volume and meter fuel accordingly:

- An airflow meter or sensor
- A manifold pressure sensor (often in combination with a barometric pressure sensor)
- An air mass sensor.

Carburetors and fuel injection systems both provide rich air-fuel ratios of 12.5 to 13.5:1 and lean ratios of 15 to 16:1 for the full range of engine operating needs. Late-model carburetors and fuel injection systems used with electronic control systems have fuel metering capabilities to maintain the stoichiometric air-fuel ratio of 14.7:1. All gasoline injection systems have three basic subsystems:

- Fuel delivery subsystem:
  - fuel pump
  - fuel filter, or multiple filters
  - fuel lines, including individual lines to port injection nozzles
  - pressure regulator to maintain the required, constant fuel pressure at the injection nozzles
  - injection nozzles.
- Air control subsystem:
  - throttle
  - air volume sensor — mechanical airflow sensor, manifold and barometric pressure sensors, or air mass sensor
- Engine sensors and auxiliary systems.

You will study these as you progress through this chapter and learn about electronic engine control systems.

Electronic Injection Nozzles

To understand fuel injection as part of a complete engine control system, you must understand the operation and control of electronic injection nozzles. An electronic injection nozzle is simply a specialized solenoid, figure 17-9. It has an armature and a needle or ball valve. A spring holds the needle or ball closed against the valve seat, and the armature opens the valve when it receives a current pulse from the system computer. When the solenoid is energized, it unseats the valve to inject fuel.

The injector always opens the same distance, and the fuel pressure is maintained at a constant value by the pressure regulator. The amount of fuel delivered by the injector depends on the amount of time that the nozzle is open. This is the injector pulse width: the time in milliseconds that the nozzle is open.

The system computer varies pulse width to supply the amount of fuel that an engine needs at a specific moment. A long pulse width delivers more fuel; a short pulse width delivers less fuel.

Injector pulse width relates to another important concept that you will use to test injection systems. This is the injector duty cycle. The duty cycle relates to any intermittently operating device. Ignition dwell, for example, is

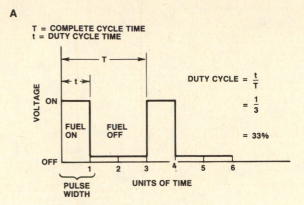

SHORT DUTY CYCLE (PULSE WIDTH)
MINIMUM FUEL INJECTION

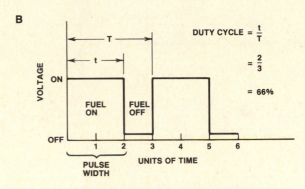

LONG DUTY CYCLE (PULSE WIDTH)
MAXIMUM FUEL INJECTION

Figure 17-10. Comparison of pulse width and duty cycle for the same cycle time.

really the ignition duty cycle. The complete operating cycle of any solenoid-operated device is the entire time from *on* to *off* to *back on* again. The duty cycle is the percentage of on-time to total cycle time.

A solenoid can operate at any number of cycles per second: 10, 20, 30, 60, or whatever the engineer chooses to design. Each complete cycle lasts the same amount of time, but duty cycle can vary as a percentage of each cycle. Pulse width varies along with the duty cycle because it is the actual *time* that the solenoid is energized. Figure 17-10 shows two different pulse widths and duty cycles for the same complete cycle time. The system computer calculates the necessary pulse width and duty cycle from information provided by system sensors. Modern digital computers operate fast enough to change injector pulse width in fractions of a second to maintain precise fuel metering.

Mechanical Fuel Injection

The only major mechanical gasoline injection system is the Bosch K-Jetronic system, figure 17-11, introduced in the mid-1970s on several European cars. The K-Jetronic system uses fuel pressure in the injector lines to open the nozzles and continuously deliver fuel to the intake manifold. The K-Jetronic system remains in use today on many imported cars and has been combined with the Bosch Motronic, or digital motor electronics (DME) system, which you will study later in this chapter.

Electronic Fuel Injection

All electronic fuel injection systems operate on the principles outlined previously, but there are two basically different system designs:

- Throttle-body injection
- Port, or manifold, injection.

Throttle-body injection

In a throttle-body system, one or two injectors are mounted in a carburetor-like throttle body on the intake manifold, figure 17-12. The fuel pump delivers fuel to the injectors by an electric fuel pump, and a pressure regulator in the throttle body maintains constant fuel pressure at the injectors, figure 17-13. The one or two injectors deliver fuel in pulses. Pulse width and duty cycle are regulated by the computer. Fuel distribution from the throttle body is similar to fuel distribution from a carburetor through the intake manifold. However, the computer-controlled injection regulates fuel metering more precisely than a carburetor and improves atomization as fuel enters the intake airflow.

Throttle-body systems have been used by all domestic carmakers since the early 1980s. Figure 17-14 shows typical throttle-body injection assemblies used by GM, Ford, and Chrysler.

From 1981 through 1983, Chrysler used a TBI system for V8 engines that injected fuel continuously, rather than in variable pulses, figure 17-15. A small variable-speed, constant-displacement pump in the throttle body receives a varying voltage signal from the computer. This pump speed changes to vary the fuel pressure and volume at the injectors, which regulates fuel metering.

Port (manifold) injection

Port, or manifold, injection systems are older designs than TBI systems. The first electronic port injection systems used in production were the Bosch D-Jetronic and L-Jetronic, introduced on several European cars in the late 1960s and early 1970s. The L-Jetronic system,

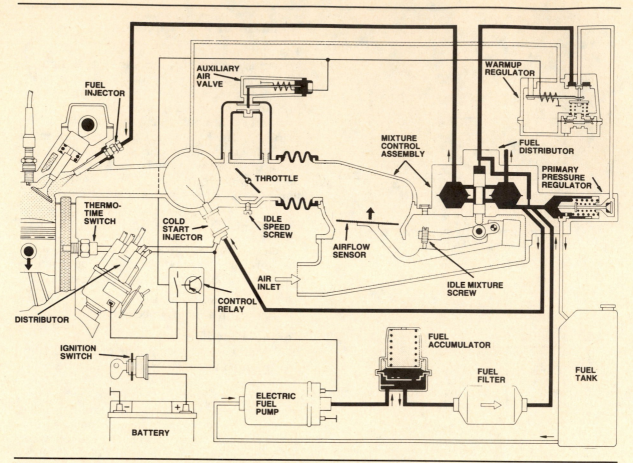

Figure 17-11. The Bosch K-Jetronic mechanical gasoline injection system. (Bosch)

figure 17-16, is the basis for several systems used by GM, Ford, Toyota, Nissan, and other carmakers in the 1980s.

Port injection systems have one injector for each cylinder, mounted in the intake manifold near the cylinder head intake port, figure 17-17. This location allows each injector to deliver fuel as closely as possible to the intake valve and to ensure equal fuel distribution to all cylinders. The intake manifold has only a throttle at its inlet (and an airflow sensor on many systems). Because the manifold does not have to hold a carburetor and distribute the air-fuel mixture to all cylinders, it can be designed to tune the airflow for desired engine performance.

Port injection systems have an injector for each cylinder, but all systems do not operate, or ''fire'' the injectors in the same way. Some systems fire the injectors in separate groups, some fire all injectors simultaneously, and others fire the injectors individually in sequence. Port injection systems can be classified in one of the four following ways to define injector control:

- Grouped, single fire
- Grouped, double fire
- Simultaneous, double fire
- Sequential.

In a grouped single-fire system, the injectors are divided into two equal groups and fired alternately. One group fires for one engine revolution; the other group fires for the next revolution. Only one injector pulse is used to deliver the entire fuel charge for each intake stroke. This kind of system is simple and economical to build, but it is not as precise as the other systems. Because only one injector in a group can fire close to the time that the intake valve opens, the fuel from the other injectors in that group must wait in the manifold until the other intake valves open. Also, because a new fuel charge is delivered only once for each engine revolution, the computer must wait longer to change the air-fuel ratio.

In a grouped double-fire system, the injector groups fire alternately, but both groups fire once for each engine revolution or twice for each intake stroke. Two injector pulses make up the fuel charge for each cylinder; each

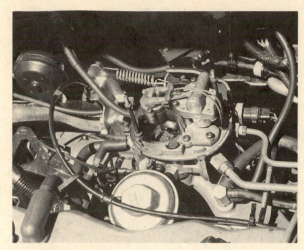

Figure 17-12. A throttle-body injection system resembles a carburetor.

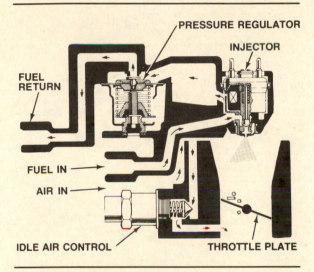

Figure 17-13. A throttle-body injection system can use one or two injectors.

pulse delivers half. The air-fuel total mixture remains in the manifold for a shorter time, and fuel metering changes can be made faster than with a single-fire system.

Simultaneous double-fire systems are common on many four-cylinder engines. All injectors fire at the same time, once for each engine revolution. Because there are two revolutions between the intake strokes for each cylinder, each injector pulse delivers half of the fuel for one intake stroke. This system is easy to program and can readjust the air-fuel ratio relatively quickly for a four-cylinder engine. Figure 17-18 is a diagram of simultaneous double-fire injector operation.

Sequential injection is the newest and most precise electronic injection control method. The computer fires each injector individually, just before the intake valve opens. The mixture

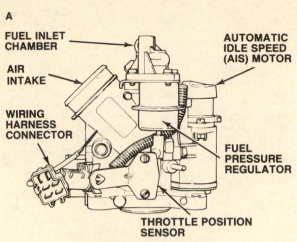

A

FUEL INLET CHAMBER

AIR INTAKE

WIRING HARNESS CONNECTOR

AUTOMATIC IDLE SPEED (AIS) MOTOR

FUEL PRESSURE REGULATOR

THROTTLE POSITION SENSOR

CHRYSLER-HOLLEY-BENDIX HIGH-PRESSURE THROTTLE BODY ASSEMBLY

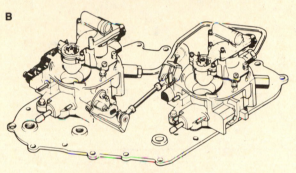

B

GM MODEL 400 CROSSFIRE INJECTION (CFI) ASSEMBLY

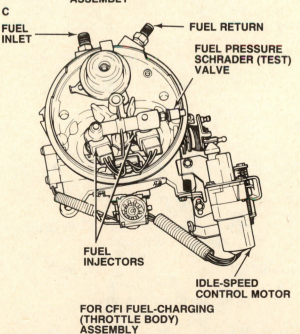

C

FUEL INLET

FUEL RETURN

FUEL PRESSURE SCHRADER (TEST) VALVE

FUEL INJECTORS

IDLE-SPEED CONTROL MOTOR

FOR CFI FUEL-CHARGING (THROTTLE BODY) ASSEMBLY

Figure 17-14. Examples of throttle-body systems used by GM, Ford, and Chrysler.

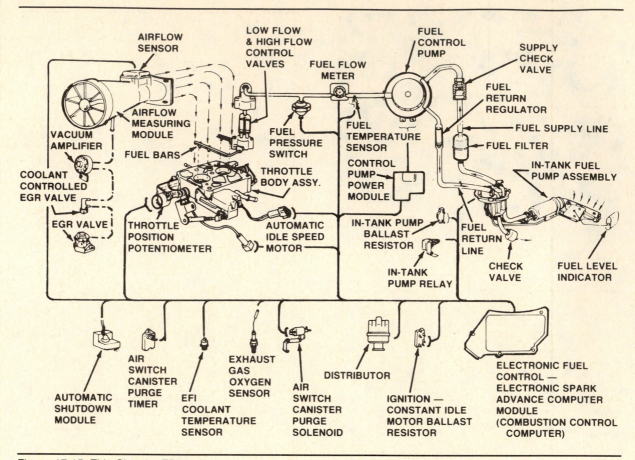

Figure 17-15. This Chrysler TBI system uses continuous, rather than variable-pulse, injection.

does not lie in the manifold, and fuel metering can be adjusted instantly from one injector to the next. Sequential systems are electronically complex and have been expensive to build. Advances in digital microprocessor technology, however, have made these systems economically available on late-model cars.

SYSTEM SENSORS

As we learned in Chapter Four, a sensor is an input device used to change temperature, motion, light, pressure, and other forms of energy into voltage signals that a computer can read. Most sensors are analog in nature; that is, they send a voltage signal proportional to the variable they are measuring. Since digital computers cannot understand analog signals, the computer must convert the analog signals to a digital form for processing. Figure 17-19 shows the most common type of sensors and their relationship to the computer.

Switches and Timers

A switch is the simplest form of digital sensor. Switches are either on (voltage signal) or off

(no voltage signal). A switch can provide the computer with either a high- or low-voltage signal, figure 17-20. In this case, input voltage from the computer is received by the switch through one of its terminals. A high-voltage signal is then returned to the computer through the other switch terminal when the switch closes, or a low-voltage signal when the switch opens. The computer is programmed to respond to the appropriate voltage signal, depending upon system design.

The switch can be combined with an integral or remote timer to delay a signal. The thermotime switch used in Bosch Jetronic and Motronic systems is typical of a combination switch-timer, figure 17-21. This type of switch is used to control the cold-start injector. Current passes through the heating element, heats the bimetal strip that holds the switch contacts, and opens the cold-start injector circuit. The time that the current takes to heat the resistance winding is the timing factor of the switch and determines the time that the circuit is closed to operate the cold-start injector. Be-

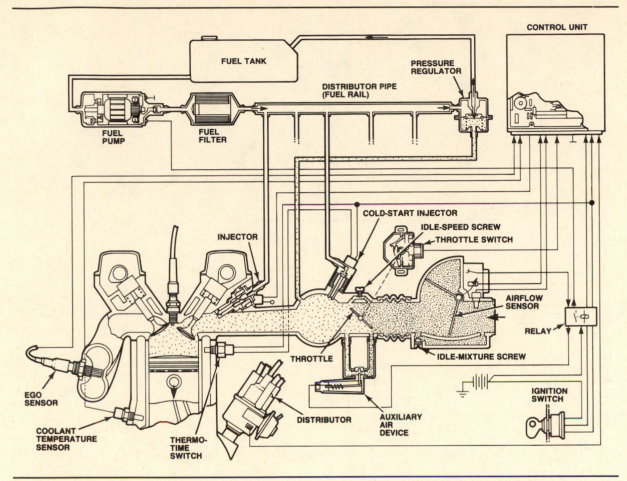

Figure 17-16. The Bosch L-Jetronic system has been used on various Japanese, European, and domestic vehicles. (Bosch)

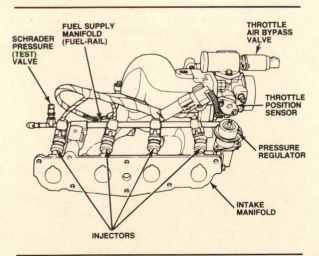

Figure 17-17. Port injection systems use one injector for each cylinder.

cause the switch is installed in the engine water jacket, coolant temperature keeps the switch bimetal strip open when the engine is warm.

Resistors

Most automotive sensors are a resistor of some type. Resistors send an analog voltage signal proportional to the variable they are measuring. Since resistors cannot generate but only modify a voltage, they require a reference voltage from the computer.

A thermistor is a two-wire variable resistor used to signal a change in temperature, figure 17-22. The computer applies reference voltage to one end of the thermistor and receives the return voltage from the other end, figure 17-19. As the temperature of the thermistor increases, its return voltage signal increases.

A **potentiometer** is a three-wire variable resistor. The computer applies reference voltage

Potentiometer: A variable resistor with three terminals. Return signal voltage is taken from a terminal attached to a movable contact that passes over the resistor.

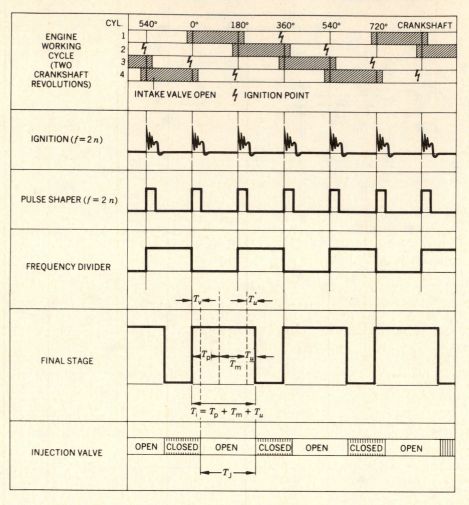

Figure 17-18. Four-cylinder engine cycles, with all injectors firing at the same time. (Bosch)

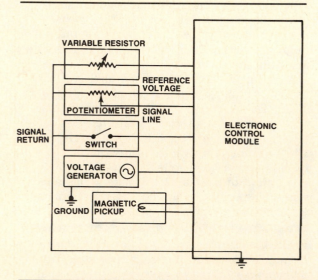

Figure 17-19. The computer (electronic control) relies on input signals from various sensors.

to one end; the other end is grounded. A movable contact that slides across the resistor connects to the third terminal, figure 17-19. Since the reference voltage remains constant, the return voltage varies only relative to the position of the movable contact. Figure 17-23 shows a potentiometer connected to a vane airflow sensor used to measure the volume of airflow in a fuel-injection system. The potentiometer is activated by the moving vane and sends an analog signal to the computer.

A piezoresistive sensor is one whose signal voltage varies according to the pressure or force applied to it. Like a thermistor, it has two connections. One terminal receives the reference voltage; the second terminal returns the signal voltage to the computer. Engine detonation sensors are piezoresistive devices, as are many barometric and manifold pressure sensors.

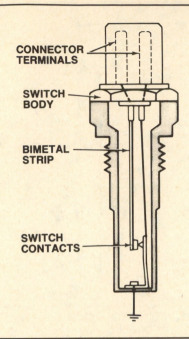

Figure 17-20. When the ground connection closes in this temperature switch, signal voltage is high. When it opens the switch, the voltage is low.

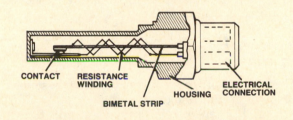

Figure 17-21. A thermo-time switch is used to limit the operation of a cold-start injector according to temperature.

Transformers

Transformer sensors, like resistors, receive a reference voltage and send an analog signal back to the computer. A transformer contains a movable core, allowing the coupling between the single input and dual output windings to vary according to core position. When the reference voltage is applied to the input winding, the signal voltage generated in each output winding is equal as long as the core remains centered, figure 17-24. As the core moves away from center, the output voltage of one winding exceeds that of the other winding. The two output winding voltages are processed by the computer into one signal voltage in direct proportion to the amount and direction of movement. The transformer is often used as a **manifold absolute pressure (MAP)** sensor.

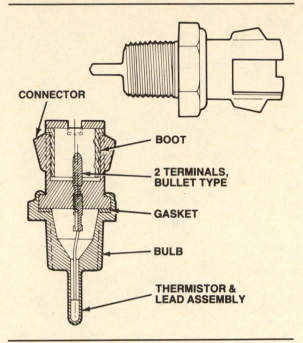

Figure 17-22. A thermistor requires a reference voltage from the computer. (Ford)

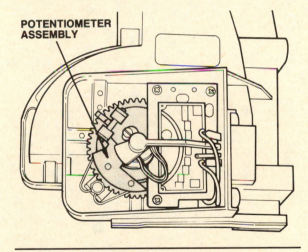

Figure 17-23. Van-type airflow meters use a potentiometer to signal the position of the vane (amount of airflow) to the computer. (Ford).

Generators

This type of sensor does not require a reference voltage. It generates its own signal volt-

---

Manifold Absolute Pressure (MAP): Pressure in the intake manifold that is a combination of atmospheric pressure and manifold vacuum or boost pressure.

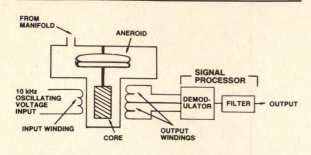

Figure 17-24. A transformer creates a voltage differential between two output windings.

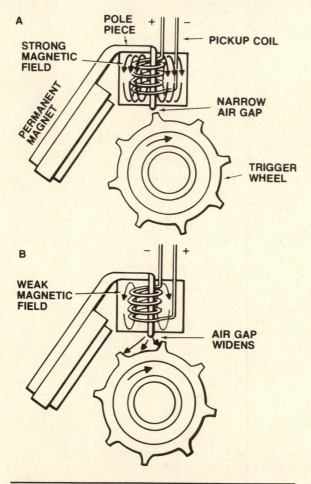

Figure 17-25. The magnetic field expands and collapses as the trigger wheel's teeth move past. This induces a varying-strength voltage in the pickup coil.

age. The magnetic pulse generator used in a breakerless distributor is one common example. The rotating trigger wheel varies the reluctance around a magnetic pole piece and pickup coil, figure 17-25. The signals produced can be used as a basic timing reference.

Pulse generators also have been used to indicate firing order, engine speed, and crankshaft

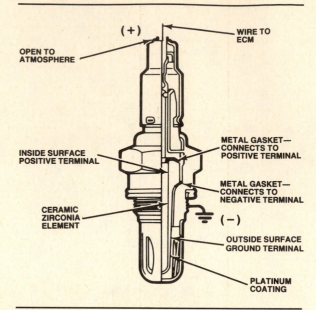

Figure 17-26. A late-model, single-wire exhaust gas oxygen (EGO) sensor. (Buick)

position. Bosch, Ford EEC-I and II, and the 1977 GM MISAR system use a pulse generator to respond to a cutout or tooth on the flywheel or harmonic balancer.

Zirconia Exhaust Gas Oxygen (EGO) Sensors

The concept of feedback fuel metering systems revolves around the exhaust gas oxygen (EGO) sensor. The sensor is basically a **galvanic battery** that generates from 0.1 to 0.9 volt by comparing the oxygen in the exhaust to the oxygen in the outside air.

The typical EGO sensor contains two platinum-surface electrodes separated by a ceramic zirconia element, figure 17-26. The inner surface (positive terminal) of the zirconia element is open to the atmosphere; the outer surface (negative terminal) is in contact with the exhaust gases. The zirconia element is an insulator when cold, and a semiconductor at operating temperature.

For comparative purposes, the atmosphere contains 21 percent oxygen; rich exhaust gases contain virtually none. A large differential in the amount of oxygen contacting the inner and outer surfaces results in greater conductivity, and causes the sensor to send a voltage signal above 0.6 volt, figure 17-27A. Lean exhaust contains approximately 2 percent oxygen. This reduces the differential, resulting in less conductivity and a voltage signal under 0.3 volt, figure 17-27B. We can summarize the operation of an EGO sensor as follows:

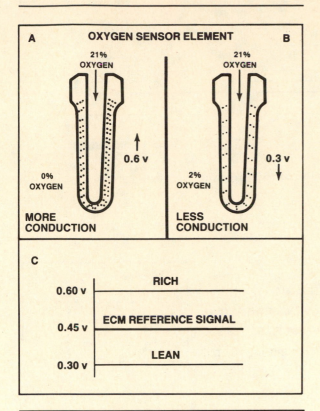

Figure 17-27. An EGO sensor measures the oxygen differential between ambient air and exhaust gases, using the ECM reference voltage as a midpoint between the two extremes. (Buick)

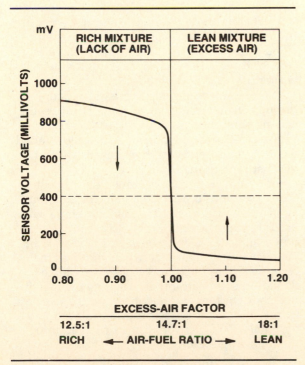

Figure 17-28. The EGO sensor provides its fastest response at the stoichiometric air-fuel ratio of 14.7.

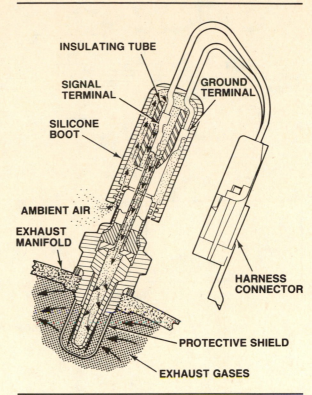

Figure 17-29. An early double-wire EGO sensor.

- When exhaust oxygen content is low (rich mixture), sensor voltage is high
- When exhaust oxygen content is high (lean mixture), sensor voltage is low.

Figure 17-28 shows the operating range of a sensor at about 1,472°F (800°C). Sensor voltage changes fastest at an air-fuel ratio of 14.7, which makes it ideal for maintaining the stoichiometric ratio.

Another important point about EGO sensors is that *they measure oxygen; they do not measure air-fuel ratio*. If the engine misfires, a large amount of oxygen remains in the unburned mixture that passes out with the exhaust. In this case, the sensor will deliver a false overly lean mixture signal. This is one example of why computer control of ignition and EGR is necessary for correct fuel metering control.

As you learned in Chapter Four and when you studied other sensors in this chapter, the computer sends a reference voltage to resistive sensors for sensor operation. The EGO sensor

Galvanic Battery: A battery that generates voltage based on a difference in oxygen content near two electrodes.

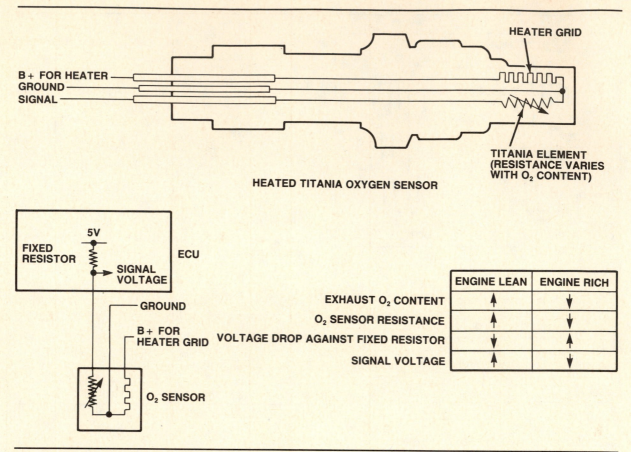

Figure 17-30. The heated titania EGO sensor used by Jeep.

is a generator and does not need a reference voltage for operation. The computer, however, uses a reference voltage as a comparison for the sensor voltage signal. Because the EGO signal voltage ranges from 0.1 or 0.3 volt with a lean mixture to 0.6 or 0.9 with a rich mixture, the computer uses an internal reference voltage of about 0.45 volt as a comparison, figure 17-27C. This internal reference voltage is also the basis for fuel metering output signals during open-loop operation when the computer ignores the EGO sensor.

All EGO sensors must warm to at least 300°C (572°) before they will generate an accurate signal. EGO sensors provide their fastest response to mixture changes at about 800°C (1472°F). This is the primary reason for open-loop fuel control on a cold engine.

The EGO sensor is installed in the exhaust manifold or header pipe directly in the path of the exhaust gas stream where it can monitor both the exhaust gas and ambient air. Some V-type engines use an EGO sensor in each manifold. The exact location and placement of the sensor vary according to engine design, because engineers position it where it will be the most efficient.

All zirconium-dioxide EGO sensors work on the principles just discussed, but they are not all built the same way. They may have one, two, or three wires that connect to the vehicle wiring harness. Early model sensors, figure 17-29, had two wires and were grounded through the computer or to some point on the chassis or engine. Some later sensors use a single wire for signal output and are grounded through the threads on their outer shell to the exhaust pipe or manifold.

Some sensors have a silicone boot to protect the sensor and to provide a vent for ambient air circulation. The positioning of a boot (when used) is important. If the boot is seated too far down on the sensor body, it can block the air vent, resulting in an inaccurate signal to the computer. The silicone boot has been abandoned on some late-model engines because it was thought that the silicone material gives off fumes that corrode electrical connections and terminals. EGO sensors can be divided into the following basic types:

- Standard unheated
- Water-resistant unheated
- Water-resistant heated
- Waterproof heated.

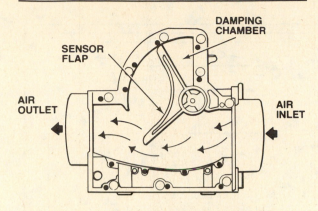

Figure 17-31. A vane-type airflow sensor.

To make EGO sensors water-resistant and waterproof, it was necessary to design them to use a different air reference source. Older designs have their air reference source at the sensor, but the water-resistant and waterproof sensors receive their air reference input through the sensor lead wires and connector.

Titania Exhaust Gas Oxygen Sensors

Zirconia EGO sensors have proven themselves during more than a decade of use, but EGO sensors containing titanium-dioxide or titania-sensing elements also are being used by Jeep, Toyota, and other carmakers. Both types of sensors provide a feedback signal indicating how rich or lean the exhaust is. Unlike the zirconia sensor, however, the titania sensor does not generate voltage. Instead, it detects exhaust oxygen content by acting as a variable resistor.

The computer provides a constant reference voltage to the sensor. As the oxygen content of the exhaust changes, the resistance of the titania-sensing element varies. Since the resistance of the sensing element also can be affected by temperature, a heating element is incorporated in the sensor to maintain a constant temperature of approximately 1,475°F (850°C).

Figure 17-30 shows the heated titania EGO sensor as used on 1987-90 4.0-liter Jeep engines. The computer provides the sensor with a five-volt reference voltage. The signal voltage is measured between the sensor and a fixed resistor in series with the sensor. As sensor resistance changes, the signal voltage also changes. With a rich mixture (low exhaust oxygen content), the sensor signal voltage is below 2.5 volts. With a lean mixture (high exhaust oxygen content), sensor signal voltage

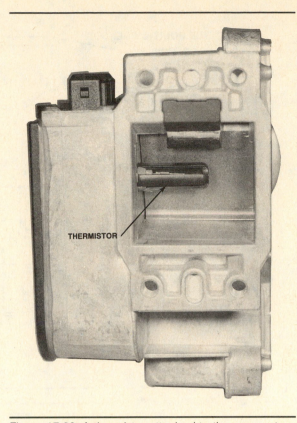

Figure 17-32. A thermistor attached to the vane acts as an air temperature sensor.

exceeds 2.5 volts. Although signal voltage direction, relative to oxygen content of the exhaust gas, is the opposite of a zirconia EGO sensor's signal, the computer's program allows it to read the signal correctly and make the necessary adjustments in fuel metering.

EGO Sensor Contamination

EGO sensor operation can be adversely affected by contamination. The following sources of contamination should be investigated in cases of multiple or repeated EGO sensor failures on the same vehicle:

- An overly rich mixture can deposit black carbon or soot on the sensor tip. Carbon deposits, however, will not cause sensor failure and can be burned off in the engine by running it at part-throttle for at least two minutes.
- Lead deposits are more serious, as they will glaze the sensor element, making it useless. Lead deposits generally result from the use of leaded fuel, although methanol in gasoline also can cause lead contamination by dissolving the terne coat inside the fuel tank. Lead contamination is hard to detect by a visual inspection.

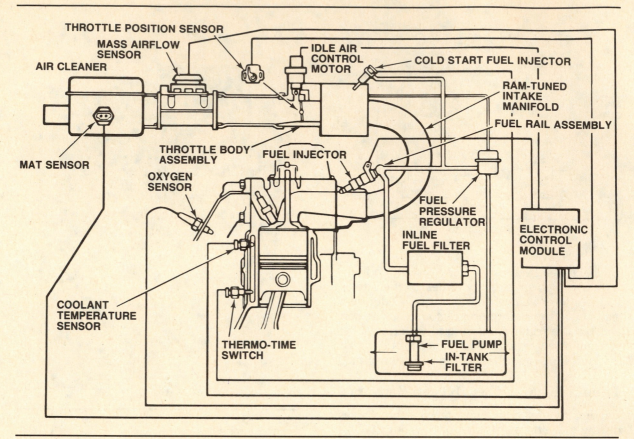

Figure 17-33. Typical mass airflow (MAF) sensor location in the fuel injection system. (General Motors)

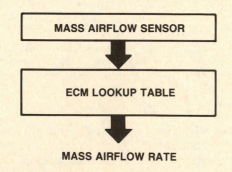

Figure 17-34. The engine control computer processes the MAF sensor signal directly through a lookup table to determine mass airflow rate. (General Motors)

• Some RTV silicone gasket materials emit silica vapors that will contaminate the EGO sensor. Sand-like particles of silica in the vapors embed themselves in the sensor element and clog its surface. This type of contamination slows down the sensor's response time, affecting engine operation. Silica contamination produces a whitish appearance on the sensor element.

• Other deposits can eventually affect sensor operation. Oil produces dark brown discoloration on the element, while antifreeze causes whitish discoloration.

Other Sensors

The following is a brief description of other sensors found in electronic engine control systems.

Vane airflow sensors
Some fuel injection systems use a vane-type airflow sensor, figure 17-31, positioned between the air filter and the intake manifold. The airflow sensor monitors the volume of air entering the intake manifold. Many systems also include a thermistor to sense air temperature. The thermistor often is an integral part of the vane, figure 17-32. Since the angular position of the vane is proportional to airflow, a potentiometer connected to the vane, figure 17-23, sends a voltage signal proportional to intake air volume to the computer.

Mass airflow sensors
A thermal measurement device, the mass airflow sensor is installed between the air intake and air throttle body to determine the molecu-

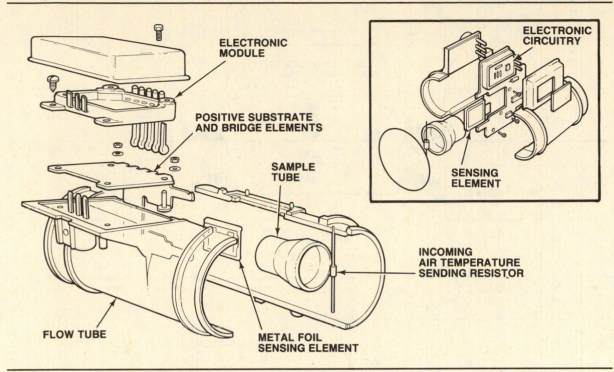

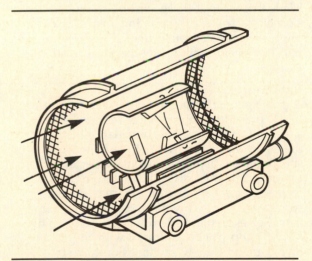

Figure 17-35. A heated thin-film MAF sensor consists of a screen or metal foil element to break up incoming airflow, a ceramic resistor to measure air temperature, and an electronic module. (General Motors)

Figure 17-36. The heated wire MAF sensor places the wire directly in the path of incoming air. (General Motors)

lar mass of combustible air entering the engine, figure 17-33. It performs the same function as a vane-type airflow sensor, but combines the airflow measurement into a single sensor, figure 17-34. Two basic types of mass airflow (MAF) sensors are used: a heated platinum wire or a heated thin-film semiconductor. Current provided by the MAF module heats the wire or film, which is cooled by incoming airflow. As the heated wire or film cools, the module increases current to keep the sensor temperature at a specified level. As the wire or film again heats up, current decreases. The module measures current changes, and converts them into voltage signals sent to the engine control computer for use in determining injector pulse width. Figure 17-35 shows the components of a typical heated thin-film MAF; figure 17-36 shows the heated wire design.

Manifold pressure, vacuum, and barometric pressure sensors

These sensors keep the computer informed about air volume and engine load, allowing it to adjust fuel metering accordingly. Their input also is used by the computer to adjust timing and EGR flow relative to load. Speed-density fuel injection systems rely on a manifold absolute pressure (MAP) sensor as the primary input in calculating mass airflow rate, figure 17-37. They may be piezoresistive devices, transformers, or potentiometers operated by an **aneroid** bellows or a vacuum diaphragm.

Aneroid: A bellows or capsule that contains a vacuum and changes its length in response to changing atmospheric pressure.

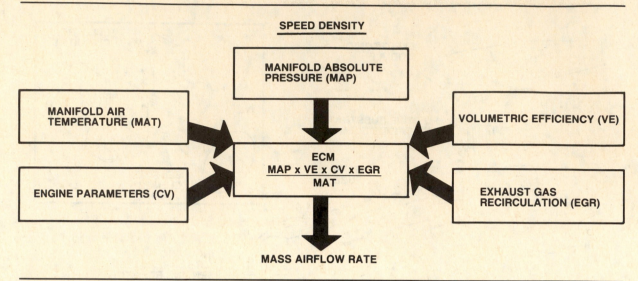

Figure 17-37. A speed density injection system uses manifold absolute pressure and temperature to calculate mass airflow rate. (General Motors)

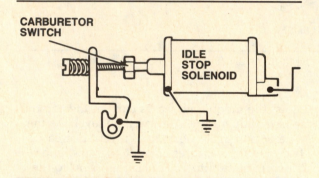

Figure 17-38. Chrysler uses a simple on/off switch to indicate throttle position. (Chrysler)

Temperature sensors

A simple bimetal switch, figure 17-20, is used when the computer is only interested in whether air or coolant temperature is above or below a specific point. If the computer requires information about temperature in a range, a thermistor is used, figure 17-22.

Throttle position sensors (TPS)

A throttle position sensor (TPS) may be a simple on/off switch, figure 17-38, used to indicate wide-open throttle or idle position with a high or low voltage.

A potentiometer can also be used to indicate the exact position and speed of throttle movement. Figure 17-39 shows a rotary-type throttle position sensor used on fuel injection assemblies. A linear-type TPS is generally used with carburetors. The two types differ physically, but both send the computer an analog signal proportional to the throttle plate opening angle. The rotary potentiometer moves on an axis with the throttle shaft, figure 17-40; the

linear potentiometer uses a plunger that rides on a throttle shaft cam.

Ignition timing, crankshaft position, and engine speed sensors

We learned about these sensors in our discussion of electronic ignitions in Chapter Sixteen. They send the computer analog and digital signals to control timing, fuel metering, and EGR.

Vehicle speed sensors

A pulse generator or an optical sensor, figure 17-41, provides the computer with vehicle speed information. This information is used by the computer in a variety of ways, including speedometer displays, torque converter lockup, and transmission shift scheduling. As vehicle systems have become more complex, some are equipped with multiple speed sensors. For example, Chevrolet and GMC light-duty pickup trucks equipped with the Turbo Hydra-matic 4L80-E transmission have both an output shaft speed sensor and an input speed sensor in addition to the main vehicle speed sensor. The PCM uses transmission input and output speeds to determine line pressure, transmission shift patterns, and torque converter clutch apply pressure, in addition to calculating turbine speed, gear ratios, and torque converter clutch slippage for diagnostic purposes.

EGR sensors

A sliding-contact potentiometer may be connected to the top of the EGR valve stem to inform the computer of EGR flow rate, figure 17-42. This information is used by the com-

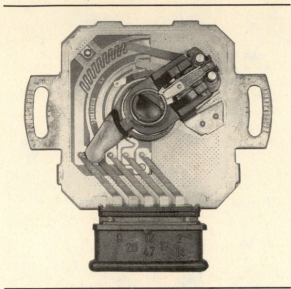

Figure 17-39. Bosch uses a rotary potentiometer as a throttle position switch.

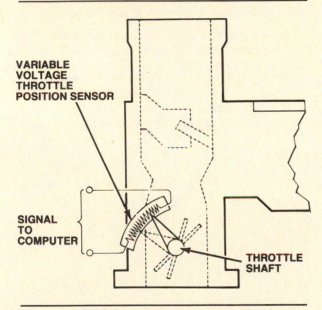

Figure 17-40. Because a rotary potentiometer moves on an axis with the throttle shaft, it can inform the computer of any change in throttle position. (Ford)

puter to control timing, fuel metering, and EGR valve operation.

Air conditioning sensors

An air conditioning compressor adds to the engine load when the compressor clutch is engaged. To allow the computer to make the necessary adjustments to compensate for the increased load, a simple on/off switch is used to tell the computer whether the compressor clutch is engaged or disengaged.

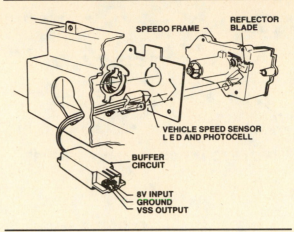

Figure 17-41. An LED and a photocell in the speedometer act as a speed sensor. (GM)

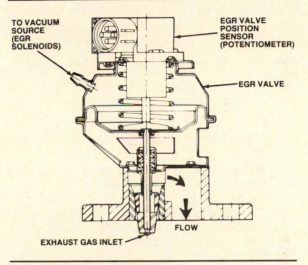

Figure 17-42. A potentiometer may be used to sense EGR flow. (Ford)

Detonation sensors

Detonation sensors generally use a piezoresistive crystal which changes resistance whenever pressure is applied to it, figure 17-43. A reference voltage from the computer is applied to one terminal. The return signal voltage from the other terminal remains at its programmed value as long as there is no detonation, and the pressure on the crystal is uniform. If detonation occurs, however, the unequal pressure on the crystal changes the sensor's resistance and the return voltage signal changes.

SYSTEM ACTUATORS

In Chapter Four, we learned that an actuator is an output device that changes the computer's voltage signal into a mechanical action. Most engine control actuators are solenoids, al-

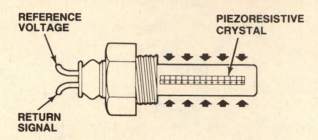

NO DETONATION—EQUAL PRESSURE

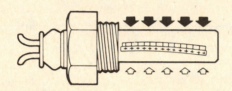

DETONATION—UNEQUAL PRESSURE

Figure 17-43. The piezoresistive crystal in a detonation sensor flexes when detonation (unequal pressure) occurs. (Audi)

though **stepper motors** are used in some applications.

A solenoid is an electromechanical device that operates much like a simple switch: voltage is applied to energize it and removed to deenergize it. For this reason, it can be considered a digital actuator. Solenoids typically are used to control a vacuum signal or to control fuel flow and air bleeds.

A stepper motor is a d.c. motor that moves in approximately 100 to 120 incremental steps as it goes from a deenergized state (no voltage) to a fully energized state (full voltage). The stepper motor functions as an analog actuator with digital signals. Stepper motors are primarily used for idle speed and mixture control.

Solenoid Operation

Most solenoids used in a computer control system are grounded through the computer. This allows the computer to control voltage to the solenoid without having to switch system voltage. The solenoid can be energized for any length of time the computer desires, or it can pulse on and off at a given rate per second.

You learned about pulse width modulation and duty cycle in Chapter Four and earlier in this chapter when you studied fuel injector solenoids. Pulse width, or the length of time that a solenoid remains energized, is not a concern with solenoids that are energized indefinitely.

However, if a solenoid is required to pulse on and off rapidly, pulse width and duty cycle become factors. Figure 17-44 illustrates the relationship between pulse width, variable duty cycle, and fixed cycle time for a mixture control solenoid used in a feedback carburetor.

As we saw earlier, a computer-controlled fuel system operating in open loop ignores the EGO sensor. It sends a predetermined, fixed duty cycle to the fuel solenoid. When the system switches into closed-loop operation, the fuel solenoid duty cycle is varied by the computer according to sensor input to maintain the 14.7 air-fuel ratio as closely as possible.

Fuel Metering Actuators

A mixture control solenoid or a stepper motor is designed to produce a 14.7 air-fuel ratio at the midpoint of its operational range (or at a 50-percent duty cycle). Such actuators usually have a $\pm$ 2 ratio leeway, making them capable of producing air-fuel ratios from 12.7 to 16.7:1.

Stepper motors
This type of actuator is used in some Motorcraft and Carter carburetors. The motor can control the air-fuel ratio by moving the metering pins into the main circuit air bleeds to reduce air and thus enrich the mixture, or moving them outward to allow more air to enter and lean the mixture. The stepper motor used in the Motorcraft 7200 VV carburetor controls the air-fuel ratio by moving a metering valve inside the carburetor. In early models of this carburetor, the metering valve opened a passage, figure 17-45. This allows control vacuum to enter the fuel bowl, lowering the air pressure on the fuel and leaning the air-fuel ratio. Later models of the 7200 VV worked differently. The valve opens air bleeds to let more air into the air-fuel mixture at the discharge jets.

The idle speed control (ISC) and idle air control (IAC) motors used on some Ford and General Motors fuel systems are other examples of stepper motors, figure 17-46.

Mixture control solenoids
All mixture control solenoids work on the variable duty cycle principle, but they can manage air-fuel ratios in different ways. The mixture control solenoid used in Rochester carburetors, figure 17-47, is an integral part of the carburetor. It operates a metering rod in the main jet, as well as a rod that controls an idle air bleed passage. Other systems use a solenoid that controls vacuum to a diaphragm installed in the carburetor. The vacuum diaphragm con-

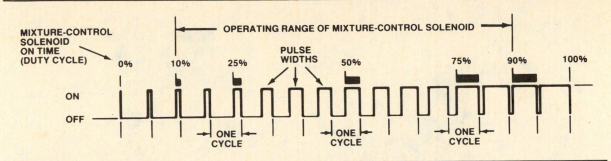

Figure 17-44. Duty cycle, or the percentage of solenoid on-time, can be altered to control fuel metering. While total cycle time remains constant, duty cycle and pulse width may vary. (GM)

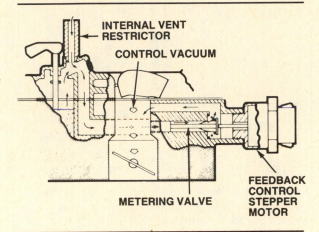

Figure 17-45. A stepper motor is used in early Ford 7200 VV carburetors to vary air pressure on the fuel bowl. (Ford)

trols the operation of the metering rods and air bleeds.

Some Carter carburetors use a pulse solenoid with a variable duty cycle to control the air bleeds, figure 17-48.

EGR Actuators

Engine control computer systems that manage EGR flow use solenoids to regulate the amount of vacuum applied to the EGR valve. Although system designs differ, figure 17-49 shows a typical system, as used in Ford's EEC-II.

Other System Actuators

In addition to controlling ignition timing and fuel metering, the newer integrated electronic engine systems control several other functions:

- Torque converter lockup or engine shifting — solenoid valves in the transmission or transaxle hydraulic circuits respond to computer signals based on vehicle speed and engine load sensors

- Air injection switching — one or more solenoids operate a valve in the vacuum line to the air switching or air control valve, figure 17-50
- Vapor canister purge — a solenoid installed in the canister-to-carburetor or manifold vapor line opens and closes as directed by the computer.

HISTORY OF ENGINE CONTROL SYSTEMS

Electronic engine controls appeared on the automotive scene with the 1977 models. The early control systems regulated only a single function: either ignition timing or fuel metering. However, they were rapidly expanded to control both systems, as well as numerous other engine functions. Most late-model engine control systems have a self-diagnostic capability, can display trouble codes for troubleshooting, and do the following:

- Open- and closed-loop operation
- Electronic ignition timing control
- Fuel metering control
- Stoichiometric air-fuel ratio control
- EGR flow control
- Air injection switching
- Vapor canister purging
- Automatic transmission or transaxle torque converter lockup.

Bosch Lambda and Motronic Systems

The Robert Bosch Company pioneered fuel injection and electronic controls used in European vehicles. The Volvo lambda-sond system

Stepper Motor: A direct-current motor that moves in incremental steps from deenergized to fully energized.

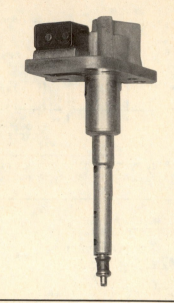

Figure 17-47. A mixture control solenoid used in Rochester carburetors.

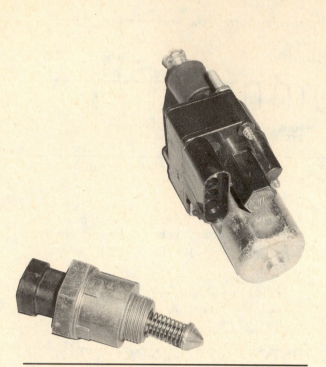

Figure 17-46. GM uses a stepper motor as an idle speed control for a carburetor (top) or to control airflow in a fuel injection throttle body (bottom).

(manufactured by Bosch) was combined with K-Jetronic fuel injection on 1977 Volvo models sold in the U.S. This was the first electronically controlled fuel metering system using a three-way catalytic converter and EGO sensor, figure 17-51.

An input signal from the EGO sensor results in an output signal to the K-Jetronic timing valve. This valve varies the injection control pressure and regulates the fuel supplied by the continuous injection nozzles. The original lambda-sond system controls only fuel metering.

The Bosch Motronic or digital motor electronics (DME) system added ignition timing and electronic spark control to the fuel metering control of the lambda-sond system. In addition to the three-way converter and EGO sensor, the DME system receives input signals from crankshaft speed and position sensors, a magnetic pulse generator in the distributor, and the L-Jetronic sensors. This allows the computer to:

- Adjust injector pulse width for air-fuel ratio control
- Adjust ignition timing for combined speed and load conditions
- Shut off injection completely during closed-throttle deceleration.

Chrysler

Chrysler introduced its electronic lean-burn (ELB) spark timing control system in 1976 on some 400-cid V8 engines, figure 17-52. The system is based on a special carburetor that provides air-fuel ratios as lean as 18:1 and a modified electronic ignition controlled by an analog spark control computer attached to the air cleaner housing. Two printed circuit boards inside the computer contain the spark control circuitry. The program schedule module receives the sensor inputs and interprets them for the ignition control module, which directs the spark timing output. The 1976 ELB distributor has dual ignition pickups and a centrifugal advance mechanism. The distributor secondary components are similar to those used with the basic Chrysler electronic ignition. A dual ballast resistor controls primary current and protects the spark control computer from voltage spikes.

In 1977, ELB became available on all Chrysler V8 engines and the centrifugal advance mechanism was eliminated. A second-generation ELB design was used on 5.2-liter V8's. The start pickup in the distributor was dropped, and the computer was redesigned so all the circuitry fit on a single board.

The second-generation system was adopted on all V8's in 1978, and a new ELB version was introduced on the Omni and Horizon four-cylinder engine. The four-cylinder system

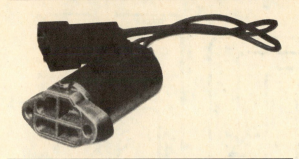

Figure 17-48. A pulse solenoid controls variable air bleeds in some Carter carburetors. (Carter)

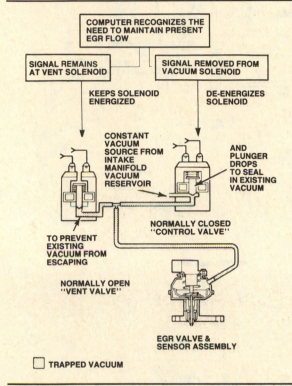

Figure 17-49. A typical computer-controlled EGR system. (Ford)

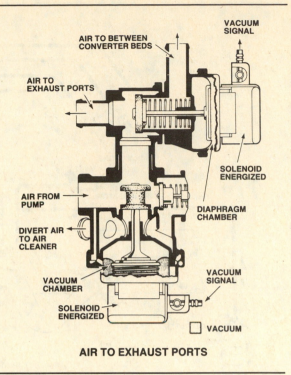

Figure 17-50. The Delco air switching valve uses two solenoids. (Delco-Remy)

uses a Hall-effect distributor instead of a magnetic pickup. It has variable dwell to control primary current and does not use a ballast resistor. The four-cylinder spark control computer is mounted on the left front fender, figure 17-53.

With the introduction of three-way converters, the ELB system was modified in 1979 to work with revised carburetors that provided air-fuel ratios closer to 14.7. The protection circuitry was integrated into the computer, and the dual ballast resistor was replaced by a single 1.2-ohm resistor to control primary current only. This third-generation system was renamed electronic spark control (ESC) and appeared on some six-cylinder inline engines

with an EGO sensor and a feedback carburetor.

The 1980 model year was a transitional one for Chrysler. All California engines received ESC with feedback fuel control. The 5.9-liter V8 and Canadian 5.2-liter four-barrel V8s continued to use ESC without the feedback system. All other engines reverted to basic electronic ignition with mechanical and vacuum advance mechanisms. Detonation sensors were introduced on some 1980 ESC systems, but the biggest change was the switch from an analog to a digital computer. Models with the digital computer in 1980 can be identified by their return to dual ignition pickups in the distributor. Systems with digital computers also eliminate the ballast resistor completely. Since 1981, all of Chrysler's domestic, carbureted, four-cylinder engines and all six-cylinder and V8 powerplants have feedback fuel control and digital ESC systems without ballast resistors.

Chrysler introduced the modular control system (MCS), figure 17-54, in late 1983 on throttle-body fuel-injected four-cylinder engines. In 1984, its use was expanded to turbocharged port-injected engines as well. The modular control system regulates vehicle functions using two separate modules whose func-

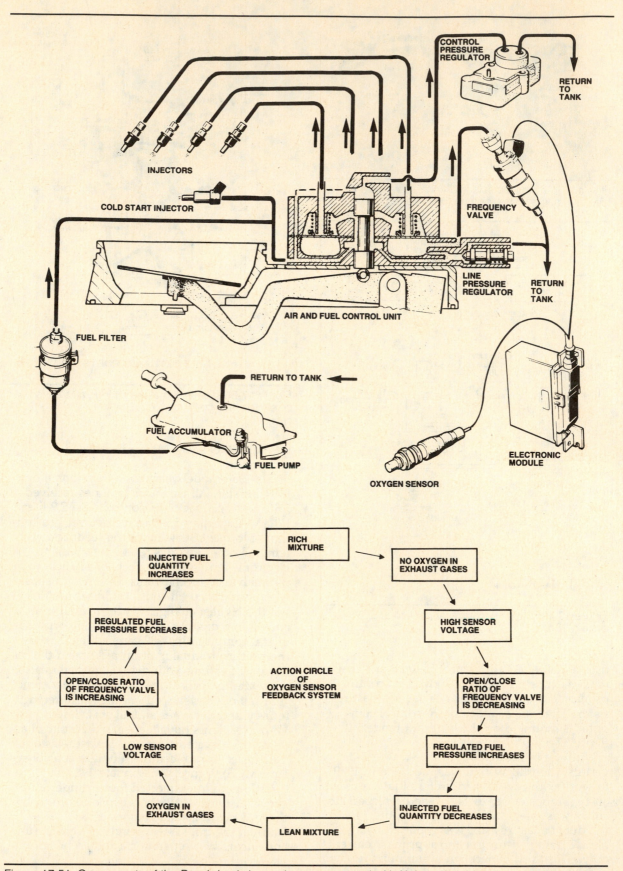

Figure 17-51. Components of the Bosch lambda-sond system as used with K-Jetronic injection on the 1977 Volvo. Bottom view shows the cycles of oxygen feedback operation. (Volvo)

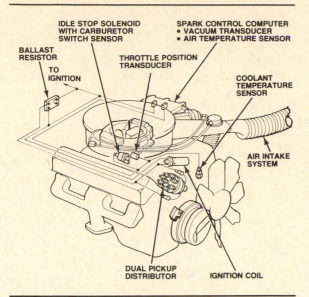

Figure 17-52. A Chrysler electronic lean-burn (ELB) system.

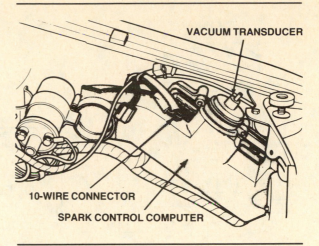

Figure 17-53. The Chrysler four-cylinder ESC spark control computer.

tions are similar to the two circuit boards in the original ELB computer. The logic module handles all of the low-current tasks within the system, including receiving the inputs and making control decisions. A replaceable PROM is mounted in the logic module housing, and a self-test program is provided to aid in system diagnosis. The logic module is mounted inside the car to avoid underhood electrical interference.

The power module handles the high-current tasks and is located in the left front fender. It looks similar to the spark control computer used in four-cylinder ESC systems. The power module contains the regulated power supply for the entire control system, along with the switching controls for the ignition coil, fuel injectors, and auto-shutdown (ASD) relay. The ASD supplies power to the coil, the fuel pump relay, and the power module when it detects a distributor cranking signal.

The modular control system (MCS) was replaced by the single-module engine control (SMEC) computer on some 1987 four-cylinder and V6 engines, figure 17-55, which brought the two circuit boards used in MCS logic and power modules under one housing. Its advanced microprocessor is smaller, faster, and more powerful than the earlier MCS microprocessor, with electrically erasable memory (EE-PROM) that can be programmed in the assembly plant. The SMEC processes instructions twice as fast as the older MCS system. This speed is important for use on the V6 engine, as the additional cylinders require the computer to process 50 percent more informa-

tion per engine revolution than a four-cylinder engine.

The use of complementary metal oxide semiconductor (CMOS) technology improves component heat resistance. When combined with the reduction in overall size of the components, the SMEC can be installed in the engine compartment with far fewer heat-related problems than the separate logic and power modules. It also includes extensive diagnostic circuitry for use in determining and correcting problems.

Further refinement of Chrysler's engine computer came in 1989 with the introduction of the single-board engine controller (SBEC) and the SBEC II in 1992, figure 17-56. The circuitry in the SBEC and SBEC II is simplified considerably from that used by previous engine controllers. This was achieved by replacing standard integrated circuits (ICs) with application-specific integrated circuits (ASICs). The ASICs are notably smaller in size than standard ICs, while providing an expanded number of functions. One ASIC takes the place of four separate input-output ICs previously used. Circuit simplification allowed the two circuit boards to be combined, forming a single board that requires less space. This resulted in a smaller and aerodynamically designed housing with improved cooling airflow through it, and reduces the number of external wiring connections from 74 to 60.

As shown in figure 17-56, the SBEC engine controller accepts a larger number of input signals and produces more output signals than earlier controllers. In addition to the controller's increased number of functions, its enlarged memory capacity incorporates expanded diagnostic capabilities.

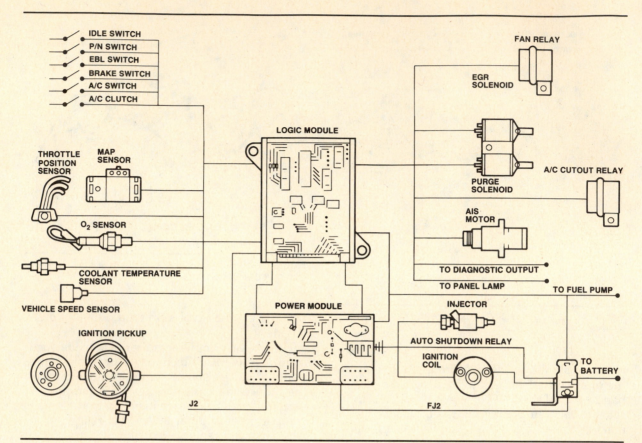

Figure 17-54. Chrysler's modular engine control system (single-point injection version).

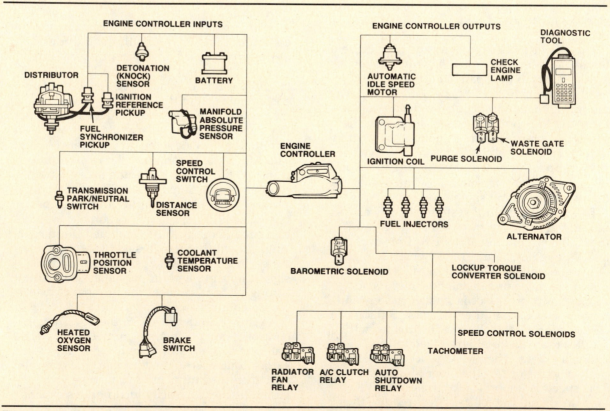

Figure 17-55. Chrysler's single module engine control system (multi-point injection version shown). (Chrysler)

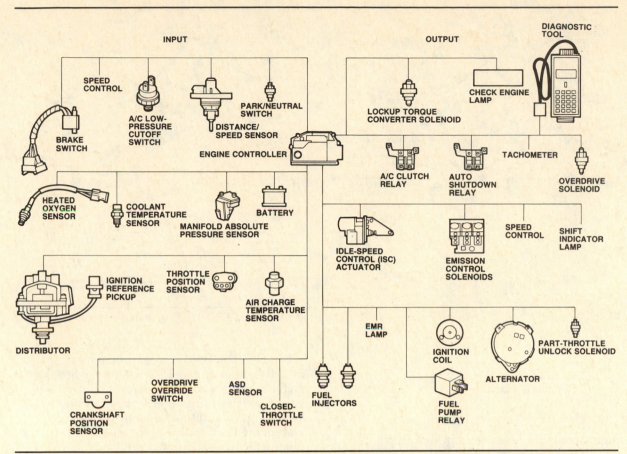

INPUT

OUTPUT

DIAGNOSTIC TOOL

SPEED CONTROL

A/C LOW-PRESSURE CUTOFF SWITCH

PARK/NEUTRAL SWITCH

DISTANCE/ SPEED SENSOR

BRAKE SWITCH

ENGINE CONTROLLER

LOCKUP TORQUE CONVERTER SOLENOID

CHECK ENGINE LAMP

A/C CLUTCH RELAY

AUTO SHUTDOWN RELAY

TACHOMETER

OVERDRIVE SOLENOID

HEATED OXYGEN SENSOR

COOLANT TEMPERATURE SENSOR

MANIFOLD ABSOLUTE PRESSURE SENSOR

BATTERY

IDLE-SPEED CONTROL (ISC) ACTUATOR

EMISSION CONTROL SOLENOIDS

SPEED CONTROL

SHIFT INDICATOR LAMP

IGNITION REFERENCE PICKUP

THROTTLE POSITION SENSOR

AIR CHARGE TEMPERATURE SENSOR

DISTRIBUTOR

EMR LAMP

IGNITION COIL

ALTERNATOR

PART-THROTTLE UNLOCK SOLENOID

CRANKSHAFT POSITION SENSOR

OVERDRIVE OVERRIDE SWITCH

ASD SENSOR

CLOSED-THROTTLE SWITCH

FUEL INJECTORS

FUEL PUMP RELAY

Figure 17-56. Chrysler's single board engine control system (multi-point injection version shown). (Chrysler)

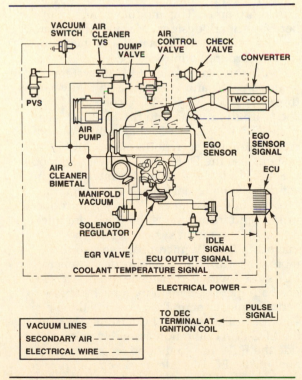

VACUUM SWITCH

AIR CLEANER TVS

DUMP VALVE

AIR CONTROL VALVE

CHECK VALVE

CONVERTER

PVS

TWC-COC

AIR PUMP

EGO SENSOR

EGO SENSOR SIGNAL

ECU

AIR CLEANER BIMETAL

MANIFOLD VACUUM

SOLENOID REGULATOR

IDLE SIGNAL

EGR VALVE

ECU OUTPUT SIGNAL

COOLANT TEMPERATURE SIGNAL

ELECTRICAL POWER

TO DEC TERMINAL AT IGNITION COIL

PULSE SIGNAL

VACUUM LINES ————
SECONDARY AIR - - - - -
ELECTRICAL WIRE — - — -

Figure 17-57. Ford's feedback electronic engine control (EEC) system.

All of these Chrysler computer control systems are designed with an emergency "limp-in" mode. In case of a system failure, the computer reverts to a fixed set of operating values. This allows the vehicle to be driven to a shop for repair. If the failure is in the start pickup or the coil triggering circuitry, however, the engine will not start.

Ford

Ford introduced its feedback electronic engine control system, figure 17-57, on some 1978 2.3-liter, four-cylinder engines. The system contains a three-way catalyst and conventional oxidation catalyst (TWC-COC) converter, an EGO sensor, a vacuum control solenoid, and an analog computer. Its control was limited to fuel metering. In 1980, a digital computer replaced the analog unit and the system was renamed the microprocessor control unit (MCU) fuel feedback system. The major change in early applications is the addition of self-diagnostics, but later designs have expanded capabilities including control over idle speedup, canister purge, and detonation spark control. They might be considered complete

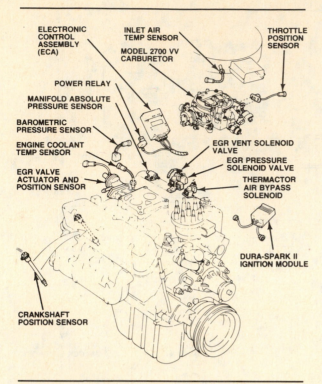

Figure 17-58. Ford's EEC-I system introduced in 1978.

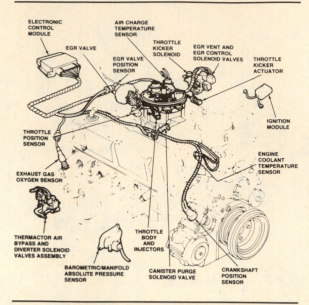

Figure 17-59. EEC-III/CFI system components.

engine control systems except that they lack continuous spark-timing control.

Ford also introduced its first generation electronic engine control (EEC-I) system, figure 17-58, on the 1978 Lincoln Versailles. This system controls spark-timing, EGR flow, and air injection. A digital microprocessor electronic control assembly (ECA) installed in the passenger compartment receives signals from various sensors. It then determines the best spark-timing, EGR flow rate, and air injection operation and sends signals to the appropriate control devices.

All 1978-79 California EEC-I systems use a variation of the blue-grommet Dura-Spark II ignition. The 1979 Federal EEC-I system has a yellow-grommet dual-mode Dura-Spark II module. Although these modules appear similar to their non-EEC counterparts, they are controlled through the ECA and cannot be tested with the same procedures.

The ignition switching signal on 1978 EEC-I systems is provided by a sensor at the rear of the engine block that detects four raised ridges on a magnetic pulse ring mounted to the end of the crankshaft. In 1979, the pickup and pulse ring were moved to the front of the engine immediately behind the vibration damper. This design is used on the later EEC-II and EEC-III systems as well.

Late in 1979, Ford's second generation EEC-II system appeared on some 5.8-liter V8 engines. EEC-II added electronic controls for vapor canister purging and air injection switching. In addition, dual three-way converters are used with a feedback carburetor for precise air-fuel mixture control.

EEC-II systems have a new Dura-Spark III ignition module that can be identified by its brown grommet. This module differs from earlier Dura-Spark designs. Many of the control circuits have been eliminated and their functions incorporated into the ECA.

Ford's third generation EEC-III system appeared in 1980 and is available in two versions through 1984. EEC-III/FBC incorporates a feedback carburetor similar to the EEC-II system; EEC-III/CFI, figure 17-59, has a throttle-body-type central fuel injection system. All EEC-III systems use the Dura-Spark III ignition module. EEC-III is the first Ford computer engine control system to have a self-test program.

Ford's EEC-IV, figure 17-60, was introduced in 1983 and incorporates the thick-film integrated (TFI) ignition system. The two-microchip EEC-IV microprocessor is much more powerful than the four- or five-microchip ECAs used with earlier EEC systems. EEC-IV has both increased memory and the ability to handle almost one million computations per second. Unlike earlier EEC systems, however, the EEC-IV's calibration assembly is located inside the ECA and cannot be replaced separately. All EEC-IV systems have an improved self-test capability with trouble codes that are stored for readout at a later date.

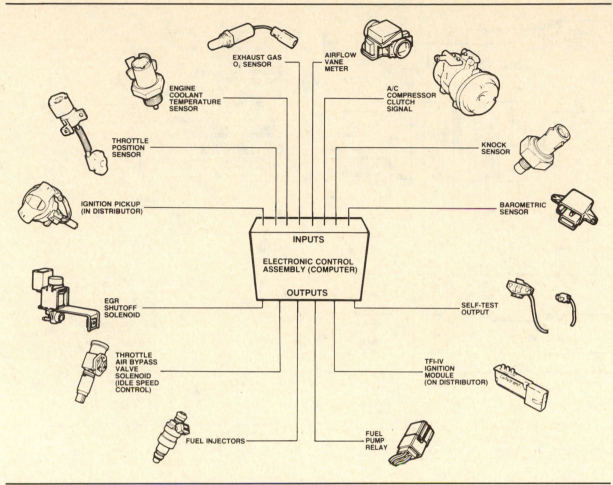

Figure 17-60. Typical components of a late-model Ford EEC-IV system.

Since 1986, Ford has made continuing and significant improvements in the processing speed, memory and diagnostic capabilities of its EEC-IV microprocessor without changing the basic designation of the system. Although the original EEC-IV microprocessor is now a dinosaur compared to the one currently used, Ford discovered that technicians in the field were intimidated by the use of I, II, III, and IV designations, and discontinued the practice of redesignating the system when improvements were made. The most recent version introduced with the 1993 Mark VIII has 56 kilobytes of RAM (versus 32 kilobytes for the previous version) and processes data at a clock speed of 18 MHz (versus 15 MHz).

Unlike Chrysler and GM, Ford did not embrace the concept of multiplexing, but has relied instead on smarter computers. Most Ford vehicles equipped with electronic automatic transmissions have the transmission control functions integrated in the ECA, which has been renamed a powertrain control module (PCM).

All Ford EEC systems have a limited operating strategy (LOS) mode in case of a failure within the system. The exact nature of the LOS varies from one system to another, but generally, the timing is fixed at 10°, and other ECA outputs are rendered inoperable.

General Motors

The first GM spark-timing control was offered on 1977-78 Oldsmobile Toronados. The 1977 system was called microprocessed sensing and automatic regulation (MISAR). MISAR is a basic spark-timing system only. A rotating disc and stationary sensor on the front of the engine replace the pickup coil and trigger wheel of the distributor. Except for this change, the 1977 MISAR system uses a standard HEI distributor with a basic four-terminal ignition module.

The MISAR system was modified in 1978 and renamed electronic spark timing (EST). The crankshaft-mounted disc and stationary sensor were dropped, and a conventional pick-

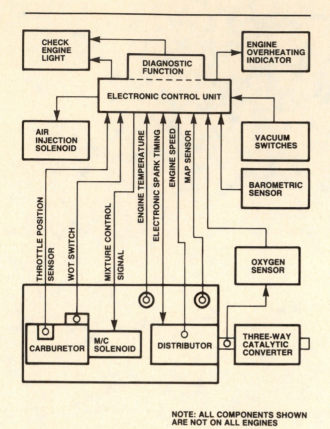

Figure 17-61. GM's computer-controlled catalytic converter (C-4) system.

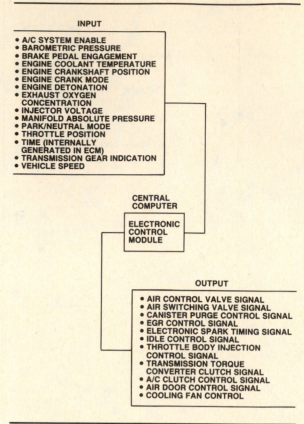

Figure 17-62. Typical CCC system sensors (inputs) and controls (outputs).

up coil and trigger wheel were again fitted in the HEI distributor. The ignition module, however, is a special three-terminal design that is not interchangeable with any other HEI system.

In mid-1979, GM introduced the computer-controlled catalytic converter (C-4) system, figure 17-61. At first, the C-4 system was purely a fuel control system used with three-way converters. But in 1980, Buick V6 engines with C-4 were also fitted with an electronic spark-timing (EST) system. Although this is the same name applied to the MISAR system just discussed, the two systems are not the same. C-4 with EST has a single electronic control module (ECM) that regulates both fuel delivery and spark timing. It was GM's first complete computer engine control system. The C-4 system was further upgraded in 1981 with EST in almost all applications, and additional control capabilities were added. The expanded system, figure 17-62, was renamed computer command control (CCC or C-3).

In 1986, GM began to update the CCC system through the introduction of a new high-speed ECM on certain vehicles. Systems using the new ECM often are called ''P-4'' systems.

The high-speed ECM is smaller than previous models, but has more functional capabilities. It operates at twice the speed of previous ECMs, is capable of 600,000 commands per second, and contains fewer IC chips and internal connections. The high-speed ECM draws less current with the ignition off, provides more diagnostic functions, and operates reliably on battery voltage as low as 6.3 volts. Service procedures for the unit allow repair and reprogramming by replacing several different integrated circuits in the controller housing.

ECMs used on vehicles with electronic automatic transmissions have the transmission control circuitry integrated in the memory and calibration (MEM-CAL) unit, and have been redesignated as powertrain control modules (PCMs). All C-4 and C-3 systems have self-diagnostic capabilities. The newer the system, the more comprehensive the diagnostic capabilities are. Several GM cars provide diagnostic readouts accessible through instrument panel displays, although the trend has clearly been to make such information available only through the Tech I scan tool in late-model diagnostic systems.

Control System Development

As you have learned in this chapter, engine systems have developed considerably since they first appeared a decade ago. Today's computer control systems, however, are undergoing an even more rapid development into a highly sophisticated electronic system composed of many microprocessors (computers) that will eventually manage all operational and convenience systems in a vehicle. The body computer module (BCM) concept which appeared on some 1986 GM luxury cars is the first generation of these "total control" systems, and their development should be more rapid than the progress we've seen with engine control systems.

When a particular vehicle arrives for service, you will have to know the system's components, understand its operation, and use the correct procedures and specifications. As described in Chapter One of the *Shop Manual*, this information is found in service manuals available from the carmaker or independent publishers such as Gousha/Chek-Chart. It is impossible for the individual technician to carry all of this information in his or her head.

However, you should not forget that the laws of electricity, physics, and chemistry have no manufacturer's trademark on them. They remain the same, and all of the systems we have studied operate on the same principles.

SUMMARY

All computers must perform four basic functions: input, processing, storage, and output. Engine control computers use various sensors to receive input data. This data is compared to lookup tables in the computer's memory. Some data may be stored in memory for future use. The computer output takes the form of voltage signals to its actuators.

A control system operates in an open-loop mode until the EGO sensor is warm enough, then the computer switches into the closed-loop mode. In open loop, the computer ignores feedback signals and functions with a predetermined set of values. Once the system switches into closed loop, the computer acts

---

■ The Rise and Fall of Gaskets in a Tube

In the 1970s, carmakers replaced many traditional cork gasket installations with room-temperature-vulcanizing (RTV) silicone sealants. RTV sealants quickly gained an unchallenged reign as "gaskets in a tube" for installing such parts as water pumps, valve covers, oil pans, transmission and differential covers, and other components.

Cork gaskets had been the industry standard for decades in these applications. Cork, however, dries out with age and loses its shape. Parts departments often found themselves with an inventory of unusable over-age gaskets. Moreover, car dealers and garages had to stock a variety of gaskets for different car models. RTV sealant seemed a revolutionary breakthrough.

When properly applied, RTV is an excellent sealer, but mating surfaces must be perfectly clean of oil and grease because oil dissolves the RTV sealant. Additionally, RTV residue in bolt holes can cause a hydraulic effect that affects torque when a bolt is installed. These are minor problems, however, that were easily overcome by professional technicians. But, RTV also has longer-term disadvantages that took time for the service industry to discover. For example, it:

- Has a short shelf life — about one year
- Does not cure properly when the shelf life is expired
- Spoils if the cap is left off the tube, because moisture in the air causes it to cure

- Is expensive to manufacture and stock for long periods.

Despite these disadvantages, carmakers used and specified RTV sealants and created a virtual depression in the cork gasket industry. In the mid-1980s, though, General Motors discovered that RTV sealants can cause long-term problems that had been unforeseen a decade earlier.

Although RTV sealant cures sufficiently to provide a firm seal in 24 to 48 hours, it can require as long as one year after installation to cure *completely*. Final curing time depends on where it is used and how thickly it is applied. During the prolonged curing time, RTV sealant gives off acidic fumes that can corrode electrical connections and sensitive electronic parts.

As solid-state electronic components increased in use during the 1980s, GM found that RTV sealant can contribute to failure of these sensitive devices. Now, GM and other carmakers are again providing cork-based gaskets for applications where RTV sealant had been used. The gasket makers, meanwhile, have learned new methods of leak control. In one method, they bond cork to both sides of thin metal, producing gaskets that meet the needs of modern vehicles and eliminate the shrinkage and deterioration problems that plagued the cork gaskets of a generation ago. In a more recent method, the thin metal is encased in a rubberized material to produce a gasket that is reuseable for the life of the vehicle (100,000 miles).

on the feedback signals and is constantly ''re-tuning'' the engine while it is running. The most recent computers have the ability to adapt their operating strategies to account for a number of conditional changes, including the wear that results from engine operation.

System sensors generally measure analog variables. Their voltage signals are digitized by the computer, which compares the signals to its program and sends an output signal to the actuators. Actuators change the computer voltage signal into electromechanical motion. Sensors are generally switches, resistors, transformers, or generators. Actuators are usually solenoids and stepper motors.

Computer-controlled engine systems began as a way of managing fuel metering for better mileage and emission control. Manufacturers used electronic ignitions with the fuel metering systems to form the basis for an engine management system. Chrysler's lean-burn, the Bosch DME system, Ford's EEC-I, and GM's C-4 system are examples of early engine control systems. The most recent systems, such as GM's CCC and Ford's EEC-IV systems, have self-diagnostic capabilities, control many more functions, and are far more efficient and powerful than their predecessors.

Review Questions

Choose the single most correct answer.
Compare your answers with the correct answers on page 431.

1. The first domestic engine control system was Chrysler's electronic lean-burn. It controls:
   a. Ignition timing
   b. Fuel metering
   c. EGR and air injection switching
   d. Throttle position

2. The engine control system used on most late-model Ford vehicles is called:
   a. Electronic Feedback Fuel Control (EFFC)
   b. Microprocessor Control Unit (MCU)
   c. Electronic Engine Control-IV (EEC-IV)
   d. Computerized Emission Control (CEC)

3. Technician A says that engine computers receive input data, process and store the data, and send output signals.
   Technician B says that late-model engine computers are based on analog microprocessors.
   Who is right?
   a. A only
   b. B only
   c. Both A and B
   d. Neither A nor B

4. NO_x emissions may be reduced best by:
   a. Enriching the fuel mixture
   b. Lowering the engine's compression ratio
   c. Recirculating exhaust gases
   d. Retarding spark timing

5. A detonation sensor is a:
   a. Transformer
   b. Resistor
   c. Potentiometer
   d. Generator

6. Technician A says that an exhaust gas oxygen (EGO) sensor with two wires is grounded to the exhaust manifold.
   Technician B says that the computer ignores a two-wire EGO sensor in closed-loop operation.
   Who is right?
   a. A only
   b. B only
   c. Both A and B
   d. Neither A nor B

7. Technician A says that a throttle position sensor (TPS) may be either a rotary or linear potentiometer.
   Technician B says that a TPS can be a simple on/off switch.
   Who is right?
   a. A only
   b. B only
   c. Both A and B
   d. Neither A nor B

8. Technician A says that the output signal from one computer can act as an input signal for another computer.
   Technician B says that late-model computers have self-diagnostic abilities and can display trouble codes.
   Who is right?
   a. A only
   b. B only
   c. Both A and B
   d. Neither A nor B

9. Technician A says that too much exhaust gas recirculation will increase HC emissions and fuel consumption.
   Technician B says that emissions are low and fuel consumption is high when timing is advanced.
   Who is right?
   a. A only
   b. B only
   c. Both A and B
   d. Neither A nor B

10. The atmosphere contains 21 percent oxygen. Rich exhaust gases contain:
    a. 6 percent
    b. 4 percent
    c. 2 percent
    d. 0 percent

11. Technician A says that duty cycle is that part of a complete cycle when the solenoid is on, or energized.
    Technician B says that pulse width is the length of time that a solenoid remains energized.
    Who is right?
    a. A only
    b. B only
    c. Both A and B
    d. Neither A nor B

12. Electronic fuel injectors are one type of:
    a. Solenoid
    b. Sensor
    c. Stepper motor
    d. Control unit

13. The first electronically controlled fuel metering system with a three-way converter and EGO sensor was the:
    a. C-4 system
    b. Lambda-sond system
    c. Bosch Motronic system
    d. Ford FEEC system

14. Technician A says that GM microprocessors have a replaceable PROM.

    Technician B says that Ford EEC-IV microprocessors have a replaceable calibration assembly.

    Who is right?
    a. A only
    b. B only
    c. Both A and B
    d. Neither A nor B

15. Technician A says that a solenoid is a digital actuator.

    Technician B says that a stepper motor works like an analog actuator with digital signals.

    Who is right?
    a. A only
    b. B only
    c. Both A and B
    d. Neither A nor B

16. The first engine control systems appeared on domestic cars in:
    a. 1979
    b. 1977
    c. 1974
    d. 1972

17. Technician A says that EEPROMs used in a GM ECM/PCM can be erased and reprogrammed.

    Technician B says that nonvolatile RAM memory is lost whenever the ignition is turned off. Who is right?
    a. A only
    b. B only
    c. Both A and B
    d. Neither A nor B

18. Technician A says that computers can be integrated through multiplexing.

    Technician B says that automatic transmission operation is controlled by the engine control computer in late-model vehicles.
    a. A only
    b. B only
    c. Both A and B
    d. Neither A nor B

PART SIX

Lighting, Accessory, and Body Electrical Systems

18

Lighting Systems

Automotive lighting circuits include important safety features. For this reason, they must be properly understood and serviced. Lighting circuits follow general patterns, according to the devices they serve. Slight variations will appear from manufacturer to manufacturer.

HEADLAMP CIRCUITS

The headlamp circuit is one of the most standardized automotive circuits, because headlamp use is regulated by laws that until recently have seen little change since the 1940s. There are two types of headlamp circuits:

- Two-lamp circuit
- Four-lamp circuit.

Manufacturers select the type of circuit on the basis of automotive body styling. Each circuit must provide both a high-beam and a low-beam light, a switch or switches to control the beams, and a high-beam indicator.

Circuit Diagrams

Most often, the headlamps are grounded, and switches are installed between the lamps and the power source, figure 18-1. Some circuits have insulated bulbs and a grounded switch, figure 18-2. In both cases, all lamp filaments are connected in parallel. The failure of one filament will not affect current flow through the others.

A two-lamp circuit, figure 18-3, uses lamps that contain both a high-beam and a low-beam filament. A four-lamp circuit, figure 18-4, has two double-filament lamps and two lamps with single, high-beam filaments. Lamp types are explained in more detail later in this chapter.

Switches and Circuit Breakers

The three operating conditions of a headlamp circuit are:

- Off — no current
- Low-beam — current through low-beam filaments
- High-beam — current through both the low-beam and the high-beam filaments.

These current paths are controlled by one or two switches. The switches may control other lighting circuits as well.

Most domestic cars have a three-position main headlamp switch. The positions, figure 18-5, are:

- First position — off, no current
- Second position — current flows to parking lamps, taillamps, and other circuits

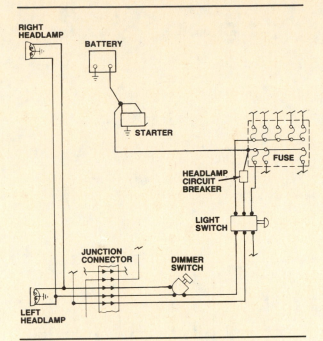

Figure 18-1. Most headlamp circuits have insulated switches and grounded bulbs.

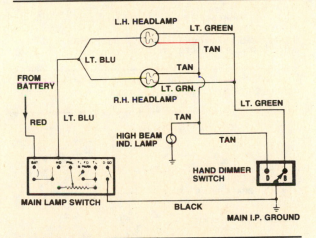

Figure 18-2. Some headlamp circuits use grounded switches and insulated bulbs. (Oldsmobile)

- Third position — current flows to both the second position circuits and to the headlamp circuit.

The headlamp switch is connected to the battery whether the ignition switch is on or off.

A two-position dimmer switch is connected in series with the headlamp switch. The dimmer switch controls the high- and low-beam current paths. If the headlamps are grounded at the bulb, figure 18-6, the dimmer switch is installed between the main headlamp switch and the bulbs. If the headlamps are remotely grounded, as shown in figure 18-2, the dimmer switch is installed between the bulbs and ground.

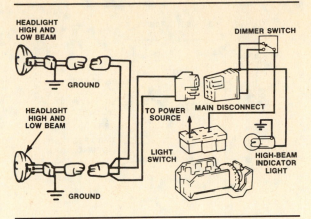

Figure 18-3. A two-lamp headlamp circuit uses two double-filament bulbs.

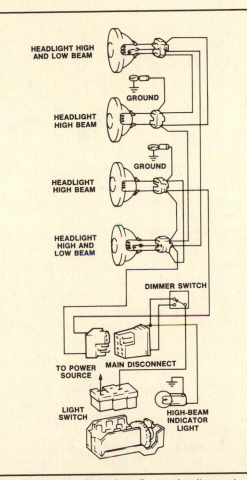

Figure 18-4. A four-lamp headlamp circuit uses two double-filament bulbs and two single-filament bulbs.

The dimmer switch on older cars and most light-duty trucks is foot operated and mounted near the pedals, figure 18-7. On late-model cars, it generally is mounted on the steering column and operated by a multifunction stalk, or lever, figure 18-8.

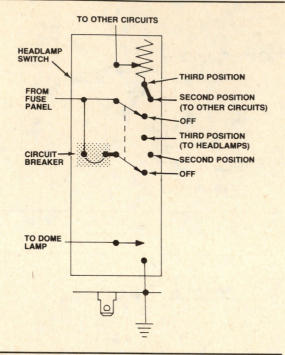

Figure 18-5. The main headlamp switch controls both the headlamp circuit and various other lighting circuits. (Chrysler)

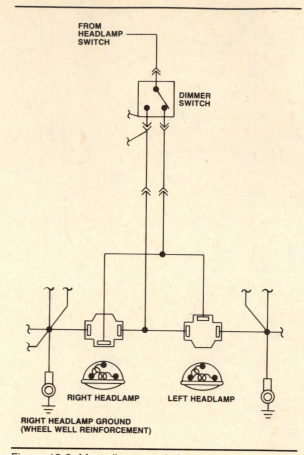

Figure 18-6. Most dimmer switches are insulated and control current flow to grounded bulbs. (Chrysler)

Some imported and late-model domestic cars use a single switch to control all of the headlamp circuit operations.

Three basic types of headlamp switches are used:

- Mounted on the steering column and operated by a lever, figure 18-9
- A push-pull switch mounted on the instrument panel, figure 18-10
- A rocker-type switch mounted on the instrument panel, figure 18-11.

All systems must have an indicator lamp for high-beam operation. The indicator lamp is mounted on the instrument panel. It forms a parallel path to ground for a small amount of high-beam current and lights when the high-beam filaments light.

Because headlamps are an important safety feature, the circuitry is protected by a Type 1, self-setting circuit breaker. The circuit breaker can be built into the headlamp switch, figure 18-5, or it can be a separate unit, figure 18-1.

Headlamps

Until 1940, a small replaceable bulb mounted behind a glass lens was used to provide light for night driving. Safety standards established in the United States in 1940 made round, sealed-beam units mandatory on domestic

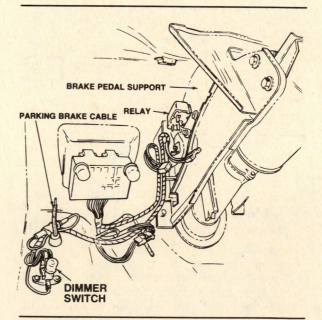

Figure 18-7. Until the mid-1970s, dimmer switches were usually mounted on the floor and were foot operated. (Ford)

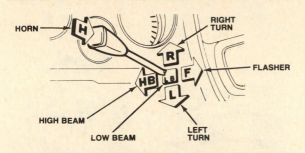

Figure 18-8. Late-model dimmer switches are operated by a steering column-mounted multifunction stalk or lever and control other lamp circuits. (Ford)

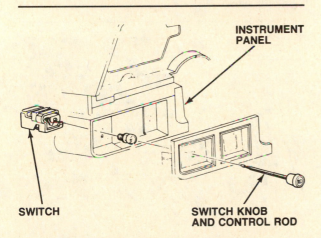

Figure 18-9. Headlamp switches may be mounted on the steering column and operated by a stalk or lever.

Figure 18-10. Push-pull headlamp switches are mounted on the instrument panel. (Ford)

cars. Repeated attempts to modify the standards after World War II were only partially successful, beginning with the introduction of rectangular sealed-beam units in the mid-1970s. The first major change in headlight design came with the rectangular halogen headlamp, which appeared on some 1980 models. Since that time, considerable progress has been made in establishing other types, such as composite headlamps which use replaceable halogen bulbs.

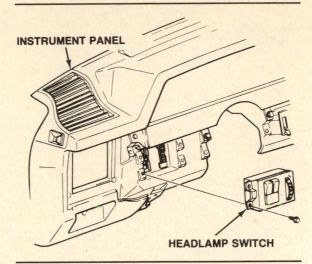

Figure 18-11. Rocker-type headlamp switches usually have a separate rotary rheostat control. (Ford)

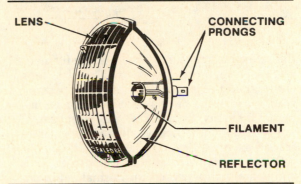

Figure 18-12. A cutaway view of a conventional sealed-beam headlamp.

Conventional sealed-beam headlamps

Sealed-beam headlamps are a one-piece, replaceable unit containing the filament, reflector, lens, and connecting terminals, figure 18-12. The position of the filament in front of

■ Headlamp Control Levers

Late-model cars are not the first to have a column-mounted lever controlling the headlamp circuit. The headlamps on the 1929 Reo Wolverine Model B were turned on and off by a lever mounted to the left of the horn button on the steering wheel. This lever also controlled the high-low beam switching. The Reo instruction book pointed out that, because each headlamp filament produced twenty-one candlepower, the headlamps should not be used when the car was standing still to avoid draining the battery.

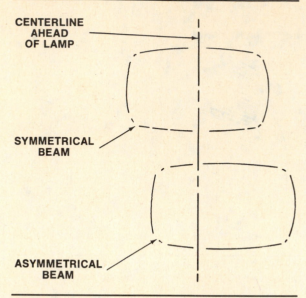

Figure 18-13. The glass lens design determines whether the beam is symmetrical or asymmetrical.

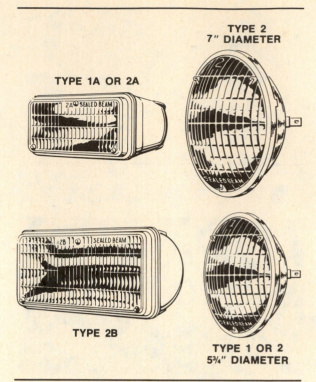

Figure 18-14. These sealed-beam bulbs used on late-model automobiles are being replaced by composite headlamps.

the reflector determines whether the filament will cast a high or a low beam. The glass lens is designed to spread this beam in a specific way. Headlamps have **symmetrical** or **asymmetrical** beams, figure 18-13. All high beams are spread symmetrically; all low beams are spread asymmetrically.

Five types of conventional sealed-beam lamps are manufactured for normal automotive use. The type code is molded into the lens of the bulb. The different types are shown in figure 18-14.

- Type 1 lamps contain a single, high-beam filament inside a circular, 5³/₄-inch (146-mm) diameter housing
- Type 1A lamps contain a single, high-beam filament inside a rectangular, 4 × 6¹/₂-inch (102 × 165-mm) housing
- Type 2 lamps contain both a high-beam and a low-beam filament inside a circular housing of either 5³/₄-inch (146-mm) or 7-inch (178-mm) diameter
- Type 2A lamps contain the same filaments as a Type 2, inside a rectangular, 4 × 6¹/₂-inch (102 × 165-mm) housing
- Type 2B lamps contain the same filaments as a Type 2, inside a rectangular housing made to metric dimensions of 142 × 200 mm (5.6 × 7.9 inches).

All of these lamps have three aiming pads, which are small glass bumps molded into the lens at specific points. These are used when the headlamps are being aimed with a mechanical aimer, as we will learn in the *Shop Manual*.

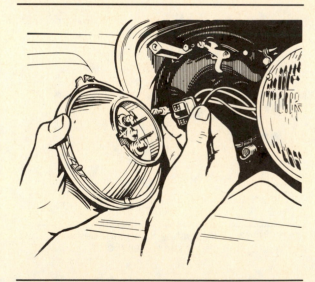

Figure 18-15. The bulbs are connected into the headlamp circuit with multiple-plug connectors.

Headlamps are installed in a circuit with multiple-plug connectors, figure 18-15. Type 1 and 1A lamps have two connecting prongs, while Type 2, 2A, and 2B lamps have three connecting prongs. One prong is a ground path; as you look at the rear of the lamp, this is the left-hand prong. The other one or two prongs conduct current from the battery to the filaments.

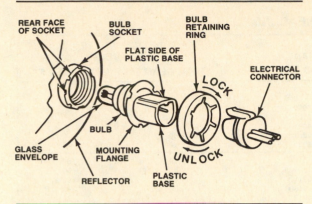

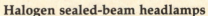

Figure 18-16. A replaceable halogen bulb is installed through the rear of the reflector and held in place with a retaining ring. (Ford)

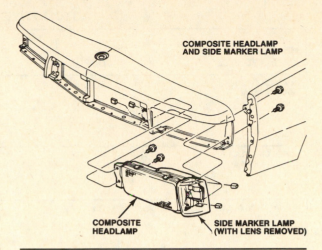

Figure 18-17. Composite headlights use a polycarbonate lens and form a permanent part of the car's styling. (GM)

Halogen sealed-beam headlamps

Halogen sealed-beam headlamps first appeared as options on some 1980 domestic cars. Their illumination comes from passing current through a filament in a pressure-filled halogen capsule, instead of through a filament in conventional evacuated sealed-beam bulbs. Halogen lamps provide brighter, whiter light than conventional headlamps.

Service and adjustment procedures are the same for halogen sealed-beam lamps as they are for conventional sealed-beams. Early bulb-type halogen lamps were not interchangeable with conventional sealed-beam headlamps, but today halogen sealed-beam lamps can be used as direct replacements for their conventional counterpart in many cases. Halogen lamps are manufactured of glass or plastic. Glass lamps carry an ''H'' prefix; plastic lamps have an ''HP'' prefix. Plastic lamps are less susceptible to stone damage and also weigh considerably less than glass lamps.

Halogen sealed-beam lamps are manufactured in the same sizes and types as conventional sealed-beams, with one additional type:

- Type 2E lamps contain both a high-beam and a low-beam inside a rectangular, 4 × 6$\frac{1}{2}$-inch (102 × 165-mm) housing.

Like conventional sealed-beams, the type code and aiming pads are molded into the lens of the bulb.

Composite headlamps

Composite headlamps first appeared on some 1984 models as a part of the aerodynamic styling concept that has characterized car design since the mid-1980s. Composite headlamp design uses a replaceable halogen headlamp bulb which fits into a socket at the rear of the reflector, figure 18-16. Since the headlamp housing does not require replacement unless damaged,

it can be incorporated as a permanent feature of automotive styling. The housing can be designed to accept a single bulb or dual bulbs.

Composite headlamps can be manufactured by two different methods. In one, polycarbonate plastic is used to form the lens portion of the headlamp housing, figure 18-17, and the inside of the housing is completely sealed. In the other, a glass lens cover is permanently bonded with a reflector housing to form a single unit. Because this type of composite headlamp is vented to the atmosphere, water droplets may form on the inside of the glass lens cover when the headlamps are off. Such condensation disappears rapidly when the lights are turned on and does not affect headlamp performance.

Replacement halogen bulbs may contain both high- and low-beam filaments for use in two-headlamp systems, or individual high- or low-beam filaments for use in four-headlamp systems. The halogen bulbs have a quartz surface which can be easily stained when handled. For this reason, the bulbs are furnished in protective plastic covers which should not be removed until the bulb has been installed.

Symmetrical: The same on both sides of center. In a symmetrical high-beam headlamp, the light beam is spread the same distance to both sides of center.

Asymmetrical: Different on both sides of center. In an asymmetrical low-beam headlamp, the light beam is spread farther to one side of center than to the other.

AUTOMOTIVE HEADLAMPS

HEADLAMP TYPE AND SIZE	ID CODE①	TRADE NO.②	DESIGN WATTS @ 12.8 VOLTS	
			HIGH BEAM	LOW BEAM
5 3/4-INCH CIRCULAR SEALED-BEAM	2C1	4000	37.5	60
	2C1	4040③	37.5	60
	2C1	H5006	35	35
	1C1	4001	37.5	
	1C1	H4001	37.5	
	1C1	5001	50	
	1C1	H5001	50	
7-INCH CIRCULAR SEALED-BEAM	2D1	6014	50	50
	2D1	H6014	60	50
	2D1	6015③	60	50
	2D1	6016④	60	50
	2D1	H6017	60	35
4 × 6 1/2-INCH RECTANGULAR SEALED BEAM	1A1	4651	50	
	1A1	H4651	50	
	2A1	4652	40	60
	2A1	H4656	35	35
	2A1	H4662	40	45
	2A1	H4739	40	50
	2E1	H4666	65	45
5 1/2 × 8-INCH RECTANGULAR SEALED BEAM	2B1	6052	65	55
	2B1	H6052	65	55
	2B1	H6054	65	35
3 × 5-INCH RECTANGULAR	H1	H4701	65	
	H3	H4703	65	
	H4	H4704	60	55④
REPLACEMENT HALOGEN BULB		9004	65	45

NOTES:
① The first character indicates the number of beams in the bulb, the second indicates the size and number of bulbs used on the car, and the third is an SAE photometric specification.   ② H indicates a halogen sealed-beam.   ③ Heavy duty.   ④ At 13.2 volts.

Figure 18-18. Common sealed-beam headlamps and replaceable halogen bulbs.

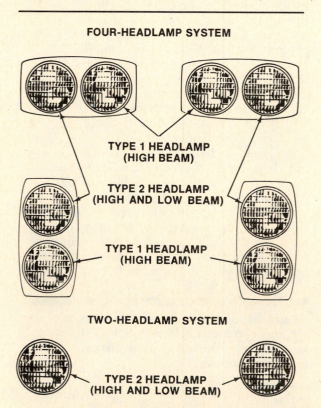

Figure 18-19. The law requires that headlamps be arranged in one of these patterns. The same requirements apply to rectangular lamps.

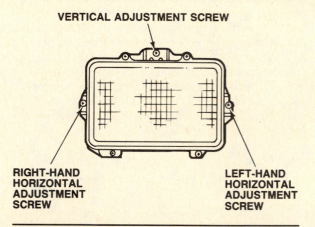

Figure 18-20. Most sealed-beam headlamps have vertical and horizontal adjusting screws. (GM)

If the quartz surface is accidentally touched with bare hands, it should be cleaned immediately with a soft cloth moistened with alcohol.

Replacing the halogen bulb in a composite headlamp does not normally disturb the alignment of the headlamp assembly. There should be no need for headlamp alignment unless the composite headlamp assembly is removed or replaced. If alignment is required, however, special adapters must be used with the alignment devices.

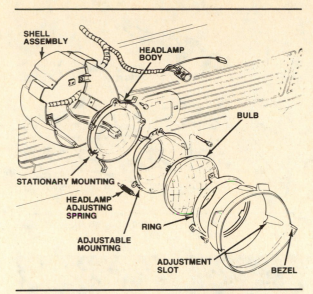

Figure 18-21. Headlamps are held in an adjustable mounting which is generally concealed by a decorative bezel.

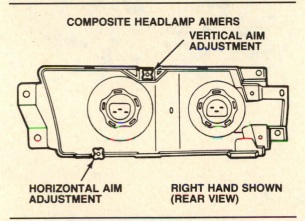

Figure 18-22. Composite headlamps also have vertical and horizontal adjustments. (GM)

Figure 18-18 describes the automotive headlamps currently in use.

Headlamp Location and Mounting

State and Federal laws control the installation of headlamps. Automotive designers must place headlamps within certain height and width ranges. In addition, two- or four-lamp systems must follow one of the patterns shown in figure 18-19.

Headlamps are mounted so that their aim can be adjusted. Most circular and rectangular lamps have three adjustment points, figure 18-20. The sealed-beam unit is placed in an adjustable mounting which is retained by a stationary mounting. Many cars have a decorative bezel that hides this hardware while still allowing lamp adjustment, figure 18-21. Composite

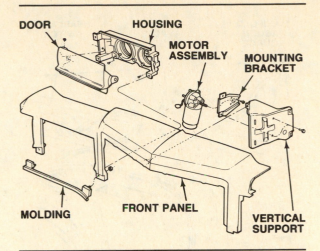

Figure 18-23. Headlamps can be concealed by a moveable door. (Chrysler)

Figure 18-24. Headlamps can be concealed by moving them into and out of the car's bodywork.

headlamps use a similar two-point adjustment system, figure 18-22, but require the use of special adapters with the alignment devices.

Concealed headlamps

Another automotive styling feature is concealed headlamps. These can be either a stationary lamp behind a moveable door, figure 18-23, or a lamp that moves in and out of the car's bodywork, figure 18-24. The doors can be metal or clear plastic.

Headlamp concealing mechanisms are operated by electric motors or vacuum actuators. Electrically operated systems usually have a relay controlling current flow to the motor. Vacuum-actuated systems work with engine vacuum stored in a reservoir, figure 18-25.

Federal law requires that the concealing mechanisms on late-model cars be controlled by the main headlamp switch and that "pop-up" headlamps that rise out of the hood must not come on until they have completed 75 percent of their travel. Switches used with electrically operated headlamp doors have additional contacts to activate the relay, figure 18-26.

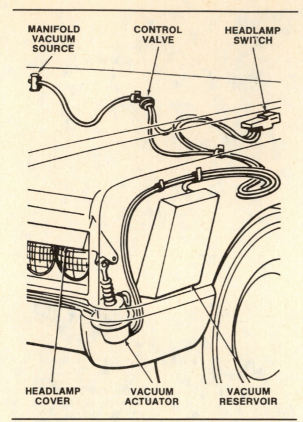

Figure 18-25. Some headlamp doors are operated by engine vacuum.

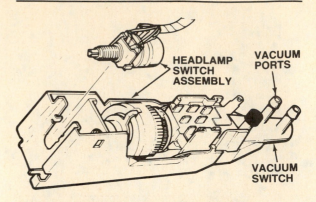

Figure 18-27. The main headlamp switch may have a built-in vacuum switch. (Ford)

Figure 18-28. Older cars often use clear covers, or fairings, over the headlamps. (British Leyland)

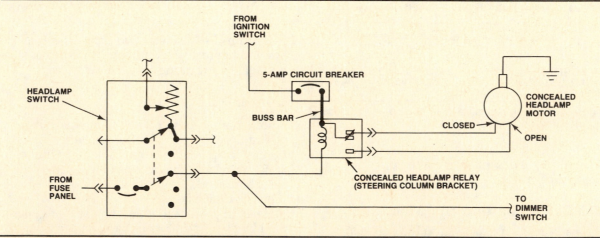

Figure 18-26. The main headlamp switch must operate the concealing mechanism. (Chrysler)

Vacuum-actuated systems usually have a vacuum switch attached to the headlamp switch, figure 18-27. Some older cars may have a separate switch to control the door. All concealed headlamp systems also must have a manual opening method, such as a crank or a lever, as a backup system.

Some 1967 and earlier cars have a clear plastic lens cover, or fairing, over the sealed-beam unit, figure 18-28. These are not legal on later model cars.

Automatic Headlamp Systems

Photocells and solid-state circuitry sometimes are used to control headlamp operation. A system either can turn the lamps on and off or can control high- and low-beam switching. Some parts can be adjusted, but defective

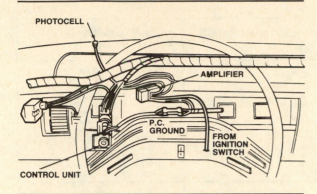

Figure 18-29. This photocell is mounted near the left side of the dash panel and reacts to outside light to control the headlight on-off operation. (Ford)

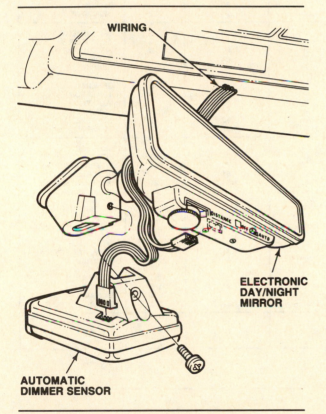

Figure 18-30. The photocell/amplifier assembly can be part of the rear view mirror assembly. (Ford)

parts cannot be repaired. All automatic systems have manual switches to override the automatic functions.

On-off control

The photocell and amplifier sensor used in this system may be mounted on top of the instrument panel, figure 18-29, facing upward so that it is exposed to natural outside light. It may also be mounted to the rearview mirror assembly, figure 18-30, facing outward for exposure to outside light. The photocell voltage

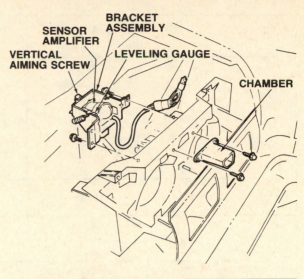

Figure 18-31. This photocell reacts to the lights of oncoming cars to control the headlamp beam switching.

is amplified and applied to a solid-state control module. Photocell voltage decreases as outside light decreases. Most photocells are adjustable for earlier or later turn-on. At a predetermined low light and voltage level, the module turns the headlamps on. The module often contains time-delay circuitry, so that:

- When the vehicle is momentarily in dark or light, such as when passing under a bridge or a streetlamp, the headlights do not flash on or off.
- When the automobile's ignition is turned off, the headlights remain on for a specified length of time and then are turned off.

High-low beam switching

In this system, the photocell is mounted behind the radiator grille, figure 18-31, so that it

■ Gas Lighting

Headlamps that burned acetylene gas were used on early cars, trucks, and motorcycles. The acetylene gas came from a pre-filled pressurized container or from a "gas generator".

One type of acetylene gas generator used a drip method. A tank filled with water was mounted above another tank containing calcium carbide. A valve controlled the dripping of water onto the calcium carbide. When water was allowed to drip onto the carbide, acetylene gas formed. The gas was routed through a small pipe to the headlamps. The headlamps were lit with a match or by an electric spark across a special lighting attachment.

BULB TYPE	BASE TYPE	TRADE NO.	AMPERAGE	CANDLE POWER	COMMON USE
T 3 1/4 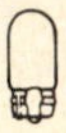	WEDGE	161①	.19	1	GENERAL
		168	.33	3	INSTRUMENT
		184	.24	1	INSTRUMENT
		193	.33	2	INSTRUMENT
		194①	.27	2	INSTRUMENT
		557	.42	2.5	WARNING
	MINIATURE BAYONET	256	.27	1.6	PARKING BRAKE
		1815	.20	1.4	INTERIOR
		1889	.27	2	INSTRUMENT
		1891	.24	2	GENERAL
		1892	.12	0.8	RADIO DIAL
		1893①	.33	2	INSTRUMENT
		1898	.33	2	INSTRUMENT
G 3 1/2 	MINIATURE BAYONET	53	.12	1	INDICATOR
		182	.18	1	GENERAL
		1445①	.135	0.7	GENERAL
G 4 1/2 	MINIATURE BAYONET	57	.24	2	INDICATOR
		257	.27	1.6	FLASHING
		293①	.33	2	GENERAL
		1895	.24	2	INDICATOR
G 6 	SINGLE-CONTACT BAYONET	61	.84	2	INSTRUMENT
		67	.59	4	INDICATOR
		89	.57	6	INSTRUMENT
		97①	.69	4	MARKER
		98	.62	6	GENERAL
		631①	.63	6	GENERAL
		1293	.40	50	GENERAL
	DOUBLE-CONTACT BAYONET	68	.42	3	INDICATOR
		90①	.57	6	MARKER
		96	.69	4	GENERAL
		99	.62	6	GENERAL
		1178①	.69	4	GENERAL
S 8 	SINGLE-CONTACT BAYONET	93	1.07	15	GENERAL
		199①	2.25	32	INTERIOR, SIGNAL
		1073	1.70	32	INTERIOR, SIGNAL
		1095	.51	4	GENERAL
		1141①	1.34	21	INTERIOR, SIGNAL
		1156①	1.70	32	INTERIOR, SIGNAL
		1159	1.60	21	GENERAL
		1295	3.00	0.5	SIDE MARKER
	DOUBLE-CONTACT BAYONET	94	1.07	15	INTERIOR
		1005	1.31	21	GENERAL
		1076	1.8	32	TAILLAMP
		1142	1.34	21	INTERIOR
		1176①②	1.31/.57	21/6	STOP, TAIL, SIGNAL
		1376②	1.6/.64	21/6	GENERAL
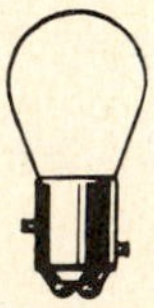	DOUBLE-CONTACT INDEXED	198①②	2.25/.68	32/4	GENERAL
		1016②	1.26/.57	21/6	STOP, TAIL
		1034②	1.8/.51	32/3	SIGNAL, MARKER
		1157①②	1.97/.51	32/3	SIGNAL, MARKER
T 4 3/4 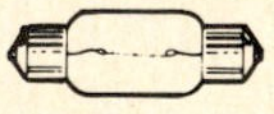	DOUBLE END CAP (FESTOON)	211	.97	12	INTERIOR
		212	.74	6	INTERIOR

① Heavy-duty bulb
② Double-filament bulb

Figure 18-32. Common automotive bulbs.

is exposed to the lights of oncoming vehicles. When a bright light strikes the photocell, the voltage developed acts upon a relay to switch from high- to low-beam current.

COMMON AUTOMOTIVE BULBS

Sealed-beam and composite headlamps are very specialized types of lamp bulbs. The other bulbs used in automotive lighting circuits are much smaller and less standardized. Figure 18-32 shows a representative sampling of commonly used bulb and base designs. Each specific bulb has a unique trade number which is used consistently by all manufacturers.

Most small automotive bulbs are clear and are mounted behind colored lenses. Some applications, however, may call for a red or an amber bulb. This is indicated by an R for red and NA for amber.

Small automotive bulbs use either a brass or a glass wedge base. Bulbs with a brass base fit into a matching socket. The single or double contacts on the base of the bulb are the insulated contacts for the bulb's filaments. A matching contact in the socket supplies current to the bulb filament, figure 18-33. A single-

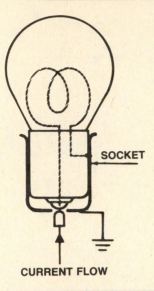

CURRENT FLOW

SOCKET

Figure 18-33. Automotive bulbs and sockets must be matched.

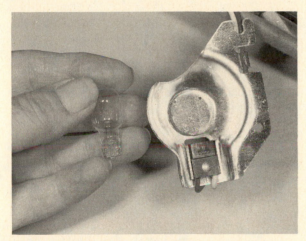

Figure 18-34. Wedge-base bulbs are increasingly used for interior lighting applications.

contact bulb contains one filament; a double-contact bulb has two filaments. The ground end of the bulb filament is connected directly to the base of the bulb, which is grounded through contact with the socket. In many cases, a separate ground wire leads from the socket to a ground connection. All double-contact bulbs are indexed so that they will fit into the socket in only one way. This is called an indexed base.

Wedge-base bulbs generally have been used for instrument cluster and other interior lighting applications. The base and optical part of the bulb are a one-piece, formed-glass shell with four filament wires extending through the base and crimped around it to form the external contacts, figure 18-34. The design locates

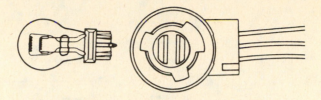

Figure 18-35. Wedge-base bulbs with plastic sockets are used for some external lighting applications. (Chrysler)

the contacts accurately, permitting direct electrical contact with the socket, which contains shoulders to hold the bulb in place. The bulb is installed by pushing it straight into its socket, with no indexing required.

Wedge-base 2358 bulbs with a new socket design were introduced in 1987 as replacements for the brass base 1157 and 2057 bulbs for exterior lighting applications. The wires of the low-profile plastic socket exit from the side instead of the rear, figure 18-35. This reduces the possibility of wire damage and permits the socket to be used in more confined areas. Since the introduction of this base-socket design, a series of these bulbs has been made available in both clear and amber versions.

TAILLAMP, LICENSE PLATE LAMP, AND PARKING LAMP CIRCUITS

The taillamps, license plate lamps, and parking lamps illuminate the car for other drivers to see.

Circuit Diagram

These lamps usually share a single circuit, because the laws of some states require that they be lit at the same time. Figure 18-36 shows a typical circuit diagram. Since the lamps are controlled by the main headlamp switch, they can be lit whether the ignition switch is on or off.

Switches and Fuses

These lamps are controlled by contacts within the main headlamp switch. They can be lit when the headlamps are off, figure 18-37. A fuse (usually 20 amperes) protects the circuit.

Bulbs

The bulb designs most commonly used as taillamps and parking lamps are G-6 single-contact bayonet and S-8 double-contact bayonet. The tail and parking lamps may be one filament of a double-filament bulb. License plate lamps are usually G-6 single-contact bayonet or T-3 1/4 wedge bulbs.

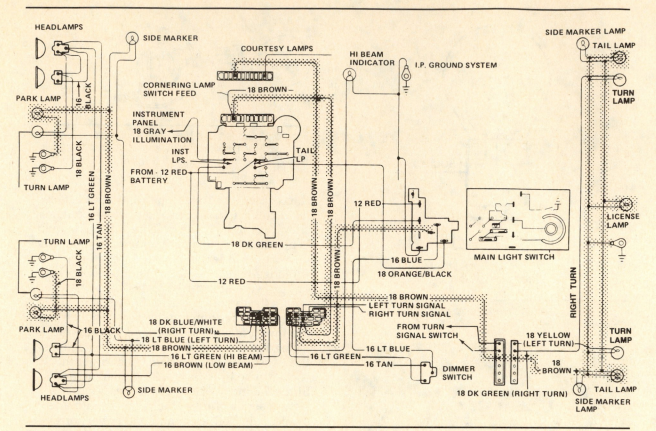

Figure 18-36. A taillamp, license plate lamp, and parking lamp circuit diagram. (Buick)

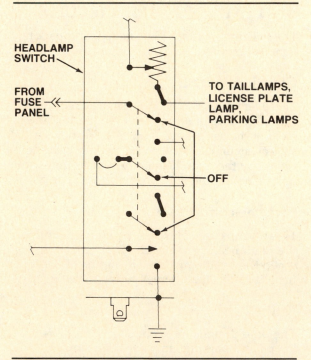

Figure 18-37. Contacts in the main headlamp switch provide current to the taillamps, license plate lamps, and parking lamps. (Chrysler)

STOP LAMP AND TURN SIGNAL CIRCUITS

Stop lamps, also called brake lamps, are always red. Federal law requires a red high-mounted brake lamp, or HMBL, on 1986 and later models. Turn signals, or directionals, are either amber or white on the front of the car and either red or amber on the rear.

Circuit Diagram

A typical circuit diagram with stop and turn lamps as separate bulbs is shown in figure 18-38A. When the brakes are applied, the brake switch is closed and the stop lamps light. The brake switch receives current from the fuse panel and is not affected by the ignition switch.

When the turn signal switch is moved in either direction, the corresponding turn signal lamps receive current through the flasher unit. The flasher unit causes the current to start and stop very rapidly, as we will see later. The turn signal lamp flashes on and off with the interrupted current. The turn signal switch receives current through the ignition switch, so that the signals will light only if the ignition switch is on.

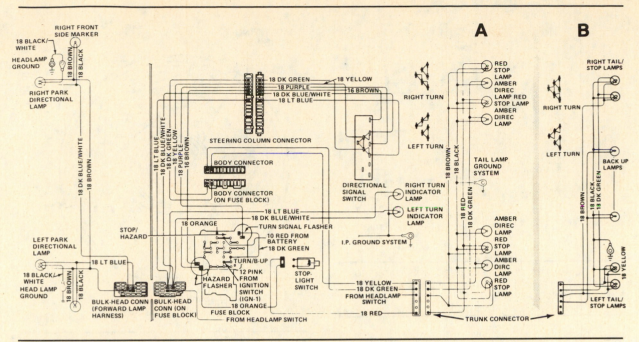

Figure 18-38. Stop lamp and turn signal circuits. The basic drawing (A) has separate bulbs for each function. The alternate view of the rear lamps (B) has single bulbs with double filaments. One filament of each bulb works for stop lamps and for turn signals. (Buick)

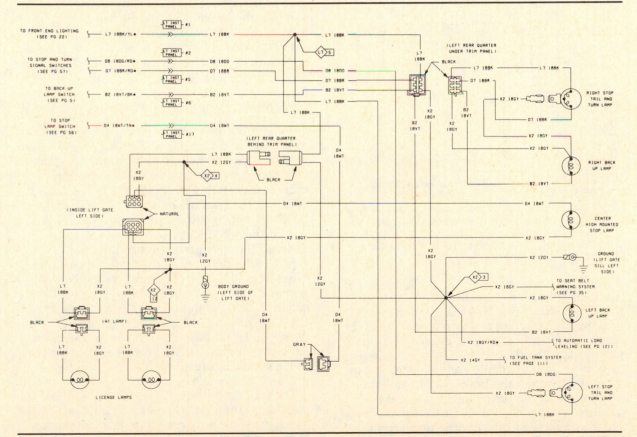

Figure 18-39. A typical rear lighting circuit diagram showing the inclusion of the high-mounted brake lamp (HMBL) mandated by law on 1986 and later models. (Chrysler)

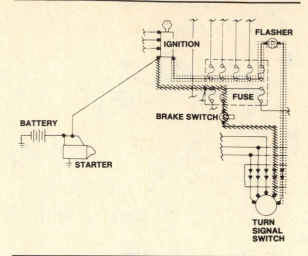

Figure 18-40. The ignition switch controls current to the turn signal switch, but does not affect current to the brake switch.

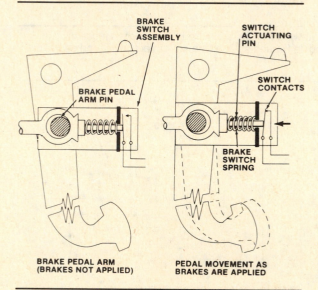

Figure 18-41. When the brake pedal is pressed, the entire brake assembly moves with it. The switch actuating pin does not move as far as the contacts do, and so it closes the contacts. (Ford)

In many cars, the stop and turn signals are both provided by one filament, figure 18-38B or figure 18-39. When the turn signal switch is closed, the filament receives interrupted current through the flasher unit. When the brakes are applied, the filament receives a steady flow of current through the brake switch and special contacts in the turn signal switch. If both switches are closed at once, brake switch current is not allowed through the turn signal switch to the filament on the signalling side. The signalling filament receives interrupted current through the flasher unit and so it flashes on and off. The filament on the opposite

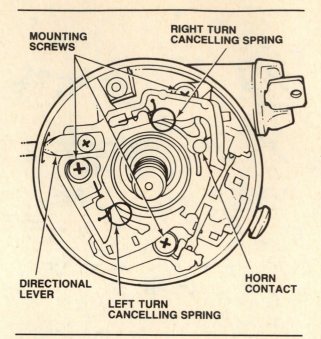

Figure 18-42. The turn signal switch includes various springs and cams to control the contact points.

side of the car receives a steady flow of current through the brake switch and the turn signal switch and so it is continuously lit.

Figure 18-39 shows the integration of the single filament center high-mounted stop lamp in a typical stop and turn signal circuit.

Switches, Fuses, and Flashers

Several units affect current flow through the stop lamp and turn signal circuits. The ignition switch is located between the battery and the turn signal switch, figure 18-40, so that the current cannot flow through the turn signal switch if the ignition switch is off. The brake switch is not controlled by the ignition switch. It is connected directly to battery voltage through the fuse panel, figure 18-40.

Before the mid-1960s, the brake switch was often located within the brake hydraulic system and operated by hydraulic pressure. Because of changes in braking system design, this type of switch is no longer commonly used. On late-model cars, the brake switch is usually mounted on the bracket that holds the brake pedal, figure 18-41. When the pedal is pressed, the switch is closed.

The turn signal switch is mounted within the steering column and operated by a lever, figure 18-42. Moving the lever up or down closes contacts to supply current to the flasher unit and to the appropriate turn signal lamp. A turn signal switch includes cams and springs that cancel the signal after the turn has been completed.

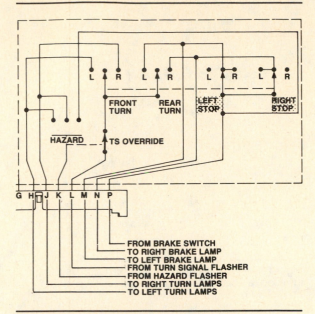

Figure 18-43. When the stop lamps and turn signals share a common filament, stop lamp current flows through the turn signal switch.

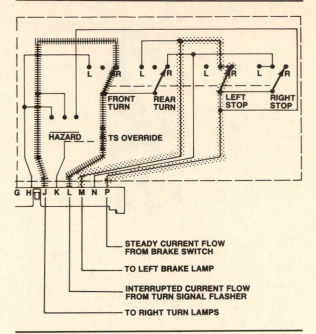

Figure 18-44. When a right turn is signalled, the turn signal switch contacts send flasher current to the right-hand filament and brake switch current to the left-hand filament.

That is, as the steering wheel is turned in the signalled direction and then returns to its normal position, the cams and springs separate the turn signal switch contacts.

In systems using separate filaments for the stop and turn lamps, the brake and turn signal switches are not connected. If the car uses the same filament for both purposes, then there must be a way for the turn signal switch to interrupt the brake switch current and allow only flasher unit current to the filament on the side being signalled. To do this, brake switch current is routed through contacts within the turn signal switch, figure 18-43. By linking certain contacts, the bulbs can receive either brake switch current or flasher current, depending upon which direction is being signalled.

For example, figure 18-44 shows current flow through the switch when the brake switch is closed and a right turn is signalled. Steady current through the brake switch is sent to the left brake lamp. Interrupted current from the turn signal is sent to the right turn lamps.

Flasher units supply a rapid on-off-on current to the turn signal lamps. To do this, they act very much like a Type 1 self-setting circuit breaker. Current flows through a bimetallic arm, figure 18-45, heating the arm until it bends and opens a set of contact points. When the current stops, the arm cools and the contact points close again. This cycle occurs rapidly so that the turn signal lamps flash on and off about once every second. Flasher units

usually are installed in the wiring harness beneath the instrument panel, figure 18-46, or in the fuse panel.

Some manufacturers, including Ford, have used an additional control unit in series with multiple turn signal lamps, figure 18-47. This transistorized module causes the three rear turn signal lamps on either side to flash in sequence, from the center of the car outward.

The turn signal circuit must include one or more indicators to show the driver that the

■ Switch the Bulbs, Not the Switch

Have you ever been stumped by a turn signal problem where the lamps on one side flashed properly, but those on the other side lit and burned steadily without flashing? The flasher checks out okay, and the panel indicator lights but doesn't flash. Both bulbs, front and rear, light; power is getting to the sockets. Sounds like trouble with the switch. Maybe it is.

However, before you tear into the steering column, try swapping the front and rear bulbs from one side to the other. Sometimes, a little corrosion on a socket and the resistance of an individual bulb can add up to cumulative resistance that unbalances the circuit and prevents flashing. Swapping the bulbs or cleaning the contacts can reduce the resistance to within limits, restore equilibrium, and get the system working correctly again.

Figure 18-45. The internal components of a turn signal flasher.

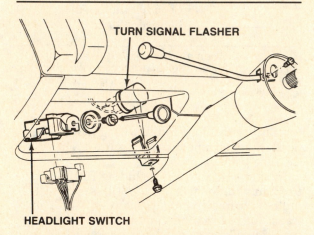

TURN SIGNAL FLASHER

HEADLIGHT SWITCH

Figure 18-46. The turn signal flasher is often mounted beneath the instrument panel. (Oldsmobile)

turn signals are operating. These indicators are small bulbs in the instrument panel that provide a parallel path to ground for some of the flasher unit current. Most systems have separate indicators for the right and left sides, although some cars use only one indicator bulb for both sides. On some models, additional indicators are mounted on the front fenders facing the driver.

The stop lamp and turn signal lamp circuits are usually protected by two separate fuses, rated at about 20 amperes.

Bulbs

The bulb types traditionally used as stop or turn signal lamps are the S-8 single- and double-contact bayonet base, although the 2358 wedge-base bulbs are being used more frequently. The stop and turn filaments may be part of a double-filament bulb.

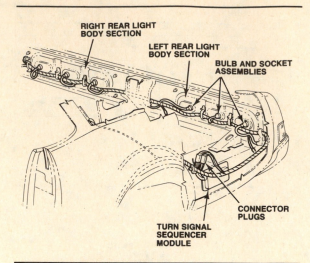

RIGHT REAR LIGHT BODY SECTION

LEFT REAR LIGHT BODY SECTION

BULB AND SOCKET ASSEMBLIES

CONNECTOR PLUGS

TURN SIGNAL SEQUENCER MODULE

Figure 18-47. When multiple rear turn signals are installed, a special sequencer module is used to control current. (Ford)

HAZARD WARNING LAMP (EMERGENCY FLASHER) CIRCUITS

All motor vehicles sold in the United States since 1967 have a hazard warning lamp circuit. It is designed to warn other drivers of possible danger in emergencies.

Circuit Diagram

The hazard warning lamp circuit uses the turn signal lamp circuitry, a special switch, and a heavy-duty flasher unit. The switch receives battery current through the fuse panel. When the switch is closed, all of the car's turn signal lamps receive current through the hazard flasher unit. An indicator bulb in the instrument panel provides a parallel path to ground for some of the flasher current.

Switches, Fuses, and Flashers

The hazard warning switch can be a separate unit or it can be part of the turn signal switch, figure 18-48. In both cases, the switch contacts route battery current from the fuse panel through the hazard flasher unit to all of the turn signal lamps at once. In most systems, the hazard warning switch overrides the operation of the turn signal switch. The hazard warning circuit is protected by a 15- to 20-ampere fuse.

The hazard warning flasher looks like a turn signal flasher when assembled, but it is constructed differently and operates differently. This allows it to control the large amount of current required to flash all of the turn signal lamps at once.

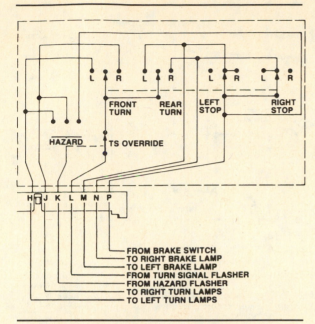

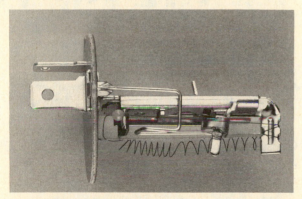

Figure 18-48. The hazard warning switch is often a part of the turn signal switch.

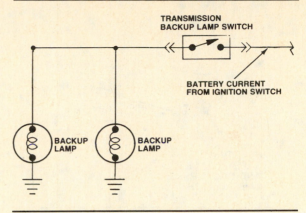

Figure 18-50. A typical backup lamp circuit. (Chrysler)

BACKUP LAMP CIRCUITS

The white backup lamps light when the car's transmission or transaxle is in reverse. The lamps have been used for decades, but have been required by law since 1971. Backup lamps and license plate lamps are the only white lamps allowed on the rear of a car.

Circuit Diagram

A typical backup lamp circuit diagram is shown in figure 18-50; figure 18-39 shows integration of the backup lamp with the stop, taillamp, and turn signals in a typical rear lighting diagram. When the transmission switch is closed, the backup lamps receive current through the ignition switch. The lamps will not light when the ignition switch is off.

Switches and Fuses

The backup lamp switch generally is installed on the transmission or transaxle housing, figure 18-51, but it may be mounted near the gear selector lever, figure 18-52, on some vehicles.

Figure 18-49. The hazard flasher is constructed to control a large amount of current.

The flasher consists of a stationary contact, a moveable contact mounted on a bimetallic arm, and a high-resistance coil, figure 18-49. The coil is connected in parallel with the contact points. The contact points are normally open. When the hazard warning switch is closed and current flows to the flasher, the high resistance of the coil does not allow enough current to light the lamps. However, the coil heats up and causes the bimetallic strip to close the contacts. The contacts form a parallel circuit branch and conduct current to the lamps. Decreased current flow through the coil allows it to cool and the bimetallic strip opens the contacts again. This cycle repeats about 30 times per minute.

■ **Installing New Bulbs**

If you replace a bulb in a parking light, turn signal, stop lamp, or taillamp, you may find that the bulb will not light unless you hold it against the socket. This may be due to weakened springs or flattened contacts. To solve the problem, apply a drop of solder to the contact points at the base of the bulb. Add more solder if necessary or file off the excess. The result will be a good solid connection. Also, for a weak spring, if the wires going to the socket are given slack, you may be able gently to stretch the spring.

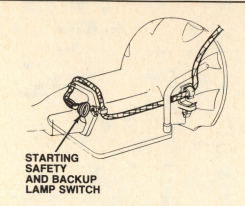

Figure 18-51. The backup lamp switch can be mounted on the transmission housing. (Chrysler)

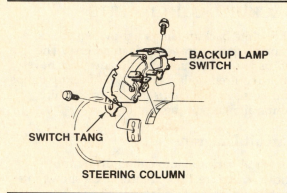

Figure 18-52. The backup lamp switch can be mounted near the gear shift lever. (Oldsmobile)

The backup switch may be combined with the neutral safety switch. The circuit is protected by a 15- to 20-ampere fuse, which often is shared with other circuits.

Bulbs

The bulb designs most commonly used as backup lamps are S-8 single-contact bayonet and double-contact indexed.

SIDE MARKER AND CLEARANCE LAMP CIRCUITS

Side marker lamps are mounted on the right and left sides toward the front and rear of the vehicle to indicate its length. Side marker lamps are required on all cars built since 1969, and are found on many earlier models as well. Front side markers are amber; rear side markers are red. On some vehicles, the parking lamp or taillamp bulbs are used to provide the side marker function.

Clearance markers are required on some vehicles according to their height and width.

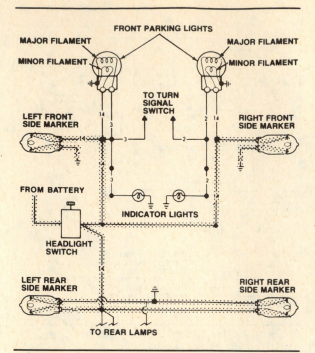

Figure 18-53. Side marker lamps can be independently grounded. (Ford)

Clearance lamps, if used, are included in the side marker lamp circuitry. Clearance lamps face forward or rearward. Like side markers, front clearance lamps are amber; rear lamps are red.

Circuit Diagrams

Side marker lamps can be either grounded or insulated, figures 18-53 and 18-54. When they are grounded, figure 18-54, the ground path for current is through the turn signal filaments. When the headlamp switch is off and the turn signal switch is on, both the turn signal and the side marker on the side being signalled will flash. When the headlamp switch is on, only enough current flows to light the side marker. The turn signal lamp does not light until the turn signal switch and flasher are closed; then the turn signal lamp will light. The side marker lamp will not light, because 12 volts are applied to each end of the filament. There is no voltage drop and no current flow. When the turn signal flasher opens, the turn signal lamp goes out. Normal headlamp circuit current lights the side marker lamp. This sequence makes the two lamps flash alternately — one is lit while the other is not.

Switches and Fuses

Side marker lamps are controlled by contacts within the main headlamp switch. Their circuit

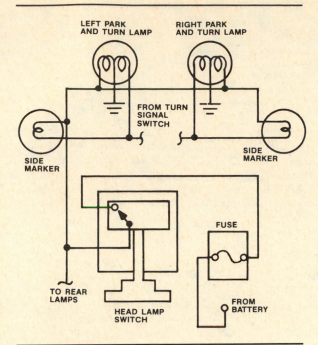

Figure 18-54. Side marker lamps can be grounded through the turn signal filaments.

is protected by a 20-ampere fuse, which usually is shared with other circuits.

Bulbs

The G-6 and S-8 single- and double-contact bayonet base bulbs commonly are used.

INSTRUMENT PANEL AND INTERIOR LAMP CIRCUITS

Instrument Panel

The lamps within the instrument panel can be divided into three categories: indicator, warning lamps, and illumination lamps. We have seen that some circuits, such as high-beam headlamps and turn signal lamps, include an indicator mounted on the instrument panel. Warning lamps, which alert the driver to vehicle operating conditions, will be discussed in Chapter Nineteen. Lamps that simply illuminate the instrument panel are explained below.

Circuit diagram

Many late-model automobiles use a printed circuit behind the instrument panel to simplify connections and conserve space, figure 18-55. The connections can also be made with conventional wiring, figure 18-56.

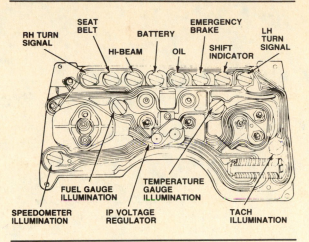

Figure 18-55. A printed circuit board is used behind most late-model instrument panels. (Ford)

Switches and rheostats

Current to the panel lamps is controlled by contacts within the main headlamp switch, figure 18-57. The instrument panel lamps receive current when the parking and taillamps are lit and when the headlamps are lit.

■ Accessory Lighting

Every car manufacturer offers unique accessory lighting circuits. These range from hand-controlled spotlights to driving and fog lamps. Each additional accessory circuit requires more bulbs, more wiring, and possibly an additional switch.

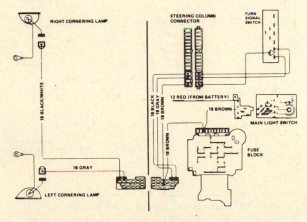

For example, cornering lamps can be mounted on the front sides of the car to provide more light in the direction of a turn. When the turn signal switch is operated while the headlamps are on, special contacts in the turn signal switch conduct a steady flow of current to the cornering lamp on the side being signalled.

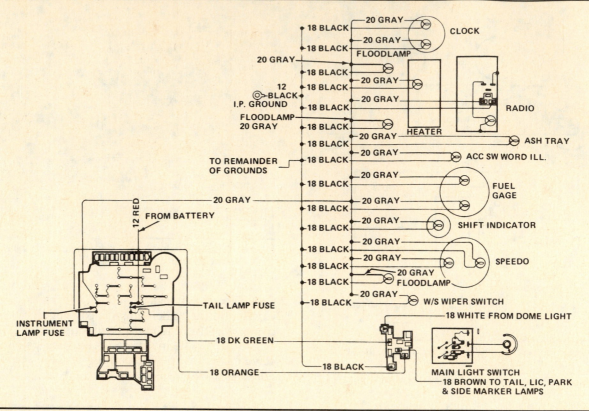

Figure 18-56. Multistrand wiring can be used behind the instrument panel. (Buick)

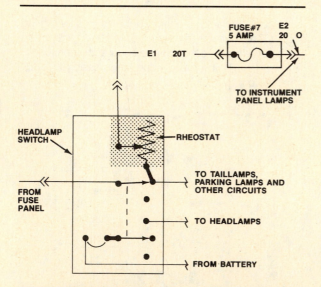

Figure 18-57. The panel lamps receive current through the main headlamp switch, which may also contain a rheostat to control the current. (Chrysler)

Rheostats and potentiometers are variable resistors that allow the driver to control the brightness of the panel lamps. The rheostat or the potentiometer for the panel lamps can be a separate unit, figure 18-58, or it can be a part of the main headlamp switch, figure 18-57.

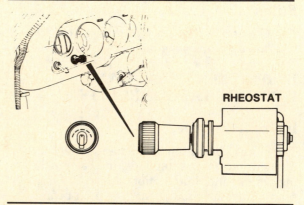

Figure 18-58. The rheostat may be a separate unit in the panel lamp circuit. (Chrysler)

Bulbs

The T-3 ¼ bulb with wedge or miniature bayonet base is a design commonly used in instrument panel illumination.

Interior Lamps

Interior, or courtesy, lamps light the interior of the car for the convenience of the driver and passengers.

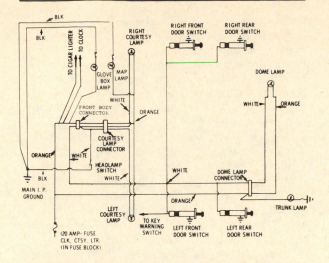

Figure 18-59. The interior (courtesy) lamp circuit may have insulated bulbs and grounded switches. (Oldsmobile)

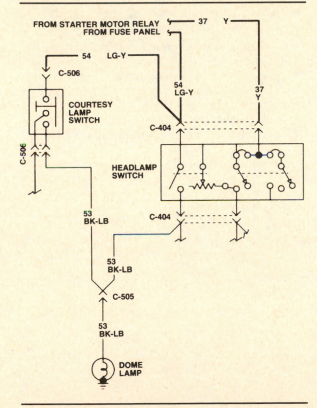

Figure 18-60. The interior lamps may be grounded and also have insulated switches.

Circuit diagram

Interior lamps receive current from the battery through the fuse panel. Switches at the doors control this current, and light the lamps when one of the doors is opened. Many manufacturers install the bulbs between the power source and the grounded switch, figure 18-59. Others,

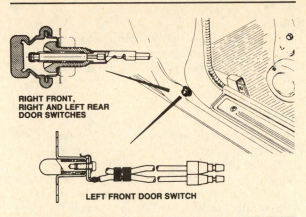

Figure 18-61. Interior lamps are controlled by switches at the door jambs. (Chrysler)

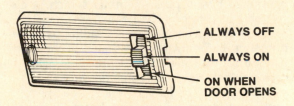

Figure 18-62. Interior lamps often have a manual switch to override the automatic operation. (Ford)

including Ford and Chrysler, install the switches between the power source and the grounded bulb, figure 18-60.

Courtesy lamp circuits also may contain lamps to illuminate the glove box, trunk, and engine compartment. Additional switches that react to glove box door, trunk lid, or hood opening control current through these bulbs.

Switches

The switches used in courtesy lamp circuits are push-pull types, figure 18-61. Spring tension closes the contacts when a door is opened. When a door is closed, it pushes the contacts apart to stop current flow. When any one switch is closed, the circuit is complete and all lamps are lit.

One or more of the interior lamps may have a manually controlled switch to complete the circuit, figure 18-62. This switch allows the driver or passengers to light the bulb even when all the doors are closed.

Rheostat: A variable resistor used to control current.

Bulbs
The S-8 bulbs are used for trunk and engine compartment lamps, with T-3 $1/4$ wedge and T-3 $3/4$ double-end-cap bulbs used as courtesy lamps.

SUMMARY

Headlamp circuits must provide low- and high-beam lights for driving, and a high-beam indicator lamp for driver use. Two or four lamps may be used. Most often, the lamps are grounded, but some circuits have insulated lamps and grounded switches. The main headlamp switch also controls other lamp circuits. The main switch sometimes controls high-low beam switching but this is usually controlled by a separate dimmer switch. A circuit breaker protects the headlamp circuit.

Conventional sealed-beam headlamps use a tungsten filament; halogen sealed-beam lamps pass current through a pressure-filled halogen capsule. Halogen headlamps provide a brighter light with less current. Sealed-beam headlamps have either a high-beam filament (Type 1) or both a high- and low-beam filament (Type 2). Headlamps are always connected with multiple-plug connectors.

Changes in Federal lighting standards have permitted sealed-beam headlamps made of plastic instead of glass. Plastic headlamps weigh considerably less and are more damage-resistant than glass. The changes also have resulted in the use of a composite headlamp in place of sealed-beams. The composite headlamp consists of a polycarbonate lens housing and a replaceable halogen bulb which contains a dual filament. Since the lens housing is not replaced, it has been integrated into vehicle styling.

Headlights are mounted so that their aim can be adjusted vertically and horizontally.

Some cars have concealed headlamps with doors or mountings that are operated by vacuum or by electric motors. The main headlamp switch controls these mechanisms, and there also is a manual control provided to open and close the mechanisms if necessary.

Photocells and solid-state modules are used to control the headlamp on-off and beam switching operation on some vehicles.

Bulbs used in other lighting circuits are smaller than sealed-beam units, and must be installed in matching sockets. These other lighting circuits include the:

- Taillamp, license plate lamp and parking lamp circuits
- Stop lamp and turn signal circuits
- Hazard warning (emergency flasher) circuit
- Backup lamp circuit
- Side marker and clearance lamp circuit
- Instrument panel and interior lamp circuits.

Review Questions

Choose the single most correct answer.
Compare your answers with the correct answers on page 431.

1. Which of the following is true concerning headlamp circuits?
   a. The circuits can have totally insulated bulbs and grounded switches
   b. The lamp filaments are connected in series
   c. All circuits use lamps that contain both a high beam and a low beam
   d. The headlamps receive power through the ignition switch

2. Because headlamps are an important safety feature, they are protected by:
   a. Heavy fuses
   b. Fusible links
   c. Type-I circuit breakers
   d. Type-II circuit breakers

3. All high beams are spread:
   a. Symmetrically
   b. Asymmetrically
   c. Either a or b
   d. Neither a nor b

4. All types of headlamps have _____ that are used when adjusting the beam.
   a. Connecting prongs
   b. Aiming pads
   c. Filaments
   d. Reflectors

5. Concealed headlamps can be operated by all of the following methods, EXCEPT:
   a. Electric motor
   b. Vacuum actuator
   c. Manually
   d. Accessory belt

6. Which of the following is *not* true of automatic headlamp systems?
   a. Can turn headlamps on or off
   b. Can control high- and low-beam switching
   c. Are easily repaired when defective
   d. Can be adjusted to fit various conditions

7. On small automobile bulbs which have only one contact, the contact is:
   a. Insulated
   b. Indexed
   c. Grounded
   d. Festooned

8. Double-contact bulbs that are designed to fit into the socket only one way are called:
   a. Miniature bayonet base
   b. Single-contact bayonet
   c. Double-contact indexed
   d. Double-contact bayonet

9. The taillamps, license plate lamps, and parking lamps are generally protected by:
   a. A Type-I circuit breaker
   b. A Type-II circuit breaker
   c. A 20-amp fuse
   d. Three fusible links

10. Turn signal flasher units supply a rapid on-off-on current flow to the turn signal lamps by acting very much like:
    a. Circuit breakers
    b. Fuses
    c. Zener diodes
    d. Transistorized regulators

11. Which of the following is *not* part of the hazard warning lamp circuit?
    a. Turn signal lamps
    b. Brake lamps
    c. Flasher unit
    d. Instrument panel

12. The only white lamps allowed on the rear of a car are:
    a. Backup lamps and turn signal lamps
    b. Backup lamps and license plate lamps
    c. License plate lamps and turn signal lamps
    d. Turn signal lamps and backup lamps

13. Brightness of the instrument panel lamps is *not* controlled by:
    a. Diodes
    b. Rheostats
    c. Potentiometers
    d. Variable resistors

14. The switches used in courtesy lamp circuits are:
    a. Compound switches
    b. Push-pull switches
    c. Three-way switches
    d. Rheostats

15. Which of the following is *not* true of composite headlamps?
    a. Use replaceable bulbs
    b. Are part of the car's styling
    c. Have a polycarbonate lens
    d. May be red or amber

16. Halogen sealed-beam lamps:
    a. Are not as damage-resistant as glass
    b. Produce 30% less light
    c. May be made of plastic
    d. Have been used since the 1940s

19

Horn, Windshield Wiper and Washer, Electric Cooling Fan, and Instrument Circuits

HORN CIRCUITS

An automobile horn is a safety device operated by the driver to alert pedestrians and other motorists. Some states require two horn systems, with different sound levels for city and country use.

Circuit Diagram

Some older automobiles used a simple series horn circuit, figure 19-1A. Battery current is supplied to the horn circuit through the fuse panel, or from a terminal on the starter relay or solenoid. The normally open horn switch is installed between the power source and the grounded horn. When the driver pushes the horn button, the horn switch closes and current flows through the circuit to sound the horn. If the car has more than one horn, figure 19-1B, each horn will form a parallel path to ground.

Most horn circuits include a horn relay, figure 19-2. The normally open relay contacts are between the power source and the grounded horn. The horn switch is between the relay coil and ground. When the horn switch is closed, a small amount of current flows through the relay coil. This closes the relay coil and allows a greater amount of current to flow through the horns.

Some Chrysler front-wheel-drive (FWD) vehicles have an air horn system which uses a compressor in its circuitry, figure 19-3. Circuit operation is similar to that shown in figure 19-2, but current flows through the relay to the compressor, which is grounded at the headlamp ground. The compressor then activates the horn.

Horn Switches, Relays, and Fuses

The horn switch is normally installed in the steering wheel or steering column, figure 19-4. Contact points can be placed so that the switch will be closed by pressure at different points on the steering wheel, figure 19-5. Some cars have a button in the center of the wheel, others have a number of buttons around the rim of the wheel, or a large separate horn ring. Many imported cars and some domestic cars have the horn button on the end of a multi-function lever or stalk on the steering column. All of these designs operate in the same way: pressure on the switch causes contacts to close. When the pressure is released, spring tension opens the contacts.

Horn relays can be mounted on the fuse panel, figure 19-6. They also can be attached to the bulkhead connector or mounted near the horns in the engine compartment. The relay is not serviceable but must be replaced if defective.

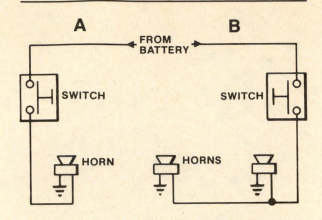

Figure 19-1. A simple circuit with a single horn in series with the switch (A), or two horns in parallel with each other and in series with the switch (B).

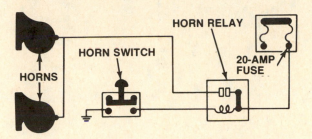

Figure 19-2. Many horn systems are controlled by a relay. (Chrysler)

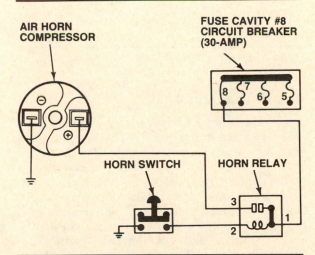

Figure 19-3. Chrysler's air horn system is a relay circuit but the relay activates an air horn compressor, which operates the horn. (Chrysler)

The horn circuit often shares a 15- to 20-ampere fuse with several other circuits. It may also be protected by a fusible link.

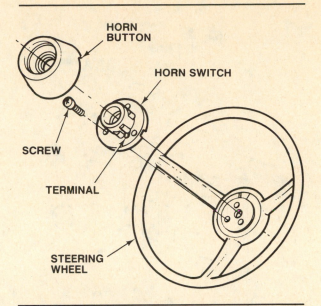

Figure 19-4. The horn switch is mounted in the steering column. (Chrysler)

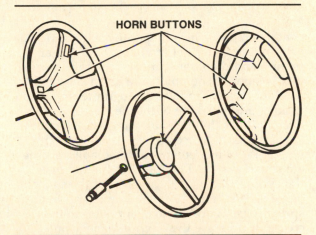

Figure 19-5. Horn buttons can be placed at various locations around the steering wheel.

Horns

Except for Chrysler's air horn, which uses air pressure from the compressor, automobile horns use electromagnetism to vibrate a diaphragm and produce sound waves. A typical horn contains normally closed contact points in series with a coil. One of the contact points is mounted on a moveable armature to which the horn diaphragm is connected.

The horn coil is in series with the horn switch or horn relay contacts. When the horn switch or horn relay contacts close, current flows through the horn coil to ground. The electromagnetic field created by the coil attracts the armature, also moving the diaphragm. The armature movement opens the

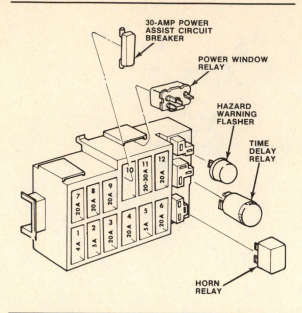

Figure 19-6. The horn relay can be mounted on the fuse panel. (Chrysler)

contact points, which open the coil circuit. With no magnetic field to hold them, the armature and diaphragm move back to their normal positions. The points are again closed, allowing current to flow through the coil. This making and breaking of the electromagnetic circuit causes the horn diaphragm to vibrate.

Since this cycle occurs very rapidly, the resulting rapid movements of the diaphragm create sound waves. The speed or frequency of the cycling determines the pitch of the sound created. This can be adjusted by changing the spring tension on the horn armature to increase or decrease the electromagnetic pull on the diaphragm. We will learn more about this procedure in the *Shop Manual*.

WINDSHIELD WIPERS AND WASHERS

Federal law requires that all cars built in, or imported into, the United States since 1968 have both a two-windshield wiper system and a windshield washer system. Wiper systems on older vehicles may be operated by engine vacuum or by the power steering hydraulic system.

Modern wiper systems are operated by electric motors. The washer system can be manually operated, or it can have an electric pump. Many vehicles also have a single-speed wiper and washer for the rear window. This is a completely separate system, but it operates in the same way as the windshield wiper and washer system.

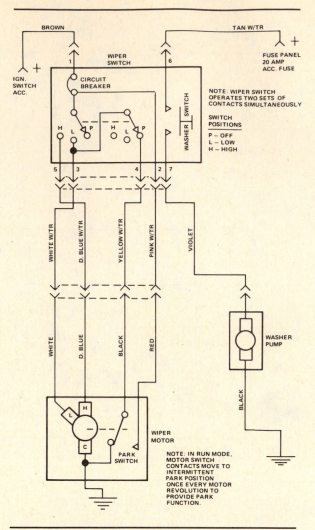

Figure 19-7. A simple two-speed wiper circuit.

Circuit Diagram

A typical two-speed wiper system circuit diagram is shown in figure 19-7. The motor fields are permanent magnets. The wiper switch controls both the wiper motor speeds and the washer pump. The park switch within the wiper motor ensures that when the wiper switch is turned off, the motor will continue to turn until the wiper arms have reached the bottom edge, or park position, of the windshield. The circuit shown has a circuit breaker built into the wiper switch. However, the circuit breaker also can be a separate unit, or it can be mounted on the wiper motor.

Figure 19-8 shows low-speed current flow through the simple circuit. Current flows through the wiper switch contacts, the low-speed brush L, and the common (shared) brush C to ground. During high-speed operation, the current flows through the high-speed

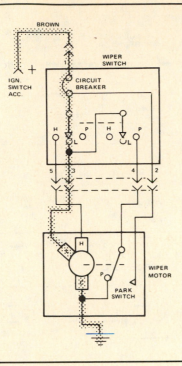

Figure 19-8. Low-speed current flow.

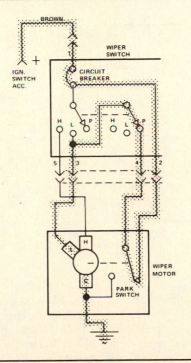

Figure 19-9. The park switch allows the motor to continue turning until the wiper arms reach their park position.

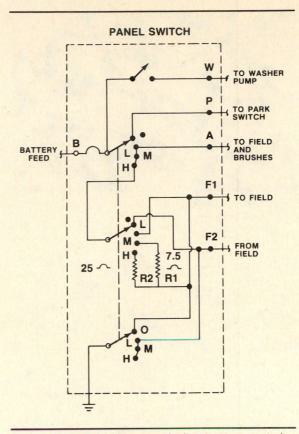

Figure 19-10. This three-speed wiper system controls motor speed by routing field current flow through various resistors. (Chrysler)

brush H and the common brush to ground. When the wiper switch is turned to park, or off, the park switch comes into the circuit.

The park switch is a two-position, cam-operated switch within the wiper motor. It moves from one position to the other during each motor revolution. When the wiper arms are at their park position, the park switch is at the P contact, as shown in figure 19-7. No current flows through the park switch. At all other wiper arm positions, the park switch is held against spring tension at the other contact. If the wiper switch is turned off while the wiper arms are not at their park position, figure 19-9, current will flow through the park switch to the low-speed brush. The motor will continue to turn until the wiper arms reach their park position. At that point, the park switch moves to the P contact and all current stops.

When extra features are added to the wiper system, the circuits become more complex. For example, many manufacturers offer three-speed wiper systems. These systems use electromagnetic motor fields. The switch contacts route field current through resistors of various values, figure 19-10, to vary the wiper motor speed. Some GM two-speed wiper circuits also use this type of motor.

Many late-model vehicles have wiper arms that retreat below hood level when the switch

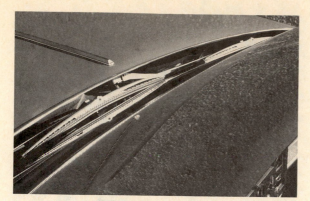

Figure 19-11. Many late-model cars have a depressed-park wiper position.

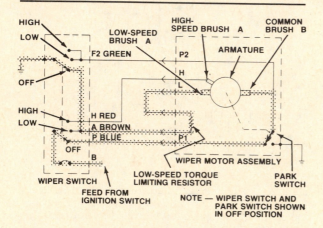

Figure 19-12. Low-speed current flow in a depressed-park system. (Chrysler)

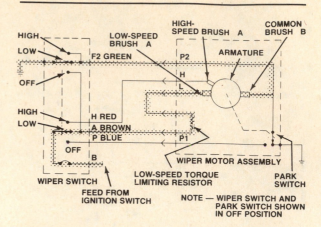

Figure 19-13. The park switch reverses current flow through the motor so that the wiper arms are pulled down into the depressed park position. (Chrysler)

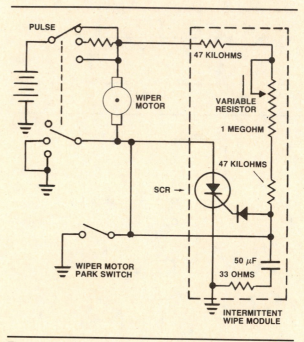

Figure 19-14. An SCR in the solid-state intermittent wiper module or control unit triggers the wiper motor for intermittent wiper arm sweeps. (Chrysler)

is turned off, figure 19-11. This is called a depressed park position and is controlled by the park switch. When the wiper switch is turned off, the park switch allows the motor to continue turning until the wiper arms reach the bottom edge of the windshield. The park switch then *reverses* current flow through the wiper motor, which makes a partial revolution in the opposite direction. The wiper linkage pulls the wiper arms down below the level of the hood during this motor reversal. The motor reversal also opens the park switch to stop all wiper motor current flow.

A depressed-park wiper system is shown in figure 19-12. During normal operation, current flows through either brush A or common brush B to ground. When the wiper switch is turned off, figure 19-13, current flows through the park switch, into brush B, and through low-speed brush A to ground. This reverses the motor's rotation until the wiper arms reach the depressed park position, the park switch moves to the grounded position, and all current stops.

Many wiper systems have a low-speed intermittent or delay mode. This allows the wiper arms to sweep the windshield completely at intervals of three to 30 seconds. Most intermittent, or delay, wiper systems route current through a solid-state module containing a variable resistor and a capacitor, figure 19-14. Once the current passing through the variable resistor has fully charged the capacitor, it triggers a silicon-controlled rectifier (SCR), which allows current flow to the wiper motor. The park switch within the motor shunts the SCR circuit to ground. Current to the motor con-

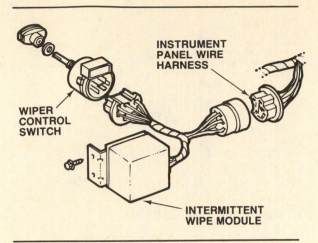

Figure 19-15. The intermittent wipe governor or module is installed between the wiper switch and the wiper motor.

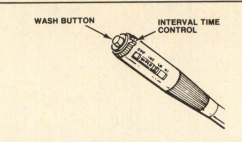

Figure 19-16. The washer switch is usually a spring-loaded pushbutton mounted on the instrument panel or on a multifunction lever. (Ford)

tinues, however, until the wiper arms reach their park position and the park switch is opened. The capacitor rate of charge, and therefore the interval between the wiper arm sweeps, is controlled by the driver through the variable resistor.

On some imported cars, the intermittent or delay mode is sensitive to vehicle speed and varies from approximately 15 seconds (at low road speed) up to the wipers' normal low speed (at moderate road speed) as vehicle speed changes. The intermittent mode can be cancelled by pressing a cancel switch, and wiper speed can be set manually with the wiper switch.

Intermittent wiper control circuitry on many cars is contained in a separate module which is installed between the wiper switch and the wiper motor, figure 19-15.

Switches

The wiper switch is between the power source and the grounded wiper motor. The wiper switch does not receive current unless the ignition switch is turned to the Accessory or the Run position. The wiper switch may be mounted on the instrument panel, or it can be mounted in the steering column and controlled by a multifunction lever or stalk, figure 19-16.

If the system has an electric washer pump, the pump is generally controlled by contacts within the wiper switch. The washer is usually operated by a spring-loaded pushbutton that is part of the wiper switch, figure 19-16. Moving the switch to its wash position or pressing the pushbutton will operate the washer pump as long as the switch is held in position or is pressed.

Motors

Most two-speed wiper motors use permanent ceramic magnets as pole pieces. Three brushes ride on the motor's commutator. One brush is a common, or shared, brush and conducts current whenever the wiper motor is operating. The other brushes are placed at different positions relative to the motor armature. Current through one brush produces a different motor speed than current through the other brush. The wiper switch contacts route current to one of these two brushes, depending upon which wiper motor speed the driver selects.

In many wiper motors, the high-speed brush is placed directly opposite the common brush, figure 19-17. The low-speed brush is offset to one side. This placement of the low-speed brush affects the interaction of the magnetic

■ **From Bell To Electric Horn**

Many types of signal alarms have been used on cars:

- Mechanical bell
- Bulb horn
- Compression whistle
- Exhaust horn
- Hand-operated horn (Klaxon)
- Electric horn.

The mechanical bell was used on very early cars. The driver operated the bell with a foot pedal. The bulb horn, similar to that on a child's bicycle, proved to be inconvenient and unreliable. The compression whistle was most often used in cars with no battery or limited battery capacity. A prefilled cylinder provided the whistle's power. Exhaust horns used gases from the engine exhaust; they, too, were foot-operated. The hand-operated Klaxon horn amplified a grating sound caused by a metal tooth riding over a metal gear. This did not work well, because the horn had to be near the driver rather than at the front of the car. Over the years, the electric horn has been the most popular type of signal alarm.

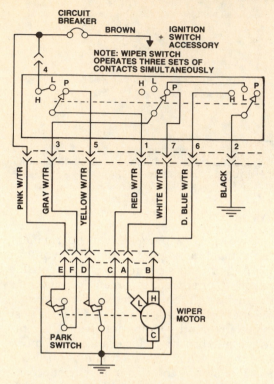

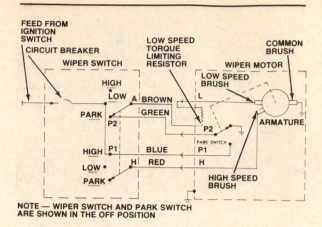

Figure 19-18. This motor has an extra resistor in the low-speed circuit, so the low-speed brush is placed directly across from the common brush. The common brush is grounded, and the two speed-control brushes are insulated.

Figure 19-17. In this system, the high-speed brush is set directly opposite the common brush. The common brush is insulated, and the two speed-control brushes are grounded through the wiper switch.

fields within the motor and makes the motor turn slowly. The placement of the high-speed brush causes the motor to turn rapidly. Chrysler and some GM two-speed motors vary from this pattern, figures 19-14 and 19-18. The low-speed brush is directly opposite the common brush and the high-speed brush is offset. A resistor wired in series with the low-speed brush reduces the motor's torque at low speed. This extra resistance in the low-speed circuit results in a lower motor speed even with the reversed brush position.

The common brush can be grounded and the two speed-control brushes can be insulated, as shown in figure 19-18. Other motors have the speed-control brushes grounded through the wiper switch contacts and the common brush insulated, figure 19-17.

Some two-speed and all three-speed wiper motors have two electro-magnetic field windings, figure 19-19. One field coil is in series with a motor brush and is called the series field. The other field coil is a separate circuit branch directly to ground and is called the shunt field. The two coils are wound in opposite directions, so that their magnetic fields oppose each other.

The wiper switch controls current through these two field coils. At low speed, about the same amount of current flows through both coils. Their opposing magnetic fields result in a weak total field, so the motor turns slowly. At medium speed (three-speed motor), current to one coil must flow through a resistor. This makes the coil's magnetic field weaker and results in a stronger total field within the motor. The motor revolves faster. At high speed, current to the coil must flow through a greater value resistor. The total magnetic field of the motor is again increased, and the motor speed increases. The resistors can act on either the shunt coil or the series coil to reduce current flow and thereby increase the motor's total field strength and speed. In figure 19-19, the resistors act on the shunt field.

Many wiper motors can be serviced to some extent, as we will learn in the *Shop Manual*.

Washer Pumps

Windshield washer pumps draw a cleaning solution from a reservoir and force it through nozzles onto the windshield. The unit can be a positive-displacement pump or a centrifugal pump that forces a steady stream of fluid, or it can be a pulse-type pump that operates valves with a cam to force separate spurts of fluid.

The washer pump is generally mounted in or on the fluid reservoir, figure 19-20. GM pulse pumps are mounted on the wiper motor, figure 19-21. Washer pumps are not usually serviceable but are replaced if they fail.

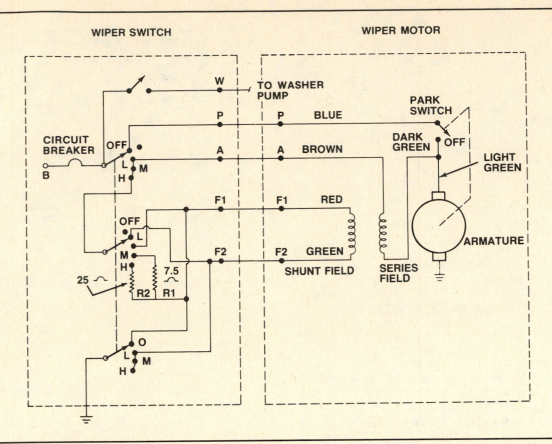

Figure 19-19. In this motor with two electromagnetic fields, the motor speed is controlled by the amount of current through one of the fields. (Chrysler)

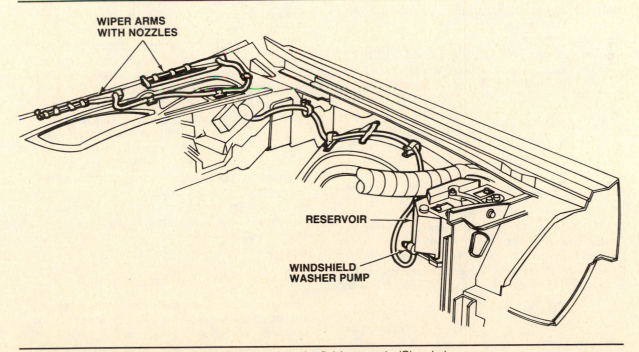

Figure 19-20. The washer pump is often mounted on the fluid reservoir. (Chrysler)

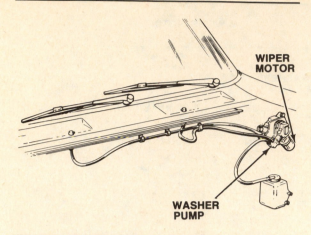

Figure 19-21. Some GM systems have a washer pump mounted on the wiper motor.

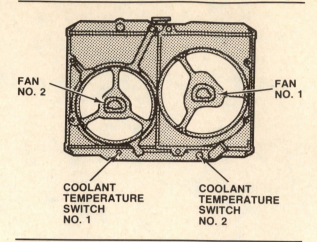

Figure 19-22. Some vehicles use dual electric cooling fans. One system cools the radiator, while the other system cools the A/C condenser. (Chrysler)

COOLING FAN CIRCUITS

There is no practical way to drive a cooling fan from the crankshaft pulley of a transversely mounted engine. Therefore, an electric cooling fan is used. Some may use one fan to cool the radiator and a separate system to cool the air conditioning condenser, figure 19-22. Vehicles with a longitudinally mounted engine and the traditional crankshaft-driven fan mounted on the water pump shaft may also use one or more electric cooling fans.

Dual electric cooling fans often are used with turbocharged and air conditioned vehicles to provide additional engine cooling and air conditioning performance at idle. They are also used with intercooled turbocharged vehicles to cool the hot compressed intake air, thus increasing its density and improving cylinder charging efficiency. When two electric fans are used, each has its individual circuit with different control temperatures. Since electric fans work when needed and shut off when they are not needed, they help increase fuel efficiency.

Circuit Diagram

Electric cooling fan circuits generally incorporate a relay and temperature switch, figure 19-23. The normally open relay contacts are located between the power source and the grounded fan motor. The temperature switch is installed between the relay coil and ground. When engine coolant temperature closes the temperature switch contacts, a small amount of current flows through the relay coil to close the relay contact points and allow a greater amount of current to activate the fan motor.

On air conditioned vehicles, the circuit is also wired through the air conditioning relay.

This bypasses the coolant temperature switch and fan relay and allows the cooling fan to run in one of two modes, depending upon the particular vehicle:

- At all times when the air conditioning compressor clutch is engaged
- When the air conditioning system is on and compressor head pressure exceeds a specified value.

An "after-run" feature found on some vehicles incorporates an air temperature sensing switch, figure 19-24. If the ambient temperature is above a specified value when the engine is shut off, the air temperature sensing switch keeps the circuit closed regardless of coolant temperature to keep the fan running for a specified time. The "after-run" timer is incorporated in the fan relay. This feature is often used with turbocharged vehicles.

Toyota uses a dual "three-stage" fan system on some vehicles which automatically switches back and forth from a parallel connection at high-speed operation to a series connection for low-speed operation, figure 19-25. Switching is controlled by air conditioning compressor operation and coolant temperature. This system reduces electrical power consumption, vibration, and noise.

Coolant Temperature Switch

The coolant temperature switch is generally mounted in the cylinder head or in a radiator header tank where it is internally isolated from the radiator, figure 19-24. The switch contains a bimetallic contact arm that closes when coolant temperature reaches the switch's calibrated value, figure 19-26. When the contact arm

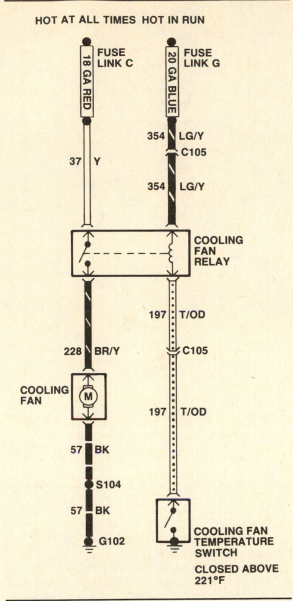

Figure 19-23. Electric cooling fan circuits are controlled by a temperature switch and relay. (Ford)

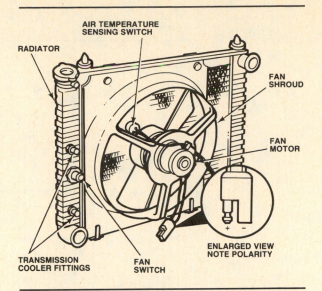

Figure 19-24. An air temperature sensing switch will keep the fan running after the engine is turned off when ambient air temperature is above a certain level. (Chrysler)

closes, the switch completes the circuit to the fan relay, which turns the fan motor on. The temperature switch is usually connected to the battery side of the ignition switch to allow the fan to operate whether the engine is on or off. For this reason, you should always disconnect the fan motor when working under the hood near it, because it can turn on without warning if the coolant temperature rises.

The air temperature sensing switch used in systems with the ''after-run'' feature, figure 19-24, is similar in construction to the coolant temperature switch, but it is designed to provide a quicker temperature change response time.

Computer Control

The electric cooling fan on late-model, four-cylinder Chrysler vehicles is controlled by the on-board computer instead of a temperature sensing switch in the radiator. The computer's temperature sensor provides the input used by the computer to switch the fan circuit on and off. The computer is programmed to:

- Prevent the fan from running during cranking regardless of coolant temperature
- Allow the fan to run whenever the air conditioning compressor clutch is engaged
- Switch the fan on at different coolant temperatures according to engine speed
- Switch the fan on for a designated length of time at idle when specified ambient air and coolant temperatures are present.

On Chrysler vehicles with on-board diagnostics, the circuitry and temperature sensor are monitored by the computer, which will set fault code 35 if the fan relay does not turn on and off when it should.

Some late-model GM cars use the continuously variable, dual-fan motor control circuit shown in figure 19-27. The fan control module transmits a voltage signal to the body control module (BCM), which switches the control line on and off with a pulse width modulation. The fan control module in turn switches the fan motor ground to control the fan speed. The longer the ground is intact, the longer the fan motors run during the pulse period.

The fan control module contains a current flow sensor so that it knows when the fan mo-

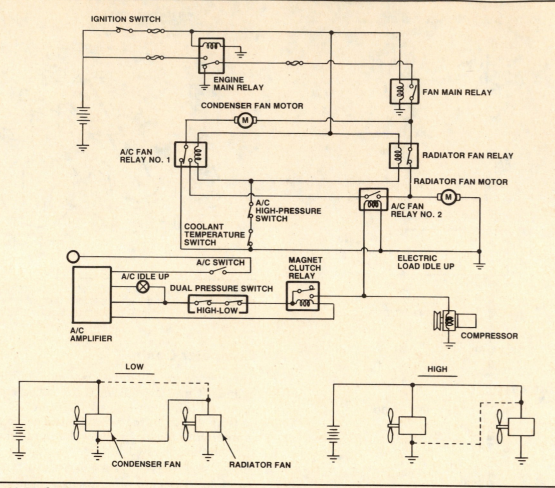

Figure 19-25. Operational and circuit diagrams for Toyota's three-stage electrical fan system. (Toyota)

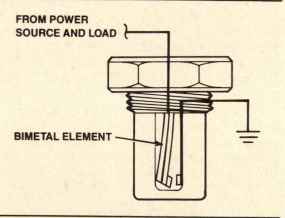

Figure 19-26. A bimetallic strip in a coolant temperature switch closes when engine coolant exceeds the switch's temperature limit. (Ford)

tors are running. The feedback generator sends a 12-volt signal to the BCM when the fans are off and drops the voltage to zero when the fans are running. This pulsing volt-

age from the feedback line tells the BCM that fan operation is correct.

The BCM can modify fan operation to correct a problem. For example, if a fan becomes stuck and will not rotate, it would cause an excessive current draw which might damage the system under ordinary circumstances. If this happens, however, the control module current sensor switches the feedback line high and low to tell the BCM that a problem exists. When it receives this signal, the BCM modifies the control circuit to reduce fan operation and prevent the excessive current draw.

Fan Relay and Motor

Cooling fan relays are similar in appearance to many other relays used in an engine compartment. Generally, however, a cooling fan relay is mounted on the driver's side of the vehicle, on the cowl, the shock tower, or along the fenderwell. Since several relays are often located together and may be housed inside a protective cover, you should check the carmaker's

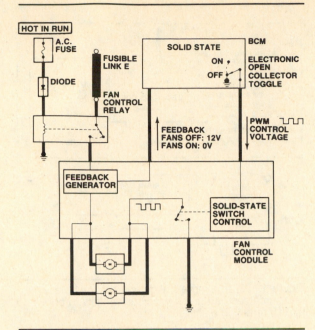

Figure 19-27. The GM body control module (BCM) operates dual cooling fans through a solid-state control module by switching current on and off to provide pulse width modulation. The feedback circuit tells the BCM what the fans are doing. (GM)

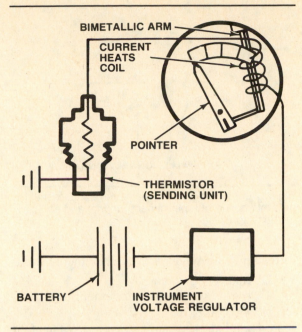

Figure 19-28. The thermal-type gauge depends upon the heat of current flow bending a bimetallic strip. (Chrysler)

factory shop manual to determine exactly which one controls the cooling fan. Cooling fan relays are not serviceable but must be replaced if defective.

Cooling fan motors are small, high-torque units with permanent ceramic magnets for poles. Like relays, they are not serviceable but are replaced if defective.

ELECTROMAGNETIC INSTRUMENT CIRCUITS

Gauges and warning lamps allow the driver to monitor a vehicle's operating conditions. These instruments differ widely from car to car but all are analog. Digital electronic instruments are explained later in this chapter. Warning lamps are used in place of gauges in many cases because they are less expensive and easier to understand, although they do not transmit as much useful information as gauges do.

The following paragraphs explain the general operation of analog gauges, lamps, and the sending units that control them.

Gauge Operating Principles

Common gauges use one of three operating principles:

- Mechanical
- Bimetallic (thermal-type)
- Electromagnetic.

Mechanical gauges are operated by cables, fluid pressure, or fluid temperature. Because they do not require an electrical circuit, they do not fit into our study. The cable-driven speedometer is the most common mechanical gauge.

Bimetallic gauges
A bimetallic gauge works because current flowing through the bimetallic strip will heat up one of the metals faster than the other, causing the strip to bend. A typical gauge, figure 19-28, has a U-shaped bimetallic piece anchored to the gauge body at the end of one arm. The other arm has a high-resistance wire, or heater coil, wound around it. Current flow through the heater coil bends the free bimetallic arm. Varying the current changes the bend in the arm. A pointer attached to the moving arm can relate the changes in current to a scale on the face of the gauge.

Ambient temperature could affect the gauge, but the U-shape of the bimetallic strip provides temperature compensation. While ambient temperature bends the free arm in one direction, the fixed arm is bent in the other direction and the effect is cancelled.

Electromagnetic gauges
The movement of an electromagnetic gauge depends on the interaction of magnetic fields.

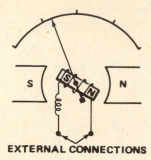

EXTERNAL CONNECTIONS

Figure 19-29. The D'Arsonval movement uses the field interaction of a permanent magnet and an electromagnet.

Three kinds of movements are commonly used:

- D'Arsonval movement
- Three-coil or two-coil movement
- Air core design.

A **D'Arsonval movement** has a moveable electromagnet surrounded by a permanent horseshoe magnet, figure 19-29. The electro-magnet's field opposes the permanent magnet's field. This causes the electromagnet to rotate. A pointer mounted on the electromagnet relates this movement to a scale on the face of the gauge.

The amount of current flow through the electromagnet's coil determines the electromagnet's field strength, and therefore the amount of pointer movement.

A **three-coil movement** depends upon the field interaction of three electromagnets and the total field's effect on a moveable permanent magnet. This type of gauge is used in GM and some late-model Ford vehicles.

The circuit diagram of a typical three-coil movement, figure 19-30, shows that two coils are wound at right angles to each other. These are the minimum-reading coil and the maximum-reading coil. Their magnetic fields will pull the permanent magnet and pointer in opposite directions. A third coil is wound so that its magnetic field opposes that of the minimum-reading coil. This is called the bucking coil.

The three coils are connected in series from the ignition switch to ground. A fixed resistor forms a circuit branch parallel to the minimum-reading coil. The variable-resistance sending unit forms a circuit branch to ground, parallel to the bucking and minimum-reading coils.

When sending resistance is high, current flows through all three coils to ground. Because the magnetic fields of the minimum-reading and the bucking coils cancel each other, the maximum-reading coil's field has the strongest effect on the permanent mag-

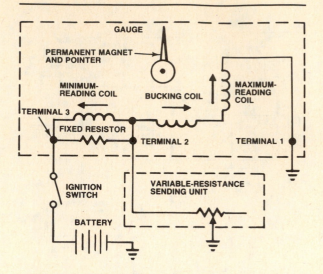

Figure 19-30. In a three-coil gauge, the variable resistance sending unit affects current flow through three interacting electromagnets.

net and pointer. The pointer moves to the maximum-reading end of the gauge scale.

As sending unit resistance decreases, more current flows through the minimum-reading coil and the sending unit to ground than flows through the bucking and maximum-reading coils. The minimum-reading coil gains a stronger effect upon the permanent magnet and pointer, and the pointer moves to the minimum-reading end of the gauge scale.

Specific three-coil gauges may have slightly different wiring, but the basic operation remains the same. Because the circular magnet is carefully balanced, it will remain at its last position even when the ignition switch is turned off, rather than returning to the minimum reading position, as does a bimetallic gauge.

The design of two-coil gauges varies with the purpose for which the gauge is used. In a fuel gauge, for example, the pointer is moved by the magnetic fields of the two coils positioned at right angles to each other. Battery voltage is applied to the E (empty) coil and the circuit divides at the opposite end of the coil. One path travels to ground through the F (full) coil; the other grounds through the sender's variable resistor. When sender resistance is low (low fuel), current passes through the E coil and sender resistor to move the pointer towards E on the scale. When sender resistance is high (full tank), current flows through the F coil to move the pointer toward F on the scale.

When a two-coil gauge is used to indicate coolant temperature, battery voltage is applied to both coils. One coil is grounded directly; the other grounds through the sending unit. Send-

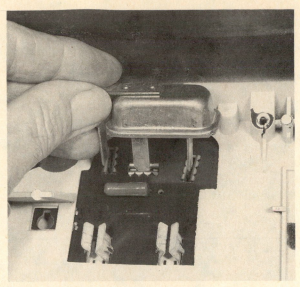

Figure 19-31. An independent instrument voltage regulator (IVR) looks like a circuit breaker and plugs into the back of the printed circuit board.

er resistance causes the current through one coil to change as the temperature changes, moving the pointer.

In the **air core gauge** design, the gauge receives a varying electrical signal from its sending unit. A pivoting permanent magnet mounted to a pointer aligns itself to a resultant field according to sending unit resistance. The sending unit resistance varies the field strength of the windings in opposition to the reference windings. The sending unit also compensates for variations in voltage.

This simple design provides several advantages beyond greater accuracy. It does not create radiofrequency interference (RFI), is unaffected by temperature, completely noiseless, and does not require the use of a voltage limiter. Like the three- and two-coil designs, however, the air core design remains at its last position when the ignition switch is turned off, giving a reading that should be disregarded.

Instrument voltage regulator

Except for the air core electromagnetic design, gauges require a continuous, controlled amount of voltage. This is usually either the system voltage of 12 volts or a regulated 5 to 6 volts. Regulated voltage is supplied by an instrument voltage regulator (IVR). The IVR can be a separate component that looks much like a circuit breaker, figure 19-31, or it can be built into one gauge, figure 19-28. Its bimetallic strip and vibrating points, figure 19-32, act like a self-setting circuit breaker to keep the gauge voltage at a specific level. Gauges that operate on limited voltage can be damaged or give inaccurate readings if exposed to full system voltage.

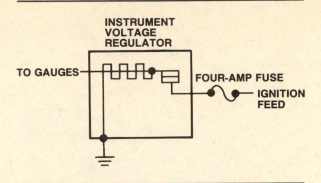

Figure 19-32. The IVR acts in the same way as a circuit breaker, but vibrates more rapidly.

To prevent radiofrequency interference (RFI) from affecting other electrical components or the radio, an IVR has a **radio choke**. This is a coil wound with fine wire that soaks up the oscillations that occur when the vibrating contacts make and break the circuit.

Warning Lamp Operating Principles

Warning lamps alert the drive to potentially hazardous vehicle operating conditions, such as:

- High engine temperature
- Low oil pressure
- Charging system problems
- Low fuel level
- Unequal brake fluid pressure
- Parking brake on
- Seat belts not fastened
- Exterior lighting failure.

D'Arsonval Movement: A small, current-carrying coil mounted within the field of a permanent horseshoe magnet. Interaction of the magnetic fields causes the coil to rotate. Used as a measuring device within electrical gauges and test meters.

Three-Coil Movement: A gauge design that depends upon the field interaction of three electromagnets and the total field effect on a moveable permanent magnet.

Air Core Gauge: A gauge design in which there is no magnetic core. A field created by the sending unit resistance moves a pivoting permanent magnet.

Radio Choke: A coil of extremely fine wire used to absorb oscillations created by the making and breaking of an electrical circuit.

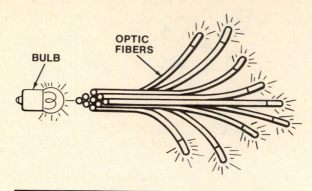

Figure 19-33. Light-carrying fibers can be used in accessory instruments.

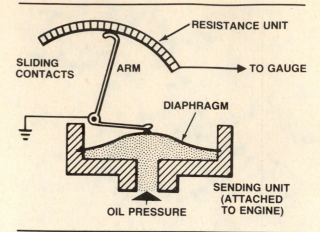

Figure 19-34. The oil pressure sending unit provides a varying amount of resistance as engine oil pressure changes.

Warning lamps can monitor many different functions but are usually activated in one of four ways:

- Voltage drop
- Grounding switch
- Ground sensor
- Fiber optics.

The first three methods are used to light a bulb or an LED mounted on the dash panel. Fiber optics is a special application of remote light.

Voltage drop
A bulb will light only if there is a voltage drop across its filament. Warning lamps can be installed so that equal voltage is applied to both bulb terminals under normal operating conditions. If operating conditions change, a voltage drop occurs across the filament, and the bulb will light. This method is often used to control charging system indicators, as we learned in Chapter Nine.

Grounding switch
A bulb connected to battery voltage will not light unless the current can flow to ground. Warning lamps can be installed so that the ground path is controlled by a switch that reacts to operating conditions. Under normal conditions, the switch contacts are open and the bulb does not light. When operating conditions change, the switch contacts close. This creates a ground path for current and lights the bulb.

Ground sensor
A ground sensor is the opposite of a ground switch. Here, the warning lamp remains unlit as long as the sensor is grounded. When conditions change and the sensor is no longer grounded, the bulb lights. Solid-state circuitry generally is used in this type of circuit.

Fiber optics
Strands of a special plastic can conduct light through long, curving runs, figure 19-33. When one end of the fiber is installed in the instrument panel and the other end is exposed to a light, the driver will be able to see that light. Changing operating conditions can cause the fiber to change from light to dark, or from one color to another. Fiber optics are usually used for accessory warning lamps, such as coolant level reminders and exterior bulb monitors.

Specific Instruments

Many different instruments have appeared in automobiles, but certain basic functions are monitored in almost all cars. Normally, a car's instrument panel will contain at least:

- An ammeter, a voltmeter, or an alternator warning lamp
- An oil pressure gauge or warning lamp
- A coolant temperature gauge or warning lamp
- A fuel level gauge.

The following paragraphs explain how these specific instruments are constructed and installed.

Charging system indicators
Ammeter, voltmeter, and warning lamp installations were studied in Chapter Nine. Ammeters usually contain a D'Arsonval movement that reacts to field current flow into the alternator and charging current flow into the battery. Many late-model cars have a voltmeter instead of an ammeter. A voltmeter indicates battery condition when the engine is off, and charging system operation when the engine is running. Warning lamps light to show an un-

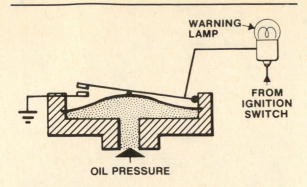

Figure 19-35. This oil pressure grounding switch has a fixed contact and a contact that is moved by the pressure-sensitive diaphragm.

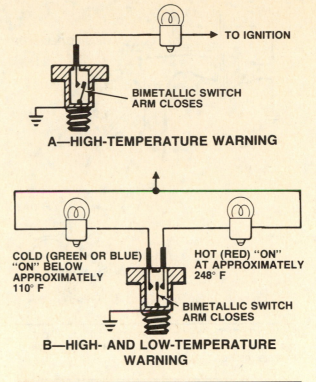

Figure 19-36. Temperature grounding switches expose a bimetallic strip to engine coolant temperature to light a high-temperature lamp or both high- and low-temperature warning lamps.

dercharged battery or low voltage from the alternator. Lamps used on GM cars with a CS charging system will light when the system voltage is too high or too low.

Some 1975 and later Chrysler rear-wheel-drive (RWD) cars with ammeters also have an LED mounted on the ammeter face. The LED works independently to monitor system voltage and lights when system voltage drops by about 1.2 volts. This alerts the driver to a discharge condition at idle caused by a heavy electrical load.

Oil pressure gauge or warning lamp
The varying current signals to an oil pressure gauge are supplied through a variable-resistance sending unit that is exposed to engine oil pressure. The resistor variation is controlled by a diaphragm that moves with changes in oil pressure, figure 19-34.

An oil pressure warning lamp lights to indicate low oil pressure. A ground switch controls the lamp, figure 19-35. When oil pressure decreases to an unsafe level, the switch diaphragm moves far enough to ground the warning lamp circuit. Current then can flow to ground and the bulb will light.

Oil pressure warning lamps can be operated by the gauge itself. When the pointer moves to the low-pressure end of the scale, it closes contact points to light a bulb or an LED.

Temperature gauge or warning lamp
In most late-model cars, the temperature gauge sending unit is a thermistor exposed to engine coolant temperature, figure 19-28. As coolant temperature increases, the resistance of the thermistor decreases and current through the gauge varies.

Temperature warning lamps can alert the driver to high temperature or to both low and high temperature. The most common circuit uses a bimetallic switch and reacts only to high tempera-

ture, figure 19-36A. A ground switch has a bimetallic strip that is exposed to coolant temperature. When the temperature reaches an unsafe level, the strip bends far enough to ground the warning lamp circuit. If the circuit also reacts to low temperature, the bimetallic strip has a second set of contacts. These are closed at low temperature, figure 19-36B, but open during normal operating temperature. The low-temperature circuit usually lights a different bulb than does the high-temperature circuit.

A temperature warning lamp or an LED also can be lit by the action of the temperature gauge pointer, as explained for the oil pressure gauge.

Fuel gauge or warning lamp
All modern cars have a fuel level gauge. Some have an additional warning lamp or an LED to indicate a low fuel level.

Current through the fuel gauge is provided by a variable resistor in the fuel tank. The tank sending unit has a float that moves with the fuel level, figure 19-37. As the float rises and falls, the resistance of the sending unit changes. If a low fuel level indicator is used, its switch may operate through a heater or bimetallic relay to prevent flicker.

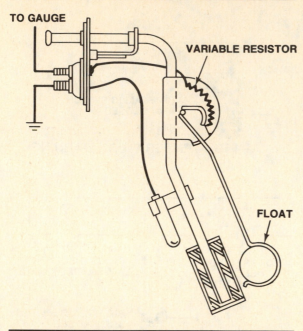

Figure 19-37. The fuel tank sending unit has a float that moves with the fuel level in the tank and affects a variable resistor.

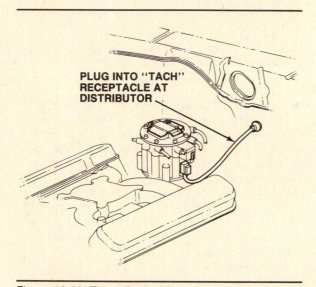

Figure 19-38. This HEI distributor has a special connector for a tachometer. (Pontiac)

Fuel level warning lamps are operated by the action of the fuel gauge pointer, as explained for an oil pressure gauge.

Tachometer

In addition to the other instrument panel displays, some cars have tachometers to indicate engine speed in revolutions per minute (rpm). These usually have an electromagnetic movement. The engine speed signals may come from an electronic pickup at the ignition coil, figure 19-38. Voltage pulses taken from the ig-

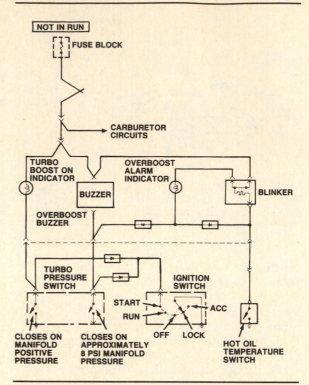

Figure 19-39. Ford's original turbo boost control circuit used a combination pressure switch to operate the boost indicator and overboost buzzer. (Ford)

nition system are processed by solid-state circuitry into signals to drive the tachometer pointer. The pointer responds to the frequency of these signals, which increase with engine speed. A filter is used to round off the pulses and remove any spikes.

Late-model vehicles with an engine control system may control the tachometer through an electronic module. This module is located on the rear of the instrument cluster printed circuit board and is the interface between the computer and tachometer in the same way the solid-state circuitry processes the ignition system-to-tachometer signals described earlier.

Turbo boost indicators

Most turbocharged engines have visual or audible indicators to inform the driver about turbo boost levels. Figure 19-39 shows the circuit diagram of the warning system used on 1979-80 Ford Mustang and Capri 2.3-liter engines with a draw-through turbocharger, where fuel is introduced upstream of the compressor. At low manifold pressure when the turbocharger starts to operate, a set of contacts in the turbo pressure switch turns on the boost indicator lamp to indicate that the turbocharger is functioning. If manifold pressure reaches approximately 8 psi (55 kPa), a second set of contacts in the switch close while the first set opens.

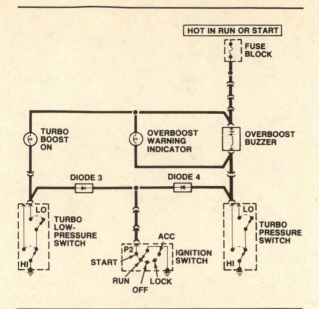

Figure 19-40. The second generation Ford turbo boost control circuit uses individual low- and high-pressure switches. (Ford)

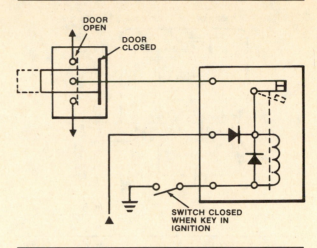

Figure 19-41. Current will flow through this warning buzzer only when both switches are closed — when the door is open and the key is in the ignition switch.

This turns off the boost indicator lamp and turns on the overboost buzzer and alarm indicator lamp. A high engine oil temperature warning indicator system is incorporated with the boost warning system. If this condition occurs during turbocharging, the oil temperature warning lamp also will flash.

Figure 19-40 shows the circuit diagram of the warning system used on 1984 and later Ford 2.3-liter engines with a blow-through turbocharger, where fuel is injected downstream of the compressor. Although this system uses separate low- and high-pressure switches, it functions in essentially the same way, but without the oil temperature warning.

Malfunction Indicator Lamp (MIL)

Vehicles with electronic engine control systems generally have a computer-operated warning lamp on the instrument panel to indicate the need for service. In the past, this was called a CHECK ENGINE, SERVICE ENGINE SOON, POWER LOSS, or POWER LIMITED LAMP according to carmaker. To eliminate confusion, all domestic manufacturers now refer to it as a MALFUNCTION INDICATOR LAMP (MIL).

The MIL has a dual function: it alerts the driver to a malfunction in one of the monitored systems, and can be used to retrieve the fault or trouble codes stored in the computer memory by grounding a test terminal in the diagnostic connector. Like other warning lamps, the MIL comes on briefly as a bulb check when the ignition is turned on.

Antilock Brake System (ABS) Warning Lamp

Vehicles with ABS have a computer-operated amber ANTILOCK warning lamp in addition to the MIL and the standard red BRAKE lamp. The ANTILOCK lamp serves the same functions for the ABS that the MIL does for engine control systems:

- Lights to warn of a system problem that inhibits ABS operation
- Retrieves trouble codes in the same way as the MIL
- Lights briefly at the beginning of an ignition cycle as a bulb check and to notify the driver that self-diagnostics are taking place.

Buzzers, Tone Generators, Chimes, and Bells

Buzzers are a special type of warning instrument. They produce a loud warning sound during certain operating conditions, such as:

- Seatbelts not fastened
- Door open with key in ignition
- Lights left on with engine off
- Excessive vehicle speed.

A typical buzzer, figure 19-41, operates in the same way as a horn. Instead of moving a diaphragm, the vibrating armature itself creates the sound waves.

In figure 19-41, two conditions are required to sound the buzzer: the door must be open, and the key must be in the ignition. These conditions close both switches and allow current to flow through the buzzer armature and coil.

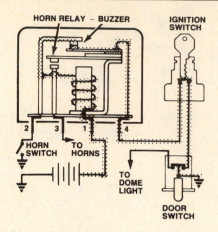

Figure 19-42. General Motors cars may have a buzzer built into the horn relay. Here, the buzzer is activated because both the door switch and the key switch are closed. (Oldsmobile)

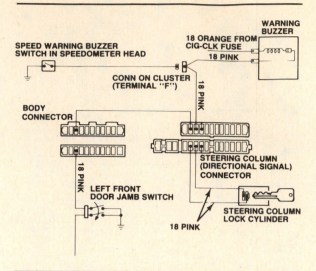

Figure 19-44. In this circuit, one buzzer responds both to excessive speed and to driver door position. (Buick)

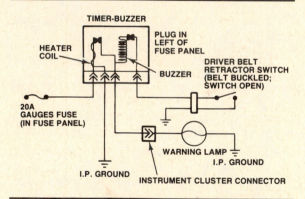

Figure 19-43. This buzzer will only sound for a few seconds each time it is activated because of the circuit breaker and heater coil built into the unit. (Oldsmobile)

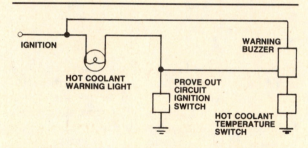

Figure 19-45. This warning buzzer will be activated if engine coolant temperature rises above a safe level. (Ford)

Most warning buzzers are separate units mounted on the fuse panel or behind the instrument panel. General Motors vehicles may have a buzzer built into the horn relay, figure 19-42. When the ignition key is left in the switch and the door is opened, a small amount of current flows through the relay coil. The magnetic field is strong enough to operate the buzzer, but it is not strong enough to close the horn contacts.

Buzzers are usually activated by grounding switches. A timing circuit can be built into the buzzer by winding a heater coil around an internal circuit breaker, figure 19-43, and connecting the heater coil directly to ground. When current flows to the buzzer, a small amount of current flows through the heater coil to ground. When the coil is hot enough, it will open the circuit breaker and keep it open. Current through the buzzer will stop even though the grounding switch is still closed.

Some typical buzzer warning circuits are shown in figures 19-44 and 19-45. Figure 19-45 includes a prove-out circuit branch. This has a manual grounding switch that the driver can close to check that the bulb and buzzer are still working. Some prove-out circuits operate when the ignition switch is at Start, to show the driver if any bulbs or buzzers have failed.

Tone generators, chimes, and bells are mechanical devices that produce a particular sound when voltage is applied across a sound bar. Various sounds are obtained by varying the voltage. Like buzzers, they are replaced if defective.

ELECTRONIC INSTRUMENT CIRCUITS

Electronic instruments used on late-model cars have the same purpose as the traditional analog instruments: they display vehicle operating information to the driver. The primary difference between the electronic and traditional systems is the way in which the information is displayed.

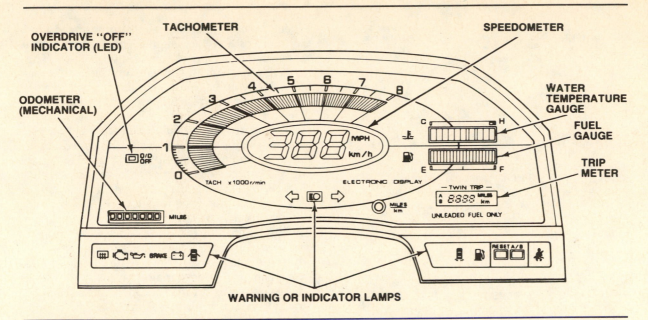

Figure 19-46. Toyota's electronic display is a digital combination meter which uses a colored liquid crystal display (LCD) panel. (Toyota)

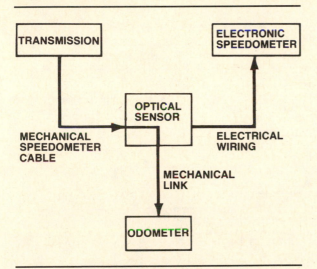

Figure 19-47. A block diagram of Ford's electronic speedometer system used in Lincolns and Mark VIs of the early 1980s. (Ford)

Like analog instruments, electronic instruments receive inputs from a sensor or a sending unit. The information is displayed in various ways, as we will see later in this chapter. Depending upon the gauge function and the manufacturer's design, the display may be digital numbers or a vertical, horizontal or curved bar, figure 19-46.

The following paragraphs give three examples of how electronic instruments function.

The first example is in figure 19-47, which shows a block diagram of a Ford electronic

■ Seatbelt-Starter Interlocks

During 1974 and early 1975, U.S. Federal safety standards required a seatbelt-starter interlock system on all new cars. The system required front-seat occupants to fasten their seatbelts before the car could be started. This particular standard was repealed by an act of Congress in 1975. Now, most interlock systems have been disabled so that only a warning lamp and buzzer remain.

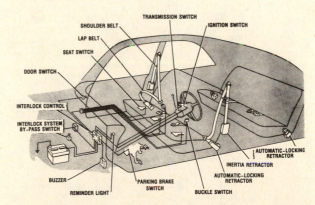

Interlock systems use a solid-state or relay module to control current flow to the starter solenoid or starter relay. Switches in the front seat cushions signal the module when someone is sitting in the seat. When the seatbelts are fastened at all occupied seats, the module will complete the starter system control circuit. In case of a module failure, a bypass switch in the engine compartment can be activated by hand to close the solenoid circuit.

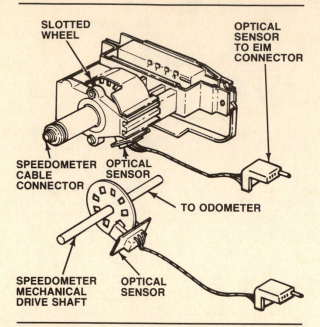

Figure 19-48. The optical sensor is used to translate mechanical movement into an electrical signal for Ford's electronic speedometer. (Ford)

speedometer system. The electronic speedometer receives a voltage signal representing vehicle speed from an optical sensor, figure 19-48. The optical sensor input comes from the speedometer cable, connected to the speedometer drive gear in the transmission case. As the cable rotates, it turns the slotted wheel through the optical sensor. This breaks the optical field and generates an electrical pulse to the speedometer display. The number of pulses generated by the optical sensor is proportional to vehicle speed. Figure 19-49 shows the electrical circuit diagram for the electronic speedometer.

The second example is shown in figure 19-50A, picturing the basic concept behind a more sophisticated electronic speedometer than the one just described. The display device used can be a quartz analog (swing needle) display or a digital readout. The speed signal in this system originates from a small a.c. voltage generator with four magnetic fields called a permanent magnet (PM) generator. This device usually is installed at the transmission or

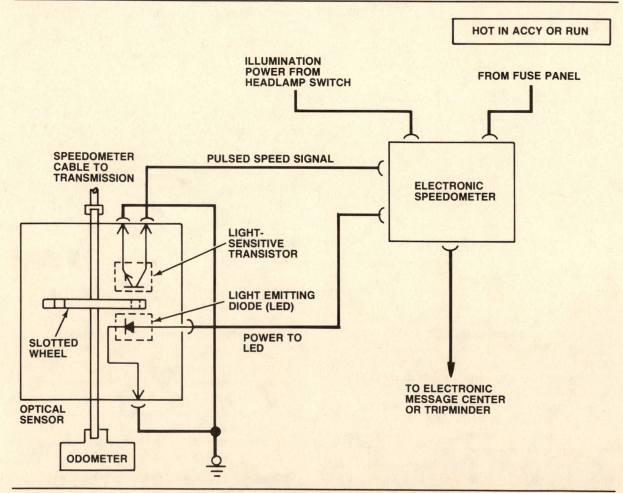

Figure 19-49. This circuit diagram shows the electrical relationship of the optical sensor to the speedometer. (Ford)

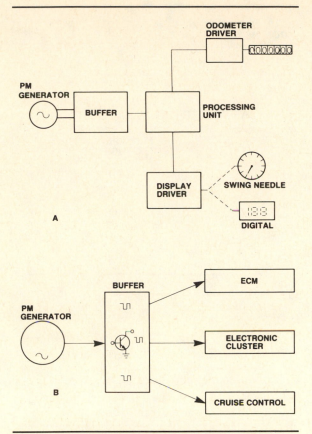

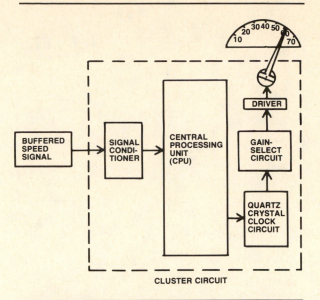

Figure 19-51. The buffered signal passes to a signal conditioner, which transmits it to the CPU where a quartz clock circuit ensures accuracy. After processing, the signal goes to a gain-select circuit, which sends it to the driver circuit for analog display.

Figure 19-50. GM's electronic speedometer uses a permanent magnet (PM) generator instead of an optical sensor. In A, the buffer translates the PM generator analog signals into digital signals for the processor, which activates the display driver to operate an analog or a digital display. In B, the buffer toggles voltage on and off to interpret vehicle speed to the electronic cluster. (GM)

transaxle speedometer gear adapter and is driven like the speedometer cable on conventional systems.

As the PM generator rotates, it generates an a.c. voltage of four pulses per turn, with voltage and frequency increasing as speed increases. The unit pulses 4004 times per mile of travel (2488 times per kilometer) with a frequency output of 1.112 oscillations per second (Hertz) per mile per hour of travel (0.691 Hertz per kilometer per hour of travel).

Since the PM generator output is analog, a buffer is used to translate its signals into digital input for the processing unit. The processing unit sends a voltage back to the buffer, which switches the voltage on and off and interprets it as vehicle speed changes. If the instrument cluster has its own internal buffer as part of the cluster circuitry, the PM generator signal will go directly to the speedometer.

On some systems, the buffer may contain more than one switching function, figure

19-50B, as it handles the ECM and cruise control systems. These secondary switching functions run at half the speed of the speedometer switching operation or 0.556 Hz/mph (0.3456 Hz/km/h).

If the instrument cluster uses a quartz analog display, figure 19-51, the gauge is similar to the two-coil electromagnetic gauge discussed earlier. This type of gauge is often called a swing needle or air-core gauge and does not return to zero when the ignition is turned off. When the car begins to move, the buffered speed signal is conditioned and sent to the central processing unit (CPU). The CPU processes the digital input using a quartz crystal clock circuit and sends it to a gain-select circuit, where it is transferred to a driver circuit. The driver circuit then sends the correct voltages to the gauge coils to move the pointer and indicate the car's speed.

Virtually the same process is followed when a digital display is used, figure 19-52, with the following minor differences in operation:

- The CPU can be directed to display the information in either English or metric units. A select function sends the data along different circuits according to the switch position.
- The driver circuit is responsible for turning on the selected display segments at the correct intensity.

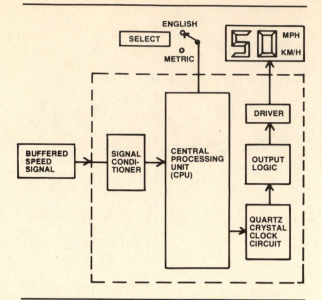

Figure 19-52. The digital cluster circuit is similar to the analog circuit, but an output logic circuit is used instead of a gain select circuit.

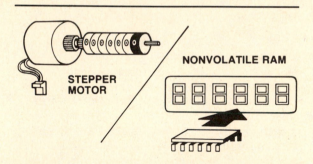

Figure 19-53. Electronic odometers may use a stepper motor or a nonvolatile RAM chip for mileage display. (GM)

The odometer used with electronic speedometers can be electromechanical using a stepper motor, figure 19-53A, or an IC chip using a **nonvolatile RAM**, figure 19-53B.

The electromechanical type is similar to the conventional odometer, differing primarily in the way in which the numbers are driven. A stepper motor takes digital-pulsed voltages from the speedometer circuit board at half the buffered speed signal discussed earlier. This provides a very accurate accounting of accumulated mileage.

The IC chip retains accumulated mileage in its special non-volatile RAM which is not lost when power is removed. Since its memory cannot be turned back, the use of this chip virtually eliminates one of the frauds often associated with the sale of used cars.

The third example is shown in figure 19-54, which is the circuit diagram for a Ford electron-

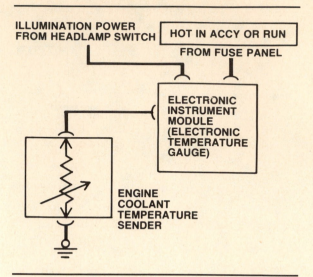

Figure 19-54. Ford's electronic temperature gauge circuit is similar to that of an analog gauge. (Ford)

ic temperature gauge. The coolant temperature sensor is a thermistor with high resistance at low temperatures and low resistance at high temperatures. When a cold engine is first started, the sensor's resistance is very high, resulting in a low voltage output to the gauge display, which translates into a low coolant temperature reading on the display. As coolant temperature increases, sensor resistance decreases. This results in a higher voltage output to the gauge display, which translates into a higher coolant temperature reading.

Trip Computers

Electronic instruments may stand alone, they may be part of a microprocessor-controlled system, figure 19-55, or they may be incorporated into an electronic "message center" often called a trip computer. Figure 19-56 shows the sensors and display devices (actuators) used in the electronic message center system on some Lincoln and Mark VI models. Figure 19-57 shows the circuit diagram for the system.

While the electronic instruments function on their own in this system, the inputs they receive are also applied to the control module, which uses them for calculations. For example, when the driver pushes the appropriate buttons or keys to activate such calculations, fuel gauge and speed indicator signals are used by

Nonvolatile RAM: Random access memory (RAM) that retains its information when current to the chip is removed.

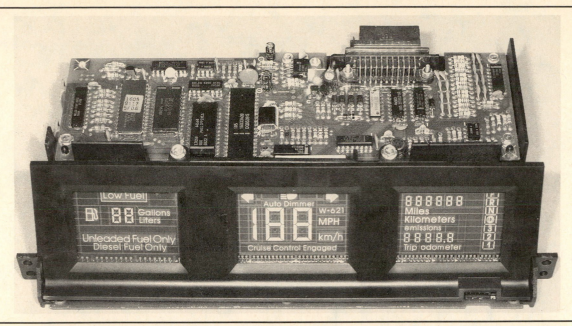

Figure 19-55. The 1986 Cadillac digital instrument cluster is a microprocessor-based system which responds to input from the ECM and BCM to provide blue-green vacuum fluorescent displays.

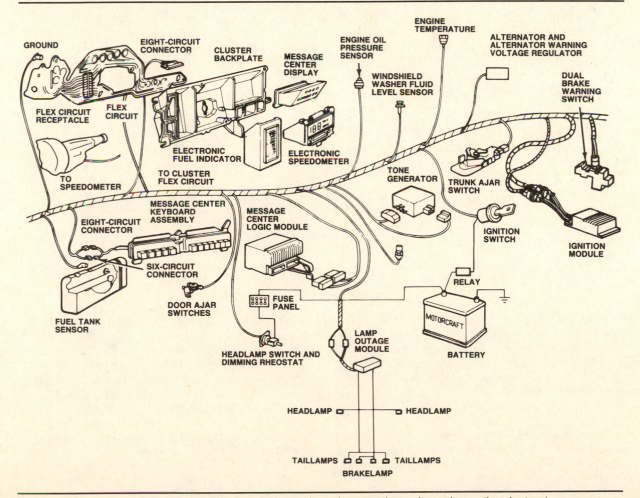

Figure 19-56. These sensors, display devices (actuators), and processing units make up the electronic message center system used on Lincolns and Mark VIs of the early 1980s. (Ford)

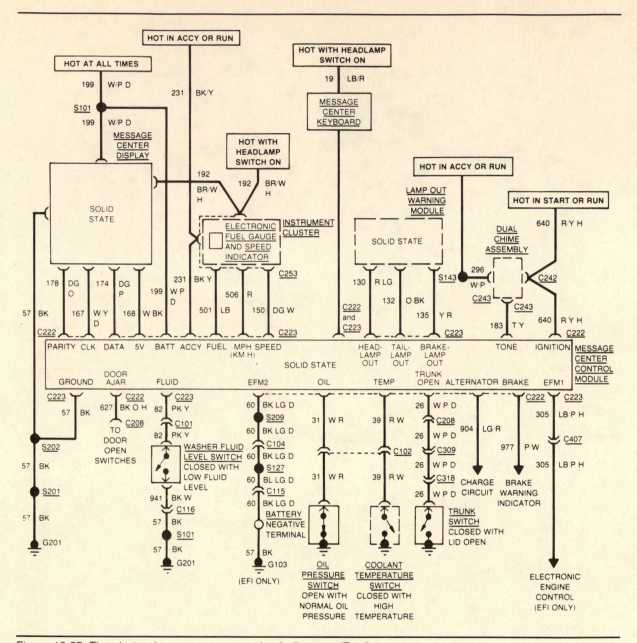

Figure 19-57. The electronic message center circuit diagram. (Ford)

the control module to calculate fuel consumption, mileage and fuel remaining. The control module processes the signals and sends an appropriate signal to the message center display.

Warning indications to the control module start with a switch closing to ground. The ground signal is interpreted by the control module as an abnormal condition and processed by the microcomputer, which then sends an appropriate signal to the message center display. On engines with fuel injection, the control module receives an additional ground signal and an input from the electronic control assembly (ECA). This allows the module to calculate

instantaneous fuel economy when desired by the driver. Pressing the proper button brings up the trip average fuel economy, followed a few seconds later by the instantaneous fuel economy reading. This lets the driver see how engine load changes affect fuel economy.

The message center keyboard contains the pushbuttons to activate the trip computer functions. Each pushbutton is a switch connected to the control module. When a switch is pressed, it provides a ground path to the control module. The keyboard performs three functions. It lets the driver:

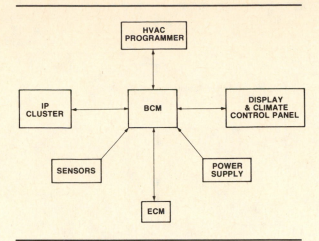

Figure 19-58. Sophisticated electronic systems are composed of several computers and use a central computer (GM calls it a body control module) to manage the system. (GM)

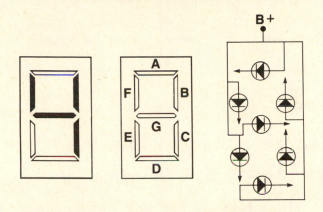

Figure 19-59. Selective application of voltage through the diodes composing a light-emitting diode (LED) result in an alphanumeric display. (GM)

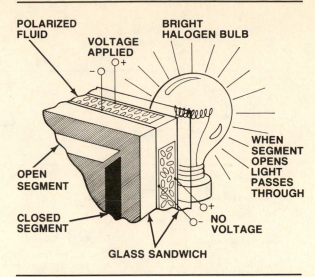

Figure 19-60. Light passes through polarized fluid to create the liquid crystal display (LCD). (GM)

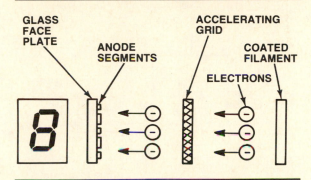

Figure 19-61. In a vacuum fluorescent display, voltage applied selectively to segment anodes makes the fluorescent material glow. (Chrysler)

- Program the control module with data about time, date, and trip information
- Select the information to be displayed on the message center
- Check all systems monitored by the electronic message center system.

Body Control Module (BCM) Computers

When more than one computer is used on a vehicle, it is often desirable to link their operations. The body control module (BCM) used on some late-model GM cars is an example. The BCM manages the communications for the multiple computer system, figure 19-58, using a network of sensors, switches, and other microprocessors to monitor vehicle operating conditions. Certain components also provide the BCM with feedback signals. These tell the BCM whether the con ponents are responding to the BCM commands properly. Like the electronic control module (ECM) which operates the engine control system, the BCM has built-in diagnostics to help locate and correct a system malfunction.

Displays
Electronic displays are used in electronic instrument clusters and other electronic readout devices. Unlike electromechanical instruments, they do not require a digital-to-analog conversion; they're compatible with the digital signals from a computer. The major types of displays that are used with electronic instruments are described in the following paragraphs.

Light-emitting diode (LED)
The light-emitting diode (LED) is a semiconductor diode that transmits light when electrical current is passed through it, figure 19-59.

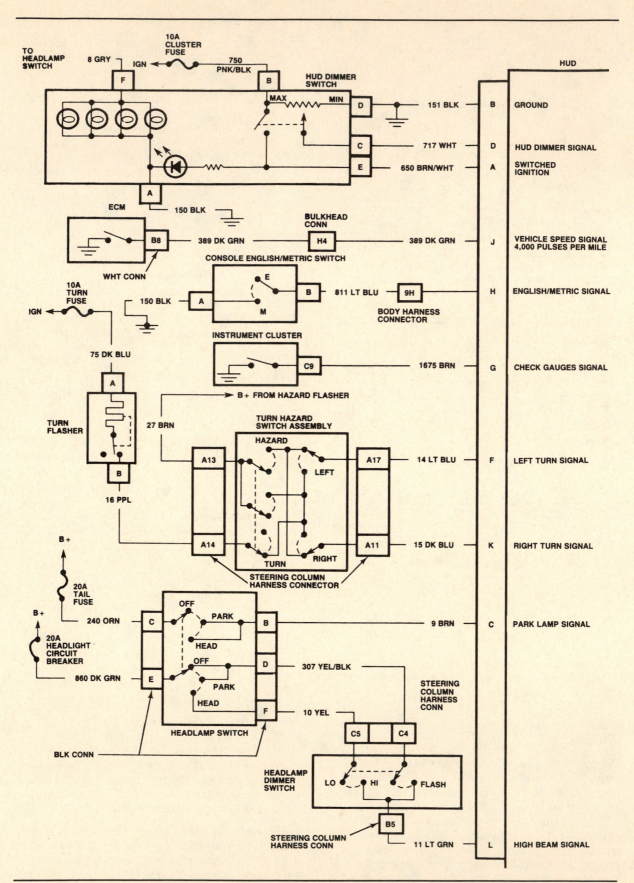

Figure 19-62. A wiring schematic of the HUD system as used by Oldsmobile. (Oldsmobile)

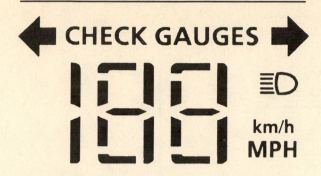

Figure 19-63. The HUD system display image. (Oldsmobile)

An LED display is composed of small dotted segments arranged to form numbers and letters when selected segments are turned on. The LED are usually red, yellow, or green. LEDs have two major drawbacks:

- While easily seen in the dark, they are difficult to read in direct sunlight.
- They consume considerable power relative to their brightness.

Liquid crystal display (LCD)

The **liquid crystal display (LCD)** uses sandwiches of special glass containing electrodes and polarized fluid to display numbers and characters. Light cannot pass through the polarized fluid until voltage is applied. The display is very dense, however, and the various special filters used to provide colors create even more density. For this reason, halogen lights are generally placed behind the display, figure 19-60. Although LCDs perform slowly in cold ambient temperatures, require proper alignment, and are very delicate, they have two big advantages:

- They consume very little power relative to their brightness.
- They can be driven by a microprocessor through an interfacing output circuit.

Vacuum fluorescent display (VFD)

This is the most commonly used display for automotive electronic instruments, primarily because of its durability and bright display qualities. The **vacuum fluorescent display (VFD)** generates light similar to a television picture tube, with free electrons from a heated filament striking phosphor material that emits a blue-green light, figure 19-61.

The anode segments are coated with a fluorescent material such as phosphorous. The filament is resistance wire, heated by electrical current flow. The filament coating produces the free electrons, which are accelerated by the electric field generated by the voltage on the accelerating grid. High voltage is applied only to the anode of those segments required to form the characters to be displayed. Since the anode is at a higher voltage than the fine wire mesh grid, the electrons pass through the grid. The phosphors on the segment anodes impressed with high voltage glows very brightly when struck by electrons; those receiving no voltage do not glow. The instrument computer determines the segments necessary to emit light for any given message and applies the correct sequences of voltage at the anodes.

VFD displays are extremely bright, and their intensity must be controlled for night viewing. This can be done by varying the voltage on the accelerating grid: the higher the voltage, the brighter the display. Intensity can also be controlled by pulse width dimming, or turning the display on and off very rapidly while controlling the duration of on-time. This is similar to the pulse-width modulation of a carburetor mixture control solenoid or a fuel injector. The on-off action occurs so rapidly that it cannot be detected by the human eye.

Cathode ray tube (CRT)

The latest display device to be used in automotive instrumentation is the **cathode ray tube (CRT)**, as used in the 1985 Lincoln Mark VII Comtech or the 1986 Buick Riviera. The CRT is essentially the same as that used in an oscilloscope or a television set. CRT's function with an electron beam generated by an electron gun located at the rear of the tube. The CRT consists of a cathode that emits electrons and an anode that attracts them. Electrons are "shot" in a thin beam from the back of the tube. Permanent magnets around the outside neck of the tube and plates grouped around the beam on the inside of the tube shape the beam. A tube-shape anode that surrounds the beam ac-

Liquid Crystal Display (LCD): An indicator consisting of a sandwich of glass containing electrodes and polarized fluid. Voltage applied to the fluid allows light to pass through it.

Vacuum Fluorescent Display (VFD): An indicator in which electrons from a heated filament strike a phosphor material which emits light.

Cathode Ray Tube (CRT): An electron beam tube with a cathode at one end and an anode at the screen end. A "ray" of electrons shot from the cathode to the anode creates a pattern on the luminescent screen.

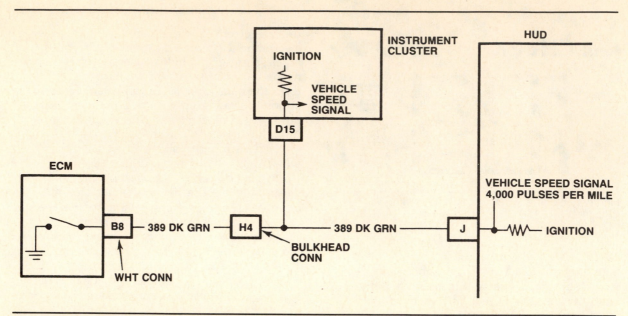

Figure 19-64. The vehicle speed sensor circuit between the ECM and HUD module. (Oldsmobile)

celerates it as it leaves the electron gun. The beam has so much momentum that the electrons pass through the anode and strike a coating of phosphorus on the screen, causing the screen to glow at these points. The control plates are used to move the beam back and forth on the screen, causing different parts of it to illuminate. The result is a display (oscilloscope) or a picture (television).

Menu-Driven Instrumentation

The CRT used in the 1986 and later Buick Riviera and other models has a touch-sensitive mylar switch panel installed over its screen. This panel contains ultrathin wires which are coded by row and column. Touching the screen in designated places blocks a light beam and triggers certain switches in the panel according to the display mode desired. The switches in turn send a signal to the control circuitry, which responds by displaying the requested information on the CRT screen. In principle, this type of instrumentation combines two personal computer attributes: it has touch-screen control and is menu driven.

By **menu-driven**, we mean that the program operating the CRT offers the driver several choices from a list or "menu" of selections regarding many areas of vehicle operation. For example, suppose you touch DIAGNOSTICS. This brings up a another menu allowing you to choose between four main and one optional categories: electrical, powertrain, brakes, vehicle, and lamp (optional). Each category displays a box that shows "OK" if the system is

working properly. If problems exist, additional display screens can be summoned to lead you through the troubleshooting routines. In other modes, the CRT menus allow you to control or check the air conditioning, radio, trip monitor, and gauge readings.

Head-Up Display System

The Head-Up Display (HUD) was introduced by Pontiac as standard equipment on the 1990 Grand Prix Turbo. After making modifications and refinements in the system, a Generation II HUD was offered as optional equipment on certain 1991 and later GM cars.

This electronic instrumentation system, figure 19-62, consists of a special windshield, a HUD unit containing a computer module, and a system-specific dimmer switch. The HUD unit processes various inputs which are part of the instrument cluster and projects frequently used driver information on the windshield area for viewing from the driver's seat. The dimmer switch provides system power for the computer module, varies the intensity of the display unit, and can change the vertical position of the display image through a mechanical cable drive system.

When the ignition is turned on, the HUD unit performs a self-check routine and projects the following image, figure 19-63, for approximately 3.5 seconds:

- Turn signal indicators
- High-beam indicator
- Check gauges indicator

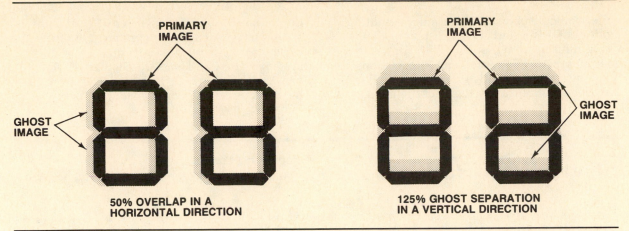

Figure 19-65. If the double image or ghosting on the windshield exceeds that shown above, the windshield should be replaced. (Oldsmobile)

- Speed (km/h or mph) indicator
- All segments of the digital speedometer.

After completing the self-check, the system begins normal operation.

The ECM provides vehicle speed information for HUD operation by completing a ground path to the HUD unit 4,000 times per mile, figure 19-64. Each time the HUD unit recognizes a voltage drop at terminal J, it counts one pulse. By counting the pulses per second, the HUD unit can determine vehicle speed and project the corresponding figure on the windshield display.

A normal problem with the HUD system is called image ghosting. This faint secondary image appears to float above or to one side of the brighter primary image, figure 19-65. The special windshields used with HUD systems are selected by testing all production windshields for the problem and selecting those that show a minimal ghosting effect. Replacing a HUD windshield with one chosen at random will likely result in an unacceptable amount of ghosting.

SUMMARY

An automotive horn circuit can be a simple series circuit, or it can use a relay to control current flow through the horns. The horn switch is a normally open push-pull switch that is operated by the driver. Horns use electromagnetism to vibrate a diaphragm and to produce sound waves.

Windshield wiper and washer circuits have many variations. They can include a permanent magnet motor or one with electro-magnetic fields. The park position can be at the bottom edge of the windshield or below the bottom edge. An intermittent wipe feature can be driver- or speed-controlled. Each of these variations requires slightly different circuitry. Washer pumps can be mounted at the cleaner reservoir or on the wiper motor. Pumps are not serviced, but are replaced.

Electric cooling fans are used on vehicles with transverse engine placement. They may also be used with the engine-driven pump on longitudinal mounted engines. Dual fan systems often are used with turbocharged vehicles. Cooling fan circuits work with a relay controlled by a coolant temperature switch. When used with air conditioning systems, the air conditioning relay also is wired into the fan circuit so the cooling fan will run whenever the air conditioning is on. Some fans have an after-run feature that keeps the fan running for a predetermined length of time after the engine is shut off. This time duration is controlled by a timer in the relay.

Instruments include gauges and warning lamps. There are various types of gauges, including mechanical, bimetallic, electromagnetic, and electronic. Warning lamps can be lit by a voltage drop, a grounding switch, a ground sensor, or fiber optics. Late-model vehicles may have a digital display instead of traditional analog gauges. Digital displays can be individual or they can be part of a more elaborate vehicle electronic system, such as a trip computer or message center. Body control module (BCM) computers act as a manager of other computers in a comprehensive vehicle system.

Menu Driven: A computer program that allows the user to select choices from a list or ''menu''. As each choice is made, another menu allows the user to make another choice to achieve the desired end result.

Electronic displays may use a light-emitting diode (LED), a liquid crystal display (LCD), a vacuum fluorescent display (VFD), or a cathode ray tube (CRT) to transmit information. Some instrumentation is menu driven, giving the user an opportunity to select the information to be displayed. Touch-sensitive screens similar to personal computers are used instead of keyboards or pushbuttons on late-model systems. The GM Head-Up Display (HUD) projects useful vehicle information in front of the driver near the windshield.

Review Questions
Choose the single most correct answer.
Compare your answers with the correct answers on page 431.

1. Horn relays are sometimes included in the horn circuit to:
   a. Allow the use of two horns in the circuit
   b. Decrease the amount of current needed to activate the horn
   c. Increase the amount of current needed to activate the horn
   d. Allow the horn button to be placed on the end of a stalk on the steering column

2. Horn circuits are generally protected by a:
   a. Fuse
   b. Fusible link
   c. Either a or b
   d. Neither a nor b

3. The _____ within the wiper motor ensures that when the motor is turned off the wiper arms will be brought to the bottom position.
   a. Wiper switch
   b. Park switch
   c. Recycle relay
   d. Park/neutral switch

4. Two-speed wiper motors generally use _____ to achieve the two speeds.
   a. Cams
   b. Reduction gears
   c. Speed-control brushes
   d. Gear reduction

5. All three-speed wiper motors have _____ fields.
   a. Electromagnetic
   b. Permanent magnet
   c. Two series
   d. Two shunt

6. Which of the following is *not* a reason why warning lamps have replaced gauges in automobiles?
   a. Cheaper to manufacture
   b. Cheaper to install
   c. More accurate
   d. Easier to understand

7. Temperature compensation in bimetallic gauges is accomplished by:
   a. Current flow through the heater coil
   b. The shape of the bimetallic strip
   c. An external resistor in the circuit
   d. Hermetically sealing the unit

8. Gauges with three-coil movements are most often used by:
   a. General Motors
   b. Ford
   c. Chrysler
   d. American Motors

9. An oil pressure warning lamp is usually controlled by:
   a. Voltage drop
   b. Ground switch
   c. Ground sensor
   d. Manual switch

10. The sending unit in the fuel gauge uses a:
    a. Fixed resistor
    b. Zener diode
    c. Float
    d. Diaphragm

11. Buzzers are a special type of warning device that are activated by:
    a. Voltage drop
    b. Ground switches
    c. Diaphragms
    d. Optical fibers

12. Which of the following is *not* used in the electric cooling fan circuit of an air conditioned vehicle?
    a. Coolant temperature switch and fan relay
    b. A/C relay
    c. Air temperature sensing switch and after-run timer
    d. Shuttle switch

13. In GM computer-controlled electric fan circuits:
    a. The BCM switches the control line voltage on/off with a pulse width modulation
    b. The fan control module switches the ground on/off
    c. Both a and b
    d. Neither a nor b

14. Electromagnetic gauges do *not* use a:
    a. Mechanical movement
    b. D'Arsonval movement
    c. Air core movement
    d. Two- or three-coil movement

15. Which type of gauge does *not* use an instrument voltage regulator (IVR)?
    a. D'Arsonval movement
    b. Air core movement
    c. Two-coil movement
    d. Three-coil movement

16. Technician A says that GM's electronic speedometer interprets vehicle speed by using a buffer to switch the voltage on/off.

    Technician B says that GM's electronic speedometer uses a buffer to translate the analog input of the PM generator into digital signals.

    Who is right?
    a. A only
    b. B only
    c. Both A and B
    d. Neither A nor B

17. Technician A says that an electronic speedometer cannot use a stepper motor to provide the display.

    Technician B says that the use of nonvolatile RAM prevents the odometer from being turned back.

    Who is right?
    a. A only
    b. B only
    c. Both A and B
    d. Neither A nor B

18. An electronic display device using electrodes and polarized fluid to create numbers and characters is called:
    a. LCD
    b. LED
    c. VFD
    d. CRT

19. Which electronic display device is most frequently used because it is very bright, consumes relatively little power, and can provide a wide variety of colors through the use of filters?
    a. LCD
    b. LED
    c. VFD
    d. CRT

20. Which electronic display device is difficult to read in daylight and consumes considerable power relative to its brightness?
    a. LCD
    b. LED
    c. VFD
    d. CRT

20

Body Electrical Systems (Accessories)

Electrical accessories provide driver and passenger comfort, convenience, and entertainment. New electrical accessories are introduced every year, but some systems have been common for many years. Such systems increasingly are being automated with computer control. This chapter will explain the electrical operation of some of the common accessory systems.

HEATING AND AIR CONDITIONING SYSTEMS

Although heating and air conditioning systems rely heavily on mechanical and vacuum controls, a good deal of electrical circuitry also is involved. Since the late 1970s, air conditioning systems have become increasingly "smart", relying on solid-state modules or microprocessors for their operation. This also has complicated the job of servicing such systems.

Heater Fan

Heating systems use a fan attached to a permanent-magnet, variable-speed blower motor to force warm air into the passenger compartment, figure 20-1. The higher the voltage applied to the motor, the faster it runs. A switch mounted on the instrument panel controls the blower operation, figure 20-2. In most heating systems, the switch controls blower speed by directing the motor ground circuit current through or around the coils of a resistor block, figure 20-3, mounted near the motor.

When the switch is off, the ground circuit is open and the blower motor does not run. Some systems used in the 1970s, however, were wired so that the blower motor operated on low speed whenever the ignition was on. When the switch is turned to its low position, voltage is applied across all of the resistor coils and the motor runs at a low speed. Moving the switch to its next position bypasses one of the resistor coils. This allows more current to the blower motor, increasing its speed. When the switch is set at its highest position, all of the resistors are bypassed and full current flows to the motor, which then operates at full speed.

In some GM systems, a relay is used between the high switch position and the blower motor. Ford incorporates a thermal limiter in its resistor block, figure 20-3. Current flows through the limiter at all blower speeds. If current passing through the limiter heats it to 212°F (100°C), the limiter opens and turns off the blower motor. When this happens, the entire resistor block must be replaced.

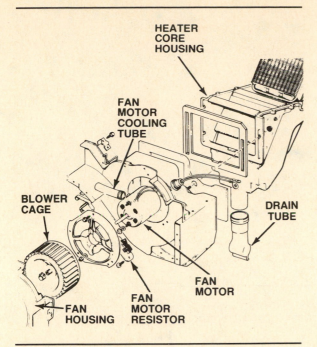

Figure 20-1. An electric motor drives the heater fan.

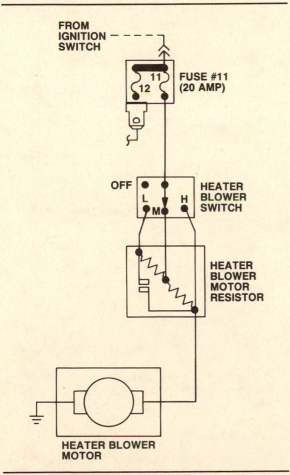

Figure 20-2. The fan control switch routes current through paths of varying resistance to control motor speed. (Chrysler)

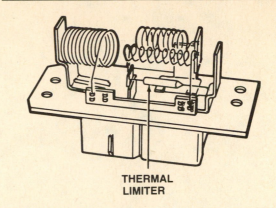

Figure 20-3. Blower motor resistors are installed on a ''block'' near the motor. Some resistor blocks have a thermal limiter. (Ford)

Air Conditioning Fan and Compressor Clutch

Air conditioning fan controls are similar to heater controls. In most cars that have both heating and air conditioning systems, the same blower motor is shared by both systems, figure 20-4. One or more switches route current through different resistors to control the blower motor speed.

In addition to the fan switch, the control assembly in the passenger compartment contains an air conditioning clutch switch and a clutch switch activated when the function selector lever is set to the Defrost position. These switches are used to operate the belt-driven compressor. A compressor that operates constantly wastes energy. To use energy most efficiently, the compressor has an electromagnetic clutch, figure 20-5. This clutch locks and unlocks the compressor pulley with the compressor shaft. The compressor will only operate when the clutch switch is closed and the electromagnetic clutch is engaged.

Earlier air conditioning systems used either a suction throttling valve or an evaporator pressure-control valve to control compressor operation. Most recent air conditioning systems use a clutch-cycling pressure switch or a pressure-cycling switch to control compressor clutch operation. This pressure-operated electric switch generally is wired in series with the clutch field coil. The switch closes when the pressure on the low side of the refrigerant system rises to a specified value, engaging the clutch. When system pressure drops to a predetermined value, the switch opens to shut off the compressor. The switch operates to control evaporator core pressure and prevent icing on the cooling coils.

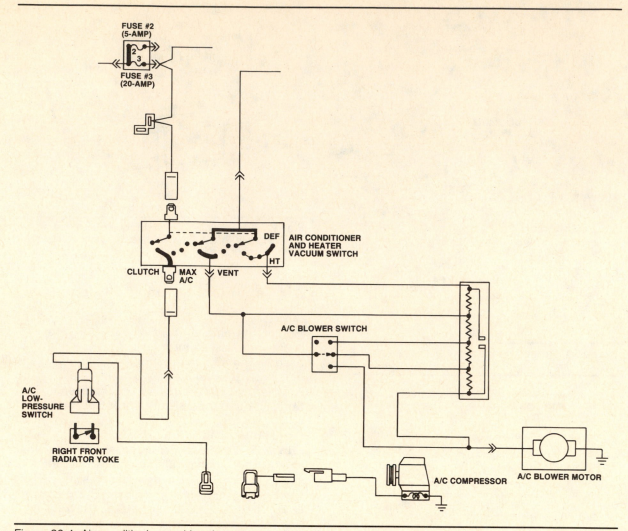

Figure 20-4. Air conditioning and heating systems share the same fan. (Chrysler)

Air conditioning systems may also use low- and high-pressure switches as safety devices:

- The low-pressure switch usually is closed during normal compressor operation and opens only when refrigerant is lost or ambient temperature is below freezing.
- The high-pressure switch usually is closed to permit compressor operation. However, if system pressure becomes excessive (generally 360 to 400 psi or 2,480 to 2,760 kPa), the switch acts as a relief valve and opens to shut off the compressor. Once pressure drops to a safe level, the switch will close again and permit the compressor to operate.
- A pressure relief valve on the compressor high-pressure side may be used instead of a high-pressure switch. Some systems have a diode installed inside the compressor clutch connector to suppress any voltage spikes that might be produced by clutch circuit interruption.

Other compressor clutch controls may include:

- A power steering pressure or cutout switch to shut the compressor off whenever high power steering loads are encountered, as during parking. The switch senses line pressure and opens or closes the circuit to the compressor clutch accordingly.
- A wide-open throttle (WOT) switch on the carburetor or accelerator pedal to open the circuit to the compressor clutch during full acceleration.
- A pressure-sensing switch in the transmission to override the WOT switch when the transmission is in high gear.

Automatic Temperature Control (ATC)

The basic underhood components of all air conditioning systems have already been described. As we have seen, they provide input to, and protection for, the refrigeration system.

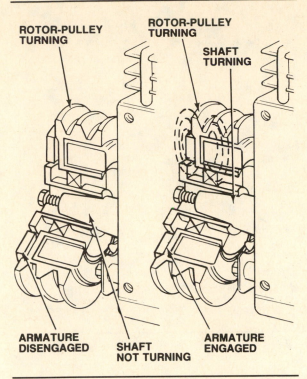

Figure 20-5. The electromagnetic clutch in this air conditioning compressor prevents the compressor from wasting energy.

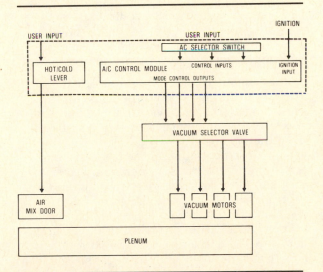

Figure 20-6. Manual air conditioning system block diagram. (GM)

All input to the air conditioning system begins with the control assembly mounted in the instrument panel. Temperature control can take three forms:

- Manual control
- Semiautomatic (programmer controlled)
- Fully automatic (microprocessor or body computer controlled).

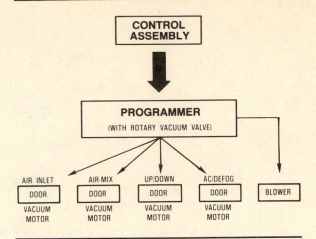

Figure 20-7. Semiautomatic A/C systems use an electronic programmer to translate mechanical control movement into actuator signals. (GM)

A manual temperature control system does not provide a method by which the system can function on its own. System input must be made by the user through the mechanical control assembly. Once the air conditioning switch is turned on, the temperature selection made, and the blower speed set, the system functions with vacuum-operated mode door actuators and a cable-actuated air-mix door. Figure 20-6 is a block diagram of such a system.

With a semiautomatic temperature control system, the user still selects the mode, but the actuators are electrically operated. Selecting the mode does not directly control the actuator; it creates an electrical input to an independent module or programmer, figure 20-7. On Chrysler vehicles, the electronic **servomotor** performs the programmer function, figure 20-8. Two sensors are added to inform the programmer of ambient temperature and in-car temperature, figure 20-9. Using its built-in power supply, the programmer calculates the resistance values provided by the temperature dial setting and the two additional sensors to move the cables or the vacuum selector valves. The semiautomatic temperature control system differs from a manual system primarily in the use of the programmer; actuators and doors are still moved by mechanical linkage and cables.

In a fully automatic temperature control system, the control assembly is electronic instead

Servomotor: An electric motor that is part of a feedback system used for automatic control of a mechanical device, such as in a temperature control system.

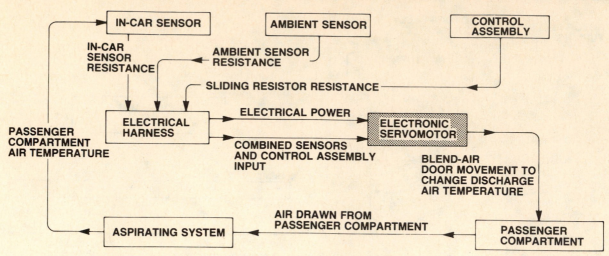

- LOW AIR TEMPERATURE AT SENSORS INCREASES RESISTANCE

- HIGH TEMPERATURE COMFORT LEVER SETTING INCREASES RESISTANCE

- HIGH RESISTANCES CAUSE SERVOMOTOR TO MOVE BLEND-AIR DOOR TO HIGHER REHEAT POSITION

Figure 20-8. An electronic servomotor takes the place of a programmer in Chrysler's semiautomatic A/C system. (Chrysler)

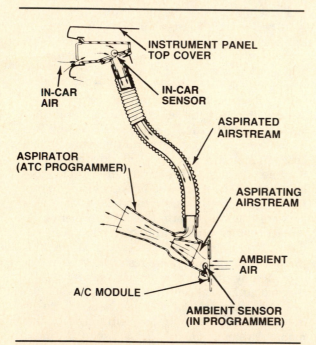

Figure 20-9. Resistance values from in-car and ambient temperature sensors are coupled with the resistance provided by the control assembly temperature dial to direct the programmer. (GM)

of manual. The user selects a mode and the temperature. The control assembly microprocessor sends the appropriate signals to the programmer to operate the system. Electric servomotors are used as actuators to send a feedback signal to the electronic control assembly, figure 20-10. This lets the control assembly monitor the system and make whatever adjustments are required to maintain the desired system temperature. Since the control assembly is constantly monitoring the system, it knows when a malfunction occurs and can transmit this information to the service technician.

Semiautomatic (programmer controlled)
The GM C61 system is representative of the semiautomatic control system. Once the mode and temperature have been selected by the user, the system automatically controls blower speed, air temperature, air delivery, system turn-on, and compressor operation. It does this with a programmer inserted between the control assembly and the actuators, figure 20-7, and two temperature sensors.

The ambient sensor installed in the programmer is exposed to ambient airflow through a hole in the module wall. The in-car sensor is located under the instrument panel top cover. Figure 20-9 shows the sensor locations. Both sensors are disc-type thermistors which provide a return voltage signal to the programmer based on variable resistance.

The programmer is built into the air conditioning control assembly, figure 20-11, and contains:

- A d.c. amplifier that receives a weak electrical signal from the sensors and control assembly and sends a strong output signal proportional to the input signal it receives

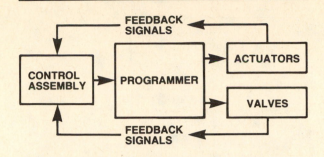

Figure 20-10. The actuators used in fully automatic A/C systems provide feedback signals which allow the control assembly to monitor system operation. (GM)

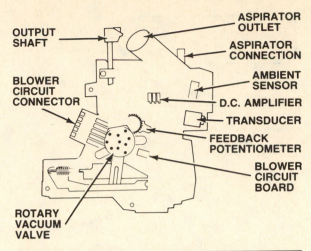

Figure 20-11. Components of the programmer used in GM's C61 A/C system. (GM)

- A transducer that converts the amplifier signal to a vacuum signal that actuates the vacuum motor
- A vacuum checking relay that has a check valve to maintain a constant vacuum signal to the vacuum motor and the rotary vacuum valve
- A vacuum motor to actuate the rotary shaft that drives the air-mix door link
- A rotary vacuum valve to route vacuum to control the mode doors and operate the heater water valve; this valve does the same job as a vacuum selector valve in a manual system
- A feedback potentiometer to inform the programmer of system corrections required by changing temperature demands.

A circuit board electrical switch is mounted on the base of the control assembly. The rotary switch contacts are positioned by the mode-select lever to provide the correct electrical path to the compressor clutch coil.

The temperature dial varies the resistance of a wire-wound rheostat installed directly above it. The programmer uses the total resistance provided by the temperature dial and temperature sensors to calculate how the system should function.

To use this type of system, the driver has only to set the control assembly in the Auto mode and select a temperature. From this point on, the programmer controls the system operation by automatically setting the mode and blower speed and adjusting the air-mix doors to maintain the desired air temperature.

Note that we have added nothing to the underhood portion of the air conditioning system. We have only modified the operation of the control system by adding a device to maintain temperature within a selected narrow range.

Fully automatic (microprocessor controlled)
The GM electronic touch climate control (ETCC) system is representative of the fully automatic control system. Once the mode and the temperature have been selected by the user, the system automatically controls blower speed, air temperature, air delivery, system turn-on, and compressor operation. It does this with an electronic control assembly containing a microprocessor.

While basic operation of an ETCC system is the same regardless of the car in which it's installed, there are several different versions of the system. The primary difference between each version is the kind of actuator and the way in which each is controlled:

- All ETCC systems use an electric servo-motor to control the air-mix door
- Systems on full-size cars use electrically operated mode door actuators
- Systems on compact and intermediate cars use vacuum-controlled mode door actuators operated by a programmer
- Luxury full-size systems use a power module to control blower speed and have a diagnostic mode to provide trouble codes for troubleshooting.

Once the user selects the operating mode and the temperature at the climate control panel, the microprocessor looks at the selected mode and temperature, the temperatures inside and outside the car, and the positioning of the mode and air-mix doors. Based on this input, the microprocessor decides what has to be done to bring the in-car temperature in line with the selected temperature. It can:

- Turn the compressor on or off as required
- Vary the blower motor speed to create the necessary air movement inside the car

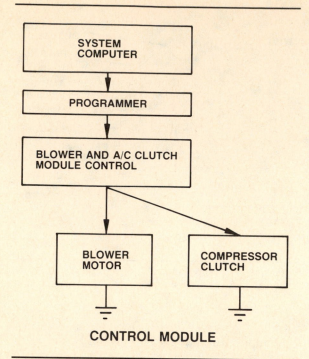

CONTROL MODULE

Figure 20-12. One ETCC system design uses a blower and A/C control module to control blower motor speed and compressor clutch operation. (GM)

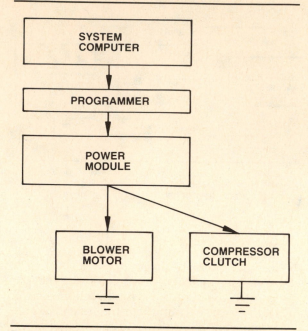

Figure 20-13. Another ETCC design controls blower motor speed and compressor clutch operation through a power module. (GM)

- Activate one or more vacuum or electric motors to open or close the doors that direct airflow in the passenger compartment.

In the ETCC system, compressor clutch cycling is controlled both by the underhood switches we looked at earlier and by the control assembly. On all but luxury systems, if the microprocessor decides to activate or deactivate the compressor or vary the blower speed, it sends a signal through the programmer to the blower and the air conditioning clutch control module, figure 20-12. A power transistor in the control module engages or disengages the compressor as required. A resistor strip in the temperature door actuator provides a control voltage to the microprocessor for infinitely variable blower motor speeds. When the luxury-series microprocessor decides to activate or deactivate the compressor or vary the blower speed, it sends a signal through the programmer to the power module, figure 20-13.

There also are differences in the way in which the compressor is cycled. If the system uses a power module, the compressor clutch is grounded through the low-pressure switch, figure 20-14A. The power module cycles power to the compressor clutch. In systems with a blower and air conditioning clutch control module, the compressor clutch power is received through a fuse and the power steering cutout switch or diode; the module cycles the ground circuit to the compressor.

ETCC systems with a diagnostic mode store a trouble code if a malfunction occurs in the system, as determined by its feedback signals. For example, if the potentiometer signal from the air-mix door tells the microprocessor that the door cannot reach the position that the system requires, the microprocessor will register a trouble code. When the service technician pushes the proper keys, the system displays a numeric code on the climate control panel. As with trouble codes in other electronic systems, the carmaker provides a specific troubleshooting chart for each code to locate the cause of the problem.

Fully automatic (BCM controlled)
The electronic climate control (ECC) system used by Cadillac is similar to the ETCC system just described. When used with a body control computer (BCM), the control assembly contains an electronic circuit board, but the BCM acts as the microprocessor. The BCM is constantly in touch with the climate control panel on the control assembly through a **data link**, or digital signal path (serial data line) provided for communication. The panel transfers user requests to the BCM, which sends the correct data to the panel for display.

Like the other semi- and fully automatic systems we have looked at, the user selects the mode and temperature. The system automati-

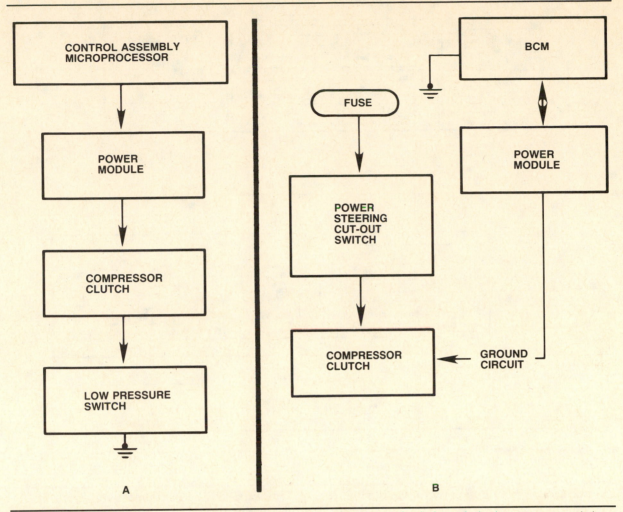

Figure 20-14. Non-BCM-controlled ECC systems ground the compressor clutch through the low-pressure switch and provide power through the power module (A). BCM-controlled ECC systems send power through a fuse and a power steering cutout switch, and cycle the ground through the power module (B). (GM)

cally controls blower speed, air temperature, air delivery, system turn-on, and compressor operation. While the ECC system functions similarly to the ETCC system, there are differences in compressor cycling methods. In a system without BCM control, the compressor clutch is grounded through the low-pressure switch. The power module thus cycles power to the compressor clutch, figure 20-14A. In a BCM-controlled system, the compressor clutch power is received through a fuse and the power steering cutout switch or diode; the power module cycles the ground circuit for the compressor, figure 20-14B.

The electronic comfort control (ECC) system used by Oldsmobile is BCM-controlled and can be used either as a fully automatic or as a manual system. When used manually, the driver can control blower speed and air deliv-

ery mode, but the system will continue to control temperature automatically. In addition to the BCM, power module, programmer and control panel assembly used in other BCM-controlled systems, the ECC system uses inputs from the engine electronic control module (ECM). This allows the BCM to check several engine and compressor conditions before it turns the compressor on.

The BCM communicates with the engine ECM, the ECC panel, and the programmer on the serial data line to transmit data serially (one piece after another). The serial data line

Data Link: A digital signal path for communications between two or more components of an electronic system.

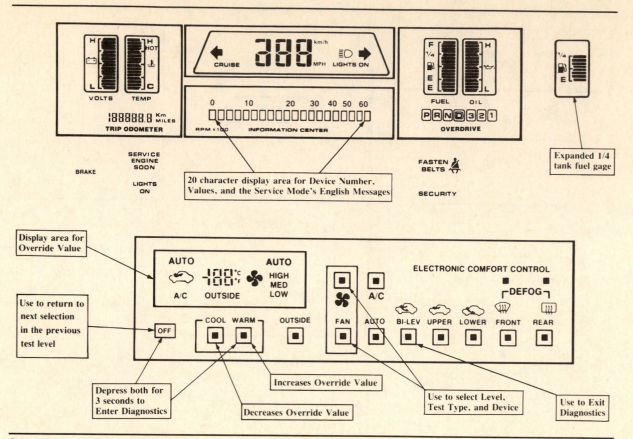

Figure 20-15. The instrument panel cluster (top) and the ECC control panel (bottom) are used to enter diagnostics and access the BCM self-diagnostic system. (GM)

acts like a party telephone line; while the BCM is communicating with the ECM, the programmer and the ECC panel can ''hear'' and understand the conversation. They also can process and use the information communicated, but they cannot cut in on the transmission. For example, suppose the ECM is sending engine data to the BCM. The ECC panel computer, which needs to display engine rpm to the driver, ''listens'' in on the conversation, picks up the data it needs and displays it on its panel. When the ECM is finished, it momentarily transmits a five-volt signal to declare the line idle and the BCM opens a conversation with the next device it needs to talk with.

The programmer controls air delivery and temperature on instructions from the BCM, using a series of vacuum solenoids that control the mode door operation. The programmer also has a motor that controls the air-mix door position to regulate temperature. When directed to change blower speed by the BCM, the programmer sends a variable voltage signal to the power module, which sends the required voltage to the blower motor.

The ECC system is the most complex of the ones we've discussed, and this is reflected in the diagnostic sequence designed into the overall system network. When any subsystem exceeds its programmed limits, the system sets a trouble code and in some cases provides a backup function. The instrument panel cluster and the EEC panel, figure 20-15, are used to access and control the self-diagnostic features. When the technician accesses the diagnostic mode, any stored BCM and ECM codes are displayed, along with various BCM and ECM parameters, discrete inputs and outputs, and any BCM output override information.

RADIOS AND SOUND SYSTEMS

The inner circuitry of radios, tape players, power amplifiers, and graphic equalizers is beyond the scope of this text. However, a technician must understand the external circuitry of sound systems in order to troubleshoot them.

Most sound units and speakers are grounded. In a few four-speaker systems, the speakers are insulated from their mountings. Current flows from the sound unit, through all of the speakers, and back to ground.

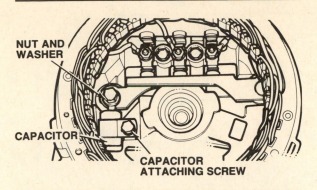

Figure 20-16. RFI capacitors can be installed inside the alternator. (Chrysler)

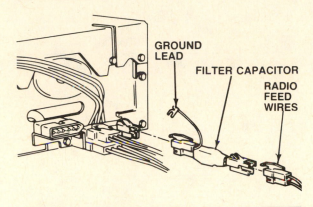

Figure 20-17. An RFI capacitor may be installed near the radio. (Buick)

In addition to resistance-type spark plugs and cables, automobiles use capacitors and ground straps to suppress radio static or interference caused by the ignition and charging systems. Capacitors may be mounted:

- Inside the alternator, figure 20-16
- Behind the instrument panel near the radio, figure 20-17
- At the ignition coil with the lead connected to the coil primary + terminal, figure 20-18A
- In a module mounted at the wiper motor and connected in series between the motor and wiring harness, figure 20-18B.

Ground straps are installed to conduct small, high-frequency electrical signals to ground. They require a large, clean, surface-contact area. Such ground straps are installed in various locations depending upon the vehicle. Some common locations are:

- Radio chassis to cowl
- Engine to cowl
- Across the engine mounts
- From air conditioning evaporator valve to cowl.

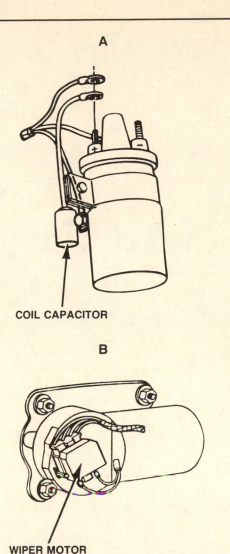

Figure 20-18. RFI capacitors may be installed on the ignition coil or on the wiper motor. (Chrysler)

The small bulb that lights the sound unit controls may be part of the instrument panel circuitry, figure 20-19, or part of the sound unit's internal circuitry.

Some cars use electrically extended radio antennas, figure 20-20. The antenna motor may be automatically activated when the radio is turned on, or it may be controlled by a separate switch, figure 20-21. A relay may control current to the antenna motor.

REAR WINDOW DEFOGGER AND DEFROSTER

Some older vehicles have a rear window defogger, figure 20-22, which is a motor-driven fan similar to that used in the heating system but

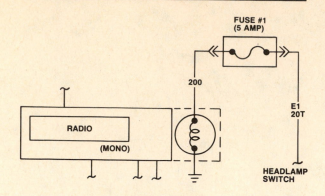

Figure 20-19. This radio illumination lamp is controlled by the panel illumination circuitry. (Chrysler)

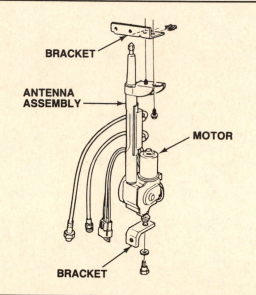

Figure 20-20. The motor of an electrically extended radio antenna is installed inside the wheelwell. (Oldsmobile)

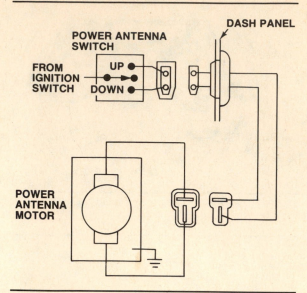

Figure 20-21. Power antennas can be controlled by a separate switch. (Chrysler)

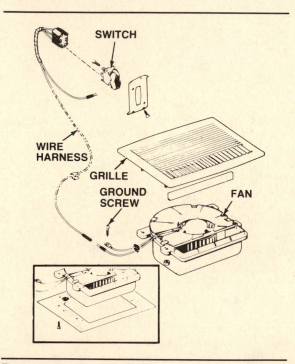

Figure 20-22. The defogger fan blows air at the inside of the rear window.

mounted behind the rear seat near the rear window. It is controlled by a separate switch that routes motor current through circuits of varying resistance (like a heater fan) to change motor speed. Heat is provided electrically by a length of resistance wire in the defogger unit. The resistance heater is connected in parallel with the motor so that it heats when the motor is running at either high or low speed, figure 20-23.

A defroster is a grid of electrical heating conductors that is bonded to the rear window glass, figure 20-24. The defroster grid is sometimes called a defogger. Current through the grid may be controlled by a separate switch and a relay, figure 20-25, or by a switch-relay combination, figure 20-26. In both designs,

when the switch is closed, the relay is energized and an indicator lamp is lit. The relay contact points conduct current to the rear window grid.

Most late-model systems have a solid-state timing module that turns off the defroster current automatically. In the system shown in figure 20-25, the switch "On" position energizes the relay's pull-in and hold-in coils. The switch

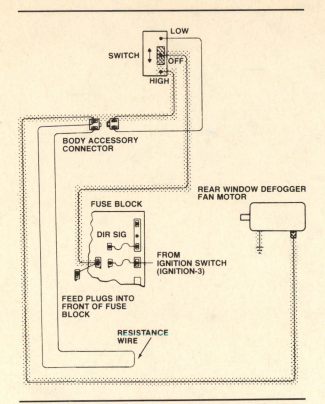

Figure 20-23. In this defroster circuit, heat is provided by a length of resistance wire. (Buick)

Figure 20-24. The grid of conductors on this rear window will heat the glass and evaporate any condensation.

"Normal" position keeps the hold-in coil energized so that the relay points remain closed.

Cleaning the inside rear glass should be done carefully to avoid scratching the grid material and causing an open in the circuit.

HEATED WINDSHIELD

Some late-model cars have a windshield containing a conductive material that can be heated to melt frost and ice rapidly. The standard three-layer laminated windshield has a silver and zinc oxide layer applied to the back of the

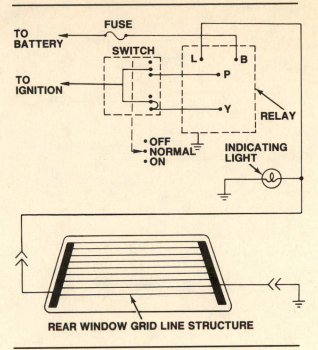

Figure 20-25. Defroster circuits often use a separate relay to control current. (Chrysler)

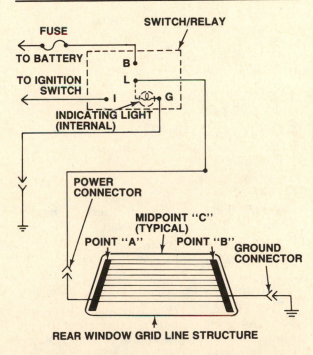

Figure 20-26. Defroster circuits can also use a combined switch and relay to control current flow. (Chrysler)

outer glass layer, to form an electrical conductor within the windshield. Silver buss bars at the top and bottom of the windshield connect the conductive layer to the power and the ground circuit.

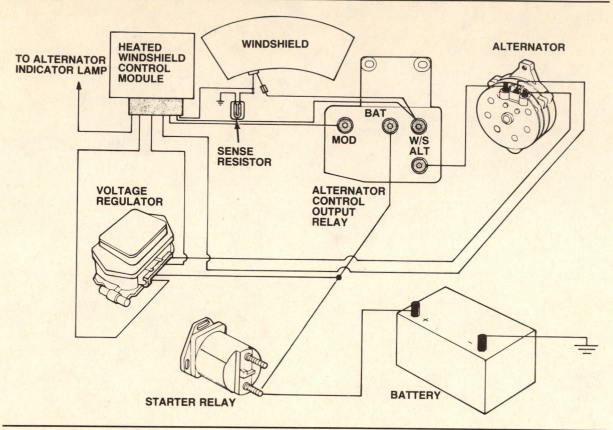

Figure 20-27. The components used in Ford's heated windshield system. (Ford)

Figure 20-27 shows the components of the system used by Ford:

- Conductive windshield
- Alternator output relay
- Control module
- On/off switch
- Sensing resistor.

Three conditions must be met before the heated windshield system will operate:

- The system must be on
- The engine must be running (alternator output)
- The interior temperature of the vehicle must be under 40°F (4°C).

The control module contains a thermistor to sense in-car temperature and to prevent system operation when it exceeds 40°F (4°C). It also contains a timing function to limit system operation to four-minute cycles. When the three operational conditions are met, the module signals the driver by turning on an indicator lamp. At the same time, it turns off the charging system voltage regulator and switches alternator output from the car's electrical system to the windshield power circuit to energize the power relay, then turns the regulator back on to restore

alternator output. This connects the windshield power circuit to the alternator output terminal through the power relay.

Once the battery is disconnected from the alternator, its voltage will drop to about 12 volts. Sensing this drop, the voltage regulator will full-field the alternator. Since the battery is out of the charging circuit and the alternator is providing full-field power, alternator output voltage increases to 30 to 70 volts, depending upon engine rpm. The control module prevents alternator output from rising above 70 volts. While the system is operating, the module also monitors battery voltage. If battery voltage drops below 11 volts, the module denies power to the power relay and reconnects the car's electrical system to the alternator.

The module also is linked to the EEC-IV engine control microprocessor by the same wiring that transmits the air conditioning compressor On signal. If the heated windshield system is turned on and the vehicle is not in gear, the module signals the EEC-IV module to increase engine speed to approximately 1,400 rpm, ensuring enough output from the alternator. Once the vehicle is shifted into gear, the EEC-IV module resumes its nor-

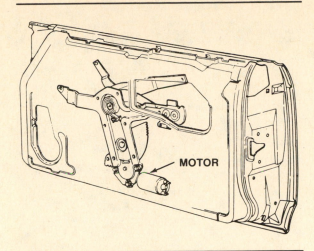

Figure 20-28. The motor within this car door can raise and lower the window glass. (Ford)

mal idle speed control function. Since they are both carried on the same circuitry, an air conditioning signal will override a heated windshield signal if they occur at the same time.

A sensing resistor connected to the module prevents system operation with a cracked or damaged windshield. The module monitors the voltage across the resistor and shuts the system off if it detects a voltage drop. A 15-ampere fuse in the fuse panel protects the low-voltage control circuit; a fusible link at the alternator output control relay protects the high-voltage power circuit.

POWER WINDOWS

Car doors can contain motors to raise and lower the window glass, figure 20-28. The motors usually are the permanent-magnet type and are insulated at their mounting and grounded through the control switch, figure 20-29, or the master switch. Each control switch operates one motor, except for the driver's door switch. This is a master switch that can control any of the motors. Some systems have a mechanical locking device that allows *only* the driver's switch to control any of the motors.

The single-motor control switches each have one terminal that is connected to battery voltage. Each of the two other switch terminals is connected to one of the two motor brushes. The window is moved up or down by reversing the direction of motor rotation. Motor rotation is controlled by routing current into one brush or the other.

Each individual window switch is connected in series with the driver's master switch. Current from the motor must travel through the master switch to reach ground.

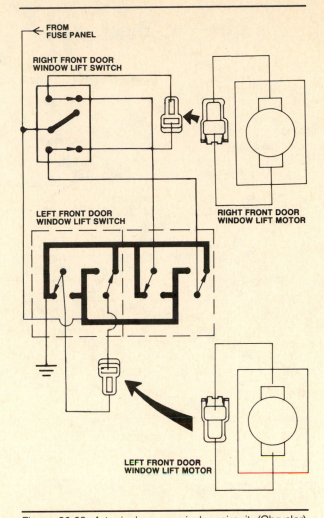

Figure 20-29. A typical power window circuit. (Chrysler)

POWER SEATS

Electrically adjustable seats can be designed to move in several ways:

- Two-way systems move forward and backward
- Four-way systems move forward, backward, and front edge up and down
- Six-way systems, used in most late-model applications, move forward, backward, up, and down, tilt forward and backward, and move front edge up and down, and rear edge up and down.

A typical two-way power seat system, figure 20-30, was made by GM. The series-connected motor has two electromagnetic field windings that are wound in opposite directions. One winding receives current from the forward switch position. The second winding receives current from the rear switch position. Current through one winding will make the motor turn in one direction; current through the opposite

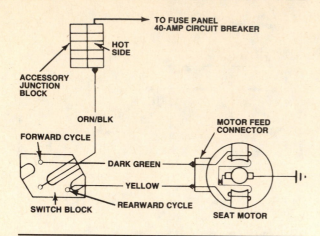

Figure 20-30. GM's two-way power seat has a motor with electromagnetic fields; current through the fields determines the direction of motor rotation. (Oldsmobile)

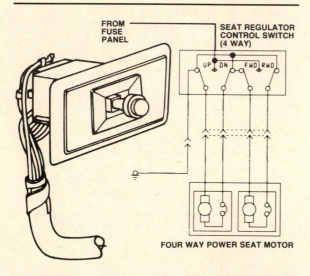

Figure 20-31. This switch controls the Ford four-way power seat circuit. (Ford)

winding will make the motor turn in the opposite direction. The motor armature is linked to the seat mounting by a transmission that translates this rotary motion into seat motion.

Ford and GM have made four-way power seat systems that contain two reversible motor armatures in one housing. Ford's motors have permanent-magnet fields, while GM's motors have series-connected electromagnetic fields. One motor is linked to a transmission that moves the seat forward and backward. The other motor's transmission tilts the front edge of the seat. Both motors are controlled by a single four-position switch, figure 20-31. The switch contacts shift current to different motor brushes (Ford) or to different field windings (GM) to control motor reversal.

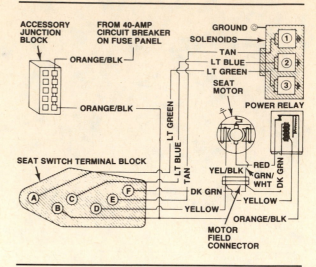

Figure 20-32. GM's early six-way power seat uses a single motor and three transmissions controlled by three solenoids. (Oldsmobile)

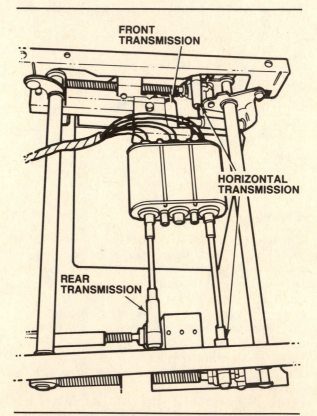

Figure 20-33. Late-model GM and Ford six-way power seats use a triple-armature motor similar to this Chrysler unit. (Chrysler)

Early GM six-way power seat systems use one reversible motor that can be connected to one of three transmissions. Transmission hookup is controlled by three solenoids, figure 20-32. The control switch is similar to that used by Ford and Chrysler, but the circuitry differs.

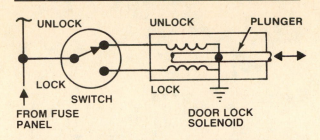

Figure 20-34. The GM power door lock system.

Current must flow through one of the solenoids to engage a transmission, then through a relay to ground. The relay points conduct current to the motor brushes. Additional switch contacts conduct current to the electromagnetic motor windings.

Chrysler, Ford, and late-model GM six-way power seat systems use three reversible motor armatures in one housing, figure 20-33. The control switches have two two-position knobs that control edge tilt and a four-position knob that controls forward, backward, up and down seat movement. The switch contacts shift the current to different motor brushes to control motor reversal. The permanent-magnet motors are grounded through the switch and may contain an internal circuit breaker.

POWER DOOR LOCKS, TRUNK LATCHES, AND SEAT BACK RELEASE

Solenoids and motors are used to control door, trunk and seat back latches, and locks. Door and trunk systems are usually controlled by separate switches mounted near the driver. Seat back latches are usually controlled by door-jamb switches.

In some GM door lock systems, current flows through a solenoid winding to ground, figure 20-34, when the driver closes the switch. The solenoid core movement either locks or unlocks the door, depending upon which switch position is selected.

Some Ford and Chrysler electric door locks use a relay-controlled circuit, figure 20-35. Current from the control switch flows through the relay coil, closing the relay contacts. The contacts route current directly from the fuse panel to the solenoid windings.

Other Ford, Chrysler, and GM power door locks use an electric motor to move the locking mechanism. The electric motor receives current through a relay, figure 20-36.

Power trunk latches use an insulated switch and a grounded solenoid coil, figure 20-37.

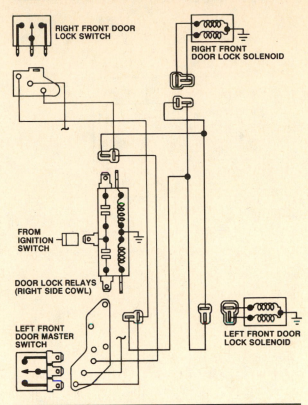

Figure 20-35. The Chrysler power door lock system. (Chrysler)

Power seat back releases can be automatically controlled by grounding door jamb switches, figure 20-38. Opening one of the front doors energizes a relay. The relay contacts conduct current to solenoids which unlatch both seat backs.

AUTOMATIC DOOR LOCK (ADL) SYSTEM

General Motors and Ford both use an automatic door lock (ADL) system in the power door lock system on some of their models as a safety and convenience feature. Ford ADL systems are an integral part of the keyless entry system, while General Motors ADL systems are available on vehicles regardless of whether they have keyless entry.

On GM vehicles with automatic transaxles, placing the gear selector in Drive automatically locks all vehicle doors when the ignition is On. All doors unlock automatically when the gear selector is returned to the Park position. Individual doors can be unlocked manually from the inside, the front doors can be unlocked with the key from outside, or all the doors can be unlocked electrically while in Drive.

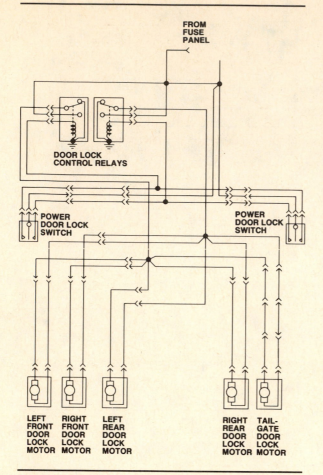

Figure 20-36. Some Ford power door lock systems use motors rather than solenoids for movement. (Ford)

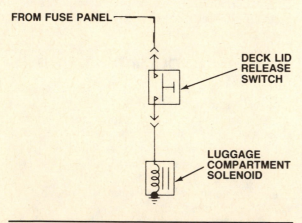

Figure 20-37. A typical power trunk lid latch system. (Ford)

System Operation

The ADL feature may be a function of the chime module, an ADL controller, or a multi-function alarm module, depending on the vehicle model. In a typical General Motors ADL

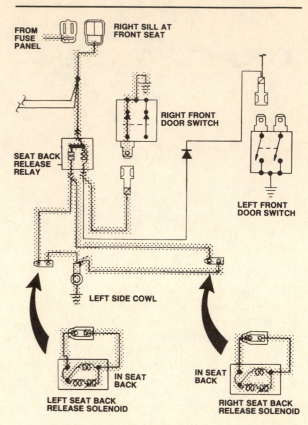

Figure 20-38. In this power seat back release system, the grounding of either door jamb switch energizes both seat back release solenoids. (Chrysler)

circuit, voltage is applied to the chime module, ADL controller, or alarm module. When the doors are closed, the ignition is in the run position, and the gear selector is placed in Drive, the module or controller sends current to ground through the lock relay coil in the ADL relay, figure 20-39. Current passes through the relay, door lock motors, and unlock relay to ground, locking the doors. The module or controller then removes current from the relay coil to prevent damage to the lock motors. When the vehicle stops and the gear selector is returned to Park, voltage is sent to the unlock relay coil in the ADL relay. The doors are unlocked by current passing through the relay, door lock motors, and lock relay to ground.

KEYLESS ENTRY SYSTEMS

The first keyless entry system used on domestic vehicles was developed by Ford in the late 1970s. Chrysler and GM both offer keyless entry options on some current models. Since their applications differ substantially in design, concept, and operation, we will look at the Ford version first.

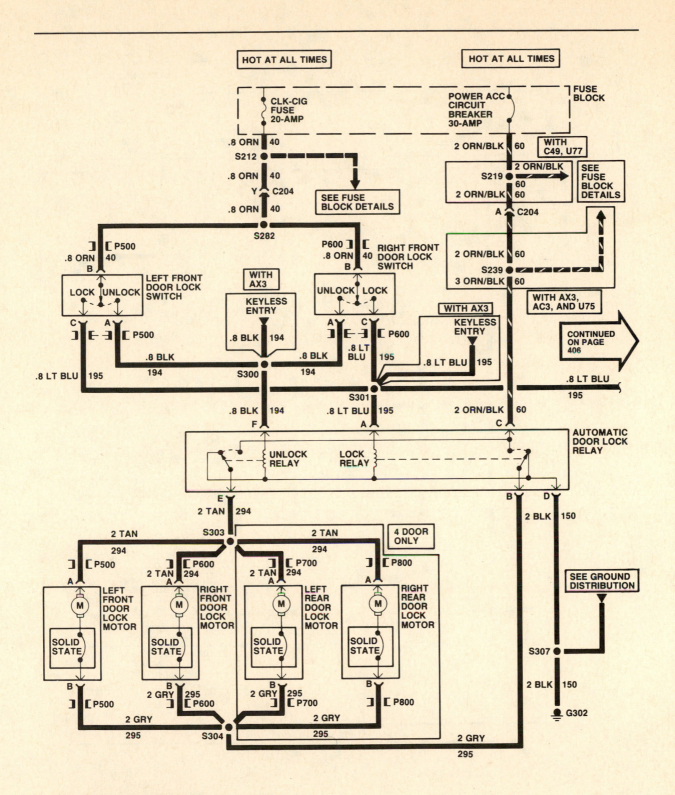

Figure 20-39. This ADL circuit diagram shows how the multifunction alarm module is integrated with the power door lock system. (Oldsmobile)

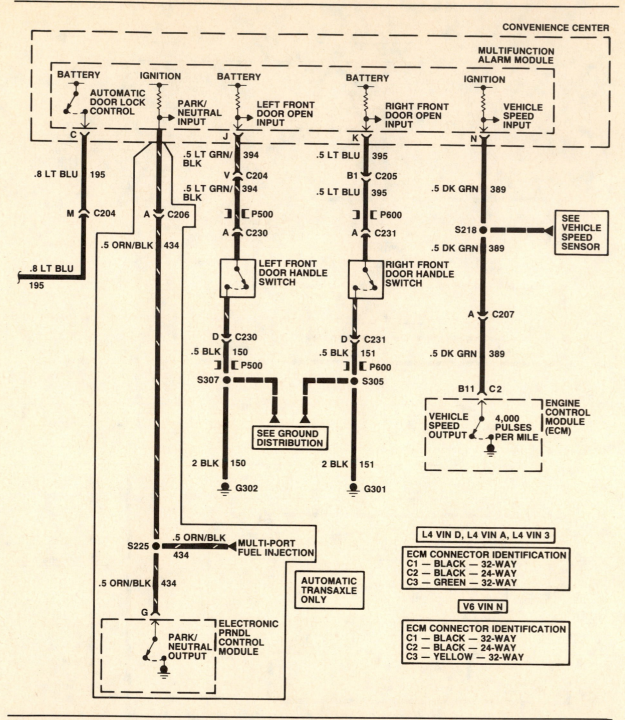

Figure 20-39. ADL circuit diagram. (continued)

Ford

Ford's present keyless entry system has remained substantially unchanged since its introduction. It provides a convenient entry method when the vehicle keys have been forgotten, or accidentally locked inside. The system consists of a five-button keypad secured to the outer panel on the driver's door, a microprocessor-relay control module, and connecting wiring, figure 20-40.

The keyless entry system incorporates two additional subsystems: one for illuminated entry and the other for automatic door locks. Operating as a single system, it performs the following functions:

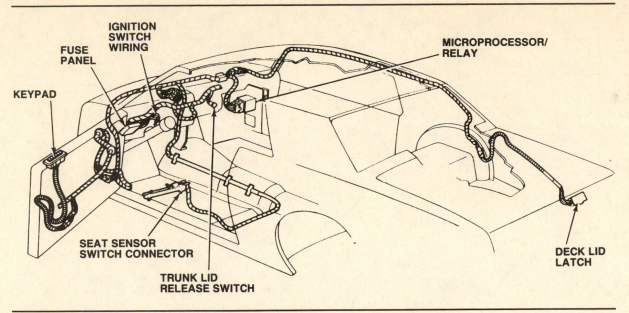

Figure 20-40. The Ford keyless entry system components and wiring harness. (Ford)

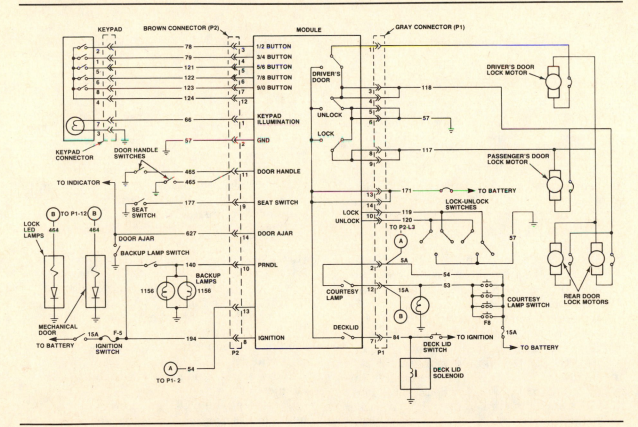

Figure 20-41. A typical schematic of the Ford keyless entry system. (Ford)

- Unlocks the driver's door
- Unlocks other doors or the deck lid when a specific keypad button is depressed within five seconds after unlocking the driver's door
- Locks all doors from outside the vehicle when the required keypad buttons are depressed simultaneously
- Turns on the interior lamps and the illuminated keyhole in the driver's door

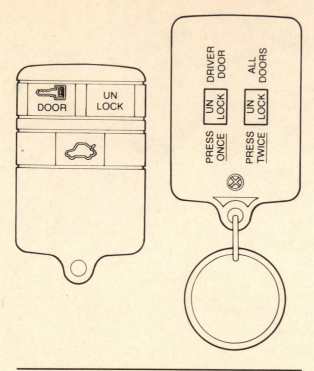

Figure 20-42. RKE or RLC transmitters differ in design from one application to another, but all have three buttons and attach to a key ring. (Oldsmobile)

- Automatically locks all doors when they are closed, the driver's seat is occupied, the ignition switch is on, and the gear selector is moved through the reverse position.

A linear keypad using calculator-type buttons is installed in the driver's door and used to input a numerical code to the control module. The five keypad buttons are numbered 1-2, 3-4, 5-6, 7-8, and 9-0 from left to right. The numerical code used to open the door, however, is a derivative of a five-digit keypad code stamped on the control module and printed on a sticker attached to the inside of the deck lid. This code refers to the location of the five buttons on the keypad, not the keypad button number. For example, if the module number is 23145, the doors will unlock only if the keys are depressed in that order. If the module requires replacement, a sticker bearing the new module number is applied over the old sticker on the deck lid.

The control module's program operates the keyless entry, illuminated entry, and ADL systems. Two 14-pin connectors (one brown and one gray) connect the wiring harness to the control module; the brown connector also connects the keypad harness to the module. The following components provide inputs to the control module:

- Keypad buttons
- Door handles
- Courtesy lamp switch
- Driver's seat sensor
- Transmission backup lamp switch
- Ignition switch
- Door lock and unlock switches
- Door ajar switch.

The following components receive output signals from the control module:

- Keypad lamps
- Interior courtesy lamps
- Door lock LEDs
- Deck lid release solenoid
- Door lock solenoids.

Figure 20-41 shows a typical Ford keyless entry circuit diagram. Ford added a remote keyless entry feature on some 1993 models. This uses a hand-held radio transmitter with three buttons for door lock control from outside the vehicle. If the vehicle is equipped with the Ford antitheft system, a four-button transmitter is used. The additional button is marked PANIC and allows the driver to activate the alarm in an emergency. The system operates essentially the same as the Delco RKE system described below.

Delco

In 1993, GM introduced a Passive Keyless Entry (PKE) system on the Corvette. In this system, a key-fob transmitter locks the doors as the person carrying it walks away from the car, and unlocks them when the carrier comes close to the car again. The owner does not even need to push a button.

Other GM vehicles use the Delco Remote Keyless Entry (RKE) or Remote Lock Control (RLC) system. A hand-held radio transmitter with three buttons, figure 20-42, allows the driver to lock or unlock the doors and trunk lid from outside the car. The transmitter contains a random 32-bit access code stored in a PROM. The same code is stored in a receiver module located in the trunk. This receiver detects and decodes UHF signals from the transmitter within a range of approximately 33 feet (10 meters).

Depressing the DOOR button on the transmitter sends a signal to the receiver. If the signal contains a valid access code (VAC), the receiver supplies battery voltage to the lock relay coil. This energizes the lock relay, which sends current to the door lock motors. The LH door lock motor is grounded through receiver terminal B and internal contacts; all other motors are grounded through the unlock relay contacts in the door lock relay, figure 20-43.

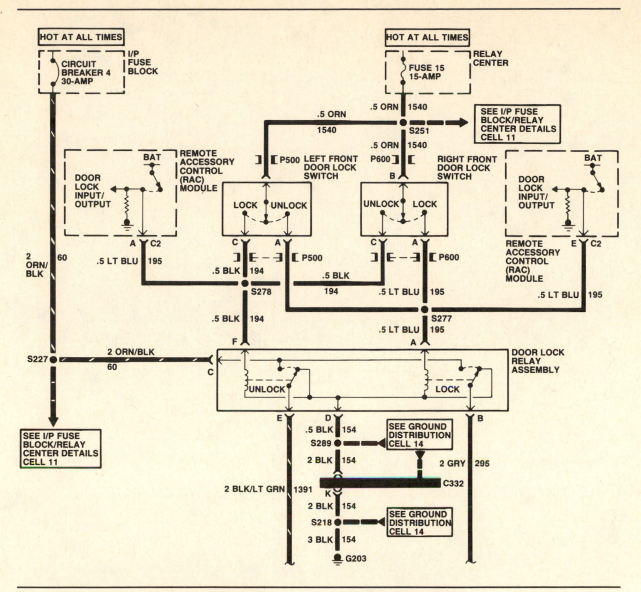

Figure 20-43. Oldsmobile Cutlass remote keyless entry circuit diagram. (Oldsmobile)

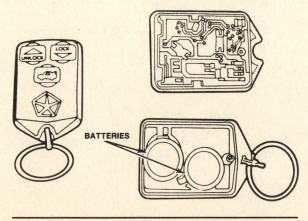

Figure 20-44. The Chrysler remote keyless entry transmitter is very similar in design and operation to the Delco RKE transmitter.

When the lock function is used, the receiver grounds circuit 156, turning on the interior lights for two seconds to indicate that the doors are locked.

If the transmitter UNLOCK button is depressed once, the receiver sends battery voltage to the LH door lock motor, which is grounded through the lock relay contacts in the door lock relay, and only the LH door is unlocked. To unlock all doors, the UNLOCK button must be depressed twice. At this signal, the receiver also sends battery voltage to the unlock relay coil in the door lock relay. This energizes the unlock relay, which sends current to the other three door lock motors. The lock relay contacts in the door lock relay provides ground for the motors, which unlock

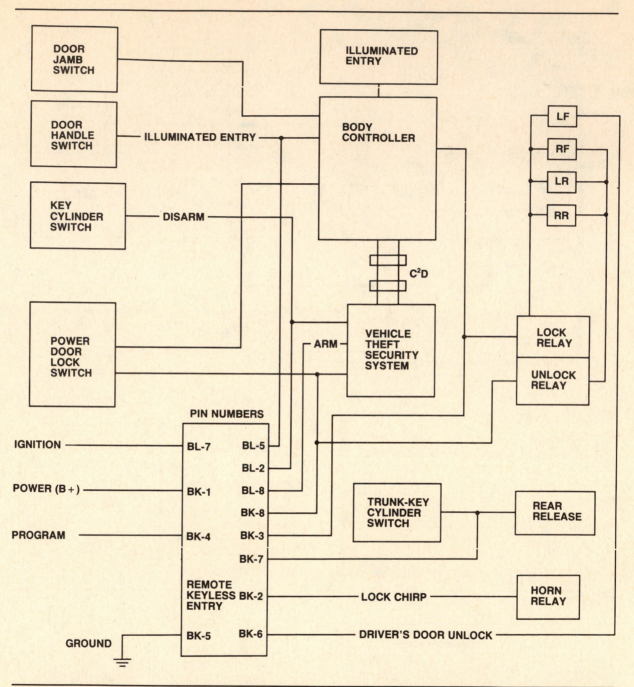

Figure 20-45. A block wiring diagram of the Chrysler remote keyless entry system shows its interrelationship with the vehicle theft security system and BCM. (Chrysler)

the doors. When the unlock function is used, the receiver also grounds circuit 156 to turn on the interior lights for approximately 40 seconds, or until the ignition switch is turned to the Run position.

Depressing the trunk lid release button on the transmitter signals the receiver to supply battery voltage at terminal H. This current energizes the trunk lid release solenoid, allowing

the trunk lid to be opened. However, if the ignition is on and the transaxle position switch is not in Park, battery voltage is not supplied and the trunk lid cannot be opened.

Chrysler

The Chrysler keyless entry system also uses a hand-held radio transmitter, figure 20-44, to unlock and lock the vehicle doors and deck lid.

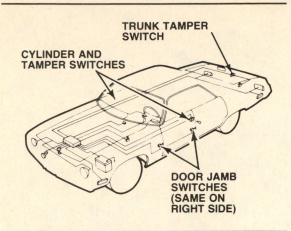

Figure 20-46. A theft deterrent system uses strategically placed switches in the door jambs, door lock, and trunk lock cylinders. (GM)

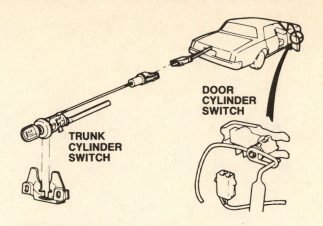

Figure 20-47. Cylinder tamper switches are activated by the lock cylinders when a forced entry is attempted. (GM)

This multipurpose system is similar to many aftermarket theft deterrent systems, since it turns on the interior lamps, disarms the factory installed theft security system, and chirps the horn whenever it is used.

The transmitter attaches to the key ring and has three buttons for operation within 23 feet (7 meters) of the vehicle module receiver. The transmitter has its own code stored in the module memory. If the transmitter is lost, stolen, or an additional one is required, a new code also must be stored in module memory. Figure 20-45 shows the integration of the keyless entry, illuminated entry, vehicle theft security, and power door lock systems with the body control module (BCM).

THEFT DETERRENT SYSTEMS

Antitheft systems are usually aftermarket installations, although in recent years, some carmakers have offered factory installed systems on the luxury vehicles in their model line. Basic antitheft systems provide a warning when a forced entry is attempted through the car doors or the trunk lid. A starter interlock feature is incorporated on some models.

System functioning relies on strategically located switches installed in the door jambs, the door lock cylinders, and the trunk lock cylinder, figure 20-46. After the system is armed, any tampering with the lock cylinders or an attempt to open any door or the trunk lid without a key causes the alarm controller to trigger the system.

Once a driver has closed the doors and armed the system, an indicator lamp in the instrument cluster comes on for several seconds, then goes out. The system is disarmed by unlocking a front door from the outside with the

key or turning the ignition on within a specified time. If the alarm has been set off, the system can be disarmed by unlocking a front door with the key.

■ When to Degauss?

Have you run into this problem yet? A customer complains that the vehicle's compass in the overhead console is malfunctioning. It either indicates North in every direction, or it constantly rotates even when the car is heading in a straight line. Should you replace the compass with a new one?

No. Chances are, the problem is not the compass.

Compasses installed in overhead consoles should never be exposed to any magnetic field, or their accuracy will be affected. A magnetic field can be generated by various sources. It may happen if an aftermarket sunroof is installed. The saw used to cut the opening in the roof can magnetize the metal around the sunroof and alter the compass operation. It may occur when the service technician troubleshooting a radio malfunction temporarily mounts a test antenna on the roof, or when someone works on the console with a magnetized screwdriver.

Diagnosing the problem may not be easy, since there is no record of a magnetic field having been near the compass, and few technicians realize the effect of a saw, test antenna, magnetized screwdriver, or the like on a compass.

But once you realize the cause of the problem, the answer is quite simple: have the roof of the vehicle "degaussed" by a radio or TV serviceman. This is similar to erasing an audio or a video tape with a bulk tape eraser. It neutralizes the magnetic field in the area of the compass and will return most "defective" compasses to working order in just a few minutes.

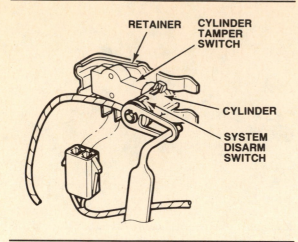

Figure 20-48. The UTD disarm switch is a part of the LH front door lock cylinder. (GM)

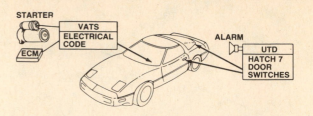

Figure 20-49. The Delco VATS system has a resistor key circuit and an ECM-controlled starter interlock with the UTD system to foil would-be thieves. (GM)

The trend in factory installed antitheft systems is to combine the operation of the exterior lights, starter, horn, power door locks, and keyless entry system with a computer module to create an integrated system of multiple circuits. Such systems are complex and require the correct circuit schematic and wiring diagrams to troubleshoot.

Delco UTD System

The Delco universal theft deterrent (UTD) system was introduced on some 1980 GM models and offered as an option until it was superseded by the personal automotive security system (PASS). The circuitry, logic, and power relays that operate the system are contained within a controller module.

When the system is armed by the driver, a security system warning lamp in the instrument panel glows for four to eight seconds after the doors have been closed, then shuts off. The system can be disarmed without sounding the alarm by unlocking a front door from the outside with a key, or by turning the ignition switch on. If the alarm has sounded, it can be shut off by unlocking one of the front doors with a key.

If the system is armed and a door is opened forcibly, a two-terminal doorjamb switch activates the alarm through one terminal. The other switch terminal operates the interior lights. On vehicles with power door locks, the circuits are separated by a diode. Tamper switches are installed in all door locks and the trunk lid lock, figure 20-47. The switches are activated by any rotation or in-and-out movement of the lock cylinders during a forced entry. A disarm switch in the LH door cylinder, figure 20-48,

allows the owner to deactivate the system without sounding the alarm before entering the vehicle. All tamper switches should be kept clean, as corrosion can cause the system to activate without apparent reason.

Exact wiring of the UTD system depends on the particular vehicle and how it is equipped. To understand just how the system works on a given vehicle, you must have the proper wiring diagram.

Delco VATS/PASS-Key II™ System

The Delco vehicle antitheft system (VATS) introduced as standard equipment on the 1986 Corvette, figure 20-49, functions as an ignition-disable system. It is not designed to prevent a forced entry, but to protect the steering column lock if an intruder breaks into the vehicle. When used on Corvettes with the UTD system, the combination was called the forced entry alarm system (FES). When used on other GM vehicles, VATS is called PASS-Key II™. The system, figure 20-50, consists of the following components:

- Resistor ignition key
- Steering column lock cylinder with resistor-sensing contact
- VATS or PASS-Key II™ decoder module
- Starter enable relay
- ECM or PCM
- Wiring harness.

A small resistor pellet embedded in the ignition key contains one of 15 different resistance values. The key is coded with a number that indicates which resistor pellet it contains. Resistor pellet resistance values vary according to key code and model year. To operate the lock, the key must have the proper mechanical code (1 of 2,000); to close the starter circuit, it must also have the correct electrical code (1 of 15).

Inserting the key in the ignition lock cylinder brings the resistor pellet in contact with the resistor sensing contact. Rotating the lock applies battery power to the decoder module, figure 20-50. The sensing contact sends the re-

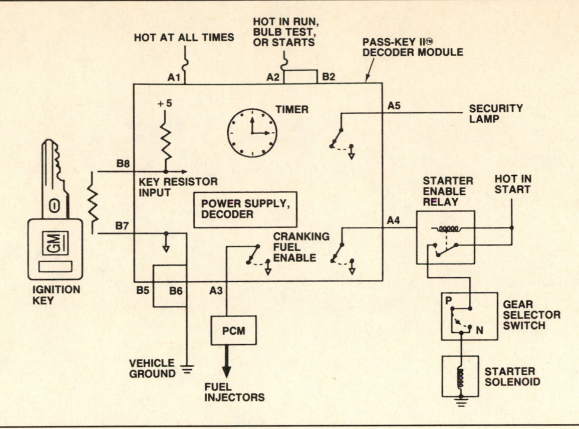

Figure 20-50. A circuit diagram of the PASS-Key II™ system. (Oldsmobile)

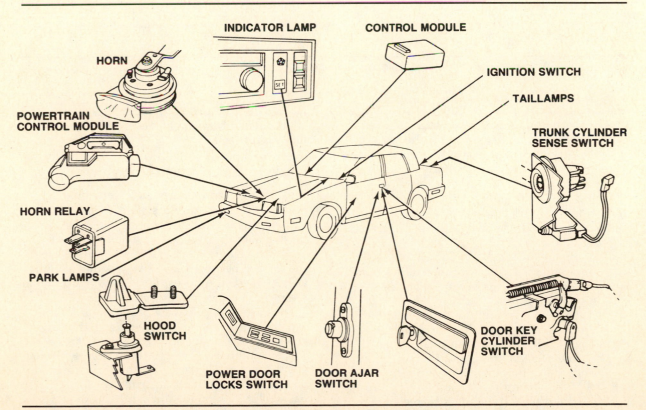

Figure 20-51. Components of the Chrysler theft security system. (Chrysler)

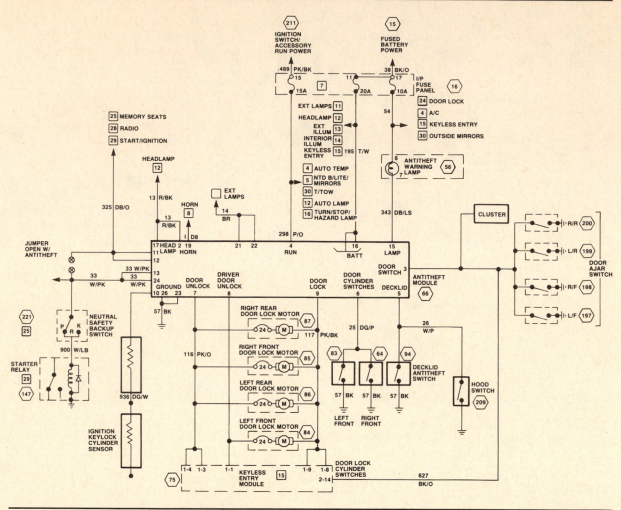

Figure 20-52. A typical Ford antitheft system circuit schematic. (Ford)

sistance value of the key pellet to the decoder module, where it is compared to a fixed resistance value stored in memory. If the resistor code and the fixed value are the same, the decoder module energizes the starter enable relay, which closes the circuit to the starter solenoid and allows the engine to crank. At the same time, the module sends a pulse-width modulated (PWM) cranking fuel enable signal to the ECM or PCM.

If the key resistor code and the module's fixed resistance value do not match, the module shuts down for two to four minutes. Repeating the attempt to start the vehicle with the wrong key will result in continued module shutdowns. During vehicle operation, the key resistor pellet inputs are continually read. If the module sees an open, short, or incorrect resistance value for 60 consecutive seconds, a SECURITY indicator lamp comes on and remains lighted until the fault is corrected. The lamp also comes on for five seconds when the

ignition is first turned on. This serves as a bulb check and indicates that the system is functioning properly.

Chrysler Theft Security System

This passive arming theft deterrent system, figure 20-51, is factory installed on high-line Chrysler models and functions like many aftermarket alarm installations. When combined with the Remote Keyless Entry, figure 20-45, the system becomes an active arming system. Once armed, the doors, hood, and trunk lid all are monitored for unauthorized entry.

The system is passively armed by activating the power door locks before closing the driver's door; it will not arm if the doors are locked manually. The system is actively armed if the doors are locked with the RKE transmitter. A SET lamp in the instrument cluster flashes for 15 seconds during the arming period. If a forcible entry is attempted while the system is armed, it responds by sounding the horn, flashing the park and tail lamps, and activating an engine kill feature.

The system is passively disarmed by unlocking either front door with the key, or actively disarmed by using the RKE transmitter. If the alarm has been activated during the driver's absence, the horn will blow three times when the vehicle is disarmed as a way of informing the driver of an attempted entry or tampering.

Ford Antitheft System

This antitheft system, figure 20-52, bears many similarities to the Delco UTD theft deterrent system. It is installed on luxury models, uses many of the same components, and functions in essentially the same way. Once the system is armed, any tampering with the doors, hood, or trunk lid signals the control module. Once triggered, the system flashes the low-beam headlamps, the parking lamps, and alarm indicator lamp on and off; sounds the horn; and interrupts the starter circuit. The system is composed of the following components:

- Antitheft control module
- Antitheft warning indicator
- Door key unlock switches
- Hood switch
- Trunk lid lock cylinder tamper switch
- Ignition key lock cylinder sensor.

It also incorporates the following components from other systems:

- Power door lock switches
- Door ajar switches
- Horn relay
- Low-beam headlamps
- Parking lamps
- Keyless entry module
- Starter relay.

SUMMARY

Heating and air conditioning systems share a motor-driven fan. The motor speeds usually are controlled by varying the resistance in the motor circuit. Air conditioning systems also have an electromagnetic clutch on the compressor. The clutch is energized by the air conditioning system control switch. The switch may be a suction throttling valve, an evaporator pressure-control valve, or a clutch-cycling pressure switch. Other switches are used in the clutch circuit to protect the system from high or low pressure, or to shut the clutch off under certain conditions such as wide-open throttle.

Older vehicles may use a fan and motor as a rear window defogger. This system is similar to the heating system. A rear window defroster or defogger on late-model vehicles is a grid of conductors attached to the rear window. A relay usually controls current to the conductors. Ford's heated windshield system uses current directly from the alternator.

The parts of a sound system that will concern most service technicians include the way the sound unit and the speakers are mounted, interference capacitors, panel illumination bulbs, and power antennas.

Power windows are moved by a reversible motor. Motor direction is controlled by current through different brushes. The driver's side master switch controls all of the windows, because each individual switch is grounded through the master switch.

Power seats can be moved by one, two, or three motors and various transmission units. Permanent-magnet motors or electromagnetic field motors can be used. Current to the motors sometimes is controlled by a relay.

Power door locks, trunk latches, and seat back releases can be moved by solenoids or motors. Relays are often used to control current to the solenoid or motor.

ADL systems are a safety feature integrated with the power door locks. They automatically lock all doors before the vehicle is driven. Keyless entry systems are both convenience and safety features. They allow a driver access to a vehicle by entering a code through a keypad on the driver's door, or by depressing a button on a key chain transmitter.

Theft deterrent systems such as the Delco UTD and Ford Antitheft System are factory installed on luxury cars. Such systems use other vehicle systems to sound an alarm when the car is tampered with. The Delco VATS/PASS-Key II™ system uses a resistor ignition key which is "read" by the lock cylinder when inserted. If the resistance and the memory value do not match, the system shuts down the ignition and the starter.

Review Questions

Choose the single most correct answer.
Compare your answers with the correct answers on page 431.

1. Technician A says that an electronic climate control (ECC) system with BCM control cycles the power to the compressor clutch.

   Technician B says that an electronic climate control (ECC) system without BCM control cycles the ground circuit to the compressor clutch.

   Who is right?
   a. A only
   b. B only
   c. Both A and B
   d. Neither A nor B

2. Technician A says that Ford's heated windshield system uses a conductive grid bonded to the outside surface of the glass.

   Technician B says that the conductive grid is applied to the back of the outer glass layer before it is laminated to the inner glass layer.

   Who is right?
   a. A only
   b. B only
   c. Both A and B
   d. Neither A nor B

3. Constant operation of the compressor in automotive air conditioning systems is prevented by:
   a. A solenoid
   b. A servomagnet
   c. An electromagnetic clutch
   d. A one-way clutch

4. Individual switches on automobile power window circuits must be connected in _____ with the driver's master switch.
   a. Series
   b. Shunt
   c. Parallel
   d. Series-parallel

5. The air conditioning compressor clutch can be controlled by:
   a. A power steering cutout switch
   b. A pressure cycling switch
   c. Both a and b
   d. Neither a nor b

6. Technician A says that the user selects the mode in a semiautomatic temperature control system, but the actuators are electrically operated.

   Technician B says that a semiautomatic temperature control system uses in-car and ambient temperature sensors.

   Who is right?
   a. A only
   b. B only
   c. Both A and B
   d. Neither A nor B

7. Technician A says that the body control module (BCM) talks to other computers in an ECC system on a serial data line.

   Technician B says that the ECC system programmer activates the actuators on a serial data line.

   Who is right?
   a. A only
   b. B only
   c. Both A and B
   d. Neither A nor B

8. GM power seat system motors use:
   a. Permanent-magnet fields
   b. Electromagnetic fields
   c. Both A and B
   d. Neither A nor B

9. The Delco vehicle anti-theft system (VATS) uses a _____ in the ignition key.
   a. Thermistor
   b. Potentiometer
   c. Magnet
   d. Resistor

10. Power window systems use:
    a. Unidirectional motors
    b. Reversible motors
    c. Stepper motors
    d. Servomotors

11. Technician A says that Ford's heated windshield system will only work if the in-car temperature is above 40°F (4°C).

    Technician B says that the heated windshield module can control the EEC-IV module under certain circumstances.

    Who is right?
    a. A only
    b. B only
    c. Both A and B
    d. Neither A nor B

12. Technician A says that a keyless entry system incorporates the function of an illuminated entry system.

    Technician B says that moving the gear selector into Drive with the ignition on activates an ADL system.

    Who is right?
    a. A only
    b. B only
    c. Both A and B
    d. Neither A nor B

13. Technician A says that the Delco Remote Keyless Entry (RKE) and the Remote Lock Control (RLC) are different keyless entry systems.

    Technician B says that the RKE and RLC systems are subsystems of the VAT and PASS systems.

    Who is right?
    a. A only
    b. B only
    c. Both A and B
    d. Neither A nor B

14. Technician A says that if the resistance value of the ignition key in the PASS system does not match the UHF value stored in the receiver's memory, the vehicle will not start.

    Technician B says that a factory installed theft deterrent system is a complex multiple circuit system.

    Who is right?
    a. A only
    b. B only
    c. Both A and B
    d. Neither A nor B

Glossary of Technical Terms

Actuator: A device which translates the computer output voltage signal into mechanical energy.

Adaptive Memory: A feature of computer memory that allows the microprocessor to adjust its memory for computing open-loop operation, based on changes in engine operation.

After Top Dead Center (ATDC): The position of a piston after it has passed top dead center. Usually expressed in degrees, such as 5° ATDC.

Air Core Gauge: A gauge design in which there is no magnetic core. A field created by the sending unit resistance moves a pivoting permanent magnet.

Air-Fuel Ratio: The ratio of air to gasoline by weight in the air-fuel mixture drawn into an engine.

Alternating Current: A flow of electricity through a conductor, first in one direction and then in the opposite direction.

Ambient Temperature: The temperature of the air surrounding a particular device or location.

Ammeter: A meter used to measure electrical current flow in amperes.

Ampere: The unit for measuring the rate of electric current flow.

Analog: A voltage signal or processing action that varies relative to the operation being measured or controlled.

Analog-to-Digital (AD): An electronic conversion process for changing analog voltage signals to digital voltage signals.

Aneroid: A bellows or capsule that contains a vacuum and changes its length in response to changing atmospheric pressure.

Armature: The movable part in a relay. The revolving part in a generator or motor.

Asymmetrical: Different on both sides of center. In an asymmetrical low-beam headlamp, the light beam is spread farther to one side of center than to the other.

Atom: The smallest part of a chemical element that still has all the characteristics of that element.

Available Voltage: The peak voltage that a coil can produce.

Bakelite: A synthetic plastic material that is a good insulator. Distributor caps are often made of Bakelite.

Ballast (Primary) Resistor: A resistor in the primary circuit that stabilizes ignition system voltage and current flow.

Base: The center layer of semiconductor material in a transistor.

Before Top Dead Center (BTDC): The position of a piston as it nears top dead center. Usually expressed in degrees, such as 5° BTDC.

Biasing: Applying voltage to a junction of semiconductor materials.

Binary System: A mathematical system containing only two digits (0 and 1), which allows a digital computer to read and process input voltage signals.

Bipolar: A transistor which uses both holes and electrons as current carriers.

Bits: A digital input or output signal. One bit roughly equals one computer keystroke, or one discrete piece of information. The word comes from *binary digit*.

Block-Learn Function: The long-term effects of integrator corrections. Block-learn complements adaptive memory. If the computer continually makes the same correction, it "learns" the correction and adapts its memory to make the correction factor part of its basic program.

Bottom Dead Center (BDC): The exact bottom of a piston stroke.

Bound Electrons: Five or more tightly held electrons in an atom's valence ring.

Breakdown Voltage: The voltage above which a zener diode will allow reverse current flow.

Breaker Points: The metal contact points that act as an electrical switch in a distributor. They open and close the ignition primary circuit.

Buss Bar: A solid metal strip, or bar, used as a conductor in a fuse panel.

Capacitance: The ability of two conducting surfaces, separated by an insulator, to store an electric charge.

Carbon Monoxide: An odorless, colorless, tasteless poisonous gas. A pollutant produced by an internal combustion engine.

Cathode Ray Tube (CRT): An electron beam tube with a cathode at one end and an anode at the screen end. A "ray" of electrons shot from the cathode to the anode creates a pattern on the luminescent screen.

Cell: A case enclosing one element in an electrolyte. Each cell produces approximately 2.1 to 2.2 volts. Cells are connected in series.

Central Processing Unit (CPU): The processing and calculating portion of a microcomputer.

Centrifugal Force: The natural tendency of objects, when rotated, to move away from the center of rotation.

Centrifugal (Mechanical) Advance: A method of advancing the ignition spark using weights in the distributor that react to centrifugal force.

Choke Coil: A coil wound with fine wire and installed in a circuit to absorb oscillations that occur when the circuit is closed or opened.

Circuit: A circle or unbroken path through which an electric current can flow.

Circuit Number: The number, or number and letter, that carmakers use to identify an electrical circuit in a diagram.

Closed Loop: An operational mode in which the computer reads and responds to feedback signals from its sensors, adjusting system operation accordingly.

Closed Loop Dwell Control: A type of distributorless ignition system in which the control module varies dwell time in response to previous coil current buildup.

Clutch Start Switch: A starting safety switch that is operated by the clutch pedal.

Collector: The outside layer of semiconductor material in a transistor that conducts current away from the base.

Color Coding: The use of colored insulation on wire to identify an electrical circuit.

Commutator: A segmented ring attached to one end of an armature in a d.c. generator or a motor, providing an electrical connection between the armature and the brushes. In a generator, it rectifies the alternating current. In a motor, it provides a direct current path to the armature.

Compound Motor: A motor that has both series and shunt field windings. Often used as a starter motor.

Concentric: Having the same center, such as two circles drawn around a common centerpoint.

Condenser: A capacitor. Usually refers to an automotive capacitor constructed of two pieces of tinfoil, separated by an insulator, within a metal can.

Conductors: Materials that allow easy electron flow because of their many free electrons.

Continuity: Continuous, unbroken. Used to describe a working electrical circuit or component that is not open.

Conventional Theory: The current flow theory that says electricity flows from positive to negative. Also called the positive current flow theory.

Counterelectromotive Force (CEMF): An induced voltage that opposes the source voltage and any change (increase or decrease) in the charging current.

Cranking Performance Rating: A battery rating based on the amperes of current that a battery can supply for 30 seconds at 0°F, with no battery cell falling below 1.2 volts.

Crossfiring: Ignition voltage jumping from the distributor rotor to the wrong spark plug electrode inside the distributor cap. Also, ignition voltage jumping from one spark plug cable to another due to worn insulation.

Cycling: Battery electrochemical action and operation from charged to discharged and back. One complete cycle is operation from fully charged to discharged and back to fully charged.

D'Arsonval Movement: A small, current-carrying coil mounted within the field of a permanent horseshoe magnet. Interaction of the magnetic fields causes the coil to rotate. Used as a measuring device within electrical gauges and test meters.

Data Link: A digital signal path for communications between two or more components of an electronic system.

Delta-Type Stator: An alternator stator design in which the three windings of a three-phase alternator are connected end-to-end. The beginning of one winding is attached to the end of another winding. Delta-type stators are used in alternators that must give high-current output.

Depletion Region: An area near the junction of a diode where P-material is depleted of holes and N-material is depleted of electrons.

Detented: Positions in a switch that allow the switch to stay in that position. In an ignition switch, the On, Off, Lock, and Accessory positions are detented.

Diaphragm: A thin flexible wall, separating two cavities, such as the diaphragm in a vacuum advance unit.

Dielectric: The insulating material between the two conductive plates of a capacitor.

Digital: A voltage signal or processing function that has only two levels, on/off or high/low.

Digital-to-Analog (DA): An electronic conversion process for changing digital voltage signals to analog voltage signals.

Diode: An electronic device made of P-material and N-material bonded at a junction. A diode allows current flow in one direction and blocks it in the other.

Direct Current: A flow of electricity in one direction through a conductor.

Discrete Device: A complete, separately manufactured, individual component with wire leads for connection into a circuit.

Doping: The addition of a small amount of a second element to a semiconductor element.

Drain: The field-effect transistor (FET) layer which collects current carriers (similar to the collector of a bipolar transistor).

Duty Cycle: The percentage of the total time that a solenoid is energized during pulse width modulation as determined by a timed voltage pulse from the computer.

Dwell Angle: The measurement in degrees of how far the distributor cam rotates while the breaker points are closed. Also called cam angle, or dwell.

Electrochemistry: In a battery, voltage caused by the chemical action of two dissimilar materials in the presence of a conductive chemical solution.

Electrolyte: The chemical solution in a battery that conducts electricity and reacts with the plate materials.

Electromagnet: A soft iron core wrapped in a coil of a current-carrying conductor.

Electromagnetic Induction: The creation of a voltage within a conductor when relative motion exists between the conductor and a magnetic field.

Electromagnetic Interference (EMI): An undesirable form of electromagnetism created by rapid changes in field strength whenever current stops and starts.

Electromagnetics: The study of the relationship of magnetic energy to electrical energy.

Electron: A negatively charged particle within an atom.

Electron Theory: The current flow theory that says electricity flows from negative to positive.

Electrostatic Field: The area around an electrically charged body resulting from the difference in voltage between two points or surfaces.

Element: A complete assembly of positive plates, negative plates, and separators making up one cell of a battery.

Elements: Chemical building blocks that make up all types of matter in the physical universe.

Emitter: The outside layer of semiconductor material in a transistor that conducts current to the base.

Engine Mapping: A process of vehicle and engine simulation used to establish variable values for the computer to work with, in determining system control.

Equivalent Resistance: The total resistance of a parallel circuit. The single mathematical equivalent of all the parallel resistance.

Extended-Core Spark Plug: Also called power tip. The insulator core and the electrodes in this type of spark plug extend further into the combustion chamber than they do on other types.

Farad: The unit of measurement of capacitance.

Field Circuit: The charging system circuit that delivers current to the alternator field.

Field Relay: A magnetic switch used to open and close the alternator field circuit or, in a charging circuit with a warning lamp, to control the lamp circuit.

Firing Order: The order in which combustion occurs in the cylinders of an engine.

Firing Voltage (Required Voltage): The voltage level that must be reached to ionize and create a spark in the air gap between the spark plug electrodes.

Fixed Dwell: The ignition dwell period begins when the switching transistor turns on and remains relatively constant at all speeds.

Flux Density: The number of flux lines in a magnetic field area. The more flux lines in a unit of area, the stronger the magnetic field at that point.

Flux Lines: Another term for magnetic flux.

Forward Bias: The application of a voltage to produce current flow across the junction of a semiconductor.

Four-Stroke Cycle: One complete operating cycle of a piston in a four-stroke engine. The four strokes of the cycle are: intake, compression, power, and exhaust.

Free Electrons: Three or fewer loosely held electrons in an atom's valence ring.

Full-Wave Rectification: A process by which all of an a.c. sine wave voltage is rectified and allowed to flow as d.c.

Galvanic Battery: A battery that generates voltage based on a difference in oxygen content near two electrodes.

Gate: The field-effect transistor (FET) layer which creates a capacitive field that lets current flow from the source to the drain (similar to the base of a bipolar transistor).

Ground Cable: The battery cable that provides a ground connection from the vehicle chassis to the battery.

Group Number: A battery identification number that indicates battery dimensions, terminal design, holddown location, and other physical features.

Half-Wave Rectification: A process by which only one-half of an a.c. sine wave voltage is rectified and allowed to flow as d.c.

Hall-Effect Switch: A signal-generating switch that develops a transverse voltage across a current-carrying semiconductor when subjected to a magnetic field.

Hardware: The mechanical and electronic components that physically make up a computer.

Heat Range: The measure of a spark plug's ability to dissipate heat from its firing end.

Hold-In Winding: The coil of small-diameter wire in a solenoid that is used to create a magnetic field to hold the solenoid plunger in position inside the coil.

Hole: The space in a valence ring where another electron could fit.

Hydrocarbon: A chemical compound of hydrogen and carbon. A major pollutant from an internal combustion engine. Gasoline itself is a hydrocarbon compound.

Ignition Interval (Firing Interval): The number of degrees of crankshaft rotation between ignition sparks.

Impurities: The doping elements added to pure silicon or germanium to form semiconductor materials.

Induced Voltage: The voltage which appears in a conductor when relative motion exists between it and magnetic flux lines.

Inductive-Discharge Ignition: A method of igniting the air-fuel mixture in an engine cylinder. It is based on the induction of a high voltage in the secondary winding of a coil.

Installation Diagram: A drawing that shows where the wires, loads, attachment hardware, and other parts of an electrical circuit are installed in a car.

Insulated, or Hot, Cable: The battery cable that conducts battery current to the automotive electrical system.

Insulators: Materials that oppose electron flow because of their many bound electrons.

Integrated Circuit (IC): A very small, complex electronic circuit that contains hundreds or thousands of transistors and other devices on a tiny silicon chip.

Integrator Function: The ability of the computer to make short-term — minute-by-minute — corrections in fuel metering.

Ion: An atom which has become unbalanced by losing or gaining an electron. It can be positively or negatively charged.

Ionize: To break up molecules into two or more oppositely charged ions. The air gap between the spark plug electrodes is ionized when the air-fuel mixture is changed from a non-conductor to a conductor.

Isolated Field Circuit: A variation of the A-circuit. Field current is drawn from the alternator output *outside* of the alternator and sent to an insulated brush. The other brush is grounded through the voltage regulator.

Junction: The area where two types of semiconductor materials (P- and N-material) are joined.

Lap Winding: A method of wiring a motor armature. The two ends of a conductor are attached to two commutator bars that are next to each other.

Left-Hand Rule: A method of determining the direction of the magnetic flux lines surrounding a current-carrying conductor, when the electron theory of current flow (– to +) is used. If the conductor is grasped with the left hand so the thumb points in the direction of current flow, the fingers will point in the direction of magnetic flux.

Light-Emitting Diode (LED): A gallium-arsenide diode that emits energy as light. Often used in automotive indicators.

Liquid Crystal Display (LCD): An indicator consisting of a sandwich of glass containing electrodes and polarized fluid. Voltage applied to the fluid allows light to pass through it.

Logic Gates: Circuit switching functions within a computer which act as routes for output voltage signals according to differing combinations of input signals.

Logic Symbol: A symbol identifying the type of gate in a digital or logic circuit.

Lookup Tables: Part of a computer's program, or instructions. One set of lookup tables is common to all microprocessors of a specific group. Another set of lookup tables is used for specific engine calibrations and is located in the PROM.

Magnetic Field: The area surrounding a magnet that is influenced by the magnet's energy.

Magnetic Flux: The invisible directional lines of force which make up a magnetic field.

Magnetic Pulse Generator: A signal-generating switch that creates a voltage pulse as magnetic flux changes around a pickup coil.

Magnetic Saturation: The condition when a magnetic field reaches full strength and maximum flux density.

Magnetic Shunt (Magnetic Bypass): A piece of metal on a voltage regulator coil that controls voltage output at varying temperatures by affecting the coil's magnetic field.

Magnetism: A form of energy caused by the alignment of atoms within certain materials. The ability of a metal to attract iron.

Manifold Absolute Pressure (MAP): Pressure in the intake manifold that is a combination of atmospheric pressure and manifold vacuum or boost pressure.

Manifold Vacuum: Low pressure in an engine's intake manifold, below the carburetor throttle.

Menu Driven: A computer program that allows the user to select choices from a list or ''menu''. As each choice is made, another menu allows the user to make another choice to achieve the desired end result.

Module: A self-contained, sealed unit that houses the solid-state circuits which control certain electrical or mechanical functions.

Minus Rule: Minus metal on the minus side of the distributor breaker points means a minus-capacity condenser.

Multiplex Wiring System: An electrical circuit in which several devices share signals on a common conductor. Signals may be transmitted in parallel form by a solid-state switching device or in serial form over a peripheral data bus or fiber optic cable.

Mutual Induction: Creation of voltage in one conductor by the rise and collapse of the magnetic field surrounding another conductor.

Negative Polarity: Also called ground polarity. A correct polarity of the ignition coil connections. Coil voltage is delivered to the spark plugs so that the center electrode of the plug is negatively charged and the grounded electrode is positively charged.

Negative Temperature Coefficient (NTC): A type of sensor (also called a thermistor) that has *less* resistance as its temperature increases.

Neutral Junction: The center connection of the three windings in a Y-type stator.

Neutron: A particle in an atom that has no charge and is electrically neutral.

N-material: A semiconductor material that has excess (free) electrons because of the type of impurity added. It has a negative charge and will repel additional electrons.

No-Load Oscillation: The rapid, back-and-forth, peak-to-peak oscillation of voltage in the ignition secondary circuit when the circuit is open.

Nonvolatile RAM: Random access memory (RAM) that retains its information when current to the chip is removed.

Nucleus: The center core of an atom that contains the protons and neutrons.

Ohm: The unit for measuring electrical resistance. When one volt pushes one ampere through a circuit, the resistance present is one ohm.

Ohmmeter: A meter used to measure resistance to current flow.

Open Loop: An operational mode in which the computer adjusts a system to function according to pre-determined instructions and does not always respond to feedback signals from its sensors.

Orifice: A small opening in a tube, pipe, or valve.

Output Circuit: The charging system circuit that sends voltage and current to the battery and other electrical systems and devices.

Oxides of Nitrogen: Chemical compounds of nitrogen and oxygen. Major pollutants produced by an internal combustion engine which combine with hydrocarbons to produce smog.

Parallel Circuit: A circuit that has more than one path through which current can flow.

Peak Inverse Voltage (PIV): The highest reverse bias voltage that can be applied to a junction of a diode before its atomic structure breaks down and allows current to flow.

Permeability: A measure of the ease with which materials can be penetrated by magnetic flux lines. Iron is more permeable than air.

Photoelectricity: Voltage caused by the energy of light as it strikes certain materials.

Piezoelectricity: Voltage caused by physical pressure applied to the faces of certain crystals.

P-material: A semiconductor material that has holes for additional electrons because of the type of impurity added. It has a positive charge and will attract additional electrons.

Polarity: Having poles, such as the north and south poles of a magnet. The poles of a battery or an electrical circuit are its positive and negative terminals.

Pole: The areas of a magnetized body where the lines of magnetic force are concentrated. One end of a magnet.

Ported Vacuum: Vacuum immediately above the throttle plate in a carburetor.

Positive Polarity: Also called reverse polarity. An incorrect polarity of the ignition coil connections. Coil voltage is delivered to the spark plug so that the center electrode of the plug is positively charged and the grounded electrode is negatively charged.

Potential: Possible, but not yet in use. The voltage between two points.

Potentiometer: A variable resistor with three terminals. Return signal voltage is taken from a terminal attached to a movable contact that passes over the resistor.

Primary Battery: A battery in which chemical processes destroy one of the metals necessary to create electrical energy. Primary batteries cannot be recharged.

Primary Windings: The coil winding made of a few turns of a heavy wire, which uses battery current to create a magnetic field.

Primary Wiring: The low-voltage wiring in an automobile electrical system.

Program: The instructions a computer uses to do its job. The program consists of mathematical instructions and may include fixed data and require variable data from vehicle sensors.

Programmable Read-Only Memory (PROM): An integrated circuit chip installed in the on-board computer which has been programmed with operating instructions and database information for a particular vehicle.

Proton: A positively charged particle within an atom.

Pull-In Winding: The coil of large-diameter wire in a solenoid that is used to create a magnetic field to pull the solenoid plunger into the coil.

Pulse Width Modulation (PWM): The continuous on/off cycling of a solenoid a fixed number of times per second.

Radio Choke: A coil of extremely fine wire used to absorb oscillations created by the making and breaking of an electrical circuit.

Radiofrequency Interference (RFI): A form of electromagnetic interference created in the ignition secondary circuit which disrupts radio and television transmission.

Random-Access Memory (RAM): Computer memory in which information can be written (stored) and read. Whatever is stored in RAM is lost whenever power to the computer is shut off.

Reach: The length of the spark plug shell from the seat to the bottom of the shell.

Read-Only Memory (ROM): The permanent part of a computer's memory storage function. The ROM can be read but not changed and is retained when power to the computer is shut off.

Reciprocating Engine: Also called a piston engine. An engine in which the pistons move up and down or back and forth, as a result of combustion on the top of the cylinder.

Recombinant: A nongassing battery design in which the oxygen released by the electrolyte recombines with the negative plates.

Rectify: To change alternating current to direct current.

Reference Voltage: Voltage applied to a sensor to which a microprocessor compares the sensor's output voltage and makes any adjustments.

Relative Motion: Movement of a conductor in relation to magnetic flux lines or movement of magnetic flux lines in relation to a conductor.

Relay: An electromagnetic switch. A relay uses a small amount of current flow to control the flow of a larger amount of current through a separate circuit.

Reluctance: The tendency of some materials to resist penetration by magnetic flux lines.

Reserve Capacity Rating: A battery rating based on the number of minutes a battery at 80°F can supply 25 amperes, with no battery cell falling below 1.75 volts.

Resistance: Opposition to electrical current flow.

Resistor-Type Spark Plug: A plug that has a resistor in the center electrode to reduce the inductive portion of the spark discharge.

Reverse Bias: The application of a voltage so that normally no current will flow across the junction of a semiconductor.

Rheostat: A variable resistor used to control current.

Right-Hand Rule: A method of determining the direction of magnetic flux lines surrounding a current-carrying conductor, when the conventional theory of current flow (+ to –) is used. If the conductor is grasped with the right hand so the thumb points in the direction of conventional current flow, the fingers will point in the direction of magnetic flux.

Schematic Diagram: A drawing of a circuit or any part of a circuit that shows how it works.

Secondary Battery: A battery in which chemical processes can be reversed. A secondary battery can be recharged so that it will continue to supply voltage.

Secondary Windings: The coil winding made of many turns of a fine wire, in which voltage is induced by the rise and collapse of the magnetic field of the primary winding.

Self-Induced Voltage: Voltage created in a conductor by the magnetic lines of a current through that same conductor.

Semiconductors: Materials that have four electrons in their valence ring and are neither good conductors nor good insulators.

Sensor: A device which provides input data in the form of voltage signals to a computer.

Series Circuit: A circuit that has only one path through which current can flow.

Series Contacts: The normally closed set of contacts in a double-contact regulator. When they open, field current must flow through a resistor.

Series Motor: A motor that has only one path for current flow through the field and armature windings. Commonly used for starter motors.

Series-Parallel Circuit: A circuit that has some parts in series with the voltage source and some parts in parallel with each other and with the voltage source.

Servomotor: An electric motor that is part of a feedback system used for automatic control of a mechanical device, such as in a temperature control system.

Shorting Contacts: The normally open set of contacts in a double-contact regulator. When closed, they short-circuit the field to ground.

Shunt: Parallel. An electrical connection or branch circuit in parallel with another branch circuit or connection.

Shunt Motor: A motor that has its field windings wired in parallel with its armature. Not used as a starter motor, but often used to power vehicle accessories.

Sine Wave Voltage: The constant change, first to a positive peak and then to a negative peak, of an induced alternating voltage in a conductor.

Single-Phase Current: Alternating current caused by a single-phase voltage.

Single-Phase Voltage: The sine wave voltage induced within one conductor by one revolution of an alternator rotor.

Sintered: Welded together without using heat to form a porous material, such as the metal disc used in some vacuum delay valves.

Software: The programs and logic functions that are stored in the computer.

Solenoid-Actuated Starter: A starter that uses a solenoid both to control current flow in the starter circuit and to engage the starter motor with the engine flywheel.

Source: The field-effect transistor (FET) layer which supplies current-carrying holes or electrons (similar to the emitter of a bipolar transistor).

Spark Voltage: The inductive portion of a spark that maintains the spark in the air gap between a spark plug's electrodes, usually about one-quarter of the firing voltage level.

Specific Gravity: The weight of a volume of liquid divided by the weight of the same volume of water at a given temperature and pressure. Water has a specific gravity of 1.000.

Starting Bypass: A parallel circuit branch that bypasses the ballast resistor during engine cranking.

Starting Safety Switch: A neutral start switch. It keeps the starting system from operating when a car's transmission is in gear.

Static Electricity: Voltage resulting from the transfer of electrons from the surface of one material to the surface of another material. The electrons are ''static'', meaning at rest.

Stepper Motor: A direct-current motor that moves in incremental steps from deenergized to fully energized.

Stoichiometric Air-Fuel Ratio: The air-fuel ratio of approximately 14.7 that provides the most complete combustion and combination of oxygen and hydrocarbon molecules.

Stroboscopic Effect: The effect caused by a rapidly flashing light as it makes moving objects appear stationary.

Stroke: One complete top-to-bottom or bottom-to-top movement of an engine piston.

Sulfation: The crystallization of lead sulfate on the plates of a constantly discharged battery.

Symmetrical: The same on both sides of center. In a symmetrical high-beam headlamp, the light beam is spread the same distance to both sides of center.

System Diagram: A drawing that shows all of the different circuits in a complete electrical system.

Television-Radio-Suppression (TVRS) Cables: High-resistance, carbon-conductor ignition cables that suppress RFI.

Thermistor (Thermal Resistor): A resistor specially constructed so that its resistance decreases as its temperature increases.

Thermoelectricity: Voltage resulting from an unequal transfer of electrons from one metal to another, when one of the metals is heated.

Three-Coil Movement: A gauge design that depends upon the field interaction of three electromagnets and the total field effect on a movable permanent magnet.

Three-Phase Current: Three overlapping, evenly spaced, single-phase currents that make up the total a.c. output of an alternator.

Thyristor: A silicon-controlled rectifier (SCR) that normally blocks all current flow. A slight voltage applied to one layer of its semiconductor structure will allow current flow in one direction while blocking current flow in the other direction.

Top Dead Center (TDC): The exact top of a piston stroke. Also a specification used when tuning an engine.

Torque: Twisting or rotating force; usually expressed in foot-pounds, inch-pounds, or Newton-meters.

Total Ignition Advance: The sum of centrifugal advance, vacuum advance, and initial timing; expressed in crankshaft degrees.

Transducer: A device that converts (transduces) one form of energy to another. A sensor is such a device, converting light or other energy into a voltage signal.

Vacuum: A pressure less than atmospheric pressure.

Vacuum Advance: The use of engine vacuum to advance ignition spark timing by moving the distributor breaker plate.

Vacuum Fluorescent Display (VFD): An indicator in which electrons from a heated filament strike a phosphor material which emits light.

Valence Ring: The outermost electron shell of an atom.

Valve Timing: A method of coordinating camshaft rotation and crankshaft rotation so that the valves open and close at the right times during each of the piston strokes.

Variable Dwell: The ignition dwell period varies in distributor degrees at different engine speeds, but remains relatively constant in duration or actual time.

Venturi: A restriction in an airflow, such as in a carburetor, that increases the airflow speed and creates a reduction in pressure.

Volt: The unit for measuring the amount of electrical force.

Voltage: The electromotive force that causes current flow. The potential difference in electrical force between two points when one is negatively charged and the other is positively charged.

Voltage Creep (Voltage Drift): Excessive voltage at high speeds due to excessive field current flow through a single-contact regulator.

Voltage Decay: The rapid oscillation and dissipation of secondary voltage after the spark in a spark plug air gap has stopped.

Voltage Drop: The measurement of the loss of voltage caused by the resistance of a conductor or a circuit device.

Voltage Reserve: The amount of coil voltage available in excess of the voltage required to fire the spark plugs.

Voltmeter: A meter used to measure electromotive force in volts.

Waste Spark: An ignition system without a distributor in which one coil in a coil pack fires two spark plugs at the same time. The spark in the cylinder on compression ignites the air-fuel mixture, while the spark in the cylinder on its exhaust stroke is wasted.

Watt: The unit of measurement for electric power. One way to measure the rate of doing work. Watts equals volts times amperes.

Wave Winding: A method of wiring a motor armature. The two ends of a conductor are attached to two commutator bars that are opposite each other.

Wire Gauge: Wire size numbers based on the cross section area of the conductor. Larger wires have lower gauge numbers.

Wiring Harness: A bundle of wires enclosed in a plastic cover and routed to various areas of the vehicle. Most harnesses end in plug-in connectors. Harnesses are also called looms.

Y-Type Stator: An alternator stator design in which one end of each of the three windings in a three-phase alternator is connected at a neutral junction. This design is used in alternators that require high voltage at low alternator speed.

Zener Diode: A junction of semiconductor materials that has been heavily doped so that the junction will allow reverse current flow without damage at any voltage above a specific value.

Index

Answers to Review Questions

Chapter 1: Basic Electricity and Basic Circuits
1-B 2-A 3-A 4-D 5-B 6-C 7-B
8-C 9-A 10-C 11-D 12-D 13-A
14-B 15-C 16-B 17-A 18-C 19-A
20-B 21-D 22-A 23-B 24-C 25-C

Chapter 2: Magnetism and Electromagnetism
1-C 2-A 3-A 4-B 5-A 6-A 7-A
8-C 9-A 10-B 11-A 12-A

Chapter 3: Semiconductors and Solid-State Electronics
1-B 2-A 3-C 4-C 5-A 6-A 7-C
8-D 9-D 10-C 11-C 12-D

Chapter 4: Automotive Computer Systems
1-D 2-B 3-C 4-A 5-D 6-A 7-C
8-A 9-C 10-C 11-D 12-A 13-C
14-B 15-A 16-C 17-D 18-C 19-C
20-B

Chapter 5: Automotive Wiring and Basic Circuit Components
1-A 2-D 3-C 4-C 5-C 6-D 7-A
8-C 9-B 10-D 11-D 12-A 13-B
14-B 15-A 16-D

Chapter 6: Introduction to Electrical Circuit Diagrams
1-A 2-A 3-C 4-B 5-D 6-C 7-A
8-D

Chapter 7: Batteries
1-C 2-B 3-B 4-A 5-D 6-B 7-B
8-A 9-C 10-B 11-A 12-D 13-D
14-C 15-A 16-D 17-C 18-D
19-C 20-D 21-B

Chapter 8: A.C. Charging Systems and Alternators
1-A 2-C 3-D 4-B 5-C 6-A 7-D
8-A 9-D 10-B 11-D 12-B 13-A
14-C 15-D

Chapter 9: Regulators and Indicators
1-C 2-D 3-D 4-A 5-D 6-B 7-B
8-C 9-C 10-D 11-A

Chapter 10: Starting System Overview
1-C 2-A 3-D 4-D 5-D 6-C 7-C
8-D 9-D

Chapter 11: Starter Motors
1-B 2-C 3-B 4-D 5-A 6-A 7-C
8-D 9-A 10-B 11-B 12-D 13-D
14-A 15-C

Chapter 12: The Ignition System and Engine Operation
1-B 2-D 3-D 4-C 5-A 6-B 7-D
8-D 9-C 10-A 11-A 12-B 13-D

Chapter 13: The Ignition Primary Circuit and Components
1-D 2-C 3-A 4-C 5-C 6-D 7-B
8-C 9-A 10-B 11-B 12-C 13-D
14-A 15-C 16-B 17-B 18-A

Chapter 14: The Ignition Secondary Circuit and Components
1-D 2-D 3-C 4-A 5-D 6-C 7-C
8-B 9-D 10-B 11-C 12-D 13-C
14-D 15-C

Chapter 15: Ignition Timing and Spark Advance Control
1-D 2-C 3-B 4-A 5-C 6-C 7-B
8-D 9-D 10-C

Chapter 16: Solid-State Electronic Ignition Systems
1-B 2-B 3-A 4-C 5-A 6-B 7-D
8-A 9-B 10-D 11-C 12-A 13-B
14-A 15-C 16-D 17-B 18-C 19-A
20-B 21-D 22-A 23-C

Chapter 17: Electronic Engine Control Systems
1-A 2-C 3-A 4-C 5-B 6-D 7-C
8-C 9-A 10-C 11-C 12-A 13-B
14-A 15-C 16-B 17-A 18-C

Chapter 18: Lighting Systems
1-A 2-C 3-A 4-B 5-D 6-C 7-A
8-C 9-C 10-A 11-B 12-D 13-B
14-A 15-D 16-C

Chapter 19: Horn, Windshield Wiper and Washer, Electric Cooling Fan, and Instrument Circuits
1-B 2-C 3-B 4-C 5-A 6-C 7-B
8-A 9-B 10-C 11-B 12-D 13-C
14-A 15-B 16-C 17-B 18-A 19-C
20-B

Chapter 20: Body Electrical Systems (Accessories)
1-D 2-B 3-C 4-A 5-C 6-D 7-A
8-C 9-D 10-B 11-B 12-C 13-D
14-B

NOTES

NOTES

NOTES

NOTES

NOTES

NOTES

NOTES